STUDIES IN
THE DEITY OF JESUS,
THE CHRIST

By
E. E. DeWitt

Disclaimer

The author of this work has quoted the writers of many articles and books. This does not mean that the author endorses or recommends the works of others. If the author quotes someone, it does not mean that he agrees with all of the author's tenets, statements, concepts, or words, whether in the work quoted or any other work of the author. There has been no attempt to alter the meaning of the quotes; and therefore, some of the quotes are long in order to give the entire sense of the passage.

Copyright © December, 2013 by Dr. Ed DeWitt
All Rights Reserved
Printed in the United States of America

REL067030: Religion: Christian Theology – Apologetics.

ISBN: 978-0-9860377-8-8

All Scripture quotes are from the King James Bible except those verses compared and then the source is identified.

No part of this work may be reproduced without the expressed consent of the publisher, except for brief quotes, whether by electronic, photocopying, recording, or information storage and retrieval systems.

Address All Inquiries To:
THE OLD PATHS PUBLICATIONS, Inc.
142 Gold Flume Way
Cleveland, Georgia, U.S.A. 30528

Web: www.theoldpathspublications.com
E-mail: TOP@theoldpathspublications.com

1.0

DEDICATION

"To my wife, Linda"

E. E. DeWitt

TABLE OF CONTENTS

DEDICATION	3
TABLE OF CONTENTS	5
FOREWORD	33
(Session One)	33
CHAPTER 1: WHAT THE CHURCHES SAY	35
(Session Two)	35
Meaning of the Word: Church	35
The Real Definition of a Church	35
The Historical Church	35
The Liturgical Churches	36
From the Westminster Confession of Faith:	36
The Lutheran Church	36
The Orthodox Church	36
The Testimony of the Pentecostal Church	37
The Testimony of the Baptist Churches	37
The Testimony of Other Various Protestant Churches	37
The Testimony of Para-church Agencies	38
The Testimonies of the Faithful	39
The Testimony of 1 John 5:7	39
CHAPTER 2: TERMS	45
(Session Three)	45
The Foundation of the Christian Faith	45
The Hope of Christian Salvation	45
Jesus Taught That He Was Divine	46
The Defining Doctrine	47
The Wisdom of Man is Mere Foolishness	48
CHAPTER 3: FALSE VIEWS OF JESUS	51
(Session Four)	51
Just Who Is Jesus	51
Eutychianism	51
Nestorianism	51
Apollianarianism	52
Arianism	52

Ebionism 52
　　Docetism 52

Chapter 4: Terminology Explained 55
　　(Session Five) 55
　　Jesus Christ 55
　　The Son of David Versus The Son of God 55
　　The Humanity and Deity of Jesus 56
　　The Messiah 56
　　The Word 56
　　The Agent in All of Creation 57
　　Firstbegotten 57
　　Melchisedec 58
　　Sonships 58
　　The Son of Man 58
　　The Son of God 58
　　First Born 59
　　Image of the Father 59
　　Christ 59
　　Second Person of the Trinity 59

CHAPTER 5: JESUS: THE SON OF GOD 61
　　(Session Six) 61
　　God Declared that Jesus is His Son 61
　　Jesus said that He is the Son of God 61
　　Jesus Identified Himself to the Father as the Son of God 62
　　Jesus Claimed before the High Priest that He is the Son of God 62
　　The Holy Spirit Assured Us that Jesus is the Son of God 62
　　The Angel Gabriel said that Jesus is the Son of God 62
　　Even the Demons Agreed that Jesus is the Son of God 62
　　John the Baptist Affirmed that Jesus is the Son of God 63
　　Matthew Said that Jesus is the Son of God 63
　　Mark Said that Jesus is the Son of God 63
　　Luke Said that Jesus is the Son of God 63
　　John Said that Jesus is the Son of God 63
　　Nathaniel Recognized Him 64

TABLE OF CONTENTS

- Andrew Said that Jesus is the Son of God 64
- The Blind Man Said that Jesus is the Son of God 64
- The Disciples in the Ship Said that Jesus is the Son of God 64
- Peter Said that Jesus is the Son of God 64
- He is the Son of God 64
- Even Judas, the Betrayer, Said that Jesus is the Son of God 64
- The Centurion Said that Jesus is the Son of God 65
- Paul Said that Jesus is the Son of God 65
- The Ethiopian Eunuch Said that Jesus is the Son of God 65
- The Empty Tomb Stands as a Testimony that Jesus is the Son of God 65
- Many Say that Jesus Never Said He Was God. This is an Error 66

CHAPTER 6: ATTRIBUTES OF JESUS 67
- (Session Seven) 67
- Traits About Jesus Which Show His Deity 67
- The Revealer 67
- The Object of the Father's Love 67
- The Father Shows Jesus All 67
- Jesus Is the One Who Quickens 67
- Jesus Is the Object of Honor 68
- Jesus Has Life In Himself 68
- He is the Liberator 68
- He is the Object of the Father's Glory 68
- Jesus is the Lover of Righteousness 68
- Jesus is the Test of Truth 68
- He is the Sent One 68
- Jesus is the Assurance of Life 68
- He is the Ticket to the Father's Abode 69

CHAPTER 7: EVIDENCES THAT JESUS IS THE SON OF GOD 71
- (Session Eight) 71
- Sixteen Evidences that Jesus is the Son of God 71
- Jesus is the Savior of the World 71
- Jesus is more than a Religious Leader or Teacher 71
- Jesus is Glorified Above All Others 71
- Jesus is the Person of the Gospel Message 71

Jesus is the Reconciler of Men 72
Jesus is our Role Model 72
Jesus is the Person of Fellowship 72
Jesus is the Deliverer from Wrath 72
The Father Spoke Through Jesus 72
Jesus Is the Creative Agent 72
He is the Propitiation for Our Sin 72
Jesus is the Cleanser From Sin 73
Jesus is the Repository of Life 73
Jesus is Known to Demons 73
Jesus is the Repository of the Promises of God... 73
Jesus is the Stronghold of Our Faith 74
Jesus is the Great High Priest 74
He is our Constant Contemporary as Well as Our Constant Companion 74
Jesus Was also Mistreated by Men 74
He is the Lord of Glory 75

CHAPTER 8: JESUS THE SON OF GOD 77
(Session Nine) 77
The Biblical Use of the Term "the Son of…" 77
Jesus Was No "Con Man".. 78
Jesus' Hearers Understood His Claims 78
The Messiah Is Recognized as the Son of God in the Old Testament 79

CHAPTER 9: JESUS IS THE ANGEL OF THE LORD 81
(Session Ten) 81
The Preincarnate Appearances of Jesus: The Angel of the Lord............................... 81
Brief Explanation of the Trinity 81
His Name is Wonderful 81
No Man Has Seen God 82
The Misdirected Worship of Lucifer 82
Jesus Is the Theme of the Bible.. 83

CHAPTER 10: JESUS IS THE THEME OF THE BIBLE 85
(Session Eleven) 85
Jesus Was in Existence Before All Things 85
Several Appearances 85

TABLE OF CONTENTS

The Angel of the Lord Was Called "God" by Hagar 86
Jacob Identifies the One with Whom He Wrestled as God 88
Gideon Called the Angel Messenger, God 88
Abraham Identifies the Angel of the Lord as Jehovah 88
The Angel Who Was the Captain of the Lord's Host 89
The Authority of the Angel to Instruct in Worship 89

CHAPTER 11: gODS WITH A SMALL "G" 91
(Session Twelve) 91
Jesus Is Not a Created god 91
Jesus, the "Monogenes" 91
Jesus is Ascribed as Having the Creative Attributes of God 92
Jesus Has Demonstrated that He Is God 92
Jesus is God - With a Capital "G." 93

CHAPTER 12: GOD: HE IS ONE 95
(Session Thirteen) 95
The Trinitarian View Is Not Pagan 95
There Is Only One God 95
We Need to Be Careful How We Say Things 95
Belief in the Trinity is Not Polytheism 96
The Trinity Is of One Essence 96
A Strong Indication of the Trinity 96
The Concept of the Unity of the Trinity is a Hard Concept 97
There is But One God 97

CHAPTER 13: ACCEPTING JESUS AS GOD 99
(Session Fourteen) 99
The Omnipresence of God 99
The Body of Jesus was The Temple where Resided the Eternal God 99
The Image of the Invisible God 100
The Concept of the Trinity is Not of Levels of Authority 100
The Meaning of The Firstborn of Every Creature 101
Kenosis 101
The Jehovah Witness Cult 101
Let There Be No Mistake. Jesus is God 102
Jesus Has a Distinct Personality; The Mystery of the Godhead 102

CHAPTER 14: GOD: HE IS PLURAL 105
(Session Fifteen) 105
God is Eternally Existent in But One Essence 105
Within this One Essence the Trinitarian Sees Three Distinct "Persons." 105
The Trinity is of the Same Essence and Nature 105
God Has Been Eternally Existent in the Triune Godhead 106
The Unity of Purpose of the Trinity 106
The Truth of the Trinity Proclaimed in Scripture From the Beginning 107

CHAPTER 15: THE ONENESS OF THE GODHEAD 109
(Session Sixteen) 109
God is a Being of Plurality Within His Oneness 109
God is Three Equals, But One Being 109
There is Only One God, He is Manifest in Three "Persons" 109
Elohim 110
Because Jesus in Not the Father, It Does Not Imply Any Lack of Deity 111
Why Jesus is Called "the Son"? 111
From John 12:45, Jesus is Equal With the Father in His Essence 112
From Titus 2:13, Jesus is the Great God and Saviour 112

CHAPTER 16: I. THE DUAL NATURE OF JESUS 113
(Session Seventeen) 113
The Concept Is Taught In Scripture 113
Jesus Possessed Certain Attributes Even Before Bethlehem 113
First, An Eternal Place of Abode 113
Second, Jesus was Possessed of Creative Power Before Bethlehem 113
Third, Jesus Possessed Knowledge Before Bethlehem 114
Fourth, Jesus Possessed Glory Before Bethlehem 114
Fifth, Jesus Possessed Riches Before Bethlehem 114
Things True Before Bethlehem 114
First, Jesus Was Foreordained 115
Second, Jesus Was With the Father Before Bethlehem 115
Third, Jesus was *"Of Old."* 116
Fourth, Jesus Was Worshipped by Angels 116
Fifth, Jesus Was Called "Lord" by David 116
Sixth, Jesus Was a "Rock of Refreshment." 116

TABLE OF CONTENTS

Seventh, Jesus Was Sent 117
Eighth, Jesus Was Known by Abraham 117
Ninth, Jesus Was Before John the Baptist 118
Tenth, Jesus' Pre-existence 118

CHAPTER 17: II. THE DUAL NATURE OF JESUS 119
(Session Eighteen) 119
His Humanity 119
The Human Nature of Jesus was United With the Divine Nature Before Bethlehem 119
The Symbiosis of His Nature 119
Although He is Fully Human, He is in His Essence God 120
Jesus' Omnipresence 120

CHAPTER 18: JESUS' VOLUNTARY SUBMISSION 123
(Session Nineteen) 123
Kenosis 123
Jesus Only Laid Aside the Outward Glory of the Godhead. He Remained God 123
Jesus Did Not Empty Himself of His Essential Glory, Only its Manifestation 123
Jesus was Fully Human 124
Jesus Came as God, but God Clothed in the Flesh of Humanity 124
The Incomprehensible has Become Comprehensible for Our Benefit 124
The Father Has Exalted Jesus 125
The Purpose of the Kenosis 125
Jesus Never Ceased Being Who He Is 125
Our Perfect Substitute 126

CHAPTER 19: KENOSIS 127
(Session Twenty) 127
The Method of His Dealing With Sinful Humanity 127
The Old Testament Sacrificial System Was Effective But It Was Not Permanent 127
Subjection to the Father 127
The Purchase of Our Redemption 128
Jesus Existed in Another Form Before Bethlehem 128
The Doctrine of the Godhead: Jesus and the Father are of the Same Essence 129
Jesus' Work was Far More Than Just the Cross 129
The Kenosis Makes Jesus the Mediator 130
Jesus is the Only Possible Mediator 130

- The Kenosis also Displayed the Great Power of Jesus 130
- The Kenosis in Action 130

CHAPTER 20: THE GLORIFICATION OF JESUS 133
- (Session Twenty-One) 133
- He is the Glorious Creator, Sustainer and King of the Universe 133
- We Have Been Influenced by the "Wealth and Prosperity Gospel" 133
- We Get Caught up in His Wonderfulness and Overlook His Greatness 133
- The Express Image 134
- Another Proof of His Glory 134
- First, God Declared His Glory; God Said It, That Settles It 135
- Second, God's Words Declare His Glory 135
- The Proof of His Glory Was Shown to the Disciples At the Transfiguration 135
- Moses' Derived Glory 136
- Another Proof of His Glory 136

CHAPTER 21: THE POWER OF THE GLORY OF JESUS 137
- (Session Twenty-Two) 137
- The Concept of "Tri theism" Is Not in the Bible 137
- The Greek Preposition "Para" and Jesus' Glory 138
- The Power of His Glory is Shown in His Performance 138
- The Glory of Jesus is Shown by His Receiving Worship 139
- Jesus is to be Glorified by These Events 139

CHAPTER 22: I. JESUS HAS THE ATTRIBUTES OF DEITY 141
- (Session Twenty-Three) 141
- Attributes Which He Shares with No Human 141
- Four Instances Where Jesus Appropriated the Attributes of God 141
- First, Thy Sins Be Forgiven 141
- Second, Jesus Knew Their Thoughts 141
- Third, Jesus Could Raise the Dead 142
- Another Attribute, Jesus' Claim to "All Power" 142
- Another Attribute, Jesus' Omnipresence 143

CHAPTER 23: II. JESUS HAS THE ATTRIBUTES OF DEITY 145
- (Session Twenty-Four) 145
- Jesus Was Always in Fellowship With the Father 145
- John 14:6 is Jesus' Claim to the Prerogatives of God 145

TABLE OF CONTENTS

John 14:6 Establishes the Claim That Jesus is Self existent 146
The Worship of Jesus By the Angels 146
The Lord's Supper is a Call by Jesus to Worship Him 146

CHAPTER 24: III. JESUS HAS THE ATTRIBUTES OF DEITY 149
(Session Twenty-Five) 149
There are Only Two Entities Who are Actually Capable of Accepting Worship 149
Nine Instances In Scripture Records of Worship Being Properly Offered to Jesus .. 149
First, The Firstbegotten, Is Worshipped 149
Second, The Wise Men Worshipped Jesus 150
Third, The Disciples Worshipped Jesus 150
Fourth, A Military Man Worshipped Jesus 150
Fifth, A Leper Worships Jesus 151
Sixth, The Woman of Tyre Worships Jesus 151
Seventh, A Handicapped Person Worships Jesus 151
Eighth, The Disciples Worshipped Jesus 151
Ninth, The Disciples of Emmaus Worshipped Jesus 151
Jesus Accepts Worship From All and Will be Worshipped by All 152

CHAPTER 25: JESUS DISPLAYED THE POWER OF HIS DEITY 153
(Session Twenty-Six) 153
The Power of Jesus Is Simply Part of Who He Was and Is 153
The Power As the Living Word 153
Observations That Jesus is Superior to All Created Beings 154
He Is Superior to Angels 154
Jesus Is Superior to Moses 154
Jesus Is Superior to King Solomon 155
Jesus Is Superior to Jonah 155
Jesus Is Superior In His Name 155
Jesus Is Superior in the One Sacrifice He Offers for All Men 156
Jesus' Offering is Superior to the Offering of Abel 156
Jesus' Blood Sacrifice Is Superior 157
Why Jesus' Blood Is Superior 157
The Necessity of the Virgin Birth 157

CHAPTER 26: THE NAME OF JESUS IS ASSOCIATED WITH GOD 159
(Session Twenty-Seven) 159

Three Areas Where the Name of Jesus Is Associated With God 159
First, the Name Is Included In the Baptismal Formula 159
Baptism Does Not Save, But Is Symbolic 159
The Gift of the Holy Spirit 159
Footwashing 160
Second, The Name of Jesus Is Used In Apostolic Benedictions 160
Jesus Is Set Apart From the Rest of Humanity 162
Jesus Is No Ordinary Human 162

CHAPTER 27: THE NAME OF JESUS IS ASSOCIATED WITH GOD IN THE VERY ESSENCE OF WHO JESUS IS 165

(Session Twenty-Eight) 165
Jesus Name Is Associated With The Very Essence Of God 165
Jesus Is One With the Godhead 165
Jesus Is God In Human Form 165
Jesus Is One With God In Image 165
The Power of God Is Assigned to Jesus 166
Jesus is One with God in Glory 166
Jesus is One with God in Honor 166
Jesus is One with God in Possessions 167
The Message of the Spirit is Jesus' Message 167
Jesus is One with God in Saving Faith 167
"Coming to God" Means "Coming to Jesus" 167
Jesus is One with God in Abiding with Believers 167
Jesus is One with God in Being Hated by the World 168
Jesus is One with God in Baptism 168
Jesus is One with God in Raising the Dead 168
Jesus is One with God in Benediction 168

CHAPTER 28: THE KNOWLEDGE OF JESUS DISPLAYS THE POWER OF GOD 169

(Session Twenty-Nine) 169
The Knowledge of Jesus Was Not an Occultic Knowledge 169
The Traditional Text Is Not a Faulty Text 169
The Supernatural Power of Jesus 170
The Greatest Need of Man is to Have his Sins Forgiven 172
Jesus Knew the Manner of His Impending Death 172

TABLE OF CONTENTS

CHAPTER 29: THE POWER OF THE LIFE OF JESUS DISPLAYS HIS ESSENTIAL DEITY 173
- (Session Thirty) 173
- Several Verses Illustrating Jesus' Power Over Life 173
- Life was Who Jesus Is 173
- Jesus Is Not From the Same Time/Space Continuum 174
- One Must Conclude That Jesus is God 174
- Jesus is the Means of Sustaining Life 174
- Jesus is the Exclusionary Way to Heaven 174
- Jesus Did Works By His Own Power and Authority 175
- Jesus' Great Compassion 175

Chapter 30: JESUS IS THE LORD OF NATURE 177
- (Session Thirty-One) 177
- Four Incidents That Jesus Is the Lord of Nature 177
- First, Water Into Wine 177
- Second, The Feeding of the Five Thousand 178
- Third, The Miracle of the Great Fishes 178
- Fourth, The Miracle of the Net 178
- Jesus' Miracles Were By The Power of His Word and Authority 179

CHAPTER 31: THE HOLINESS OF JESUS DISPLAYS THE POWER OF HIS PERSONAL DEITY 181
- (Session Thirty-Two) 181
- Four Instances Point to The Holiness of Jesus That Displayed His Personal Deity .. 181
- First, Jesus was Holy from Before the Foundation of the World 181
- Second, Jesus' Very Nature Is Holy 182
- Third, Jesus was Holy at His Birth in Bethlehem 182
- Fourth, Jesus was Holy as a Child 183
- Jesus Never Rebelled Against God 183

CHAPTER 32: TESTIMONIES FROM SCRIPTURE AS TO THE HOLINESS OF JESUS 185
- (Session Thirty-Three) 185
- Eight Testimonies 185
- First, The Testimony of God, the Father 185
- Second, The Testimony of Unclean Spirits 186
- Third, The Testimony of Judas, the Betrayer 186

Fourth, the Testimony of Pilate	187
Fifth, The Testimony of the Wife of Pilate	187
Sixth, The Testimony of the Cross	188
Seventh, The Testimony of the Centurion	188
Eighth, The Testimony of Jesus	189

CHAPTER 33: I. THE WORKS OF JESUS DISPLAY THE POWER OF GOD 191

(Session Thirty-Four)	191
Jesus Calms the Great Storm	191
Three Other Instances	192
First, The Man Sick With Palsy	192
Second, Jesus Healed Disease and Cast out Demons	193
Third, Jesus Laid Down His Life and Reclaimed It Again	193

CHAPTER 34: II. THE WORKS OF JESUS DISPLAY THE POWER OF GOD 195

(Session Thirty-Five)	195
Jesus the Creator	195
Jesus Has the Title Deed to the Earth	196
Jesus Is the Messiah	196
Jesus Holds Together the Universe	196
Jesus' Place of Power and Authority Over Death and Life	197

CHAPTER 35: IN JESUS IS DISPLAYED THE ATTRIBUTES OF GOD 199

(Session Thirty-Six)	199
Jesus said, I and My Father Are One	199
Jesus Is Wisdom	199

CHAPTER 36: THE ESSENCE OF JESUS CONTAINS THE ATTRIBUTES OF GOD 201

(Session Thirty-Seven)	201
These Attributes of Deity Are Beyond the Capability of Mere Humans	201
The Immortality of Jesus	201
Jesus Has the Keys to Hell and Death	202
Three Other Attributes	202
First, Jesus Is From Eternity	202
Second, Jesus is the Sustainer of All	203
Thirdly, Jesus is Everything	203

CHAPTER 37: THE OMNISCIENCE OF JESUS 205

(Session Thirty-Eight)	205

TABLE OF CONTENTS

Several Instances of the Omniscient Nature of Jesus Displayed 205
First, Jesus Knows All 205
Second, Jesus Knows the Thoughts of Man 206
Third, Jesus Knows the Hearts of Men 206
Fourth, Jesus Knows the Lives of Men 207
Fifth, Jesus knows the Craftiness of Men 207
Sixth, Jesus Knows the Love of Man 208
Seventh, Jesus Knows the Whereabouts of Man 208

CHAPTER 38: JESUS ALSO KNOWS THE FUTURE 211
(Session Thirty-Nine) 211
Jesus' Knowledge Was Absolute 211
Jesus Knew the Catch of Fish 212
Jesus Knew of the Denial of Peter 212
Jesus Knew What Sort of Death Awaited Peter 213
Jesus Knew of His Own Death 213
Jesus Knew What Was Going to Happen on the Day of His Crucifixion 213
Jesus Knew of the Betrayal of Judas 214
Jesus Knew the Reaction of the Disciples to His Arrest 214
Jesus Knew of the Passover Accommodations 215
Jesus Knew of His Ascension into Heaven 215
Jesus Knew Who Would Betray Him 216
Jesus Knows What is in All Men 216

CHAPTER 39: ATTRIBUTES OF JESUS, CONTINUED 217
(Session Forty) 217
Jesus Is Immutable 217
Jesus is Self-existent 217
Jesus is Truth 218
Jesus is Holy 218
Jesus Our High Priest 219
Jesus Is the Only Mediator 219

CHAPTER 40: JESUS AS CREATOR 221
(Session Forty-One) 221
First, Jesus Is the Creator 221
Jesus Is Omnipotent 222

Jesus Created All Things Out of Nothing 222
Jesus Created All Things in Heaven and in Earth 222
Jesus Created the Worlds 223

CHAPTER 41: THE OMNIPRESENCE OF JESUS 225
(Session Forty-Two) 225
This is an Attribute of God 225
Jesus Fills All things 226
Jesus Is Near to All 227

CHAPTER 42: MORE ATTRIBUTES CONFIRMING JESUS IS GOD 229
(Session Forty-Three) 229
Jesus Is Our Constant Contemporary 229
Jesus is life 229
Man Was Not the Product of Evolutionary Mutations 229
Jesus, the Repository, Not the Depository, of Life 230
Jesus is Truth 230
Jesus is the Way to God 230
The Eternality and Love of Jesus 231
Jesus is the "Alpha and Omega" 232

CHAPTER 43: THE ALL POWERFULNESS OF JESUS 233
(Session Forty-Four) 233
The Attribute of Omnipotence 233
Jesus Has the Power of Life and Death 233
Jesus the Great Physician 233
Jesus Healed the Blind 234
Jesus Healed Sicknesses 234
Jesus is the Creator God 235
Jesus Healed the Withered Hand 236
Jesus is Lord of the Sabbath 236
Jesus Healed a Man with "Dropsy" 236
Jesus Healed Paralysis 237

CHAPTER 44: THE POWER OF JESUS TO HEAL 239
(Session Forty-Five) 239
Jesus Healed Leprosy 239
Jesus Healed Palsy and Fever 239

TABLE OF CONTENTS

Jesus Healed the Insane 240
Jesus Healed the Woman With the Issue of Blood 240
Jesus Healed Infirmity 240
Jesus Healed the Ear of the Soldier Who Came to Arrest Him 241

CHAPTER 45: OBSERVATIONS OF THE DIVINE POWER OF JESUS 243
(Session Forty-Six) 243
Jesus Exhibited This Divine Power from His Own Person 243
Consider the Fig Tree 243

CHAPTER 46: JESUS EXHIBITED POWER OVER SATAN 245
(Session Forty-Seven) 245
God Cannot Be Tempted 246
Satan Can Never Defeat God 246
Jesus Has Power Over the Works of Satan 246
Jesus Has Power Over Satan, the Destroyer of Life 246
False Religious Systems are Tools of Satan 247
Jesus Displayed His Power Over Satan at Calvary 247

CHAPTER 47: JESUS HAS POWER OVER DEATH AND THE GRAVE 249
(Session Forty-Eight) 249
Several Scriptural Instances 249
Jesus Rose From the Dead Himself 249
Jesus' Death Was a Glorious Culmination of His Planned Ministry to Humanity 249
Jesus Is Shown to Have Ultimate Authority Over Death 250

CHAPTER 48: JESUS' POWER OVER DEATH 253
(Session Forty-Nine) 253
Several Examples 253
The Son of the Widow of Nain 253
The Matter of Jarius' Daughter 254
Jesus Raised Lazarus From the Dead 255

CHAPTER 49: JESUS HAS ALL POWER IN HEAVEN AND IN EARTH 257
(Session Fifty) 257
First, Jesus Has All Power in Heaven and in Earth 257
Jesus Has a Displayed Power Over the Elements 258
Jesus Has the Power of Upholding the Entirety of the Created Universe 258
Jesus Has the Power to Change Our Bodies 259

Jesus Has Power Among Humanity 260

Jesus Has Power of Hell and Death 260

CHAPTER 50: THE AUTHORITY OF JESUS 263

(Session Fifty-One) 263

The Teaching of Jesus Exhibited This Authority 263

Jesus Exercised His Authority in All Situations 263

Jesus Displayed Trust In the Scripture 264

Jesus Answers to Religious Leaders Displayed His Authority 264

Jesus Exercised His Authority in His Ministerial Life 264

Jesus Retrained Control, Authority, At His Trial 265

The Authority of Jesus Displayed Even in His Physical Death 266

The Death of Jesus Was Not an Accident 266

CHAPTER 51: JESUS DISPLAYED IN HIS ACTIONS THE TRUTH THAT HE WAS AND IS GOD 267

(Session Fifty-Two) 267

Jesus Simply Proved the Point by His Actions and Authority 267

The Authority of Jesus to Judge Humanity 267

Jesus Displayed His Authority in His Miracles 268

He Displayed Authority Over Time and Space as the Creator of Time and Space ... 269

Jesus Said, "My words..." 269

CHAPTER 52: THE ETERNALITY OF JESUS 271

(Session Fifty-Three) 271

Two Instances When Jesus Claimed Full Deity 271

First 271

Second 271

Jesus Claims to Have Existed Before Abraham 272

The "Name" of "I Am" denotes the One Who is Existent Within Himself 272

CHAPTER 53: MORE COMMENTS ON THE ETERNALITY OF JESUS 275

(Session Fifty-Four) 275

Jesus Is Not a Created God 275

The Firstborn, Its Meaning 276

Kenosis 276

"Mount of Transfiguration" The Glory That Was His 277

The Baptism of Jesus 277

TABLE OF CONTENTS

The One Who Is God 277

CHAPTER 54: THE OLD TESTAMENT ATTESTS TO THE ETERNALITY OF JESUS 279
    (Session Fifty-Five) 279
    Proverbs 8 279
    Wisdom Is Jesus 279
    Isaiah 9:6 279
    Micah 5:2 280
    John 1:1 280
    Philippians 2:6 280

CHAPTER 55: JESUS IS THE CREATOR 283
    (Session Fifty-Six) 283
    Genesis 1:1 Compared to John 1:1-3 283
    The Logos 283
    He Is THE Creative Force of the Godhead 283
    Jesus Is No Part of Creation, He Is the Creator 284

CHAPTER 56: JESUS IS THE CREATOR AND MIRACLE WORKER 287
    (Session Fifty-Seven) 287
    Most of the Miracles Jesus Performed Were a Restoration 287
    Jesus Miracles Were the Setting Aside of the Laws of Nature 287
    Sin Causes All the Ill That Befalls Mankind 288
    Jesus the "Great Physician." He is More. He is God Almighty 288
    Colossians 1:16-17: The Glory Which Is His 288
    Revelation 1:11, 3:14, 4:11 289

CHAPTER 57: THE PERSONALITY OF JESUS 291
    (Session Fifty-Eight) 291
    Three Errors 291
    The Arian Error 291
    Sabellians 292
    His Messiahship 293
    This Oneness of Jesus with Jehovah is Necessary to Our Very Salvation 293

CHAPTER 58: JESUS' TEACHING REVEALS THE DIVINE MIND 295
    (Session Fifty-Nine) 295
    The Truths of the Illumination of the Spirit 295
    The Teaching of Jesus Was Personal and Pointed 296

STUDIES IN THE DEITY OF JESUS, THE CHRIST

- The Authority That Jesus taught was Either Divine or He Was an Egomaniac 296
- Jesus Teaching to Pilate 296
- Jesus Teaching That He Had Authority Over Demons 296
- Jesus Taught Authority Over the Religious Leaders of the Jewish People............. 296
- Jesus Taught Authority Over Religious Observances 297
- Jesus Taught Authority Over Sickness.. 298
- Jesus Taught Authority Over Human Relationships 298
- Jesus Taught Authority Over Heavenly Things... 298
- The Teaching of Jesus Was Factual 299
- The Lie That Jesus Taught What He Knew to Be Error 299

Chapter 59: THE CHARACTER OF JESUS REVEALS THE DIVINE MIND 301
- (Session Sixty) 301
- The Character of Jesus Compared With the Claims of Jesus 301
- The Character of Jesus Displays the Marks of the Divine 301
- His Miracles Display His Divine Character 302
- John 5:19 Explained 302
- Two Prophecies in One Verse 302
- Jesus Character Displayed in the Announcement: Animal Sacrifice Is Out............ 303

Chapter 60: JESUS ADMITS HIS DIVINITY 305
- (Session Sixty-One) 305
- Christianity Is Different From All Other Religions of the World........................... 305
- Is Jesus a Liar? 305
- On the Basis of the Claims of Jesus, We Must Either Accept Him or Reject Him ... 305
- Others Understood the Claims of Jesus to Deity 306
- The Demons Understood 306
- Jesus' Antagonists Understood 307
- The Jewish Leaders Understood Jesus 307
- Thomas Understood... 308

CHAPTER 61: JESUS STRONGLY INFERS HIS DEITY.. 309
- (Session Sixty-Two) 309
- Passages Where Jesus Infers His Deity 309
- Matthew 14:33 309
- Mark 2:1-11 309
- Matthew 28:19-20.. 310

TABLE OF CONTENTS

John 16:28 310
John 10:17-18 310
John 16:15 311
Matthew 5:21-22 311

CHAPTER 62: JESUS' ESSENCE PROCLAIMS THE POWER OF HIS DEITY 313

(Session Sixty-Three) 313
Examples 313
John 3:31 & 8:23: Jesus Is Above All 313
John 3:12-13: Jesus Makes the Claim That He Is From Heaven 313
John 6:38: Jesus Claims to Be From Heaven For a Purpose 313
John 8:42: Jesus Claims to Be From God 314
Matthew 28:18 & John 17:2: Jesus Claims Omnipotence 314
Luke 9:47 & John 2:24-25, 1:1-3: Jesus Claims to be Omniscient 314
Matthew 18:20, 28:20, & John 3:13: Jesus Claims to be Omnipresent 314
Mark 14:61-62 & John 9:35-37: Jesus Claims to Be the Son of God 315
John 4:25-26: Jesus Claims He Is the Messiah 315
John 14:6: The Way to God 315
John 10:9: Jesus Claims to Be the Door to Heaven 315
John 10:10, 28: Jesus Claims to Be the Giver of Life 316
John 14:27: Jesus Claimed to Be the Giver of Peace 316
Matthew 11:28: Jesus Claims to Be the Giver of Rest 316
John 8:34, 36: Jesus Claims to Be the Giver of Liberty 317
John 1:9, 8:12: Jesus Claims to Be the Light of the World 317
Luke 19:10, John 3:17: Jesus Claims to Be the Savior of the World 317
Matthew 20:28 7 John 10:11: Jesus Claims to Be the Substitute of the World 317
John 5:22: Jesus Claims to Be the Judge of the World 318
Matthew 16:18: Jesus Claims to Be the Builder of the Church 318
Matthew 16:27 & Revelation 22:12: Jesus Claims to Be the Rewarder of Men 318
John 11:25: Jesus Claims to Be the Resurrection 319
Mark 2:10-11: Jesus Claims to Be the One Who Forgives Sin 319
John 14:14: Jesus Claims to Be the One Who Answers Prayer 319
John 15:26: Jesus Claims to Be the One Who Sent the Holy Spirit 319
John 14:3: Jesus Claims to Be the One Who Would Come Again 319

CHAPTER 63: JESUS CLAIMED DEITY IN HIS VERY WORDS 321

STUDIES IN THE DEITY OF JESUS, THE CHRIST

(Session Sixty-Four) 321
Two Verses to Consider 321
John 10:30: Jesus Said That He and the Father Were One 321
Hebrews 1:3: The Shared Glory of the Father and the Son 321
Jesus Claims the Authority of God In Three Specific Areas 322
Mark 2:10 Jesus Said "The Son of Man Hath Power on Earth to Forgive Sin" 322
John 5:22: All Judgment Is Committed Unto the Son 322
John 5:21, 6:39-40, 54; John 10:17-18: Jesus Has Authority to Raise the Dead .. 322
Matthew 26:63-64: Jesus Tells the Truth About Who He Was and Is 323
John 10:30; Jesus Said, "I and the Father Are One" 323
Revelation 1:8; 21:6-7: Jesus Claims the Be Deity With Authority 323
All the Claims Leave Us With a Choice 324

CHAPTER 64: OTHERS ADMIT TO THE DEITY OF CHRIST 325
(Session Sixty-Five) 325
Many Persons Recognized Who Jesus Was 325
The Claim That Scripture Has Changed So Much We Cannot Know is False 325
Nine Instances of Contemporaries Who Recognized His Divinity 325
First, John 1:36: John the Baptist 325
Second, Matthew 16:16: The Apostle Peter 326
Third, John 20:28: The Apostle Thomas 326
Fourth, John 20:31; The Apostle John 326
Fifth, John 4:29: The Samaritan Woman 326
Sixth, John 9:33: The Blind Man Healed 327
Seventh, Matthew 27:54: The Centurion and His Men 327
Eighth, John 7:46: The Enemies of Jesus 327
Ninth, Matthew 26:59-66: The Witnesses 327
Eight Example of Those Who Testified to the Deity of Jesus 328
First, Hebrews 1:8: God Himself 328
Second, John 10:30; Jesus Himself 328
Third, Isaiah 9:6: Isaiah 328
Fourth, Luke 1:46-47: Mary 328
Fifth, John 20:28: Thomas 329
Sixth, John 1:1; Revelation 19:13: The Apostle John 329
Seventh, Ephesians 2:6; Colossians 2:9; 1 Timothy 3:16: Paul 329

TABLE OF CONTENTS

Eight, Jude 25: Jude 329
CHAPTER 65: THOSE WHO KNEW JESUS BEST KNEW HE WAS GOD 331
   (Session Sixty-Six) 331
   First, Nathanael 331
   Second, John 332
   Third, Peter 332
   Fourth, Thomas 332
   Fifth, Pilate 333
   Sixth, One of the Men Crucified with Jesus 333
   Seventh, the Apostle Paul 334
   Eighth, The Executioner 334
   Ninth, The Writer of Hebrews 334
   The Testimony of Zacharias and His Wife, Elizabeth 335
   The Testimony of Thomas 336
CHAPTER 66: HIS ENEMIES UNDERSTOOD THE CLAIMS OF JESUS TO DEITY 337
   (Session Sixty-Seven) 337
   The Scribes 337
   The Jews Who Tried to Stone Him 338
   The Demons 338
   Most of the Jews 339
   The Magistrates at the Trial of Jesus 340
   The Religious Elite 340
   The Antagonists of Jesus 340
   Jesus' Executioners 340
   Judas 341
CHAPTER 67: THE PROPHETS SPEAK OF THE MESSIAH 343
   (Session Sixty-Eight) 343
   John the Baptist, a Preacher of Righteousness 343
   Elijah 344
   OT Prophecies of the Ministry of the Messiah 345
   Psalm 2:8-9 345
   II Samuel 7 346
   The Times of the Gentiles 346
   Psalm 93:2 346

Isaiah 9:7 347

Psalm 45:6 347

Hebrews 1:8 347

Revelation 22:16 348

Isaiah 53 with John 3:16 348

Acts 8:26-39 348

Romans 9:5 348

Isaiah 9:6 348

CHAPTER 68: THE OT AND THE NT SPEAK OF THE DIVINITY OF JESUS 351

(Session Sixty-Nine) 351

Isaiah 40:3 With Matthew 3:3 351

Isaiah 6:1 With John 12:41 351

Isaiah 53:1 With John 12:37-43 351

The "Rock" in Various OT Passages With 1 Cor. 10:4 & Other NT Passages 352

Genesis 49:10 With Psalm 2:7 354

Proverbs 30:4 With John 3:13 355

Isaiah 9:6 355

Daniel 3:23, 25 355

CHAPTER 69: I. JEHOVAH AS SHOWN IN THE OT IS COMPARED WITH JESUS AS SHOWN IN THE NT 357

(Session Seventy) 357

First, the Unchanging Nature of Jehovah: Psa. 102:24-27 With Heb. 1:10-12 357

Second, A Messenger Goes Before Him: Isa. 40:1-4 357

Zacharias Prophesied About John, the Baptist: Luke 1:68-76 358

Third, Jesus Fulfills those OT Statements In His Own Actions: Jer. 17:10 358

Revelation 2:23 358

Fourth, Jesus Fulfills the Statements About Light and Glory From the OT 359

Isaiah 60:19 359

Luke 2:32 & John 1:9 359

Revelation 21:23 359

Fifth, Jesus Fulfills the Statements of Temptation 359

Numbers 21:6-7 Is Considered. 359

John 3:14 360

1 Timothy 2:5 360

TABLE OF CONTENTS

Sixth, Jesus Is Called the "Stone of Stumbling" 360
Isaiah 8:13-14 With 1 Peter 2:7-8 360
Seventh, Jesus Fulfills the OT Statements as Shepherd 361
Luke 18:19 & Hebrew 13:20 With John 10:18 361
1 Peter 5:4 361
Eighth, Jesus Fulfills the OT Statements That He Seeks and Saves the Lost 361
Ezekiel 34:11-12 With Luke 19:10 362
Jer. 2:13 & 17:13 With John 4:10 & 17:13 362

CHAPTER 70: II. JEHOVAH AS SHOWN IN THE OT IS COMPARED WITH JESUS AS SHOWN IN THE NT 363

(Session Seventy-One) 363
First, Jehovah In the OT and Jesus In the NT are From Everlasting 363
Second, Both Shall Remain Even After Heaven and Earth Perish 363
Third, Jehovah and Jesus Are From the Beginning 364
Fourth, Jehovah and Jesus Speak of Themselves as Being The First 365
Fifth, Jehovah and Jesus Are The Creator 365
Sixth, Jehovah and Jesus Are the Supporter and the Preserver 366
Seventh, Jehovah and Jesus Are Unchanging 366
Eighth, Jehovah and Jesus Are Almighty 366
Ninth, Jehovah and Jesus Are to Whom the Angels Cry 367
Tenth, Jehovah and Jesus Are Righteous 367
Eleventh, Jehovah and Jesus Are the Only Savior 367
Twelfth, Jehovah and Jesus Are Above All 368
Thirteenth, Jehovah and Jesus Are to Whom Every Knee Shall Bow 368
Fourteenth, Jehovah and Jesus Are the Last 368

Chapter 71: THE SCRIPTURES DECLARE THAT JESUS IS DIVINE 369

(Session Seventy-Two) 369
Jesus Is God 369
Isaiah 9:6-7 369
The Divinity of Christ 370
Matthew 1:23: Emmanuel 370
Melchizedek 370
Matthew 18:20 372
John 1:1 372

John 1:14 373
John 1:18 373
Monogenes 373
John 5:23 374
John 8:56 374

CHAPTER 72: JESUS IS THE ANOINTED KING 375
(Session Seventy-Three) 375
John 12:45: He That Seeth Me Seeth Him That Sent Me 375
Acts 17:22-27: How Paul Preached 376
Romans 1:3, 4: Jesus Declared to Be the Son of God 376
Romans 1:20: Jesus Eternal Power as God 377
Romans 9:5: Jesus Is God 377
1 Corinthians 12:4-6: Jesus is One of the Trinity and Thus God 378
Philippians 2:6: Speaks of the Kenosis of Christ 378

CHAPTER 73: JESUS IS THE IMAGE OF THE INVISIBLE GOD 379
(Session Seventy-Four) 379
When We Look at Jesus We See the Person of God Who Is Invisible 379
Colossians 1:15-17 379
Jesus Is the Author of All Creation 379
Is There Nothing That God Cannot Do? 379
All Things Were Created *For* Him 380
The Disconnect of Humanity to the Realities of the Spiritual 380
All Things Consist by the Power of Jesus 380
New *Translations* on the Market Have Changed This Verse 380
Titus 2:13 381
The Phrase "Great God and Our Saviour" Apply As One to "Jesus Christ 381
Hebrews 1:3 381
The Brightness of the Glory of God Emanates from Jesus, Himself 381
Hebrews 1:8 382
Wrong Interpretations 382
A Phrase Shows Jesus to be Divine in His Very Being and Existence 383
The Theories of "Theistic Evolution" and "Deism" Fall by the Wayside 383
Hebrews 1:8-14: The Messiah Will Have an Eternal Throne and Dominion 383

Chapter 74: JESUS WAS GOD IN THE FLESH 385

TABLE OF CONTENTS

    (Session Seventy-Five) 385
    Hebrews 2:14: The Self-Existent Jesus Took On Flesh and Blood 385
    The Mystery of Godliness 385
    Hebrews 3:1-4: The Apostle and High Priest 385
    The Ultimate Builder 385
    1 John 5:7: The Verse, One of the Clearest Statements, Was In the Early Writings 386
    1 John 5:20: The True God and Eternal Life 386
    John 1:4: In Him Was Life 386
    Revelation 1:8: The Beginning and the conclusion 386
    Revelation 4:8: Note the Singular Verb 387
    Matthew 3:17: The Special Connectedness of Jesus and the Father 387
    Three Instances Where the Son Is Specifically Called God 387

Chapter 75: THE TRUTH OF HIS DIVINITY 389
    (Session Seventy-Six) 389
    Some Facts About Jesus Which Point to His Deity 389
    The Times of the Nations 389
    Second, Scriptural Prophecies Concerning Jesus 389

CHAPTER 76: CIRCUMSTANTIAL EVIDENCE THAT POINTS TO THE DIVINITY OF JESUS 395
    (Session Seventy-Seven) 395
    Mark 6:2-3: Jesus Came From Relative Obscurity 395
    Jesus Came from Adversity and Opposition 395
    Real Authority Comes From the Words of God 396
    Jesus Is the Word of God and Is God and Therefore the Real Authority 396
    Jesus Is the Spirit of Prophecy 396
    Jesus Lived a Sinless Life 398
    Jesus Became Sin, He Was Not a Sinner 398
    Dr. DeWitt's Commentary on Luke 16:19 399
    The Sinlessness of Jesus Proves His Divinity and Saves Our Souls! 400

CHAPTER 77: THE MIRACLES WHICH JESUS PERFORMED POINT TO THE FACT OF HIS DIVINITY 403
    (Session Seventy-Eight) 403
    Several Reasons to Believe Jesus Is Divine 403
    The Miracles 403
    The Fulfilled Prophecies About Jesus 403

Must Consider That Jesus Said He Was Divine 404

Most Important Is the Fact of His Resurrection 404

The Attributes of Jesus Illustrate That He Is God 405

CHAPTER 78: THE IMPORTANCE OF THE SONSHIP OF JESUS 407

(Session Seventy-Nine) 407

Several Examples 407

First, The Sonship Is Important to Our Understanding of the Trinity 407

Second, The Concept of the Eternal Sonship of Jesus Is Very Important 408

Third, The Sonship Is Important to Jesus' Sinlessness 408

Fourth, The Sonship of Jesus Is Important to Jesus' Ability to Save Sinners 409

Things Inferred, Stated, or Contained Within Any Denial of the Sonship of Jesus .. 409

First, To Deny the Sonship Is to Call God a Liar 409

Second, The Severity of Refusing to Accept Jesus as the Son of God 410

Third, To Deny the Sonship Is to Die in Sin 410

Fourth, Even the Demons Admit That Jesus Is Divine 411

Fifth, The Delegation of Power By Jesus Is A Sign of His Deity 412

CHAPTER 79: THE FACTS OF JESUS' LIFE AND BIRTH POINT TO THE FACT THAT HE IS DIVINE 413

(Session Eighty) 413

Fact One, The First Prophecy of Jesus Points to His Deity 413

Fact Two, The Names of Jesus Are the Names of God 414

Fact Three, Jesus Would Do a Perfect and Supernatural Work 414

Fact Four, The Eternality of Jesus Is a Statement of His Full Deity 415

Fact Five, The Announcements of His Birth Were Supernatural Events 416

Fact Six, Jesus Came Into the World In "the Fullness of Time" 417

CHAPTER 80: WHY WE BELIEVE IN THE DEITY OF CHRIST 419

(Session Eighty-One) 419

The Supernatural Star 419

The Temptation of Jesus 420

John the Baptist's Announcement 420

The Compassionate, Sinless, Sacrifice of Himself Displayed Love 420

Jesus Never Wavered 421

Jesus Never Dismissed the Words of the OT 421

Jesus Unsurpassed Understanding of Scripture 421

TABLE OF CONTENTS

    The Lord of the Sabbath 422
    Jesus Proclaims the Preservation of the Scripture 422
    Supernatural Miracles 423
    His Knowledge of Future Events: The Divine Mind and Power of Jesus 423
    The Prophecy of His Triumphal Return 423
    The Betrayal 423
    The Future Kingdom 424
    Disciples Scattered 424
    His Return 424
    The Understanding of the Rotating Earth 424
    The Warning About Persecution 424
    The Manner of His Death 425

CHAPTER 81: OTHER PROOFS THAT JESUS WAS GOD 427
    (Session Eighty-Two) 427
    Jesus' Resurrection Is Incontrovertible Proof of His Deity 427
    Jesus' Flesh Was A "Temple" Where God Dwelt 427
    Even the Death of Christ Is Proof of His Divinity 427
    More Comments On Jesus' Resurrection 428
    Over 520 Individuals Saw Jesus After He Rose From the Dead 428
    Jesus' Present Life Saves Us From Sin 428
    Jesus' Ability to Forgive Sin 428
    Forgiveness Is Proof of the Divinity of Jesus 429

BIBLIOGRAPHY 431
OUTLINE STUDIES 435
    In The Deity of Jesus, The Christ 435
    Prepared, 1989, by Dr. E. E. DeWitt, D.D. 435
    Revised 2012 435

ABOUT THE AUTHOR 477
INDEX OF WORDS AND PHRASES 479

FOREWORD
(Session One)

We begin today a study in the Person of Jesus Christ. We will look at the historical references to His Divine nature. Most importantly, we will also look into the Scriptural record of His Divine nature. There are many views of Jesus and His nature within history; some of these are heretical while the majority of them are based on the Scriptural record.

The important thing to understand is that our beliefs and conjectures are not in the end result very important. What is of utmost importance is "What saith the Scripture." That is where our study will go. Upon the Rock of Scripture is where our study will rest.

This study was prepared some years ago to be used in the television ministry of Dr. E. E. DeWitt. As such the study was intended to be as understandable as possible. "Big words," or theological jargon, were kept to a minimum and are explained where such terms were used. The intent was to make this study usable for the student of the Bible irrespective of his or her educational background. It is our intention of course that the educational background might be stronger from a theological standpoint after this study is completed.

The outline being used contains the following chapter headings.

What the Churches Say
Terms
Jesus: The Son of God
Jesus as The Angel of the Lord
gods With a Small "g"
God: He is One
God: He is Plural
The Dual Nature of Jesus
His Voluntary Submission
The Glorification of Jesus
Jesus Has the Attributes of Deity
The Authority of Jesus
The Eternality of Jesus
Jesus is the Creator
The Personality of Jesus
Jesus Admits His Divinity
Others Admit to the Deity of Jesus
The Prophets Speak of the Messiah
The Old Testament, and the New Testament, Speak of the Divinity of Jesus
The Scriptures Declare that Jesus is Divine
The Truth of His Divinity

This study will also, of necessity, speak of the nature of God.

Some things are hard to understand. God speaks to us from the vantage point of eternity and Spirit. We are beings of time and physicality. As such, we are prone to accept that which we are able to fully understand and to reject that which differs from our natural frame of references. True Christianity, however, is a medium of faith. We are to accept what God says as Ultimate Truth even when we have problems grasping the content of that Truth.

A few weeks after I had left the war zone of South Viet Nam in 1969, I was home in the kitchen of our apartment. As I reached for the cookie jar my wife decided to sneak up behind me and scare me. She, as a civilian, could have not understood what war was like. She could not have understood the defense mechanisms which were built into a soldier in a time of war. But, she began to understand rather abruptly that one must not sneak up upon a soldier less than a month removed from a war zone.

We cannot understand all the things which God has for us. Besides the above references to time/eternity and physicality/Spirit, we are creatures born with a nature which is blinded by the fact of sin. As we go through this study I would caution that you not believe something is so simply because I wrote a sentence. Check all the Scriptural references. Only God is Truth and that Truth has been given to us in His inspired and preserved Words.

It is my intention to keep each session short at an easily digestible amount of words for the average person of the twenty-first century. Further length would detract from the value of what was written.

CHAPTER 1
WHAT THE CHURCHES SAY
(Session Two)

When I propose to write about "What The Churches Say" about the Divinity of Jesus in today's section I intend to be very broad in my definition of "Church."

Meaning of the Word: Church

The meaning of the word we use, "Church," comes from a New Testament word which describes "a called out assembly of persons." In a sense, my unit in the Viet Nam War was a "church" by the New Testament definition. The group which assailed Paul at Ephesus was a "church" by the New Testament definition. A group of juror's called out of the general population to determine the guilt or innocence of a man at a trial is a "church" by the New Testament definition.

In general society our use of the term Church is defined from an ecclesiastical dictionary rather than a strict Biblical understanding. We use the term to define denominations, groups of various denominations (as in "the church world") and even the building where the people meet to worship together on a Lord's Day morning.

The Real Definition of a Church

The real definition of a church, in the religious sense, is that it is a body of believers whom God has called out of the general population. They have been given the purpose to fulfill the Great Commission. Rightly speaking, with the literal interpretation of the word, we can have local churches but we can have no "Church."

A true church, Biblically speaking, is a local group of believers who have banded together, under God, with the express purpose of worshiping Him in a corporate body and taking His teachings and message out into the larger world.

I wrote the above just so I would not confuse anyone with a false description of the concept of "Church" as I, somewhat, misuse it here. My purpose here is to speak of the broad concept of "the church world" and note how various organizations which are religious, specifically Christian, in nature have viewed the Person of Jesus.

For the most part I am simply going to list the writings of these various groups. I will not attempt to add my comment, except as it may be necessary to explain some term, as it would be superfluous to the discussion.

The Historical Church

First, Cole (*Basic Christian Faith*) describes the testimony of the historical church. From the Council of Chalcedon 451 AD:

> "We acknowledge one and the same Christ so to be perfect God and perfect man; of the same substance with the Father as regards His Godhead, and of the same substance with us as regards His manhood - in all things like unto us, sin only excepted; begotten of the Father from everlasting, but in the last days born of the Virgin; subsisting of separation; the distinction between the natures not being destroyed by the union, but each preserving its own properties and both culminating in one Person and Hypostasis: one and the same Christ, not divided into two Persons."

From the early part of the 20th century, in a series of position papers which shaped early Fundamentalism (*The Fundamentals*), Prof. Benjamin B. Warfield, D.D., LL.D., wrote the section on "The Deity of Christ."

> Luke 15:10 - In answering the Pharisees murmurings at His meetings with sinners, Jesus points out that the very nature of the Heavenly, which He Himself is, is to meet and call sinners.

The Liturgical Churches

Second, about the testimony of liturgical churches, Cole (*Basic Christian Faith*) again writes:

> From the Thirty-ninth Article of the Church of England, 1563: "The son, which is the Word of the Father, begotten from everlasting of the Father, the very and eternal God, and of one substance with the Father, took man's nature in the womb of the Blessed Virgin, of her substance, so that the two whole and perfect natures, that is to say, the Godhead and manhood, were joined together in one Person, never to be divided."

From the Westminster Confession of Faith:

"The Son of God, the second Person of the Trinity, being very and eternal God, of one substance, and equal with the Father, did, when the fullness of time was come, take upon him man's nature, with all the essential properties and common infirmities thereof, yet without sin, being conceived by the power of the Holy Ghost, in the womb of the Virgin Mary, of her substance. So that the two whole, perfect, and distinct natures, as Godhead and manhood, were inseparably joined together in one person, without conversion, composition, or confusion, which is the very God and very man, yet one Christ, the only Mediator between God and Man."

The Lutheran Church

Luther's Small Catechism sets forth the teaching of the Lutheran Church. This volume says:

> "I believe that Jesus Christ is true God because the Scriptures ascribe to Him A. Divine names... B. Divine Attributes... C. Divine Works... D. Divine honor and glory."

Further, Luther's Small Catechism argues that it is necessary that Christ be Divinity so that:

A. His fulfilling of the Law would be efficacious for all men (Ps. 49:7-8; Rom. 5:19).

B. His life and death would be sufficient for our redemption (Mk. 10:45),

C. He could defeat both death and Satan (II Tim. 1:10; Heb. 2:14; I Cor. 15:57)

The Orthodox Church

Coniaris (*Introducing the Orthodox Church: Its Faith and Life*) speaks of the Orthodox Church:

> "Jesus is Lord - absolute and undisputed creator and possessor of the entire universe... When the title 'Christ' (meaning the Anointed One or the Messiah) is applied to Jesus it becomes a confession of faith indicating our faith that Jesus, the Son of God, the Second Person of the Trinity, is the Messiah."

CHAPTER 1: WHAT THE CHURCHES SAY

The Testimony of the Pentecostal Church

Third, the testimony of the Pentecostal Church. The Full Gospel Christian Church Constitution and By-Laws, state:

> "The Full Gospel Christian Church gladly accepts the fact that the Bible emphatically and unequivocally teaches the union of three (3) persons in the Godhead, correctly called in theology, the Trinity. The Three (3) persons of the Godhead are (1) God, The Father, (2) Jesus Christ, The Son, (3) The Holy Spirit, The Comforter."

In "The Pentecostals," Nichol writes, in Statement number 2 from the Statement of Truth adopted by the Pentecostal Fellowship of North America:

> We believe that there is one God, eternally existent in three persons: Father, Son and Holy Ghost."

The Testimony of the Baptist Churches

Fourth: the testimony of Baptist Churches. A special note here: Properly speaking, there is no Baptist denomination. There may be Conventions and Associations, but no denominations. One of the hallmarks of the Baptist movement is that each church is independent and accountable only to God.

Under Article of faith "a," the New Hyde Park Baptist Church Articles of Faith assert that:

> "We believe that the Godhead eternally exists in three persons: Father, Son and Holy Spirit, and that these three are One God."

The Confession of Faith of the Leonard Street Baptist Church states that:

> "We believe that there is (a) one, and only one, living and true God, an infinite, intelligent Spirit, the maker and supreme ruler of the heaven and the earth; (b) inexpressibly glorious in holiness, and worthy of all possible honor, confidence and love; (c) that in the unity of the Godhead there are three persons, the Father, the Son, and the Holy Ghost, equal in every divine perfection, and executing distinct but harmonious offices in the great work of redemption...(C) Matt. 28:19; John 15:26; I Cor. 12:4-6; I John 5:7; John 10:30; 17:5; Acts 5:3-4; Phil. 2:5-6; Eph. 2:18; II Cor. 13:14."

The Constitution and Articles of Faith of the General Association of the Regular Baptist Churches affirms that:

> "...in the unity of the Godhead there are three persons, the Father, the Son and the Holy Spirit, equal in every divine perfection, and executing distinct but harmonious office in the great work of redemption (Exod 20:2,3; I Cor. 8:6; Rev. 4:11)."

Bogard (*The Baptist Way Book*) says:

> "We believe... that in the unity of the Godhead there are three persons, the Father, the Son, and the Holy Spirit; (Matt. 28:19; John 15:26) equal in every divine perfections (John 10:30), and executing distinct but harmonious offices in the great work of redemption. (Eph. 2:18; II Cor. 13:14)

Cross (*What is the American Baptist Association?*) has listed under "Belief's," at number 5,

> "The Deity of Jesus Christ."

The Testimony of Other Various Protestant Churches

Fifth: the testimony of other various Protestant churches.

The Constitution of the Berean Fundamental Church lists Article of Faith, number II.

"We believe that the Godhead Eternally exists in three persons: the Father, the Son, and the Holy Spirit. These three are one God, having precisely the same nature, attributes, essence and perfections, and worthy of precisely the same homage, confidence and obedience. (Mark 12:29; Gen. 1:26; Matt. 28:19; John 14:16, 17, 26; II Cor. 13:14)"

"This is the Church of the God of Prophecy" says that:

"The trinity is recognized as one Supreme Godhead in three persons - the Father, the Son, and the Holy Ghost."

In a tract, "Have You Ever Walked Through These Doors?," The Missionary Church asserts that:

"We believe that Jesus Christ was and is both God and man, and that He came to earth in the form of a man to pay the penalty of sin. By faith in His sacrificial death, man is forgiven of his sin and is reunited into fellowship with God."

In an 1891 book, *"The Iowa Yearly Meetings of Friends Book of Discipline"* the Friends affirm that:

"Meetings on Ministry and Oversight shall be careful to recommend no one to be recorded as a minister or elder whose doctrinal view are not clearly in accord with the affirmation of the following question. [Question number 3] Did thou believe in the Deity and Manhood of the Lord Jesus Christ...?"

The 1968 Book of Discipline of the United Methodist Church, says that:

"The Son, who is the Word of the Father, the very eternal God, of one substance with the Father, took man's nature in the womb of the blessed Virgin; so that two whole and perfect natures, that is to say the Godhead and Manhood, were joined together in one person, never to be divided; whereof is one Christ, very God and very Man..."

The 1972 Discipline of the Wesleyan Church agrees that:

"There is but one living and true God, everlasting, of infinite power, wisdom and goodness; the Maker and Preserver of all things, visible and invisible. And in unity of this Godhead there are three persons of one substance, power, and eternity - the Father, the Son (the Word), and the Holy Ghost. (Gen 1:1; 17:1; Ex. 3:13-15; 33:20; Deut. 6:4; Ps. 90:2; 104:24; Isa. 9:6; Jer 10:10; John 1:1-2; 4:24; 5:18; 10:30; 16:13; Acts 5:3-4; Rom. 16:27; I Cor 8:4, 6; II Cor. 13:14; Eph. 2:18; Phil. 2:6; Col. 1:16; I Tim. 1:17; I John 5:7, 20; Rev. 19:13)."

Ludwig (Manual of the Church of the Nazarene) writes that:

"We believe in Jesus Christ, the Second Person of the Triune Godhead; that He was eternally one with the Father..."

The Testimony of Para-church Agencies

Sixth: the testimony of para-church agencies.

Doctrinal Statement number 2 of the Chosen Peoples Ministries says:

"We believe in the Triune nature of the one true God, and in the Deity of the Lord Jesus Christ, the only begotten Son of God, born of a virgin."

The Prison Fellowship Statement of Faith declares,

"We believe in one God, Creator and Lord of the Universe, the co-eternal Trinity: Father, Son and Holy Spirit... We believe that Jesus Christ... [is] truly God and truly man..."

CHAPTER 1: WHAT THE CHURCHES SAY

The Statement of Faith of the Toledo Home Fellowship contains these words:

> "We believe in the Trinity of the Father, Son and the Holy Spirit, one God and Creator of all things, seen and unseen. (Matt 28:19; I John 5:7)"

Billy Graham's *"A Biblical Standard for Evangelists,"* gives the following standard:

> "The proof that Jesus was Who He said He was is: His perfect life (He was without sin); His power over nature at the storm on Galilee (Matt. 8:23-27), over sickness and death; the prophecies which were fulfilled in His life; His resurrection from the dead; and, the lives that have been changed by Him."

The Testimonies of the Faithful

Seventh: the result of the testimonies of the faithful argue for the divinity of Jesus. Read (*The Christian Faith*) went so far as to assert that:

> "...Christianity is Christ..." This is a completely reasonable statement. If we were to remove reference to Christ our "Christianity" would be no more than another philosophy for living life in this world. Eternal Salvation comes through Jesus. Without Him we have no faith, no hope, no reason for the existence of the Christian churches.

May (*Christian Unity*) argues for the truth of the divinity of Jesus as the linchpin of the entire Christian faith:

> "Christian unity demands acceptance of His perfect deity and at the same time His perfect humanity... Jesus' mother, Mary, is a bona fide member of the human race, and His Father, God, is the one, true, and living God... [Those] who consider Him to be a great prophet and the greatest teacher who ever lived, but deny His deity, are not eligible for Christian Fellowship. Likewise, those who consider Jesus to be divine but who deny His humanity are also ineligible to be a part of the Christian community."

This week's session has probably seemed somewhat tedious and dry. It was, after all, simply a recitation of various Statements of Faith. This was groundwork. But, it was important groundwork. I hope that we have shown that the acceptance of the Deity of Jesus is not an aberrant doctrinal point. This is a doctrine which is central to the historic Christian faith.

Also, the various doctrinal statements have given a wealth of Scriptural references to bolster the argument for the Deity of Jesus. We can say anything we want; it is the Scripture which is the final authority on faith and practice for the Christian.

The Testimony of 1 John 5:7

As an aside, I John 5:7 was mentioned several times as a proof text on the Deity of Jesus. Many have dismissed this verse as a "gloss;" as something added which is not part of the true Body of Scripture. They are wrong!

The following is added in regards to this verse from my own work on inspiration:

> This session will concern itself with I John 5:7. I would like to give this verse in its immediate context below. I will underline the seventh verse.
>
> *"Who is he that overcometh the world, but he that believeth that Jesus is the son of God? This is he that came by water and blood, even Jesus Christ; not by water only, but by water and blood. And it is the Spirit that beareth witness, because the Spirit is truth. <u>For there are three that bear record in heaven, the Father, the word, and the Holy Ghost: and these three are one.</u> If we receive the witness of men, the*

witness of God is greater: for this is the witness of God which he hath testified of his Son." (I John 5:5-8)

As we look at the extended passage we will see that verses five and six make mention of the Trinity. In verse five Jesus is mentioned as "the Son of God;" this is a mention, albeit by inference, of the Father. Verse six picks up on the point of the miraculous incarnation. This verse also speaks of the "third" member of the Trinity in that it says that the Spirit gives His witness to these facts.

Verse seven, the verse in question, is an outright affirmation of the Trinity.

Verse eight speaks of three witnesses on earth that bear witness to the same Truth, that of the incarnation of Jesus. These three are the Spirit, the water which is an intimation of the physical birth of Jesus, and the blood which is an intimation of the divine pre-existence of Jesus, which is once again an intimation of the Father.

This is three instances of mention of the Trinity of the Godhead. This just seems an interesting formula to me. The formula also, as it appears here, is the belief of the churches on earth, as based in the reality in Heaven. We are then, in the final verse, given the fact that the witness of Heaven is even greater than the witness of man on earth.

This is a verse, however, which has been under constant attack in "church" circles. Some of the reasons for the attack are, I would believe, quite valid. Still, I accept this verse as part of the preserved Words of God.

Most of the information I will present here is a defense of the verse from the negative. "It is because something lacks in the dismissal." This is a concept which bothers me. Some of the facts presented, quite frankly, concern me.

It is at times like this that I must resort to "Jonah faith." Jonah was a man who was called of God to do a specific task. Jonah didn't want to perform that task. His entire cultural upbringing and rational argued that this was the wrong thing to do. Jonah ran from the call of God. God had "prepared a great fish" (Jonah 1:17) and Jonah was prepared as a great fish food.

God got the attention of Jonah. Jonah did that which he was called to do. But, as we read the Book of Jonah we will see that Jonah never did get around to agreeing with God. I have always considered this a great act of faith. Even though Jonah did not agree with God, Jonah did the bidding of God. Even when everything in his life said "NO!," Jonah acted simply because, well with a little prodding, God had said "YES!"

Folks, that is great faith. When everything we've ever learned argues against doing the known will of God, we need to do it anyway. God said so. That settles it.

What it all boils down to is that I accept this verse as part of the Scripture simply because this verse is included in the Scripture which bears the stamp of the approval and preservation of God.

Hills (The King James Version Defended [pp. 212-213]) argues for the verse. There are manuscripts which do not contain this verse. Of them Hills would argue that, if, during the 2nd and 3rd centuries, this phrase were dropped through carelessness, it might be continued to be omitted because of the Sabellian heresy. The Sabellian's held that the members of the Trinity are identical; they are but different views of the One Being, rather than the orthodox view that, while The Members of the Trinity are of the same *essence*, They are individual Personalities. The orthodox would see the copies which contained this phrase as being favorable to the heresy of the Sabellian and would consider those which did not contain it to be the pure text.

CHAPTER 1: WHAT THE CHURCHES SAY

We often use the illustration of the Trinity that it is like a man who is a father, husband, and son. He is the same man in whatever place he stands. It is just that he is viewed in different lights by different people. This is not, however, an accurate representation of the Trinity. If it were we would have the absurdity of Jesus praying to Himself in the Gospels. At the stoning of Stephen we would see Jesus sitting at His Own right hand.

Granted, if God said that those things were true in the Spiritual realm, they would be true. But, we understand the Trinity to be three distinct Persons Who are of One Essence. In John 1:1 we read, "In the beginning was the Word, and the Word was with God, and the Word was God." The picture here is of two equals sitting face to face.

When we speak of the Trinity, as it is revealed in the Bible, we are often at a loss to explain a concept of Spirit and Eternity as we work within the confines of the physical and of time. There are things we will not understand until we are passed from this existence into our eternal existence. "For *as* the heavens are higher than the earth, so are my ways higher than your ways, and my thoughts than your thoughts." (Isaiah 55:9)

A better illustration of the concept of the Trinity might be sitting near me right now. It is a simple cup of coffee with sugar and cream. The three elements are distinct elements. I can taste them each as I drink the coffee. But, they are joined together to produce just one beverage. They are inseparable even as they are diverse.

This is an admittedly poor illustration. But, it is the best I have to offer for us to consider the Spiritual things of God with our finite minds.

Faith remains the medium of the Christian.

Hills [p. 210] also argues that the "Johannine comma" might have actually dropped out of the Greek manuscripts only to be preserved by the Western Church in the Latin Text. "...on the basis of the external evidence it is at least possible that the *Johannine comma* is a reading that somehow dropped out of the Greek New Testament text but was preserved in the Latin Text..."

> "It is found in r an Old Latin manuscript of the 5th or 6th century, and in the **Speculum**, a treatise which contains the Old Latin text. It was not included in Jerome's original edition of the Latin Vulgate, but around the year 800 it was taken into the text from the Old Latin manuscripts...[p. 210]"

It is very important to note of the above. This verse was not originally in Jerome's Vulgate. It was, however, in a writing which was based on the Old Latin text. The Old Latin Vulgate, the word "Vulgate" simply meaning "common," and was applied to a translation made around 157 A.D., would give the verse the imprimatur of antiquity. Such a translation, obviously a translation of an even older document, would argue for Apostolic authority for the verse.

Hills further argues in the negative for the inclusion of the verse in our Bibles today.

> "If the *comma* originated in a trinitarian interpretation of I John 5, why does it not contain the usual trinitarian formula, namely, the Father, the *Son*, and the Holy Spirit? Why does it exhibit the singular combination never met with elsewhere, the Father, the *Word*, and the Holy Spirit? According to some critics, the unusual phraseology was due to the efforts of the interpolator who first inserted the *Johannine Comma* into the New Testament text. In a mistaken attempt to imitate the style of the Apostle John, he changed the term *Son* into the term *Word*. But this is to attribute to the interpolation, which was

> surely to uphold the doctrine of the Trinity, including the eternal generation of the Son, a flawed concept. With this as the main concern, of any supposed forger of the verse, it is very unlikely that he would abandon the time-honored formula, Father, *Son*, and Holy Spirit, and devise an altogether new one, Father, *Word*, and Holy Spirit. [p. 209]"

This argument from the negative is that, if a forger had wanted to make this verse only *seem* to be part of the original, he would not have written it as it is written. A forger who wanted his fake money to be accepted would not substitute my picture on a one dollar bill for that of George Washington. Even though my hair is approaching the color of Mr. Washington's powdered wig, it would not be accepted.

Finally, Hills argues that God has worked with man, specifically through the Spirit's influence upon the churches, to preserve the Canon of Scripture.

> "...the Textus Receptus has both its human aspect and its divine aspect, like the Protestant Reformation itself or any other work of God's providence. And when we consider the manner in which the *Johannine Comma* entered the Textus Receptus, we see the human element at work. Erasmus omitted the *Johannine Comma* from his first edition (1516) of his printed Greek New Testament on the ground that it occurred only in the Latin version and not in any Greek manuscript. To quiet the outcry that arose, he agreed to restore it if but one Greek manuscript could be found which contained it. When one such manuscript was discovered soon afterwards, bound by his promise, he included the disputed reading and thus it gained a permanent place in the Textus Receptus. The manuscript which forced Erasmus to reverse his stand was written at Oxford about 1520 for the special purpose of refuting Erasmus, and this is what Erasmus himself suggested in his notes. [p. 209]"

Some have disputed the veracity of the story about the "specially prepared manuscript" above. The story, however, is unimportant. What is important is the great outcry about the lack of one verse. It seems that the Spirit of God moved upon the people of God in the churches of God in defense of the proper reading.

The Words of God have been preserved for us in exactly this manner. The true churches, peopled by the true Blood bought believers, have been gifted to "try the spirits." "Beloved, believe not every spirit, but try the spirits whether they are of God: because many false prophets are gone out into the world." (I John 4:1)

The Words of God had been preserved in many old manuscripts. A fresh supply of them flooded Europe after the fall of Constantinople. Those Words were brought into the Protestant Reformation. This was an area where the Latin of Jerome had held sway for hundreds of years. The dominant Roman Church had decreed that the populace could not have Bibles in their own languages. The Roman Church had kept the precious Words of God, the Words meant for all humanity, under the lock and key of Church control and tradition.

Now that a new day had dawned, the people wanted the True, and Pure, Words which God had inspired and preserved. I believe that the Spirit acted strongly upon the people to rescue the Words of this verse from power of Satan as he attempted to "downgrade" Jesus in the eyes of the people. A less than Divine Christ would be a false Christ. A false Christ would be a weak Christ in the eyes of the people. This could be used as a wedge to drive the emerging movement back into the error of Catholicism which proclaimed herself as the power of God on earth and her pontiff as the true representative of Christ, through the chair of Peter, on earth.

CHAPTER 1: WHAT THE CHURCHES SAY

In conclusion, many of the disputed passages are the result of copyist errors. The most common error was to see a word, or a set of words, on one line and then to look back after copying that passage and seeing same words or set of words at another place on the page. In this manner words, sentences, even paragraphs could be left out (or more uncommonly, copied twice) through fatigue or carelessness of the copyist. I have caught myself doing that very thing as I copy from my note cards onto these pages.

The point, here, is that it would be quite easy for a passage, such as I John 5:7, to be dropped from some manuscripts. It is not anywhere near as easy for a copyist to insert such a passage.

[*God Keeps His Word*; E. E. DeWitt; Wordclay; Bloomington, IN; 2009; *The King James Version Defended*, Edward F. Hills; The Christian Research Press; Des Moines, IA; 1984]

We would also do well to consider that the verse was quoted as Scripture by some of the early "Church Fathers." This is not to claim that their works were inspired. Far from that, but this does give evidence when one such as Tertullian (*Apology, Against Praxeas*) makes reference to the verse in @ 200 A.D. we must admit that the verse was in current use prior to that time.

In our next session we will begin to look at some of the terms of our study.

CHAPTER 2
TERMS
(Session Three)

Hopefully this section will be a little more interesting than the last section. In our last section we simply looked at what the various church statements of faith had said about the Divinity of Jesus. It was a necessary section, used to establish that the Deity of Christ is not an aberrant doctrine. The doctrine is, rather, one of the foundational doctrines of the entire historic Christian churches.

The Foundation of the Christian Faith

Lindsell (*Harper Study Bible*) says that the Deity of Jesus is the foundation of the Christian Faith. That it is. John 20:28 gives the great statement of Thomas upon seeing the risen Christ. The assessment is foundational to the Christian faith:

> "The deity of Christ is the foundation of the Christian faith. The denial of it invalidates the entire structure of Christian theology."

Indeed, I would question whether or not there can be any "Christian" theology which denies this cardinal doctrine. In our day, especially in this election season, we are confronted with a cultic "church" claiming that they are another branch of the Christian faith. This cult, Mormonism, was founded on the principle that, they believed, the entire Christian world was in apostasy and had been since very early in the existence of the churches.

Their "Christology" denies the absolute deity of Jesus. Since they teach that God was once a man, in a sort of parallel universe, or world, and *"became"* a god, Jesus is simply the "Spirit child" of this deity. This makes Jesus simply a god, with a small case "g," who is no more than another man in substance and potentiality.

This doctrinal stance, all by itself, is enough to deny that the Mormon Church is a Christian Church in the historic, and the Biblical, sense.

Josh McDowell (*Answers to Tough Questions*) argues for the special place which Jesus has, as an Individual and Deity, in the true Christian faith. The Deity of Jesus is the center of the Christian Faith.

> "Confucianism is a set of teachings; Confucius is not important. Islam is the revelation of Allah, with Mohammed being the prophet, and Buddhism emphasizes the principles of Buddha, not Buddha himself. This is especially true of Hinduism, where there is no historical founder. However, at the center of Christianity is the person of Jesus Christ. Jesus did not just claim to be teaching mankind the truth. He claimed that **He** was the Truth (John 14:6)."

The Hope of Christian Salvation

It is in the Deity of Jesus where the hope of Christian salvation resides. This is about as central a doctrine as there is in Christian theology. If Jesus were not Divine, it follows that He is only a man. In such a case His death cannot be substitutionary. If Jesus were simply another human being, He could only die for His own sins. He would not have the capacity to die for anyone else's sin.

If Jesus was not Divine He would be unable to atone for even His own sins. (He is Divine and He never committed any sin. This is a simple "supposition" in which we are engaging for the sake of argument.) Neither, in such a case, could He atone for the sins of anyone else. One born a sinner, as all are (The only exception to this is Jesus via the Virgin Birth!), can only die in his sins – never for his own sins or the sins of anyone else. Any act of an individual while in a state of sin becomes sin. This is true even of seemingly benign acts. (see Proverbs 21:4)

Any possible atonement must be made by one who is both sinless and has the "standing" to be a "representative" of the one to whom such atonement is proffered. Only Jesus, as the Divine/human substitute, can offer full atonement through His representative sacrifice.

If Jesus was not Divine then His teaching stems from a false basis of authority. Five times in the fifth chapter of Matthew Jesus says, "Ye have heard it said, but I say..." In doing this Jesus was claiming authority to teach even beyond the teaching of the religious leaders of the day and, more importantly, beyond the very Words of the received Scripture of the Old Testament. Jesus was displaying this authority by exercising His Divine right to illumine the true meaning of that Scripture.

In Mark 2:28 Jesus declares: *"Therefore the Son of man is Lord also of the sabbath."*

Jesus made the claim that even the Sabbath, the day dedicated especially to God, was under His control. He was the "ruler," if you will, of even the Sabbath.

In John 10:30 Jesus says: *"I and my Father are one."*

Now, there are those who make this verse to only read that Jesus and the Father are one in purpose. This wasn't the way the people of the day understood His Words. Verse thirty three records that, *"The Jews answered him, saying, For a good work we stone thee not; but for blasphemy; and because that thou, being a man, makest thyself God."*

This is a very clear statement. Jesus did not correct this view. Instead He called into question the religious leaders own understanding of God. But at no time did He back away from the argument that He and God were equal.

The point here is that Jesus claimed Divine authority for His teaching. Even at the Last Supper He noted that a New Testament was established in His Blood at the coming crucifixion. If Jesus were not Divine, His entire teaching stems from a false basis of authority.

This understanding, that if Jesus were not really God in the flesh, means that His entire leadership role is flawed. He is false; therefore, His teaching is false.

But, of course, such is not the case. Jesus is Divine and His teaching has the authority of Deity to undergird what it is He taught.

We must also argue that if Jesus were not Divine, He cannot be considered a good man. He cannot be considered to be a religious leader.

Jesus Taught That He Was Divine

Jesus taught that He was Divine. This is clear from just those few passages above. If He believed that He was Divine, and He was not, then He was insane. There is no moral compulsion to follow His ethical teaching if those teachings are based in the deluded mind of a mad man. There is no religious compulsion to follow His religious teachings if those teachings are based in the mind of a man who was not in control of

CHAPTER 2: TERMS

his own fantasies. His religious teachings would be false because they would not have the leading of the Spirit of God; rather those teachings would have insanity at their very base.

Jesus taught that He was Divine. It must be seen that if He knew that this was false He was guilty of deceiving the masses. His mind would then be clear of insanity, but his teaching would not be clear. His teaching would be flawed by His own flaw of character. The words of a liar cannot be trusted. The words of a liar cannot claim that they are true, except it be done to lead confusion into the minds of his listeners.

Such a one as this *cannot* lead anyone to the Truth of God. A person such as this might claim to lead people to God. But such cannot be the case. To disregard the truth about one's own person is to sin.

> "He that saith, I know him, and keepeth not his commandments, is a liar, and the truth is not in him." (I John 2:4)

Since, however, Jesus is Divine, He is God. Anyone who would disagree with this assessment is himself a liar of the first rank. This person who denies the full Deity of Jesus might not understand his own error. Sin may have darkened his mind. But, the truth remains that to teach the denial of the Divine nature of Jesus Christ is to teach error.

So what should we understand of those who reject the Divinity of Jesus? There are few issues that I could make about their statement, but I think the Bible compels us to consider that the acceptance or rejection of the Divinity of Jesus ought to be a test of fellowship.

The full Deity of Jesus Christ is such a seminal doctrine of Christianity that I cannot conceive the possibility that a person who would reject the full Deity of Jesus Christ could be considered a Christian in the Biblical sense of the word.

> "And every spirit that confesseth not that Jesus Christ is come in the flesh is not of God: and this is the spirit of antichrist, whereof ye have heard that it should come, and even now already is it in the world." (I John 4:3)

The Defining Doctrine

Commenting on the above verse, Spurgeon (*The Spurgeon Devotional Bible*) considers of the doctrine of the Divinity of Jesus as a defining doctrine for the Christian.

> "This is a very useful test in many cases. If any form of doctrine denies or dishonours the Godhead or Messiahship of the Lord Jesus, or makes his incarnation to be a mere myth, it is to be rejected with abhorrence. Errors which touch the person or work of Jesus are fatal."

The bottom line is that we are called to faith in the Person of Jesus, and of His substitutionary death on the Cross of Calvary, as a condition of our salvation and fellowship. If the view held of the Person of Christ is faulty, then the faith *cannot* reside in the true Person of Jesus. If Jesus is not accepted as Who He is, the faith so directed is not directed at Jesus.

It is true that there are those who do not accept the Divinity of Jesus. Zeoli (*Is Jesus God, Book Number One*) accepts that there are many who do not believe such. He notes that many also do not accept the Virgin Birth because it is often

> "...not believed by present day scholars."

That, Zeoli reminds us, is simply not the truth in its totality. There are many conservative scholars who do accept the Virgin Birth. By the same token, many conservative scholars do accept the Divinity of Christ.

The final fact is however, is that it does not matter what the "scholar" believes. What is important is where truth resides. Truth is truth simply because it is truth. We may firmly believe that the doctor is wrong when he tells us that we have a cancer. Our acceptance, or denial, of the fact of the cancer does not argue against the reality of the disease.

Lack of faith in the reality of the Person, and Deity, of Jesus Christ is a cancer which will doom our soul to an eternity far from His presence.

Those who accept the Bible must accept the Deity of Jesus Christ because the Bible teaches such is the truth. It is a simply matter of placing trust in the Biblical record as we place trust in the Savior.

Sure, such a happenstance as the Virgin Birth, and the Divinity of Jesus, are events beyond the scope of the natural human experience. That is certain. It has only happened on one occasion. But, when we accept the fact that God is the God of miracle, and of control of the events and times of human history, it is not a hard thing to consider the truth. When we consider that God is the creator of both the physical universe and the laws that operate therein, it is not a far stretch to believe that He is easily the God of Miracle.

When considering the Divinity of Jesus, the important point is not what one does, or does not, accept as doctrine. What is important is what God has said is true in His Own Book. Man's acceptance of this - simply put - is that we either take the Word of God as Truth or we accept the theory of man as truth.

It is true that worldly wisdom might not accept the Divinity of Jesus. Worldly wisdom is centered in the illusions of the physical and of time. The wisdom of God is centered in the realities of eternity and the spiritual.

The Wisdom of Man is Mere Foolishness

Orr (*Can We Be Sure That Jesus Is God?*) finds fault with the wisdom of man. The Scripture declares that the wisdom of man is mere foolishness.

> *"Professing themselves to be wise, they became fools." (Romans 1:22) "Where is the wise? where is the scribe? where is the disputer of this world? hath not God made foolish the wisdom of this world?" (I Corinthians 1:20)*

Orr also sees that the Scripture refers to the wisdom of man as a conceited wisdom. Conceit is a trait that is either unfounded or whimsical. It is not the wisdom of Truth.

> *"Be of the same mind one toward another. Mind not high things, but condescend to men of low estate. Be not wise in your own conceits." (Romans 12:16)*

Zeoli (*Is Jesus God – Book Number One*) says that those who trust in their own wisdom are deceived.

> *"For the wisdom of this world is foolishness with God. For it is written, He taketh the wise in their own craftiness." (I Corinthians 3:19)*

When man devises plans and theologies without regard to the revealed Words of God, he is playing a game he is destined to lose. It is a foolish game.

Orr (*Can We Be Sure That Jesus Is God?*) again notes the obvious when he says that the wisdom of God is above that of man.

> "If Jesus is not God, the world is irreparably lost. If He is not God, the entire structure of truth collapses. If He is not God, the Bible is a lie, the Gospel is a farce. And heaven is just a jest."

Praise God, such is not reality. Jesus is, as the Scripture declares, God in human flesh. He is our sacrifice, our perfect sacrifice, and He is our Savior.

There are many other false views of Jesus. We will begin to look at some of these in our next session.

CHAPTER 3
FALSE VIEWS OF JESUS
(Session Four)

Just Who Is Jesus

When we speak of Jesus we must consider just who He is. There are probably thousands of persons in the world who bear the name "Jesus." This is a fairly common name among the Latin population. When we speak of Jesus Christ we are speaking of Jesus, the Messiah. The point is that when we consider just Who Jesus is we are not, or should not be, defining Him. We should be acknowledging just Who He is in fact.

There are many who speak of a false Jesus because they have defined the name, "Jesus," to rest upon their concept of who they wish Him to be. We need to be specific on this point. A false view of Jesus will produce a false Christ. As only the True Christ can offer salvation to mankind, a false view must lead to damnation.

When Acts 4:12 says that there is no other name by which we must be saved, the concept of His Name is not a talisman. The name "Jesus" is not magic. The Name, properly used, is descriptive of the Savior.

This is really an important point. Any view which denies Jesus, Himself, to be just Who He Is, will give false views of other truths as well. Christianity, both as a religion and as a means of salvation begins rises and falls upon the Truth of the Person of Jesus Christ.

Bancroft (*Elemental Theology*) gives several false pictures of Jesus which have been held throughout the ages.

> "Cerinthianism held that there was no union of the two natures [of Jesus] until after baptism, thus establishing Christ's Deity upon His baptism rather than His birth."

This is a very common error in our day as well. When the phrase "The Christ Spirit" is used it will generally refer to this error. Under this reasoning, Jesus was only one of many "Ascended Masters." He is generally lumped, by this group, with such as Buddha, Zoroaster, Mohammed and others.

The Bible gives a different picture of Jesus. From His miraculous Virgin Birth, to His substitutionary death, and in His miraculous resurrection from the dead, Jesus is pictured as "One of a Kind." Nowhere does the Bible ascribe a Deity thrust upon Jesus. Deity was, and is, part of His essential nature.

Eutychianism

Eutychianism held that the two natures of Christ were mingled into one which was predominantly divine, though not the same as the original divine nature." This is a picture of a "lesser God" in the Person of Jesus. This view would deny Him His essential Deity even as it denies Him his full humanity. Either of these would disqualify Him from being the effective substitute for the sins of the world.

Nestorianism

Nestorianism denied the union of human and Divine natures, making Christ two persons." This very nearly lowers the concept of the duality of nature of Jesus into a sort of Divine Possession on the same order as demon possession. Again, such a view would not allow Jesus to be an actual representation of humanity. As such He could not have been our substitute as a sin bearer. This view would also deny Jesus the full extent of His Divinity in the body of human flesh. His death, as a human, would then be just that - a death of a human. He could not be the Savior of any other.

Apollianarianism

Apollianarianism made Christ only two parts human, denying to Him a human soul, which they claimed is sinful." Further, as the soul is that portion of human emotion, this would have meant that He could not have been actually tempted. Therefore He could not have actually defeated sin for us. Again, this would disqualify Him as our Savior.

Arianism

Arianism regarded Christ as the highest of created beings, thus denying His Deity and misinterpreting His temporary humiliation." The Bible teaches that all things were created by Jesus. He is the active force of creation. This being so, He could not have been a created being. As a created being He could not have been truly Divine.

If Jesus were only a created being, even the highest of the created beings, He would have been only a messenger of God on the order of the angels. Without that full, and essential, Deity from eternity past, He would not have had the ability to die in the place of another as more than a simple "sin bearer." He would not, then, be The "sin eradicator." Jesus destroyed the works of Satan, including the sin nature which is part of the human nature. Since He, Jesus, had no sin, He did this in our place as our substitute.

Without the full Deity which resided within and as Him, He could not have accomplished this work.

Ebionism

Ebionism denied the divine nature of Christ and held Him to be only man." This is also the view of most theological liberals. They are able to accept Jesus as a great teacher and religious leader. This view does not allow them to accept Him as Savior.

Docetism

Docetism denied the reality of Christ's body on the ground that His purity could not be linked with matter, which was thought by Docetists to be inherently evil." The body of humanity which was Jesus was without evil. While sin may have rested on others, the Virgin Birth allowed Jesus to be born as a human but without the defect of sin upon Himself. It was necessary that He be one of us, a human, in order to die for our sins.

There are also those few in our time who would argue that the Person of Jesus Christ never existed. They claim the entire concept was fable. This is not a reasonable assumption. The entire history of Western Civilization is bound to the fact that Jesus did exist. His death and resurrection were motivating factors for the spread of Christianity throughout the world in just a few centuries. Jesus is an historical fact.

More importantly, Jesus is the Savior of the World to those who would accept Him.

The one volume Commentary Practical and Explanatory on the Whole Bible, looks at Colossians 2:9, which says:

CHAPTER 3: FALSE VIEWS OF JESUS

"For in him dwelleth all the fulness of the Godhead bodily," and observes that Jesus is not simply "God-Like," He is God.

In our next session we will consider, and explain, some confusing terminology.

Chapter 4
Terminology Explained
(Session Five)

In this session we are going to look at some of the terminology used to explain the Person of Jesus Christ. Some of this terminology will be obvious. Some of it will be that which has often caused confusion to the person engaged in Bible study.

Jesus Christ

The first term is that which is used in His very Name: Jesus Christ. Jesus is His earthly Name. It is the Greek equivalent of the Old Testament name of Joshua. The name simply means "God with us." Well, that is Who He is in reality. The "Name" of Christ is actually a title. Christ means, "The anointed one." With reference to Jesus, this has to do with His Messiahship. He is, as Pilate wrote over the Cross, The King of the Jews. He is also, of course, the King over the Christian.

When we used the name, Jesus, with the title, Christ, we are referring to Him by his title and name. It is akin to saying, King David. The first name of David was not "King," of course. It is a way of differentiating King David from any other David. Jesus was a common name at the time of His earthly birth. To refer to Him as Jesus Christ is to differentiate Him from all others and to show respect for His Office.

Jesus is also referred to as "Son." There are several verses we need to see in relation to this fact.

> *"Concerning his Son Jesus Christ our Lord, which was made of the seed of David according to the flesh; and declared to be the Son of God with power, according to the spirit of holiness, by the resurrection from the dead." (Romans 1:3-4)*

The Son of David Versus The Son of God

The Commentary Practical and Explanatory on the Whole Bible, asks that we consider that Jesus was **made** the son of David but **declared** the Son of God. The former applies to His humanity while the latter refers to His Divinity.

The human body of Jesus was a "new" thing. He, Himself, is eternal. So, as the body was prepared within the womb of the Virgin, He became, or was made, the son of David. This refers to His earthly lineage. It is this human lineage which gives Him legal right to claim, and to accept, the Throne of the line of David. He is the King of the Jews by right of lineage.

But, as to the actual Person of Jesus, He was declared to be the Son of God. He was not "made" into the Son of God; He did not receive the "God Spirit" at any time. He simply was declared, it was said of Him - or it was noted about Him - would be another way to say the same thing, that He was the Son of God.

It was the Spirit that made this declaration. It was His resurrection which provided the proof of the declaration of the Holy Spirit.

The Humanity and Deity of Jesus

This simple passage destroys the arguments of those who claim that Jesus "became a god" at some point. He was declared to be that which He was. Also, those who would argue to His divinity and yet ignore His humanity are thereby answered. He was human even as He was, and is!, Divine.

> "And the angel answered and said unto her, The Holy Ghost shall come upon thee, and the power of the Highest shall overshadow thee: therefore also that holy thing which shall be born of thee shall be called the Son of God." (Luke 1:35)

Dake (*The Dake Annotated Bible*) says that Luke 1:35 speaks of this humanity of Christ as well as His Divinity:

> "Sonship with Christ always refers to humanity, not to deity. As God, He had no beginning (Mic. 5:2; Jn. 1:1-2); was not begotten or He would have had a beginning, was begotten, and was God's Son (Ps. 2:7, 12; Mt. 1:18; Lk. 1:35; Heb. 5:5)."

Scripture teaches that there was a day in history when the Father had a Son and the Son a Father. Yet the same Scripture teaches the eternality of the Son. Rather than a contradiction, this is a clear teaching of the Biblical concept of the dual nature of Jesus Christ. As God, the Son He is eternal; as the Son of God, He is human with beginning.

Not to "split hairs" with my source, but doing so anyway: I believe when the term "Son of God" is used that it does refer to the Divinity of Jesus. Properly speaking, from our human standpoint, there is a distinction between His Deity and His humanity in the terms "God, the Son" and "the Son of God." But both refer to His essential Deity. The term "son of man" (even though via the Virgin Birth He was the son of woman) more accurately refers to His humanity.

The Messiah

It's a matter of semantics. The bottom line is that Dake is correct. The verse does point out both the humanity and deity of Jesus.

> "But thou, Bethlehem Ephratah, though thou be little among the thousands of Judah, yet out of thee shall he come froth unto me that is to be the ruler of Israel; whose goings forth have been from of old, from everlasting." (Micah 5:2)

This verse is a prophecy of the coming Messiah. This coming One was to be the ruler, yet not the ruler as were other kings. It is said that his activity has been "from old." The meaning here is that of something in the most extreme of the distant past. Lest anyone miss the meaning a clause "from everlasting" is added. This ruler, Messiah, will be eternal in His essence. That little distinction can be made of no one but God, Himself. Any other person, or even heavenly or angelic being, would be created. To have existed from eternity is to place the attribute of God upon the Person so named.

The Word

> "In the beginning was the Word, and the Word was with God, and the Word was God. The same was in the beginning with God. All things were made by him; and without him was not any thing made that was made." (John 1:1-3)

I've added one verse beyond where Dake went. I believe that it makes the sense even more clearly about the full divinity of Jesus.

CHAPTER 4: TERMINOLOGY EXPLAINED

This passage does not say that the Word (Jesus) started at the beginning. The verse simply states that in the beginning Jesus was already existent. This verse, speaking of Jesus, is reminiscent of Genesis 1:1, "In the beginning God..." Both have the same frame of the nexus of time and eternity. Both say that deity existed at that point.

Only, of all the various versions, translations and commentaries that I have seen, the cult of the Jehovah's Witnesses make this verse say substantially anything different. They say that the Word became a god. This is a mistranslation made only for the sake of doctrine from their standpoint. The preserved Words of God refer to Jesus (the Word) as being God.

A prospective pastor at a church I attended once used this passage to indicate that Jesus was not eternal. He said that the passage only intimates that Jesus was in existence by the time the creation began. He made Jesus into a created god in his use of this verse. The problem with his view is that Jesus, the Son, is Himself called "God" in the passage. Under the understanding of this man the creation could not have happened because, again in his view, God was not created until creation began. Such a view removes the eternality of not only the Father but also of the Son. Such a view is heretical as well as indefensible from the spiritual point of view.

The Agent in All of Creation

The third verse speaks of the creation. Jesus was the active agent in all of creation. He, Himself, was not a created being.

> "I will declare the decree: the LORD hath said unto me, Thou art my Son, this day have I begotten thee. ... Kiss the Son, lest he be angry, and ye perish from the way, when his wrath is kindled but a little. Blessed are all they that put their trust in him" (Psalm 2:7 & 12)

This passage is another Messianic prophecy. It speaks of the human nature of Jesus. This has to do with His kingship as the verses immediately following proclaim. I see this verse as having millennial implications as well. The kiss could refer to either a person's love for Jesus, or for the reverence extended toward a monarch. I would argue for the latter at this point as his wrath, especially in the Old Testament, speaks of judgment. Those who are blessed are they that have trusted Him. For the Christian, the judgment is past in regard to eternal salvation.

> "Now the birth of Jesus Christ was on the wise: When as his mother Mary was espoused to Joseph, before they came together, she was found with child of the Holy Ghost." (Matthew 1:18)

Again, this is a verse which speaks of the humanity of Jesus. But, even here, note that the Name used is "Jesus Christ." This is a dual reference to Him. As "the Christ" He is entitled to be called the "King of the Jews" since His lineage traces back to King David. Also, as Messiah (the meaning of the word), He is acknowledged as Divine.

Firstbegotten

We have already dealt with Luke 1:35 above. About the only thing I would add is that He is called "holy." This is a phrase used of God as only He is holy. All men born of the flesh are born sinners. Obviously Jesus was the lone exception to this rule.

> "For unto which of the angels said he at any time, Thou art my Son, this day have I begotten thee? And again, I will be to him a father, and he shall be to me a Son?

And again, when he bringeth in the firstbegotten into the world, he saith, And let all the angels of God worship him." (Hebrews 1:5-6)

Jesus is here called the "firstbegotten." We will get to that phrase a little later. For now, I'd just like to note that this is a legal phrase giving Jesus the right of preeminence over all the other humans.

What I would like to note is that the angels were called to worship Jesus. Only God is rightfully allowed to accept Worship in the universe. Others may, as Satan, accept worship from others. But, they are doing this illegally. Since this is Scripture, and the Father is speaking, the call to worship is a clear reference to the Deity of the Son.

Melchisedec

We could also consider Hebrews 5:6:

"As he saith also in another place, Thou art a priest forever after the order of Melchisedec."

The only time we see Melchisedec in Scripture is in Genesis 14:18-20. In this place we see that Abram offers tithe to Melchisedec. Melchisedec is seen as a "type" of Jesus in that Melchisedec has no, Theophany. He is a shadow, or type, of Christ who was to come. The bread and wine offered to the "army" of Abram was not offered as a religious symbol but only as a refreshment for these men. Jesus also offers rest for the weary soldier of the cross. (see Matthew 11:28-30)

Melchisedec did accept tithes of Abraham. Melchisedec was a priest of the Most High God. Since Jesus is God He would not have been a priest unto Himself. Also, not that in Genesis 14:19 Melchisedec said, "Blessed be Abram of the most high God." Had this been a preincarnate appearance of Jesus the phrase would simply have been "Blessed by Abram."

Sonships

There are different "sonships" ascribed to Jesus. He is called the "Son of David." This refers to His Messiahship. It is a phrase which speaks of His Messianic office in the Redemptive plan. Secondarily, this phrase also speaks of His legal right to assume the literal Throne of David. This will be seen during the Millennial Reign of Christ.

The Son of Man

Jesus is also called, "The Son of Man." This speaks of His humanity. He is the perfect Representation of human beings in the Redemptive plan.

The Son of God

Jesus is also called, "The Son of God." This is said in reference to His Deity. This also speaks of His Authority in the Redemptive plan.

"Who is the image of the invisible God, the firstborn of every creature." (Colossians 1:15)

Halley (*Halley's Bible Handbook*) says of this verse that the term "First Born" does not relate to beginnings. Rather, it relates to the position of honor which is the right of Jesus. We in this nation are prone to call the wife of the president "The First Lady." It is obvious that we are not calling her the first woman born in this country. It is an honorary title. It is somewhat the same with Jesus except that in His case the honor is not conferred. It is part of Who He is in reality.

CHAPTER 4: TERMINOLOGY EXPLAINED

First Born

Also, this term, "First Born," is a term which applies to His position of eminence over all creation. It would be good to note that the overall the "creatures" would put Him outside their line of sin while still admitting Him entrance into their race as the Representative in His Work of Redemption. This is yet another verse in which both His humanity and His deity are found.

Image of the Father

God, the Father, is called "invisible." He has not been seen by the eyes of humanity as He is Spirit. So, also, is the Son Spirit. But the Son condescended to become one of us so that He could become our Savior from sin. To say that Jesus is the "image" of the Father is to equate Jesus to full equality with the Father. Jesus, simply put, is God.

Christ

Jesus is often referred to as "Christ." As stated above, this is not a name. It is an office, or a title. Christ is the New Testament Greek equal to the Old Testament Hebrew word "Messiah." It simply means that He is the promised Savior.

Second Person of the Trinity

Quite often we speak of the "First, Second, or Third" Person of the Trinity. This is not reflective of the rank of the Father, Son or Holy Ghost. All Three are equally God. There is no difference in Their Divine Status. The reference, when it is used, is only in relation to Their manifestation to mankind.

The term "Trinity" refers to that essential truth that there is only One God. That One God, however, has the Essence of Three distinct "Persons." The Father is God; but the Father is neither the Son nor the Holy Spirit. The Son is God; but the Son is neither the Father nor the Holy Spirit. The Holy Spirit is God; but the Holy Spirit is neither the Father nor the Son.

The Three are distinct, yet they remain **ONE**. How? I do not even begin to understand this. However, the Bible makes this concept very clear. Therefore, I accept the Trinity.

We are creatures of time and physicality. God is a Being of eternity and Spirit. We have no frame of reference to understand the things of His eternal spirituality. What we do have is His Words to us in His inspired and preserved Scripture. We must accept on faith that which God has revealed unto us.

In our next session we will begin to look at Jesus: The Son of God.

CHAPTER 5
JESUS: THE SON OF GOD
(Session Six)

Zeoli (*Is Jesus God? – Book Number One*) found twenty two persons and places which declared that Jesus is the Son of God. I will list these below and, sometimes, make a brief comment.

God Declared that Jesus is His Son

First, and most importantly, God declared that Jesus is His Son. It is important to note that the Spirit did not say that Jesus had *become* His Son. Jesus was not "endowed with the Christ Spirit" at His baptism. Jesus was born as the Son of God. The Spirit is merely giving voice to the reality of the situation as it already exists.

> "And Jesus, when he was baptized, went up straightway out of the water: and, lo, the heavens were opened unto him, and he saw the Spirit of God descending like a dove, and lighting upon him: And lo a voice from heaven, saying, This is my beloved Son, in whom I am well pleased." (Matthew 3:16-17)

Jesus said that He is the Son of God

Also, quite importantly, Jesus said that He is the Son of God. Had He not made these statements we might be out of bounds to make such a suggestion. But, He did say so.

Jesus told the woman at the well that He was the Son of God.

> "The woman saith unto him, I know that Messias cometh, which is called Christ: when he is come, he will tell us all things. Jesus saith unto her, I that speak unto thee am he." (John 4:25-26)

To make a claim that He was the Messiah, the Christ, is to make a claim to be the Son of God.

Jesus told the blind man whom He had healed of his blindness, that He is the Son of God.

> "Jesus heard that they had cast him out; and when he had found him, he said unto him, Dost thou believe on the Son of God. He answered and said, Who is he, Lord, that I might believe on him? And Jesus said unto him, Thou hast both seen him, and it is he that talketh with thee." (John 9:35-37)

Jesus told His disciples that he is the Son of God.

> "When Jesus heard that, he said, This sickness is not unto death, but for the glory of God, that the Son of God might be glorified thereby." (John 11:4)

Jesus told the Jews that He is the Son of God. Time and again in these New Testament histories we will see that Jesus is attacked by the religious leaders, not generally does this happen among the Jewish people but by their leaders only, on a charge of "blasphemy" because they are convinced that He has claimed Divinity. Never does Jesus dispute this claim as either incorrect or a misunderstanding of His words.

> "But Jesus answered them, My Father worketh hitherto, and I work. Therefore the Jews sought the more to kill him, because he not only had broken the sabbath, but

said also that God was his Father, making himself equal with God." (John 5:17-18)

"Say ye of him, whom the Father hath sanctified, and sent into the world, Thou blasphemest; because I said, I am the Son of God?" (John 10:36) "The Jews answered him, We have a law, and by our law he ought to die, because he made himself the son of God." (John 19:7)

Jesus Identified Himself to the Father as the Son of God

Jesus identified Himself to the Father as the Son of God. This was not to make a claim to God. Jesus was simply agreeing with the Father as to His place and mission.

"These words spake Jesus and lifted up his eyes to heaven, and said, Father, the hour is come; glorify thy Son, that thy Son also may glorify thee: As thou hast given him power over all flesh, that he should give eternal life to as many as thou hast given him. And this is life eternal, that they might know thee the only true God, and Jesus Christ, whom thou hast sent. I have glorified thee on the earth: I have finished the work which thou gavest me to do. And now, O Father, glorify thou me with thine own self with the glory which I had with thee before the world was." (John 17:1-5)

Jesus Claimed before the High Priest that He is the Son of God

Jesus claimed before the High Priest that He is the Son of God.

"But held his peace, and answered nothing. Again the high priest asked him, and said unto him, Art thou the Christ, the Son of the Blessed? And Jesus said, I am: and ye shall see the Son of man sitting on the right hand of power, and coming in the clouds of heaven." (Mark 14:61-62)

The Holy Spirit Assured Us that Jesus is the Son of God

The Holy Spirit assured us that Jesus is the Son of God.

"And declared to be the Son of God with power, according to the spirit of holiness, by the resurrection from the dead." (Romans 1:4)

The Angel Gabriel said that Jesus is the Son of God

The angel Gabriel said that Jesus is the Son of God. An angel is simply a messenger of God. That is who an angel is and what an angel does. Since the angels do not sin and do convey their messages as messengers of God, this is a tacit admission that God has sent the message which is delivered by Gabriel.

"And in the sixth month the angel Gabriel was sent from God unto a city of Galilee, named Nazareth, To a virgin espoused to a man whose name was Joseph, of the house of David; and the virgin's name was Mary. ... And the angel answered and said unto her, The Holy Ghost shall come upon thee, and the power of the Highest shall overshadow thee: therefore also that holy thing which shall be born of thee shall be called the Son of God." (Luke 1:26-27 & 35)

Even the Demons Agreed that Jesus is the Son of God

Even the demons agreed that Jesus is the Son of God. The demons certainly did not wish to "build up" the reputation of Jesus. Consider how Satan had attempted to pull Him down in the fourth chapter of Matthew. The demons were simply speaking out of anguish at a fear of punishment. They simply addressed Jesus as Who He Is.

"And, behold, they cried out, saying, What have we to do with thee, Jesus, thou Son of God? art thou come hither to torment us before the time." (Matthew 8:29) "And

CHAPTER 5: JESUS: THE SON OF GOD

unclean spirits, when they saw him, fell down before him, and cried, saying, Thou art the Son of God." (Mark 3:11) "And devils also came out of many, crying out, and saying, Thou art Christ the Son of God. And he rebuking them suffered them not to speak: for they knew that he was Christ." (Luke 4:41)

John the Baptist Affirmed that Jesus is the Son of God

John the Baptist, the forerunner, affirmed that Jesus is the Son of God. John was a prophetic preacher of righteousness. Here he admits that even he, a prophet of God, did not realize just Who Jesus was. Such truth was revealed unto John by the Spirit of God.

"And John bare record, saying, I saw the Spirit descending from heaven like a dove, and it abode upon him. And I knew him not: but he that sent me to baptize with water, the same said unto me, Upon whom thou shalt see the Spirit descending, and remaining on him, the same is he which baptizeth with the Holy Ghost. And I saw, and bare record that this is the Son of God." (John 1:32-34)

Matthew Said that Jesus is the Son of God

Matthew said that Jesus is the Son of God. This is inspired Scripture. The only possible misunderstanding at this point is to misunderstand what He Who inspired Scripture has said.

"But while he thought on these things, behold, the angel of the Lord appeared unto him in a dream, saying, Joseph, thou son of David, fear not to take unto thee Mary thy wife: for that which is conceived in her is of the Holy Ghost. Behold, a virgin shall be with child, and shall bring forth a son, and they shall call his name Emmanuel, which being interpreted is, God with us." (Matthew 1:20 & 23)

Mark Said that Jesus is the Son of God

Mark said that Jesus is the Son of God.

"The beginning of the gospel of Jesus Christ, the Son of God." (Mark 1:1)

Again this was written by the inspiration of God.

Luke Said that Jesus is the Son of God

Luke said that Jesus is the Son of God. Inspiration says that this is the Word of God in this matter.

"And the angel answered and said unto her, The Holy Ghost shall come upon thee, and the power of the Highest shall overshadow thee: therefore also that holy thing which shall be born of thee shall be called the Son of God." (Luke 1:35)

John Said that Jesus is the Son of God

John said that Jesus is the Son of God. "But these are written, that ye might believe that Jesus is the Christ, the Son of God; and that believing ye might have life through his name." (John 20:31) The purpose of the Scripture of God is to reveal the glory of God. Scripture always says what is meant and means what is said.

Nathaniel said that Jesus is the Son of God.

"Nathaniel answered and saith unto him, Rabbi, thou art the Son of God; thou art the King of Israel." (John 1:49)

Nathaniel Recognized Him

Nathaniel met the Master and recognized to Whom he was speaking.

Andrew Said that Jesus is the Son of God

Andrew said that Jesus is the Son of God.

> "He first findeth his own brother Simon, and saith unto him, We have found the Messias, which is, being interpreted, the Christ." (John 1:41)

Andrew admitted the truth of his own understanding. He was correct.

The Blind Man Said that Jesus is the Son of God

The blind man said that Jesus is the Son of God. Even the blind man could see that the One Who had healed him was not just another man.

> "Jesus heard that they had cast him out; and when he had found him, he said unto him, Dost thou believe on the Son of God. He answered and said, Who is he, Lord, that I might believe on him? And Jesus said unto him, Thou hast both seen him, and it is he that talketh with thee. And he said, Lord, I believe. And he worshipped him." (John 9:35-38)

The Disciples in the Ship Said that Jesus is the Son of God

The Disciples in the ship said that Jesus is the Son of God.

> "Then they that were in the ship came and worshipped him, saying, Of a truth thou art the Son of God." (Matthew 14:33)

These disciples had just experienced a miracle in that Jesus had stilled **both** the wind and the waves. Their own experience and eyes proved the Divinity of Jesus.

Peter Said that Jesus is the Son of God

Peter said that Jesus is the Son of God.

> "He saith unto them, But whom say ye that I am" and Simon Peter answered and said, Thou art the Christ, the Son of the living God." (Matthew 16:15-16)

He is the Son of God

The disciples had lived and ate with Jesus for months. They had seen Him in every situation. They knew that He was not just another man; He is the Son of God.

Martha said that Jesus is the Son of God.

> "She saith unto him, Yea, Lord: I believe that thou art the Christ, the Son of God, which should come into the world." (John 11:27)

In the depths of her despair over the death of her brother Martha still understood the wonder of the Person of Jesus Christ. Not understanding the purpose of his delay in arriving, she was disappointed that He had not come earlier but she still acknowledged Him as Who He is.

Even Judas, the Betrayer, Said that Jesus is the Son of God

Even Judas, the betrayer, said that Jesus is the Son of God.

> "Then Judas, which had betrayed him, when he saw that he was condemned, repented himself, and brought again the thirty pieces of silver to the chief priests and elders, Saying, I have sinned in that I have betrayed the innocent blood. And they said, What is that to us? see thou to that. And he cast down the pieces of silver in

CHAPTER 5: JESUS: THE SON OF GOD

the temple, and departed, and went and hanged himself." Matthew 27:3-5)

It is important to note, here, that Judas understood that Jesus was not guilty of sin. He knew that he, himself, had sinned. However, his repentance was unto himself. He was sorry for what he had done. At no point do we ever see that he repented toward God and accepted Jesus as his own, personal, Savior.

To understand all about Christ, without accepting Him as Savior, is to die in sin. Salvation comes not from simply understanding the facts. Salvation comes from accepting the Savior.

The Centurion Said that Jesus is the Son of God

The centurion, who was one of the executioners of Jesus, said that Jesus is the Son of God.

> *"Now when the centurion, and they that were with him, watching Jesus, saw the earthquake, and those things that were done, they feared greatly, saying, Truly this was the Son of God." (Matthew 27:54)*

There is some debate as to whether this centurion understood the importance of what he had said, or whether he was simply comparing Jesus to the gods of the Romans. Since Jesus was a well-known Person, He had been preaching and sending out the twelve to further His influence. John the Baptist, who spoke of Jesus as The Lamb of God (John 1:29), had also been quite well known - even to the point of being a prisoner who was murdered for his ministry. It is entirely possible that this centurion, and maybe some of those with him, understood and were saved.

I don't know. I would like to think it is so.

Paul Said that Jesus is the Son of God

Paul said that Jesus is the Son of God.

> *"And straightway he preached Christ in the synagogues, that he is the Son of God." (Acts 9:20)*

The Ethiopian Eunuch Said that Jesus is the Son of God

The Ethiopian eunuch said that Jesus is the Son of God.

> *"And Philip said, If thou believest with all thine heart, thou mayest. And he answered and said, I believe that Jesus Christ is the Son of God. And he commanded the chariot to stand still: and they went down both into the water, both Philip and the eunuch; and he baptized him." (Acts 8:37-38)*

The Empty Tomb Stands as a Testimony that Jesus is the Son of God

The empty tomb stands as a testimony that Jesus is the Son of God.

> *"And declared to be the Son of God with power, according to the spirit of holiness, by the resurrection from the dead." (Romans 1:4)*

Once again, as at His baptism, the empty tomb is not the point where Jesus is first endowed as "Christ." The empty tomb only stands as proof that Jesus is the very Son of God. The word "declared" is simply an acknowledgement of the truth of His Divinity.

There are many resurrections detailed in Scripture. The difference between them and the Resurrection of Jesus is that there was no one praying for Him to be resurrected. He simply rose from the dead of His own will and power. Jesus is the Son of God.

This is another picture of His deity. All the other resurrections in the Bible were effected when the power of God came upon a human instrument. There was no such "attending physician" when Jesus rose from the dead. It was His power which caused His resurrection. Since a resurrection is always a manifestation of the power of God, and Jesus displayed this power in His Own Person, Jesus is God.

Many Say that Jesus Never Said He Was God. This is an Error

Many have said that they *cannot* believe that Jesus is divine because He never said that He was. This is an error. He said, often, that He was the Son of God. This was understood by the people of the day of His earthly walk to be a claim to deity. It is also possible to see that attributes of Who Jesus was during his earthly sojourn. Those attributes are expressions of His divinity.

In our next session we will look at some of those attributes of Jesus.

CHAPTER 6
ATTRIBUTES OF JESUS
(Session Seven)

This week's session will follow the example of our last session. Once again, Zeoli (Is Jesus God? - Book Number One) has listed fifteen things about the Person of Jesus which testify that He is the Son of God. I will list these and, sometimes, make short comments.

Traits About Jesus Which Show His Deity

In our last session, just to review, Evangelist Zeoli had listed twenty-two persons and events which testified about Jesus. In this session the focus is on those traits about Him which show His Deity.

The Revealer

Jesus is portrayed as the One Who is the revealer of the Father.

> "All things are delivered unto me of my Father: and no man knoweth the Son, but the Father; neither knoweth any man the Father, save the Son, and he to whomsoever the Son will reveal him." (Matthew 11:27)

The Object of the Father's Love

Jesus is the object of the Father's love. "The Father loveth the Son, and hath given all things into his hand." (John 3:35)

Jesus is the object of faith.

> "He that believeth on the Son hath everlasting life: and he that believeth not the Son shall not see life; but the wrath of God abideth on him." (John 3:36)

> "Let not your heart be troubled: ye believe in God, believe also in me." (John 14:1)

> "And brought them out, and said, Sirs, what must I do to be saved? And they said, Believe on the Lord Jesus Christ, and thou shalt be saved, and thy house." (Acts 16:30-31)

The Father Shows Jesus All

Jesus is the One to Whom the Father shows all.

> "For the Father loveth the Son, and sheweth him all things that himself doeth: and he will shew him greater works than these, that ye may marvel." (John 5:20)

Jesus Is the One Who Quickens

Jesus is the One Who quickens. The word "quicken" means to make alive.

> "For as the Father raiseth up the dead, and quickeneth them; even so the Son quickeneth whom he will." (John 5:21)

Jesus is the Judge.

> "For the Father judgeth no man, but hath committed all judgment unto the Son." (John 5:22)

Jesus Is the Object of Honor

Jesus is the Object of Honor.

> "That all men should honour the Son, even as they honour the Father. He that honoureth not the Son honoureth not the Father which hath sent him." *(John 5:23)*

Jesus Has Life In Himself

He is the One Who has Life in Himself.

> "For as the Father hath life in himself, so hath he given to the Son to have life in himself." *(John 5:26)*

He is the Liberator

He is the Liberator.

> "If the Son therefore shall make you free, ye shall be free indeed." *(John 8:36)*

He is the Object of the Father's Glory

He is the object of the Father's Glory.

> "And whatsoever ye shall ask in my name, that will I do, that the Father may be glorified in the Son." *(John 14:13)*

It might be well to add at this point that "in my name" is not intended as a magical phrase. To pray "in His name" means to pray in His will. It is akin to a man who really is a policeman and one who is not. Both may say, "In the name of the law." Only one really is speaking in the name of the law. The authority in prayer lies in the will of Christ.

Jesus is the Lover of Righteousness

Jesus is the Lover of Righteousness.

> "But unto the Son he saith, Thy throne, O God, is for ever and ever: a sceptre of righteousness is the sceptre of thy kingdom. Thou hast loved righteousness, and hated iniquity, therefore God, even thy God, hath anointed thee with the oil of gladness above thy fellows." *(Hebrews 1:8-9)*

Jesus is the Test of Truth

Jesus is the Test of Truth.

> "Who is a liar but he that denieth that Jesus is the Christ? He is antichrist, that denieth the Father and the Son." *(I John 2:22)*

The acceptance of the deity of Jesus Christ is a test of both orthodoxy and true Christianity.

He is the Sent One

He is the Sent One.

> "And we have seen and do testify that the Father sent the Son to be the Saviour of the world." *(I John 4:14)*

Jesus is the Assurance of Life

Jesus is the Assurance of Life.

> "He that hath the Son hath life; and he that hath not the Son of God hath not life." *(I John 5:12)*

CHAPTER 6: ATTRIBUTES OF JESUS

He is the Ticket to the Father's Abode

He is the Ticket to the Father's abode.

> *"Whosoever shall confess that Jesus is the Son of God, God dwelleth in him, and he in God."* (I John 4:15)

In these post Christian days of ecumenical fervor, we often lose sight of the fact that true Christianity is somewhat exclusive. Oh, anyone can become a Christian. But, to gain eternal life and peace with God - forgiveness of sins - one must accept Jesus as his Savior. There is no other way. While other "religious traditions" might lead one to an exemplary life on this earth; only a relationship with Jesus Christ *cannot* only insure, but guarantee, salvation from sin, peace with God and an eternal home in Heaven.

All other paths are false and will lead to an eternal Hell. This is not a message which the world wants to hear. Still, they do need to hear the eternal truth that Jesus Christ died in time so that they might live in eternity.

We have one more session to address Evangelist Zeoli's books. These are so good, as far as pointing out that Divine Nature of Christ, that I wanted to share them. Our next session will be much like these last two. We will look at the fact that the actions of Jesus also testify that He is the Son of God.

CHAPTER 7
EVIDENCES THAT JESUS IS THE SON OF GOD
(Session Eight)

We will conclude during this session with our look at the work of Evangelist Zeoli (*Is Jesus God – Book Number One*). We will continue in the same manner as we have in the last two sessions. Zeoli has given sixteen evidences that Jesus is the Son of God in his examination of the actions of Jesus during His earthly sojourn.

Sixteen Evidences that Jesus is the Son of God

As in the past two sessions, I will look at these actions and make occasional comment. In each instance I will list the supporting Scripture.

Jesus is the Savior of the World

Jesus is the Savior of the world.

> "For God sent not his Son into the world to condemn the world; but that the world through him might be saved." (John 3:17)

Notice that this verse is a companion to John 3:16 as it states the intention of God to offer salvation through the work of the Son. Notice, in the very next verse, why this is a necessity.

> "He that believeth on him is not condemned: but he that believeth not is condemned already, because he hath not believed in the name of the only begotten Son of God." (John 3:18)

Jesus is more than a Religious Leader or Teacher

Jesus is more than a religious leader or teacher. Our very salvation depends upon our relationship with this risen Lord. That statement could not be made of any other religious leader. The other religious leaders came to show what they believed to be the way to placate God. They gave rules and regulations to follow to find salvation. Only of Jesus may it be rightly said that He did not come to simply show us how to live. He came to be the atonement which enabled us to live in fellowship with The God of Love.

Jesus is Glorified Above All Others

Jesus is glorified above all others.

> "The God of Abraham, and of Isaac, and of Jacob, the God of our fathers, hath glorified his Son Jesus, whom ye delivered up, and denied him in the presence of Pilate, when he was determined to let him go." (Acts 3:13)

Jesus is the Person of the Gospel Message

Jesus is the Person of the gospel message.

> "For God is my witness, whom I serve with my spirit in the gospel of his Son, that without ceasing I make mention of you always in my prayers." (Romans 1:9)

Again, Jesus did not come to simply show a way of religious observance. He, Himself, is the focal point of the entire gospel message since this message emanates from His passion on the Cross of Calvary. Jesus is the reason for more than just a season; He is the reason for the salvation which He has imparted unto us.

Jesus is the Reconciler of Men

Jesus is the Reconciler of men.

> "For if, when we were enemies, we were reconciled to God by the death of his Son, much more, being reconciled, we shall be saved by his life." (Romans 5:10)

Jesus rose from the dead that first Easter morning as a surety of our own salvation. He did more than simply "walk the walk and talk the talk." He gives unto us the means to walk boldly to the Throne of Grace in prayer because of the Salvation He has purchased on our account.

Jesus is our Role Model

Jesus is our Role Model.

> "For whom he did foreknow, he also did predestinate to be conformed to the image of his Son, that we might be the firstborn among many brethren." (Romans 8:29)

Jesus is the Person of Fellowship

Jesus is the Person of fellowship.

> "God is faithful, by whom ye were called unto the fellowship of his Son Jesus Christ our Lord." (I Corinthians 1:9)

We must never forget that Jesus founded a church. It is our duty, to Him, to be faithful in attendance with other born again persons. That concept of fellowship is for our edification. To feel that one can worship God as well in a forest as in a sanctuary is to evidence a belief that one does not have to honor Christ and the brethren. It is a prideful consideration completely out of context with the New Testament record.

Jesus is the Deliverer from Wrath

Jesus is the Deliverer from wrath.

> "And to wait for his Son from heaven, whom he raised from the dead, even Jesus, which delivered us from the wrath to come." (I Thessalonians 1:10)

We have been saved from the wrath of God through the sacrifice of His Son. This is not a thing we could accomplish on our own. No amount of "church" works, or ethical detail, can erase the sin in our lives; this is only accomplished by the sacrifice of Jesus on the Cross of Calvary.

The Father Spoke Through Jesus

Jesus is the One through Whom the Father spoke.

> "Hath in these last days spoken unto us by his Son, whom he hath appointed heir of all things, by whom also he made the worlds." (Hebrews 1:2)

Jesus Is the Creative Agent

As we notice, again, that Jesus is the Creative Agent of the Godhead, we are drawn to His teachings in the gospel message.

He is the Propitiation for Our Sin

Jesus is the propitiation for our sin.

> "Herein is love, not that we loved God, but that he loved us, and sent his Son to be

CHAPTER 7: EVIDENCES THAT JESUS IS THE SON OF GOD

the propitiation for our sins." (I John 4:10)

That word, "propitiation," simply means that He is the appeasement, or the satisfaction of the payment, for our sins. God counts the sacrifice of Jesus as the basis on which we are saved.

(Quick aside: That definition is from <u>The Defined King James Bible</u>. You would do well to obtain a copy. If there is no copy at your local bookseller just tell them that it is published by *The Bible for Today* located in Collingswood, New Jersey, USA. In the interest of full disclosure, I have very limited contact with this publisher and do not profit from the sale of this edition. You, however, will profit - spiritually - from the purchase.)

Jesus is the Cleanser From Sin

Jesus is the cleanser from sin.

> "But if we walk in the light, as he is in the light, we have fellowship one with another, and the blood of Jesus Christ his Son cleanseth us from all sin." (I John 1:7)

Again we are commanded to exercise a fellowship one with another. That's church attendance! We also need to note that this is not salvation; the sacrifice of Jesus on Calvary is the basis of our salvation. Our fellowship, one with another, is a response, our love returned to Him, to that great salvation.

Jesus is the Repository of Life

Jesus is the Repository of Life.

> "And this is the record, that God hath given to us eternal life, and this life is in his Son. He that hath the Son hath life; and he that hath not the Son of God hath not life." (I John 5:11-12)

Jesus is Known to Demons

Jesus is known to demons.

> "And, behold, they cried out, saying, What have we to do with thee, Jesus, thou Son of God? art thou come hither to torment us before the time." (Matthew 8:29)

It is a sad commentary on the state of humanity that even the demons know more of Christ than do most men!

Jesus is the Repository of the Promises of God

Jesus is the Repository of the Promises of God.

> "For it is written, I will destroy the wisdom of the wise, and will bring to nothing the understanding of the prudent. Where is the wise? where is the disputer of this world? hath not God made foolish the wisdom of this world?" (I Corinthians 1:19-20)

The gospel message is simple: Accept Jesus and live with your sins forgiven. Still, the world tries to make salvation into something hard which they must do. In doing so they are rejecting God's plan. They are, in effect, telling Him that they do not value the death of His Son great enough to save their souls; so they seek to do better.

Folks, this demands a new paragraph. THERE AIN'T NOTHING BETTER!

Jesus is the Stronghold of Our Faith

Jesus is the Stronghold of our faith.

> "I am crucified with Christ: nevertheless I live; yet not I, but Christ liveth in me: and the life which I now live in the flesh I live by the faith of the Son of God, who loved me, and gave himself for me." (Galatians 2:20)

It is He who saved us. It is He who keeps us in the faith.

Jesus is the Great High Priest

Jesus is the Great High Priest.

> "Seeing then that we have a great high priest, that is passed into the heavens, Jesus the Son of God, let us hold fast our profession." (Hebrews 4:14)

Jesus is called the Great High Priest. The duty of a priest is to present the petitions of humanity to God. Jesus is our advocate with the Father. His sacrifice has brought us to the place where our sins are remembered no more. We now are allowed fellowship with God.

The Psalmist tells us that,

> "As far as the east is from the west, so far hath he removed our transgressions from us." (Psalm 103:12)

North and South will meet at the poles but East and West are constantly running away from each other. This is the imagery used to point out that Jesus forgives all our sins. In Him those sins are wiped from the record of God.

He is our Constant Contemporary as Well as Our Constant Companion

Jesus is presented as passed into Heaven. He is well able to address our needs at any time and at any place. He is not bound by time or location. He is our Constant Contemporary as well as our Constant Companion. This should give us pause. We must realize that the Savior is ever with us. May our actions be always pleasing unto Him.

The Son of God, of course, is Jesus.

Jesus Was also Mistreated by Men

Jesus was also mistreated by men.

> "Of how much sorer punishment, suppose ye, shall he be thought worthy, who hath trodden under foot the Son of God, and hath counted the blood of the covenant, wherewith he was sanctified, an unholy thing, and hath done despite unto the spirit of Grace." (Hebrews 10:29)

Jesus endured the mistreatment of men while He walked this earth because they hated Him. Men still hate Him. I've just read where a television personality spoke of Jesus with an obscene epithet. There has not been much reporting on the incident. No one, really, seems to care. The sad fact is that Jesus is still a despised figure.

That is sad. Sadder still are those who are born again by the Blood of Jesus Christ who refuse to treat Him as Lord. The "Great Commission" was not a suggestion; it was the lawful order of the Lawful Commander of the Army of the Redeemed.

Even past this, too many of us spend our days blissfully unaware of His presence. Oh, we remember Him on Sunday morning, or when we have problems, but we ignore Him - treat Him as completely unimportant to our lives - at other times.

He is the Lord of Glory

He is the Lord of Glory. May we be ever cognizant of this reality.

In our next session we will return to our normal method of study as we begin to look at the concept of "sonship" within Scripture.

CHAPTER 8
JESUS THE SON OF GOD
(Session Nine)

In this session we continue to look at the issue of Jesus as the Son of God. In order to do this properly we must consider the Biblical use of the term "the son of..." Ryrie (*Basic Theology*) has given us several illustrations of how this term has been used in Scripture.

The Biblical Use of the Term "the Son of..."

Generally the phrase "son of" refers to "offspring." But is can also mean other things.

In I Kings 20:35 the phrase "sons of the prophets" used. The meaning here has nothing to do with the physical generation of these persons. The phrase means "...of the order of the prophets." In other words, the meaning is applied to a group. We use the same general idea quite often when speaking of our military. We speak of "our boys" when we mean "our nation's soldiers."

Nehemiah 12:28 also follows this pattern when it speaks of "sons of the singers." The meaning is that group of persons who were of the order of the singers.

Sometimes, as Ryrie points out, the term "son of" can apply to a recognition of the essential nature of an individual. In Acts 4:36 we see this term applied to Joses. He was called "The son of consolation." We could use more "Joses'" in our churches today!

In Mark 3:17 we see that James and John were called "the sons of thunder." The meaning is that these were men of thunderous personalities.

When Jesus, as Ryrie also points out, was called the "Son of Man," this had reference to His representing us before the Father. This phrase also points out that Jesus is to be our Example of how we ought to relate toward God.

However, when the Scripture speaks of Jesus as the "Son of God," this is with reference to His Divinity.

Kelly (*The Deity of Christ*) realizes that Jesus said that He was Divine in words about Himself.

> "In no summary [of Jesus claiming full divinity] should one omit the testimony of the fifth, the divinity chapter of John's Gospel, where our Lord Himself cites six testimonies to His sonship..."

In this chapter Jesus references His own claim, the claims of John the Baptist, the witness of the Father, the very works which Jesus did, the testimony of the Scripture about Him, and the testimony of Moses.

In John 5:31 Jesus admits, *"If I bear witness of myself, my witness is not true."* This is true, of course. Many have "admitted" to great acts of heroism during war time. Many who have so claimed this are guilty of "stolen valor." "Stolen Valor" refers to those who claim to be military heroes for some sort of personal gain who have never performed the acts which they claim. They are deceivers and liars. They are, in popular parlance, "con men."

Jesus Was No "Con Man"

Jesus did make claims about His Deity in verses 17, 24, 26. He was no "con man." Nonetheless it is important that He made such claims. Had He never claimed such we would have no logical reason to assume that He was, and is, the Son of God. But, by His Own admission His claims demand verification from other sources.

Jesus lists these affirming claims of others as to His Deity. He lists John the Baptist in verses 33-34. John the Baptist was a respected prophet. His word carries much weight. Still, it is possible that John may have been mistaken.

Jesus also makes an appeal to Moses and his writing in verses 46-47. Moses is respected as a virtual "founding father" of the Jewish faith in his penning of the first five books of the Pentateuch. Still, Moses was a man. It is possible that even Moses may have been mistaken.

Jesus also made appeal to His works in verses 16-17, 19, 25 and 29. I believe that the boxer, Muhammad Ali once said, "It ain't bragging if you can do it." There is some truth in that statement. Many of the miracles of Jesus, such as raising Lazarus from the dead, are beyond the scope of "magic" and duplicity. These miracles and wonders, such as stilling the wind *and* the waves during a storm at sea, are profound testimonies to the truth of His claims.

The appeal of Jesus to the Scripture in verse 39 is an uncontestable confirmation of His Deity.

Even the Father, in verses 19, 21, 22, 23, 26, 27, 37 and 43, is a Collaborative Witness to the claim of Deity by Jesus.

Even discounting the two witnesses of human origin, which I do not believe we have the right to discount!, Jesus presents a compelling case for His full Divinity as The Son of God.

Jesus' Hearers Understood His Claims

Kelly also noted the "I am" use of Jesus.

> "I only cite further the 'I am's' of this Gospel [John], as identifying Him with Jehovah in His infinite, unfathomable nature; note but one, 'Before Abraham was, I am,' and reflect upon it." (John 8:58)

As to this last reference, also reflect upon the actions of His hearers. They understood exactly what He had claimed. Clarke (*Adam Clark's Commentary*) spoke of the understanding of the hearers of Jesus on another occasion. This one is referenced in John 19:7.

> "When Christ called himself the Son of God, they [the religious leaders] understood it to imply positive equality to the Supreme Being; and, if they were wrong, our Lord never attempted to correct them."

Had the understanding of these religious leaders to the intent of the words of Jesus been wrong, His failure to correct them means that He believed it to be true. This is all the more compelling when one considers the possible punishment for such a claim, were it false. Therefore, the statement was true. He displayed His Own belief that it was a true understanding of what He had said. Therefore this is either true, His equality with God, or Jesus was Himself in error to the extent of madness.

Had the understanding of these religious leaders to the intent of the words of Jesus

CHAPTER 8: JESUS THE SON OF GOD

been a misunderstanding of His meaning, He failed to correct their misconceptions. If this were the case, we must consider Jesus to be a deceiver and false teacher whose pronouncements cannot be trusted.

If, however, this understanding on the part of these religious leaders is not a misconception, and He did not correct them and He was neither insane nor a deceiver it must be true that Jesus is God!

The Messiah Is Recognized as the Son of God in the Old Testament

The Scriptures also declare that Jesus is the Son of God. Zeoli (*Is Jesus God? Book Number One*) sees that the Messiah, who Jesus clearly was, is recognized as the Son of God in the Old Testament.

> "I will declare the decree: the LORD hath said unto me, Thou art my Son; this day have I begotten thee." (Psalm 2:7)

> "Then Nebuchadnezzar the king was astonied, and rose up in haste, and spake, and said unto his counsellors, Did not we cast three men bound into the midst of the fire? They answered and said unto the king, True, O king. He answered and said, Lo, I see four men loose, walking in the midst of the fire, and they have no hurt; and the form of the fourth is like the Son of God. Then Nebuchadnezzar came near to the mouth of the burning fiery furnace, and spake, and said, Shadrach, Meshach, and Abednego, ye servants of the most high God, come forth and come hither. Then Shadrach, Meshach, and Abednego, came forth of the midst of the fire." (Daniel 3:24-26)

Now, I don't know if the king understood what he was saying. I am rather certain that he had no concept of Jesus of Nazareth. I do believe, however, that the Spirit of God anointed his mouth with this observation. God can anoint the mouth of whosoever He wills in His working to teach the truths of eternity. As we consider that this is part of the inspired Record, we must consider these facts.

In the same light as this statement of Nebuchadnezzar is the statement of the High Priest, Caiaphas, from John 11:50-51 which took place near the beginning of the plans to have Jesus executed.

> "Nor consider that it is expedient for us, that one man should die for the people, and that the whole nation perish not. And this he spake not of himself: but being high priest that year, he prophesied that Jesus should die for the nation."

Jesus is often recognized in the New Testament as the Son of God. I will only reference John 20:31 at this time.

> "But these are written, that ye might believe that Jesus is the Christ, the Son of God; and that believing ye might have life through his name."

In our next session we will begin to discuss the concept of Jesus as The Angel of the Lord. These are pre-incarnate appearances of Jesus. That term just means that these are appearances of Jesus before He took upon Himself a human body in Bethlehem.

CHAPTER 9
JESUS IS THE ANGEL OF THE LORD
(Session Ten)

In this session we will consider that the same Jesus of the New Testament is "The Angel of the Lord" as mentioned in the Old Testament. This is a reasonable conjecture since we realize that Jesus did not come into existence in Bethlehem. Bethlehem was the place where Jesus chose to accept a human body so that He could identify with us. But, Bethlehem was not the place where Jesus began to exist. We have already considered His eternality at other places in this study.

The Preincarnate Appearances of Jesus: The Angel of the Lord

Neither should we consider that Jesus was an angel, such as Gabriel, in His pre-existent state. His Deity has already been discussed. Jesus is not a created Being; rather, He is, Himself, the Creative Agent by whom all was created.

> *"All things were made by him; and without him was not any thing made that was made." (John 1:3)*

Consider Exodus 3:2 and 6.

> *"And the angel of the LORD appeared unto him in a flame of fire out of the midst of a bush: and he looked, and, behold, the bush burned with fire, and the bush was not consumed. ...*

Moreover he said,

> *I am the God of thy father, the God of Abraham, the God of Isaac, and the God of Jacob. And Moses hid his face; for he was afraid to look upon God."*

Also, compare this passage with John 1:18.

> *"No man hath seen God at any time; the only begotten Son, which is in the bosom of the Father, he hath declared him."*

That which we see in these two passages shows this "Angel of the Lord," from the passage in Exodus, to be Jesus in His pre-incarnate state. We see in Exodus that "The Angel of the Lord" is the same as the "God of the Fathers." When this fact is compared with the passage from John, (No one has seen God except as He is revealed by Jesus.) we are led to conclude that "The Angel of the Lord" in Exodus is an appearance of Jesus as the second "Person" of the Trinity.

Brief Explanation of the Trinity

A very quick aside is in order here. When the phrase "The first Person, or second, or third, of the Trinity" is used, we are not speaking of an order of rank. Each is fully God. God is fully One. We only speak of first, second, and third as to the order of appearance in the Scripture.

His Name is Wonderful

The Pulpit Commentary notes that the Angel of the Lord identified His Name as "secret" to the parents of Sampson in Judges 13:18. The name is secret because it is wonderful. That is the meaning of the word "secret." It is thus translated in Isaiah 9:6

in reference to Jesus. The name, the implication thereof, is so "transcendently wonderful (cf. II Cor. 12:4)," that it could not be uttered.

We may compare this concept with the custom of the ancient Jew in which he felt compelled not to speak the name of Jehovah.

Strong (*Systematic Theology*) points out that The Angel of the Lord identified Himself as God when He revealed Himself to Abraham as Abraham was preparing to sacrifice Isaac.

> *"And the angel of the LORD called unto him out of heaven, and said, Abraham, Abraham: and he said, Here am I. ... And said, By myself have I sworn, saith the LORD, for because thou hast done this thing, and hast not withheld thy son, thine only son." (Genesis 22:11 and 16)*

Strong also sees this self identification of God as "The Angel of the Lord" made to Jacob at the camp of Laban.

> *"And the angel of God spake unto me in a dream, saying, Jacob: And I said, Here am I. And he said, Lift up now thine eyes, and see, all the rams which leap upon the cattle are ringstaked, speckled, and grisled: for I have seen all that Laban doeth unto thee." (Genesis 31:11-12)*

No Man Has Seen God

Once again, as we consider that John informs us that no man has seen God except as by the Son in a physical body, we must consider these self identified references to God as "Theophanies." This is an appearance of God in the form of a human. Before Bethlehem Jesus would sometimes appear in the form of a man in the Old Testament. At Bethlehem He came in the form of man. Before Bethlehem Jesus would appear, or look like, a man to certain individuals at certain times. At Bethlehem Jesus became a man in the incarnation.

At no point did Jesus ever cease to be God, however. We need to understand this fact. We have discussed this dual nature of Jesus in our study on the Virgin Birth. This book, *Study in the Virgin Birth*, is available from the same publisher as is this volume.

Strong also referred to verses wherein "The Angel of the Lord" received, and more importantly accepted worship from men.

> *"And the angel of the LORD appeared unto him in a flame of fire out of the midst of a bush: and he looked, and, behold, the bush burned with fire, and the bush was not consumed. And Moses, said, I will now turn aside, and see this great sight, why the bush is not burnt. And when the LORD saw that he turned aside to see, God called unto him out of the midst of the bush, and said, Moses, Moses. And he said, Here am I. And he said, Draw not nigh hither: put off thy shoes from off thy feet, for the place whereon thou standest is holy ground." (Exodus 3:2-5)*

> *"For it came to pass, when the flame went up toward heaven from off the altar, that the angel of the LORD ascended in the flame of the altar. And Manoah and his wife looked on it, and fell on their faces to the ground. But the angel of the LORD did no more appear to Manoah and to his wife. Then Manoah knew that he was an angel of the LORD. And Manoah said unto his wife, We shall surely die, because we have seen God." (Judges 13:20-22)*

The Misdirected Worship of Lucifer

The only angel in Scripture which accepts worship is that "angel of light," Lucifer.

CHAPTER 9: JESUS IS THE ANGEL OF THE LORD

The deceiver accepted worship from humans. This worship is misdirected due to the sin nature and leads to destruction.

The order of the angels of God does not accept worship. They give, as should we, their worship to God. That "The Angel of the Lord," in these instances, did receive worship as though it was His right, and the program of God was hastened because of these actions, we must conclude that this was an appearance of God to Moses, and then to the parents of Samson.

We conclude, therefore, that these were appearances of Jesus prior to His entry into the human race at Bethlehem.

Please, well note the truth as to both the Divinity of Jesus and the concept of the Triune Nature of the Godhead that is shown in these instances. Even in the Old Testament, hundreds of years before the events of Bethlehem, Jesus is shown to be God. His pre-incarnate appearances also point to His identification with the human race by which He provided us with the Perfect Sacrifice for sin.

Jesus Is the Theme of the Bible

The Bible is One Book. Jesus is the Theme throughout the sacred page.

We will continue this discussion in our next session.

CHAPTER 10
JESUS IS THE THEME OF THE BIBLE
(Session Eleven)

We saw in our last session that "The Angel of the Lord" often identified Himself as God. We also saw that no man has seen God except as the Son has revealed Him. Therefore, we are led to conclude that "The Angel of the Lord" was a pre-incarnate (before birth at Bethlehem) appearance of Jesus.

Jesus Was in Existence Before All Things

Since the New Testament as well as Old Testament references to Messiah agree that Jesus was in existence before all things, and is in fact the Creative Agent of the Godhead (see John 1:1-3) rather than Himself a created being, this assessment is well grounded in Scripture.

There are others who identify the Angel of the Lord as Jehovah. Remembering the caveat above, the no one has seen God except as He was revealed in the Person of Jesus, to thus identify the Angel of the Lord is to identify Jesus in a pre-incarnate appearance.

Several Appearances

Let us consider several of these appearances where this has happened.

> "And the angel of the LORD found her by a fountain of water in the wilderness, by the fountain in the way to Shur. And he said, Hagar, Sarai's maid, whence camest thou? and wither wilt thou go? And she said, I flee from the face of my mistress Sarai. And the angel of the LORD said unto her, Return to thy mistress, and submit thyself under her hands. And the angel of the LORD said unto her, I will multiply thy seed exceedingly, that it shall not be numbered for multitude. And the angel of the LORD said unto her, Behold thou art with child, and shalt bear a son, and shalt call his name Ishmael, because the LORD hath heard thy affliction. And he will be a wild man; his hand will be against every man, and every man's hand against him, and he shall dwell in the presence of all his brethren. And she called the name of the LORD that spake unto her, Thou God seest me: for she said, Have I also here looked after him that seeth me? Wherefore the well was called Beerlahairoi; behold, it is between Kadesh and Bered." (Genesis 16:7-14)

Zeoli (*Is Jesus God? – Book Number One*) has made several observations about this passage. The first, of course is that Hagar identifies the Angel of the Lord as Jehovah. Zeoli looks past Hagar's observation and focus on the acts of this Angel of the Lord. Hagar, after all, could have been mistaken. The acts of this Angel of the Lord argue that she was correct in her assessment.

First, we see that the Angel claims the power to multiply Hagar's seed. This is followed by the Angel's understanding that Hagar was pregnant with a male child. In those long ago, pre sonogram days, the pregnancy might have been obvious; the gender of the child would have been pure speculation except to God.

Further, in verse twelve we see that this Angel prophesied about the life and lineage of this son to be. More than this, the Angel seemed, to me at least, to make this prophecy as a promise to Hagar in her time of despair.

The Angel of the Lord Was Called "God" by Hagar

Finally, in this passage the Angel was called "God" by Hagar. There was no rebuke from the Angel over this. A being from the order of created angels would have been quick to own up to his own status and direct all worship toward God.

> "And the angel of the LORD appeared unto him in a flame of fire out of the midst of a bush: and he looked, and, behold, the bush burned with fire, and the bush was not consumed. And Moses said, I will now turn aside, and see this great sight, why the bush is not burned. And the LORD saw that he turned aside to see, God called unto him out of the midst of the bush, and said, Moses, Moses. And he said, Here am I. And he said, Draw not nigh hither: put off thy shoes from off thy feet, for the place whereon thou standest is holy ground. Moreover he said, I am the God of thy father, the God of Abraham, the God of Isaac, and the God of Jacob. And Moses hid his face, for he was afraid to look upon God. And the LORD said, I have surely seen the affliction of my people which are in Egypt, and have heard their cry by reason of their taskmasters; for I know their sorrows." (Exodus 3:2-7)

Zeoli once again notices that Moses has identified the Angel of the Lord as Jehovah. This is done both without rebuke and under inspiration as Moses was the human instrument who wrote these words.

We further notice that this Angel appeared to Moses in a supernatural manner. In the appearances of angels in the Scripture, they are normally appearing as mere men. The people in Lot's day mistook the angels for casual strangers in their city.

The Angel also called out to Moses with authority. This Angel did not preface his remarks with, "The Lord says unto you," as is the case with beings from the order of angels. This Angel just spoke under His Own authority.

We must also note that this Angel gave Moses instruction in worship. Again, this was done on the Angel's Own authority rather than appealing to the authority of God. As such, unless this were a wicked angel, this was God speaking. The outworking of events since this time show that this was God. A wicked angel's counsel would have caused havoc rather than the chain of events which culminated in the coming of Messiah.

Besides all this, the Angel claimed to be God in verse six.

> "And it came to pass, when Joshua was by Jericho, that he lifted up his eyes and looked, and, behold, there stood a man over against him with his sword drawn in his hand: and Joshua went unto him, and said unto him, Art thou for us, or for our adversaries? And he said, Nay; but as captain of the host of the LORD am I now come.. And Joshua fell on his face to the earth, and did worship, and said unto him, What saith my lord unto his servant? And the captain of the LORD's host said unto Joshua, Loose thy shoe from off thy foot for the place whereon thou standest is holy. And Joshua did so." (Joshua 5:13-15)

Dake (*The Dake Annotated Bible*) sees that, once again, this Angel of the Lord is identified by the one to whom He was speaking, as Jehovah.

Dake also drew the parallel that the Angel claimed to be the Captain of the Host of the Lord while God is identified as the Captain of Israel in II Chronicles 13:12.

The Angel also accepted Worship from Joshua and allowed Joshua to call Him "Lord." (Scofield's notes on Malachi 3:18 states that where the all capital letter form of "LORD" is used in the King James Bible, the meaning is the English equivalent of "Jehovah.")

CHAPTER 10: JESUS IS THE THEME OF THE BIBLE

Further, again as Dake has brought out, the Angel commanded Joshua to remove his shoes in the same manner as had God done with Moses at the burning bush.

> *"But he said unto me, Behold, thou shalt conceive, and bear a son; and now drink no wine nor strong drink, neither eat any unclean thing: for the child shall be a Nazarite to God from the womb to the day of his death. Then Manoah intreated the LORD, and said, O my Lord, let the man of God which thou didst sent come again unto us, and teach us what we shall do unto the child that shall be born. And God hearkened to the voice of Manoah; and the angel of God came again unto the woman as she sat in the field: but Manoah her husband was not with her. And the woman made haste, and ran, and shewed her husband, and said unto him, Behold, the man hath appeared unto me, that came unto me the other day. And Manoah arose, and went after his wife, and came to the man, and said unto him, Art thou the man that spakest unto the woman? And he said, I am. And Manoah said, Now let thy words come to pass. How shall we order the child, and how shall we do unto him. And the angel of the LORD said unto Manoah, Of all that I said unto the woman let her beware. She may not eat of any thing that cometh of the vine, neither let her drink wine or strong drink, nor eat any unclean thing: all that I commanded her let her observe. And Manoah said unto the angel of the LORD, I pray thee, let us detain thee, until we shall have made ready a kid for thee. And the angel of the LORD said unto Manoah, Though thou detain me, I will not eat of thy bread: and if thou wilt offer a burnt offering, thou must offer it unto the LORD. For Manoah knew not that he was an angel of the LORD. And Manoah said unto the angel of the LORD, What is thy name, that when thy sayings come to pass we may do thee honour? And the angel of the LORD said unto him, Why askest thou after my name, seeing it is secret? So Manoah took a kid with a meat offering, and offered it upon a rock unto the LORD: and the angel did wondrously; and Manoah and his wife looked on. For it came to pass, when the flame went up toward heaven from off the altar, that the angel of the LORD ascended in the flame of the altar. And Manoah and his wife looked on it, and fell on their faces to the ground. But the angel of the LORD did no more appear to Manoah and to his wife. Then Manoah knew that he was an angel of the LORD. And Manoah said unto his wife, We shall surely die, because we have seen God." (Judges 13:7-22)*

Zeoli, again, sees that Manoah knew Who he had seen and verbalized the same. Note, especially, the last sentence (v. 22) of the passage. Again, this is a pre-incarnate appearance of our Lord Jesus Christ in which He is referred to as "God."

> *"And Jacob was left alone; and there wrestled a man with him until the breaking of the day. And when he saw that he prevailed not against him, he touched the hollow of his thigh, and the hollow of Jacob's thigh was out of joint, as he wrestled with him. And he said, Let me go, for the day breaketh. And he said, I will not let thee go, except thou bless me. And he said unto him, What is thy name? And he said, Jacob. And he said, Thy name shall be called no more Jacob, but Israel: for as a prince hast thou power with God and with men, and hast prevailed. And Jacob asked him, and said, Tell me, I pray thee, thy name. And he said, Wherefore is it that thou dost ask after my name? And he blessed him there. And Jacob called the name of the place, Peniel: for I have seen God face to face, and my life is preserved." (Genesis 32:24-30)*

First, the Old Testament often presents real events which have happened in history in a physical sense. We are to learn spiritual lessons from these physical events. At this event I see the concept of "prevailing prayer." There are times when it is God's will for us to "wrestle" with Him in prayer. This exercise builds our spiritual, and faith facilities, lives so that we can be stronger Christians for Him and His great work in the world.

Jacob Identifies the One with Whom He Wrestled as God

It is Dake (*Dake Annotated Bible*), here, who recognizes the fact that Jacob identifies the One with Whom he wrestled as God. Jacob recognized Him as the Blesser. Only God can give us real blessing.

We see a physical miracle as the "Wrestler" shrunk the sinew of Jacob.

The fact that Jacob claimed to have seen God is a recognition of what had happened.

The new name of Jacob is recorded, revered, and vilified, down through history.

> "And the angel of the LORD put forth the end of the staff that was in his hand, and touched the flesh and the unleavened cakes, and there rose up fire out of the rock, and consumed the flesh and the unleavened cakes. Then the angel of the LORD departed out of his sight. And when Gideon perceived that he was an angel of the LORD, Gideon said, Alas, O Lord GOD! for because I have seen an angel of the LORD face to face. And the LORD said unto him, Peace be unto thee, fear not: thou shalt not die." (Judges 6:21-23)

Gideon Called the Angel Messenger, God

Zeoli (*Is Jesus God? – Book Number One*) points out that Gideon was not corrected when he called this Messenger, "God." He was, rather, comforted.

We must also note at this place the Angel of the Lord received sacrifice from Gideon. This is an act of God only. Others who would do so are false. The end thereof would not be good or triumph as was seen in the events surrounding Gideon and this Visitation.

> "And the angel of the LORD called unto him out of heaven, and said, Abraham, Abraham: and he said, Here am I. And he said, Lay not thine hand upon the lad, neither do thou any thing unto him for now I know that thou fearest God, seeing thou hast not withheld thy son, thine only son from me. And Abraham lifted up his eyes, and looked, and behold behind him a ram caught in a thicket by his horns: and Abraham went and took the ram, and offered him up for a burnt offering in the stead of his son. And Abraham called the name of that place Jehovahjireh: as it is said to this day, In the mount of the LORD it shall be seen. And the angel of the LORD called unto Abraham out of heaven the second time, And he said, By myself have I sworn, saith the LORD, for because thou hast done this thing, and hast not withheld thy son, thine only son: That in blessing I will bless thee, and in multiplying I will multiply thy seed as the stars of the heaven, and as the sand which is upon the sea shore; and thy seed shall possess the gate of his enemies; And in thy seed shall all the nations of the earth be blessed; because thou hast obeyed my voice." (Genesis 22:11-18)

Abraham Identifies the Angel of the Lord as Jehovah

In this passage Abraham identifies the Angel of the Lord as Jehovah. This Angel also gives instruction in worship. Given the relationship which Abraham enjoyed with God, for Abraham to accept instruction in worship, even under these circumstances, is a strong indication that Abraham really did accept that this Angel was Jehovah.

Further events, down to this day, have proved the correctness of Abraham's

CHAPTER 10: JESUS IS THE THEME OF THE BIBLE

understanding in this instance of just to Whom he was speaking.

In verse sixteen we see that the Angel identifies Himself as "Lord." Verses seventeen and eighteen give credence to this identification as the Angel shows a knowledge beyond that of any mere human.

We hearken back now to Genesis 32:24-30 and consider the time that Jacob wrestled with the Angel of the Lord.

> *"And Jacob was left alone; and there wrestled a man with him until the breaking of the day. And when he saw that he prevailed not against him, he touched the hollow of his thigh; and the hollow of Jacob's thigh was out of joint, as he wrestled with him. And he said, Let me go, for the day breaketh. And he said, I will not let thee go, except thou bless me. and he said unto him, What is thy name? And he said Jacob. And he said, Thy name shall be called no more Jacob, but Israel: for as a prince hast thou power with god and with men, and hast prevailed. And Jacob asked him, and said Tell me, I pray thee, thy name. And he said, Wherefore is it that thou dost ask my name? And he blessed him there. And Jacob called the name of the place Peniel: for I have seen God fact to face, and my life is preserved."*

Zeoli points out that this "Wrestler" gave Jacob a new name which was more than normal. It was normal that the name by which a person in these times was known would be an indication of his character. But, this new name given to Jacob was a name which had a prophetic consideration about it. This requires a knowledge of future events which is limited to God.

That this "Wrestler" also blessed Jacob gives credence to the fact that the "Wrestler" was God.

The Angel Who Was the Captain of the Lord's Host

At this point we revisit Joshua 5:13-15 where Joshua came upon the Angel Who was the Captain of the Lord's Host. This could be none other than God. The fact that this Angel accepted Worship is a further proof that He was God.

> *"And it came to pass, when Joshua was by Jericho, that he lifted up his eyes and looked, and, behold, there stood a man over against him with his sword drawn in his hand: and Joshua went unto him, and said unto him, Art thou for us, or for our adversaries? And he said, Nay; but as captain of the host of the LORD am I now come. And Joshua fell on his face to the earth, and did worship, and said unto him, What saith my lord unto his servant? And the captain of the LORD'S host said unto Joshua, Loose thy shoe from off thy foot; for the place wherein thou standest is holy. And Joshua did so."*

The Authority of the Angel to Instruct in Worship

Zeoli notes that this Angel also had the authority to instruct in worship.

While we often consider that Jesus is only relevant to the New Testament. The fact, however, is that God did often visit the Old Testament saints. He did so in the form of a man. That man was Jesus Christ.

The Pulpit Commentary tells us that the early church father's considered that Joshua 5:13-15 speaks of the pre-incarnate Jesus.

We are led, from the evidence such as above, including that Jesus is the Medium by which the unseen God was shown to the world, that Jesus is "The Angel of the Lord" in these Old Testament encounters. This being true, and we believe it is, then Jesus is

God. His Deity is proven beyond any question.

Ryrie (*The Ryrie Study Bible*) also accepts this consideration. He considers Genesis 16:10 and agrees that this is a physical manifestation of God. Part of our argument is based on inference. Ryrie says, "Since the angel of the Lord ceases to appear after the incarnation, it is often inferred that the angel in the O. T. is a preincarnate appearance of the Second Person of the Trinity [Jesus]."

I would like to note, once again, because it is important. When we speak of the "First," "Second," and "Third" Persons of the Trinity, we are not speaking of any sort of ranking order. All, and Each, are fully God. The numerical designations only refer to the order of revelation of Each in the progressive and unfolding teaching of Scripture. "The Father" was first referenced in Scripture. Then "The Son." And, lastly, "The Holy Spirit."

Much of our view of the Identity of "The Angel of the Lord" is based on Scriptural principles. Leupold (*Exposition of Genesis*) argues, from Genesis 16:7, that "The organic unity of Scripture would be broken if ... the central point in the Old Testament revelation was a creature angel, while that of the New is the Incarnation of the God-Man."

In other words, it would be strange if a mere "person" from the created order of angels was so dominant in the Old Testament revelation while the "Person" of the New Testament is Jesus Christ, very God and very Man. It is more reasonable, from Scriptural principle that Jesus, pre-existent from before the beginning, is the Divinely presented Angel of the Lord.

The Pulpit Commentary also speaks of this Scriptural principle. This commentary looks at I Corinthians 10:4 and sees a Scriptural pronouncement which backs up our contention that the Angel of the Lord of the Old Testament is the same Jesus of the New Testament. "As a matter of [historical] fact, the Word, the Wisdom of God, was the Angel of the Church in the Wilderness."

I believe that we have shown "The Angel of the Lord" to be Jesus in several pre-incarnate appearances. Since this "Angel" was identified as God, this should - all by itself - settle the question of the full Deity of Jesus Christ.

In our next session we will begin to consider the concept of "gods With a Small "g."

CHAPTER 11
gODS WITH A SMALL "G"
(Session Twelve)

Jesus Is Not a Created god

A few years ago I was engaged in a "battle" of sorts with a man I never met. He was writing a weekly religious column in a local newspaper. I would disagree in the "letters to the editor" section. His argument was that Jehovah of the Old Testament is the God of the Bible. He was correct in that. He also argued that the Christ, Jesus, of the New Testament was a created being who had been given the title "God." He was way wrong on that!

His argument was that while Jesus had taught the way to God, He was not, Himself, God in the flesh. The writer was incorrect in that statement as well.

Part of his argument centered on the fact that other people in the Bible had been addressed as "god." I felt it necessary to present the Bible truth of this consideration lest there be any confusion.

Burrell (*Jesus: Son of God*) has well noted that Jesus is called "God" in a unique sense in the Bible. Adam, for instance, is called the son of God by the fact of his creation. The nation of Israel was called God's son by their special election as God's Chosen People. In the New Testament all Christians are children (sons) of God by the regeneration of the New Birth.

Jesus, the "Monogenes"

However, when one considers Jesus, He is called the Son of God in an entirely differing manner. Only Jesus is described as that "monogenes," the unique and one of a kind, only begotten Son of God. "For God so loved the world, that he gave his only begotten Son, that whosoever believeth in him should not perish, but have everlasting life." (John 3:16)

There were others in Bible times that were referred to as "gods." This was one of the troubles associated with the infant church and the Roman government. The Caesars were, by imperial law, to be worshipped as deities; the Christians refused to do this.

Even earlier, the Egyptian people considered their pharaohs to be real gods. This was not an unusual situation in some cultures.

The Egyptian's, however, expected others to address their pharaoh as "God." The Concordia Study Bible notes this. "The pharaohs of Egypt were sometimes addressed as 'my god' by their vassal kings in Palestine, as evidenced by the Amarna letters.

Since the ancient Jews saw themselves as special representatives of the True God, it is not surprising that they would follow the linguistic traditions of the day by using the term "god" to address their own king who ruled, albeit temporally and temporarily, over the chosen people of God.

But, if this were done, the central truth of the Jewish religion is that there is only One True Creator God would not be cast aside. Thus, these Jewish people would not have considered their kings as divine. That these same people would have considered that their kings ruled as representatives of God is admitted. But, their religious observances would have recognized the difference.

To dismiss the many Messianic passages in the Psalms (example: *"Thy throne, O God, is for ever and ever: the sceptre of thy kingdom is a right sceptre." (Psalm 45:6)*, for instance, as simply cultural statements made about temporal rulers - or, worse yet, as mistaken religious observations - is both unwarranted and unwise. More to the point, such a suggestion is wrong!

Strong (*Systematic Theology*) has weighed in on the subject. Religious leaders (as well as political leaders in the near Theocracy of the people of Israel and Judah) were sometimes called "god." Often Scripture calls those who are representatives of God, "god," themselves. This is done since they stand in the place of representing God (Example: Exodus 4:16; 7:1; Ps. 82:6). The connection, however, leaves no doubt as to what is meant. These are examples of men standing as representatives of God.

Jesus is Ascribed as Having the Creative Attributes of God

Jesus, however, is ascribed as having the creative attributes of God.

> *"And to make all men see what is the fellowship of the mystery, which from the beginning of the world hath been hid in God, who created all things by Jesus Christ." (Ephesians 3:9)*

This is clearly a higher reference than any made of mere man. This referenced verse does not say that Jesus was not fully God. The verse states that Jesus was the Creative Agent of the Godhead.

Jesus Has Demonstrated that He Is God

Jesus stands far above any sense of merely being called "god." He has demonstrated that He IS God.

> *"Jesus answered them, Is it not written in your law, I said, Ye are gods? If he called them gods, unto whom the word of God came, and the scripture cannot be broken; Say ye of him, whom the Father hath sanctified, and sent into the world, Thou blasphemest, because I said, I am the Son of God?" (John 10:34-36)*

The reference, here, is back to Psalm 82:6 as we have already seen.

Jesus was here defending Himself from the religious leaders. Note in verse 38 that He does not back away from His unique position. He does not merely work for God; He claims equality. For this He is nearly stoned.

The Concordia Study Bible sees the truth of His statement. "If there is any sense in which men can be spoken of as 'gods' (as Ps. 82:6 speaks of human rulers and of judges), how much more may the term be used of him whom the Father set apart and sent!"

Falwell (*The Annotated Study Bible*) sees that, although Jesus is alluding to the Hebrew judges who interpret God's Law and justice, He is not denying His Own Deity.

Notice that Jesus has just shown that His words did not necessarily constitute blasphemy. In doing this He has demonstrated "...His superior knowledge of Scripture."

Back in verse thirty-three of this tenth chapter of John, we see that the reason the religious leaders were willing to stone Jesus was because, "...*thou, being a man,*

CHAPTER 11: gODS WITH A SMALL "G"

makest thyself God." They still understood that He had claimed equality with God even after His defense. Verse thirty-nine says that they were still willing to stone Him.

Had these men been mistaken in the meaning of the words of Jesus, it would have been incumbent upon Him to correct their view. Since He did not do so we must conclude that He is equal with God. Or, He is mistaken about His Own nature. Or, He is a liar in that He allowed men to believe that which He knew to be untrue.

Jesus is God - With a Capital "G."

The "bottom line truth" is, however, that Jesus is God - with a capital "G." He is the God of Eternity and Creation. He is our Lord and Savior.

When the Scripture calls Jesus, "God," there is no reference to either title or position. This exception, had it been used, would not have raised the extreme ire of the religious leaders which led to the crucifixion.

The term "God," when applied to Jesus, speaks of His Person. This Is Who He Is!

In our next session we will consider that God is One.

CHAPTER 12
GOD: HE IS ONE
(Session Thirteen)

The Trinitarian View Is Not Pagan

There are those who will call the Trinitarian view (The Father, The Son, and The Holy Ghost) a pagan view of multiple gods. This is, of course, not true. We see the One Eternal God eternally manifesting Himself in three distinct Personalities. But, we do see only One God.

There Is Only One God

I am not going to try to explain how this could be. I don't believe that any person on this earth can totally explain the concept of The Triune God. This is a concept of eternity and Spirit. Our only experience in this life is among physicality and time. We, the race of humanity, have no ability to conceptualize that which is so far beyond our experience and understanding.

I have often used the illustration of a cup of coffee with cream and sugar to try to explain this concept. Each of the elements - the coffee, cream and sugar - is detectable. But, the three have merged into one in that none of us, with average learning and materials, can ever separate those three parts. Each is distinctly different; yet each is part of the whole.

The illustration breaks down when we consider that the three elements were in different containers before they were merged in the cup. We cannot say that about God. He has been, from eternity unto eternity, God in Three distinct Personalities. God did not begin and become. God has always just "been."

I also cannot understand, or explain, the concept of eternality. It is foreign to my life experiences. We call eternity a "time without end." Yet, eternity is not time. Neither is it stasis. God acted in eternity to create time and the universe. I do not understand eternity. However, I am sure thankful that God has promised to keep me through that experience.

Simmons (*A Systematic Study of Bible Doctrine*) notes that the Bible teaches, over and over, that there is only One God. He cites Deuteronomy 6:4, Isaiah 44:6; John 17:3; I Corinthians 8:4; and I Timothy 1:17 as examples of this Bible teaching.

We Need to Be Careful How We Say Things

I am trying to break myself of a real bad habit that I find common to the Christian. We say that God is a God of power. We say that God is a God of love. We say that God is a God of grace and mercy. We are wrong! There is only One God. We should say that God is The God of Power. We should say that God is The God of Love. We should say that God is The God of Grace and Mercy.

To say "a God" is to imply that there is more than One. This term argues that the God of the Bible is merely the best of the lot. That is a false teaching. God isn't the best of the lot; He is The Lot!

Belief in the Trinity is Not Polytheism

Cole (*Basic Christian Faith*) says that the belief in the Trinity is not polytheism, a belief in more than one God. Such a concept is foreign to Christianity. The concept of the Bible is Trinitarianism not Tri-Theism. There is only one God. "The three Persons of the Trinity are one as to substance, yet three as to individuality. ... There are ... no inequalities ... each of the three is God." Yet there is only One God.

Once again, the Trinitarian view, the Bible view, is that there is but One God. He is eternally manifest in three distinct, but not disparate, individual Personalities. A way to explain the central idea is to say that in the singleness of the Godhead there is a unity of multiplicity.

There are three "Persons," but only One God.

Simmons, again, sees that we use the term "Person" in a figurative sense when we speak of the Godhead. We speak of the Father, and the Son, and the Holy Ghost. "In the case of three human beings there is a division of nature, essence, and being... Such a conception of God is forbidden by the teaching of the Scripture as to the unity of God."

The point is that we cannot consider God as three separate "Persons." On this earth there are three persons in my family since the death of my wife. I am the father. Ethan is the son. Amy is the daughter. We, the three of us constitute a family. But, we are not gathered together as one organism. Ethan works in the health care field. Amy is now working in a bank. The old and fat guy, me, is retired. We are a family; but we are not a unified organism.

The Trinity Is of One Essence

God, meanwhile, in the three "Persons" of the Godhead - The Father, The Son, and The Holy Ghost - is One in essence. Yet He remains three distinct Personalities. We use the term "Person" as a shorthand way of understanding, as best we can, with our limited human experience and intellects.

Orr (*Can We Be Sure That Jesus Christ is God*) writes of the Old Testament example of the unified multiplicity of God. In Genesis 1:1, the word for God is plural (There are three tenses in the Hebrew: singular - pertaining to one; dual - pertaining to two; and plural - pertaining to three or more.), yet the verb translated "created" is singular. One God in three Persons equals one act in harmony.

A Strong Indication of the Trinity

Alford (*The New Testament for English Readers*) finds the New Testament parallel of this Genesis insight into the nature of God. He sees Matthew 28:19 (*"Go ye therefore, and teach all nations, baptizing them in the name of the Father, and of the Son, and of the Holy Ghost."*) as teaching a unified Being of the three "Persons." "Baptizing them **in** the name" speaks of a singular act by the "Father, Son, and Holy Ghost."

This often overlooked phrase from Matthew is actually, to me at least, a stronger intimation of the Trinity than is the passage from Genesis. It could be argued, although unsuccessfully I would assert, that the passage in Genesis could have been three individuals working as a team. But, there is no question about this in the statement from Matthew. His Name **IS** (singular) "The Father, The Son, and The Holy Ghost" (Triune).

CHAPTER 12: GOD: HE IS ONE

The Concept of the Unity of the Trinity is a Hard Concept

As we have stated above, the concept of the unity within the unity of the Trinity is a hard concept for human man to grasp. Simmons has tried to explain the reasonableness of the Trinity. He has said, "...the unity of God does not preclude His trinity, and His trinity is in no way inconsistent with His unity."

I like to take a little more direct course to explain the truth of the trinity of God even when our minds might rebel at the idea. "He's God. He can do whatever He wants to do!" That isn't as flippant it might seem. God is on a completely different level of existence than are we. Just because we do not understand, with our finite minds, how a thing might be does not mean that God does not understand. The fact is that the Trinity is taught in the Scripture. It is so. God has said it is so. It is not our intellect which makes truth to be Truth. It is His will which is Sovereign.

"Hear, O Israel: The LORD our God is one LORD." (Deuteronomy 6:4)

Falwell (*The Annotated Study Bible*) has well noted that there cannot be two who are absolute. In such a case, **neither** would be **absolute**. While understanding that the Father is God, and Jesus is God, and the Holy Ghost is God, we must consider that the Three constitute but One God. Each is a separate Personality but each is united in One Essence.

There is But One God

There is but one God. We are Trinitarians because the Bible teaches this Truth. We also are Monotheist because the Bible also teaches this Truth.

In our next session we will discuss the concept of accepting Jesus as God.

CHAPTER 13
ACCEPTING JESUS AS GOD
(Session Fourteen)

We do accept that Jesus of Nazareth is God in human flesh. That's a pretty well known historic belief of the Christian churches. But, what does the Word say? Does the Word of God make the claim that God resided in the body of the Babe of Bethlehem? Our belief system must be founded on the Words which God placed in our hands through inspiration. If the Scripture does not agree with our belief, no matter how historic that belief might be, the belief if wrong and the Scripture is right.

This is so every single time!

I believe that the Scripture will show that the historic Christian claim of the divinity of Jesus is not an argument of theologians. This is an assured fact of the Truth of Who God is.

In John 2:19 Jesus answers several religious leaders. They were questioning by what right He had cleansed the Temple of the money changers and such. They wanted to know by what authority He had done so. Jesus answered, *"...Destroy this temple, and in three days I will raise it up again."* The Bible tells us that *"...he spake of the temple of his body."* (John 2:21)

What was the Temple to the Jewish people of that day? Remember, this was not a local Synagogue; this was <u>the</u> Temple in Jerusalem. The yearly feasts were celebrated at this location. Even the earthly family of Jesus made a pilgrimage to this Temple.

The Omnipresence of God

The ancients understood the concept of the omnipresence of God. God is everywhere. David, the Psalmist of Israel knew this fact.

> *"Whither shall I go from thy spirit? or whither shall I flee from thy presence? If I ascend up into heaven, thou art there: if I make my bed in hell, behold thou art there. If I take the wings of the morning, and dwell in the uttermost parts of the sea; Even there shall thy hand lead me, and thy right hand shall hold me. If I say, Surely the darkness shall cover me; even the night shall be light about me. Yea, the darkness hideth not from thee; but the night shineth as the day: the darkness and light are both alike to thee."* (Psalm 139:7-12)

The Body of Jesus was The Temple where Resided the Eternal God

Still, to the devout of the day, the Temple was the special place of residence of God. It was to the Temple that they would seek His presence. There was placed the "Holy of Holies" in which the annual sacrifice for sin was placed before the "Face" of God. Only one priest and he only once a year, could enter into this place.

This is why we see that the Veil of the Temple (see Matthew 27:51) *"was rent in twain."* at the death of Jesus on the Cross. This signified that no longer would it be only the privilege and duty of that priest to come into the presence of God; now, with the New Covenant in the Blood of Jesus, this would be the privilege and duty of all who would call upon the Name of the Savior.

As to the answer of Jesus that He would raise the Temple in three days, and the Scriptural assertion that this was the Temple of His body, Jesus was saying that the very God these people professed to worship was standing before them in His Own body. Jesus was stating His Own Deity before these men.

Adam Clarke (*Adam Clarke's Commentary*) also notes this fact. He says that the body of Jesus was **The Temple** where resided the **Eternal God**.

Without this understanding the words of Jesus make no sense in relation to the question asked.

"*For in him dwelleth all the fulness of the Godhead bodily.*" (Colossians 2:9)

We speak of accepting Jesus into our lives when we are born again. We speak of the indwelling of the Holy Spirit within the Christian. These are both true. But, the sense that true Divinity resided within the Person of Jesus is much deeper. The Spirit may dwell within us. But, as the *Pulpit Commentary* says, men may have God in their lives, but Jesus has **all of God** (the fulness of Him) in His body.

We may be "indwelt" by God; Jesus simply is God.

Clarke also notes the many representations, such as the "Mercy Seat," of God in the Temple. But, the reality of God was, and still is, in Jesus.

The Image of the Invisible God

The Pulpit Commentary, again, says that this verse means that not simply as an image did God exist in the Body of Jesus. God is bodily in the Babe of Bethlehem. This, Jesus is true God Himself.

"*Who is the image of the invisible God, the firstborn of every creature.*" (Colossians 1:15)

Of this verse, Alford (*The New Testament for English Readers*) says, "...the term 'image' ... Must not be restricted to Christ corporeally visible in the Incarnation, but understood of Him as the manifestation of God in His Whole Person and work..."

When I say that my grandson is the "image" of my son, I do not mean that they are the same. I might argue that they both stem from the same "essence." Even this is not true. Both, obviously, have different mothers so that as an illustration would fail. But, the illustration also fails because they are separate human entities.

Father to son to grandson is the normal human progression. God, however, has always been existent in the Trinity. The Trinity is not a concept of progression. The Trinity is a concept of stasis of individuality within the reality of complete unity. There is One God eternally present in the corporate unity of three individual "Person." "They" is not the proper term to use when speaking of God. "He" denotes the unity as One God.

The terms "Father" and "Son" when used to describe the first and second Persons of the Trinity seem more constructed toward our imperfect understanding of Spiritual things. The Son, in His humanity, is an example of how the human should live his life. Thus, the Son would always defer to the will of the Father. This does not place Jesus on a lower plain. This concept was part of His teaching ministry to us.

The Concept of the Trinity is Not of Levels of Authority

The concept of the Trinity is not of levels of authority. There is but One God. Each of the three "Persons" (in our understanding) of the Trinity is fully God. While separate

CHAPTER 13: ACCEPTING JESUS AS GOD

Individuals each is of the same Essence. Thus when the verse above speaks of Jesus as being "the image" of God, the full meaning is that when we look upon Jesus we are actually looking upon The Eternal God.

The Meaning of The Firstborn of Every Creature

The fact that Jesus is here called *"the firstborn of every creature"* does not denote any sort of beginning. This is a twofold reference. The first is that He is positionally above all other creatures as the firstborn was above his siblings in the families of this time. There is also a more time centric understanding of this verse. Jesus is the "firstborn," or "first," of the resurrection from the dead of the Christian - or New Covenant.

> "Who, being in the form of God, through it not robbery to be equal with God." (Philippians 2:6)

The Jerusalem Bible note at this passage says, "Lit. 'Who subsisting in the form of God': Here 'form' means all the attributes that express and reveal the essential nature of God: Christ, being God, had all the divine prerogatives by right."

Kenosis

This verse begins a section where the Kenosis is considered. The Kenosis is a theological term used to describe the fact that Jesus laid aside the outward glory of His essential Godhood. In doing this He took upon Himself the form of humanity. This "emptying" of His outward glory would not have been necessary had He not been God. Thus the extended passage speaks of the full Deity of Jesus.

> "I and my Father are one." (John 10:30)

The Jehovah Witness Cult

The Jehovah's Witness cult, among others, argues that Jesus was just talking about being consistent with the mission to which God had called Him. If this were true, Jesus *cannot* be our Savior as He would be just another man. The following Scriptures argue that this view of the Jehovah's Witness cult is not true. In verse thirty-three the reason given for these men planning to stone Jesus to death is, "...because that thou, being a man, makest thyself God."

Jesus never corrected these men. Had this been a misconception on their part, had this not been what He meant, He would have been honor bound to correct them. Failing to do so would have made Him a liar. This would have disqualified Him from being a moral, or a religious, leader.

Believing this to be true, had it not been true, would have made Jesus a lunatic. This would also have disqualified Him from being either a moral or religious leader.

Thus, Jesus is God. There is no other argument which can be made from this passage.

Matthew Henry (*Matthew Henry's Commentary*) argues against the theology of the Jehovah Witness cult, as well when he comments upon this verse.

> "This speaks more than the harmony, and consent, and good understanding that were between the Father and the Son in the work of man's redemption... It must be meant of **the oneness of the nature** of the Father and Son, that they are the same in substance, and equal in power and glory."

This verse would also argue against the Mormon concept of Jesus being a "spirit child" of Jehovah.

> *"Thus saith the LORD the King of Israel, and his redeemer the LORD of hosts; I am the first, and I am the last; and beside me there is no God." (Isaiah 44:6)*

The simple connective work "and" tells us that there are two Persons mentioned in this verse. These Two are the "The Lord, the King of Israel," and "The Redeemer, the Lord of Hosts." As Falwell (*The Annotated Study Bible*) points out, Both are called by the personal name of "Yahweh." [This author does not use the term "Yahweh," it is a corruption of Jehovah.] Yet, there is only One ("...beside me there is no god."). The Father and the Son equal One God.

Added to the above, although we are not considering this in this study, is the fact that the Father, and the Son, and the Holy Spirit equal One God!

> *"And we know that the Son of God is come, and hath given us an understanding, that we may know him that is true, and we are in him that is true, even in his Son Jesus Christ. This is true God, and eternal life." (I John 5:20)*

Pendleton (*Christian Doctrine*) argues from this verse the truth that there are not three Gods. Jesus is the "one, true God."

There is really not much other argument that can be made from the above verse. Even considering the context of the entire chapter, we are seeing a picture given of the work of Jesus of Nazareth. The concluding verse then asserts that this (which is the subject of the entire passage - Jesus) is true God.

To bolster the fact that this verse is speaking of Jesus, we also note that the passage denotes the One identified as "true God" as "eternal life." This is a phrase which is continually used of Jesus, by Whose death had come the salvation which assures eternal life. This verse can only be speaking of the complete Deity of Jesus Christ.

Let There Be No Mistake. Jesus is God

We, again, revisit Colossians 2:9,

> *"For in him dwelleth all the fulness of the Godhead bodily."* The Pulpit Commentary agrees that Jesus is fully God. Then, this source also adds that we do not worship a plurality of Gods. In Jesus is the fullness of God.

This is an important point. In this section of our study we are considering the Biblical teaching that there is only ONE GOD. There is no question, from the Biblical standpoint, that this is true. If, therefore, we are asserting the Deity of Jesus we are claiming the fullness of that Deity is His nature. Let there be no mistake. Jesus is God.

> *"In the beginning was the Word, and the Word was with God, and the Word was God." (John 1:1)*

Note this verse in relation to Jesus. "The Word was with God;" this speaks of the distinct personality of Jesus. Meanwhile, "The Word was God;" this speaks of the unity of the Godhead.

Jesus Has a Distinct Personality; The Mystery of the Godhead

Jesus is fully God. Yet, it is also true that He has a distinct Personality. This same thing must be said of the Father, and of the Holy Spirit. Each is fully God. Each has a distinct Personality. This is the mystery of the Godhead. There is but One God. Yet He - fully of One Essence – exists eternally as Three distinct Personalities.

In our next session we will begin to study this mystery as we consider that,

CHAPTER 13: ACCEPTING JESUS AS GOD

although God is One, God is Plural. It is the math of eternity and Spirit. I do not profess, as a person of time and physicality, to completely understand. I do know that this is a Bible teaching which we should consider.

CHAPTER 14
GOD: HE IS PLURAL
(Session Fifteen)

God is Eternally Existent in But One Essence

Clarke (*An Outline of Christian Theology*) asserts that, "The Divine Trinity is God's triune mode of existence."

Caird (*The Truth of the Gospel*) adds the argument of Augustine to the equation. Augustine noted that the Scriptures declare that, "God is Love." Love requires a lover, and an object of that love, and love itself. Since God existed before the creation of all things we know and understand (from eternity), the fact that He is love suggests the Trinity.

Within this One Essence the Trinitarian Sees Three Distinct "Persons."

The stock argument against the concept of the Trinity is that it introduces a concept which is foreign to monotheism. At first glance this argument seems reasonable. But, the argument of the Trinitarian is that God is eternally existent in but One Essence. Within this One Essence, however, the Trinitarian sees three distinct "Persons."

"Persons" is actually a faulty construct to consider. When we consider three "Persons," from our experience in time and physicality, we see three distinct individuals who are not gathered together into one being. My grandson, my son, and I, constitute the male part of our family unit. We are one family. But, this unity is of three separate individuals. My grandson is a little three year old ball of energy with blue eyes and short blond hair. In my family we were all blond until puberty. My son is a robust young man with fairly long hair and a beard. I am an old and fat man with graying hair. We constitute a family unit. But we are not a unit of essence.

This is not a picture of the Triune nature of God.

I am seen in three different lights. My grandson sees me as this rather large old guy who enjoys playing with him and his "G. I. Joe's." My son sees me as an ageing father. The people at church see me as a senior citizen with an annoying habit of pontificating on Biblical matters. I am but one person; but I present a different "face" to different people.

This is not a picture of the Triune nature of God.

The Trinity is of the Same Essence and Nature

God is three distinct Individuals. But, all three of the Individuals are of the same essence and nature. The Three are distinct; but the Three are One. I *cannot* really explain it. The concept of the Trinity is beyond our human comprehension. A cup of coffee, with cream and sugar, gives the best illustration that I can understand. Each ingredient may be tasted distinctly, yet not as though it were the entire cupful in and of itself. Together they form one drink and *cannot* be divided. Yet, each is a distinct ingredient.

Such, on a much grander scale of course, is the Trinity.

God Has Been Eternally Existent in the Triune Godhead

There are holes in my analogy, of course. Each of the coffee ingredients was once separate. God, meanwhile, has been eternally existent in the Triune Godhead.

Again, we cannot understand this because this is a concept of Eternity and Spirit. The only experience we have in which to understand anything is colored by our life encased in time and physicality.

Thus, the Scripture begins to teach us concepts which are far beyond our human comprehension. I am fond of appealing to John 3:13 at this point. Jesus, speaking to Nicodemus in first century Jerusalem, said,

> "And no man hath ascended up to heaven, but he that came down from heaven, even the Son of man which is in heaven."

How could Jesus be in heaven while He was speaking with Nicodemus? I do not know. I do know that the Bible says this is so. Therefore, even though the concept is beyond my comprehension, it is so.

There are those who approach the Bible with the attitude that everything within must be reasonable to their human reasoning. This is folly. God is explaining the things of eternity to people of time. True faith is to understand that God might know something a little more than we. True faith is to accept what God says simply because He has said it is so.

This is the only way I can deal with the issue of the Trinity. God said it in His Word. It is so.

Pendleton (*Christian Doctrines*) tells us that the use of the term, "Three Persons in One God," is misleading. Our concept of "person" is "individual." However, God is three personalities in One Individual.

Quite often the Bible will give us physical illustrations of the things we need to understand in the spiritual. Henderson (*Our Eternal God*) gives us several illustrations from Scripture where several persons were considered as one.

Genesis 2:24 gives us the illustration of Adam and Eve.

> "Therefore shall a man leave his father and his mother, and shall cleave unto his wife: and they shall be one flesh."

The Unity of Purpose of the Trinity

Although we often miss the point, this is a prophecy - one of the first in Scripture. There had been no fathers or mothers up to this point. Adam and Eve were singular in their existence. God said, "It's going to happen. You two are the template for those to follow."

This was also part of the teaching ministry of God to His creature. The two were considered as one even as the Trinity in actuality is One. This was basic in the foundation of the human race.

The people at the Tower of Babel were also called one.

> "And the LORD said, Behold, the people is one, and they have all one language; and this they begin to do: and now nothing will be restrained from them, which they have imagined to do." (Genesis 11:6)

Here the people were joined in a joint effort. Their work was as one. In this, although these people were wickedly employed, God was displaying the unity of

CHAPTER 14: GOD HE IS PLURAL

purpose which is resident within the Three of the Trinity. They (plural) are (singular) working throughout history.

In the New Testament Paul writes of the minister's of the Gospel message.

> "I have planted, Apollos watered; but God gave the increase. So then neither is he that planteth any thing, neither he that watereth; but God that giveth the increase. Now he that planteth and he that watereth are one: and every man shall receive his own reward according to his own labour." (I Corinthians 3:6-8)

Even though the passage understands that there are individuals involved (every man shall receive his own reward), the message is that those involved in the ministry is one ("*he that planteth and he that watereth are one*").

This same consideration is made of the ministry of the churches which Jesus founded. Although each of the churches is local (the church at Corinth, the church at Rome, the church at Galatia, etc), being many individual churches, Jesus said that He would build "my church." (see Matthew 16:18) This is a singular statement made of a plural reality.

The presenting of the Gospel message is <u>ONE</u> <u>WORK</u>. It may be carried forth by many persons at many locations, but there is One Gospel, One Lord, One Salvation. The old saw that there are "thousand's of churches so which one is right," does not understand. Yes, there are thousands of churches, each independent unto the Lord. Therein is the unity; all true churches are united in subjection to ONE LORD. This concept is a picture of the Triune nature of the Godhead.

Over and over the Scripture gives us physical illustrations of these great spiritual truths. The things of the Spirit and Eternity are not of our understanding. God says, "The truths are *like this*," thereby giving us "pictures" from which we can extrapolate the lessons He is teaching.

When you see Adam and Eve's aprons of leaves in the Garden being replaced by the coats of skins which God prepared for them, you are seeing a picture of the concept of the blood atonement as effective whereas the works of man are not effective.

When we consider Jacob wrestling with God we are reminded that we need to be prevailing in prayer. Prayer is not a flippant talisman. Prayer is a dialogue with God. It is often a pleading for that which we need. It is never a simple ritual.

When we see Joseph thrown into the pit by his brothers, sold into slavery, and then becoming the magistrate of Egypt, we are given a picture of Jesus being rejected by His Own, humanly speaking, people, killed, and then raised to sit in majesty in Heaven.

We view David as the shepherd boy who became king. This is a prophecy, and a picture of Jesus Who is the Shepherd of our Faith and the King of our lives.

The Truth of the Trinity Proclaimed in Scripture From the Beginning

Scripture begins with the proclamation of the truth of the trinity. Clarke (*Adam Clarke's Commentary*) shows us this from the very first verse of Scripture. Genesis 1:1, "In the beginning God...." "The original word [Hebrew] **Elohim**, God, is certainly the plural form of El, or Eloah, and has long been supposed, by the most eminently pious men, to imply a **plurality** of Persons in the Divine nature."

Indeed it is. There are three tenses in the Hebrew. The singular speaks of one. The dual speaks of two. But the plural, of which is Elohim, speaks of at least three. Some argue that this is "the plurality of majesty." This is not the picture which

Scripture paints of God. His Glory and His majesty stem from His Person.

Hogan (*Trinitarian Adumbration*) argues that we see the Trinity in Genesis, chapter one.

> "...God is viewed as creating...the 'Spirit' is seen hovering, and...the 'Word' is heard speaking."

The thrust of this session has been to argue that there is but One God. This is a concept which is taught over and over in the Scripture. By the same token, we see that there are three "Persons," a poor choice of terms but the best that our limited human mind can grasp, are all are of the Same Individual Essence, yet Distinct Personalities with the Oneness of the Godhead.

We will continue with this same general theme in our next session as we consider that God has presented Himself to us in this Trinitarian construct.

CHAPTER 15
THE ONENESS OF THE GODHEAD
(Session Sixteen)

God is a Being of Plurality Within His Oneness

When we speak of the "plurality" of God, we are not speaking of "plural gods." There is just one God. He, however, is a Being of Plurality within His Oneness. The Trinity is the theological term which is used to describe this manner of presentation of which God has taken of Himself.

God is Three Equals, But One Being

Read (*The Christian Faith*) has described God in this manner. God is Three Equals, but only One Being. Read does admit what all of us must, that

"There is that in God which defies all human thought and formulae..."

There is Only One God, He is Manifest in Three "Persons"

Although there is only one God, He is manifest in three "Persons." Again, as we have noted before, the term "Person" is an incorrect analogy. Our human minds rebel at the thought of three distinct persons within one body of essence. We cannot understand this because we have no frame of reference to understand this.

We do know, however, that the Bible does teach the complete unity of God. He is One. Still, the Father, the Son, and the Holy Spirit are each recognized as God. This is shown in their attributes, their abilities, and their willingness to accept worship.

Simmons (*A Systematic Study of Bible Doctrine*) points out that the Father, the Son, and the Holy Spirit are each recognized as equal. But, even realizing this does not give us the information as to how it is so. We may never gain that understanding this side of Glory.

There is but One God.

But, the Scripture, which is the Words and Teaching of God to humanity, expresses the Trinity. The Scripture recognizes that the Three are God. The Scripture teaches that the Three are described as distinct Persons.

Still, the same Scripture teaches that within this Trinity there are not three Gods. Within this Trinity is but One Holy Essence. Each of the "Persons" are completely equal.

When I was at the first college I attended I was a member of the school basketball team. My ability was such that my being on the team only meant that I had a good first row seat on the bench. If you have trouble understanding the doctrine of the Trinity there's plenty of room on the end of the bench. Almost all of us are in the same situation.

This is just the condition of most of us. We have to simply trust that what God says is so whether we understand it or not. We go on the theory that He might understand just a little bit more than we do!

Strong (*Systematic Theology*) simply says that the concept of the Trinity is "Inscrutable yet not self-contradictory, this doctrine furnishes the key to all other doctrines."

Newton (*An Outline of Christian Theology*) says only that,

"The Divine Trinity is God's threefold self-manifestation."

So, if we cannot understand this concept, if the concept goes against all human reasoning, how do we know that such a situation actually exists? Well, we go back to the old children's Sunday School song. "How do I know? / The Bible tells me so!"

Scripture does proclaim the truth of the Trinity in intimation and in illumination.

John R. Rice (*The Rice Reference Bible*) finds the Trinity in Matthew 28:19.

"Go ye therefore, and teach all nations, baptizing them in the name of the Father, and of the Son, and of the Holy Ghost."

Rice asks that we note the Trinity. People are to be baptized in the Name (Singular) of the Father, the Son, and the Holy Ghost (Plural).

Hogan (*Trinitarian Adumbration*) finds the Trinity in the very opening of the Bible narrative, *"In the beginning God created the heaven and the earth." (Genesis 1:1)*

"Not only does the opening text of the Word of God allow for a trinity of Persons in the Godhead, but it also supplies its own proper emphasis to that essential unity of the true and living God. This is implied in the fact that the very verb 'created' (**bara** in Hebrew) is in the singular. Hence our Bible commences with the sublime peculiarity of a plural substantive with a singular verb, thus laying the groundwork for the progressive unfolding of the grand truth concerning the one infinite, unique, eternal, and transcendental God who subsists as a trinity of divine Persons."

Elohim

The Word translated "God" in that verse (Elohim) is in the plural. I am not a Hebrew scholar, but every resource I searched referred to three tenses in the Hebrew. There is a singular - meaning one. There is a dual - meaning two. And, there is a plural - meaning three or more. Thus "God (Plural) created (Singular)" equates to one work being cited as having been done by a Plurality of Deity. Since the Bible consistently says that there is but One God, we have a picture of the Trinitarian concept of God.

The Three is One. That isn't just bad grammar. That is accurate representation.

Lindsell (*The Harper Study Bible*) cites Genesis 1:26.

"And God said, Let us make man in our image, after our likeness: and let them have dominion over the fish of the sea, and over the fowl of the air, and over the cattle, and over all the earth, and over every creeping thing that creepeth upon the earth."

The earlier readers of Scripture, before God had unfolded all His mystery revealed in the Scripture, might have confused "us" with being a case of speaking as a plurality of majesty. They may have even envisioned God as "...consulting with his angelic court..." Neither of these are correct interpretations of God's teaching.

As to the Plurality of Majesty, it is possible that this may be one meaning. But, by comparing Scripture with Scripture (as II Peter 1:20 commands), we find a deeper and fuller meaning.

"Knowing this first, that no prophecy of the scripture is of any private interpretation."
(II Peter 1:20)

Although this does mean that no single person can simply "find" something in the Scripture which is not warranted. The Holy Spirit, after all, does speak to the entire Body of Christ. This is a mistake of some of the more "top heavy" denominational

CHAPTER 15: THE ONENESS OF THE GODHEAD

churches; their leader gives out by fiat his "pontification" of his view and will not even allow the Holy Spirit to disagree.

On the other hand, there are those who build doctrine in their own minds and press it forward. From such comes the cultists and their followers.

The meaning of the verse has, primarily, to do with the comparing of Scripture with Scripture. Another fault of too many is to try to build a doctrine on one obscure passage. Such is not the case; the Scripture is a unified Book. We must take it; we must understand it in total.

As we compare Scripture with Scripture, as we examine the entire Holy Record, we find ample evidence that the concept God was beginning to teach, even at the very beginning of Scripture, had to do with His Own Triune Nature.

That some of the earlier people, who had not yet had the advantage of the unfolding of more Scripture, might not have understand this does not detract from the Truth.

As to the idea of a consultation with the Angelic Court, we must also differ. The creation was the Work of His Will alone. He needed no "suggestion box" sitting near those Heavenly Gates.

Unger (*Unger's Bible Handbook*) finds evidence for the Trinity from Deuteronomy 6:4. *"Hear, O Israel: The LORD our God is one LORD."* "'The Lord (YHWH) [This author believes "YHWH" is a corruption; it should be Jehovah] our Elohim is one Lord (YHWH) [Jehovah],' the **one 'dhadh**, expressing **compound unity** not **yahid**, meaning a **single** one, thus not supporting [any] ... denial of the Trinity."

Because Jesus in Not the Father, It Does Not Imply Any Lack of Deity

Jesus is not the Father. This in no way would imply any lack of deity within His essence.

Hogan (*Trinitarian Adumbration*) looks further at Genesis 1:1. He notes that the Hebrew word translated "God" in Genesis 1:1 is "Elohim" which is the plural form of "Eloah."

> "Being in the specific Hebrew plural form which applies to more than two, it lays the foundation at the very commencement of revelation for the subsequent disclosure of three divine Persons in the one Godhead."

The point is that it is not necessary for Jesus to be the Father. Jesus is God by His Own right.

Zodhiates (*God in Man*) looks at John 1:14.

> "And the Word was made flesh, and dwelt among us, (and we beheld his glory, the glory as of the only begotten of the Father,) full of grace and truth."

This passage states that Jesus is a separate personality from the Father. He is not the Father but is in constant "fellowship and proximity with the Father."

Why Jesus is Called "the Son"?

We are left with a question as to why Jesus is called "the Son," if He is full Deity in His own right. Part of the reason is that Jesus came to earth in the body of a human being. He lived as one of us while on this plane of existence. As such, He was our example of how we should also live as human beings on this earth. Part of His teaching ministry dealt with His voluntary submission.

Strong (*Systematic Theology*) explains the situation a little more fully than have I.

> "The Son is not God as such; for God is not only Son, but also Father and Holy Spirit. 'The Son' designates that distinction in virtue of which God is related to the Father, is sent by the Father to redeem the world and with the Father sends the Holy Spirit."

The term "Son of God" has more to do with giving us an understanding, and with the role assumed in the salvation of humanity from sin, than it does with "rank" as we understand that term to be.

Jesus is God. Make no mistake about that!

Jesus is described as equal with the Father in the passions of humanity. Barnes (*Barnes' Notes on the New Testament*) comments on John 15:23 in relation to this fact.

> "He that hateth me hateth my Father also."

The Two, Barnes argues, are One. To hate One is to hate the Other.

Likewise, to love One is to love the Other. That is part of the Christian experience.

Barnes also points this out from Ephesians 6:23.

> "Peace be to the brethren, and love with faith, from God the Father and the Lord Jesus Christ."

Both the Father and the Son are equally the givers of peace, love and faith.

As faith is described earlier in this Book (Ephesians 2:8-9) as a gift from God, we cannot suppose that Paul was talking of God, and then of Jesus, as giving these gifts. Paul put the two together in one phrase because they are One God.

From John 12:45, Jesus is Equal With the Father in His Essence

Barnes also argues from John 12:45 that Jesus is equal with the Father in His essence.

> "And he that seeth me seeth him that sent me."

> "In no other can it be true that he who saw Jesus saw him that sent him, unless he were the same in essence. To have said this of anyone else, even of a prophet, would be blasphemy." [Barnes]

For those who would claim that Jesus never claimed deity in the Scripture, I would ask one simple question. What was He saying in this place? Sometimes our children look much like us. I have an old college friend who said her daughter looked just like her. Even if her daughter appeared to be her twin, to see her daughter is not to have seen her. They are different persons. Jesus didn't say, "If you've seen Me, you know what God looks like." He said, "If you've seen Me, you've seen God."

From Titus 2:13, Jesus is the Great God and Saviour

We've one last verse to look at in this section. This insight comes from the *"Commentary Practical and Explanatory on the Whole Bible."*

> "Looking for that blessed hope, and the glorious appearing of the great God and our Saviour Jesus Christ." (Titus 2:13)

There is but one **Greek** article to 'God' and 'Saviour,' which shows that both are predicated on one and the same Being..."

Any "translation" which has altered this verse to suggest two Persons rather than One God is a flawed and untrustworthy translation.

In our next session we will begin a new section. We will begin to consider the dual nature of Jesus.

CHAPTER 16
I. THE DUAL NATURE OF JESUS
(Session Seventeen)

The Concept Is Taught In Scripture

When we consider the Person of Jesus Christ we must consider that His was a dual nature. The old catechism says that He is very God and very man. We often say that He is the Son of God as well as God, the Son. We see this concept taught about Jesus in the Scripture.

One of the ways in which Scripture teaches this fact is that the nature of Jesus is shown to be eternal. Since the only Eternal is God, Jesus is God.

Zeoli (*Is Jesus God? Book Number One*) makes note that Jesus possessed certain attributes even before Bethlehem.

Jesus Possessed Certain Attributes Even Before Bethlehem

First, An Eternal Place of Abode

First, Zeoli notes that Jesus has an eternal place of abode.

"What and if ye shall see the Son of man ascend up where he was before." (John 6:62)

Jesus was giving a prophecy of His ascension in this place. In the Book of Acts we see that He did, literally, ascend back into Heaven. Angel's announced the Event.

Likewise, Zeoli notes John 14:2.

"In my Father's house are many mansions: if it were not so, I would have told you. I go to prepare a place for you."

In this verse Jesus speaks of His Father's house. This was His "home" before he came to earth at Bethlehem to live among us. Now the time of His return to that home was near. It would soon be the time when He would be sacrificed.

While saying that He was returning to the Heavenlies, He also promised that we would be able, because of His soon coming sacrifice at Calvary, to be partakers of this home in Heaven. What a glorious promise. It is also a promise that could be made by none other than the "Owner" of that "Inn." Again, this is an intimation of the full Deity of Jesus.

Second, Jesus was Possessed of Creative Power Before Bethlehem

Second, Zeoli notes that Jesus was possessed of creative power before Bethlehem. He cites John 1:3-4.

"All things were made by him; and without him was not anything made that was made. In him was life, and the life was the light of men."

"He who created all things must have existed **before** all things, or otherwise He could not have created all things."

Note, also, in this verse that "In him was life." This is an important phrase. We, all of us are a derived life. Life, even human life, comes from life. We can trace this progression all the way back to Adam who God specially created. Even the angels are created beings. It can only be said of God that "in him was life." Only God is self existent. Everything else exists only at His good pleasure. This is a statement of the Deity of Jesus.

Third, Jesus Possessed Knowledge Before Bethlehem

Third, Zeoli says that Jesus possessed knowledge before Bethlehem.

> "But there are some of you that believe not. For Jesus knew from the beginning who they were that believed not, and who should betray him." (John 6:64) "Notice please that Jesus knew this from the beginning, from all eternity."

Although not part of our subject matter, I must comment that Jesus knew that Judas would betray Him. Yet, Jesus never displayed any hostility toward Judas, only love. How do we react toward those who are outside the household of faith? Are we "Christ like," the meaning of the word "Christian?" Or, are we mean and cross toward them? Our outlook toward others is the color of our Christian commitment.

Fourth, Jesus Possessed Glory Before Bethlehem

Fourth, Zeoli sees that Jesus possessed Glory before Bethlehem.

> "And now, O Father, glorify thou me with thine own self with the glory which I had with thee before the world was." (John 17:5)

There are two things to be noticed in this passage. The first is that Jesus possessed this glory from before the world was. In other words, He possessed the glory before creation. Once again, this is a clear statement of the Divinity of Jesus.

In this verse we can also see that the glory requested by Jesus was the Glory of God. Jesus says that this Glory was His before the world was. Since the Glory of God was the possession of Jesus, Jesus is God.

Fifth, Jesus Possessed Riches Before Bethlehem

Fifth, Zeoli finds that Jesus possessed riches before Bethlehem.

> "For ye know the grace of our Lord Jesus Christ, that, though he was rich, yet for your sakes he became poor, that ye through his poverty might be rich." (II Corinthians 8:9)

The passage is not, of course, speaking of any human riches. God did say, in Psalm 50:10,

> "For every beast of the forest is mine, and the cattle upon a thousand hills."

Still, the riches to which were referred were spiritual riches. As we are in Him, these are our possession. Jesus died in time so that we might live in eternity.

Ryrie (*The Ryrie Study Bible*) cites John 8:58 when speaking about the eternality of Jesus.

> "Jesus said unto them, Verily, verily, I say unto you, Before Abraham was, I am."

> "The 'I am' denotes absolute eternal existence, not simply existence prior to Abraham. It is a claim to be Yahweh [This author believes "Yahweh" is a corruption of Jehovah] of the O. T. That the Jews understood the significance of this claim was clear from their reaction (v. 59) to the supposed blasphemy."

Things True Before Bethlehem

Zeoli (*Is Jesus God? Book Number One*) lists several things which were true of

CHAPTER 16: I. THE DUAL NATURE OF JESUS

Jesus even before Bethlehem.

First, Jesus Was Foreordained

The first thing Zeoli mentions is that Jesus was foreordained.

> "Who verily was foreordained before the foundation of the world, but was manifest in these last times for you." (I Peter 1:20)

In Revelation 13:8 we see that Jesus is the Lamb slain before the foundation of the world. Our salvation was not an act of expediency.

> "And all that dwell upon the earth shall worship him, whose names are not written in the book of life of the Lamb slain from the foundations of the world." (Revelation 13:8)

When the verses before Revelation 13:8 are read one will see that the "him" being worshipped by the lost was the Antichrist. These are lost people. Of the saved, God knew that Adam, and though him all men, would sin. God knew that a sacrifice for the sin of humanity would be necessary. Before the foundation of the world, before man had sinned, before man had even been created God had determined that Jesus would go to the cross to effect salvation for a humanity which had turned its collective back upon Him.

> "But God commendeth his love toward us, in that, while we were ye sinners, Christ died for us." (Romans 5:8)

We can never earn a love this all encompassing. We can only accept, and glory in the One Who loves us.

Second, Jesus Was With the Father Before Bethlehem

Second, Zeoli sees that Jesus was with the Father before Bethlehem.

> "The LORD possessed me in the beginning of his way, before his works of old. I was set up from everlasting, from the beginning, or ever the earth was. When there were no depths, I was brought forth, when there were no foundations abounding with water. Before the mountains were settled, before the hills was I brought forth: While as yet he had not made the earth, nor the fields, nor the highest part of the dust of the world. When he prepared the heavens, I was there: when he set a compass upon the face of the depth: When he established the clouds above: when he strengthened the fountains of the deep: When he gave to the sea his decree, that the waters should not pass his commandment: when he appointed the foundations of the earth: Then I was by him, as one brought up with him: and I was daily his delight, rejoicing always before him." (Proverbs 8:22-30)

> "In the beginning was the Word, and the Word was with God, and the Word was God." (John 1:1)

These passages report that Jesus was with the Father even before the creation of all things. Some might mistake part of the poetry of the passage in Proverbs to suggest that Jesus was a created Being. Such is not the case. This section is poetry. As we compare Scripture with Scripture, we will find that Jesus was that very Creative Agent.

> "All things were made by him, and without him was not anything made that was made." (John 1:3)

The picture in John 1:1 is of two equals sitting facing one another. The passage in Proverbs is celebrating that Second Person of the Trinity. It is not relegating Jesus to a lower role; it is celebrating the Love of the Father.

Third, Jesus was *"Of Old."*

Third, Zeoli sees that Jesus was *"Of Old."*

> *But thou, Bethlehem Ephratah, though thou be little among the thousands of Judah, yet out of thee shall he come forth unto me that is to be ruler in Israel, whose goings forth have been from of old, from everlasting." (Micah 5:2)*

This verse identifies Jesus as a Being from eternity (from everlasting) which could only be said of God. All others are created. All humans are created, or birthed (life from life), in time. Even the angels are an order of created beings.

Fourth, Jesus Was Worshipped by Angels

Fourth, Zeoli finds that Jesus was worshipped by angels.

> *"In the year that king Uzziah died I saw also the Lord sitting upon a throne, high and lifted up, and his train filled the temple. Above it stood the seraphims: each one had six wings; with twain he covered his face, and with twain he covered his feet, and with twain he did fly. And one cried unto another, and said, Holy, holy, holy, is the LORD of hosts: the whole earth is full of his glory. And the posts of the door moved at the voice of him that cried, and the house was filled with smoke. Then said I, Woe is me! for I am undone; because I am a man of unclean lips, and I dwell in the midst of a people of unclean lips: for mine eyes have seen the King, the LORD of hosts." (Isaiah 6:1-5)*

Isaiah said that he had seen the Lord. Once again comparing Scripture with Scripture, we must conclude that Isaiah saw a preincarnate appearance of Jesus. John 1:18 tells us that no one has seen the Father. Only Jesus has revealed the Father to anyone. Therefore we must conclude that Isaiah saw Jesus.

If this is true, and Scripture would support this contention, then these seraphim were praising, and giving worship to, Jesus. This would mean that Jesus was either God or Satan. Only these two, in all the spiritual realms will accept worship. Since this scene was in Heaven, and the One being worshipped was called "Holy," we must accept that this was Jesus.

We might also note the triune nature of the praise, "Holy, holy, holy." This is an intimation of the Trinity of God.

Fifth, Jesus Was Called "Lord" by David

Fifth, Zeoli saw that Jesus was called "Lord" by David.

> *"While the Pharisees were gathered together, Jesus asked them, Saying, What think ye of Christ? whose son is he? They say unto him, The son of David. He saith unto them, How then doth David in spirit call him Lord, saying, the LORD said unto my Lord, Sit thou on my right hand, till I make thine enemies thy footstool? If David then call him Lord, how is he his son? And no man was able to answer him a word, neither durst any man from that day forth ask him any more questions." (Matthew 22:41-46)*

This passage speaks of the mystery of the incarnation and of the Virgin Birth. The salient point, however, is that David called Jesus "Lord." The position in which David placed his Lord was in a position of power which could only apply to God.

Sixth, Jesus Was a "Rock of Refreshment."

Sixth, Zeoli argues that Jesus was a "Rock of Refreshment."

CHAPTER 16: I. THE DUAL NATURE OF JESUS

> *"Moreover, brethren, I would not that ye should be ignorant, how that all our fathers were under the cloud, and all passed through the sea; And were all baptized unto Moses in the cloud and in the sea; And did all eat the same spiritual meat; And did all drink the same spiritual drink: for they drank of that Spiritual rock that followed them: and that Rock was Christ." (I Corinthians 10:1-4)*

Let us compare Exodus 17:6 and Numbers 20:8.

> *"Behold, I will stand before thee there upon the rock in Horeb; and thou shalt smite the rock, and there shall come water out of it, that the people may drink. And Moses did so in the sight of the elders of Israel." (Exodus 17:6) "Take the rod, and gather thou the assembly together, thou, and Aaron thy brother, and speak ye unto the rock before their eyes: and it shall give forth his water and thou shalt bring forth to them water out of the rock: so thou shalt give the congregation and their beasts drink." (Numbers 20:8)*

When we understand that the "Rock" of the Old Testament was a type of Christ we can make some comparisons. Jesus is the "Living Water." The water from the Old Testament was a "type," or physical prophecy of Jesus. That type was salvation to those who were thirsting in the desert. We can see in this that Jesus was the means of safety and sustenance to the Israelites as they moved from slavery to freedom.

I might just note a second thing as well. Moses was told to strike the first rock. He was told to only speak to the second rock. Jesus was once crucified for our sins. In the matter of salvation we do not seek to crucify Him again. We simply speak, in faith, acceptance of His offered gift of redemption.

Seventh, Jesus Was Sent

The seventh thing which Zeoli mentioned was that Jesus was sent.

> *"That all men should honour the Son, even as they honour the Father. He that honoureth not the Son honoureth not the Father which hath sent him." (John 5:23)*

Again, the fact that Jesus was sent by the Father speaks of His pre-existence. Before Bethlehem, He was. Notice, also importantly, that the honor due to Jesus is the same honor as is due to the Father. This is another statement of the Divinity of Jesus.

Eighth, Jesus Was Known by Abraham

The eighth thing about Jesus which Zeoli notes is that Jesus was known by Abraham.

> *"Your father Abraham rejoiced to see my day: and he saw it, and was glad: Then said the Jews unto him, Thou art not yet fifty years old, and hast thou seen Abraham?" (John 8:56-57)*

In Matthew 17:1-8 we see the Mount of Transfiguration event. At this event Moses was seen as speaking with Jesus. Also, amazingly enough, the disciples there knew the Old Testament persons who were speaking with Jesus. I believe that they knew these men through the spiritual sense rather than via any introduction. Paul said,

> *"For now we see through a glass, darkly; but then face to face: now I know in part, but then shall I know even as also I am known." (I Corinthians 13:12)*

I believe that this passage strongly suggests that we will know others in Heaven. And, we will be known as well.

Also, in chapter eighteen of Genesis the Lord appeared to Abraham. This was an appearance of Jesus before Bethlehem. At this time Abraham also saw the "day" of Jesus.

These events speak of the eternality of Jesus even as they speak of His full Deity.

Ninth, Jesus Was Before John the Baptist

The ninth thing Zeoli notes of Jesus was that He was before John the Baptist.

> "John bare witness of him, and cried, saying, This was he of whom I spake, He that cometh after me is preferred before me: for he was before me." (John 1:15)

We know that John the Baptist was about six months older, from the human standpoint, than was Jesus. But John acknowledges, as was his mission as the "forerunner of the Messiah," that Jesus was before him. This is another mention of the eternality of Jesus.

Tenth, Jesus' Pre-existence

The tenth thing about Jesus, as noted by Zeoli, is that Jesus is in the past.

> "Jesus Christ the same yesterday, and to day, and for ever." (Hebrews 13:8)

This is a point where I would take issue with Zeoli's statement. This verse in Hebrews is not simply a mention that Jesus existed long before Bethlehem. It is more. The term "Yesterday" speaks to His pre-existence. The term "Today" speaks to His present existence. I might make note here that this passage was written after the crucifixion but still speaks of Jesus in the present tense. The term "Forever" speaks of His permanent existence.

Hebrews 13:8 speaks of the eternality of Jesus. In doing so the verse speaks of His Divinity.

We close out this section on the Divine Nature of Jesus by looking at Romans 1:4.

> "And declared to be the Son of God with power, according to the spirit of holiness, by the resurrection from the dead."

Alford (*The New Testament for English Readers*) asks that we see that the Divine nature of Jesus is holy. "The Spirit of Holiness" is not the same as the Holy Spirit. The intent of the verse is to show that the essence of the Spirit of Jesus is holiness; that is, He is Divine, in opposition of, as well as in amplification to, His human nature as shown in verse three immediately preceding. Thus, the dual nature of Jesus is shown.

I think it also important that we consider that His manifestation of Divine Power "declared" His deity. This power did not cause, or begin, his Deity. The power only made reference to, and gave evidence to, that Deity.

Continuing with the Dual Nature of Jesus, we will consider His humanity in our next session.

CHAPTER 17
II. THE DUAL NATURE OF JESUS
(Session Eighteen)

His Humanity

In our last session we discussed the Divine nature of Jesus. Jesus is God. The Scripture declares this fact by both intimation and direct attestation. The full Deity of Jesus is not a church doctrine. It is an eternal fact.

In this session we will discuss the other side of the coin. Jesus has been described as the Son of God and God the Son. The old catechism declares that Jesus is very God and very man. This, the fact of the humanity of Jesus, is the subject of discussion for this session.

Mary went to visit her cousin Elisabeth (Luke 1:36), when Elisabeth was in her sixth month of pregnancy with the child who was to become John the Baptist. The Spirit of God revealed to Elisabeth the nature of the Child Who was being carried by Mary. Elisabeth said,

> "And whence is this to me, that the mother of my Lord should come to me?" (Luke 1:43)

The Human Nature of Jesus was United With the Divine Nature Before Bethlehem

From this prophetic word of Elisabeth we can understand that the human nature of Jesus was united with the Divine nature even before the events of Bethlehem. This is a picture that Jesus developed, in the natural, as a normal child. This was the human nature of Jesus.

But, Jesus was already acknowledged as "Lord" before His birth. He was the Savior even before His birth. This is His Divine Nature.

Thus, we can see that the Divine Nature of Jesus is now united with His humanity. He has become one of us, while retaining all the fullness of His full Divinity, so that He could become our representative and our Savior. Jesus died a human death, taking the full measure of the just punishment for sin which should have been upon us, so that we could be born spiritually.

We are born again, spiritually, when we accept His sacrifice for our sins. It is the Holy Spirit Who draws us to this decision by means of His convicting work upon our hearts. He, as one of us died in our place as payment for our sins. His sacrifice on the Cross is accepted on our account by the Father. Thus, the entire Trinity of the Godhead is involved in the salvation of sinners.

The Symbiosis of His Nature

Pendleton (*Christian Doctrine*) has described this symbiosis of His nature. "Divinity and humanity are united in Him, but they are not blended. Humanity is not deified and divinity is not humanized. ... Divinity cannot take into its essence anything finite, and the human is finite."

There are two things I need to explain. The word "symbiosis" suggests a duality where both sides are benefited by the act. God desired that man would be given a way out of sin. This was accomplished by the work of Jesus. The desire was based in the Love of God. There was, IS, no goodness in man which would have elicited this response from God.

Man benefited by being given a means of salvation from his sin. This is not a benefit which man would have desired. Lost, as he was, in sin, man would not have understood his need. When the spiritual eyes of man are opened, through the convicting agency of the Holy Spirit, man is allowed to see the spiritual realities of Heaven and Hell, sin and salvation. With this salvation man is permitted to become fully human as was the program of the original creation.

Thus, we see a double reason to praise God for our salvation. Not only has He given us a free salvation, we are also called to this salvation before our humanity would even acknowledge the need of salvation.

Although He is Fully Human, He is in His Essence God

The other thing I would need to explain is that Jesus, although He is fully human, is in His essence God. The humanity of Jesus is complete in His physical attributes. But, His Spiritual being is fully God. Deity is the essence of Who He is.

Ryrie (*Basic Theology*) explains this in a much better manner.

> "There is no mixture of divine and human attributes (as Eutchians taught), no change in either complex (as Appollinarians taught), no dividing of them, and no separating them so as to have two Persons (as Nestorianism taught). Orthodoxy says two natures comprising one Person or hypostasis forever. It is correct to characterize Christ as a theoanthropic Person. But not accurate to speak of theoanthropic nature [since that would mix the divine and human attributes]."

In His incarnation, Jesus Christ is One Person with both a complete and an unadulterated Divine nature and a complete and unadulterated human nature: Two natures - one individual.

What we see in Jesus is that God is manifested to humanity in the physical Person of Jesus Christ.

Criswell (*The Criswell Study Bible*) looks at John 1:18.

> "No man hath seen God at any time; the only begotten Son, which is in the bosom of the Father, he hath declared him." In other words, "...God choose to reveal Himself physically in Christ."

What we really have in the salvation allowed to us through the Person of Jesus Christ is a spiritual restoration of that physical fellowship between man and God which was present in the Garden before the fall of man.

Actually, this spiritual fellowship is even more personal, to us, than were the walks in the cool of the evening to Adam and Eve.

Jesus' Omnipresence

Alford (*The New Testament for English Readers*) looks at Ephesians 4:10.

> "He that descended is the same also that ascended up far above all heavens, that he might fill all things."

Jesus fills all things with His Sovereignty and workings by the Spirit. As God, Jesus can be everywhere; yet as man, He can be anywhere.

CHAPTER 17: II. THE DUAL NATURE OF JESUS

Jesus can be with us as we pray during our private devotions or our public worship services. He can be, in a personal relationship, with thousands and millions, at these times. As I pray in the central part of Illinois, old friends of mine are praying back at my old church in Louisiana. Others are praying throughout the world - all at the same time. Jesus is with all of us at the same time; yet, He is with each of us in a personal manner.

Look at the last part of Matthew 28:20. Jesus had just given the Great Commission. Then He said,

"...lo, I am with you alway, even unto the end of the world. Amen."

In this short sentence Jesus has asserted His full Divinity. He has promised to be with us, no matter where we are. This is an attestation of His Omnipresence. Omnipresence means to be everywhere at one time. It doesn't mean to quickly move about. It means to actually be all places at the same time.

Jesus literally fills the universe with His presence. This is an attribute of God.

Jesus also says that He will be with them (us, as part of the body of believers) until the end of the world. This speaks of His eternality. This is another attribute of God. We have the promise of an eternal salvation. This eternity of existence is not predicated on our own selves. It is a gift from God. Thus our eternality is a derived eternality which comes from God. Only God is Eternal in His essence. Thus Jesus was saying that He is God.

The Commentary Practical and Explanatory on the Whole Bible makes reference to Jesus based on Micah 5:2.

"But thou, Bethlehem Ephratah, though thou be little among the thousands of Judah, yet out of thee shall he come forth unto me that is to be ruler in Israel; whose goings forth have been from of old, from everlasting."

The human side of Jesus is shown by the phrase "out of thee shall come." The Divine side of Jesus is shown by the phrase "goings forth from everlasting." This is a picture of the dual nature of Jesus.

Jesus is God. The Bible says this is so. Jesus is also human. The Bible says this is so. We can rejoice in His humanity. But, we were redeemed by His Divinity. He was one of us. Yet, He is so much more than us.

Let us never fail to praise His glory and greatness!

In our next session we will begin to consider the Voluntary Submission of Jesus.

CHAPTER 18
JESUS' VOLUNTARY SUBMISSION
(Session Nineteen)

Kenosis

With this session we begin a study of one of the incomprehensible facts about Jesus. He emptied Himself of the outward glory that was His as God. How? Well, the simple answer is that He is God and can do whatever it is that He desires to do.

The "why" He did so is also incomprehensible to us. It was His Divine Love for sinful humanity that caused Him to take upon Himself a body of humanity. He did this for the express purpose of presenting Himself to the Roman executioners so that He could sacrifice His mortal life as a substitute for us. Jesus intended to die for our sins. This was His plan and purpose.

The process of laying aside His outward glory as God is known as the Kenosis. It is this concept that we are preparing to study in this session.

> "Let this mind be in you, which was also in Christ Jesus: Who, being in the form of God, thought it not robbery to be equal with God: But made himself of no reputation, and took upon him the form of a servant, and was made in the likeness of men: And being found in fashion as a man, he humbled himself, and became obedient unto death, even the death of the cross. Wherefore God hath highly exalted him, and given him a name which is above every name: That at the name of Jesus every knee should bow, of things in heaven, and things in earth, and things under the earth; And that every tongue should confess that Jesus Christ is Lord, to the glory of God the Father." (Philippians 2:5-11)

Jesus Only Laid Aside the Outward Glory of the Godhead. He Remained God

Please note that Jesus only laid aside the outward glory of the Godhead. His very essence is God. That is Who He is. This He remained, and remains.

Scofield (*The Scofield Reference Bible*) references verse six and also sees this. Scofield says that Jesus only removed the "outward and visible manifestation of the Godhead." He did not empty "...Himself of either His divine nature or His [divine] attributes..."

We will see later that Jesus exhibited these divine attributes at His Own volition. This in itself is another indication of the complete Deity of Jesus. In the Old Testament the prophets would often have the Spirit of God come upon them so that they would be empowered to produce some miracle or mighty act. In these New Testament times the Holy Spirit indwells and will, at His discretion, empower the Christian to complete an act which is miraculously beyond the ability of that person to have done on his own merit.

But, Jesus performed His miracles, and even restored Himself to physical life, by His Own right and power.

Jesus Did Not Empty Himself of His Essential Glory, Only its Manifestation

Alford (*The New Testament for English Readers*) mirrors the thought of Scofield, albeit in reference to verse seven, above. He notes that Jesus did not empty Himself of His

"...essential glory, but [of] its manifested [or visible to humankind] possession..."

The point here is that Jesus was a representative of humanity. He looked, acted, grew in physical stature, and even died, as a human being. The exception was that He was without sin. Even this latter point, that He was without sin, would have left Him unable to be a sacrifice for the sins of humanity. Every human person born of man has an inherited sin nature. In sin are we born.

Jesus was Fully Human

Jesus was fully human. But He was born of a woman via the Virgin Birth. Therefore He did not have the inherited sin nature. Thus Jesus had no sin in His life, either inherited or performed. Thus, being perfect, and perfectly obedient to the Law, He is able to impart His Own perfections and grace to sinful humans who accept His sacrifice as the basis for their salvation. He could do this on the basis of His Own Deity. Only God, to Whom sin is an affront, could offer forgiveness of sin to humanity.

There are no sacraments in the churches. A sacrament is something that we can do which will impart a measure of grace to our souls. The only "sacrament" which can impart grace to us is the sacrifice of Jesus. No other work, nothing!, can cleanse our souls and proclaim us worthy to approach the Throne of Grace.

Adam Clarke (*Adam Clarke's Commentary*) looks at verse six and pronounces Jesus as God. Jesus did not, could not as God, give up the prerogatives and power of Deity. Jesus only gave up that "...visible glorious light in which the Deity is said to dwell..." as evidenced by the many Old Testament presentations - i.e. the Burning Bush; Isaiah's vision; Ezekiel's visions; etc."

Jesus Came as God, but God Clothed in the Flesh of Humanity

When we remember that God is Spirit, He would not be recognizable to humanity even if humanity were allowed to view His glory. Jesus came as God, but God clothed in the flesh of humanity. When we look upon the Humanity of Jesus we are allowed to see God in a form that is identifiable to our physical eyes.

The Incomprehensible has Become Comprehensible for Our Benefit

Much like the teaching of the Scripture, the Written Word of God, Jesus in His physical form, the Living Word of God, teaches us of God in a manner that we are allowed to understand. The Incomprehensible has become Comprehensible for our benefit and understanding.

"The Commentary Practical and Explanatory on the Whole Bible" speaks, also, of this passage, above.

> "...He never empties Himself of the fulness of His Godhead, or His 'Being **on an equality with God**;' but between His being 'in the FORM (i.e., the outward glorious self-manifestation) of God,' and His 'taking on Him **the form of a servant**,' whereby He in a great measure emptied Himself of His precedent 'form' or outward self-manifesting glory as God."

The point that we are trying to establish here is that Jesus was God; He remained God even as He laid aside some of the Glory which is rightfully His. The passage from Philippians above states that Jesus did not consider it robbery to be equal with God. The reason this is so is that He is God.

We are told that He took upon Himself the form of a servant. He became as one of

CHAPTER 18: JESUS VOLUNTARY SUBMISSION

us, from all outward appearances. In His humanity He was an example to us of how humanity ought to live. This is often overlooked. We stumble at His subjection to the Father. This was part of His mission in becoming one of us. He placed Himself, voluntarily, in subjection to the Father even as we ought to place ourselves in subjection to Him.

The Father Has Exalted Jesus

You will notice, also, from the above verse that the Father has exalted Jesus. This does not mean that the Father "promoted" Jesus to Deity. Such is a false notion held by some who do not understand the great sacrifices which Jesus made for our salvation. The Father has simply glorified the Son with the glory that rightly belonged to the Son.

I helped my grandson put on his windbreaker this morning as he was getting ready for his preschool. The windbreaker was already his. I only placed upon him what was already his possession. That is a poor illustration. But, this is essentially what the Father did when He glorified the Son. The Father acknowledged what was already the possession of the Son.

The Purpose of the Kenosis

Now that we all understand the mechanics of the Kenosis... I don't, either. But I do understand the great love which the Savior has for me and you in that He went to these great lengths to purchase our salvation!

This speaks to the purpose of the Kenosis. This is the "why" that Jesus emptied Himself of His outward glory as God. The Kenosis is the manifestation of His dealing with sinful humanity.

Pendleton (*Christian Doctrine*) uses an illustration of the Presidency. Officially, the President of the United States is superior to us, but his nature, being human, is essentially ours. As the old saying goes, the President puts on his pants one leg at a time just like us. Now, if Hillary Clinton is elected we'll have to being to say "Pantsuit." The principle remains.

We are watching the silly season, this time "season**s**!," it's been going on for so long! The presidential primaries are being held. In November there will be an election. One of these people who have been running around, eating poorly cooked chicken dinners and shaking hands with complete strangers, will be elected. In January that person will be inaugurated.

It is an amazing scene when we consider it. One minute this person is simply another person in a crowd- of course the crowd is comprised of Secret Service agents. That person says a few words with one hand on a Bible and one hand in the air. The very next moment this person is recognized as the most powerful single person in the world.

Meanwhile, the former president, at that same moment, becomes nearly anonymous. The news people no longer shout out his name and seek his ear.

Still, through it all, these people retain their humanity. They are flesh and blood human beings of the same physical essence as are we.

Jesus Never Ceased Being Who He Is

Likewise, Jesus never ceased being Who He Is. The essential nature of Jesus, even during the Kenosis, remained Divine in this incarnation. He was still God even if the outward appearance, to the casual observer might not have shown this fact. The Fact remained.

Our Perfect Substitute

It is that human nature, which Jesus assumed in the incarnation, which allows Him to be our Perfect Substitute.

"For in him dwelleth all the fulness of the Godhead bodily." (Colossians 2:9)

Of this verse, Alford (*The New Testament for English Readers*) says,

"Before His incarnation [the fulness of the Godhead] dwelt in Him, as the Word non-incarnate, but not bodily, as now that He is the Word Incarnate."

These terms "incarnate" and "non-incarnate" are really pretty simple. Naturally, being an old and fat guy, I will use an illustration from food. You all know what "Chili Con Carne" is, don't you? It is chili with meat. "Carne" means "meat," or "flesh." That's all these words "incarnate" and "non-incarnate" mean. Jesus was in the flesh of humanity in His Incarnation. Before this incarnation He was not residing in human flesh; He was non-incarnate.

Clarke (*Adam Clarke's Commentary*) points out something about this incarnation of Jesus that I had touched briefly earlier.

"Our Lord sometimes speaks of Himself as God, and sometimes as the ambassador of God. As He had a human and a Divine nature, this distinction was essentially necessary. Many errors have originated from the want of attention to this circumstance."

If we fail to consider this dual nature of Jesus in the Incarnation, and if we fail to understand His purpose in coming into humanity, we will be sure to drift into serious error.

In our next session we will consider that this Kenosis is the method of His dealing with sinful humanity.

CHAPTER 19
KENOSIS
(Session Twenty)

The Method of His Dealing With Sinful Humanity

The Kenosis is the means used by Jesus in His dealing with sinful humanity. He became one of us as a means of being our substitute. As one of us He died as a sacrifice for sin. His sacrifice did not offer a covering for sin as had the animal sacrifice of the Old Covenant.

> "For it is not possible that the blood of bulls and of goats should take away sins." (Hebrews 10:4)

The Old Testament Sacrificial System Was Effective But It Was Not Permanent

When we read the above verse in its context we see that the Old Testament sacrificial system was effective but it was not permanent. The process had to be repeated over and over. The sacrifice of Jesus on the Cross of Calvary is both effective and permanent.

> "So Christ was once offered to bear the sins of many; and unto them that look for him shall he appear the second time without sin unto salvation." (Hebrews 9:28)

Moreover, the sacrifice of Jesus is the basis under which the former animal sacrifice's gained their own authority. It was a derived authority looking forward to the actual sacrifice which should come at Calvary.

> "For Christ is not entered into the holy places made with hands, which are the figures of the true; but in heaven itself, now to appear in the presence of God for us." (Hebrews 9:24)

Subjection to the Father

Pendleton (*Christian Doctrine*) sees that the Son, by virtue of being in subjection to the Father, assumes an "...inferiority ... in office, not in nature; the subordination is official and does not touch the divine substance."

Jesus never was not God. What we see of Him, in a subordinate role, in the New Testament is the result of the Kenosis whereby He divested Himself of the outward glory of Deity. When Jesus took upon Himself the robes of humanity, in order to be one of us and thereby become the sin substitute in our place, He placed Himself in subjection to the Father as our Representative.

> "But we see Jesus, who was made a little lower than the angels for the suffering of death, crowned with glory and honour; that he by the grace of God should taste death for every man." (Hebrews 2:9)

Jesus did not lay aside His essential Being. He was never at any point not God. But, He became as one of us. His Person was always Deity; that is Who He is. But, His position was as a human while walking those dusty roads some two thousand years ago.

Let me try to explain this construct. I am a human being beset with all the frailties and faults of humanity. My wife would have said I have a few extra of those! But, when I assume the office of pastor I become a representative of God while I am in that pulpit. I am still me. But, I assume an office. The assumption of office does not make me something I am not. If I fail to properly fulfill the mandates of that office it is I who am at fault.

Jesus assumed the office of humanity, so to speak, via the Kenosis so that He could become the Perfect Sacrifice for sin. He acted in that office as a human, because He was human. But, even while in that office, His essential Personhood was Deity.

It is from this construct that we get the dichotomy of Jesus being fully God and yet subservient to the Father. A misunderstanding of this duality of nature is the cause of many errors and the springboard for many cultists.

The Purchase of Our Redemption

Orr (*Can We Be Sure that Jesus Christ is God*) says that Jesus laid aside an equity with God to purchase our redemption. Let us be very clear, again, on this subject. The lack of equity regarded the office of Jesus as the representative of humanity. This does not reflect upon the Person of Jesus as Deity in His Own right.

Orr cites several verses in support of his words.

Philippians 2:5-11 is cited.

> *"Let this mind be in you, which was also in Christ Jesus: Who, being in the form of God, thought it not robbery to be equal with God: But made himself of no reputation, and took upon him the form of a servant, and was made in the likeness of men: And being found in fashion as a man, he humbled himself, and became obedient unto death, even the death of the cross. Wherefore God hath also highly exalted him, and given him a name which is above every name: that at the name of Jesus every knee should bow, of things in heaven, and things in earth, and things under the earth, And that every tongue should confess that Jesus Christ is Lord, to the glory of God the Father."*

Jesus Existed in Another Form Before Bethlehem

We have commented on this passage during past sessions. Nonetheless, I would again make reference to the fact that Jesus "took upon him the form of a servant," and "was made in the likeness of man," and "being found in the fashion as a man..." These words make a claim that Jesus existed in another form before Bethlehem. That "form" was as God. That is why He did not think it wrong to be considered as equal with God.

That He did not claim the glory associated with His divine existence was His choice. "...he humbled himself..."

That the Father exalted Him after the cross is not a reference to any new assumption of characteristic on the part of Jesus. It is an acknowledgment, by the Father, of the essential Deity of Jesus.

Still, the passage does take into account the subservience of Jesus during His time on this earth.

John 10:29 is cited.

> *"My Father, which gave them me, is greater than all; and no man is able to pluck them out of my Father's hand. I and my Father are one." (John 10:29-30)*

You might notice that I've added verse thirty. This is a definite statement that

CHAPTER 19: KENOSIS

Jesus is God. If you will look at the following verses you will that this is exactly what the people believed He meant. That He did not correct their view means that this was His meaning.

But, even verse twenty nine speaks of the Divinity of Jesus. At no place in Scripture do we see God placing His chosen ones at any place but in His Own Hands. For the Father to place the redeemed in the Hand of Jesus, "...which gave *them* me...," is a clear declaration of the Divinity of Jesus.

Some might argue that the verse says that the Father gave Jesus to the people. Such a view is not warranted by either the text or the context of the Words.

The fact that the believers were placed into the Hands of Jesus is a picture of His subordination to the Father due to the Kenosis.

John 16:28 is cited.

> "I came forth from the Father, and am come into the world: again, I leave the world, and go to the Father."

Jesus speaks of coming from the Father and then returning to the Father. This pictures both His subjection in the kenosis and His glorification regained.

The Doctrine of the Godhead: Jesus and the Father are of the Same Essence

John 17:21 is cited.

> "That they all may be one, as thou Father, art in me, and I in thee, that they may also be one in us: that the world may believe that thou hast sent me."

This verse very clearly sets for the doctrine of the Godhead. Jesus and the Father are of the same essence. Yet, Jesus claims a subservient position on this earth due to the kenosis.

Matthew Henry (*Matthew Henry's Commentary*) cites Matthew 3:17. This is the scene at the baptism of Jesus.

> "And lo a voice from heaven, saying, This is my beloved Son, in whom I am well pleased."

This verse also speaks to the kenosis. Jesus is pleasing to the Father. Yet, the fact that Jesus is called *"my beloved Son"* by the Father speaks of the essential Deity which was Jesus.

Jesus' Work was Far More Than Just the Cross

All of these references to the subjection of Jesus to the Father are pictures of the great sacrifice of Jesus in redeeming us from sin. He went to greater lengths than just the cross in order to save us. He laid aside the great glory which was His by nature of His essential deity.

In this He became one of us so that He might die as one of us. Thus His death is able to be counted as our death. His sacrifice may be accounted to us. We can be free of sin because of the kenosis. Jesus died in our place as one of us.

It was His essential righteousness, as Deity which made this death effective. It was His essential humanity, via the virgin birth, which allows us to access the salvation He offers.

The Kenosis Makes Jesus the Mediator

It is also the Kenosis which makes Jesus the Mediator between the Father and a sinful world.

Matthew Henry (*Matthew Henry's Commentary*) looks at Hebrews 1:10 and sees that Jesus had original title to govern the world as He is the Creator. This also means that He has the right of mediator by commission.

> "And Thou, Lord, in the beginning hast laid the foundation of the earth; and the heavens are the works of thine hands." (Hebrews 1:10)

If we would look back to the first three verses of John's Gospel we would see that Jesus is the Creative Agent of the Godhead.

Jesus is the Only Possible Mediator

It is through the kenosis that Jesus is able to bridge the gap between humanity and Divinity. He is the only possible Mediator because He is the Only God Man.

Barnes (*Barnes' Notes on the New Testament*) references the Great Commission of Matthew 28:18 and then ties this in with John 1:2, Colossians 1:16-17, and Hebrews 1:8. By comparing these passages Henry notes that as God, the Son - Jesus, had created all things and, therefore, had title right to all things. The authority which Jesus cites in Matthew is that of an office He had just assumed. With His death and resurrection Jesus had become the Mediator.

In this Jesus could both take the needs and problems of man to the Father. But He could also take the Authority of God to the creature, man. Thus, our witness and works for God are done in concert with His Authority and Power. When we try to do this work on our own, we will fail!

The Kenosis also Displayed the Great Power of Jesus

The Kenosis also displayed the great power of Jesus.

Pendleton (*Christian Doctrine*) understood that Jesus exercised great power even before Bethlehem. Jesus was free from creatureship as God. Still, by His Own volition, He could place Himself under the Law (see Galatians 4:4-5). In this way He could then satisfy the Law and yet still be able to offer grace as the One Who administered the Law.

This is yet another reason why Jesus is the only possible Savior of humanity. Only He could be under the Law, die as The Sacrifice to the demands of the Law, and then give absolution from the penalty of that same Law.

Again, Jesus is not a guide to Heaven. He, through His death, burial and resurrection, is the Very Conveyance of our souls to the Heavenly realms! Salvation is all, completely, about Him and His Work. He allows us, unworthy though we are, to access this salvation by trusting Him!

The Kenosis in Action

Dake (*The Dake Annotated Bible*) finds another illustration of the Kenosis in action. Jesus exercised great power while on earth. In John 5:19 we see a picture of the Trinity in action. The Godhead acts in unison. While on earth Jesus acted in union with the Father and His will. Meanwhile, the Spirit acts to put conviction upon the heart of man and open that person to the Words of God.

CHAPTER 19: KENOSIS

We might note that Jesus continues to exercise great power after His resurrection. When we consider John 17:6 with Philippians 2:6-11 we are able to consider the great Work which Jesus did in the Kenosis. Jesus did take up again the glory which He had laid aside in the incarnation.

This seems an often arcane doctrine. It is not. The Kenosis not only opens an uncerstanding of the New Testament ministry of Jesus to our eyes and ears it is also a basis of our very salvation. To consider the Kenosis is to consider the great love which Jesus had for us.

We have looked at the voluntary submission of Jesus. In our next session we will begin to consider the glorification of Jesus.

CHAPTER 20
THE GLORIFICATION OF JESUS
(Session Twenty-One)

He is the Glorious Creator, Sustainer and King of the Universe

In our last session we talked about the voluntary submission of Jesus as both our Savior and our example of how we ought, also, to walk in this world. Jesus also gave us a perfect example of submission as the way that we should approach our relationship with God.

This really is an important point. My son has just, about two months ago, gotten a bull dog. That dog understands who the master is in his relationship. "Louie," (That's what my son named the beast!) is a loveable dog who is very gentle with Ethan's children; he loves to just sit in front of someone so they can scratch his head. But, the dog knows that Ethan is the master.

When Ethan comes into a room the dog will perk up and run to Ethan's side. If I try to walk the beast he will drag me by his leash. Ethan doesn't even have to use the leash. The dog follows him and already obeys every command.

We Have Been Influenced by the "Wealth and Prosperity Gospel"

We need to be like that dog. Unfortunately, too many of us have been influenced by the "Wealth and Prosperity Gospel." We seem to believe that God exists to do our bidding. NO! God does grant blessings to His people. But, this is not because we are deserving. He grants out of His love, not our desire or worthiness. May we never get, or give, the impression that God is the Great Department Store in the Sky.

He is the Glorious Creator and Sustainer of the Universe. He is The King. Let us never forget our place as servants of the King! He gives us a wonderful relationship in that we are allowed to approach His throne with our supplications. But we approach in our need and for His Glory. I may often want. Often He may see that I do not need.

We know that Jesus is as the man described in Proverbs 18:24,

> "...a friend that sticketh closer than a brother."

We Get Caught up in His Wonderfulness and Overlook His Greatness

Sometimes we get caught up in His wonderfulness and overlook His greatness. The writer of Hebrews speaks of Jesus.

> "God, who at sundry times and in divers manners spake in time past unto the fathers by the prophets, Hath in these last days spoken unto us by his Son, whom he hath appointed heir of all things, by whom also he made the worlds; Who being the brightness of his glory, and the express image of his person, and upholding all things by the word of his power, when he had by himself purged our sins, sat down on the right hand of the Majesty on high." (Hebrews 1:1-3)

This verse speaks of the Glory that shines from the Person of Jesus Christ. One of the proofs of His Glory is that His Glory shines from His Person. His Glory is What, and Who, He is. You will notice that the term "...being the brightness of *his* glory..." does not speak of a reflection, or of a binary Glory. The Glory which is Jesus is the Glory of God.

The Express Image

When the term "...express image of his person..." is used the meaning is that Jesus is of the very same essence as is the Father. The phrase was not "image like His Person;" (Capital letters added. I just don't feel comfortable not capitalizing terms in reference to God!) the phrase is "...express image of his person..."

When one looks at a picture of me, why I do not know!, he will see a picture of me. When I look at a mirror I see an image of myself. But when someone else looks at me, they see me rather than a duplication. That is the meaning of the phrase used here. Looking at Jesus is the same, because He is of the same essence, as looking at God. The image is not a reflection, not a picture, not a duplication. The image is of God's very Person.

One proof of His glory shines through His sinless life and resurrection. None other has ever lived a sinless life. No one. Although there are Biblical examples of others who have risen from the dead, none of these did so on their own volition as did Jesus. He was raised from the dead in His Own power. He defeated death and walked in His Own life at His Own discretion.

Another Proof of His Glory

Another proof of this glory shines through the lives He touches yet today. I have great respect for the work done by Alcoholics Anonymous. But Jesus only needs one step to change a person's life from sinner to saint. His salvation can give a new meaning to an old life. His salvation can give a lifetime of purpose to a young life. His salvation can raise a person from the sickbed of sin and whisk them through the stars to a Home in Heaven. His salvation can give meaning and contentment in the direst of circumstance.

In an age of superstition and a myriad of religious observance, it was men and women who had an experience with the Master who "turned the world upside down" (see Acts 17:6) in the Name of Jesus. Even the great empire that persecuted them had to eventually come to an accommodation with those who claimed His Name. Time, be it BC/AD which acknowledges Him or the BCE/CE which does not, is dated from an approximation of His birth.

Even those who would deny and defame our Savior pay Him homage each time they write out checks for their monthly bills.

The verse above spoke of the "Brightness of His Glory." The *Concordia Study Bible* sees this and comments that one cannot look at the sun and not see the light. The light is of the same essence as is the sun.

The Glory of Jesus is of His eternal essence as God.

Zodhiates (*God in Man*) speaks of this glory.

> "Skeptics ask, 'Why did not Jesus by reasoning prove His deity?' But amid the blaze of His miracles, this would be like placing a label on the sun. Does the sun need a label?"

There are places in Scripture where Jesus very clearly spoke of His Deity. We have already discussed some of these. We will look at more instances in future sessions.

CHAPTER 20: THE GLORIFICATION OF JESUS

First, God Declared His Glory; God Said It, That Settles It

When skeptic's and cultist's look at the Gospel record and demand that words be put in Jesus mouth before they will accept His full Divinity, I am reminded of two things. The first is simple: God said it. That settles it whether I believe it or not!

Second, God's Words Declare His Glory

The second is the words of the rich man in hell and the reply of Abraham.

> "The he said, I pray thee therefore, father, that thou wouldest send him to my father's house: for I have five brethren; that he may testify unto them, lest they also come into this place of torment. Abraham saith unto him, they have Moses and the prophets; let them hear them. And he said, Nay, father Abraham: but if one went unto them from the dead, they will repent. And he said unto him, If they hear not Moses and the prophets, neither will they be persuaded, though one rose from the dead." (Luke 16:27-31)

The unalterable, eternal, inspired and preserved Words of God have declared that Jesus is God. Any who will not accept those Words from God will not accept any other reasoning. It will take an act of the Spirit upon their hearts to convince them of the Glory that is Jesus.

The Proof of His Glory Was Shown to the Disciples At the Transfiguration

The proof of this glory was also shown to the disciples. On the Mount of Transfiguration the disciples were allowed to see some of the Glory which Jesus had laid aside in the kenosis as He assumed the clothing of humanity so that He might become the sacrifice which would save from sin.

> "And was transfigured before them: and his face did shine as the sun, and his raiment was white as the light." (Matthew 17:2)

The interesting thing here is that Peter, James, and John, the three disciples who were allowed to accompany Jesus at this event, knew to whom Jesus was speaking.

> "And, behold, there appeared unto them Moses and Elias talking with him." (Matthew 17:3)

These men had been gone from the earthly scene for hundreds of years. It is certain that the three disciples did not know these men from the effect of their earthly eyes.

Jesus had allowed these three a glance into the spiritual realm of eternity. The three saw, and knew, by the power of the Spirit upon their spiritual understanding.

The Scripture does not say that these two also radiated light as did Jesus.

There was, however, a time when the face of Moses shined.

> "And it came to pass, when Moses came down from mount Sinai with the two tables of testimony in Moses' hand, when he came down from the mount, that Moses wist not that the skin of his face shone while he talked with him. And when Aaron and all the children of Israel saw Moses, behold, the skin of his face shone; and they were afraid to come nigh him. And Moses called unto them; and Aaron and all the rulers of the congregation returned unto him: and Moses talked with them. And afterward all the children of Israel came nigh: and he gave them in commandment all that the LORD had spoken with him in mount Sinai. And till Moses had done speaking with them, he put a vail on his face." (Exodus 34:29-34)

Notice the difference in the two accounts. When Moses came down from Mr. Sinai, after being in the presence of God, his face shone with the glory of God to such an extent that his face had to be hidden from even Aaron with a cloth.

Moses' Derived Glory

But, on the Mount of Transfiguration, even the clothes of Jesus shone with this Holy Glory and Light. The difference is that Moses was a servant of God. Moses spoke the oracles of God and transmitted the commandments of God to the people. His "glory," such as it was, was not his own. It was a derived glory which had more to do with the Words of God which he spoke and his position as the messenger of God.

With Jesus, as Henry (*Matthew Henry's Commentary*) points out, the glory was much more than just His face. The glory of Jesus was not a derived glory, having to do only with his mission. The Glory of Jesus was His Own Glory by His right as God.

Not only was the Glory of Jesus shown to His disciples; that glory was also shown through His disciples.

These disciples were not a fearless bunch of world changers. At His death these disciples scattered in fear. But, after His resurrection those same disciples became fearless propagators of His story. They braved beatings and martyrdom for their Master. From the time of Pentecost on, this band of followers were energized by the glory of the Lord.

It is interesting to note just who these disciples were. His disciples were mostly not drawn from the religious elite. They came from the working class. This was a working class whose status was of a nation occupied by a foreign power. They were, themselves, subjects of that foreign power. They did not live in a mobile society. They could have been expected to travel very little. They could have been expected to rarely travel out of sight of their childhood homes and families.

Yet, these same people, with all the cultural and social disadvantages, took His Message of sin and salvation to the corners of the world. Not only did they take the message. The argued the message so compellingly that they made converts wherever they went. So persuasive was this message that the converts became, themselves, fearless propagators of the Truth that Jesus Christ died in time so that others might live in eternity.

Another Proof of His Glory

Another proof of the glory of Jesus is shown in this day by the work He has done for us.

The Pulpit Commentary comments on Philippians 2:6.

"Who, being in the form of God, thought it not robbery to be equal with God."

In order to fully understand the great magnificence of what Jesus did for us in coming into this world, we need to understand the glory which He voluntarily laid aside.

We, ourselves, need to give Him the Glory though our praise and through our obedience. He came to save sinners. We were sinners which he has saved. Now, to show Him obedience and glory we need to search out others who need to hear the old story of Jesus and His love.

In our next session we will begin to consider the power of the Glory of Jesus.

CHAPTER 21
THE POWER OF THE GLORY OF JESUS
(Session Twenty-Two)

In this session we will consider the power of the Glory of Jesus. That power of the Glory of Jesus was His Own Glory.

Alford (*The New Testament for English Readers*) looks at Philippians 2:6,

"Who, being in the form of God, thought it not robbery to be equal with God."

Alford sees that in His preincarnate existence, Jesus was God. Therefore, He was equal with the Father.

A thing we often overlook is that Jesus was equal with the Father even while He was on this earth as a human person. He never ceased to be God. In the kenosis He laid aside the outward glory of His Divinity. But, He never stopped being Divine. He remained God even while He resided in the body of humanity.

This was necessary. For His sacrifice to be sufficient for all people of all ages who would accept Him, it was an absolute necessity that He retain the essence of His being. Had He been sacrificed as an ordinary Human His sacrifice would not have been sufficient.

Again, I caution you not to discount His humanity in the above statement. Born of a woman, He was fully human even while retaining the essence of the Godhead in His being. Without this humanity He could not have died as our substitute.

This is a great mystery of the synthesis of His nature. In order for Him to complete His task of becoming the sacrifice for the sins of humanity, it was necessary for Him to be fully human and fully God. It is only the power of His Own Glory which would allow such a thing as this.

Barnes (*Barnes' Notes on the New Testament*) accesses Colossians 2:9.

"For in him dwelleth all the fulness of the Godhead bodily."

"The language is such as would be obviously employed on the supposition that God became incarnate, and appeared in human form; and there is no other idea which it so naturally expresses, nor is there any other which it can be **made** to express without a forced construction." "Theotas," the word translated "Godhead," does not simply mean an attribute (morality, holiness, knowledge, etc.), "...but that whole Deity thus became incarnate, and appeared in human form."

The Concept of "Tri theism" Is Not in the Bible

The Bible nowhere even suggests a concept of "tri theism," the idea of a "council of "Persons" being the One God. The Bible picture is that there is but One God. This One God is eternally existent in three distinct "Persons." These Three are different Personalities yet the Three consist of but One Essence.

I know, "Clear as mud." I do not believe that this is a concept we can begin to grasp with our physical and time centric minds. We will understand when we reach the eternal realms of spirit in Heaven. For now we must simply accept on faith that which God has said because He has said it is so.

Such acceptance is called "Faith." This is the medium of our relationship with God.

The Greek Preposition "Para" and Jesus' Glory

Zodhiates (*God in Man*) explains that the power of His Glory was in His "Para." In John 1:14 and 17:5, the Greek preposition, "para." is used in speaking of the glory of Jesus. "Para" means "beside, alongside." We, therefore, see that the Glory of Jesus was not derived from the Father but His [Jesus'] Own Glory which was **alongside** that of the Father.

The meaning here is that Jesus did not derive His Glory from the Father. The Glory of Jesus was His Own Glory. This, of course, also speaks to the Deity of Jesus.

While we have looked at the concept that the power of the Glory of Jesus was His Own Glory, we must consider that Jesus, as God, is eternal. What was, is. And it always will be. Therefore, we must also consider that the power of the Glory of Jesus **IS** His Own Glory.

Barnes (*Barnes' Notes on the New Testament*) also speaks of Philippians 2:6. He sees that the power is His in His Own Person. It is part and parcel of What and Who He is. Form, in this verse, can mean only either splendor, majesty, glory or nature as in essence.

Thus, when the verse says that Jesus was "in the form of God," the meaning is that He **IS** very God in the essence of His Own Being.

The Power of His Glory is Shown in His Performance

The power of His Glory is shown in His performance - in what He did. Matthew 17:3 begins the narrative of the Transfiguration. In this we catch a glimpse, although a veiled glimpse, of the glory which was the property of Jesus before He "laid it aside" in the Kenosis.

> *"And now, O Father, glorify thou me with thine own self with the glory which I had with thee before the world was." (John 17:5)*

At this stage Jesus is yet within His own voluntary submission to the Father. This is part of the Kenosis. He has not yet gone to the Cross to fulfill His task as sacrifice for the sins of the world. Therefore, He speaks to the Father.

Note the eternality of Jesus in this verse. He was God before the world was. He still is God or He could not make this prophecy that He would reverse the process of the Kenosis and regain that which was His, His outward Glory as God, by right. What He has laid aside He has the power, and right, to gather to Himself again.

What Jesus was, God, He is still. This never changed even during His voluntary submission in the Kenosis.

We are also able to see the performance of the Glory of Jesus. Clarke (*Adam Clarke's Commentary*) references John 1:18 –

> *"No man hath seen God at any time, the only begotten Son, which is in the bosom of the Father, he hath declared him."*

The glory of Jesus is seen in that He gave the message of God to man. The Word has "...announced the Divine oracles unto men..."

In His life, His teaching, His manner of miracle, and His miraculous death, burial and resurrection, Jesus has actually shown the truth of God to humanity. Of no one, but God, could it be said that "...he hath declared him." We might be able to declare

CHAPTER 21: THE POWER OF THE GLORY OF JESUS

facts about God. Indeed, the penmen who have passed the inspired and preserved Scripture down through the ages to us, have done this. But only God, Himself, could have declared the essence of the Father unto men.

The Glory of Jesus is Shown by His Receiving Worship

The Glory of Jesus is also shown in the fact that He received worship.

> "Being made so much better than the angels, as he hath by inheritance obtained a more excellent name than they. For unto which of the angels said he at any time, Thou art my Son, this day have I begotten thee? And again, I will be to him a Father, and he shall be to me a Son? And again, when he bringeth in the firstbegotten into the world, he saith, And let all the angels of God Worship him." (Hebrews 1:4-6)

About this passage, Adam Clarke (*Adam Clarke's Commentary*) has said that the ancient Jews had the highest regard for the angels. They considered them the highest council of God. The angels could even be worshipped as God's representatives [although not for themselves). None but God was thought to be entitled to the worship of angels. The writer of Hebrews, in saying that Jesus is above the angels, and that the angels are instructed to worship Jesus, is claiming Deity for Jesus. [Reference is made by Clarke to the **Targum** of Jonathan ben Uzziel]

This passage is speaking of relationships. In relationship, the Son and the Father are distinct. This passage does not suggest that Jesus began at Bethlehem. Such a construct would be foreign to the rest of Scripture. The Father said these things. Through the medium of the Virgin Birth Jesus *was* "brought into the world." But, it is equally true that Jesus existed in Glory and as Deity, before these events.

If Jesus were not God, to suggest that the angels must worship Him would be considered the highest of blasphemy. Since Jesus is God, this is simply His right by virtue of Who He is.

Jesus is to be Glorified by These Events

In John 11:4 Jesus was speaking of Lazarus.

> "When Jesus heard that, he said, This sickness is not unto death, but for the glory of God, that the Son of God might be glorified thereby."

Since Jesus is God, the statement of this verse is perfectly reasonable. The events are intended to give glory to God. Jesus is to be glorified by these events. The glory that was intended for God is properly applied to the Son. By that action the glory does go to God.

For those who would claim that Jesus never claimed to be God, this verse must be misapplied. Properly applied, this verse is a direct claim of Deity made by Jesus.

In our next session we will begin to examine that Jesus has the attributes of Deity. In other words, the essence of what makes God, God, is applied to Jesus.

CHAPTER 22
I. JESUS HAS THE ATTRIBUTES OF DEITY
(Session Twenty-Three)

Attributes Which He Shares with No Human

What do we mean when we say that Jesus has the attributes of Deity? An attribute is something that makes a person who he is. For instance, when people ask, "How are you?" I always answer, "Old and fat." Those are attributes that describe the physicality of who I am.

There are many people with whom I share those attributes. But, when we speak of the attributes of Jesus we are speaking of attributes which He shares with no human. Jesus claimed, as Personal attributes, the rights and privileges which belonged to God, alone.

There are those who argue that Jesus never claimed Deity for Himself. These persons are wrong. Every time that Jesus exercised those attributes which were of God, and acted upon those claims, He was asserting His Deity. He claimed, both through His words and His actions, that He was not simply another man. His words and actions made the claim that He was (IS!) God in human flesh.

Four Instances Where Jesus Appropriated the Attributes of God

Christianson (*Why We Believe in the Deity of Christ*) noted four instances where Jesus appropriated the attributes of God as He ministered to the people of those long ago days. One of these is in the familiar incident where a man was let down, by his friends, through a roof. These men were seeking healing.

First, Thy Sins Be Forgiven

Jesus looked upon this man and said,

> "...be of good cheer; thy sins be forgiven thee." (Matthew 9:2)

The religious scribes who were present were aghast as this statement. Verse three says that,

> "...certain of the scribes said within themselves, This man blasphemeth."

These men knew that no mere man could forgive sin; this was the prerogative of God, Alone.

Second, Jesus Knew Their Thoughts

In verse four we see that Jesus knew the thoughts of these men. Surely this was not a parlor trick of "reading minds." This was an exercise of Deity in that Jesus knew the thoughts of these scribes.

Jesus went beyond this understanding of thoughts. Verse six records Jesus as saying,

> "But that ye may know that the Son of man hath power on earth to forgive sins, (then saith he to the sick of the palsy,) Arise, take up thy bed, and go unto thine house."

Anyone could have claimed to have forgiven sin. To just say such a thing is no great feat. But, Jesus said that He would prove the fact that He had forgiven sin by immediately healing this lame man. Verse seven gives the proof of the claim of Jesus. "And he arose, and departed to his house."

Third, Jesus Could Raise the Dead

Beyond the simple, if we can really say such a thing!, of the healing of the lame man, Jesus also said that He could raise the dead.

> *"For as the Father raiseth up the dead and quickeneth them; even so the Son quickeneth whom he will." (John 5:21)*

There are many instances in the Scripture where people have been brought back to physical life. Jesus promised to do this. His promise was different from those others who were used of God to restore physical life. Each of these persons was energized by the Spirit of God to restore life. Jesus said that He would perform these miracles by His Own volition. It would be by His Own will that the miracle would occur.

Further, Jesus said that He would restore physical life in the same manner as the Father did so. This is an obvious claim of absolute equality with the Father. In this Jesus was stating His Own Deity.

> *"For the Father judgeth no man, but hath committed all judgment unto the Son: That all men should honour the Son, even as they honour the Father: He that honoureth not the Son honoureth not the Father which hath sent him. Verily, verily, I say unto you, He that heareth my word, and believeth on him that sent me, hath everlasting life, and shall not come into condemnation; but is passed from death unto life. Verily, verily, I say unto you, The hour is coming, and now is, when the dead shall hear the voice of the Son of God: and they that hear shall live. For as the Father hath life in himself; so hath he given the Son to have life in himself; And hath given him authority to execute judgment also, because he is the Son of man." (John 5:22-27)*

Christianson has made the point that Jesus claimed that He would be the Judge of the World. That is a prerogative of God. Again, Jesus was making the claim of absolute Deity for Himself.

There is even more in this passage which are claims of Jesus to deity. The honor given to Jesus is necessary for one to honor God. The honor to One is honor to Both. Jesus also claimed that He had life within Himself. Each of us is born from our parents. That original spark of the breath of God into Adam has continued. Life springs from life. Jesus said that He was Life. His Life did not spring from any other human; He was Life and this life was part of His Own makeup. This is a claim of deity.

Christianson also noted the claim of Jesus as given in the Great Commission.

> *"And Jesus came and spake unto them, saying, All power is given unto me in heaven and in earth." (Matthew 28:18)*

Another Attribute, Jesus' Claim to "All Power"

Jesus spoke to His disciples. He said that all power, both in Heaven and in earth, was in Him. This is a certain claim to the Deity of Jesus.

There can be two who are powerful. But, there cannot be two who are "all powerful." If Jesus were not God in the flesh He could not have "all power." If God had decreed that His Own power were to be transferred to Jesus, God would cease to be God because He would no longer be all powerful.

CHAPTER 22: I. JESUS HAS THE ATTRIBUTES OF DEITY

Only a realization of the Triune nature of God, and the deity of Jesus, could make the statement of Matthew to be true.

A further notification of the Deity of Jesus is given in the very last verse of the Book of Matthew.

> "...and, lo, I am with you alway, even unto the end of the world. Amen." (Matthew 28:20)

Another Attribute, Jesus' Omnipresence

As we consider this verse we must note that the teaching is that Jesus would be with His churches, and the people of those churches, in whatever place they assembled and worked. This is the attribute of Omnipresence. Simply put, this means that Jesus was claiming that He could be in every place at the same time.

We see this same attribute of Jesus as He spoke with Nicodemus in the third chapter of John's Gospel.

> "And no man hath ascended up to heaven, but he that came down from heaven, even the son of man which is in heaven." (John 3:13)

No mere man can be in more than one location at any given time. Not even the angels have this ability. This is an attribute of God, alone. Jesus was fully stating His Deity when He made this prophecy and promise.

There is more. Notice that Jesus promised this support "...unto the end of the world..." In this Jesus was stating His Own eternality. Again, this is an attribute of God, alone. We may live in Heaven for all eternity; we will have this ability through the power of Jesus. Jesus had already, in this verse, claimed all power for Himself. Thus, His eternality is dependent only upon His Own Personal attributes.

He is God!

We will continue with this same theme in our next session - God willing.

CHAPTER 23
II. JESUS HAS THE ATTRIBUTES OF DEITY
(Session Twenty-Four)

Jesus Was Always in Fellowship With the Father

On one of the occasions when Jesus healed a man, actually more than on one occasion, the Jewish leadership accused Him of violating the Sabbath. The answer of Jesus was to the point.

"But Jesus answered them, My Father worketh hitherto, and I work." (John 5:17)

Alford (*The New Testament for English Readers*) spoke about the verse. He contended that there was no need for Jesus to rest (on the Sabbath) as must a mortal human. Mortal man is in danger of losing his attentiveness to God. Jesus, however, was engaged in worship as the operative stance of even His work.

I would agree, substantially, with Alford. However, I would make an amplification. Worship is adoration of God. But, worship is also a state of communion with God. Jesus was always in fellowship with the Father.

We could also argue that Jesus is both God and man. As God He is worthy of our worship, Himself. As man He is our example of the worship of the Triune God. To misunderstand this application of His example of humanity for us is to misunderstand the totality of His mission to this earth in that first century. He came to die as our sacrifice. He came to show us the reality of God in ways that we could understand. He also came to live as one of us; in this He was our example of how we ought to walk as human beings.

There was another time when these Jewish leaders castigated Jesus because He, and His disciples, was gleaning a field to eat. After making a short defense, Jesus made an astounding, to the Pharisees, assertion. He said,

"For the Son of man is Lord even of the sabbath day." (Matthew 12:8)

Again, for those who would claim that Jesus never claimed deity for Himself I would suggest they look at this verse very carefully. The Sabbath is the Covenant Day. It is a day dedicated to the worship of God. Rest is part of the day. Rest, however, means a cessation of normal daily activity. This is so that the mind and soul may meditate upon the things of God.

For Jesus to claim that He is the Lord of the Sabbath is a clear and unmistakable attestation of His Deity.

The fact is that, as God, Jesus has the right to do whatever He wishes in relation to the Sabbath. It is a day dedicated to Him. He no more breaks the Sabbath in doing good than He does in His sustaining of the universe.

John 14:6 is Jesus' Claim to the Prerogatives of God

There is another well known verse where Jesus claims the prerogatives of God.

"Jesus saith unto him, I am the way, the truth, and the life: no man cometh unto the Father, but by me." (John 14:6)

Again, this is a very clear pronouncement of His Own Deity which was made by

Jesus. He does not make a claim that He will show anyone the way to the Father. He, Himself, is The Way. No mere human man could make such a claim in truth. Jesus also claims to be Truth, Itself. Only God is ultimate Truth. Therefore, Jesus has made the case that He is God.

John 14:6 Establishes the Claim That Jesus is Self existent

Only God is self existent. All other life has been given by Him. For Jesus say that He is life, is a certain claim of His Own Deity. He is God. The only other explanation for these statements is that He was mistaken - or a liar, which would negate all. His life of miracle, His resurrection from the dead, His great spiritual influence in the succeeding centuries all show that He was neither liar nor mistaken. He is God. There is no other rational conclusion which can be reached.

Jesus also taught mankind how to worship.

Simmons (*A Systematic Study of Bible Doctrine*) notes that worship is an honor due to God alone. Yet, Jesus received worship. This is another place in which Jesus has claimed Deity as He has claimed the rights associated with Deity.

> *"That all men should honour the Son, even as they honour the Father. He that honoureth not the Son honoureth not the Father which hath sent him." (John 5:23)*

To fail to give due honor to Jesus is to fail to give honor to the Father. Both are then due the same honor. This is an indication of the triune nature of God.

> *"And again, when he bringeth in the firstbegotten into the world, he saith, And let all the angels of God worship him." (Hebrews 1:6)*

The Worship of Jesus By the Angels

The worship by the angels, which belongs only to the Creator (Remember, the basic sin of Satan was to seek the honor which belongs only to God.) is to be given to Jesus.

> *"And when he had given thanks, he brake it, and said, Take, eat: this is my body, which is broken for you: this do in remembrance of me. After the same manner also he took the cup, when he had supped, saying, This cup is the new testament in my blood: this do you, as oft as ye drink it, in remembrance of me." (I Corinthians 11:24-25)*

The Lord's Supper is a Call by Jesus to Worship Him

Despite our many "days" on the "church calendar," this is the only place in the New Testament that I find the Christian being told to commemorate any day or event. Jesus called us to honor His death on the Cross. This is instruction in worship which only God could institute.

> *"But grow in grace, and in the knowledge of our Lord and Saviour Jesus Christ. To him be glory both now and for ever. Amen." (II Peter 3:18)*

Again, honor and glory, not to mention grace and a need to learn more of Him, are to be given to the Person of Jesus. This would be simple sacrilege were it not directed toward the Creator God. Thus, Jesus is shown as God.

> *"And the Lord shall deliver me from every evil work, and will preserve me unto his heavenly kingdom: to whom be glory for ever and ever. Amen." (II Timothy 4:18)*

Compare the first part of this verse with the Psalms of David. The Protector of David is always described as being God. The same inspired and preserved Scripture,

CHAPTER 23: II. JESUS HAS THE ATTRIBUTES OF DEITY

here, identifies Jesus as the Protector. They are the same Protector.

Also, the eternal glory is ascribed to Jesus. Again, Jesus is shown as God. Pendleton (*Christian Doctrine*) cites Matthew 4:10.

> "The saith Jesus unto him, Get thee hence, Satan: for it is written, Thou shalt worship the Lord thy God, and him only shalt thou serve."

And we see that Jesus claimed that only God could be worshipped. Yet Pendleton also notes John 5:23,

> "That all men should honour the Son, even as they honour the Father. He that honoureth not the Son honoureth not the Father which hath sent him."

This is where Jesus calls for worship from men. Thus, Jesus made the claim of His Own Divinity.

We will pick up on this theme in our next session where we will consider just ten instances where Jesus accepted worship from others. Remember, when Jesus accepts worship, He is accepting that which properly belongs to God. He is either claiming full Divinity for Himself, or He is blaspheming the very Name and Person of God.

Either we must admit that Jesus is God or we must reject Him as a heretic and charlatan unworthy of being a spiritual leader.

CHAPTER 24
III. JESUS HAS THE ATTRIBUTES OF DEITY
(Session Twenty-Five)

One of the many things we point to with regard to the Deity of Jesus is the fact that He accepted worship. This is an act that is only properly permitted by God. For Jesus to have accepted worship, had He not been convinced of His Own Deity, would have been an act passing pride and reaching sacrilege. Such an acceptance on His part would disqualify Him from being either a religious or a moral guide for humanity.

There are Only Two Entities Who are Actually Capable of Accepting Worship

My understanding of Scripture is that there are only two entities in the entire universe who are actually capable of accepting worship: God, Almighty and Satan, the deceiver.

Satan comes in many disguises. Thus, any worship which is not directed toward the Lord of the Universe is worship of Satan. Such is, even if not intended to be so, a form of false religious devotion. Many false cultists are engaged in "Devil Worship" even when they would both believe and argue that such is not the case. If Jesus were not Divine and accepted worship He would be guilty of taking that glory and privilege which belongs to God and delivering it to Satan.

Since Jesus is Divine, His acceptance of worship would be proper in every way. Further, to deny Him this worship would be a sin against the God Who created us.

Nine Instances In Scripture Records of Worship Being Properly Offered to Jesus

Evangelist Anthony Zeoli (*Is Jesus God? Book Number Two*) has listed nine instances where Scripture records worship being properly offered to Jesus. The first of these is listed in Hebrews 1:6.

First, The Firstbegotten, Is Worshipped

"And again, when he bringeth in the firstbegotten into the world, he saith, And let all the angels of God worship him."

We have already considered this term, "first begotten." It is a positional term rather than a chronological term. A simple look back to John 3:16 will show that Jesus is the "only begotten" of God.

My son, Ethan, is my only son. If I were to call him my first begotten son it would indicate that there was another son. Since there is not another, such a statement would confuse rather than illuminate.

In the culture of the day in which the Bible was written, the "first begotten" was a term which designated a position of power and privilege within the family. Since there is no distinction of position among the "Persons" of the Triune Godhead, this concept of understanding would be faulty on our part.

But, as we read the term, and understand the term, in the Scripture we must understand just to whom that Scripture was written. It was written to us. It is, to us, the Name of Jesus which is powerful unto salvation. God, the Father, may forgive us. The Spirit may call us into salvation through His convicting work. But, it is Jesus Christ, and His Work on Calvary which has purchased that salvation for us.

Again, speaking to humanity, God's Word says of Jesus,

> "Wherefore God also hath highly exalted him, and given him a name which is above every name: That at the name of Jesus every knee should bow, of things in heaven, and things in earth, and things under the earth." (Philippians 2:9-10)

Notice that this last mentioned verse also spoke of Heavenly entities, as well as human, and sinful entities as well ("Under the earth" seems to indicate that even the demons of Hell must ultimately admit that worship rightly belongs to Him.) are to give Him worship. The last two denote His power and position. The first, "in heaven," denotes the angels of God as did also Hebrews 1:6. These angels understand to Whom worship is to be given. They would not make the "mistake" of offering worship to any but God.

Second, The Wise Men Worshipped Jesus

Second, Zeoli notes that the wise men worshipped Jesus.

> "And when they were come into the house, they saw the young child with Mary his mother, and fell down, and worshipped him: and when they had opened their treasures, they presented unto him gifts, gold, and frankincense, and myrrh." (Matthew 2:11)

The fact that the Spirit of God spoke to these men in the very next verse, and did not chide them for improper worship, would say that this worship was acceptable unto God. This acceptance would only be possible because Jesus is Deity. Jesus is God.

Third, The Disciples Worshipped Jesus

Third, Zeoli note that the disciples in the ship worshipped Jesus.

> "Then they that were in the ship came and worshipped him, saying, Of a truth thou art the Son of God." (Matthew 14:33)

This is worship which Jesus very plainly accepted. As noted above, this is an indication of the full Divinity of Jesus. In accepting this worship Jesus was admitting that He is God.

Fourth, A Military Man Worshipped Jesus

Zeoli finds another place where Jesus accepted worship. This time the worship came from a military man.

> "While he spake these things unto them, behold, there came a certain ruler, and worshipped him, saying, My daughter is even now dead: but come and lay thy hand upon her, and she shall live." (Matthew 9:18)

More than simply worshiping Jesus, this military man ascribed to Jesus the power of life. This echo's the words of John:

> "In him was life; and the life was the light of men." (John 1:4)

Jesus did not refuse the worship. Neither did Jesus dispute the fact that in Him was life. In just a few short verses we see that Jesus was powerful even unto the giving of temporal life. To us in this day He offers spiritual life. The same power to perform is available because Jesus is God in the flesh.

CHAPTER 24: III. JESUS HAS THE ATTRIBUTES OF DEITY

Fifth, A Leper Worships Jesus

Just a chapter earlier Zeoli brings our attention to a leper;

> "And, behold, there came a leper and worshipped him, saying, Lord, if thou wilt, thou canst make me clean." (Matthew 8:2)

Jesus does not consider men as do we. There was no class distinction in His mind. From the power of a Roman soldier to the outcast leper, Jesus was powerful. We also see that from both persons He received worship without any apology or restraint. To receive worship from all is His right as God, Incarnate.

Sixth, The Woman of Tyre Worships Jesus

Sixth, Zeoli also shows us that Jesus accepted worship from the Woman of Tyre. This was a woman who was not, humanly speaking, of His race.

> "Then came she and worshipped him, saying, Lord, help me." (Matthew 15:25)

Not only did Jesus receive worship from this woman, He also greatly commended her faith as He answered her prayers of petition.

> "Then Jesus answered and said unto her; O woman, great is thy faith: be it unto thee, even as thou wilt. And her daughter was made whole from that very hour." (Matthew 15:28)

Seventh, A Handicapped Person Worships Jesus

Zeoli also references that Jesus accepted the worship of a handicapped person, a blind man.

> "And he said, Lord, I believe. And he worshipped him." (John 9:38)

Though this man could not see Jesus with his physical eyes, the eyes of his spirit were attuned to the power of Deity in his presence.

Eighth, The Disciples Worshipped Jesus

There were also the disciple's of Jesus. These were devout men who worshipped Jesus.

> "And when they saw him, they worshipped him: but some doubted." (Matthew 28:17)

That last phrase, "but some doubted," is a very important phrase in the text. The worship of these men was not a "mass hysteria." These men gave worship to Jesus from a reasoned heart. Their worship was not offered by men merely being swept up in the crowd's emotional wave. They worshipped because they believed that Jesus was very God. Pious men of their background would not have otherwise offered worship.

Ninth, The Disciples of Emmaus Worshipped Jesus

The disciples on the road to Emmaus also worshipped Jesus.

> "And they said one to another, Did not our heart burn within us, while he talked with us by the way, and while he opened to us the scriptures." (Luke 24:32)

This is also an important point. The worship offered was centered in the message of the Scripture. Whenever we move outside the Scripture we are prone to error. A reliance upon the inspired and preserved Words of God is a guard against mindless fanaticism. Fanaticism is not wrong if it is centered in the Words of the Spirit.

Jesus Accepts Worship From All and Will be Worshipped by All

Finally, Zeoli looks to Philippians 2:10-11 and shows us that Jesus accepts worship from all.

> *"That at the name of Jesus every knee should bow, of things in heaven, and things in earth, and things under the earth; And that every tongue should confess that Jesus Christ is Lord, to the glory of God the Father."*

The importance of this verse is the assertion that all will ultimately bow in worship before Jesus Christ. Some will do this to their everlasting damnation. But, worship Him they will! For the Christian, saved through the Blood of Jesus, the worship will be joyful.

Notice, also, that this worship brings glory to God, the Father. There is but One God. He is eternally manifested in three distinct "Persons." Thus giving glory to Jesus is giving glory to the Father, and to the Spirit., as well as giving glory to Jesus.

We have looked at the concept of worship being received by Jesus. This is part of His privilege as God. Indeed, were Jesus not God this would be profane and sinful. Since the Spirit of God has inspired and preserved the Words of Scripture, and that Scripture speaks in the affirmative about this worship directed to Jesus, we must conclude that Jesus is God.

In our next session we will consider that Jesus displayed the power of His Deity.

CHAPTER 25
JESUS DISPLAYED THE POWER OF HIS DEITY
(Session Twenty-Six)

My little grandson has been "house broken" (we also have puppies) for some time now. Still, he is quite proud of the skill. I will be out shopping with him when he tells me he needs to "go." Upon entering the men's room, or small boy's room in his case, he will loudly proclaim to one and all, if there are others in the room, that "I am a big boy. I can go potty all by myself."

This was a "rite of passage" for Eli. But, in the grand scheme of things this is not a great skill. Our puppies understand the concept of "there is a time and a place." Sadly, the dogs often forget their lessons; but they do know.

There are skills that each of us have learned. When I was working as a teacher I always told the children that not everyone is automatically a good student. But, all can learn the skills to being a student. "It's like baseball," I told them, "Or working on cars. We all have interests and it is to those interests that we devote our time and become better at these endeavors." But, these things are skills.

There are other things that are just "part and parcel" of who we are. I am about the same height as was my father at the same age. My son inherited an aptitude, because he's worked at it this has been nourished, at mechanical things. He has inherited this, mostly by watching, from his mother. She was the "fixer" in our family.

My height is part of who I am. My son's interest in mechanical things is another example of interests feeding a person; it isn't a part of his physical makeup.

The Power of Jesus Is Simply Part of Who He Was and Is

There were things that were simply part of the makeup of who Jesus was, and is, that displayed the power of Deity which was part of Who He is. These were not things He "learned." These were just manifestations of Who He was, and is.

John 1:1 says of Jesus that He is God.

> "In the beginning was the Word, and the Word was with God, and the Word was God."

Alford (*The New Testament for English Readers*) has noted this as part of the makeup of Jesus.

> "'The Word' is not an attribute of God, but an acting reality, by which the eternal and Infinite is the first great cause of the created and finite."

The Power As the Living Word

What Alford is saying is that the designation of Jesus as "the Word" is not simply to describe part of the picture of God. "The Word" is the power of God in Creation. If the next few verses are consulted one will see that Jesus is the 'Creative Agent" of the Triune Godhead.

In this Jesus is described as possessing, and displaying, His Own unique power as God. Thus, when John 1:1 is considered in conjunction with the rest of the chapter Jesus is shown as God. He isn't simply displaying the acts of God; those acts are showing that He, Himself, is God.

Rice (*Rice Reference Bible*) makes the interesting observation that both the Written and the Living Word came through human instrumentation. God gave us the Written Word via the prophets. That Word remains of Him and His eternal essence; He only used the prophets as instruments to bring His Words from the eternal realms into the created world.

Jesus, likewise, came into the physical world through human instrumentation. The Living Word was presented into the physical world via Mary. Still, He is God in His essence. The mode of conveyance does not change the character of that which is conveyed.

Observations That Jesus is Superior to All Created Beings

Zeoli (*Is Jesus God? Book Number Two*) has listed several observations which reveal that Jesus is superior to all created beings. This is to be expected as He is the Creative Agent of those beings.

He Is Superior to Angels

First, in Hebrews 1:4-9 Jesus is shown to be superior to the angels.

> *"Being made much better than the angels, as he hath by inheritance obtained a more excellent name than they. For unto which of the angels said he at any time, Thou art my Son, this day have I begotten thee? And again, I will be to him a Father and he shall be to me a Son? And again, when he bringeth in the firstbegotten into the world, he saith, And let all the angels of God worship him. And of the angels he saith, Who maketh his angels spirits, and his ministers a flame of fire. But unto the Son he saith, thy throne, O God, is for ever and ever: a sceptre of righteousness is the scepter of thy kingdom. Thou hast loved righteousness, and hated iniquity, therefore God, even thy God, hath anointed thee with the oil of gladness above thy fellows."*

If there is any confusion due to the references to Jesus being "begotten," I would encourage you to go back to our last session and look at the reasons these phrases appear. Basically, these have to do with Jesus as the representative of humanity - not with His Own essential Deity.

Notice that worship is demanded, even of the angels, to be given to Jesus. Since proper worship may only be directed toward God this is an indication of the Deity of Jesus.

Besides this, Jesus is shown to be superior to the angels in His administrative ("Thy throne, O God), judgment, and holiness.

Jesus Is Superior to Moses

Two chapters later in the Book of Hebrews Zeoli asks us to consider that Jesus is also superior to Moses.

> *"Wherefore, holy brethren, partakers of the heavenly calling, consider the Apostle and High Priest of our profession, Christ Jesus; Who was faithful to him that appointed him, as also Moses was faithful in all his house. For this man was counted worthy of more glory than Moses, inasmuch as he who hath builded the house hath more honour than the house. For every house is builded by some man; but he that built all things is God. And Moses verily was faithful in all his house, as a servant, for a testimony of those things which were to be spoken after; But Christ as*

CHAPTER 25: JESUS DISPLAYED THE POWER OF HIS DEITY

a son over his own house; whose house are we, if we hold fast the confidence and the rejoicing of the hope firm unto the end." (Hebrews 3:1-6)

You will note that Moses is given his full respect and due. He is called a great man. But, he is shown to be inferior to Jesus. Notice the difference between Moses and Jesus. Moses, a human instrument of God, is credited as being part of the "house" of God. Jesus is cited as the "builder" of the house. In other words, Jesus is shown to stand outside the structure of even Israel. He is shown, although born into the race of man as a Jew, to be the Founder and Constructor of the Jewish people.

This trait shows Jesus to be more than simply another human being. He is shown to be God.

Jesus Is Superior to King Solomon

Zeoli also shows Jesus to be superior to the Old Testament King Solomon.

"The queen of the south shall rise up in the judgment with this generation, and shall condemn it: for she came from the uttermost parts of the earth to hear the wisdom of Solomon; and, behold, a greater than Solomon is here." (Matthew 12:42)

Solomon is known to the world, primarily, for two things: His great wealth and His great wisdom. Jesus is superior in His wisdom. In John 3:12-13, Jesus is speaking to Nicodemus. He says, "If I have told you earthly things, and aye believe not, how shall ye believe, if I tell you *of* heavenly things? And no man hath ascended up to heaven, but he that came down from heaven, *even* the Son of man which is in heaven."

Jesus was able to describe Heavenly things of which Solomon had no idea. Jesus, in His eternal existence and understanding, is superior to Solomon.

Jesus is also superior to Solomon in the riches of His creative Glory as God. Jesus needs no accounting of His wealth for He owns all by right of creation.

Jesus Is Superior to Jonah

Zeoli also mentions that Jesus is superior to Jonah.

"The men of Nineveh shall rise in judgment with this generation, and shall condemn it: because they repented at the preaching of Jonas; and, behold, a greater than Jonas is here." (Matthew 12:41)

Jonah is an interesting character. I don't believe he ever completely agreed with God. The faith of Jonah was shown, after God got his attention in the specially prepared fish, in that he did the bidding of God even when he might have violently disagreed. In other words, he trusted God beyond his own prejudices. That is a great faith!

Jonah was a preacher of righteousness. Jesus IS Righteousness. The people responded to the message of Jonah. Jesus Is the Message of Salvation. Jonah showed the sign of repentance to the people of Nineveh. By His life, death, burial and resurrection, Jesus showed the sign of True Salvation to the people of the New Testament day and forward until this very day.

Jesus Is Superior In His Name

Zeoli also shows that Jesus is superior in the essence of Who He is. Even His name is superior.

"Wherefore God also hath highly exalted him, and given him a name which is above

every name." (Philippians 2:9)

Consider this verse in relation to the above.

"Neither is there salvation in any other: for there is none other name under heaven given among men, whereby we must be saved." (Acts 4:12)

I have just read a report that nearly 70% of "Christians" believe that there are many ways to Heaven than just faith in Christ. I question the true salvation of every one of these persons. The salvation experience is tied to faith in Jesus as being the ONLY sacrifice for the remission of sins. For one to believe that there are other ways of salvation is to lack faith in the sacrifice of Jesus.

Jesus Is Superior in the One Sacrifice He Offers for All Men

Zeoli also points out that the Scripture tells us that this sacrifice of Jesus is superior.

"Nor yet that he should offer himself often, as the high priest entereth into the holy place every year with blood of others; For then must he often have suffered since the foundation of the world: but now once in the end of the world hath he appeared to put away sin by the sacrifice of himself. And as it is appointed unto men once to die, but after this the judgment: So Christ was once offered to bear the sins of many; and unto them that look for him shall he appear the second time without sin unto salvation." (Hebrews 9:25-28)

"And every priest standeth daily ministering and offering oftentimes the same sacrifices, which can never take away sins: But this man [Jesus], after he had offered one sacrifice for sins for ever, sat down on the right hand of God." (Hebrews 10:11-12)

The former sacrificial system was a teaching tool to prepare the way for an understanding of the sacrifice of Jesus. This is not to denigrate the former sacrificial system. It was effective for the Old Testament saints because they were responding in faith to the revelation which God had given to them. But, in the light of eternity, these sacrifices only covered the sins of the people.

"For it is not possible that the blood of bulls and of goats should take away sin." (Hebrews 10:4)

The ultimate, legal in the light of eternity, removal of the sin of the Old Testament saints waited for the ultimate sacrifice of Jesus Christ on the Cross of Calvary. Their faith was counted to them as personal righteousness; but there were those who only performed the sacrifices as a sort of "civic duty." They had no real faith. The faithful were counted as saved for eternity by the sacrifice of Jesus Christ. They might not have understood this, probably didn't, at the time. But, God counted their faith and applied the Blood of Jesus to their accounts.

Jesus' Offering is Superior to the Offering of Abel

Indeed, as Zeoli mentions, the blood of Jesus is superior to that of the offering of Abel.

"And to Jesus the mediator of the new covenant, and to the blood of sprinkling, that speaketh better things than that of Abel." (Hebrews 12:24)

Just a chapter earlier Abel is mentioned as offering a "more excellent sacrifice..."

By faith Abel offered unto God a more excellent sacrifice than Cain, by which he obtained witness that he was righteous, God testifying of his gifts: and by it he being dead yet speaketh. (Hebrews 11:4)

CHAPTER 25: JESUS DISPLAYED THE POWER OF HIS DEITY

By comparing Scripture with Scripture, these two verses specifically, we see that the Old Testament sacrificial system was able to give witness to the righteous heart. But, it was the sacrifice of Jesus which gave access to the New Birth experience and true salvation.

Jesus' Blood Sacrifice Is Superior

Zeoli also references Hebrews 9:12 to show the superiority of the Blood of Jesus.

"Neither by the blood of goats and calves, but by his own blood he entered in once into the holy place, having obtained eternal redemption for us."

Again, this speaks of a onetime salvation, a onetime sacrifice, and the full superiority of the Blood of Jesus in the salvation of souls for eternity.

Why Jesus' Blood Is Superior

Zeoli also references that John explains the superiority of the Blood of Jesus.

"...and the blood of Jesus Christ his son cleanseth us from all sin." (I John 1:7b)

I have written about the fact that all this is so in my commentary on Genesis 3:15.

The verse also indicates that the ultimate salvation of humanity from sin would need to come through the agency of a human. Although God gave the symbol of the blood sacrifice when He made coats of skins to cover the nakedness of Adam and Eve, this could not effect their ultimate salvation. The coats could only cover. They would not eradicate that sin which was hidden beneath.

Their nakedness remained under the coats of skins.

It would be necessary for a human to shed his blood to offer an escape from the sin nature. This human could not come from the actions of the male who had willingly given control of himself over to Satan. Neither could this human be a female as Adam was the head of the race. Also, it was the sin of Adam which caused the eyes of them both to be opened. Although a sinner, and thus doomed by her sin, Eve seemed to have no such realization as she offered the fruit to Adam.

The Necessity of the Virgin Birth

We are, therefore, presented with the need that a human male be sacrificed for the sins of humanity. Yet, this male could not come through the effort of man. The birth could not be of the normal human progression. Also, this male could not have the taint of sin in his own nature. Further, it would be necessary that the male would have power over the tempter. Only God could have that power.

That this is a prophecy of the Virgin birth of Jesus Christ, the very Son of God, Who would be human while retaining His Own Deity, is contained within the verse and its context within Scripture.

The ultimate superiority of Jesus is contained in His Person. While fully human, through the medium of the Virgin Birth, Jesus is also God. This is why salvation can only be accessed through faith in Him and His sacrifice at the Cross of Calvary.

These are more than simple indications. These are evidences to the fact that Jesus is God, Eternal, in the flesh of humanity.

In our next session we will see that even His Name is associated with God.

CHAPTER 26
THE NAME OF JESUS IS ASSOCIATED WITH GOD
(Session Twenty-Seven)

In Acts 4:12 we are instructed that the Name of Jesus is the Only Name under which we can find salvation. The Name of Jesus speaks of Who He is in reality. Quite often we find the Name of Jesus uttered by the pious in Scripture in ways that could only relate to His Identification as God.

Three Areas Where the Name of Jesus Is Associated With God

Strong (*Systematic Theology*) points out three areas where the Name of Jesus is associated with God in the prayers of devout men. Jesus is seen to be on equal footing with the Father in the prayers and statements of these devout men.

I might add that these Jewish persons had a history of multiple centuries of the teaching of one essential consideration of God. These were monotheistic people because they fervently believed that there was but ONE GOD. For them to equate Jesus with the Father is to say that they believed Him to Be God. They did not see Him as a usurper, or an exalted human being; they saw Him as God in the flesh.

First, the Name Is Included In the Baptismal Formula

The first instance of which Strong speaks is that the Name of Jesus is included in the Baptismal formula. It would be absurd and profane to speak of baptizing in the name of the Father and of Moses. Moses was a great leader; the mistake was never made in equating him as God.

> "Go ye therefore, and teach all nations, baptizing them in the name of the Father, and of the Son, and of the Holy Ghost." (Matthew 28:19)

It is interesting, and instructive, to note that this baptismal formula is "in the name (singular) of" and yet gives multiple names. This is a picture of the Triune God.

> "Then Peter said unto them, Repent, and be baptized every one of you in the name of Jesus Christ for the remission of sins, and ye shall receive the gift of the Holy Ghost." (Acts 2:38)

Baptism Does Not Save, But Is Symbolic

The repentance came before the baptism. The custom of the day was for the convert to be immediately baptized into the fellowship of the church. Neither of these two latter acts saved the individual as he was saved at the point of his repentance. The baptism and the church membership were signs to all of his change in heart.

As an aside, I'd like to see this ancient custom resurrected for our time. This identification makes it easier, from a human standpoint, for one to follow the Master.

The Gift of the Holy Spirit

Another aside, unlike many in the Pentecostal style churches, the Bible does not say that we must seek and labor for the "gift" of the Holy Ghost. This gift comes as part of the salvation experience when we are indwelt with the Spirit. The depth of the individual Christian understanding and acceptance of the leading of the Spirit may be discussed. But, the indwelling comes as part of the New Birth experience.

> *"Know ye not, that so many of us as were baptized into Jesus Christ were baptized into his death?" (Romans 6:3)*

The baptism of the Christian is an identification with Jesus. The next verse explains that we are then, as representatives of Jesus to the world - each and every one of us!, to walk in this new life of submission to God and holiness before the world. I John 2:1 explains that we may fail in this from time to time. We are told not to fail; but God understands our human frailty in that He has prepared a way for us to receive cleansing and continue in the Christian walk.

Footwashing

Jesus explained this concept of the Christian who fails his Master. In John, chapter thirteen, the symbolism of "foot washing" is given.

> *"Then cometh he to Simon Peter: and Peter saith unto him, Lord, dost thou wash my feet? Jesus answered and said unto him, What I do thou knowest not now, but thou shalt know hereafter. Peter saith unto him, Thou shalt never wash my feet. Jesus answered him, If I wash thee not, thou hast no part with me. Simon Peter saith unto him, Lord, not my feet only, but also my hands and my head. Jesus saith unto him, He that is washed needeth not save to wash his feet, but is clean every whit: and ye are clean, but not all." (John 13:6-10)*

That last part has, I believe, a dual meaning. The most obvious, as it is explained in the very next verse, is that all of the disciples except Judas were truly born again.

The second meaning I find has to do with the dusty roads. A person might take a bath and be clean; but walking those unpaved and dusty roads would cause his feet to become dirty. The custom of the time was for a servant to wash the feet of traveler who came to the home.

Jesus explained that Peter didn't need a complete bath. He only needed that foot washing. Likewise, our souls are cleansed by the Blood of Christ at the time of our salvation experience. We do not need to do this again. I John 2:1 informs us that our failures and sins do need to be washed. It's not renewing salvation; it is renewing our fellowship and commitment with the Savior.

The above verse, from Romans 6:3, tells us that we are identified as followers of Jesus at our baptism into a local church. Thus, we should remain dead to the things and enticements of the world as we walk in a newness of life that bears the Good News that Jesus Christ has died in time so that others might live in eternity.

Please, do not misunderstand. We are not saved by our baptism. Our baptism is symbolic to the world that our lives have been washed clean - that we have died to our sins through the sacrifice of Jesus Christ, been buried with Him as dead to our former lives, and are risen anew to a new life with Him. Baptism, to put it more simply, is a sign to the world of the newness of our hearts in Christ, Jesus. Baptism is not a means of salvation; baptism is a means to witness that we have already been saved from our sins.

Second, The Name of Jesus Is Used In Apostolic Benedictions

Strong also relates that the Name of Jesus is used in apostolic benedictions.

> *"The grace of the Lord Jesus Christ and the love of God, and the communication of the Holy Ghost, be with you all." (II Corinthians 13:14)*

CHAPTER 26: THE NAME OF JESUS IS ASSOCIATED WITH GOD

I call your attention to the Trinitarian formula in this verse. Grace is said to be the province of Jesus. Love is attributed to the Father. Communication is the sphere of the Spirit. But, each of these is linked by a conjunctive word: "And." Thus these attributes are not exclusive to the each, as I have suggested by closing each short sentence with a period as mark of punctuation.

"And" implies that Each is endued with the same qualities as is the Other. This is a picture of the unity of the Trinity while still expressing the unique manifestation of Each Member of the Triune Godhead.

> "Grace be unto you, and peace from God our Father, and from the Lord Jesus Christ." (I Corinthians 1:3)
>
> Grace be to you and peace from God the Father, and from our Lord Jesus Christ." (Galatians 1:3)
>
> "For this cause I bow my knees unto the Father of our Lord Jesus Christ." (Ephesians 3:14)
>
> "Peace be to the brethren, and love with faith, from God the Father and the Lord Jesus Christ." (Ephesians 6:23)

Here is the Name of Jesus uttered in the same breath as is the Name of the Father. Remember, once again, that the writer was a committed monotheist. He understood the concept of One God and the extreme holiness of the Name of God. To equate another name with that of the Father would be blasphemy unless Paul was convinced that Jesus was God in the Flesh!

Finally, Strong sees that the Name of Jesus fits in other miscellaneous passages.

> "That all *men* should honour the Son, even as they honour the Father. He that honoureth not the Son honoureth not the Father which hath sent him." (John 5:23)

Here it is shown that Jesus is deserving of the same honor as is the Father. Again, this would only be considered if Jesus were on equality with the Father. Again, since there is only ONE GOD, this is an admission that Jesus is God in the Flesh. Any other argument would be an affront to the Father.

> "Let not your heart be troubled: ye believe in God, believe also in me." (John 14:1)

With this verse Jesus is considered as equal with the picture of God revealed especially in the Psalms. Jesus is the God Who Comforts the afflicted righteous man.

> "And this is life eternal, that they might know thee the only true God, and Jesus Christ whom thou hast sent." (John 17:3)

When Moses asked the Name of He Who spoke from the burning bush, God replied, "I AM." God is the only Self Existent One.

In today's newspaper I read the obituary of a lady I have known for nearly my entire life. Death is the constant enemy lurking in the shadows of our lives. We have life only because God breathed life into Adam. Since the time of Adam we have seen that all human life is dependent upon another. Only God has life as a self contained attribute of Himself. This verse says that life, eternal, is a gift bestowed upon the Christian from Jesus Christ. This is a statement which addresses the fact that Jesus is God.

> "All things are delivered unto me of my Father: and no man knoweth the Son, but the Father, neither knoweth any man the Father, save the Son, and he to whomsoever the Son will reveal him." (Matthew 11:27)

Jesus Is Set Apart From the Rest of Humanity

In this verse Jesus claims to be the Only means of revealing the truth of God to humanity. Also, He says that only the Father truly understands Him. These facts set Jesus apart from the rest of humanity. Jesus is God in the Flesh.

> "Now there are diversities of gifts, but the same Spirit. And there are differences of administrations, but the same Lord. And there are diversities of operations, but it is the same God which worketh all in all." (I Corinthians 12:4-6)

Again we are given a picture of the diversity in union of the "Members" of the Trinity. One God Who is eternally revealed in three distinct "Persons."

> "I have therefore whereof I may glory through Jesus Christ in those things which pertain to God." (Romans 15:17)

Paul said that he could "glory through Jesus Christ." In this glory he would be glorying in "those things which pertain to God." Once again, a picture of Jesus being God as the glory through Him actually pertains to God.

> "And whatsoever ye do in word or deed, do all in the name of the Lord Jesus, giving thanks to God and the Father by him." (Colossians 3:17)

We are commanded to be active for Jesus. In this spiritual activity we are reminded that we are to give Him thanks; this "thanks," or praise, is then - at the same time - being given to the Father. Once again we are shown that connection of Jesus and the Father.

Jesus Is No Ordinary Human

> "Now our Lord Jesus Christ himself, and God, even our Father, which hath loved us, and hath given us everlasting consolation and good hope through grace, Comfort your hearts and stablish you in every good word and work." (II Thessalonians 2:16-17)

This close concert of the work of the Son and the Father is never shown to exist between mere man and God. Jesus is God. The facts of this passage could never have been said of an ordinary human born with the nature of sin.

> "For this ye know, that no whoremonger, nor unclean person, nor covetous man, who is an idolater, hath any inheritance in the Kingdom of Christ and of God." (Ephesians 5:5)

In this passage we see that the "Kingdom" is both of Christ and of God. This makes no sense unless Jesus is God.

> "If ye then be risen with Christ, seek those things which are above, where Christ sitteth on the right hand of God." (Colossians 3:1)

This verse does not speak so much in spatial terms as it does in terms of authority, glory, and power. He we see that Jesus is equated with that Authority, Glory, and Power which is reserved for the Father.

> "And sware by him that liveth for ever and ever, who created heaven, and the things that therein are, and the earth, and the things that therein are, and the sea, and the things which are therein, that there should be time no longer." (Revelation 10:6)

The first chapter of John says,

> "All things were made by him; and without him was not any thing made that was made." (John 1:3)

CHAPTER 26: THE NAME OF JESUS IS ASSOCIATED WITH GOD

It tells us that Jesus is the Creative Agent of the Godhead. In this verse we see His power as God displayed into the eternal realms.

> "And there shall be no more curse: but the throne of God and of the Lamb shall be in it; and his servants shall serve him." (Revelation 22:3)

This is a very important verse. The "throne" (singular) is possessed by "God and ... the Lamb..." This verse very strongly says that Jesus is God.

> "I Jesus have sent mine angel to testify unto you these things in the churches. I am the root and the offspring of David, and the bright and morning star." (Revelation 22:16)

In this place we see that Jesus asserts His humanity. But, we also see that He claims the angel as His possession. The angels are the messengers of God. Therefore, for Jesus to claim that they are His messengers is for Him to claim to be God.

This is a good stopping place for this session as the next portion might be a little long. In our next session we will consider that the Name of Jesus is associated with God in the very essence of Who Jesus Is.

CHAPTER 27
THE NAME OF JESUS IS ASSOCIATED WITH GOD IN THE VERY ESSENCE OF WHO JESUS IS

(Session Twenty-Eight)

Jesus Name Is Associated With The Very Essence Of God

Evangelist Anthony Zeoli (*Is Jesus God? Book Number Two*) has found several instances where the Name of Jesus is associated with God in the very essence of Who Jesus is.

Jesus Is One With the Godhead

Jesus is One with the Godhead.

> "For in him dwelleth all the fulness of the Godhead bodily." (Colossians 2:9)

To any unbiased person this verse would seem to settle the matter of the Deity of Jesus. He is described as fully God in a human body. We've already discussed the necessity of such an arrangement in order for He to be our Savior. He was fully human in His humanity; born of the Virgin, He had a fully human body yet it was not tainted by the inherited trait of the original sin of Adam which was passed down to the offspring of that first human man.

Jesus Is God In Human Form

Yet, Jesus is also God encased in that human form. This does not mean that He is any less God. Even the term, "encased in that human form," does not denote a lessening of His Divine nature. We see that Jesus even while He was walking the earth in that human body, still had the attributes of God in that He was omnipresent.

> "And no man hath ascended up to heaven, but he that came down from heaven, even the Son of man which is in heaven." (John 3:13)

Jesus was fully human, yet He was not limited in His essential Deity by that humanity.

These twin traits mean that Jesus was fully representative of humanity. He was positionally able to die for our sins as a representative of the race of man. Yet, He had no sin of His Own. As God Jesus has the authority to take upon Himself the sins of all who would believe. In this manner He is able to offer Righteousness in the place of our reprobate lives. He has the power, more importantly the authority, to set us free from sin.

No one except God in human flesh could have had the authority, ability, or power to complete this task.

Jesus Is One With God In Image

Jesus is One with God in Image.

> "Who being the brightness of his glory, and the express image of his person, and upholding all things by the word of his power, when he had by himself purged our sins, sat down on the right hand of the Majesty on high." (Hebrews 1:3)

We see several things in this verse about Jesus. The first is that the glory is "his glory." To suggest that Jesus had any "glory" would be a problem were He not God. For a devout, monotheistic Jew, who had centuries of cultural baggage pointing to the religious view of but "One God," to have suggested that a mere mortal had a glory about him would be preposterous unless he were convinced that Jesus was, indeed, God.

The "express image of his person" takes us back to verse two where the conversation is about God. Therefore, Jesus is said to be the exact image of God. He is not said to "look" like God, or to be a "duplicate" of God. Jesus is said to be the certain image of that God.

The Power of God Is Assigned to Jesus

Even the power of God is assigned to Jesus as He is seen "upholding all things by the word of his power." The power of the Father is not referenced. As Jesus sits "on the right hand of the Majesty on high," we must not suppose that this means that He and the Father are separate entities. The picture is of a position of power rather than a spatial situation.

> "And he that seeth me seeth him that sent me." (John 12:45)

> "Jesus saith unto him, Have I been so long time with you, and yet hast thou not known me, Philip? he that hath seen me hath seen the Father; and how sayest thou then, Shew us the Father." (John 14:9)

Jesus argues, rather forcefully I might add, that He, Himself, is the Deity which men seek.

He was either right in His assertion or He was wrong. If He were wrong He was either a liar or crazy. Either of these would disqualify Him from a position of moral authority such as He possessed. The only consideration is that He was correct: Jesus is God.

Jesus is One with God in Glory

Jesus is One with God in Glory.

> "And now, O Father, glorify thou me with thine own self with the glory which I had with thee before the world was." (John 17:5)

We have earlier discussed the Kenosis whereby Jesus laid aside the outward glory of His Deity while He sojourned as a man on this earth; in this place we see that Jesus was ready to take up that glory once more. Notice, especially, that the glory which Jesus sought to recover was the Glory of God. This had been His even before the creation of the world.

Jesus is One with God in Honor

Jesus is One with God in Honor.

> "That all men should honour the Son, even as they honour the Father. He that honoureth not the Son honoureth not the Father which sent him." (John 5:23)

Jesus is shown to be due the exact same honor as is the Father. As to the phrase "which sent him," we must recall that part of the work of Jesus on this earth was to be our example of submission to God. The human Jesus was always ready to bow to the Father. The Divine Jesus is God; men must bow to Him.

CHAPTER 27: THE NAME OF JESUS IS ASSOCIATED WITH GOD IN HIS ESSENCE

Jesus is One with God in Possessions

"All things that the Father hath are mine: therefore said I, that he shall take of mine, and shall shew it unto you." (John 16:15)

Jesus claims the right of the cattle on a thousand hills. This is not the "prosperity gospel" of which we hear in our day. This is Jesus saying that every thing that the Father possesses is His. I do not believe that the primary reference here is to anything physical. This has not been the thrust of His speech in the preceding portion of this chapter. Jesus was speaking of Spiritual realities.

The Message of the Spirit is Jesus' Message

Even the work of the Holy Spirit is said to have to do with Jesus. That is the meaning of "he shall take of mine, and shall shew it unto you." This refers to the message and story of Jesus Christ which is the primary message of the Spirit.

Jesus is One with God in Saving Faith

Jesus is One with God in Saving Faith.

"Let not your heart be troubled: ye believe in God, believe also in me." (John 14:1)

"And this is life eternal, that they might know thee the only true God, and Jesus Christ, whom thou hast sent." (John 17:3)

"Coming to God" Means "Coming to Jesus"

Folks, the simple truth is that "coming to God" means "coming to Jesus."

It is at this very place that all false religious systems fail. One cannot "find God" through religious contemplation. God is not available in a mosque. The local synagogue is not the repository where God may be found. Good works, religious devotion, purity of life, a moral character, altruism, public service, self-mortification, and on and on... None of these can lead to God.

The Bible informs us that,

"Jesus saith unto him, I am the way, the truth, and the life: no man cometh unto the Father, but by me." (John 14:6)

Would you have salvation from your sins? Come to Jesus at the cross. Would you have peace with God? Come to Jesus at the cross. Would you have a home in Heaven? Come to Jesus at the cross.

Would you want to live the most fruitful life possible in helping your fellow human being? Take them the old story of Jesus at the cross!

Jesus is One with God in Abiding with Believers

Jesus is One with God in Abiding with Believers.

"Jesus answered and said unto him, If a man love me, he will keep my words: and my Father will love him, and we will come unto him, and make our abode with him." (John 14:23)

Here is another picture of the omnipresence of Jesus. It is easy to conceive that God can abide in the heart and life of the righteous. Consider that Jesus, as God, has just promised to do the same. That means being in many, many places at the same time. Actually, the meaning is that Jesus is in **ALL** places at the same time. It is not possible for any man; no matter how great a "person" he may be, to do this. But,

Jesus is God. What He has promised He is able to accomplish.

Jesus is One with God in Being Hated by the World

Jesus is One with God in being hated by the World.

> "He that hateth me hateth my Father also." (John 15:23)

The identification of Jesus with the Triune Godhead extends even to the emotions of the created human who would hate Him. Since the concept of the sin of Adam is a conscious turning of his back to God, it is only reasonable that sinful humankind would hate the God of the Bible. Jesus is included in this hatred.

It is only the miracle of the power of God the Spirit that any respond to the Gospel message that Jesus Christ died in time so that others could live in eternity.

Jesus is One with God in Baptism

Jesus is One with God in Baptism.

> "Go ye therefore, and teach all nations, baptizing them in the name of the Father, and of the Son, and of the Holy Ghost." (Matthew 28:19)

We have noticed this already. "Baptizing them in the 'name,'" singular, of the Father, Son, and Holy Ghost. One God is eternally existent in the Triune Godhead.

Jesus is God.

Jesus is One with God in Raising the Dead

Jesus is One with God in Raising the Dead.

> "For as the Father raiseth up the dead, and quickeneth them; even so the Son quickeneth whom he will." (John 5:21)

It is interesting to note that the Old Testament saints also performed miracles, as did Jesus. However, in the Old Testament we see that the Spirit came upon these prophets and empowered them to perform these mighty acts. In the New Testament we see Jesus performing miracles at His Own choice and power.

> "For whether is easier, to say Thy sins be forgiven thee; or to say, Arise, and walk? But that ye may know that the Son of man hath power on earth to forgive sins, (then saith he to the sick of the palsy,) Arise, take up thy bed, and go unto thine house." (Matthew 9:5-6)

Jesus is One with God in Benediction

Jesus is One with God in Benediction.

> "The grace of the Lord Jesus Christ, and the love of God, and the communion of the Holy Ghost, be with you all. Amen." (II Corinthians 13:14)

Once again, the Name of Jesus is given the same devotion as that of the Father. The entire Trinity is seen in this verse: The grace of Jesus, the love of the Father, and the fellowship of the Spirit are all mentioned.

In this session we have seen that the Name of Jesus is given the same honor, and recognized as having the same power, as the Father. Again, Jesus is God.

In our next session we will consider that the knowledge of Jesus displays the power of God.

CHAPTER 28
THE KNOWLEDGE OF JESUS DISPLAYS THE POWER OF GOD.
(Session Twenty-Nine)

We will consider that the knowledge of Jesus displayed the power of God. Orr (*Can We Be Sure Jesus Christ is God*) wrote on this subject. We will be drawing from the Scripture references to which he deferred in offing his insight into the Divinity of Jesus.

The Knowledge of Jesus Was Not an Occultic Knowledge

We will also consider the fact that the knowledge which Jesus displayed was not that of a "fortune teller." In Exodus we are told that the command given to Moses was, "Thou shalt not suffer a witch to live." (Exodus 22:18)

We need to understand that all witches are not Samantha Stevens. When the title "witch" was given the subject covered a range of occultic activities. The operative sin of the witch, and this includes the fortune teller, is that they seek "hidden knowledge." This, actually, is at the root of the word "occult."

When King Saul went to inquire of the witch of Endor (I Samuel 28:7-25), his actual intent was to speak to the departed prophet Samuel. Saul was seeking the Word of God. In doing so, however, Saul was directly disobeying the revealed Word of God as had already been given through Moses.

We can never find the leading of God by frequenting the place He has said for us not to go!

This time, I believe, the witch actually did see the deceased person she was asked to produce. I believe that Samuel did return from the grave, his spirit at least, to confront Saul in the Name of the Lord. The reaction of the witch in verse 12, and the counsel given by Samuel, lead me to believe that God allowed this interaction at this one place.

Lest one be tempted to attempt to search out the will of God, while being outside the will of God, as did Saul, we must consider that the message given was one of death.

This "sooth saying" is actually a repudiation of the Words of God in that it rejects as incomplete the message which God has given and accepts another message over that of the message given by God.

That is the danger, and the sin, of occultism. It is a rejection of God.

The early Gnostic sect was guilty of occultism in that they sought out special knowledge as a condition of their view of salvation. Salvation, to them, is not available to everyone. Salvation is only available, as they said, to those who have gained these "spiritual" insights.

The Traditional Text Is Not a Faulty Text

There is a danger of leading toward occultism when one considers the newer English language version translations. These are united in the argument that the

Traditional Text is a faulty text. They argue that the true text of Scripture was lost for a thousand years, corroded over time, and only in the last 150 years, or so, has man been able to piece the true message of God back into a resemblance of the original words.

This is a lack of faith in the preserving power of God coupled with a ferocious faith in the ability of man to reconstruct, nearly, what God has allowed to be lost. I would argue that attempting to reconstruct that which God allowed to be lost, if that were true that those words had been lost and it is not!, is an exercise in attempting to thwart the revealed will of God.

The seeking of a text which would supercede that which God had preserved in history is a seeking of "hidden" spiritual knowledge. In that sense it could be considered as occult.

The Supernatural Power of Jesus

Getting back to the topic at hand... The knowledge of Jesus possessed was not an occultic knowledge. He didn't move into trance, or use magic potions. He simply spoke from His Own knowledge as God.

Orr notes that Jesus knew what was thought under the fig tree by Nathanael.

> *"Nathanael saith unto him, Whence knowest thou me? Jesus answered and said unto him, Before that Philip called thee, when thou was under the fig tree, I saw thee." (John 1:48)*

In the verse previous Jesus had said,

> *"Behold an Israelite indeed, in whom is no guile."*

Jesus mentioned the mindset of Nathanael when he was sitting in the shade of the tree. Jesus mentioned the fact that Nathanael was sitting under the tree. Jesus said that this is where Philip had spoken to Nathanael about Jesus.

Any one of these observations, by themselves, would have been a picture of the Supernatural power of Jesus to see incidents and hear thoughts at a great distance. All three of them piled one upon another are a sure indication that the claims of Jesus to absolute Deity are true claims.

Orr also notes the fact that Jesus even knew that He had performed a healing without seeing the person He healed.

> *"So Jesus came again into Cana of Galilee, where he made the water wine. And these was a certain nobleman, whose son was sick at Capernaum. When he heard that Jesus was come out of Judaea into Galilee, he went unto him, and besought him that he would come down, and heal his son: for he was at the point of death. Then said Jesus unto him, Except ye see signs and wonders, ye will not believe. The nobleman saith unto him, Sir, come down ere my child die. Jesus saith unto him, Go thy way, thy son liveth. And the man believed the word that Jesus had spoken unto him, and he went his way. And as he was now going down, his servants met him, and told him saying, Thy son liveth. Then enquired he of them the hour when he began to amend. And they said unto him, Yesterday at the seventh hour the fever left him. So the father knew that it was at the same hour, in the which Jesus said unto him, Thy son liveth: and himself believed, and his whole house." (John 4:46-53)*

We are, perhaps, a little jaded in that we have heard this story so often in Sunday

CHAPTER 28: THE KNOWLEDGE OF JESUS DISPLAYS THE POWER GOD

School and church service. We've even read the story several times in the Scripture. We tend to look at these episodes in the Bible and consider them as inspiring stories.

Folks, consider: What if it was your son? A couple of days ago a young person was hit by a foul ball at a professional baseball game. The youngster suffered a fractured skull, if I remember correctly. Suppose that were your son. Would you be worried? Would you be concerned?

Of course you would. Probably the happiest point in the ordeal would be when the doctor said, "He's going to be alright. Don't worry."

That is the situation in the above narrative. A man had a son who was dying. This was a time when people were very familiar with death from disease. Young people were not immune to death. The father was frantic. He found Jesus and poured out his story. Jesus, the Great Physician, said, "He is going to alright. Don't worry."

The boy did live. Upon investigation the father found that the boy had been healed of the malady at the exact hour which Jesus had said, "Go thy way, thy son liveth."

Folks, think about this in real time because it happened in real life. Jesus didn't anoint the boy with oil. Jesus didn't lay hands on the boy. Jesus didn't even examine the boy. Jesus simply, at a distance, healed the boy.

This is certainly the power of God wielded by the Person of God. We look at this and consider it a great miracle. Jesus looked at it and considered it part of His work in the world.

Jesus knew, Orr reminds us, the need of Nicodemus.

> "There was a man of the Pharisees, named Nicodemus, a ruler of the Jews: The same came to Jesus by night, and said unto him, Rabbi, we know that thou art a teacher come from God: for no man can do these miracles that thou doest, except God be with him. Jesus answered and said unto him, Verily, verily, I say unto thee, Except a man be born again, he cannot see the kingdom of God. Nicodemus saith unto him, How can a man be born when he is old? can he enter the second time into his mother's womb, and be born? Jesus answered, Verily, verily, I say unto thee, Except a man be born of water and *of* the Spirit, he cannot enter into the kingdom of God. That which is born of the flesh is flesh; and that which is born of the Spirit is spirit. Marvel not that I said unto thee, ye must be born again. The wind bloweth where it listeth, and thou hearest the sound thereof, but canst not tell whence it cometh, and whither it goeth: so is every one that is born of the Spirit. Nicodemus answered and said unto him, How can these things be? Jesus answered and said unto him, Art thou a master of Israel, and knowest not these things? Verily, verily, I say unto thee, We speak that we do know, and testify that we have seen; and ye receive not our witness. If I have told you earthly things, and ye believe not, how shall ye believe, if I tell you *of* heavenly things? And no man hath ascended up to heaven, but he that came down from heaven, *even* the Son of man which is in heaven. And as Moses lifted up the serpent in the wilderness, even so must the Son of man be lifted up: That whosoever believeth in him should not perish, but have eternal life. For God so loved the world, that he gave his only begotten Son, that whosoever believeth in him should not perish, but have everlasting life." (John 3:1-16)

It seemed that Nicodemus had come to Jesus to discuss theology. Jesus knew that the need of the heart of Nicodemus was that he needed to be born again. This is exactly where Jesus began His interview with Nicodemus.

The Greatest Need of Man is to Have his Sins Forgiven

The greatest need of man is to have his sins forgiven. The greatest Love of God was to call men and women to repentance. Jesus understood the need. Jesus provided the power to furnish the answer to the need when He "set his face towards Jerusalem" so that He could endure the Cross to purchase salvation for any who believe.

Orr reminds us that Jesus even knew the answer to His antagonist.

> *"And Jesus answering said unto them, Render to Caesar the things that are Caesar's, and to God the things that are God's. And they marvelled at him."* (Mark 12:17)

These men came to Jesus with a question they felt He could not answer. "Is it right to pay taxes." If Jesus had answered, "No," He would have been considered a traitor to the occupying armies of Rome. If Jesus had answered, "Yes," He would have been considered a traitor to the Jewish people.

Jesus displayed the wisdom of God in His answer. His answer was neither traitor to one, nor friend to the other. His answer was simple, direct, and correct in every detail.

Barnes (*Barnes' Notes on the New Testament*) references Mark 5:30.

> *"And Jesus, immediately knowing in himself that virtue had gone out from him, turned him about in the press, and said, Who touched my clothes?"*

If the entire passage is read (v.24-34) we find the story of a lady who was ill. She had spent every bit of money she had, probably an inheritance, on physicians and her sickness had not abated. When she simply touched the hem of the garment which Jesus was wearing she was immediately healed.

This is the miracle associated with the story. And, a great miracle it is!

The question of Jesus hearkens back to Adam and Eve in the Garden. The request was not made so that He could receive information. As with Adam ("And the LORD God called unto Adam, and said unto him, Where *art* thou?" - Genesis 3:9) the question was asked so that the woman, in this case, would have an opportunity to make a public confession.

Jesus Knew the Manner of His Impending Death

Jesus even knew the manner of His impending death. "From that time forth began Jesus to shew unto his disciples, how that he must go unto Jerusalem and suffer many things of the elders and chief priests and scribes, and be killed, and be raised again the third day." (Matthew 16:21)

To me, the most amazing thing about the fact that Jesus knew the manner of His death, was that this was the reason He had come into this earth. He came to die for our salvation.

In all these matters about which Jesus had supernatural understanding we do not see one case where He asked the Father to open His eyes to them. Jesus knew these things in Himself. That is the power of God. These are further proofs that Jesus is God.

In our next session we will consider that the power of the life of Jesus displays His essential Deity.

CHAPTER 29
THE POWER OF THE LIFE OF JESUS DISPLAYS HIS ESSENTIAL DEITY
(Session Thirty)

Several Verses Illustrating Jesus' Power Over Life

Orr (*Can We Be Sure That Jesus Christ Is God?*) sees that the power of the life of Jesus displays the power of God. Orr then references several verses to illustrate his claim.

John 1:4, "In him was life; and the life was the light of men."

There are two things that this verse says that point out the Divinity of Jesus. The first of these is the fact that "In him was life." I have life within my own being. This is a borrowed life in that it came from, originally, Adam and was then passed down to my own children. This isn't what the verse suggests about Jesus. The verse does not say that life was in Him; the verse says that in Him was life.

Life was Who Jesus Is

This is really a startling concept. Life was in Him. This means that He is the repository of life. Back in Exodus 3:14 Moses was informed just Who had spoken to him from the burning bush. God said, "I am that I am." What God was saying was that He was the Self Existent Eternal One. Life was not a facility passed on to Him. Life was Who He Is.

He, God, is Life Eternal. We were given life by Him at the point of creation. This life is never our possession, or part of our own personhood. Our physical lives are simply continuation passed on from our ancestors. Life is not our possession; life is a gift given by God.

I gave a friend of mine a book tonight. I could only do this because I purchased the book at a store. It was mine to give. Life is never ours to, actually, give. Life is simply a gift originally given by God which flows down through the generations of humanity as a gift of God. We are not the bearers, nor the givers of the gift. Life simply transfers through natural processes which God set in motion.

By saying that "In Him was life," John's Gospel is saying that Jesus is the Self Existent One. This means that Jesus is God, Eternal. Had Jesus been a created being, He would not be Self Existent as His Own life would also have flowed from the gift of God. As the Self Existent One Jesus was not given a gift of life; He IS life.

With this fact in mind we can see that Jesus did not begin in time. He has existed from eternity as the First Cause of all that is, or can be. Evolutionary theory, in speculating that life somehow "spontaneously generated" from lifeless materials will never be a satisfactory explanation of "beginnings" as it discounts the original Gift of Life from the Giver of Life.

This verse also says that his "life was the light of men."

Many years ago my wife and I had a fourteen foot travel trailer. Late one night I pulled this trailer into a state park to camp for the night. This park offered "primitive" camping. This meant that there was no hook ups for electricity, water or sewage. All that is offered is fairly level ground on which to set up camp for the night.

It was a moonless night. As I pulled into the camping area I saw a very flat section of ground about thirty yards ahead of where we stopped. I asked Linda is she wanted me to pull further forward to this area. She said, "No. There isn't a single camper there so something must be wrong with the ground. In the morning we found what was wrong with the "ground." It was a small lake.

Why hadn't we noticed this the night before? Partly, we were very tried and needed to get some sleep. But, the real reason is that in the light of day we could see the reality that we had missed in the dark of night.

Jesus Is Not From the Same Time/Space Continuum

Jesus came to shed light upon spiritual realities. No mere man could do this. The realities of spirit and eternity are not possible for man to ascertain because he has no possible understanding of that which he has not, and *cannot* in his naturally physical and time centric state, observe.

The fact that Jesus came to enlighten, by the force of His Self Existent Life, means that Jesus is not, in His essence, from the same time/space continuum. He is from the spiritual and the eternal; without this reality He could not show humanity the facts of this Heavenly abode.

One Must Conclude That Jesus is God

Couple this with the aforementioned facts of His Self Existent state and one must conclude that Jesus is God.

John 6:48, Jesus said, "I am the bread of life."

Bread, to the ancients, was the "staff of life." Bread is that which made it possible for life to be sustained. There were, to be sure, other food stuffs available. But, bread was the most basic staple of meals. We may remember that at the Last Supper the elements were bread and wine.

Jesus is the Means of Sustaining Life

For Jesus to say that He was the "Bread of Life," is for Him to say that He is the means of sustaining life. When we recall that life is a gift from God, we are struck by the fact that Jesus said that He was the One Who made the continuation of life possible. Again, He claimed the absolute role of Deity when He said this.

John 14:6, "Jesus saith unto him, I am the way, the truth, and the life: no man cometh unto the Father, but by me."

Jesus is the Exclusionary Way to Heaven

I have often heard it said that there are many ways to Heaven. The Bible nowhere condones this falsehood. Jesus is the Exclusionary Way to Heaven. He doesn't show the way to Heaven; He is the Way to Heaven. We access salvation by accepting Him and His sacrifice on the Cross of Calvary. It is not possible that a mere man, born of the union of man and woman and thus a partaker of the nature of sin, could ever be the substitute for anyone else. Such a mere man would have his own sin; thus he would be unable to save even himself.

Only the Perfection of Jesus, the Son of God, could offer salvation from sin. It took

CHAPTER 29: THE POWER OF THE LIFE OF JESUS DISPLAYS HIS ESSENTIAL DEITY

the perfection of God to offer the remission of sins. Jesus is God.

> Matthew 9:18-25, "While he spake these things unto them, behold, there came a certain ruler, and worshipped him, saying, My daughter is even now dead: but come and lay thy hand upon her, and she shall live. And Jesus arose, and followed him, and so did his disciples. And, behold, a woman, which was diseased with an issue of blood twelve years, came behind him, and touched the hem of his garment: For she said within herself, If I may but touch the hem of his garment, I shall be whole. But Jesus turned him about, and when he saw her, he said, Daughter, be of good comfort; thy faith hath made thee whole. And the woman was made whole from that hour. And when Jesus came into the ruler's house, and saw the minstrels and the people making a noise, He said unto them, Give place: for the maid is not dead, but sleepeth. And they laughed him to scorn. But when the people were put forth, he went in, and took her by the hand, and the maid arose."

Jesus Did Works By His Own Power and Authority

There are many healings listed in the Bible. The difference between the healings of Jesus and those of the prophets is that the Spirit came upon the prophets to empower them for mighty works. Jesus, instead, did these works on His Own Authority as God.

It is obvious that Jesus did not seek special "permission" to heal the woman with the issue of blood. This healing is all the more remarkable because He did nothing. The faith of the woman, in Him, facilitated the healing. The simple narrative here would suggest that Jesus did not know that the woman needed healing. Such is not the case. Jesus knew, as God, the thoughts and intents of the heart - including this woman as evidenced by the fact that He knew her need and the provision He had provided.

In the raising of the young girl Jesus displayed His life giving power. Remember, life is from God. Therefore, Jesus is God.

At this time in history there were "professional mourners." These were probably the ones making the noise at the death bed. Jesus dismissed the false and the "professionals" and proceeded to raise the dead.

What a picture this is of salvation. There are false religious concepts, and often false religious professionals. These leave the lost soul dead in sin. Only the entrance of Jesus can provide eternal life to the soul dead in sin.

> Luke 7:12-15, "Now when he came nigh to the gate of the city, behold, there was a dead man carried out, the only son of his mother, and she was a widow: and much people of the city was with her. And when the Lord saw her, he had compassion on her, and said unto her, Weep not. And he came and touched the bier: and they that bare him stood still. And he said, Young man, I say unto thee, Arise. And he that was dead sat up, and began to speak. And he delivered him to his mother."

Jesus' Great Compassion

One thing that should always be noticed about Jesus is His great compassion. This was a time when women had few rights and fewer privileges in society. I don't know if this was the case at this time, but I would guess that this dead son was the only means of income for this woman. His work provided her sustenance. Since the father of the young man is not mentioned, I would hazard a guess that this was the case.

This is an instance where Jesus had compassion on both the living and the dead.

> "And hope maketh not ashamed, because the love of God is shed abroad in our

hearts by the Holy Ghost which is given us." (Romans 5:5)

"For God so loved the world, that he gave his only begotten Son, that whosoever believeth in him should not perish, but have everlasting life." (John 3:16)

God loves the world so much that He offers the Savior. This is an offer of Eternal Life from Jesus. God loves the Christian so much that He sends the Holy Ghost to the Christian. This is an offer of a fuller life for the redeemed.

Since Jesus is the means of salvation, both offers of life are given upon His Authority as God.

I John 5:11, "And this is the record, that God hath given to us eternal life, and this life is in his Son."

Once again we see that the concept of salvation is exclusionary in the Scripture. Jesus is the only Savior available to humanity. No work, no worship, no other way is it possible to come to God. Only Jesus can offer salvation from sin, a relationship with God, and a home in Heaven.

We see here that the eternal life is a gift from God. We also see that this gift is encased in Jesus. This fact, from Scripture, attests to the full Divinity of Jesus Christ.

Jesus is God. This is a fact as recorded in the inspired and preserved Book of God.

In our next session we will consider that Jesus is the Lord of Nature.

Chapter 30
JESUS IS THE LORD OF NATURE
(Session Thirty-One)

Four Incidents That Jesus Is the Lord of Nature
First, Water Into Wine

Orr (*Can We Be Sure That Jesus Christ Is God*) argues that Jesus is the Lord of Nature. Orr cites four incidents from the New Testament to back up his claim. We will first look at these four and then consider the issue from further perspective.

> "This beginning of miracles did Jesus in Cana of Galilee, and manifested forth his glory, and his disciples believed on him." (John 2:11)

This is the well-known "water into wine" miracle. The text says that this miracle was a manifestation of His glory. This is so. This was so in even more of a sense than we normally will consider.

My grandchildren have two cups sitting on the ledge above their kitchen sink. In each of these cups the little ones (six and four years old) has a small plant. One plant is thriving. One plant is nearly dead. I'll consider the thriving plant first.

The one plant has been regularly watered with fresh water. It is thriving. No one has ever given any plant food to this plant. No one has ever tried to "feed" the plant with anything. All that has been done is to add water. The miracle of life, as far as the natural perception is seen, is that the water has caused this plant to grow.

Water will also cause the grape vines to grow. As these vines mature they will produce grapes. The vintner will take these living, growing grapes and squeeze the fluid out of them. This fluid is produced from the water flowing through the grape vines. From this source is made the sweet grape juice.

Jesus took the water, bypassed the grape vine and the vintner, and produced wine for the feast. This was a miracle of creation in that He produced the nutrients that the grapes would have supplied, and time in that He didn't take four months growing time to produce the liquid.

Jesus is the Master of time and botany. He could do more quickly, and better, than the grape vine, itself, could have ever done. There is a spiritual lesson here in that Jesus is all we need. What we lack He, Himself, will provide. He has done this with His passion at the cross; He continues to do this through the Spirit in guiding our lives into deeper fellowship as the days go by. He will do this when we enter the valley of the shadow as He gives us safe transport unto an eternal Home in the Halls of Heaven.

The second plant on the shelf is nearly dead. The problem? It was directly below where the sponge is hung which is used to wash the dishes. This means that the plant has been attacked by dripping water from this sponge. Now, water, as we've seen above, is a good thing. The problem here is that this water is not pure water. It is soapy water as it falls from the "dish sponge."

We need to pure Words of God. Any mixture of man's "soap" of philosophy, or even religiosity, will cause us soul sicknesses. This is true as we try to live for Christ in our Christian lives. It is even "more true" as we consider the conversion of the sinner. It has been well said that Jesus and nothing else equals everything we need for salvation. Meanwhile, Jesus and anything else equals nothing when it comes to our salvation.

Salvation is a total faith and commitment that Jesus paid the entire penalty for our sin on the Cross of Calvary. Any other work added to this, church work or church doctrine, means that our complete trust is not placed wholly upon Him. The little addition, even a pious addition, means that we do not have full faith in Him. This negates any possibility of a saving faith.

In our back yard we have a grape vine. Several years ago a "wild grape" vine attacked our little arbor. The entire arbor is now worthless as far as producing usable grapes. Let us never forget that Jesus is everything. Anything else, as far as salvation is concerned, will be a detriment to salvation.

Second, The Feeding of the Five Thousand

Even in our Christian lives we need to keep our spiritual eyes on Him. Following a preacher is allowable only if that following leads to Jesus. We must keep all others to the side as we fix our eyes upon the True Master.

> "Therefore they gathered them together, and filled twelve baskets with the fragments of the five barley loaves, which remained over and above unto them that had eaten." (John 6:13)

This incident is often called the feeding of the five thousand. This is not accurate. Verse ten says that there were about five thousand men. The crowd, when women and children are added in, probably totaled closer to twenty thousand.

For this multitude, Jesus had five loaves of bread and two fish. When all the people had eaten, there was much more than just this left over.

Again, consider time. Time is a creation of the Creator. Had time been allowed to pass, the fish would have multiplied (had they been alive) and the barley would have (had it not already been baked) produced more seeds that would have made more barley.

But, this isn't what happened. Jesus performed a miracle of multiplication. He created more bread, much more, and more fish, much more, in order to feed the crowd. As from the rib of Adam God had produced another complete person, Eve, even so did Jesus produce more food from the little available.

Third, The Miracle of the Great Fishes

A miracle isn't really a hard thing for God. God created all; to create a little more is not a daunting task for Him.

> "Simon Peter went up, and drew the net to land full of great fishes, an hundred and fifty and three: and for all there were so many, yet was not the net broken." (John 21:11)

Fourth, The Miracle of the Net

Jesus performed two miracles, here. First, Peter had been fishing for some time with no notice given that he had caught anything. Verse five really suggests that Peter had caught nothing. Suddenly, at the word of Jesus, many fish were suddenly caught were no fish were previously available.

CHAPTER 30: JESUS IS THE LORD OF NATURE

Fishing "luck" is one thing; the evidence of another miracle of Jesus is quite another thing!

The second miracle is that the net, which should have burst from the weight of so many fish, was able to draw them in.

Again a spiritual application: We are well able to accomplish more than we should be able to accomplish for Jesus because the Spirit goes with us. In our own power we will fail as did Peter in his fishing. With the Lord we can never fail.

My wife was a very good fisherman. We would drive past ponds where the fish would get out and block our car so they could ask if Linda had brought a rod and reel. I never did catch any fish. If I wanted fish caught I had to bring my wife. If you would have "success" in your Christian life you'd better make sure the Spirit is at your side!

The many incidents of healing, the mental and physical restorative works of Jesus, the casting out of the demons, etc., these all display the power of God through the Person of Jesus Christ. Every one of these miracles is a testament to the fact that Jesus is God in the flesh.

Jesus' Miracles Were By The Power of His Word and Authority

Remember, the prophets who performed mighty works did so only as the Spirit came upon them especially for these isolated incidents. Jesus performed miracles on the power of His Own word and authority.

This is really what we mean when we speak of Jesus as the Lord of Nature. He had power over nature; that is demonstrated by His miracles and mighty acts. We haven't even mentioned his power over the wind and the waves as He was in the boat on the Lake of Galilee. These were displays of His absolute authority over His Own creation.

To still the wind was a mighty act of authority. To still the waves, even as the wind was stilled, is an absolute astonishment to our ears. The inertia of the movement of the waves would have worked to keep them going as they slowly used the stored energy of the wind. To still the waves was also a mighty act of authority.

Jesus has this authority over nature because He is the Creator of Nature. He is God.

In our next session we will consider that the Holiness of Jesus displays the power of His Personal Deity.

CHAPTER 31
THE HOLINESS OF JESUS DISPLAYS THE POWER OF HIS PERSONAL DEITY
(Session Thirty-Two)

The Holiness of Jesus is beyond the holiness of mere men. His Holiness is more than a simple outward impression given to His followers and foes. His Holiness was a part of His Being. Even in the case of His driving the money changers out of the Temple, His Holiness was displayed in the act of His seeming anger. In this instance He displayed His Holiness in that He would brook no act which would cast disrepute upon the worship of God.

Four Instances Point to The Holiness of Jesus That Displayed His Personal Deity

In point of fact, the Holiness of Jesus displayed His Personal Deity. Zeoli (*Is Jesus God? – Book Number Two*) lists four Scriptural instances which point out the fact of the Holiness of Jesus.

First, however, I think we need to consider just what the word "Holy" means.

At first glance we might consider this to be another "what is the meaning of 'is'" questions. Holy, after all means "holy." The first consideration as we look at the word is in the negative. "Holy" is separate from "profane." The primary meaning of profane is something which is in juxtaposition to "Holy."

Not a lot of help?

Profane speaks of the physical things. I don't mean human physical; the meaning is the physical, natural, world around us. God is of the spiritual dimensions. We are of the physical dimensions while we are living on this world. Holy is that which is concerned with the spiritual dimensions. We use the word "sanctuary" in this sense. We consider the Bible to be "The Holy Bible" because the Words therein are gifts from God.

While profane can refer to the sacrilegious, the primary connotation is that it speaks of something that is not holy. We can act holy, from time to time. But, Jesus is Holy. He was of this earth; but, He is also otherworldly in that He is God.

First, Jesus was Holy from Before the Foundation of the World

Zeoli points out that Jesus was Holy from before the foundation of the world.

> "But with the precious blood of Christ, as of the lamb without blemish and without spot: Who verily was foreordained before the foundation of the world, but was manifest in these last times for you." (I Peter 1:19-20)

Even forging past the fact that Jesus was already in existence before the Creation (John 1:3 reminds us that He created all things and was, therefore, not any part of the Creation except as The Creator.), we see that Jesus was Holy from before the foundation of the world. This means that He has always been Holy.

Always. Never anything but. No other human could make that simple claim.

Every single human being born on this planet, with the exception of Adam and Eve, was born with a nature that was profane. We are all born with a sin nature, inherited from Adam.

Adam and Eve began holy; but they sinned and became sinners. In becoming a sinner Adam, as head of the human race, passed this "sin gene" down to every descendant of his. That means every person born of man and woman.

Jesus, however, was born via the virgin birth. He had no sin at Bethlehem. He was Holy at the point of His physical birth. This was a different situation from that of any other human ever born. It was not the goodness of His mother; it was the goodness of His Father which produced the physical body which was Holy.

Just above, when I said that Adam and Eve began holy, I did not mean that they were Divine in any sense. They were, however, set apart as a special creation. God breathed life into Adam. This was not done with any of the creatures of the land, air, or sea. God imparted a certain holiness unto them so that they could have fellowship with Him. The two had a holiness but it was not of their own; it was a derived holiness bestowed upon them by God.

Second, Jesus' Very Nature Is Holy

The Holiness of Jesus, however, is part of Who He Is. His very nature is Holy. Hebrews 7:26 reminds us that Jesus is Holy. When speaking of His Office as High Priest, the following comment is made.

"For such an high priest became us, who is holy, harmless, undefiled, separate from sinners, and made higher than the heavens."

This verse speaks of Jesus. We must note that the "was made" does not refer to a promotion, His being created, or His sudden ascension to a post. The meaning has to do with His innate status of Creator God. The "was made" speaks of His humanity united with His Deity.

Hebrews 13:8 reminds us that, "Jesus Christ the same yesterday, and to day, and for ever."

He was Holy before all creation. He is Holy as He fulfills the Office of High Priest for the Christian. He will be Holy for all eternity. There is none about this could be said except God. Jesus is God!

Third, Jesus was Holy at His Birth in Bethlehem

Zeoli also points out that Jesus was Holy at His birth in Bethlehem.

"And the angel answered and said unto her, The Holy Ghost shall come upon thee, and the power of the Highest shall overshadow thee: therefore also that holy thing which shall be born of thee shall be called the Son of God." (Luke 1:35)

"That holy thing" is, of course, Jesus. This does not mean that He was a "thing." He was a fully human as any of us. But, with this being true, He is also fully God.

This verse is actually very important. All of the verses are! This verse, however, points up the difference between Jesus and all other men born of women. He was Holy at His birth. All others are born with a sin nature transmitted from their fathers back to Adam. This is why the verse is very careful to make note that the Father of Jesus was God, the Spirit. The Human body of Jesus was placed into Mary and gestated there.

The physical body of Jesus was fully human, yet without sin. He, even His physical

CHAPTER 31: THE HOLINESS OF JESUS DISPLAYS THE POWER OF HIS PERSONAL DEITY

body, was always Holy.

Fourth, Jesus was Holy as a Child

Zeoli points out that Jesus was Holy as a child.

> "By stretching forth thine hand to heal; and that signs and wonders may be done by the name of thy holy child Jesus." (Acts 4:30)

I understand that this verse uses the word "child" as an indication of the virgin birth. The point I want us to understand is that Jesus never ceased being Holy. A lot of otherwise "good" kids have done a lot of "bad" things during their teen age years. The teen age years are often called years of rebellion.

Jesus Never Rebelled Against God

Jesus never rebelled against God. When he stayed behind to talk with the learned priests at Jerusalem during His youth, this was not a rebellion. This was "being about His Father's business." (see Luke 2:49)

This attitude of Holiness was to mark the entire earthly life of Jesus. This attitude of Holiness also marked the death of Jesus.

> "And Peter, fastening his eyes upon him with John, said, Look on us. And he gave heed unto them, expecting to receive something of them. Then Peter said, Silver and gold have I none; but such as I have give I thee: In the name of Jesus Christ of Nazareth rise up and walk. And he took him by the right hand, and lifted him up: and immediately his feet and ankle bones received strength. And he leaping up stood, and walked, and entered with them into the temple, walking, and leaping, and praising God. And all the people saw him walking and praising God: And they knew that it was he which sat for alms at the Beautiful gate of the temple: and they were filled with wonder and amazement at that which had happened unto him. And as the lame man which was healed held Peter and John, all the people ran together unto them in the porch that is called Solomon's, greatly wondering. And when Peter saw it, he answered unto the people, Ye men of Israel, why marvel ye at this? or why look ye so earnestly on us, as though by our own power or holiness we had made this man to walk? The God of Abraham, and of Isaac, and of Jacob, the God of our fathers, hath glorified his Son Jesus; whom ye delivered up, and denied him in the presence of Pilate, when he was determined to let him go. But ye denied the Holy One and the Just, and desired a murderer to be granted unto you; And killed the Prince of life, whom God hath raised from the dead; whereof we are witnesses." (Acts 3:4-15)

This is the well known incident where Peter and John came upon a lame man begging at the gate of the Temple. This man was healed in the power of Jesus. The people who were witnesses were astonished. To their credit, the people did give the glory to God.

But, Peter using this for an evangelistic endeavor reminded the people that Jesus had been crucified just a few days previous. Peter told the people that this healing was in the power of Jesus. The same Jesus Who had been crucified was Holy in His death. It was the Holiness of the now risen Savior which had empowered the miracle.

Jesus died a Holy death to cleanse us of our own sins. He rose from the dead, still Holy, to empower us to carry forth His work of seeking the sinners for salvation. This scenario could only be spoken about God in the Flesh.

Jesus is God. In our next session we will consider some testimonies from Scripture as to the Holiness of Jesus.

CHAPTER 32

TESTIMONIES FROM SCRIPTURE AS TO THE HOLINESS OF JESUS

(Session Thirty-Three)

Eight Testimonies

In our last session we looked at the fact of the Holiness of Jesus as a testimony to His Deity. In this session we will consider some of the testimonies made to the Holiness of Jesus. Evangelist Anthony Zeoli (*Is Jesus God? – Book Number Two*) has listed eight such testimonies.

It might be instructive to note that not all of these testimonies come from supporters of Jesus.

We are currently in the "silly season" of presidential politics. It is interesting to note that any person can be always right in whatever he does if he has the correct party affiliation. The other candidate, of the other party, will be considered wrong even if he advocates the exact same thing.

In politics this is called "partisanship." This spirit can paralyze a nation. Even among the news organization, which are expected to inform rather than instruct, this spirit of partisanship political "analysis" is exhibited.

Those who would be statesmen are rarely given a chance in the political world.

This is an attitude which extends far beyond politics. It is seen in religion. It is seen in education. And, it is often seen in personal interactions. This concept is why the testimony to the Holiness of Jesus is so remarkable and ultimately forceful testimony to the affirmative fact of the Divinity of Jesus.

First, The Testimony of God, the Father

The first of these testimonies which Zeoli mentions is not one of the detractors of Jesus. Zeoli makes reference to the testimony of God, the Father, to the Holiness of Jesus.

> "But unto the Son he saith, Thy throne, O God, is for ever and ever: a sceptre of righteousness is the sceptre of thy kingdom. Thou hast loved righteousness, had hated iniquity, therefore God, even thy God, hath anointed with the oil of gladness above thy fellows." (Hebrews 1:8-9)

Once again, as we have noticed before, the Father was speaking of the Son in reference to the Office of Jesus as the substitute for sinners. As such Jesus was fully human. As to the eternal makeup of Jesus, He is God and fully so. But in His Office as the substitute for sinners the Bible will consider the humanity which He took upon Himself in the incarnation.

Many false doctrines have come because Christians have not considered that Jesus is fully God while being fully human. The Bible will often make a distinction between the position of His Office as Savior - which He willingly assumed in the Kenosis (see Philippians 2:6-8) - and His Deity in which He is the Creator of all (see John 1:1-3).

In the passage in question at this time we see that the Father called the Son God.

"...Thy throne, O God..." This would be an amazing inconsistency if the Trinitarian understanding of the Triune Godhead were not an established Scriptural truth.

The Father spoke of the Son in this passage as righteous, i.e. Holy, in all things and at all times.

Second, The Testimony of Unclean Spirits

The second person, actually group, which Zeoli mentions would not be suspected of being supporters of Jesus. Zeoli references the testimony of the unclean spirits to the Holiness of Jesus.

> *"And there was in their synagogue a man with an unclean spirit; and he cried out, Saying, Let us alone; what have we to do with thee, thou Jesus of Nazareth? art thou come to destroy us? I know thee who thou art, the Holy One of God. And Jesus rebuked him, saying, Hold thy peace, and come out of him." (Mark 1:23-25)*

I think it instructive to note that the unclean spirits were not privy to the plans of Jesus. They had no idea what He had in store for them. Sometimes we give Satan too little respect in that we do not consider his great power. We need to fear him when we are on our own. This is why we need to be in prayer, often, to the Lord!

With the above in mind we should be thankful that,

> *"...greater is he that is in you, than he that is in the world." (I John 4:4b)*

These demon entities were in fear of Jesus. They knew, as Satan knows, that the Lord is more powerful than any other entity in all the physical and spiritual worlds. Jesus is in charge.

These demons also understood the utter holiness of Jesus!

Third, The Testimony of Judas, the Betrayer

The third person Zeoli references might come as a bit of a surprise. Zeoli references the testimony of Judas to the Holiness of Jesus.

> *"Then Judas, which had betrayed him, when he saw that he was condemned, repented himself, and brought again the thirty pieces of silver to the chief priests and elders, Saying I have sinned in that I have betrayed the innocent blood. And they said, What is that to us? see thou to that. (Matthew 27: 3-4)*

There are many possibilities as to why Judas betrayed Jesus into the hands of the authorities. Some argue that Judas was a Zealot and didn't believe that Jesus was moving fast enough to dislodge the Roman occupation. Judas may have intended that Jesus be made a martyr for Jewish independence.

Some argue that Judas, a high ranking member of the Disciples as the treasurer, may have thought he could take the place of Jesus as leader of the group. Some argue that it was simply avarice; Judas wanted the money. It may be that Judas had observed Jesus simply walking away from other crowds who would have stoned Him to death, such as John 10:39, and simply thought that Jesus would walk away from this trap as well. Jesus would be safe and Judas would have thirty more pieces of silver.

Who knows, for sure, what were the motives of Judas? What we do know is that it was all within the plan of God. Jesus can never be surprised!

Consider this fact in your own life. That little sin that you figure no one knows about; Jesus knows. He knew about it before you became entangled within it. If this is true, and we know that it is, we need to work all the more for Him in appreciation of His

CHAPTER 32: TESTIMONIES FROM SCRIPTURE AS TO THE HOLINESS OF JESUS

great love for us.

Repent of the sin, of course. But do not let the fact of sin, past, overcome your witness today! You have been forgiven. God is in the forgiving business! That is a point that can add fervency to your witness for Him.

About forgiveness: Many somewhat overlook this passage. They see a seeming contradiction between the phrase that Judas "repented himself" in verse three above and John 17:12 where Jesus alludes to the fact that Judas was a "lost" person.

There is no contradiction. Judas repented in that he was sorry that the events had worked out in the manner they had. Judas never really repented of his sin. Rather than seek forgiveness from the Savior, Judas committed suicide. Suicide never solves any problems; it only solidifies them. The person who commits suicide can never seek forgiveness from either man or God; he can never seek to rectify the problem. He has passed from life unto death.

Nevertheless, Judas admitted that he had betrayed an innocent, a holy, man. That much of a testimony he did leave behind.

Fourth, the Testimony of Pilate

The fourth testimony Zeoli notes is that of Pilate. Pilate gave a testimony to the Holiness of Jesus.

> "Pilate therefore went forth again, and saith unto them, Behold, I bring him forth to you, that ye may know that I find no fault in him." (John 19:4)

I have heard, way too many times, that "the Jews killed Jesus." Theologically this is incorrect; it was our sins for which He died. Emphatically, spiritually, it was us - every single one of us - who was responsible for the death of Jesus. Our sins nailed Him to the Cross. Somehow this realization ought to make us more and more grateful that Jesus Christ died in time so that we could live in eternity.

Ain't He a Wonderful Savior! There is no word in my vocabulary, or even group of words, which can even begin to describe the glory and thanks due to Him! The songwriter tried, "Isn't He wonderful, wonderful, wonderful..." We'd need every "wonderful" ever spoken or written in all the languages of all the history of the world; and we'd still fall far short!

Also, from the strictly historical setting, Pilate *cannot* be found without fault. Pilate may have found Jesus to be without fault; but Pilate lifted not one finger to stop the crucifixion. As a point of fact, Pilate gave the official sanction for the Roman soldiers to carry out the execution.

Nonetheless, it must be noted that Pilate found Jesus faultless. That is the essence of the Holiness of Jesus. He is without fault before God and man - even the men who had Him killed.

Fifth, The Testimony of the Wife of Pilate

The fifth testimony which Zeoli notes is of the wife of Pilate. Pilate's wife speaks to the Holiness of Jesus Christ.

> "When he was set down on the judgment seat, his wife sent unto him, saying, Have thou nothing to do with that just man: for I have suffered many things this day in a dream because of him." (Matthew 27:19)

God does not normally speak in dreams in this age. We now have His complete record of Scripture through which He speaks to us. But, I believe that He could do so anytime He pleases. That being said, I do not believe that this was a case of the Spirit of God speaking. I believe the speaker in the dream was Satan.

Why? The first reason is to whom the dream was directed. Had God wanted to stop this travesty of justice, He might have spoken with Pilate. But, why? Consider,

> "Jesus answered [Pilate], My kingdom is not of this world: if my kingdom were of this world, then would my servants fight, that I should not be delivered to the Jews: but now is my kingdom not from hence." (John 18:36)

Did you catch that "now" from the lips of Jesus? His kingdom is not "now" of this world. Jesus came the first time to be the "Suffering Savior." He will come back again to assume the Throne of David and reign as Absolute Monarch over the entire world!

Had the Father wanted to stop the Crucifixion He would not have needed to send a dream to the wife of the secular ruler. The truth is that the coming Crucifixion was central in the plan of God from before the foundations of the world.

> "But God commendeth his love toward us, in that, while we were yet sinners, Christ died for us." (Romans 5:8)

Satan may have tried to find a way to stop the events set in motion. I really don't know if this is the source of the dream. It could have been bad pepperoni pizza too late at night at Mr. and Mrs. Pilate's house. But, I do know that God wanted this crucifixion to take place. This was a vindication of the Holiness of Jesus that He was the One Who died in payment for the sins of the world.

Sixth, The Testimony of the Cross

Sixth, Zeoli notes that the thief on the cross testified to the Holiness of Jesus.

> "And we indeed justly; for we receive the due reward of our deeds: but this man hath done nothing amiss." (Luke 23:41)

The "jail house talk" had certainly centered upon this "special" prisoner, Jesus. Everyone must have known that He was being given some "special" treatment. He was being hurriedly judged and hurriedly executed. It was obvious that some "high ups" wanted Him dead. And dead quickly!

It is also probable that this thief had heard of Jesus. It is very likely, given the location in Jerusalem, that this thief had heard much, both pro and con, about Jesus. It is even possible that this thief had heard Jesus speak.

Zeoli argues that this statement was the thief's testimony to the Holiness of Jesus. I disagree. I believe that the next verse was the testimony of this thief that Jesus was the Holy One of Israel.

> "And he said unto Jesus, Lord, remember me when thou comest into thy kingdom." (Luke 23:42)

This thief placed his dying soul in the Hands of the dying man next to him. This thief acknowledged the Holiness of Jesus with his faith.

Seventh, The Testimony of the Centurion

The seventh testimony to which Zeoli makes note is that of the Centurion. The Centurion gives testimony to the Holiness of Jesus.

> "Now when the centurion, and they that were with him, watching Jesus, saw the earthquake, and those things that were done, they feared greatly, saying, Truly this

CHAPTER 32: TESTIMONIES FROM SCRIPTURE AS TO THE HOLINESS OF JESUS

was the Son of God." (Matthew 27:54)

Tradition tells us that this Centurion became a solid Christian. Tradition is a very fragile witness. The Words of the Scripture are true at every time. I don't know if the Centurion was a follower of Jesus. He could have been. Jesus was well known to the military. Some were believers.

Would this Centurion have taken part in the crucifixion had he been a believer? Probably. Military men are not given much choice in whether or not to obey orders. If he were a believer he would have known that there was nothing within his power that could stop the execution. However, if he could be there he might be able to give some comfort to the dying Savior.

Again, I just don't know. The Scripture is silent on this point. My conjecture is simply guess work!

I do know that the events of the crucifixion had an effect on these soldiers. Whether these men were simply talking about their own Roman gods, or whether they were referencing the true God in Heaven, I do not know. I do know that they knew, beyond any shadow of a doubt, that Jesus was not just another execution victim.

That these hardened soldiers, they were the "execution detail" and this was - it would appear - their normal duty, were so affected by the death of Jesus is testimony to His Holiness.

Eighth, The Testimony of Jesus

The last mention of a testimony to the Holiness of Jesus, as mentioned by Zeoli, is that of Jesus, Himself.

This is rather more important that we might consider at first blush. Several years ago I was sitting out at the local mall when an elderly gentleman came and sat beside me on the bench. I was impressed by the man's flowing, silver white beard. Although no match for my girth, he was slightly rotund. A young child came up to him and said, "Santa, when did you get in town." The man laughed and said that he wasn't really Santa. "Santa is up at the North Pole making toys for you. I just look like him."

I may consider someone to be something; that is just my opinion. Many people may consider someone to be something; that is just their opinion. If the person in question ever claims to be that "something," at that point we must examine whether or not he is as advertised. Until he makes that claim, we have no real basis to expect our "guesses" to be "truth."

Had Jesus never claimed this Holiness, we might have had reason to doubt. But He did.

> *"Which of you convinceth me of sin? And if I say the truth, why do ye not believe me?" (John 8:46)*

Jesus claimed Holiness, freedom from sin, because this was His right. He was Holy. He IS Holy. Others agreed with Him.

This could only be said of Deity. Jesus is God.

In our next session we will consider that the works of Jesus display the power of God.

CHAPTER 33
I. THE WORKS OF JESUS DISPLAY THE POWER OF GOD
(Session Thirty-Four)

We have been discussing the various aspects of the personality of Jesus which point out the fact of His Deity. We have looked at His holiness, His power over death, disease and nature itself, that He lived a sinless life, that His very Name is associated with God, and have concluded that each of these speak to His absolute Deity.

In this session we are going to consider the works of Jesus. These display the power of God. In all these things we see that Jesus exhibited the attributes of Deity. Each, of itself, points to the Deity of Jesus. All, put together in one Man, actually in one God/Man, give us the picture that Jesus is very God while being very man.

Jesus Calms the Great Storm

Jesus performed the miraculous with an air of expectation. There was no "hoopla" about His miracles. He didn't publish them about. Indeed, even the writers of the Gospel accounts didn't spend time looking at these miracles. Those miracles were simply performed by Jesus, as a matter of course, because of Who He Is.

> "And when they had sent away the multitude, they took him even as he was in the ship. And there were also with him other little ships. And there arose a great storm of wind, and the waves beat into the ship, so that it was now full. And he was in the hinder part of the ship, asleep on a pillow; and they awake him, and say unto him, Master, carest thou not that we perish? And he arose, and rebuked the wind, and said unto the sea, Peace, be still. And the wind ceased, and there was a great calm. And he said unto them, Why are ye so fearful? how is it that ye have no faith? And they feared exceedingly, and said one to another, What manner of man is this, that even the wind and the sea obey him?" (Mark 4:36-41)

Can't you almost see Jesus and this little flotilla of ships? Jesus had already had a long day. He was undoubtedly up early in prayer. Then He spent the day preaching righteousness to the crowd of hearers.

He had apparently been preaching from one of these ships. The sway of the sea would have rocked the boat gently. This would have made it difficult for Jesus to speak to the large crowd which had probably gathered. The New Testament accounts inform us that Jesus would frequently speak to crowds of thousands.

There were no microphones or loud speakers. In order to be heard by a large crowd it would be necessary for Jesus to strongly project His voice. It would have been necessary that He keep up this projected voice for hours at a time. This day, to add to the general work of teaching, He had to find His "sea legs" and rock with the boat as He spoke to the crowd.

Is it any wonder that the disciples found Him asleep in the back of the boat? He must have been physically exhausted. What the disciples felt was a storm which threatened their very lives, Jesus saw as a cradle rocking Him into slumber. He was at peace.

When the disciples woke Jesus, He stirred Himself, stood and said, "Peace. Be still," to the winds and waves. I believe that, after chiding the disciples for their fear, He simply went back to His place and went back to sleep.

Notice the love and care of Jesus in this event. There were no really large boats in this "naval" excursion to the other side of the lake. The other boats with the disciples were called "other little ships." My impression is that these were very small vessels. When Jesus calmed the storm it would appear that His boat was at peace. The other, smaller, boats had also been at jeopardy from the waves which swept over them. Now, after Jesus spoke, all was at peace as the boisterous winds and crashing waves were quieted at the voice of the Master.

Jesus calmed the wind and the waves for the small boats.

Both of these were great miracles. Both display the power of God over the creation of God. If He had only stopped the winds it would have taken some time for the sea to calm. But, in an instant, at His Divine Word, Jesus stilled both the wind and the waves.

This is a mighty power of the Almighty God!

Three Other Instances

Orr (*Can We Be Sure That Jesus Christ Is God*) looks at three other instances where the mighty works of Deity were performed by Jesus.

First, The Man Sick With Palsy

One of these examples concerns a certain man with some persistent friends. This man was sick; he was confined to a bed. His friends, hearing Jesus was in town - and having heard of the miracle of His healings - took their friend to Jesus.

Well, they tried to take their friend to Jesus. There were so many people thronging about Jesus that they could not find a way to get to Him. Finally, since Jesus was preaching inside a building at this point, they devised a plan. They went to the roof of the building and tore back part of the tiles of the roof. They then lowered their friend down for an audience with the Savior.

Jesus healed the sick man. But, Jesus did this in an unexpected manner.

> "When Jesus saw their faith, he said unto the sick of the palsy, Son, thy sins be forgiven thee." (Mark 2:5)

Some of the religious leaders did not appreciate this being done. They argued, in their hearts,

> "Why doth this man thus speak blasphemies? who can forgive sins but God only?" (Mark 2:7)

In another miracle, one we often overlook in this passage, Jesus understood what these religious leaders were thinking. He knew their very thoughts.

Consider, for just a second, the enormity of that fact! This wasn't the "slight of hand" of a stage master; this was the power of God displayed by the Saving Master! Jesus replied to the doubt of the religious leaders.

> "But that ye may know that the Son of man hath power on earth to forgive sins, (he saith to the sick of the palsy,) I say unto thee, Arise, and take up thy bed, and go thy way into thy house." (Mark 2:10-11)

Jesus, displaying the power to forgive sins, took upon Himself that which was

CHAPTER 33: I. THE WORKS OF JESUS DISPLAY THE POWER OF GOD

rightfully His: He forgave sins. Only the God of the Bible has the authority to forgive sins! In saying this Jesus was announcing Himself as God.

Second, Jesus Healed Disease and Cast out Demons

Jesus also healed disease and cast out demons. Orr appeals to Matthew 10:1 on this point.

> *"And when he had called unto him his twelve disciples, he gave them power against unclean spirits, to cast them out, and to heal all manner of sickness and all manner of disease."*

Actually, I think that Orr undersold his point, here, about the mighty works of Jesus displaying the power of God.

In the Old Testament the prophets had been empowered of God to perform mighty works. The Spirit came upon them to do the miraculous. In this passage it is Jesus Who gives to the disciples the power to perform mighty works.

Consider for just a moment the importance of this fact. Jesus gave, on the basis of His Own authority, the power to others so that they could cast out demons and heal disease. This means that the power to do these things was originally the power of Jesus. He could not give what He did not possess. If He originally possessed this power, it means that Jesus is God!

Don't let anyone tell you that Jesus never claimed deity. By His very life and works He did so - and He claimed this Deity often!

Third, Jesus Laid Down His Life and Reclaimed It Again

The last work mentioned by Orr is the most assertive that Jesus is God. He lay down His life and reclaimed it again at His volition.

> *"Therefore doth my Father love me, because I lay down my life, that I might take it again. No man taketh if from me, but I lay it down of myself. I have power to lay it down, and I have power to take it again. This commandment have I received of my Father." (John 10:17-18)*

Jesus could easily have avoided the cross had He so desired. The song reminds us that "He could have called ten thousand angels." Indeed, he could have done so. He also could have simply walked away from His accusers.

At one time Jesus had announced His Deity to the religious leaders. The result?

> *"Then took they up stones to cast at him: but Jesus hid himself, and went out of the temple, going through the midst of them, and so passed by." (John 8:59)*

Some have suggested that this event, and probably several more that weren't recorded in Scripture, was on the mind of Judas when he betrayed Jesus. He thought Jesus could just walk away and was horrified when such did not happen.

I don't know if that is true or not. Two things I do know. Jesus could have walked away from His crucifixion. He had the power to do so! And, Jesus intended to die the death of the cross simply because He did love us. He went to the cross willingly because His plan was to become the Redeemer of all who would accept Him.

Not only did Jesus die because He intended to allow others to live free from sin, He also took back His Own life at His Own choosing.

Again, the Old Testament saints had raised the dead back to life. But, they had only done so as the Spirit came upon them for the task. Many in the New Testament had been raised back to life. But, only Jesus reclaimed His Own physical life. Others were raised back to life by Him. Still others were raised by to life, by the apostle's through the Power of Jesus' Name.

Jesus is God. His works prove this is a true statement!

We will continue with this same subject in our next session.

CHAPTER 34
II. THE WORKS OF JESUS DISPLAY THE POWER OF GOD
(Session Thirty-Five)

As we look at the works of Jesus we will see that His works display His Deity. We continue this portion of our study from our last session.

Simmons (*A Systematic Study of Bible Doctrine*) points out that the works of God are performed by Jesus. Simmons cites several verses which point out that to Jesus is ascribed the work of creation. We will list several of these below and make short comments.

Jesus the Creator

John 1:3 - "All things were made by him; and without him was not any thing made that was made."

There are those who argue that Jesus was a "created god." The argument made is that, while Jesus is "a god," He is not The God. Besides the Biblical pronouncements that there is but One God, this is not a philosophically tenable position. If Jesus is, as the Scripture plainly states, The Creator of all things, and He is Himself a created being, we are left with the absurdity that He is His Own Creator.

This passage, quite simply, leaves no room for any other conclusion than that Jesus is the very Creator God. He is, Himself, eternal as He stands before all of creation as the First Cause, and Producer, of all of Creation.

The *"New World Translation of the Holy Scriptures,"* a Jehovah's Witness publication, seems to try to tie this third verse in with verse four and argue that Jesus is only the Creator of Life. That just isn't what the text says. The text argues that Jesus is the Creator of all things. That would, of course, include life.

Life comes from the Creator God. In Genesis 2:7 we see that God, the Creator, breathed life into Adam. This means that Jesus, The Creator, gave life to humanity. The two processes cannot be divided between two entities. Therefore, Jesus is God!

I Corinthians 8:6 argues,

"But to us there is but one God, the Father, of whom are all things, and we in him; and one Lord Jesus Christ, by whom are all things, and we by him."

The argument of this verse, as in John 1:3, is that Jesus is the Creator. Notice the picture of the unified Godhead in this verse. One God, the Father; all things are in Him. One Lord, Jesus; all things are by, or produced by, Him. The Two, to our eyes, are both described as "ONE" with exclusive jurisdiction over all. Therefore, Jesus is God!

Colossians 1:16 - "For by him were all things created, that are in heaven, and that are in earth, visible and invisible, whether they be thrones, or dominions, or principalities, or powers: all things were created by Him, and for him."

In this case Jesus is again cited as the Creator of all. But, in this verse Jesus is specifically noted as the Creator of both the physical ("in earth") <u>and</u> the spiritual ("in heaven"). Thus, there is no room for any argument that Jesus may be a "created," or "secondary," "god." He is The (singular) Creative Agent.

Jesus Has the Title Deed to the Earth

Also, please note that Jesus is also described as the One Who has title deed to the history of the earth. The nations and governments of the earth are all placed under His creative power. Therefore, Jesus is God!

> *Hebrews 1:10 - "And, Thou, Lord, in the beginning hast laid the foundation of the earth; and the heavens are the works of thine hands." In verse eight, above, the writer had given the identification of whom he was speaking."*
>
> *Hebrews 1:8 "But unto the Son he saith, Thy throne, O God, is for ever and ever: a sceptre of righteousness is the sceptre of thy kingdom."*

Jesus Is the Messiah

This eighth verse hearkens back to Psalm 45:6.

> *"Thy throne, O God, is for ever and ever: the sceptre of thy kingdom is a right sceptre."*

This Psalm is a prophecy of the Messiah. Jesus is that Messiah. The human penman of Hebrews is, once again, ascribing the entire creation to the work of Jesus. Therefore, Jesus is God.

> *Hebrews 3:3-4 - "For this man was counted worthy of more glory than Moses, inasmuch as he who hath builded the house hath more honour than the house. For every house is builded by some man; but he that built all things is God."*

In this passage Jesus is said to have more honor than Moses. Moses was a great leader of Israel. Jesus is the Creator of Israel. This puts Jesus in control of the affairs of man about fifteen hundred years before the events of Bethlehem. This passage speaks both the eternality of Jesus and His power to dictate the affairs of men and nations. Therefore, Jesus is God.

> *Revelation 3:14 - "And unto the angel of the church of the Laodiceans write; These things saith the Amen, the faithful and true witness, the beginning of the creation of God..."*

We know, from other places in the Scripture that all things were created by Him. Because of this we understand that this verse is not saying that Jesus is the first of the created beings. The meaning is that Jesus is the One Who began the creation of God.

Again, this is a statement that Jesus is God.

Jesus Holds Together the Universe

Strong (*Systematic Theology*) sees that Jesus does the work of the upholding of the universe. Strong cites two passages of Scripture to illustrate this teaching.

> *Colossians 1:17 - "And he is before all things, and by him all things consist."*

The "Defined King James Bible" notes that the word "consist" is an archaic English form of "hold together."

What we have in this verse, then, are two statements to the full Divinity of Jesus. The first is that the verse speaks of His eternality in that "...he is before all things..."

The second statement of His Deity is that He is the force which holds the universe together. I just watched a television show about a gigantic "accelerator" in Europe. They are using this "machine" to try to figure out why everything in the universe seems to be flying further apart (the concept of an expanding universe) and yet some things

CHAPTER 34: II. THE WORKS OF JESUS DISPLAY THE POWER OF GOD

(such as the earth) seem to hold together. The answer is real easy: Jesus holds the universe in place. He holds the things of the universe together! Therefore, Jesus is God.

> Hebrews 1:3 - "Who being the brightness of his glory, and the express image of his person, and upholding all things by the word of his power, when he had by himself purged our sins, sat down on the right hand of the Majesty on high."

Again, Jesus holds the universe in His power. Therefore, He is God.

Jesus' Place of Power and Authority Over Death and Life

That phrase, "sat down on the right hand of the Majesty on high," speaks of the place of power and authority. It does not, as is clear when we compare Scripture with Scripture, assume that Jesus is in any way inferior to the Father.

Pendleton (*Christian Doctrine*) notes that Jesus does the work of bringing life.

> John 5:28-29 - "Marvel not at this: for the hour is coming, in the which all that are in the graves shall hear his voice, And shall come forth; they that have done good unto the resurrection of life; and they that have done evil, unto the resurrection of damnation."

Without getting bogged down in other theological arguments, we know that no one can do "good works" until they are saved by the grace of Jesus. Therefore we understand that this passage is not at variance with the Bible teaching of salvation freely given by the grace of God. This passage does not speak to the "mode" of salvation. This passage speaks of the blessing of salvation.

Our purpose in this session is to address the Deity of Jesus. Under this heading we may look and see that the voice of Jesus calls these deceased persons to judgment. The same voice which originally created the world is the One Who calls even the deceased people of the world to stand before Him in life.

Therefore, Jesus is God.

We may also note that Jesus does the work of raising and judging the dead.

> "And hath given him authority to execute judgment also, because he is the Son of man." (John 5:27)

Immediately following this verse is the passage above about Jesus calling the deceased to judgment. The very fact that Jesus is judging sinners means that He is the One Who was offended by their sin. This is not the judgment of a temporal judge; this is the judgment of the Eternal Judge deciding matters of eternity. Jesus has this authority and power. Therefore, Jesus is God.

> "When the Son of man shall come in his glory, and all the holy angels with him, then shall he sit upon the throne of his glory: And before him shall he gather all nations: and he shall separate them one from another, as a shepherd divideth his sheep from the goats." (Matthew 25:31-32)

This is the judgment of the nations at the end of this age. Again, only God has the right and privilege to make this judgment. Only God has the power to enforce this judgment. Therefore, Jesus is God.

The works of God are performed by Jesus because He is God. It may be true that anyone may compose music. But, only Chopin could compose a work of Chopin. There may be many composers but there is only One God. I almost put "only one **True** God," but that would be a false statement. There is only **One** God. Were there any others who would try to assume the title, they are - by definition - **false** gods.

In our next session we will begin to discuss the fact that in Jesus is displayed the attributes of God.

CHAPTER 35
IN JESUS IS DISPLAYED THE ATTRIBUTES OF GOD
(Session Thirty-Six)

Any unbiased reader of the New Testament accounts must admit that the picture of Jesus given by His biographers in the Gospels is one in which the attributes of God are attributed to Jesus. Further, since the Bible teachers that there is but One God, if it is true that the attributes of God are attributed to Jesus, the only conclusion is that Jesus is God.

Jesus said, I and My Father Are One

Barnes (*Barnes' Notes on the New Testament*) uses John 10:30 to show that Jesus claimed the power of God. This answer, which Jesus gave to the Jewish leaders, was occasioned by a discussion not of plan or of purpose, but of power. Jesus was claiming the Omnipotent Power of God - an attribute of God. He was, therefore, claiming Deity.

The hearers (v. 31) understood this. If it were not His intention to say this He is guilty of moral dishonesty in that He did not correct the hearers.

The power which Jesus claimed at this point was the power to give eternal life to whomsoever He chose. (see v. 28) The hearers were a group of persons who were accustomed to themselves as being the exclusive recipients of the favor of God. Jesus has, in verse 26, argued that they were not the favored of God simply because they had failed to accept Him.

Thus, the power which Jesus claimed was more than simply the power to give salvation to whomever He would. The power He claimed extended over the Covenant People as well. They were to be judged in relation to their acceptance of Him. This was a direct usurpation of the power of God. His hearers knew this.

Jesus Is Wisdom

Matthew Henry's Commentary looks at the wisdom chapter of Proverbs, Proverbs eight. He sees that Wisdom, especially in verses 22-30, is more than merely an attribute of God. This Wisdom "...has personal properties and actions..." This passage refers to Jesus and places Him before any of the creation was begun.

We often fail to understand the great love which God has shown forth upon the world. In eternity past, if we may use that term improperly yet so as to be understandable to our time- centric ears; before the creation, God knew that mankind would sin and stand in need of a Savior. God knew the events of Calvary before the world was begun. Revelation 13:8 speaks of Jesus as a Lamb slain before the foundations of the world.

Before creation was begun God, the Son, understood that the events of Bethlehem would lead to the events of Golgotha. In that sense Jesus is the eternally begotten Son of the Father. This isn't a "rank" within the Godhead; this is a statement of purpose. This passage in Proverbs takes this truth into account.

We need to understand this point of doctrine as we read this passage from

Proverbs. Jesus is not a created Being. He is, in fact and as we see in various Scriptures, the very Creator of all that was created.

In our next session we will begin to see that the essence of Jesus contains the attributes of God.

CHAPTER 36

THE ESSENCE OF JESUS CONTAINS THE ATTRIBUTES OF GOD

(Session Thirty-Seven)

These Attributes of Deity Are Beyond the Capability of Mere Humans

We are still looking into the attributes of Jesus. The attributes of Jesus, the very essence of What and Who He is, are the attributes of God.

When people ask me, "How are you?" I generally reply with, "Old and fat." These are attributes which describe my physical appearance. This is not what we mean when we speak of the attributes of Deity within the Person of Jesus.

When I say that I am old it is only relatively so. There are people who are older than me. There are less and less of these every year; but they do exist. The same could be said about my physical girth. There are people, few people!, who are even heavier than am I. I know; it's hard to believe. But, it is true.

When we speak of these attributes of Deity in regard to Jesus we are speaking of attributes which are singularly His. These attributes of Deity are not simply in degree; they are beyond the capability of mere humans to possess.

The Immortality of Jesus

Zeoli (*Is Jesus God? – Book Number Two*) has spoken of the immortality of Jesus. We, as born again believers, have an immortality which comes to us via the gift of God. Jesus, we see this in John 1:4, is the Repository of Life.

> "*In him was life; and the life was the light of men.*" The immortality of Jesus is a trait of His; it is part of just Who He is.

Zeoli references several verses to illustrate this fact.

> "*Who [Christ] only hath immortality, dwelling in the light, which no man can approach unto; whom no man hath seen, nor can see: to whom be honour and power everlasting. Amen.*" (I Timothy 6:16)

This particular verse is a strong statement of the Divinity of Jesus. If it is only Jesus who "hath immortality," and this is a singular trait of God, it must follow that Jesus is God.

This verse is speaking of Jesus. The middle part of the verse gives a very "Old Testament" view of man being unable to see the One about Whom Paul is writing. We know that Jesus was seen by many people while He walked this earth. Paul even saw Jesus after His resurrection and ascension. Therefore, the concept that Jesus is One "whom no man hath seen, nor can see," is not accurate unless one factors in the preincarnate (before His birth in Bethlehem) Person of Jesus.

The second chapter of Philippians informs us that Jesus laid aside the outward glory of His Godhead when He came to earth to offer Himself as the atonement for sin. This means that it is true that no man has seen Him in His Glorious splendor as God.

The last third of this verse from I Timothy bolsters the argument that Jesus is God in that the benediction ("to whom be honour and power everlasting. Amen.") is a benediction of praise which would only have been uttered about God.

> "Wherefore he is able also to save them to the uttermost that come unto God by him, seeing he ever liveth to make intercession for them." (Hebrews 7:25)

This particular verse can be confusing at first glance. The appearance is there that God and Jesus are separated. This is not so. The Trinity of the Godhead is three distinct Personalities Who eternally exist as One. In this verse Jesus is being spoken of in His office as Savior. Thus, sinners come to Him in faith and He presents them to the Father as saved individuals.

Since the verse also says that "he is able also to save them," making the salvation experience under the power of Jesus, we see that He is God - even in this verse. Only God has the privilege of pardoning the sin of the sinner.

Jesus Has the Keys to Hell and Death

> "I am he that liveth, and was dead; and, behold, I am alive for evermore, Amen; and have the keys of hell and of death." (Revelation 1:18)

Again, this verse is obviously in reference to Jesus. His death and resurrection are referenced in such a way that the verse could refer to no one else.

This verse also gives Jesus the keys of both hell and death. This is a clear reference to His full Divinity. None but God could have the responsibility and authority which those keys indicate.

The point we are discussing in this study, at this time, has to do with the immortality of Jesus. Each of these references states that the work of Jesus is eternal. Therefore, He is eternal. Therefore, He is God.

Three Other Attributes

Little (*Know What and Why You Believe*) points out three other attributes of Jesus which point to His absolute Divinity.

First, Jesus Is From Eternity

First, Jesus is from eternity.

> "Then said the Jews unto him, Thou art not yet fifty years old, and hast thou seen Abraham? Jesus said unto them, Verily, verily, I say unto you, Before Abraham was, I am." (John 8:57-58)

Two things are at play in this verse as regards the Divinity of Jesus. I believe that the most important was His use of the Covenant Name. Jesus said, "I am." This was the Name by which God identified Himself to Moses from the burning bush.

That Jesus used this phrase as an assertion of Deity is made obvious by the remainder of the Chapter. That is the way the Jewish leaders understood it to have been used. Jesus never, at any point, argued that this is not what He meant.

For those who would argue that Jesus never claimed to be God, look again at this verse. This is exactly what He did. The Jewish leaders understood this. That Jesus did not correct them, had they been wrong in their understanding, is a proof that this is, indeed, exactly what He meant.

The other point in this verse is that Jesus made an obvious claim to have existed before His birth in Bethlehem. He argues that He has seen Abraham. Couple this with

CHAPTER 36: THE ESSENCE OF JESUS CONTAINS THE ATTRIBUTES OF GOD

the "I am" statement and we see Jesus fully assert His Divinity.

Second, Jesus is the Sustainer of All

Second, Jesus is the Sustainer of All.

> "Who being the brightness of his glory, and the express image of his person, and upholding all things by the word of his power, when he had by himself purged our sins, sat down on the right hand of the Majesty on high." (Hebrews 1:3)

In verse two, just previous to this verse, Jesus is again, as in John 1:3, described as the Creative Agent Who made the universe and all that is therein. Now, in verse three, this same Jesus is described as the One Who "sustains" that very creation. It is He Who upholds "all things."

Since all means all; there just ain't nothing left over, Jesus is the Ultimate Power of the universe. This means that He is God.

Again, the picture of Jesus sitting "on the right hand of the Majesty on high," is not ascribing an inferior position to Him. This is an anthropomorphism which gives to us a picture of Him sitting in the place of power. This is actually a picture of Jesus as the Lord of Glory.

Again, Jesus is God.

Thirdly, Jesus is Everything

Thirdly, Jesus is everything.

> "For in him dwelleth all the fulness of the Godhead bodily." (Colossians 2:9)

There is no need to further comment upon the revealed Words of God. Jesus is God.

In our next session we will begin to view the fact of the Omniscience of Jesus.

CHAPTER 37
THE OMNISCIENCE OF JESUS
(Session Thirty-Eight)

There are times when the Spirit will impart specific information, otherwise unknowable, to a human. An example of this is with the Old Testament prophet Elisha. The Syrian king had set a siege around Dothan with the aim of capturing the prophet. The servant of Elisha was very worried about this situation. Elisha was not worried.

> "And when the servant of the man of God was risen early, and gone forth, behold, an host compassed the city both with horses and chariots. And his servant said unto him, Alas, my master! how shall we do? And he answered, Fear not: for they that be with us are more than they that be with them. And Elisha prayed, and said, LORD, I pray thee, open his eyes, that he may see. And the LORD opened the eyes of the young man; and he saw: and, behold, the mountain was full of horses and chariots of fire round about Elisha." (II Kings 6:15-17)

This is an example of a word of knowledge whereby God imparts special knowledge to an individual for a specific purpose.

Another example was given me a few years ago at a denominational meeting. An evangelist related that many years before he had been holding meetings in a church in Indianapolis. The host pastor asked that this evangelist stay over his scheduled time. The evangelist said that the Lord did not give him freedom to do so. God told him to pack his belongings and move on.

The church where this evangelist had been preaching was pastored by Jim Jones of People's Temple infamy before he moved his base of operations to California. Who knows what Satan may have had in store for the Godly evangelist had God not intervened with this word of knowledge.

I believe that these are rare occurrences. The point is that God will, sometimes, let us know things which are beyond the capability of a mere human person to know. With Jesus this was an everyday occurrence because Jesus knew all.

Several Instances of the Omniscient Nature of Jesus Displayed

The Spirit did not need to come upon Jesus because Jesus is, Himself, Deity and carries the Divine attribute of omniscience. "Omniscience" is one of those "seminary" words; it simply means "All Knowing." Specifically this refers to the nature of God to know and understand all things.

Evangelist Zeoli (*Is Jesus God? – Book Number Two*) lists several instances of this omniscient nature of Jesus displayed.

First, Jesus Knows All

First, Jesus knows all.

> "Now are we sure that thou knowest all things, and needest not that any man should ask thee: by this we believe that thou camest forth from God." (John 16:30)

Jesus had been speaking to His disciples about His coming passion. The disciples understood that He had knowledge which no mere human might have. In inspiration, the Spirit, let us understand - perhaps even more than did the disciples at this time - that Jesus knows all.

Second, Jesus Knows the Thoughts of Man

Second, Jesus knows the thoughts of man.

> "But when Jesus perceived their thoughts, he answering said unto them, What reason ye in your hearts?" (Luke 5:22)

This passage is from the well known incident where a man was let down through the roof so that he might receive healing from Jesus. Jesus had forgiven the man's sins at this point. Although the scribes and Pharisees said nothing, they reasoned within their thought that this was a blasphemy because no mere man had the right to forgive sin.

This was no "parlor trick." Jesus didn't simply "read their minds." Jesus knew the very thoughts of these men. This was something which no mere man could have accomplished.

This was a certain statement by Jesus of His Divinity. He knew the thoughts of the religious leaders. But, even more importantly, while understanding their abhorrence to His having forgiven the sin of this man, He proved that this act of Deity was an act of His prerogative. In both of these Jesus displayed the truth that He is God.

Third, Jesus Knows the Hearts of Men

Third, Jesus knows the hearts of men. This is somewhat different than knowing the thoughts of men. And, it is a much deeper consideration. This consideration centers on the very character of men. In this area Jesus was also omniscient.

> "And they prayed, and said, Thou, Lord, which knowest the hearts of all men, shew whether of these two thou hast chosen." (Acts 1:24)

This consideration had to do with choosing an apostle to take the place of Judas. We could talk all day about whether this was a proper thing for these men to have done. This is especially so when we consider the soon emergence of Paul.

I think one thing we need to consider is the timing of God. We should never embark upon a course because we think it expedient that we do so. Let us prayerfully consider. As an example, our church is currently searching for a new pastor. We had found a man who seemed to be perfect until we found some disturbing facts about his background.

We had prayerfully waited upon the Lord. The Lord rewarded that faith in His leadership with needed instruction when it was needful for us to have that instruction.

God has patience. It is always best that we search out His will even when this seems counter to human reason. God is always better than go if the go is of simple expedience rather than the clear leading of the Spirit. Jesus know more about situation.

> "And immediately when Jesus perceived in his spirit that they so reasoned within themselves, he said unto them, Why reason ye these things in your hearts?" (Mark 2:8)

This passage covers the same ground as did Luke 5:22 above. The difference in this verse is that Jesus not only is shown to have understood the thoughts of these men, He also, at this place, shown to have understood the reasoning behind those thoughts.

CHAPTER 37: THE OMNISCIENCE OF JESUS

The reasoning of these men was that Jesus was not the promised Messiah. Therefore, they further reasoned that He was sinful. This, in turn, they believed was shown by an act of perceived heresy on His part. Jesus understood this flaw in their reasoning was predicated in unbelief.

His response was to confront the very base of their reasoning. He provided proof, the healed man, that His forgiveness of sin was actual. In so doing He proclaimed His Deity.

Fourth, Jesus Knows the Lives of Men

Fourth, Jesus knows the lives of men.

> "Jesus saith unto her, Go, call thy husband, and come hither. The woman answered and said, I have no husband. Jesus said unto her, Thou hast well said, I have no husband: For thou hast had five husbands; and he whom thou now hast is not thy husband: in that saidst thou truly. The woman saith unto him, Sir, I perceive that thou art a prophet." (John 4:16-19)

This narrative, of course, is the well know "Woman at the Well," episode. I think that there are two things to be noticed in this account. The first, and the subject of our current study, is that Jesus had the Divine knowledge which no man could have. Jesus had never met this woman. In such a situation one is tempted to say that He did not know her. However, the facts show that Jesus knew this woman, whom He had never met in the flesh, more intimately than did many of her close associates.

As the Creator God, Jesus knows all about us. We will never surprise Him with our faults. We will never impress Him with our altruism or piety. We need to simply live our lives in subjection to His will as is our reasonable service. He knows the depth of our love for Him, whether shallow or deep. May we live so as to gain that deeper love for Him even as we thank Him for His great Love for us!

The second thing to note in this passage is that Jesus did not attack this woman's immoral life style. He didn't condone that life style, either. But, He was calling her to forsake wickedness and embrace the salvation He offered. In doing this He was both tender and compassionate as well as truthful in all His remarks.

May we learn to be more Christlike in our relationship with those both within and without the household of faith!

Fifth, Jesus knows the Craftiness of Men

Fifth, Jesus knows the craftiness of men.

> "And the chief priests and the scribes the same hour sought to lay hands on him: and they feared the people: for they perceived that he had spoken this parable against them. And they watched him, and sent forth spies, which should feign themselves just men, that they might take hold of his words, that so they might deliver him unto the power and authority of the governor. And they asked him, saying, Master, we know that thou sayest and teachest rightly, neither acceptest thou the person of any, but reachest the way of God truly: Is it lawful for us to give tribute unto Caesar, or no? But he perceived their craftiness, and said unto them, Why tempt ye me? Shew me a penny. Whose image and superscription hath it? They answered and said, Caesar's. And he said unto them, Render therefore unto Caesar the things which be Caesar's, and unto God the things which be God's. And they could not take hold of his words before the people: and they marvelled at his answer, and held their peace." (Luke 20:19-26)

The scribes and priest's had presented Jesus with, they thought, the proverbial "Do you still beat your wife" question. They thought to have both sides of the issue covered. If Jesus had said, "Yes. Pay the tribute money," He would have been seen as a collaborator with the Roman occupation. The people who followed Him would have left in droves.

If, however, Jesus said, "No. Don't pay the tribute money," He would have been held liable to Rome for rebellion. Either way, the scribes and would have removed Him from the people.

Jesus perfectly understood these facts. Jesus knew all about the traps that had been laid for Him. Jesus simply answered, truthfully, that the things of the Spirit are not necessarily the things of physical existence. Jesus used the craftiness of these men to show the truth of the Heavenly.

Sixth, Jesus Knows the Love of Man

Sixth, Jesus knows the love of man.

"But I know you, that ye have not the love of God in you." (John 5:42)

Jesus actually knows us better than we know ourselves.

Again, our local church is currently looking for a new pastor. A couple of men have come to us, in all sincerity, with the news that God has most definitely called them to be our pastor. The problem is that, so far, God has not confirmed this assertion in the church.

To be in the pastorate is a heady thing, in the natural. If a person really longs for the office of a pastor, this might be an indication that he is not called. We come to this position with fear and trembling that God has demanded that we take this responsibility upon ourselves.

Pastoring is not a "fun" thing; it is a solemn responsibility. We hold, speaking in the natural, the responsibility for leading others into a deepening walk with Jesus. This demands that our own walk be deeper still.

Anyone can preach. Only those who are God called can pastor.

The point I am making here is that our own piety can be tied to our own wants. Sometimes this is tied so closely that we do not notice the connection. God, however, does.

Do you really love God? Then do His will! Be faithful in that task He has given. Also, be faithful in prayer and study of His Words. Even all this, if our attitude be one of self glorification rather than self prostration before the Throne of God, is wrong when the object of our purpose is our own ego rather than faithfulness to the leading of God.

Jesus knows whereof we want to walk, and why we want to walk. May our walk always be following the Master's leading.

Seventh, Jesus Knows the Whereabouts of Man

Jesus knows the whereabouts of man.

"Nathanael saith unto him, Whence knowest thou me? Jesus answered and said unto him, Before that Philip called thee, when thou wast under the fig tree, I saw thee." (John 1:48)

This feat of Jesus is impressive even when considered spatially. This is a

CHAPTER 37: THE OMNISCIENCE OF JESUS

knowledge which is beyond the capacity of mere humanity. But, beyond this, Jesus also knows where we are spiritually. He knows whether we are part of the household of believers. He also knows our situation within that household. Are we faithful stewards of the task He has given us? Or, are we in the "Break Room" long after the back to work bell has rung?

All of these things which Jesus knows are part of His attributes as God. Each of these points to the fact that Jesus is God.

We will continue this theme in our next session as we consider that Jesus also knows the future.

CHAPTER 38
JESUS ALSO KNOWS THE FUTURE
(Session Thirty-Nine)

We continue this section of our study on the Deity of Jesus by considering that He knows the future. This concept differs slightly from saying that He understands the future. Understanding a thing implies a general knowledge about the entity under discussion. Knowing a thing would imply an such an intimate relationship with the subject that it is known experientially, or first hand, rather than objectively, or through a third party - be it book or witness related - information.

I lived through the "Watergate Era." I believe that my understanding of the abuses of both President Nixon and some of his congressional adversaries has given me an understanding of some of the current partisan political posturing. I can understand both the abuse and the opportunism of the political mindset with which Watergate has poisoned the present political climate.

My son, born in 1981, has only read about the era. Most of that which he has read has centered on the abuse of the Nixon administration. Little is said about the political posturing which was also used, and abused, by both the pro and anti Nixon elements.

Much of the political discourse in recent years has centered on a "gotcha" politics. If your side loses it is possible to simply make the claim, often, of impropriety among the winners. A focus is made upon the laxity of the "other" party. Little notice is taken of moral, or ethical, laxity among those of one's own party as the "other guy" is painted as "corrupt." The purpose isn't to reveal and remove corruption; the purpose is to jockey for political standing. Both the conservative and the liberal have become very adroit at this "game" to the detriment of real discourse and the legitimate needs of the population.

My understanding of Watergate and observation of the political process since, have led me to see these actions in focus. This is simply an illustration of knowing about a thing as opposed to simply understanding a thing. Understanding is the application of knowledge. Knowledge remains the seed of understanding.

Jesus' Knowledge Was Absolute

Jesus did not simply "know" things in the sense that He was a fortune teller, as we see these people today. First of all His knowledge was absolute. A modern "psychic" will often be wrong in his prognostications. Jesus was never in error. Recent events in the financial markets have driven home the truth that simply understanding the present, and the trends of the past, will not present a perfect understanding of future events. The "predictions" of Jesus were not forecast, they were newscasts before the news had even taken place.

As God, Jesus was from eternity. Jesus knew all the events, as He knows all events, because He is God. Time is simply a medium in which He came to exist in a human body in order to offer Himself as Sacrifice for our sins. Jesus knew from eternity the events even before they transpired.

Zeoli (*Is Jesus God? Book Number Two*) looks at some of these future events, recorded in Scripture, about which Jesus had knowledge.

Jesus Knew the Catch of Fish

Jesus knew the catch of fish.

> "Now when he had left speaking, he said unto Simon, Launch out into the deep, and let down your nets for a draught. And Simon answering said unto him, Master, we have toiled all the night, and have taken nothing: nevertheless at thy word I will let down the net. And when they had this done, they inclosed a great multitude of fishes: and their net brake. And the beckoned unto their partners, which were in the other ship, that they should come and help them. And they came, and filled both the ships, so that they began to sink. When Simon Peter saw it he fell down at Jesus' knees, saying, Depart from me; for I am a sinful man, O Lord. For he was astonished, and all that were with him, at the draught of the fishes which they had taken." (Luke 5:4-9)

If you have your "Defined King James Bible" handy (I encourage you to go to your local bookstore and order this edition. I have no real connection with this edition but I find it invaluable in Bible study!), you will see that the word "draught" simply means one draw of the net. Peter said, in effect, "I've been drawing the net in all day and haven't caught anything. Now you want me to try one more time? O. K. If you say so."

I am not a fisherman. If my wife were driving by a lake the fish would block the car and ask if she'd brought her pole with her; I *cannot* catch anything except old tree limbs and some shoes - not even that very well. Linda was the fisherman of the family. Still, I do understand that, generally speaking, if a net is not drawing in fish it is because there are no fish in the area.

When Peter put in the net, in this situation, at the request of Jesus, he caught not just a few "stragglers" of fish; he caught a large school of fish.

How did Jesus know that this school of fish was going by at this time? It was not a matter of "super vision" through the water. Jesus had heavenly knowledge, as God, of the fish at that time and that place.

Jesus Knew of the Denial of Peter

Jesus also knew of the denial of Peter.

> "And Peter remembered the word of Jesus, which said unto him, Before the cock crow, thou shalt deny me thrice. And he went out, and wept bitterly." (Matthew 26:75)

Take just a minute to consider when Jesus had told Peter about this denial.

> "Peter answered and said unto him, Though all men shall be offended because of thee, yet will I never be offended. Jesus said unto him, Verily I say unto thee, That this night before the cock crow, thou shalt deny me thrice. Peter said unto him, Though I should die with thee, yet will I not deny thee. Likewise also said all the disciples." (Matthew 26:33-35)

All of the group had pledged their loyalty to Jesus. Peter had said that he would die with Jesus before he denied Him. The only disciple we can find at the cross is John. The rest had, apparently, scattered. They were probably worried that as followers of Jesus they might well be the next to die. After all, they had supported Jesus in His ministries throughout the land.

CHAPTER 38: JESUS ALSO KNOW THE FUTURE

Peter was a rambunctious fellow. The fact that he followed Jesus to the judgment hall is indicative of his personality. He was not a man to be easily deferred when his mind was set to a task. Fishing was a hard job in this time. The boats were hard to handle on the water and the constant tossing and pulling of the nets was an act which built up the muscles. Not only did the inclination of Peter to go to that judgment hall indicate his willingness to follow Jesus, his physical presence would have been one to suggest he could back his claim to follow Jesus to the death.

But, Jesus said that Peter would deny Him.

After Peter's brave act of following Jesus to the first trial, Peter wavered. This was so unlike him. But, this was exactly what Jesus had said would happen. Jesus knew what would happen even when it was unlikely that such an event would occur. He had heavenly knowledge as God.

Jesus Knew What Sort of Death Awaited Peter

Jesus also knew what sort of death awaited Peter.

> "Verily, verily, I say unto thee, When thou was young, thou girdest thyself, and walkedst whither thou wouldest: but when thou shalt be old, thou shalt stretch forth thy hands, and another shall gird thee, and carry thee whither thou wouldest not. This spake he, signifying by what death he should glorify God. And when he had spoken this, he saith unto him, Follow me." (John 21:18-19)

Peter had said that he would die for Jesus. Despite his early denial of his Lord, Peter was prepared to keep that promise. He did die as a martyr in the faith. Jesus had told him that this would happen. Peter did not shrink from the prospect. His life marched toward the earthly end in the confidence of the heavenly reward.

The knowledge which Jesus had of Peter's willingness to become a martyr, as shown in this passage, makes the previous prediction of the denial of Peter all the more remarkable.

Jesus Knew of His Own Death

Jesus also knew of His Own death.

> "And they shall mock him, and shall scourge him, and shall spit upon him, and shall kill him: and the third day he shall rise again." (Mark 10:34)

> "And when they had platted a crown of thorns, they put it upon his head, and a reed in his right hand: and they bowed the knee before him, and mocked him, saying, Hail, King of the Jews! And they spit upon him, and took the reed, and smote him on the head. And after that they had mocked him, they took the robe off from him, and put his own raiment on him, and led him away to crucify him." (Matthew 27:29-31)

Jesus Knew What Was Going to Happen on the Day of His Crucifixion

I would like to add one other verse to those Zeoli referenced.

> "And it came to pass, when the time was come that he should be received up, he stedfastly set his face to go to Jerusalem." (Luke 9:51)

Jesus knew exactly what was going to happen on the day of His crucifixion. It was for this purpose that He had come into the world. It was going to be a terrible day in every single way. He knew that He would die on the cross. More than this, He knew the terrible agony which would befall Him even before the cross.

Yet, when the time came the Bible informs us that He resolutely, with purpose and courage, "set his face to go to Jerusalem." He turned toward the agony He knew was coming and did not look back. He "set his face to go to Jerusalem."

An amazing man is Jesus, our Lord! I put the word "man" in small letters realizing that Jesus is both fully human and fully Divine. It was His humanity at this time at which I marveled. If I knew, beyond any shadow of a doubt, that I would die in a car crash I would begin to walk every place I went. Jesus knew the mode, and the time, of His death. He "set his face to go to Jerusalem."

Jesus Knew of the Betrayal of Judas

Jesus also knew of the betrayal of Judas.

> "But there are some of you that believe not. For Jesus knew from the beginning who they were that believed not, and who should betray him." (John 6:64)

We can look at this from the human standpoint and marvel that Jesus was never abusive to Judas even though He knew that Judas, humanly speaking, would be responsible for Him being turned over to those who would crucify Him. More, Jesus made Judas the treasurer of the group. He gave honor to Judas.

Could any of us, with advance knowledge that a man would betray us to our death, treat that man with love and compassion? May we keep this picture of the character of Jesus in our minds as we witness to the world of the love of Jesus. We never berate, attack or abuse the sinner. We call them in love to the Lord Who loves. "God so loved the world..." (John 3:16)

Can we really call ourselves "Christian" and do otherwise?

We also need to understand that the phrase "from the beginning" is used to speak of the foundations, in eternity "past," of the world. As Jesus knew, from the beginning, that He would be the Perfect Sacrifice to set men free from sin (Even before Adam had sinned, or was even created, Jesus knew this! Oh, the Love and Grace which God bestows to us!), He also knew who it was which would betray Him into the hands of His murderers.

Yet, Jesus still called and bestowed honor upon this man.

Jesus Knew the Reaction of the Disciples to His Arrest

Jesus also knew the reaction of the disciples to His arrest.

> "Behold, the hour cometh, yea, is now come, that ye shall be scattered, every man to his own, and shall leave me alone: and yet I am not alone, because the Father is with me." (John 16:32)

> "But all this was done, that the scriptures of the prophets might be fulfilled. Then all the disciples forsook him, and fled." (Matthew 26:56)

My home church is currently searching for a new pastor. The former pastor returned to his home to look after his ailing parents. By the way, for all that I hated to see him go; this was almost a pastoral sermon on his part: Responsibility means doing what needs to be done when it needs to be done, and,

> "Honour thy father and mother..." (Ephesians 6:2)

While we are searching we have noticed that several people have begun to waver in their commitment to the local church.

CHAPTER 38: JESUS ALSO KNOW THE FUTURE

The disciples seemed to be like this. When Jesus was arrested the disciples scattered like a fleet of cockroaches in the kitchen when the light it turned on. They scattered. It seemed that the only commonality as to their destination was "anywhere but here!"

As we saw, Peter followed Jesus to the judgment hall and then denied that he was one of the disciples. John came back to stand with Jesus' mother at the crucifixion.

Jesus knew that those closest to Him, in the natural, would forsake Him when the hour of His crucifixion came. This was a knowledge which was beyond the comprehension of any other man. One would have supposed that His closest followers would have stood by Him. Jesus knew such was not to be.

Another indication of the character of Jesus was that, after His resurrection when He returned to His disciples, He never accused them or berated them for their cowardice. In effect, He said, "I know where you've been. Here is where you need to be going." He continued to teach them even as He promised them the empowerment of the Spirit.

Jesus Knew of the Passover Accommodations

Jesus also knew of the Passover accommodations.

"And he said unto them, Behold, when ye are entered into the city, there shall a man meet you, bearing a pitcher of water; follow him into the house where he entereth in. And ye shall say unto the goodman of the house, The Master saith unto thee, Where is the guestchamber, where I shall eat the passover with my disciples? And he shall shew you a large upper room furnished: there make ready." (Luke 22:10-12)

We seem to have a need to find excuses to remove the miraculous from the Bible record. We always, it seems, look for a natural reason. We are told that Jesus had made previous arrangement with this "goodman of the house" for the Passover meal. We are told that this man was a follower of Jesus. I suppose that both of these are possible. But, we are never told how Jesus knew that the man was carrying a pitcher of water. This was often "woman's work" in this day; still there were probably many carrying such pitchers from the community well. We are never told how the disciples happened to find the man doing this particular chore at this particular time or how they found the right man.

The many miracles of Jesus are hard to dismiss when one considers His Deity!

If we recall that at the birth of Jesus there was "no room at the inn" because the city of Bethlehem was so full of people, consider just how full was the city of Jerusalem at this important time. There were many people who could find no room at **any** inn at that time.

I have often marveled at the amazing symmetry of Scripture.

Yet Jesus sent His disciples into the greatly overcrowded city, to a specific man who was carrying water, to a specific house which had a room already prepared.

The knowledge of Jesus as to these specific events is so far outside the knowledge of any mere human that we must concede that Jesus is very God!

Jesus Knew of His Ascension into Heaven

Jesus also knew of His ascension into Heaven.

"...ye shall see the Son of man ascend up where he was before?" (John 6:62)

"Which also said, Ye men of Galilee, why stand ye gazing up into heaven? this same Jesus, which is taken up from you into heaven, shall so come in like manner as ye have seen him go into heaven." (Acts 1:11)

Jesus Knew Who Would Betray Him

Again, I would like to add one more verse to those Zeoli has referenced.

"And no man hath ascended up to heaven, but he that came down from heaven, even the Son of man which is in heaven." (John 3:13)

Jesus knew who would betray Him. Jesus knew who would follow Him. Jesus knew both the manner, the surrounding, and the time of His earthly death. Jesus knew of His resurrection from the dead. Here we see that Jesus also knew that He would be removing Himself from His earthly ministry - and the manner in which this would be revealed to the disciples.

When Jesus used the phrase "where he was before" in John 6:62, He was speaking in a frame of reference which the disciples could understand. In a greater sense, Jesus was in Heaven even as He was on earth. One of the attributes of God is Omnipresence. This means that God is everywhere, and in all, at the same time. God fills His creation.

When we see that Jesus was in Heaven even as He was speaking with Nicodemus in the third chapter of John, we see an absolute declaration that Jesus is God.

Jesus is no longer a physical presence on this earth. He is still real on this earth. His work still goes forth. He founded His churches to carry out His work on the earth and in time. He goes with us in this work, showing us the way we should follow, even as the Spirit empowers us.

Jesus Knows What is in All Men

Finally, Zeoli shows that Jesus knows what is in all men.

"And Jesus did not commit himself unto them, because he knew all men; And needed not that any should testify of man: for he knew what was in man." (John 2:24-25)

This passage is from a time shortly after a cleansing of the Temple. Many professed to believe on Jesus because of His miracles. These were not committed to His message. Jesus understood that these people were professing to be followers simply because of physical manifestations. They were of the stony ground. They were not true followers. They were those who would walk away as soon as His message of grace was communicated.

Sometimes people can fool us. We may believe that they are Christians. Jesus knows the heart. Many become "social christians" because they like the music at the Church; they like the people at the Church; they like the chance to be "important" in the small pond of the Church; they may even like the politics of the Church. But, folks, none of these have anything to do with the saving grace of Jesus Christ.

Jesus knows those who are spiritually born again by His grace. He also know those who are merely "hangers on." Only God could so know the human heart as this!

Jesus is God.

CHAPTER 39
ATTRIBUTES OF JESUS, CONTINUED
(Session Forty)

We continue with a look at the attributes of Jesus which declare Him to be very Deity. These attributes, as we have previously noted, are pictures of just Who Jesus is in reality. He is God Who took upon Himself the reality of human existence, while retaining His position and Person as God, in order to effect our salvation from sin.

Jesus Is Immutable

We now consider some things which Simmons (*A Systematic Study of Bible Doctrine*) notes about the attributes of Jesus which are the attributes of God. Jesus is immutable. "Immutable" is one of those theological words. It simply means that Jesus is unchanging.

> "Jesus Christ the same yesterday, and to day, and for ever." (Hebrews 13:8)

This verse informs us of the eternality of Jesus. The word "yesterday" reaches back. The word "today" touches upon the very day of the writing as well as the very day of our reading. The word "forever" touches upon all the succeeding days; it stretches from eternity and into eternity.

This verse speaks of Jesus in the present tense even as it describes Him in the past tense and future tense. Since the Book of Hebrews was written approximately thirty years after the physical death of Jesus it speaks of His immortality as it speaks of Him as a present entity in that time frame. In truth, this verse speaks of Jesus in the eternal sense. Jesus came into time but He is not of time. He, as God, is of eternity where there is no "today, tomorrow, or yesterday."

Thus, this verse attests to the fact that Jesus is eternal. This means that He is God. So often we speak of "Jesus was." I fall into this trap myself. It is wrong. Jesus **IS**!

We too, as born again believers, are promised an eternal existence with God. That this eternality of Jesus is also stretched back to "eternity past" places Him as The Creator rather than a Created Being. Thus, once again, Jesus is God.

Jesus is Self-existent

Jesus is Self-existent.

> "For as the Father hath life in himself; so hath he given to the Son to have life in himself." (John 5:26)

As we look, superficially, at this verse, we see a dichotomy of Persons between the Father and the Son. Such is not the case. We must recall that Jesus laid aside the outward glory of His Deity in the Kenosis. We have discussed this earlier. Jesus came to live as one of us, as a Human, through the Virgin Birth so that He could become the Perfect Sacrifice for our sins. When we fail to consider this dual role we are prone to theological error.

Jesus could not have been our Savior had He been a subordinate "god." Jesus had to l ve as one of us in order to be sacrificed in our place. This is the only way His perfect sacrifice became substitutionary for us. Jesus had to remain God or His death would have only been another human being dying; thus not effective for salvation.

As God Jesus died to take away our sins. As man Jesus lived to show us how we ought to live as humans on this earth. The Bible takes both of these into account when speaking of Jesus. Therefore there are times that we see His humanity. Let us never forget that His Deity is also an absolute of His Person.

Jesus is Truth

Jesus is Truth.

> "Jesus saith unto him, I am the way, the truth, and the life: no man cometh unto the Father but by me." (John 14:6)

Many complain that Christianity is exclusionary in that it considers itself as the only way to salvation. There is a reason for this exclusionary nature; Jesus is the only way to heaven. All other paths end in destruction.

> "There is a way that seemeth right unto a man, but the end thereof are the ways of death." (Proverbs 16:25)

Notice that Jesus did not say that He would *show* the way, or the truth, or life. Jesus said that he *was (IS)* those things. Thus, salvation is only through Him and His work on Calvary.

We are considering that He is Truth. Man is prone to error. Any short talk about me with my wife would prove my point! Seriously, we are prone to error. That is why we seek, as a race of man, so many divergent ways to appease God. God does not need to be appeased. He needs to be accepted!

Jesus is Truth in that He is never in error. What He has said is always so. Jesus never makes a mistake because He is the Author of the Universe and all that is therein.

Jesus is Holy

Jesus is holy. Scripture is cited to establish this fact.

> "And the angel answered and said unto her, The Holy Ghost shall come upon thee, and the power of the Highest shall overshadow thee: therefore also that holy thing which shall be born of thee shall be called the Son of God." (Luke 1:35)

Here the Spirit says that Jesus was holy at His physical birth. How different this is from the assessment of David as to his own birth. "Behold, I was shapen in iniquity; and in sin did my mother conceive me." (Psalms 51:5) David did not mean that his mother was immoral; he simply meant that he was born with a sin nature.

Jesus, on the other hand, was virgin born of woman. He did not inherit the sin nature from Adam. We have spoken of this earlier in this study.

When Adam was first created from the dust of the ground, God breathed life into him. From that first life, every other human life has come. Life from life. Even Eve, created from the rib of Adam, derived her life from Adam.

The sin of Adam came after the creation of Eve. Eve first sinned. At this point we see nothing adverse in the pages of Scripture. Eve was doomed from that moment, of course, as God had said. But Eve was not the federal head of the race. Adam, the first created, was that federal head of the race.

When Adam sinned we see that all creation was cursed with the curse of sin. Through Adam, then, was passed the "gene," if you will, of sin. Every male since has imparted this inherited sin into all the offspring of the race of humanity. But, Jesus was

CHAPTER 39: ATTRIBUTES OF JESUS, CONTINUED

Virgin Born. Even as He was fully human, this sin nature was not part of His make up because He was not born of man.

Let us be clear on this point. The human Jesus was born from the life of Adam. But, this life from the original breath of life came from the "seed" of woman. In terms we might more readily understand, women do not carry the "sin gene." That is passed on from man to his offspring. Women are also, as daughters of Adam, born with this "sin gene." They are born, as are men, as sinners. But, while women carry this "sin gene," they do not impart this malady onto their offspring. The male carriers of this "sin gene" are those who impart the "sin gene" to their offspring. Life, from the breath of life given to Adam by God, is passed on by the woman as children are born of her. Thus we are able to see that Jesus, virgin born of a woman, was born - humanly speaking – from that same breath of life as energized Adam. But, as virgin born from the woman, Jesus would not have the blemish of the sin nature passed on to His human body.

Thus, when the Bible says that Jesus is holy, this is a picture of His special birth. His life as God was from eternity rather than from Adam. Yet, His humanity was assured as His birth was through Mary, a woman of the species.

> "For such an high priest became us, who is holy, harmless, undefiled, separate from sinners, and made higher than the heavens." (Hebrews 7:26)

Jesus Our High Priest

Of course the fact is emphasized that Jesus is holy. We can also consider that Jesus is our High Priest. Jesus is also Prophet, of course. The office of prophet is to deliver the Words of God to man. Every pastor should be a prophet rather than a mere moralizer. But, the office of priest is to bring the needs of the people before the throne of God.

Jesus brings the needs of the people before God in a way that is both unique and singular. His Priesthood is unique in that He is the Only Begotten of God. He is the promised Messiah. He is the Savior Who died in our place. He is God with the authority and power to bring our needs to the Throne and to provide the answer to those needs.

Jesus Is the Only Mediator

His Priesthood is singular in that He is the only mediator. "For *there is* one God, and one mediator between God and man, the man Christ Jesus." (I Timothy 2:5) This verse, of course, speaks of Jesus in His mediatorial office as the Representative of humanity. The salient point is that He is not only the Only Savior, He is also the Only Mediator.

A pastor, or really any Christian, may pray *for* a person. We can invoke the Spirit to work upon their hearts and needs. But, neither the man in the pew nor the person in the pulpit or denominational headquarters can ever pray *in place of* a person. That personal relationship between the Spirit and the people is one of the principles of God.

Likewise, no person can take his petition to a church official, a Christian brother or sister, a pastor, or anyone else with the expectation that the prayer of those other people will relieve that person of the responsibility of approaching the Throne of Grace on his own behalf.

Only Jesus is authorized to act as Mediator between God and man. To ask another to take that responsibility is against the principles of Scripture and an attempt to lead another to sin as it is asking them to take the place of Jesus.

We can pray for others, and we should. But we can never remove our own responsibility, as individuals, to take our cares and needs to Jesus for ourselves. Group prayer is good and effective. However, private prayer is needful and a blessing to the petitioner. Private prayer is also Scriptural!

In our next session we will consider the attribute of Jesus as Creator.

CHAPTER 40
JESUS AS CREATOR
(Session Forty-One)

We again look into Evangelist Anthony Zeoli's book of 1943, *"Is Jesus God – Book Number Two"* as we consider that Jesus is the Creator God. Zeoli makes several assertions about the fact that Jesus was the Active Agent of the entire Creation. He backs his points with an appeal to Scripture. We will look at the Scripture passages referenced and add our own commentary.

First, Jesus Is the Creator

First of all, Zeoli asserts that Jesus is the Creator.

> *"All things were made by him; and without him was not any thing made that was made." (John 1:3)*

Although the *"New World Translation of the Holy Scriptures,"* published by "The Watchtower Bible & Tract Society of Pennsylvania (1961)" would try to tie this verse in with verse four and assert that "What has come into existence by means of him was life..," the verse argues that Jesus made "all things."

Certainly life, as the primarily Jehovah's Witness version above says, was made by Jesus. I believe that it was Jesus who breathed the breath of life into Adam and thus began the human experience. But, the verse quoted goes beyond this. The verse quite plainly says that Jesus created "all things." The wording is not, "all things except," nor is it, "a few specific things." The Bible plainly says that Jesus created "ALL THINGS." Since the creation accounts argue that the Creative Agent was God, this verse is a plain statement that Jesus is God.

There is no theological "wiggle room" here. Either Jesus did create all things and is, therefore, God or John made a mistake - under inspiration! - when he penned this passage. In this passage not only is the doctrine of the Deity of Jesus asserted, we also must consider that the entire doctrine of inspiration and preservation comes into play.

> *"And to make all men see what is the fellowship of the mystery, which from the beginning of the world hath been hid in God, who created all things by Jesus Christ." (Ephesians 3:9)*

There are those who would argue that God, the Father, created Jesus, the Son, and then gave Jesus the task of creating the rest of the physical universe. There are two problems with this interpretation. The first is that Genesis 1:1 begins with, "In the beginning God created the heaven and the earth." This verse very clearly says that God created. It does not say Jesus. The only alternative, again, would be that Jesus is God or the Scripture is wrong.

Second, as we've just seen in John, Jesus created "ALL." This means, obviously, that Jesus cannot be a created Being. Such a construct would argue that Jesus did not create all in that this would make Him a created Being.

Jesus Is Omnipotent

As a corollary, God is an omnipotent, all powerful, "Person." Had He created a "Tonto" God to His "Lone Ranger" Godhood, He would cease to be all powerful and thus would not be God. Jesus cannot be "a god" with creative power and be, Himself, created. Genesis tells us that God created; John tells us that Jesus was the Agent of Creation. The only logical conclusion is that Jesus is, Himself, God.

Jesus Created All Things Out of Nothing

Second, Zeoli argues that Jesus created all things out of nothing.

> *"Through faith we understand that the worlds were framed by the word of God, so that things which are seen were not made of things which do appear." (Hebrews 11:3)*

There is an old joke that several scientists approached God's Throne and said, "We have discovered how to make life. We can make a man from the elements of the earth and impart life to him."

God said, "Go ahead."

The scientists began to take their chemicals and pour them into measuring cups when God said, "Not so fast. Make your own 'dirt' like I did in Genesis." The fact is that God, in the Person of Jesus, made the entire universe from nothing except the power of His majesty.

But, there is a deeper meaning to that verse. This would not have been understood by the human penman of Hebrews. All things that are seen are made from things which are not seen. God gave the concept of molecular biology and sub atomic particle construction of all elements some twenty centuries before humanity caught on to the idea.

The Bible is replete with illustrations such as this.

Jesus Created All Things in Heaven and in Earth

Third, Zeoli sees that Jesus created all things in Heaven and in Earth.

> *"For by him were all things created, that are in heaven, and that are in earth, visible and invisible, whether they be thrones, or dominions, or principalities, or powers: all things were created by him, and for him." (Colossians 1:16)*

This verse goes far beyond the surface. The phrase "visible and invisible" could be another reference to the atomic construction. I believe that this verse goes far beyond even this. Have you ever used a "dog whistle?" The dog can hear it but we can't. God knew this concept of the limitations of man's senses long before mankind had any inkling of such a possibility. There are color spectrums which we cannot see. Did Paul know this when he was penning Colossians. No; but God did!

The Spirit also led Paul to consider that Jesus had created thrones, or kingdoms. Dominions of men are in the Hand of God. He sets up rulers and pulls them down.

I believe that the reference to dominions and principalities - and powers - speak of spiritual entities. When the Bible says that Jesus created all, as it does in the first chapter of John, the meaning is all.

When we confine our arguments about creation to the physical aspect, we are not giving full voice to the glory and majesty of The Almighty God!

CHAPTER 40: JESUS AS CREATOR

Jesus Created the Worlds

Fourth, Zeoli mentions that Jesus created the worlds.

> *"Hath in these last days spoken unto us by his Son, whom he hath appointed heir of all things, by whom also he made the worlds." (Hebrews 1:2)*

Again, as we have mentioned several times already, this verse is speaking of the office of Jesus as Savior of the World. He is positionally appointed heir of all things in His Office of Redemptive Agent. In this office He is representative of humanity. This concept of "heir" is a legalistic concept meaning that He is worthy, as the representative of humanity, to assume this right.

This is a matter of God teaching spiritual realities to people in a picture that we are able to understand. It is not a picture of a subservient Jesus. It is a picture of the great glory and honor which is due Him.

We also need to consider, from this verse, that Jesus created more than this one little planet. There is a vast universe which was also created by Him. Our view of the majesty of Jesus does not begin to reach past the very superficial. He is Almighty God. Almighty beyond even our wildest dreams and considerations!

> *"He was in the world, and the world was made by him, and the world knew him not." (John 1:10)*

When Jesus laid aside the Glory of Deity which was rightfully His, so that He could enter into this world as a child at Bethlehem, the people were well able to understand that He was a very special man, few grasped the concept that He was more than a mere teacher. He was the Promised Redeemer!

Again, the glory and love of God is shown in the Person of Jesus. Even His submissive attitude that led Him to take upon Himself the robe of human flesh, is a picture of His Deity in that this shows a love beyond the ability of a mere human being.

> *"But God commendeth his love toward us, in that, while we were yet sinners, Christ died for us." (Romans 5:8)*

Also, Zeoli reminds us that Jesus laid the foundation of the world.

> *"And, Thou, Lord, in the beginning hast laid the foundation of the earth; and the heavens are the works of thine hands." (Hebrews 1:10)*

That phrase, "in the beginning," is often used in the Scripture. As a general rule this refers back to eternity when the creation was first considered by God. To use a basketball illustration, "in the beginning" would not refer to the opening jump ball. It would refer back to before the time Dr. Naismith invented the game.

"In the beginning" refers back to when there was nothing yet of the physical created universe.

> *"And all that dwell upon the earth shall worship him, whose names are not written in the book of life of the Lamb slain from the foundation of the world." (Revelation 13:8)*

This verse begins by speaking of the world following the beast during the Tribulation era. The verse also speaks of those who are saved, in the book of life, by the "Lamb slain from the foundation of the world."

Before Adam sinned, before Adam was even created, God knew that Adam would fall from grace. Before the world was even created God knew every single act of every single person who has ever, or will ever, lived upon this earth. Jesus knew that Calvary was a waiting experience before He created the world. And, yet, He created the world so that He might save some.

Again, the Love of God is far beyond our comprehension. We, the Blood Bought believer are blessed beyond measure or comprehension!

In our next session we will consider the omnipresence of Jesus.

CHAPTER 41
THE OMNIPRESENCE OF JESUS
(Session Forty-Two)

This is an Attribute of God

In this session we will consider the fact that Jesus is omnipresent. "Omnipresent" is one of those "professional" theological words. All it really means is the attribute of being in all places at the same time.

Many stories are told of the old "Negro League" great James "Cool Papa" Bell for his amazing speed. Satchel Paige once said this man was so fast that he could turn off the light in a hotel room and be in bed before it got dark. This idea of speed is not what is meant by omnipresence. Omnipresence isn't being able to travel from point A to point B very quickly. Omnipresence is actually being at point A and point B, and everywhere else, at the exact same time.

This is an attribute of God. The angels are said to travel from place to place. Only of God is it said that He inhabits all places at the same time. As we see this attribute about Jesus we must agree that He is God.

Zeoli (*Is Jesus God? Book Number Two*) has listed several verses that illustrate this attribute of Jesus.

Jesus is where two or three are gathered.

> *"For where two or three are gathered together in my name, there am I in the midst of them." (Matthew 18:20)*

It would be interesting for one to look at the number of churches in just his own hometown and consider this verse. The town I live in is probably under 30,000 in population. In this town there are 59 churches listed in the local newspaper. I would venture to say that there are probably a few more house churches which are not listed. Also not listed are the religious services at the local prison and jail, as well as those at the various nursing homes. Consider, also, that there are some family worship groups, much like religious "home schools," and the number climbs.

We must account that not all of these assemblies are Biblically based and must be discounted from the number of those where the gathering is actually in the Name of Jesus. Also, admittedly, the beginning times for these various church services will vary. Counting just those in the newspaper the times of service will begin from 9:00 A. M. to 11:00 A. M.

What I am getting at is that it would not be possible for Jesus to be with even all of those Biblically based services unless He was able to inhabit multiple locations at the same time. This is very close to the definition of omnipresence. When we count in all the various Biblically based services around the world the number of places where Jesus must be - at the same time! - is staggering. Either He was mistaken in His assertion that He would be with even the smallest of these groups or He is God.

More than this, Jesus promises to be with His people at all times. At the conclusion of the "Great Commission" Jesus says,

> *"...and, lo, I am with you alway, even unto the end of the world. Amen." (Matthew 28:20b)*

There are Christians, Biblically based born again Christians, literally all over this world. An acquaintance of mine several years ago went into the heart of the Muslim world a few years ago to assist in the ordination of a Baptist minister, an Iraqi national, in Baghdad. There are churches, some sanctioned by the State and some simply meetings of born again individuals, in the heart of communist China. It is obvious, therefore, when Jesus promised to be with the Christian at all times, wherever they might be, that He was announcing His full Godhead.

Jesus announced this full Deity in even more impressive terms than the spatial ability to be in all places at the same time. He promised this would be until the "end of the world." This is an announcement of the eternality of Jesus. He is not limited by space; neither is He limited by time. Jesus is of the "time" of eternity. Again, this is an indication of His deity.

Jesus is also both in Heaven and in Earth. We could "spiritualize" this concept and say that He is in the heart of the believer. This would not diminish the fact of His omnipresence. But, Zeoli leads us to John 3:13.

> "And no man hath ascended up in heave, but he that came down from heaven, even the Son of man which is in heaven."

Jesus made the claim, while on earth in about 30 A.D. speaking with a man named Nicodemus, to be in Heaven - at that very instant! Consider this! Can a stronger claim be made to the eternality, omnipresence, and Deity of Jesus ever have fallen from His lips!

How anyone can say with a straight face that Jesus never claimed to be God is far beyond my reasoning power!

Jesus is in the Father and in the believer.

> "At that day ye shall know that I am in my Father, and ye in me, and I in you." (John 14:20)

Jesus claims to be in the Father. That is the Trinitarian concept. Jesus and the Father are of One essence. Jesus also claims to be in us, as Christians. That is salvation. He also says that we are in Him. This is positional righteousness.

At the Cross Jesus sacrificed Himself to be our Savior. As our Savior He has taken our sin upon Himself and paid the penalty for those sins so that we can have the benefit of His Own righteousness applied to our unworthy souls. This is a positional righteousness which we enjoy. We are not righteous; He is righteous. He has taken away our sins and counted His righteousness unto us as children, adopted children, of God.

> "But as many as received him, to them gave he power to become the sons of God, even to them that believe on his name." (John 1:12)

Jesus Fills All things

Jesus also fills all things.

> "Which is his body, the fulness of him that filleth all in all." (Ephesians 1:23)

> "He that descended is the same also that ascended up far above all heavens, that he might fill all things." (Ephesians 4:10)

I mentioned above that Matthew 18:20 was very close to the definition of omnipresence. These verses in Ephesians are the very definition of omnipresence.

CHAPTER 41: THE OMNIPRESENCE OF JESUS

Jesus is everywhere, and in every thing, at every instance. The universe, indeed, would neither function nor exist were Jesus not in all and at all. He fills the void between eternity and time.

Jesus Is Near to All

Jesus is also near to all.

> *"That they should seek the Lord, if haply they might feel after him, and find him, though he be not far from every one of us."* (Acts 17:27)

Strictly speaking this verse does not speak to omnipresence. This verse speaks to the availability of salvation to all. Any person, wherever that person may be, is invited to partake of the salvation available in Jesus Christ. Jesus died for us because He loves us and calls us to Himself. This is, of course, positionally in that we are called to accept Salvation from the Savior Who stands ready to grant that salvation.

While, as I said, not directly speaking to the concept of omnipresence, this verse certainly alludes to the fact of the omnipresence of Jesus.

This attribute of Jesus to exhibit omnipresence is a clear indication of His full Deity. Jesus is God even as He claimed to be by His statements about Himself.

CHAPTER 42
MORE ATTRIBUTES CONFIRMING JESUS IS GOD
(Session Forty-Three)

Jesus Is Our Constant Contemporary

In the session we continue to consider the fact that Jesus has the attributes of Deity. We can easily consider His human, physical, existence and consider that He is true man. But, as we consider these attributes that are also the specific province of God, we are able to consider that He is also True God.

Notice, please, that I spoke of Jesus in the present tense. He is our Constant Contemporary. He lives in the eternal now. This isn't to simply say that His "memory" is always with us, or that the story of His meaning and life is always with us. The meaning is that He is both of the physical and the spiritual. As man He was exhibited at a certain point in history. But, as God, He is always exhibited at every point in history and eternity.

Jesus is life

We begin this session with the work of Augustus Strong (*Systematic Theology*) and consider that in Jesus is life. Strong references two verses from John's Gospel to illustrate this point.

"*In him was life; and the life was the light of men.*" (John 1:4)

We've spoken on this verse before in this study. We have noted that this particular verse does not say that life was in Jesus. The verse says that in him was life. A small distinction; but it is an important distinction.

In the Garden we see that God breathed into Adam the breath of life. This was not done unto any of the other created entities. Only into Adam was this "breath of life" imparted. This means that man was a special creation. Thus, the concept of "theistic evolution" fails at this point.

Man Was Not the Product of Evolutionary Mutations

Man was not the product of evolutionary mutations. Man was created distinctly to be man. This gives to man a special and noble standing among all the creatures upon the earth. The fact that man and some other primates share over 90% of the same basic DNA means only that God had a basic building plan in mind. This is the same as a craftsman who may make a couch, bed, table, chair, and even workbench from the same basic "four legs and flat top" design. Small modifications to the basic design determine the use of the object.

The major modification which God made to humanity was that "breath of life." With that God changed the basic structure of man from beast to "living soul." As such we were given an immortality. We were also given a morality. We were also given a certain amount of creativity.

It is the creativity which allows us to consider our actions. We do not construct our lives fully on instinct. We judge and consider alternatives. We also create works of art that are beyond the capacity of mere brute beasts. The simple fact that I am writing and you are reading is evidence of our special status as human beings.

This morality means that we are able to make decisions based on a set of core beliefs rather than relying on the simple hunger, pleasure, or pain of the moment. We choose our lives to an extent far beyond that of even the most intelligent of the animal kingdom.

We are a "living soul" because God gave us this breath of life. It is something which was added to the basic structure of the human race. Eve, "born" from the rib of Adam, had this trait passed on to her. Each human being born into the world has had this gift of life added from his, or her, parents.

Jesus, the Repository, Not the Depository, of Life

Jesus, however, was the repository, not the depository, of life. That is a monumental difference.

At the burning bush Moses asked the Name of God. God's answer was, "I AM." The basic meaning of that Name is "The Self Existent One." Primarily, this is what was said of Jesus in John 1:4. He is called the Fount of Life. In Him resided life. Therefore, Jesus is God.

> *"Jesus saith unto him, I am the way, the truth and the life: no man cometh unto the Father, but by me." (John 14:6)*

This is an often overlooked verse. Please note that Jesus did not say that He was the Guide to anything. He specifically said that He was certain things. In our study we should note that He is life. This sets Him apart from mere humans who contain a derivative life. He is not the recipient of life; He is the Author of life.

Jesus is Truth

He also says that He is Truth. We may know truth. We may understand truth. We may even practice truth. But, Jesus is Truth. This simply means that there can be no falseness, no error, and no sin within Him. Such would be foreign to His Divine nature.

Jesus is the Way to God

Jesus also says that He is the Way to God. To our ears in this day the statement seems rather exclusionary. It is! Remember that Jesus is Truth. Therefore this statement is a statement of fact rather than of opinion. There is simply no salvation afforded unto mankind apart from Jesus Christ and His substitutionary death on the Cross of Calvary.

Strong also notes that Jesus is eternality.

> *"In the beginning was the Word, and the Word was with God, and the Word was God." (John 1:1)*

The phrase "In the beginning" simply means before anything of the physical universe was, or at the point of its beginning. Jesus, therefore, predates any created being.

This argument is highlighted in verse three when we find that Jesus, Himself, was the Creative Agent Who made all things. This precludes the possibility of Jesus being a created being. Therefore, Jesus is God.

> *"Jesus said unto them, Verily, verily, I say unto you, Before Abraham was, I am." (John 8:58)*

CHAPTER 42: MORE ATTRIBUTES CONFIRMING JESUS IS GOD

We can look upon this verse and argue, from a surface reading, that Jesus was only claiming to have existed before Abraham existed.

The above, all by itself, would point to the Deity of Jesus. But, we also see that Jesus used the covenant name "I am" of Himself. This is proven by the reaction, in verse 59, of the religious leaders. They rose up to stone Jesus for blasphemy.

It should also be noted that Jesus was miraculously saved from their hands. He "hid himself" among the crowd. Considering that He was the object of discussion, it is obviously a miracle of God which hid Him in the crowd. He did this Himself. Jesus is God.

The Eternality and Love of Jesus

> "And now, O Father, glorify thou me with thine own self with the glory which I had with thee before the world was." (John 17:5)

We have discussed the Kenosis, whereby Jesus laid aside the outward glory of His Own Divinity while He resided on this earth. At this time Jesus asked that His Own glory, which He had already worn, be returned to Him. Note also that this was a glory which He shared with the Father. This is another indication of the Deity of Jesus and the Trinitarian concept.

This verse also, of course, speaks to the existence of Jesus in the eternal realms. He did not begin at Bethlehem.

> "According as he hath chosen us in him before the foundation of the world, that we should be holy and without blame before him in love." (Ephesians 1:4)

Again, this verse speaks of the eternality of Jesus.

This verse also says something about the love of Jesus. He has chosen before the foundation of the world. I've had more than a few people tell me that they are unworthy of salvation because of something they might have done, or the way they've lived their lives.

Not so! Jesus knew every single thing we would ever do in our lives. We have no surprises to offer Him. Still He loves us and calls us to His offered salvation. Then, again knowing all of our faults, He presents us as holy and without blame. This is entirely based on His love and sacrifice at the Cross of Calvary.

Does this mean that we should not live to our fullest ability to be worthy of this great love? Of course not! Jesus calls the Christian to live up to the standard of holiness. We fail. We fail often. Still, Jesus calls us to strive. He also lifts us up when we cry out in our unworthiness. We are told not to sin in I John 2:1; but we are offered a remedy when we do fail our Lord.

> "My little children, these things write I unto you, that ye sin not. And if any man sin, we have an advocate with the Father, Jesus Christ the righteous."

> "And he is before all things, and by him all things consist." (Colossians 1:17)

This verse also reminds us of the eternality of Jesus. Whereas John 1:3 informs us that Jesus was the Creative Agent of the Trinity. This verse goes further. This verse informs us that Jesus is the Sustaining Force of the entire creation. Not only is it true that without Him there would be no creation, it is also true that creation would fail were it not for the work of Jesus.

Only a cultist with a preconceived view of his theology could argue that Jesus is anything less than God Almighty! The Bible, over and over, states the obvious: Jesus is God, the Son, even as He is the Son of God.

Is this beyond our comprehension? Yes. To be honest, yes. What of God is not beyond our comprehension? God, His ways and plans, is explained to us in the pages of His Book. What we learn of Him within those pages is true even if our time centric and physical minds *cannot* fathom the Truth of eternity and the spiritual!

Jesus is the "Alpha and Omega"

"And he said unto me, It is done. I am the Alpha and Omega, the beginning and the end. I will give unto him that is athirst of the fountain of the water of life freely." (Revelation 21:6)

Note a subtlety in this verse. Jesus is the "Alpha and Omega." The verse does not read "The Alpha and The Omega."

The "alpha," of course, is the first letter in the Greek alphabet while the "omega" is the last. This verse does not say that Jesus is the First and the Last. The verse asserts that Jesus is <u>from</u> the first even unto the last. He fills all eternity and spans all the ages of creative history.

Jesus is not said to just create the world and then return at the end to see how it all turned out. He is presented as The One Who cares about His creation. His love shines forth through the eternality of His Person. Jesus is the Love of God Personified!

This eternality of Jesus about which we've considered in this session is one more illustration of the Deity of Jesus. In our next session we will begin to consider the omnipotence, or the All Powerfulness, of Jesus.

CHAPTER 43
THE ALL POWERFULNESS OF JESUS
(Session Forty-Four)

The Attribute of Omnipotence

In this session we will be considering the attribute of omnipotence. This simply means that Jesus is all powerful. Once again we turn to the outline study of Zeoli, *"Is Jesus God? – Book Number Two."* Zeoli has listed references which point to the attribute of power in the life of Jesus. We will list those references and comment upon them.

Jesus Has the Power of Life and Death

Jesus has the power of life and death. John 10:7-10.

> *"Then said Jesus unto them again, Verily, verily, I say unto you, I am the door of the sheep. All that ever come before me are thieves and robbers: but the sheep did not hear them. I am the door: by me if any man enter in, he shall be saved, and shall go in and out, and find pasture. The thief cometh not, but for to steal, and to kill, and to destroy: I am come that they might have life, and that they might have it more abundantly."*

Primarily this passage is speaking of salvation, of course. The teaching is that Jesus is the only means of eternal life. No other plan or method can produce salvation except the substitutionary death of Jesus on the Cross of Calvary.

But, this verse also speaks of fulfillment in our physical life. We often forget, in our reasonable majoring on the eternal life offered in Christ, that God is the "Manufacturer" of our physical bodies. Alexander the Great wept because there were no more worlds left to conquer. Only the life dedicated to the worship of the True God can be truly fulfilling.

God knows, more intimately than even we can know, what it is that will give us true peace and contentment in this physical life. Mankind tries all manner of substitutes to fill the needs of his life. Man will try drugs, sex, a drive for material and professional success in order to give his life meaning. Ultimately none will fill the void. Only the Bible, rejected by man because of his innate sin nature, will remind us to find the "Manufacturer's specifications" which will make the machine of our physical life to run at its full potential.

Only salvation in Jesus will allow us to find, and use, the wisdom of the Book. We must find God to find true peace. We can only do this through a relationship with Jesus based on a saving faith in Him.

Jesus the Great Physician

I've been visiting a friend in the hospital for the past few weeks. The older I get the more frequently this unhappy task become a necessity. We discuss health among our ancient selves and among our offspring. The doctors come by and make tests and give treatments. Even the doctor will admit that his ministrations can heal no one. He can only treat symptoms and wait for the body to heal itself.

Jesus, however, is the Great Physician who can heal by the power of His Word. He had the power to heal the deaf and dumb.

> *"And he took him aside from the multitude, and put his fingers into his ears, and he spit, and touched his tongue; And looking up to heaven, he sighed, and saith unto him, Ephphatha, that is Be opened. And straightway his ears were opened, and the string of his tongue was loosed, and he spake plain." (Mark 7:33-35)*

This is a mighty miracle of Jesus. Just healing the man's maladies was a miracle. But, Jesus went beyond mere healing. Jesus made it so the man was able to hear, and understand, speech. Jesus made it so the man could speak plainly. Giving these skills to the man was miracle. Giving the man command of these skills, without any study or practice on the man's part, to my mind was an even greater miracle.

If I am "color blind" I may understand what red is supposed to look like. But, I would have no real frame of reference to understand the gradations of red, orange, pink, etc. The same principle would apply to the concept of hearing to this formerly deaf man.

If my arm is withered I may understand the concept of throwing a football thirty yards. But, I would need to practice for some time to be able to do that with any proficiency. The same principle would apply to the concept of speech to a man who had an impediment in his speech.

Jesus Healed the Blind

Jesus also healed the blind.

> *"And when Jesus departed thence, two blind men followed him, crying, and saying, Thou Son of David, have mercy on us. And when he was come into the house, the blind men came to him: and Jesus saith unto them, Believe ye that I am able to do this? They said unto him, Yea, Lord, then touched he their eyes, saying, According to your faith be it unto you. And their eyes were opened, and Jesus straitly charged them, saying, See that no man know it." (Matthew 9:27-30)*

What a picture this is of the conversion experience. These men came to Jesus and voiced their sickness. They acknowledged Him as Lord. He healed their eyes. Their eyes were opened so that they could see the reality of the world about them.

It is a touch from the Master that we need to open our sin darkened eyes to the reality of the spiritual needs around us. This all was not predicated on the righteousness of these men. The medium of faith in Jesus and His all sufficiency was the *salve* that opened their eyes.

Jesus Healed Sicknesses

Jesus healed sicknesses.

> *"And a certain man was there, which had an infirmity thirty and eight years. When Jesus saw him lie, and knew that he had been now a long time in that case, he saith unto him, Wilt thou be made whole? The impotent man answered him, Sir, I have no man, when the water is troubled, to put me into the pool: but while I am coming, another steppeth down before me. Jesus saith unto him, Rise, take up thy bed, and walk. And immediately the man was made whole, and took up his bed, and walked: and on the same day was the sabbath. The Jews therefore said unto him that was cured, It is the sabbath day: it is not lawful for thee to carry thy bed." (John 5:5-10)*

How often it is that formal religion will tell us that the cure of Jesus is wrong. This

CHAPTER 43: THE ALL POWERFULNESS OF JESUS

man was healed by doing nothing at all except obeying the words of Jesus.

We have too many doctors of religion telling us how to take our journey through life. We need more attention to Jesus telling how to walk. The journey will take care of itself if we walk with the Spirit.

We have too many self-help courses telling us how to live. We need more of Jesus simply giving us life for the living.

We have too many preachers telling us what, and how, to believe. We need more faith in the Words of Jesus to impart faith into our hearts.

This man was healed at a spoken word from the Eternal Word. He carried his bed even though it was the Sabbath. We need to follow the leading of the Spirit rather than the traditions of man.

> "So Jesus came again into Cana of Galilee, where he made the water wine. And there was a certain nobleman, whose son was sick at Capernaum. When he heard that Jesus was come out of Judaea into Galilee, he went unto him, and besought him that he would come down, and heal his son: for he was at the point of death. Then said Jesus unto him, Except ye see signs and wonders, ye will not believe. The nobleman saith unto him, Sir, come down ere my child die. Jesus saith unto him, go thy way, thy son liveth. And the man believed the word that Jesus had spoken unto him, and he went his way. And as he was now going down, his servants met him, and told him, saying, Thy son liveth. Then enquired he of them the hour when he began to amend. And they said unto him, Yesterday at the seventh hour the fever left him. So the father knew that it was at the same hour, in the which Jesus said unto him, Thy son liveth: and himself believed, and his whole house. This is again the second miracle that Jesus did, when he was come out of Judaea into Galilee." (John 4:46-54)

The power of Jesus to effect healing was so great that He did not need to travel to the site where the sick was laying in his bed of affliction. This particular example shows two of the attributes of God which Jesus displayed. The first is Omnipresence. We've already considered this attribute. The meaning is that Jesus can be talking to a man in one location and be in another location at the same time effecting a cure for the man's son.

Jesus is the Creator God

The second is, of course, the healing itself. Jesus is the Creator God. For Him to heal a person is as simple, more so actually, than it would be for me to replace a thumb tack on my bulletin board. He simply makes right what had gone wrong. Only God can do this!

> "And Jesus went about all Galilee, teaching in their synagogues, and preaching the gospel of the kingdom, and healing all manner of sickness and all manner of disease among the people." (Matthew 4:23)

I am under the health care system of the Veteran's Administration. Every few months I am called back to the Iowa City Veteran's Medical Facility. I go for my heart. I go for a skin condition. I go for my eyes. I go for respiratory problems. Basically, I am a total wreck.

Not really. I am a combat veteran and the military takes very good care of me by looking to find potential problems before they get worse.

I also go to a local clinic in my home town. Here a very good General Practitioner looks over my complete body and schedules trips to the various specialist's at Iowa City. Jesus was a General Practitioner. He didn't need any specialist to back up His work. Jesus healed all manner of disease. It didn't matter to Him what the problem was. He had the power to heal!

This is, of course, more than a simple physical healing. He was displaying His mastery over the course of nature. He was giving ample proof that He had the cure for the malady of sin.

Jesus Healed the Withered Hand

Jesus healed the withered hand.

> *"And, behold, there was a man which had his hand withered. And they asked him, saying, Is it lawful to heal on the sabbath days? that they might accuse him. And he said unto them, What man shall there be among you, that shall have one sheep, and if it fall into a pit on the sabbath day, will not law hold on it, and lift it out? How much then is a man better than a sheep? Wherefore it is lawful to do well on the sabbath days. Then saith he to the man, Stretch forth thine hand. And he stretched it forth; and it was restored whole, like as the other."* (Matthew 12:10-13)

Now, there is a passage with "a ton of truth" in it.

Several years ago I read an article that in a certain Eastern state there were still laws on the books which forbid any working on Sunday. A man read about this and began to attempt to make citizen's arrests of toll booth workers. He was arrested under the same law he was attacking. The upshot was that these laws were finally removed from the books.

Jesus saw through this attempt to trick Him. His reply to those who asked if it was lawful to do good on the sabbath included a reference to the hypocrisy of those who had asked the question. His reply also pointed out the fact that man and animal are different creatures. Man is the apex of the creation of God. No evolutionary argument can annul this truth.

Jesus is Lord of the Sabbath

Jesus also asserted His Deity in two more ways. In the first He asserted His absolute claim to be the Lord of the Sabbath Who could make decisions about the Laws of God because He is God.

Second, he proved His thesis by healing the man of his malady. This was not a matter where anyone could claim that the healing was simply the result of making the man feel better because of manipulation of his moods. This was an obvious healing of an obvious physical malady.

Jesus Healed a Man with "Dropsy"

Jesus also healed a man with "dropsy." This is an unnatural accumulation of fluids in any body cavity.

> *"And, behold, there was a certain man before him which had the dropsy. And Jesus answering spake unto the lawyers and Pharisees, saying, Is it lawful to heal on the sabbath day? And they held their peace. And he took him, and healed him, and let him go."* (Luke 14:2-4)

This is somewhat akin to the previous verse. The difference here is that Jesus asked the question of the religious leaders at this instance. Jesus knew their answer, of

CHAPTER 43: THE ALL POWERFULNESS OF JESUS

course, before they gave it. Jesus was being gracious to them in this case. He was not overly concerned with the response of the men. He wanted them to understand that what was about to happen was a manifestation of His Deity and power.

Jesus was reaching out to these men, even this group who most bitterly opposed Him, and offering them an illustration and invitation to His grace to save. I John 4:8 informs us that God is love; let us realize that Jesus is God.

Jesus Healed Paralysis

Jesus healed paralysis.

> "And they come unto him, bringing one sick of the palsy, which was borne of four. And when they could not come nigh unto him for the press, they uncovered the roof where he was: and when they had broken it up, they let down the bed wherein the sick of the palsy lay. When Jesus saw their faith, he said unto the sick of the palsy, Son, thy sins be forgiven thee. But there were certain of the scribes sitting there, and reasoning in their hearts, Why doth this man thus speak blasphemies? who can forgive sins but God only? And immediately when Jesus perceived in his spirit that they so reasoned within themselves, he said unto them, Why reason ye there things in your hearts? Whether is it easier to say to the sick of the palsy, Thy sins be forgiven thee; or to say, Arise, and take up thy bed, and walk? But that ye may know that the Son of man hath power on earth to forgive sins, (he saith to the sick of the palsy,) I say unto thee, Arise, and take up thy bed, and go thy way into thine house. And immediately he arose, took up the bed, and went forth before them all, insomuch that they were all amazed, and glorified God, saying, We never saw it on this fashion." (Mark 2:3-12)

Here again we see that Jesus heals another ailment. This man was bedridden due to his paralysis. We might note that the men who carried this ill man are pictures of what we ought to be as witnesses. We take the presence of Jesus out into the crowded world with our life and witness. With our prayers for the power of the Spirit, we use these means to allow sinful men an audience with the Master.

The crush of the world can never keep the love of Jesus from reaching those who approach Him in faith!

The Deity of Jesus was displayed, once again, in two ways. The most obvious was the physical healing. The less obvious, made obvious by the healing, was that Jesus had the power to forgive sin.

Only God can do this!

We will continue to consider the power of Jesus to heal as an attribute of His deity in our next session.

CHAPTER 44
THE POWER OF JESUS TO HEAL
(Session Forty-Five)

We have been considering the healings of Jesus. Evangelist Anthony Zeoli (*Is Jesus God? – Book Number Two*) has provided a very good inventory of the healings of Jesus. We have been considering these.

Jesus Healed Leprosy

We continue and see that Jesus healed leprosy.

> "When he was come down from the mountain, great multitudes followed him. And, behold, there came a leper and worshipped him, saying, Lord, if thou wilt, thou canst make me clean. And Jesus put forth his hand, and touched him, saying, I will; be thou clean. And immediately his leprosy was cleansed. And Jesus saith unto him, See thou tell no man; but go thy way, shew thyself to the priest, and offer the gift that Moses commanded, for a testimony unto them." (Matthew 8:1-4)

This is a nice story, isn't it? We look at these verses and find reference to "The Touch of the Master's Hand." We need to move beyond the "story book" setting our minds have prepared for us. We need to look at the hot, dusty road where this took place in human history. Consider the crowds that were following Jesus. We see these crowds thronging around in "Hollywood" splendor as Jesus reached out to this man.

It didn't happen that way. More likely, as soon as this leper approached the crowds did their best "cockroach impersonation" and scattered away in horror. The leper was an "unclean" person. No one would accept the contamination of even being seen with him. To have touched the leper, as Jesus did, was completely unthinkable. To touch a leper was to make one an outcast himself.

And, yet, Jesus not only healed this leper, He also reached out - even before the healing had taken place - and gave that human to human contact of a touch. This touch is something that was far beyond the scope of human kindness in that day.

The power of God was shown through the healing. The Love of God was shown through the simple touch. The fidelity of Jesus to the revealed Scripture is shown by His insistence that the now former leper go and present himself to the priest.

Jesus Healed Palsy and Fever

Jesus also healed palsy and fever. "And when Jesus was come into Peter's house, he saw his wife's mother laid; and sick of a fever. And he touched her hand, and the fever left her: and she arose, and ministered unto them." (Matthew 8:14-15)

Again we see this touch of the Master's Hand. How tender, how loving, and how powerful is the touch of Jesus. The illness was immediately healed.

The touch of Jesus allowed this woman, the mother of Peter's wife, to begin to serve the Lord. There is a simple lesson for us. Jesus did not heal as part of a traveling medicine show. Jesus healed so that those healed might be of service to others. Such is always the story of the Christian. We are saved that we might serve. When we lose sight of this we have lost sight of Jesus. He was constantly going forth to serve others.

Jesus Healed the Insane

Jesus healed the insane.

> "Lord, have mercy on my son: for he is lunatick, and sore vexed: for ofttimes he falleth into the fire, and oft into the water." (Matthew 17:15)

This is, of course, a miracle of the casting out of demons (see verse 18) but the incident shows us that Jesus was powerful over the mind as well as the body.

So many Christians seem to believe that once they obtain salvation they are to put their minds in neutral and just swim along downstream like a dead fish. NO! God commands us to be active with our minds. We are to study the Scripture. We are to learn of Christ. We are to put our minds in subjection to the Spirit, to be sure. But, the Spirit comes to illumine our minds that we might learn more of Jesus.

Jesus Healed the Woman With the Issue of Blood

Jesus also healed the woman with the issue of blood.

> "And, behold, a woman, which was diseased with an issue of blood twelve years, came behind him, and touched the hem of his garment: For she said within herself, If I may but touch his garment, I shall be whole. But Jesus turned him about, and when he saw her, he said, Daughter, be of good comfort; thy faith hath made thee whole. And the woman was made whole from that hour." (Matthew 9:20-22)

The power of Jesus was so great that this woman was healed simply by touching the hem of His garment. We see the miracle as in the healing. Indeed, that is so. But, consider the miracle that Jesus knew, even in the press of this crowd, who it was that had touched Him.

Just to understand that a certain person had touched Him in this crowd is a miracle of immense proportions. But, Jesus even understood the purpose for which His clothing had been touched.

Jesus is never far from us. He is available to uphold us in our hour of need. When our resources are gone, His resources remain at our fingertips if we will but reach out to Him. He will understand and respond.

What the physicians of the day had not been able to diagnose and heal for twelve years Jesus healed while walking on a mission to another place. Jesus is never too busy to be available for our needs. This can only be said of God. Others would have to follow a list and do things in order; God can do all things at any - or all - times.

Jesus Healed Infirmity

Jesus healed infirmity.

> "And, behold, there was a woman which had a spirit of infirmity eighteen years, and was bowed together, and could in no wise life up herself. And when Jesus saw her, he called her to him, and said unto her, Woman, thou art loosed from thine infirmity. And he laid his hands on her: and immediately she was made straight, and glorified God." (Luke 13:11-13)

Here was a woman who had been bound by a muscular illness for eighteen years. She was completely unable to straighten out her body. We do not even have a record that she called out to Jesus. Now, I am certain that she did call out to Him. It may have only been the cry of her spirit; but I do believe that she called out to Him.

CHAPTER 44: THE POWER OF JESUS TO HEAL

As Jesus approached her, her despair was replaced with rejoicing. Again, we see the loving touch of the Master's Hand. Again we see the power of God through the healing action of Jesus.

Jesus comes to the sinner in His convicting power. Before the sinner even completely realizes his need Jesus comes with the answer for the disease of sin. The sinner responds to the love of Jesus and Jesus applies the healing balm of His Shed Blood to heal the malady of sin.

Jesus Healed the Ear of the Soldier Who Came to Arrest Him

Jesus even responded in love to heal the ear of the soldier who had come to arrest Him in the Garden.

> *"And one of them smote the servant of the high priest, and cut off his right ear. And Jesus answered and said, Suffer ye this far. And he touched his ear, and healed him." (Luke 22:50-51)*

The love of Jesus never fails. Here that love is displayed at the hour of His arrest. Jesus did not want to be "rescued" from this arrest. It was for this purpose that Jesus had come into the world. The greatest healing of all was soon to come as He shed His Blood so that we might be healed of our sin.

The healings of Jesus display His great power as the Lord of Glory. Only the Creator God could have the power to heal the results of sin.

CHAPTER 45
OBSERVATIONS OF THE DIVINE POWER OF JESUS
(Session Forty-Six)

We continue with Zeoli's (*Is Jesus God – Book Number Two*) observations of the Divine power of Jesus.

The Old Testament was replete with prophets who evidenced the power of the Divine in the course of their ministries. Natural forces had been controlled, illnesses had been healed, miracles had been wrought, unknowable knowledge had been exhibited by these prophets of old. These Old Testament prophets produced mighty acts as the Spirit of God moved upon them.

The acts of Jesus were also evidences of supernatural power. But, those acts of Jesus were on a different plane than were the mighty acts of the Old Testament prophets.

The acts of the Old Testament prophets are illustrated by Samson, one of the early prophets of Israel mentioned in the Book of Judges.

"And the Spirit of the LORD came upon him...." (Judges 14:19a)

These prophets of the Old Testament were able to produce their mighty works because the Spirit of God came upon them and empowered them.

Jesus Exhibited This Divine Power from His Own Person

Jesus, meanwhile, exhibited this Divine power from His Own Person at every event of His life. Zeoli asks that we consider the incident of the power of Jesus displayed over the fig tree.

Consider the Fig Tree

"And when he [Jesus] saw a fig tree in the way, he came to it, and found nothing thereon, but leaves only, and said unto it, Let no fruit grow on thee henceforward for ever. And presently the fig tree withered away. And when the disciples saw it, they marvelled, saying, How soon is the fig tree withered away." (Matthew 21:19-20)

It would be good to also consider this account as given by the Gospel of Mark.

"And seeing a fig tree afar off having leaves, he came, if haply he might find any thing thereon; and when he came to it, he found nothing but leaves; for the time of figs was not yet. And Jesus answered and said unto it, No man eat fruit of thee hereafter for ever. And his disciples heard it. ... And in the morning, as they passed by, they saw the fig tree dried up from the roots." (Mark 11:12-13, 20)

With Mark's slightly amplified narrative of this incident we find that the disciples found the tree withered the following day.

We should note that this tree was on a public "right of way" rather than on private ground. Jesus was not destroying someone's private property; He was giving an object lesson to His disciples. Although it was early in the season, the tree was "advertising" that its fruit was ready. The coming of the leaves was an indication of the coming of the fruit.

It is not my intention to give a full exegesis but I would like to note three things about this passage as to its teaching. First, for one to evidence an outward display of "religion" without an inward possession of God's indwelling love is to feign holiness to the detriment of any who might have a hope to follow such a one into the presence of God. This would be an indictment of any "Christian" hypocrite of our day. This would also have been understood as an indictment of the false religion of the "professional" religious person of the disciple's day.

A show of "leaves" without the fruit would never be spiritually fulfilling.

Second, the curse was not immediate. A person may proceed for long periods of time with his false religious system. But, the words of Jesus are certain even when they are delayed for a time. Longfellow quoted von Logau when he wrote, "The mills of the gods grind slowly, yet they grind exceedingly small."

Because God does not act as quickly as we often reason He should we are prone to miss the fact that God does act. Has God brought you to despair?

> "...all things work together for good to them that love God, to them who are the called according to his purpose." (Romans 8:28b)

One of the works of faith is to trust that God will bless His children; our impatience does not defeat the love of God!

Even as God works according to His Own good will in our lives, so also does He often give grace for a season to the lost that they may be induced to come to repentance. As surely as God is good in His grace, He is certain in His judgment of those who would despise His love.

Finally, we see that the curse of the tree came from its roots upward. In the final analysis, we must realize that God is not the Author of Evil. Evil flows from below not from above. The curse and judgment of God comes in response to the sin, inbred and outworked, of a lost humanity who has abandoned the True Author of life and blessing.

For our purposes in the present discussion of course it is enough to see that Jesus did have power over the life, destiny, and death of even the vegetable kingdom. This means that He is the Ruler of the vegetable kingdom. This means that He was the Creator of that vegetable kingdom. This fact shows that Jesus is God.

In our next session we will consider that Jesus had power over Satan.

A quick note: In this session, as well in several past sessions, I have been using the term "Jesus had..." This is accurate in that we are considering incidents as recorded in the Scripture. However, this phrasing is inaccurate in that it implies that the power of Jesus is a thing of the past. Please understand that Jesus is the God of the Present. He is not bound by time. What He was, He is. What He is, He will be. And, though we often miss this fact, what He will be, He is even now.

As the Eternal God, Jesus is not a creature of the past, or even of the future. Jesus is the eternal "Now;" our Constant Contemporary. Jesus, even though we tend with our human eyes to see Him as an historical Person, is not merely historical. Jesus is eternal. He is as real in this day as He was in those past days. And, He will continue to be real, and powerful, in the halls of eternity. Jesus is not bound by time; He is the Author and Keeper of time as time is of His construction.

CHAPTER 46
JESUS EXHIBITED POWER OVER SATAN
(Session Forty-Seven)

Once again we are following the general outline of Zeoli (*Is Jesus God - Book Number Two*) as we consider that Jesus exhibited power over Satan.

> "Then was Jesus led up of the Spirit into the wilderness to be tempted of the devil. And when he had fasted forty days and forty nights, he was afterward an hungered. And when the tempter came to him, he said, If thou be the Son of God, command that these stones be made bread. But he answered and said, It is written, Man shall not live by bread alone, but by every word that proceedeth out of the mouth of God. Then the devil taketh him up into the holy city, and setteth him on a pinnacle of the temple, And he saith unto him, If thou be the Son of God, cast thyself down: for it is written, He shall give his angels charge concerning thee: and in their hands they shall bear thee up, lest at any time thou dash thy foot against a stone. Jesus said unto him, It is written again, Thou shalt not tempt the Lord thy God. Again, the devil taketh him up into an exceeding high mountain, and sheweth him all the kingdoms of the world, and the glory of them; And saith unto him, All these things will I give thee, if thou wilt fall down and worship me. Then saith Jesus unto him, Get thee hence, Satan: for it is written, Thou shalt worship the Lord thy God, and him only shalt thou serve. Then the devil leaveth him, and, behold, angels came and ministered unto him." (Matthew 4:1-11)

The above is the well-known occurrence of the temptation of Jesus on the mountain top. When we consider this incident we are compelled to consider the duality of the nature of Jesus, as the God/Man, and the duality of His purposes upon this earth. An understanding of this concept may be gleaned from Galatians 4:4-5. "But when the fulness of the time was come, God sent forth his Son, made of a woman, made under the law, To redeem them that were under the law, that we might receive the adoption of sons."

This verse speaks of the Virgin Birth of Jesus. To get a fuller examination of this concept I would invite you to consider my book, "*Study on the Virgin Birth*."

We must understand the Jesus never became "not God." Even while being fully human, the offspring of a woman by virtue of the Virgin Birth, Jesus retained His essential quality of Divinity. He was, as the old catechism reminds us, fully God while being fully human. This particular passage in Galatians informs us of both of these natures.

Both of these natures were necessary in order for Jesus to be the Savior. As a human He was able to represent us in that He was one of us. As God He was able to redeem us in that His holiness was applied to us through faith in His sacrifice at Calvary. We understand this only poorly and only through His inspired and preserved Words from the Scripture.

But, what more does His identification with us, as a representative of humanity, inform us of His mission on earth?

When Linda and I were newlyweds she went to a store and bought several yards of cloth. She brought the cloth home and fashioned it into a sports jacket for me. The cloth never stopped being cloth even though Linda fashioned it into that jacket. Admittedly this is a poor illustration. But it may help our finite minds to understand the great Glory of the fact that Jesus was "made" under the law.

Jesus took upon Himself the form, the actual body, of a human being. As such the God Who was Lord of the Law placed Himself under subjection to that law. In this Jesus became our example as to how we should live - as human beings - in our own bodies of humanity.

This was also a purpose of His while He walked those dusty roads of first century Israel. As to our present consideration, Jesus displayed His mastery over Satan by an appeal to the Scriptural record.

God Cannot Be Tempted

We see in James 1:13 that God cannot be tempted. Still, here in this fourth chapter of Matthew we see that Jesus is tempted. This is a temptation of the humanity of Jesus. Satan attempted to gain control of the mission of Christ by several devious temptations.

The reaction of Jesus to the temptations of Satan was on a human plane. Jesus resorted to Scripture. So should we. Scripture defeated Satan. This was an example of the humanity of Jesus teaching the human of this world how to withstand the power and provocation of Satan.

Satan is knowledgeable. Satan is devious. Satan will use lie and deception to overcome the human. Satan is a powerful being. Satan is more powerful than are any of us. Satan even knows the Scripture better than any of us; he will twist the Scripture to fulfill his own purposes. This all being true the Christian is often at an intellectual loss as to how to defend against the adversary.

God has given us the Scripture as a bulwark of defense against the wiles of Satan.

Satan Can Never Defeat God

Satan can never defeat God. Since the Scripture is inspired by God, this means that the Scripture is the very Words of God, when Satan is confronted with Scripture he is confronted by the very Voice of God. Thus, the Scripture is both a defense against Satan and an offensive strategy for the Christian witness in the world at large.

Jesus Has Power Over the Works of Satan

Jesus also has power over the works of Satan.

> "He that committeth sin is of the devil; for the devil sinneth from the beginning. For this purpose the Son of God was manifested, that he might destroy the works of the devil." (I John 3:8)

We see this power most readily observable in the salvation of a soul. That which Satan had controlled is converted into a follower of Jesus.

Jesus Has Power Over Satan, the Destroyer of Life

Jesus also has power over Satan, the destroyer of life.

> "Forasmuch then as the children are partakers of flesh and blood, he also himself likewise took part of the same; that through death he might destroy him that had the power of death, that is, the devil." (Hebrews 2:14)

To the Christian who has been redeemed by the Blood of Jesus, death is no longer

CHAPTER 46: JESUS EXHIBITED POWER OVER SATAN

the enemy. Death is not the cessation of existence. Death is not, for the Christian, the entry way into an eternity of separation.

When I was in the army I often had to transfer from place to place. Sometimes I would board an airplane. Sometimes I would board a passenger train. Sometimes I would get upon a bus and be taken to my next duty station. Often I would simply drive myself. Death to the Christian is simply that: It is a conveyance from one duty station to another. We might dread the carriage; but the glory of the Heavenly barracks of mansion, with the Commanding Officer of the Creator of the Universe, will make all our worries and pain seem trivial, and even joyful, in comparison!

Because of Jesus death is no longer our enemy! We wait, of course, for God's time - to do otherwise would be to abrogate His Own Will for our own! - but we can joyfully enter into His halls with praise and thanksgiving.

> "Therefore doth my Father love me, because I lay down my life, that I might take it again. No man taketh it from me, but I lay it down of myself. I have the power to lay it down, and I have the power to take it again. This commandment have I received of my Father." (John 10:17-18)

At the beginning of our last session I noted the difference between the mighty acts of the Old Testament prophets and the miracles of Jesus. The Old Testament prophets acted as the Spirit came upon them while Jesus acted of His Own volition. Even in the matter of the death of Jesus upon the Cross of Calvary, we see that Jesus was in charge. Even in His resurrection that first Easter morning, we see that Jesus was in charge.

Jesus was speaking of false religion when He said,

> "The thief cometh not, but for the steal, and to kill, and to destroy..." (John 10:10a)

False Religious Systems are Tools of Satan

The false religious systems are tools of Satan used to deceive men. Jesus destroyed these in His victory over Satan. All may freely come to the Savior Who has defeated death and Satan by His Own Power.

Jesus Displayed His Power Over Satan at Calvary

Jesus also displayed His power over Satan at Calvary.

> "Blotting out the handwriting of ordinances that was against us, which was contrary to us, and took it out of the way, nailing it to his cross; And having spoiled principalities and powers, he made a shew of them openly, triumphing over them in it." (Colossians 2:14-15).

You may recall that Pilate put a sign on the cross of Jesus. This was regularly done to all the convicted criminals who were thus put to death. Upon that sign was listed the offense for which the person was being executed. It is with this in mind that Paul wrote that our sins were nailed to the cross.

Jesus died in our place, bearing the penalty for our sins, so that the hold of Satan upon us was defeated! We are free in Christ because Jesus displayed His power over Satan at the Cross of Calvary!

CHAPTER 47
JESUS HAS POWER OVER DEATH AND THE GRAVE
(Session Forty-Eight)

Several Scriptural Instances

Zeoli (*Is Jesus God - Book Number Two*) gives several Scriptural instances where Jesus is shown to have power over death and the grave.

Jesus Rose From the Dead Himself

Most powerfully, we must first note that Jesus rose from the dead Himself.

First of all we must observe that Jesus understood that He would die. Along with this natural understanding was the prophetic, and to us unnatural, understanding that He would rise from the dead.

> "Jesus answered and said unto them, Destroy this temple, and in three days I will raise it up. Then said the Jews, Forty and six years was this temple in building, and wilt thou rear is up in three days? But he spake of the temple of his body. When therefore he was risen from the dead, his disciples remembered that he had said this unto them: and they believed the scripture, and the word which Jesus had said." (John 2:19-22)

Jesus' Death Was a Glorious Culmination of His Planned Ministry to Humanity

This incident happened very early in the earthly ministry of Jesus. Some would argue that the death of Jesus on the Cross of Calvary was an inglorious end to His teaching ministry. Such is not the case. The death of Jesus, as horrible a death as it was, was a glorious culmination of His planned ministry to humanity. Jesus came to die in time so that others could live in eternity!

There are also those who would argue for a sort of "Divine Suicide" in the death of Jesus. The argument is correct in that Jesus came to earth with the express purpose of dying for the sins of humanity. Such an argument is not correct in that Jesus did not actively deliver Himself into the hands of His killers. Sinful humanity, in the person of Judas, delivered Jesus to the Cross. False religion, in the person of religious leaders opposed to Him, delivered Jesus to the Cross. Sinful world systems, in the person of the Roman government, delivered Jesus to the Cross. Sinners such as I delivered Jesus to the Cross in order for Him to offer free and full salvation from those sins.

Jesus, from the natural perspective, died from the very hands He had come to deliver from sin and death.

This death, however, seen from this perspective would not have effected our salvation. Zeoli looks further to John 10:18. I add a look at the preceding verse as well as a matter of clarification.

> "Therefore doth my Father love me, because I lay down my life, that I might take it again. No man taketh it from me, but I lay it down of myself. I have power to lay it down, and I have power to take it again. This commandment have I received of my

Father." (John 10:17-18)

We see in this passage two very important points. The first is that Jesus came to live among humanity with the express purpose of giving His human life as a sacrifice for sinful mankind. Although He allowed events to conspire to send Him to the cross, His death was not as a victim. His purpose was to offer Himself as a sacrifice for sin among the very race of humanity who, humanly speaking, caused His death.

Luke 23:34 records Jesus as saying,

"...Father, forgive them; for they know not what they do..."

Indeed, neither the soldiers who actively crucified Him, nor the religious leaders who gave Him over for that crucifixion - nor the crowd who jeered Him at His hour of death, understood the greater purpose of His ultimate sacrifice. Jesus came to this earth to die in time so that others might live in eternity!

Speaking of Himself and His mission on earth, Jesus said,

"Even as the Son of man came not to be ministered unto, but to minister, and to give his life a ransom for many." (Matthew 20:28)

This verse adds an important consideration to our contemplation upon this great sacrifice of Jesus. Jesus did not die for all. This is a great theological "sticking point." Positionally Jesus did die, of course, for the sins of the world. Practically we must admit that this sacrifice is only effective upon those who have accepted Him as Savior.

This should be a great cause for reflection. Even as we study doctrine we must not neglect the necessity for our own soul's salvation! Jesus says that His sacrifice was of more importance than was His "ministry." His ethical and religious teaching *cannot* save a soul from the just judgment for sin. It is His death on the Cross of Calvary by which we are brought into salvation by His shed blood.

As to the second point in our discussion of John 10:18, we see that Jesus had power even over His Own death. More specifically, we see that Jesus raised Himself from the dead. This is an act only possible by the God of the universe. Remember, we said before that the Old Testament prophets acted when the Spirit came upon them? Jesus was not a prophet while on this earth; Jesus was (and is!) God.

John said (John 1:4), speaking of Jesus, "In him was life..." Jesus is the Author of Life. Therefore Jesus is the Very God of the Universe.

Jesus Is Shown to Have Ultimate Authority Over Death

Jesus is also shown to have ultimate authority over death.

"Who [Jesus] hath saved us, and called us with an holy calling, not according to our works, but according to his own purpose and grace, which was given us in Christ Jesus before the world began, But is now made manifest by the appearing of our Saviour Jesus Christ, who hath abolished death, and hath brought life and immortality to light through the gospel." (II Timothy 1:9-10)

It is a reality that Jesus has abolished death as a foe for the Christian. Death has become, for the Christian, nothing more than an entryway from the trials and turmoil of our human existence into the glories of an eternal existence with our Lord and Savior.

This is a glorious thought that too many of us have trouble accepting. It isn't a hard concept to grasp when the dying person is someone else. When it is us it is often not so easy a concept.

CHAPTER 47: JESUS HAS POWER OVER DEATH AND THE GRAVE

Why?

Well, there are several possible answers to this. One concerns the creation of our race in Adam. We were created as persons of time and physicality. This truth is spoken, "before the world began," from the spiritual and eternal. We have no experiential human basis to understand. But, as we draw closer to Jesus we are compelled to begin to see things from the perspective of faith. In faith we are allowed to accept that which we cannot understand simply because God said it was so.

Another reason we might have problems is more spiritual in nature. When Linda and I were working we would long for that two week period every summer which we called "vacation." This did not mean that we could ignore the fact, for the other fifty weeks of the year, that we had jobs which needed to be done.

God has given us work to do on this earth. We have an obligation to Him, as well as to those other humans with whom we come in contact, to spread the peace of the Gospel message. We need to be about the Father's work until He calls us to our rest.

The point here is that Jesus has taken control of what humanity might consider the greatest foe - death is defeated by Jesus Christ. In this He has displayed His divine authority as the mighty God of the Universe.

CHAPTER 48
JESUS' POWER OVER DEATH
(Session Forty-Nine)

We continue examining the Deity of Jesus. We continue to consider the Scripture passages as referenced in the work of Zeoli (*Is Jesus God - Book Number Two*) as our guide.

Several Examples

There are several examples in Scripture where Jesus displayed His power over death.

The Son of the Widow of Nain

The first of these examples is that of the son of the widow of Nain.

> *"And it came to pass the day after, that he went into a city called Nain; and many of his disciples went with him, and much people. And when he came nigh to the gate of the city, behold, there was a dead man carried out, the only son of his mother, and she was a widow: and much people of the city was with her. And when the Lord saw her, he had compassion on her, and said unto her, Weep not. And he came and touched the bier and they that bare him stood still. And he said, Young man, I say unto thee, Arise. And he that was dead sat up, and began to speak. And he delivered him to his mother. And there came a fear on all: and they glorified God, saying, That a great prophet is risen up among us; and, That God hath visited his people."* (Luke 7:11-16)

Notice the situation at this funeral. The dead man was the only son of his widow mother. There was no welfare available for this poor woman. She was in a terrible situation. The mourners, actual and professional, who attended this procession were sobbing and lamenting the fact of the death of this dear son. This was chaos.

But into the chaos came the compassion of Christ.

I was at the visitation before the funeral of a dear friend a few weeks ago. There, lying in the casket was the body of a man I loved and respected. I had known him nearly my entire life. We had gone through school together. We had often walked to school together. I had played with him as a youth. I had been in his boyhood home. He had been in my home. I felt the pain of the moment as happy memories mingled with the grief of the moment.

Suddenly I felt a strong hand on my shoulder. A voice I knew well said, "It's going to be alright. We'll all get through this." I looked at the one who was comforting me. It was the brother of the man in the casket. In his own hour of intense grief, with his younger brother in that casket, this man took the time to console me.

I might well have asked, "What manner of man is this that comforts others even through his own grief and pain?" I knew the man who comforted me. I knew his family. This was just the way they operated in life. They continued to consider others.

But, this man who comforted me could offer nothing except his words of comfort. Jesus had the ability to set the situation aright. Jesus not only told the widow to not weep, He gave her back the son of her youth. Jesus restored this young man to useful life.

None but the God Who originally created life could have worked this miracle of consolation and celebration. Jesus is God Almighty!

The Matter of Jarius' Daughter

Jesus also displayed His power over death in the matter of Jarius' daughter.

> *While he spake these things unto them, behold, there came a certain ruler, and worshiped him, saying, My daughter is even now dead: but come and lay thy hand upon her, and she shall live. And Jesus arose, and followed him, and so did his disciples. And, behold, a woman, which was diseased with an issue of blood twelve years, came behind him, and touched the hem of his garment. For she said within herself, If I may but touch his garment, I shall be whole. But Jesus turned him about, and when he saw her, he said, Daughter, be of good comfort; thy faith hath made thee whole. And the woman was made whole from that hour. And when Jesus came into the ruler's house, and saw the minstrels and the people making a noise, He said unto them, Give place: for the maid is not dead, but sleepeth. And they laughed him to scorn. But when the people were put forth, he went in, and took her by the hand, and the maid arose. And the fame hereof went abroad into all that land. (Matthew 9:18-26)*

We could spend time discussing the healing of the woman who touched the hem of His garment. This is a tremendous miracle. The woman didn't talk to Jesus. Jesus didn't talk to the woman. The woman was just healed in response to her own response of faith. That is enough to infer that Jesus is Deity incarnate.

But, let us consider the daughter of Jarius. We must recall that this incident did not happen in our own day. Distances were covered by foot. No one called this man, Jarius, on his cell phone to tell him that his daughter had just died. No one rushed Jesus to the girl's side in an ambulance with lights flashing and siren wailing.

The girl was dead when Jarius left the house. The girl remained dead while Jarius walked those dusty streets in his grief.

While Jarius was walking, probably in a daze of anguish, he saw a crowd thronging around a man. Jarius looked at the tumult and saw Jesus. Whether Jarius recognized Jesus or someone pointed Him out we do not know. Surely Jarius at the least knew about Jesus. He may not have had all his theology straight but Jarius knew that Jesus could fulfill his deepest need. At this point the deepest need of Jarius was to see his daughter alive.

I doubt that Jarius walked to Jesus. Surely he ran with all the speed his sandal clad feet could muster. "Jesus! My daughter is dead. A simple touch from You can restore her to life. I believe that You can work this miracle!"

With thoughts such as this Jarius made his way quickly to Jesus. Jarius heard the blessed words that Jesus would come with him. What joy must Jarius have felt.

Then Jesus suddenly stopped. He questioned His disciples about a woman touching Him. Jarius must have thought, "With all this crowd about Him? He's looking for one woman. Good grief! She's alive! My daughter is dead! We need to get back to my house!"

Sometimes we get like that don't we? We get anxious about things over which we have no control. We trust God. But, we'd sure like to trust Him a little quicker!

Jesus didn't worry about the small side trip. The daughter of Jarius was dead.

CHAPTER 48: JESUS POWER OVER DEATH

He'd fix that. For now Jesus was concerned about healing another lady. This wasn't a picture of callousness toward Jarius. This was a matter of compassion on the lady who touched the hem of His garment. Let us never worry about time. The God of eternity will do His work. Our faith in Him may be tried and perfected as we wait upon His touch.

What of the daughter of Jarius? When Jesus finally reached the house He said, "She's not dead; she's only sleeping." The mourners knew better - at least they thought they did. They laughed at the assessment of Jesus. The derided Him. Jesus ordered these people out of the room.

Faith is an often derided aspect about the Christian life. People are fond of saying that we have our heads in the clouds rather than on the firm earth of reality. The people do not understand real reality. When our heads are in the clouds we are closer to the abode of God. We are closer to His reality and power.

Jesus took this dead girl, who had been dead for some time, by the hand. He said, "Wake up child." This was not a release from a coma. The girl had been dead for some time. This was not a mass hallucination. The crowd was gone. The proof was that the dead girl was raised back to life by the touch of the Master's hand.

Jesus is God Almighty.

Jesus Raised Lazarus From the Dead

Most people are familiar with the incident where Jesus raised Lazarus from the dead. The central part of the narrative is found in John 11:32-35:

> *"Then when Mary was come where Jesus was, and saw him, she fell down at his feet, saying unto him, Lord, if thou hadst been here, my brother had not died. When Jesus therefore saw her weeping, and the Jews also weeping which came with her, he groaned in the spirit, and was troubled, And said, Where have ye laid him? They said unto him, Lord, come and see. Jesus wept."*

As we read this entire history we are struck by the great faith, and the great doubt, of those present at this grave site. Mary displayed a great faith when she said, in verse 32, "...Lord, if thou hadst been here, my brother had not died."

Forget for a moment that this is nearly an accusatory statement. "Jesus," she seemed to say, "It's too bad you didn't come quickly to the side of my ailing brother." She knew that Jesus could have healed Lazarus from whatever sickness had ended his life. This woman knew that Jesus had healed others. She knew He could have healed her brother.

Just a few verses previous, verse 23, Jesus had told Martha that her brother would live again. The faith of Martha replied that she did know that Lazarus would live again at the resurrection of the last day.

Later, at the grave in verse 39, Jesus asked that the stone which covered the grave crypt be removed. The faith of Martha would only allow her to say, "Lord, it's been four days. He has begun to decompose. 'He stinketh.'"

The tears of Jesus were not for Lazarus. Jesus knew what was going to shortly happen. Jesus didn't weep in sympathy for those mourners at the grave site. He wept because of the unbelief of those who would do anything except put faith in Him.

So hostile to the Lord were some that they would do anything to remove His message of love and forgiveness. "But the chief priests consulted that they might put

Lazarus also to death." (John 12:10) If Lazarus would cause anyone to accept Jesus, then Lazarus must die as well!

This particular incident could not be passed off as a simple "resuscitation." Lazarus had been dead for four days. Decomposition had already begun on his body. This was a resurrection. Lazarus had not passed out and awakened; he had died and was resurrected by the Power of Almighty God. The same God who had breathed life in Adam in the Garden had restored life to Lazarus in a grave yard.

Jesus is that God.

The blessed hope, the blessed reality, for the Christian is that this same Jesus will raise all the redeemed.

> "And this is the Father's will which hath sent me, that of all which he hath given me I should lose nothing, but should raise it up again at the last day. And this is the will of him that sent me, that every one which seeth the Son, and believeth on him, may have everlasting life: and I will raise him up at the last day." (John 6:39-40) "Jesus said unto her, I am the resurrection, and the life: he that believeth in me, though he were dead, yet shall he live." (John 11:25) "For the Lord himself shall descend from heaven with a shout, with the voice of the archangel, and with the trump of God: and the dead in Christ shall rise first." (I Thessalonians 4:16)

These are not simply words to be uttered at the funeral of a saint of God. It is good that we have this assurance from God. Paul did write the inspired words,

> "But I would not have you to be ignorant, brethren, concerning them which are asleep, that ye sorrow not, even as others which have no hope." (I Thessalonians 4:13)

We sorrow and grieve at the temporary loss of a loved one who has gone on to heaven. But, unlike the world at large, we have the great hope of the power of God. We are not separated from those loved ones. We are only parted for a season. They have gone on the same trip we must some day take if the Lord tarries His coming. We will meet them in "the sweet bye and bye."

Paul understood this fact. Paul knew that his hope would be rewarded with the reality of Heaven.

> "...for I know whom I have believed, and am persuaded that he is able to keep that which I have committed unto him against that day." (II Timothy 1:12b)

Only the Great God Who created all things could give that certain guarantee. John 1:3 tells us that Jesus is that Creator God. He has already displayed His power on earth. We can trust Him to display His power, as He promised - and He does not lie! - on that day just as He has prophesied and promised!

CHAPTER 49
JESUS HAS ALL POWER IN HEAVEN AND IN EARTH
(Session Fifty)

With today's session we close this section on the Attributes of Deity which were incumbent upon Jesus as God. We continue to follow the "stick outline" as presented by Zeoli.

First, Jesus Has All Power in Heaven and in Earth

The first thing to note in this session is that Jesus has all power in heaven and in earth.

> "And Jesus came and spake unto them, saying, All power is given unto me in heaven and in earth." (Matthew 28:18)

The English word "given" might give us pause in our consideration of the Deity of Christ were it not for the realization of His dual role while physically on this earth. Jesus came to be a human so that He could be The Perfect Sacrifice for our sins. As a human He accepted certain limitations on His essential Deity, through the kenosis, so that He might be representative of our humanity. We realize this even as we realize that He, at no point, ever was divested of His essential Godhood.

This being said, we also realize that He acted fully in His humanity as our Representative. In this we see that He was our example of a Godly life for humanity. Although co-equal with the Father in His Godhood, Jesus nonetheless deferred to the Father as a human. In this Jesus taught us that we should always be in subjection to God.

Jesus was not given anything "new." His power and authority as God was now being assumed, as was His right, as the human Jesus. He had completed His role as example and sacrifice and was now assuming His rightful role, even in His humanity, as God.

The fact is easily seen when we consider that this power was both in Heaven and in Earth. One who would deny His full Deity might argue that Jesus had all power in Earth, the created and time-centric arena of human capabilities. But Jesus was also asserting that He had all power, and the authority of this power, in Heaven.

Heaven is the abode of God. No one would argue that fact. For Jesus to assert that He had all power in this spiritual and eternal realm is a full statement of His essential Deity. A "created god," as claimed by the Jehovah Witness cult, would be forever subservient to the "Creator God." For Jesus to be equal with this "Creator God" would raise the absurd impossibility that both would have <u>all</u> power and <u>all</u> authority. One would be naturally "superior" to the other under that unbiblical scenario.

Since Jesus was this "Creator God," see John 1:3, Jesus is not a created "sub God." He is the very God of eternity. Jesus is fully of the eternal essence of God. He is fully resident within the triune Godhead.

Upon consideration of this verse we should consider that the Great Commission is a lawful order from God. It is the authority of God, given to us, to propagate the Christian religion into the world as a whole. Two things stand out in this regard.

First, we are bound, as soldiers of the Cross to comply with our lawful order from our superior. To fail to send forth the message that Jesus died in time so that others could live in eternity is our bound duty. Simply put, if we do not do this it will not be done. The fault lies at our door.

As a corollary of this charge, we are to instruct those converts in the doctrines of Jesus so that they can begin to take their own place in heralding the truth of the Gospel. A companion with this corollary is that we are to "baptize" believers. This constitutes an order to maintain the churches which Jesus first founded.

The second thing which stands out is that the power to fulfill that witness required of us continues to reside in Jesus. Our responsibility is to carry forth the message. His authority is the empowerment of that message.

Jesus Has a Displayed Power Over the Elements

We also must note that Jesus has a displayed power over the elements.

> *"And he saith unto them, Why are ye so fearful, O ye of little faith? Then he arose, and rebuked the winds and the sea; and there was a great calm. But the men marvelled, saying, What manner of man is this, that even the winds and the sea obey him?" (Matthew 8:26-27)*

We are all familiar with this incident. Jesus and the disciples were out in the sea in one of the small boats of the time. A great storm arose. The disciples were afraid that they would be swamped. They went to Jesus and found Him sleeping in the midst of the storm.

The disciples woke up Jesus and said, "Ain't you scared you're gonna drown?" O. K. They didn't say exactly that! You'll only find those words in the ODM Version; that's the Original DeWitt Mistranslation Version! Still, having been in a few serious storms in my time I would guess that this is pretty much what they meant.

Jesus wasn't worried in the least. I'll bet that He just looked at these disciples, shook His head with a wry smile, and said, "Wind! Waves! You're scaring these guys! Cut it out!" Again, the ODM Version.

As soon as Jesus said this the wind and the waves just stopped. There was a great calm. Now, I've seen the wind just stop on a dime. One minute the wind is carrying your kite from Pittsburgh to Philadelphia. The next minute you are running out to pick up a broken kite that just fell out of the sky. That, sometimes, happens.

You know what never happens? The waves never stop that abruptly. Never! But, they did at the Word of Jesus. Even with the wind stopped the inertia of the waves would mean that they will continue to run for a while - probably a long while if the winds were as bad as in a severe storm! But here, the winds stopped at the command of He Who had created the wind, wave, inertia and all those other physical laws.

Jesus is God.

Jesus Has the Power of Upholding the Entirety of the Created Universe

Jesus also has the power of upholding the entirety of the created universe.

> *"Who being the brightness of his glory, and the express image of his person, and upholding all things by the word of his power, when he had by himself purged our*

CHAPTER 49: JESUS HAS ALL POWER IN HEAVEN AND EARTH

sins, sat down on the right hand of the Majesty on High..." (Hebrews 1:3)

There is quite a bit in this little verse. Jesus is called the glory of, and the express image of, the Godhead. He is shown to be this in His Own Person. He has purged our sins. He is now seated on the right hand, a symbol of power and honor, on high; this means in heaven.

What we sometimes just gloss over in reading this verse is that Jesus upholds all things by the word of His power. This is the express power of Jesus which upholds over all of the time and physicality of the creation.

Jesus is The Great God!

Jesus Has the Power to Change Our Bodies

We also see that Jesus has the power to change our bodies.

"For our conversation is in heaven; from whence also we look for the Saviour, the Lord Jesus Christ: Who shall change our vile body, that it may be fashioned like unto his glorious body, according to the working whereby he is able even to subdue all things unto himself." (Philippians 3:20-21)

Jesus has already done this in part. He has saved our souls from the old nature of sin and presented us unto the Father as persons holy and acceptable unto eternal life.

What glory and praise we should render to Jesus that even our physical bodies will be changed.

"For this corruptible must put on incorruption, and this mortal must put on immortality." (I Corinthians 15:53)

In the past few months I have developed a close personal relationship with a gent named Arthur. "Arthritis" is his full name. I think he likes me a whole bunch more than I like him! I have diabetes. I have breathing problems. I have a bad heart. (No one can say, "He's old, fat, and ugly, but he's got a good heart!" I don't!) The doctor said that I have Congestive Heart Failure. I tried to get him to use the word "potential" in there somewhere but he wouldn't do it.

I'll be honest. Most of my medical problems are from my heredity. My parents just had me far too long ago! I find it wonderful that Jesus will heal all my maladies and even give this old body and overhaul. What glories await us as the Children of God!

It is only the power of God, Almighty, which can do this work. Jesus is God.

Jesus also has power over principalities and powers.

"And ye are complete in him, which is the head of all principality and power." (Colossians 2:10)

The *Defined King James Bible* defines "principality" as, "princely rank, dignity, or jurisdiction; princely territory or country." This simply means that Jesus is the Ultimate King of Kings. It is He that is in ultimate charge of even these earthly nations.

"Let every soul be subject unto the higher powers. For there is no power but of God: the powers that be are ordained of God." (Romans 13:1)

We may not agree with all the rulers that are, civilly, over us. God has set these persons in power for the working out of His Own great prophetic plans. In our form of representative government (in theory!) we have a duty to seek out Godly persons with Godly agenda when we enter those voting booths. That is our duty to God and Country. Still, the ultimate distribution of earthly power lies in the prerogatives of God.

Sometimes our highest duty is to live as Godly people in an ungodly nation. We then let our "light" shine (Matthew 5:16) of Christian witness and responsibility. Sometimes the beacon is brightest where the night is darkest.

Jesus Has Power Among Humanity

Jesus has power among humanity. Many of the dictators and politicians have displayed this type of power. But, Jesus also has power over demons.

> "When even was come, they brought unto him many that were possessed with devils: and he cast out the spirits with his word, and healed all that were sick." (Matthew 8:16)

Very little comment is needed at this point. Jesus had authority over the demons in that He was able to cast them out. They had to obey His voice and demand. This does not mean that they were subservient to Him in the sense of Master / subject. The demons are His adversaries. His authority over them was, however, complete when He spoke the word. This is because when Jesus spoke He spoke the Word of God.

These demon entities knew that their time was short to perform their nefarious deeds. Their time on this earth is both a training aid to show the superiority of God's glory and a punishment upon sinful humanity.

> "And, behold, they [the demons] cried out, saying, What have we to do with thee, Jesus, thou Son of God? art thou come hither to torment us before the time?" (Matthew 8:29.

Ultimately they knew that Jesus was Divine and had complete authority over them.

An interesting incident is reported in Acts.

> "And God wrought special miracles by the hands of Paul. So that from his body were brought unto the sick handkerchiefs or aprons, and the diseases departed from them, and the evil spirits went out of them. Then certain of the vagabond Jews, exorcists, took upon them to call over them which had evil spirits the name of the Lord Jesus, saying, We adjure you by Jesus whom Paul preacheth. And there were seven sons of one Sceva, a Jew, and chief of the priests, which did so, And the evil spirit answered and said, Jesus I know, and Paul I know; but who are ye? And the man in whom the evil spirit was leaped upon them, and overcame them, and prevailed against them, so that they fled out of that house naked and wounded." (Acts 19:11-18)

Paul had been preaching under the authority of Jesus as given in the Great Commission. It was not Paul to whom the demons subjected themselves. When the ungodly men attempted to simply use the "name" of Jesus as a talisman, they were rebuked by those same demons.

The demons are subject to Jesus because Jesus is God and has authority over them. Jesus may grant this authority to His agents. Others who attempt to "counterfeit" the Majesty and Power of Jesus will do so at their own risk!

We have already noted that Jesus has the power over Hell and death.

> "I am he that liveth, and was dead; and, behold, I am alive for evermore, Amen; and have the keys of hell and of death." (Revelation 1:18)

Jesus Has Power of Hell and Death

Only He Who created would have the power of both Hell and death upon the creature. Jesus is God.

CHAPTER 49: JESUS HAS ALL POWER IN HEAVEN AND EARTH

As we have seen in this section, Jesus has all the attributes of Deity. I have certain physical attributes: I am short. I am fat. I am old. I am ugly. But, more than this, I am also sometimes short tempered. I am also generally vain - although there is scant evidence to substantiate any basis for this particular character flaw! I am alternately talkative and quite. There is more. It is these "attributes" of mine that are the make up of who I am.

The attributes of Jesus were those of Deity. Jesus is God.

CHAPTER 50
THE AUTHORITY OF JESUS
(Session Fifty-One)

In our last section we discussed the attributes of Divinity which were displayed in the Person of Jesus. In this session we will consider the authority which Jesus exhibited based upon that authority.

The Teaching of Jesus Exhibited This Authority

Even the teaching of Jesus exhibited this authority.

> "And they were astonished at his doctrine: for he taught them as one that had authority, and not as the scribes." (Mark 1:22)

This, His teaching ministry, was not necessarily founded on demands, as such. The demands of the teaching of Jesus were tied to His Own authority; He did not appeal to either the authority of man or antiquity. His teaching authority was tied to Scripture. Even here He did not quote the opinion of others as to the meaning of Scripture. As the Author of the Scripture, He was able to give the true - often overlooked or overlaid by tradition - meaning of that Scripture.

Alford (*The New Testament for English Readers*) appeals to Philippians 2:7.

> "But made himself of no reputation, and took upon him the form of a servant, and was made in the likeness of men."

Alford notes that Jesus used His equality with God as an opportunity for "...self-abasement." In other words, Jesus chose to use His authority as a servant in the form of a man.

His authority was then more than the simple, or not so simple!, spoken word. He exercised the authority of example as He lived His earthly life as an example of how mankind ought to live their own lives in subjection to God.

Jesus Exercised His Authority in All Situations

Jesus exercised His authority in all situations. In His private life He withstood the temptations of Satan as referenced in Matthew 4:1-11.

> "Then was Jesus led up of the Spirit into the wilderness to be tempted of the devil. And when he had fasted forty days and forty nights, he was afterward an hungered. And when the tempter came to him, he said, If thou be the Son of God, command that these stones be made bread. But he answered and said, It is written, Man shall not live by bread alone, but by every word that proceedeth out of the mouth of God. Then the devil taketh him up into the holy city, and setteth him on a pinnacle of the temple, And he saith unto him, If thou be the Son of God, cast thyself down: for it is written, He shall give his angels charge concerning thee: and in their hands they shall bear thee up, lest at any time thou dash thy foot against a stone. Jesus said unto him, It is written again, Thou shalt not tempt the Lord thy God. Again, the devil taketh him up into an exceeding high mountain, and sheweth him all the kingdoms of the world, and the glory of them; And saith unto him, All these things will I give thee, if thou wilt fall down and worship me. Then saith Jesus unto him, Get thee hence, Satan: for it is written, Thou shalt worship the Lord thy God, and him only

shalt thou serve. Then the devil leaveth him, and, behold, angels came and ministered unto him."

Once again, referencing that Jesus displayed His authority as an example to humanity, we must note that in every one of these listed temptations Jesus appealed to the authority of preserved Scripture.

As we have seen previously Jesus had personal authority over the demonic elements. This authority He did exercise on the behalf of those to whom He ministered. In His humanity, however, Jesus did not resort to this Divine authority. Instead, He gave the example that we must follow. He appealed to the power of Scripture.

I would note two things in this example. First, of course, is that we are not divine in our own natures. We cannot of ourselves exercise power over the demonic elements. We can, however, appeal to both Scripture, and the God of that Scripture, as refuge and resource in temptation and trial. This is our manner of Spiritual Battle.

Jesus Displayed Trust In the Scripture

Second is the attitude of Jesus toward that Scripture. He did not see Scripture as a "maybe' which was subject to the whims of time and humanity. He displayed a trust, as an example to us in this instance, in the Scripture as the Words of God. That is important. A lost, even a somewhat "recovered" Scripture is not sufficient in the Spiritual arena. A lost, even a somewhat "recovered" Scripture is become - at its heart - the words and works of man.

Inspired Scripture is the voice of God. As such it is The Voice of eternity and not subject to decay of time or humanity. The inspired Scripture of God is also the preserved Scripture of God by its very nature as "God breathed."

When we mentioned above the "private life" of Jesus we did not mean private in the sense as hid from public view. What was meant was the Jesus exhibited His authority at all times. Even when there was no thronging crowd He acted as God. His authority was not for a "show" or "teaching" only. His authority as God was simply Who He was - and still is!

Jesus Answers to Religious Leaders Displayed His Authority

Jesus withstood the wiles of His accusers in His public life. We see many examples of Jesus being questioned by the religious leaders. Always His answers were such as to display His authority.

We may reference a point during the Triumphal Entry of what we call "Palm Sunday."

> *"And some of the Pharisees from among the multitude said unto him, Master, rebuke thy disciples. And he answered and said unto them, I tell you that if these should hold their peace, the stones would immediately cry out." (Luke 19:39-40)*

The argument of Jesus was that there was honest joy in the fact that the Messiah was entering into the holy city of Jerusalem. I don't believe that these religious leaders understood just what it was that Jesus was saying at this point. This does not detract from the authority of His statement about Himself and the fulfillment of prophecy.

Jesus Exercised His Authority in His Ministerial Life

Jesus exercised His authority in His ministerial life. When Nicodemus came to speak with Jesus, Jesus gave him authoritative teaching about the meaning of the "New Birth."

CHAPTER 50: THE AUTHORITY OF JESUS

"There was a man of the Pharisees, named Nicodemus, a ruler of the Jews: The same came to Jesus by night, and said unto him, Rabbi, we know that thou art a teacher come from God: for no man can do these miracles that thou doest, except God be with him. Jesus answered and said unto him, Verily, verily, I say unto thee, Except a man be born again, he cannot see the kingdom of God. Nicodemus saith unto him, How can a man be born when he is old? can he enter the second time into his mother's womb, and be born? Jesus answered, Verily, verily, I say unto thee, Except a man be born of water and of the Spirit, he cannot enter into the kingdom of God. That which is born of the flesh is flesh; and that which is born of the Spirit is spirit. Marvel not that I said unto thee, ye must be born again. The wind bloweth where it listeth, and thou hearest the sound thereof, but canst not tell whence it cometh, and whither it goeth: so is every one that is born of the Spirit. Nicodemus answered and said unto him, How can these things be? Jesus answered and said unto him, Art thou a master of Israel, and knowest not these things. Verily, verily, I say unto thee, We speak that we do know, and testify that we have seen; and ye receive not our witness. If I have told you earthly things, and ye believe not, how shall ye believe, if I tell you of heavenly things? And no man hath ascended up to heaven, but he that came down from heaven, even the Son of man which is in heaven. And as Moses lifted up the serpent in the wilderness, even so must the Son of man be lifted up: That whosoever believeth in him should not perish, but have eternal life. For God so loved the world, that he gave his only begotten Son, that whosoever believeth in him should not perish, but have everlasting life. For God sent not his Son into the world to condemn the world; but that the world through him might be saved. He that believeth on him is not condemned: but he that believeth not is condemned already, because he hath not believed in the name of the only begotten Son of God. And this is the condemnation, that light is come into the world, and men loved darkness rather than light, because their deeds were evil. For every one that doeth evil hateth the light, neither cometh to the light, lest his deeds should be reproved. But he that doeth truth cometh to the light, that his deeds may be made manifest, that they are wrought in God." (John 3:1-21)

Nicodemus asked Jesus a religious question. Jesus answered with more than mere religion. Jesus answered with the formula of life. He told Nicodemus that the need was not to find "religious" teaching but to find eternal life through the new birth.

Jesus argued that a true relationship with God was more than simple adherence to a religious rite. What was needed was a radical departure from life as usual. Even religious life as usual was of no consequence. What was needed was a new birth beyond the physical birth of sin and carnality. Jesus used His authority to teach of a life above sin and unto God.

Jesus Retrained Control, Authority, At His Trial

The Life Application Bible notes that Jesus retrained control even at His trial.

"Then saith Pilate unto him, Speakest thou not unto me? knowest thou not that I have power to crucify thee, and have power to release thee?" (John 19:10)

In the very next verse Jesus corrected this misunderstanding of Pilate.

"Jesus answered, Thou couldest have no power at all against me, except it were given thee from above..." (John 19:11a)

At the first during His interrogation by Pilate, Jesus had not spoken. This was in answer to prophecy.

> *"He was oppressed, and he was afflicted, yet he opened not his mouth: he is brought as a lamb to the slaughter, and as a sheep before her shearers is dumb, so he openeth not his mouth." (Isaiah 53:7)*

Jesus, the Living Word, spoke of His authority to Pilate even as He had refrained from speaking in asserting the authority of His Written Word.

The Authority of Jesus Displayed Even in His Physical Death

Alford (*The New Testament for English Readers*) sees the authority of Jesus displayed even in His physical death. His death was due to His command.

> *"And when Jesus had cried with a loud voice, he said, Father, into thy hands I commend my spirit: and having said thus, he gave up the ghost." (Luke 23:46)*

Even the Romans were surprised at how quickly Jesus had died from their crucifixion. One of the number of those who were physically responsible for the crucifixion had to thrust Him through with a spear in order to be certain of His death.

The Death of Jesus Was Not an Accident

The death of Jesus was not an accident. Neither was His death a simple miscarriage of human justice, although it was certainly this. Beyond the plans of the religious leaders, beyond the cruelty of the Roman legions, the death of Jesus was the plan of God whereby redemption was offered to sinful humanity.

Jesus did not die a victim. He died The Victor. His Own authority and love, as The Great Creator God, sent Him to the Cross of Calvary. Jesus died in time so that we might live in eternity!

CHAPTER 51
JESUS DISPLAYED IN HIS ACTIONS THE TRUTH THAT HE WAS AND IS GOD
(Session Fifty-Two)

We would note that Jesus displayed His authority. Many have argued that they doubt the full Divinity of Jesus because "He never said He was God." This is a ridiculous charge. It is a charge which fails to examine the simple evidence of the New Testament narrative. Jesus didn't simply say, "I am God," He displayed that Truth in His actions.

Actions not only speak louder than words, actions prove their point without a need to access mere words. I could say that I could run a mile in four minutes or less. For me that is bragging without the possibility of producing. If I were to attempt to run a mile at all I would be gasping for breath and carted off in an ambulance within the first two hundred yards.

I can say; but I can't do!

Jesus Simply Proved the Point by His Actions and Authority

Jesus, meanwhile, did not have to say He was Divine. He simply proved the point by His actions and authority over the time/physicality arena of the created world. His authority, as Creator, over the created realms proved that Jesus is, indeed, God.

The Authority of Jesus to Judge Humanity

> "When the Son of man shall come in his glory, and all the holy angels come with him, then shall he sit upon the throne of his glory: And before him shall be gathered all nations: and he shall separate them one from another, as a shepherd divideth his sheep from the goats: And he shall set the sheep on his right hand, but the goats on the left. Then shall the King say unto them on his right hand, Come, ye blessed of my Father, inherit the kingdom prepared for you from the foundation of the world." (Matthew 25:31-34)

John R. Rice (*The Rice Reference Bible*) comments on this passage. He notes that this is not the Great White Throne Judgment spoken of in Revelation 20:11-15. Rather this is the judgment at the conclusion of the Tribulation period. Notice that Jesus is the Judge of humanity as He allocates blessing and judgment upon humanity.

Rice concludes that this is not a judgment of nations, as such, but a judgment of individuals. He sees that the word "nations" is "ethnos" which means "Gentiles." These people are being judged by Jesus Christ.

Listen to Psalm 50:6,

> "And the heavens shall declare his righteousness: for God is judge himself. Selah."

The inspired and preserved Scripture demands of humanity that they not act as judge of others.

> "Judge not, that ye be not judged." (Matthew 7:1)

This is an interesting passage if Jesus be not God in the flesh.

Isaiah 14:12-14 says of Satan,

> "How art thou fallen from heaven, O Lucifer, son of the morning! how art thou cut down to the ground, which didst weaken the nations! For thou hast said in thine heart, I will ascend into heaven, I will exalt my throne above the stars of God: I will sit also upon the mount of the congregation, in the sides of the north: I will ascend above the clouds; I will be like the most High."

We also read of an interesting offer made to Jesus from Satan.

> "Again, the devil taketh him up into an exceeding high mountain, and sheweth him all the kingdoms of the world, and the glory of them; And saith unto him, All these things will I give thee, if thou wilt fall down and worship me." (Matthew 4:8-9)

Satan wants to be worshipped. Satan wants to sit in the Throne of God. That pride was the first sin as recorded in Scripture. If Jesus were not God He would be guilty of sin to assume the office of Judge in the above passage from the twenty-fifth chapter of Matthew. But, prophecy declares that Jesus will sit in the seat of the Judge of Humanity. Even the angels come to assist Him in this task. If Jesus were not God this would not be possible.

This authority of Jesus to judge humanity is based on His full Deity as God. You will note that mankind, elements of mankind, are being judged. The angels are not there as a judge as they only accompany Him Who is the Judge. The representation of humanity is among those being judged. Jesus stands above these as the Authority of Judgment. Therefore He is God.

Jesus Displayed His Authority in His Miracles

Beers (*The Life Application Bible*) shows that Jesus displayed His Authority in His miracles. Making reference to John 4:51

> "And as he was now going down, his servants met him, and told him, saying, Thy son liveth."

We can understand Beers argument as we see this verse in context.

> "So Jesus came again unto Cana of Galilee, where he made the water wine. And there was a certain nobleman, whose son was sick at Capernaum. When he heard that Jesus was come out of Judaea into Galilee, he went unto him, and besought him that he would come down, and heal his son: for he was at the point of death. Then said Jesus unto him, Except ye see signs and wonders, ye will not believe. The nobleman saith unto him, Sir, come down ere my child die. Jesus saith unto him, Go thy way, thy son liveth. And the man believed the word that Jesus had spoken unto him, and he went his way. And as he was now going down, his servants met him, and told him, saying, Thy son liveth. Then enquired he of them the hour when he began to amend. And they said unto him, Yesterday at the seventh hour the fever left him. So the father knew that it was at the same hour, in the which Jesus said unto him, Thy son liveth: and himself believed, and his whole house." (John 4:46-53)

Beers notes that the miracles of Jesus were not simply illusions or done by the power of suggestion. Jesus was twenty miles from the nearly dead child He healed. We could further argue against the "power of suggestion" as an explanation of this miracle by the fact that neither the child nor those who saw the child were anywhere near Jesus when the healing took place.

Jesus, the God of Eternity, was able to heal the child at a distance because Jesus

CHAPTER 51: JESUS DISPLAYED IN HIS ACTIONS THE TRUTH THAT HE WAS AND IS GOD

was not bound by the restrictions of space as are ordinary created humans. We are reminded that while Jesus was speaking with Nicodemus He was resident in Heaven.

> *"And no man hath ascended up to heaven, but he that came down from heaven, even the Son of man which is in heaven." (John 3:13)*

He Displayed Authority Over Time and Space as the Creator of Time and Space

Jesus displayed authority over more than just illness. He displayed a Divine authority over time and space as the Creator of time and space. Again, Jesus did not simply say He was God; He proved His full Divinity by the Authority displayed in His actions.

A distinction must be here noted between the acts of the prophets of the Old Testament and Jesus. The Old Testament prophets were able to perform mighty acts as the Spirit of God came upon them and empowered those actions and miracle. Jesus performed miracles in the Authority which was His by right of His innate Divinity.

Jesus Said, "My words..."

The Commentary Practical and Explanatory on the Whole Bible looks to the authority which Jesus displayed in His commands. In John 8:37 Jesus is engaged in a discussion with the religious leaders of the nation. He says,

> *"I know that ye are Abraham's seed; but ye seek to kill me, because my word hath no place in you."*

Notice, very carefully, that Jesus said, "My words..." The prophets always said, "The Word of the Lord," but here was The Lord, The Word, speaking. Jesus assumed the authority of God over the acknowledged Word of God. If that is not construed as an acknowledgment, from the very lips of Jesus, that He was God in the flesh, what is it? He said, quite simply and emphatically, that the Words of God were His Words. He made no claim that He simply agreed with those Words; He said that those Words were His.

The apostle Paul says of Jesus, the He "...made himself of no reputation..." (see Philippians 2:7) Jesus never "bragged," or made wild claims about Himself. He simply stated the Truth. More importantly, He acted as the Truth in the displaying of His authority as the Creator God of the Universe.

His actions and authority prove that Jesus is God.

In our next session we will consider the eternality of Jesus.

CHAPTER 52
THE ETERNALITY OF JESUS
(Session Fifty-Three)

The eternality of Jesus speaks of His Deity.

Two Instances When Jesus Claimed Full Deity

There are many who will deny the full deity of Jesus with the old claim of, "Just show me one place in the entire Scripture where Jesus ever claimed to be God." Many can be shown. Just look at two of these instances.

First

In John 14:9 Jesus answers Philip's question. Philip had asked nearly the same question as the skeptic above. He had said, "Come on Jesus, show us the Father. Just one time. That's all we ask." Now, this is from the EPT (Ed's Paraphrased Translation, but I don't believe it does any violence to the question actually asked by Philip in verse 8.) Jesus answered, "...Have I been so long time with you, and yet hast thou not known me, Philip? he that hath seen me hath seen the Father; and how sayest thou *then* Shew us the Father."

Second

Another time Jesus said,

> "I and my Father are one." (John 10:30)

Both of these are plain statements that Jesus is God. No room for doubt is really given. "You looking at me? You're seeing God." Again, the EPT. Nonetheless, that is essentially what Jesus said. Still, the doubter will argue that Jesus was simply saying that He worked in agreement with the Father.

What did Jesus say about this argument that He was only speaking of a "oneness of purpose?" What He did was allow for His critics to give their own interpretation of His words.

> "The Jews answered him, saying, For a good work we stone thee not; but for blasphemy; and because that thou, being a man, makest thyself God." (John 10:33)

At this point the skeptics will argue that Jesus spent the next several verses of this passage pointing out that there had been times in the past where the Scripture had given the appellation of "God" to others in Scripture. Thus, they will assert, that He denied His Own essential deity.

What the skeptic will not be so quick to point out is that Jesus never, at any time in this discourse, denied that He was God. It was for this accusation that the Jewish leaders wanted to stone Him. To have not denied this fact was a strong admission that this was in fact true. They were not wrong; He did claim to be God. He only argued that they were hypocritical in allowing others, who only stood in the place of God to the people, to be called "god." Meanwhile these same people were willing to stone Him Who stood AS God for admitting the Truth of the situation.

The crux of the matter is that Jesus is guilty of misleading these people by not correcting them if they were wrong. This would disqualify Him as a religious or moral guide. If, however, He could not correct them because they were correct in accusing Him of claiming to be God because it was Truth, He is very God as He claimed.

As to the earlier verse, John 14:9, Jesus said that those who had been with Him for some time should understand that He was God. Perhaps the problem of the skeptic at this point is that he has not been with the Savior.

Jesus Claims to Have Existed Before Abraham

Orr (*Can We Be Sure That Jesus Christ Is God*) argues from John 8:58,

> "Jesus said unto them, Verily, verily, I say unto you, Before Abraham was, I am.,"

that Jesus claimed eternality. This is an attribute of God alone. In this verse He claimed to have existed prior to Abraham.

This was more than a simple, or not so simple!, claim to predate Abraham - a man who lived nearly two thousand years before the time in question. Note the tense change: "...before Abraham was (past tense) I am (present tense)." As a man Abraham has a place in history - both past; and present as a contemporary and an historical figure. Jesus as God is presented as the Constant Contemporary in all the periods of time.

The phrase "Verily, verily," in our King James Bible's denotes that Jesus was strongly emphasizing the truth of what He was saying. "Be careful. Listen. What you are being told is truth. Don't even consider doubting this!"

The "Name" of "I Am" denotes the One Who is Existent Within Himself

"I am" is, as we all know, one of the Covenant names of God. When Moses asked for the Name of the One Who spoke from the burning bush he was told,

> "And God said unto Moses, I AM THAT I AM: and he said, Thus shalt thou say unto the children of Israel, I AM hath sent me unto you." (Exodus 3:14)

The "Name" of "I Am" denotes the One Who is existent within Himself. John 1:4 says of Jesus, "In him was life." Life did not flow <u>to</u> Jesus as it does from father to son and daughter among the children of man and woman. Life flows <u>from</u> Jesus. This could only be said of the One Who originally created life.

Therefore, by using this phrase, "I AM," Jesus was speaking to the religious sensibilities of His accusers. He was also speaking to the Truth the He <u>is</u> God. He is not bound by the constraints of time. Time, instead, is subject to Him as the Creator of time.

The Commentary Practical and Explanatory on the Whole Bible speaks on this passage.

> "'Before Abraham was I am' - the words rendered 'was' and 'am' are quite different. The one clause means 'Abraham was *'brought into being'*; the other '*I exist.*' The statement therefore is not that *Christ came into existence before Abraham did*..., but that He never *came* into being at all, but existed before Abraham had a being; in other words, existed before *creation* or *eternity*..."

He Spoke as the One Who Has Always Existed

This is an important point. Jesus did not "begin" to exist at any time. Otherwise He would have said, "I existed before Abraham." He spoke as the One Who has always existed. This makes Jesus of eternity rather than time. This, as does the fact of John

CHAPTER 52: THE ETERNALITY OF JESUS

1:3 that He created all things, also removes any possibility that Jesus was a created Being.

In point of fact Jesus was not created He <u>is</u> The, singular and emphatic, Creator.

A preacher at a service I attended recently said that, "When God created Jesus..." Worse, when I questioned him on this point he was offended that I had questioned his theology. Folks, we are not talking simple theology; we are looking at the Person of Jesus, the Christ. He is God, not simply "from eternity," but "of eternity." Jesus could not have been created and still be the Savior of humanity. He is **THE**, singular and emphatic, God Who created all things.

When we speak of the First, Second, and Third Person of the Trinity we are not speaking of order of creation or importance. As to importance, Each is singularly and emphatically God. The designation only speaks to the appearance of Each in the Scriptural record.

One God means that this entire Godhead has always existed. I cannot completely understand that fact but I can recognize that God has amply explained the Truth of that fact in His inspired and preserved Record of His teaching to humanity: The Scripture.

This attribute of eternity is the exclusive attribute of Deity. This attribute can only be existent within the One Who was, and is!, The Creator. Jesus, therefore, is God.

CHAPTER 53

MORE COMMENTS ON THE ETERNALITY OF JESUS

(Session Fifty-Four)

Jesus Is Not a Created God

The local church that I presently attend had been without a pastor for some time. Our former pastor was a very good and Godly man; I really hated to see him leave. The truth of the matter is that God sets the times and the seasons of His servants. God had decreed that this man's time was over at our local church.

Still, I hated to see him go. He was a real pastor and friend to me and I was sure that no one could replace him. That sentence says something about me. I was deficient in my view of God. In essence I had made an idol of my friend, my pastor. Once again my pastor had pastored me; he pointed out that it was time for another shepherd to feed this flock, me included.

As a retired pastor myself I did fill in "pulpit supply" from time to time. Since God at no time ever placed the burden upon me to fill that pulpit I did not. I often said, even while preaching, that we should continue to find the "man of God" for our situation.

Recently that man has come to our church door. We have welcomed him as a "long lost brother." Indeed, he is our brother in the Lord. More to the point, he is the man God has called to lead us into further fellowship. The church has taken on a lively spirit of joy at the preaching of this man of God.

While waiting for the right man we met with a few wrong men. One of them I was never really very excited about. For some reason The Spirit did not bear witness with my spirit that this was the man God had sent to us.

I tried to ignore this uneasy feeling. There were several arcane theological issues upon which the prospective pastor and I were not in agreement. None of these went to the heart of the Scriptural message so I stood aside. Then this prospective pastor said, "When God created Jesus..."

My ears were shocked into full attention. I asked if he had really said that Jesus was a created being. (Small case letters demanded in such a case as this!) He said, "Yes." At a hastily called pastoral search committee meeting I pressed the issue. He was aghast that I would question his orthodoxy over this aberration of doctrinal standards.

His argument centered upon John 1:1. He said that the verse said, "In the beginning the word..." "This means that He began at the beginning of creation," was his argument. We did not, but well could have, accessed Genesis 1:1, "In the beginning God..."

This prospective pastor was of the belief that we should accept his view because the Baptist churches have never dictated what one must believe. It is true that the various Baptist churches have always given a wide latitude over some doctrinal issues.

This has never been the case when the aberration touches the Savior. Jesus is God, eternal, not a sort of "created" God.

Isaiah 42:8 says,

> "I am the LORD: that is my name: and my glory will I not give to another, neither my praise to graven images."

We could argue that this verse pertained to idols. It does, of course. But the general principle is that God does not "share" His glory with another. This would have been the outcome if Jesus were a "created god" as the Jehovah Witness group would teach.

We could then move into a discussion of the Holy Spirit. I, somewhat, wish we had done that so I would have understood this man's thinking on the Spirit.

The Firstborn, Its Meaning

To make Jesus, and possibly the Spirit, as created beings is to diminish both their glory and the glory of God. It is to make the One God of the Holy Trinity into three separate Gods.

> "Who is the image of the invisible God, the firstborn of every creature: For by him were all things created that are in earth, visible and invisible, whether they be thrones, or dominions, or principalities, or powers: all things were created by him, and for him: And he is before all things, and by him all things consist. And he is the head of the body, the church: who is the beginning, the firstborn from the dead; that in all things he might have the preeminence." (Colossians 1:15-18)

There are a couple of things that must be said about this passage. First, we must look at the word "firstborn." The first time this word is used it speaks to His power as the Creator. This does not speak to His generation; this speaks to His position of power and privilege. This is easily understood as we look at the culture of the day. The status of the "firstborn" meant that he would be the head of the family. Indeed, the passage makes this point as to the body of the church.

The second use of the term "firstborn" speaks to His resurrection. There had been several persons raised from the dead even during the ministry of Jesus. To call Him "firstborn" cannot speak of the chronology of the event. This also speaks of His position of leadership, power, and privilege in the New Testament churches.

The passage also says that Jesus is "before" all things. Now, as far as I know "all" means "all" and that's "all" that "all" means. Jesus is not only "before" all things; He is the Creator of those elements. Therefore Jesus *cannot* be a created being.

Both the fact that He is the Creative Agent and "by him all things consist" means that Jesus has always existed. His eternality shows the fact of Deity upon Him.

Kenosis

One verse we often overlook when considering the deity of Jesus comes during His prayer from the seventeenth chapter of John. Jesus was praying for His disciples when He said,

> "And now, O Father, glorify thou me with thine own self with the glory which I had with thee before the world was." (John 17:5)

We have already discussed the "Kenosis." If you will recall, "Kenosis" is a theological term relating to the fact that Jesus emptied Himself of the outward glory of

CHAPTER 53: MORE COMMENTS OF THE ETERNALITY OF JESUS

His essential Deity when He took upon Himself the form of humanity. Philippians 2:5-11 speaks of this fact. Jesus did this so that He could become one of us in order to be the Perfect Sacrifice for sins on our behalf.

"Mount of Transfiguration" The Glory That Was His

In the first part of the seventeenth chapter of Matthew we get a picture of the obverse of the Kenosis when we observe Jesus at the "Mount of Transfiguration." We get a picture of the glory which is rightfully His. In the passage from John we see that Jesus is ready to reclaim that glory.

Two things must be noticed about this glory. First, the glory is the same glory as of the Father. Second, Jesus had this glory before the world was in existence.

Henry (*Matthew Henry's Commentary*) concludes the obvious. Both the glory and the existence of Jesus are from everlasting.

Again, this is an argument that Jesus has the attribute of eternality. This is an attribute of God. Therefore: Jesus is God.

The Baptism of Jesus

The Pulpit Commentary comments upon the baptism of Jesus as recorded in the Gospel of Matthew.

> "And Jesus when he was baptized, went up straightway out of the water: and lo, the heavens were opened unto him, and he saw the Spirit of God descending like a dove, and lighting on him: And lo a voice from heaven, saying, This is my beloved Son, in whom I am well pleased." (Matthew 3:16-17)

The Pulpit Commentary likens this event as a consecration of Jesus which exhibits eternality. The Holy Spirit descended upon Him. As parts of the "...indissoluble union of the Divine Persons, the Holy Three are one." Thus He did not *become* God (or 'a god') at this point as *He always was God*. This was consecration of the "God/Man" to His sacred office of Redeemer.

We might note that the Father also spoke from Heaven. Thus we have the entire Trinity displayed at the baptism of Jesus. John 1:32 informs us that it was John the Baptist who baptized the Son, Saw the Spirit, and heard the voice of the Father. This was a picture of the trinity shown to John the Baptist as the forerunner of Messiah.

Some have argued that Jesus, the man, was endued with the "Christ Spirit" at the baptism. This view of Jesus seems to see Him as more of a "member" of a "club" than the eternal Son of God as those who hold this view will generally argue that Jesus was only one of many "ascended master's" who were thus endowed.

A look at Matthew 1:23 should help to dispel this misconception.

> "Behold, a virgin shall be with child, and shall bring forth a son, and they shall call his name Emmanuel, which being interpreted is, God, with us."

The One Who Is God

From His birth, actually from eternity, Jesus is not the One Who *became* a God. He is the One Who *is* God.

In our next session we will take a look at the fact that even the Old Testament attests to the eternality of the One of Whom it prophesied.

CHAPTER 54
THE OLD TESTAMENT ATTESTS TO THE ETERNALITY OF JESUS
(Session Fifty-Five)

In this session we begin to consider that the Old Testament attests to the eternality of Jesus.

Proverbs 8

Merrill Unger (*Unger's Bible Handbook*) looks at the eighth chapter of Proverbs and sees that "wisdom" speaks of the pre-incarnate Jesus. Wisdom is the subject of the chapter. The first twenty-two verses of the chapter speak of the excellency of wisdom while the final fourteen verses attest to the timelessness of wisdom.

> "The LORD possessed me in the beginning of his way, before his works of old." (Proverbs 8:22)

We might note in this verse that Jesus was in communion with The Father "before his works of old." That phrase removes any argument that Jesus was a created Being in that His communion came "before" any works of God.

Wisdom Is Jesus

Unger equates Wisdom with Jesus in much the same way as does John in John 1:1. He specifically notes that Wisdom, in verse 22, is spoken of as "possessed" rather than "created" by God. Wisdom (Jesus) is eternally (the beginning, "...an absolute and timeless beginning.") co-existent with the Father.

This thesis of Unger finds some support in Revelation 13:8 where Jesus is said to be the Lamb "slain before the foundation of the world." The reference from Revelation speaks of the facts of the plan of salvation as being considered the remedy for sin even before the fact of the sin of Adam and Eve has entered into human history.

Isaiah 9:6

Lindsell (*Harper Study Bible*) looks at Isaiah 9:6:

> "For unto us a child is born, unto us a son is given: and the government shall be upon his shoulder: and his name shall be called Wonderful, Counsellor, The mighty God, The everlasting Father, The Prince of Peace."

In this prophecy of the coming of Jesus, "Everlasting Father" could be translated as "Father of Eternity" which would designate the role of the Son in creating all things, establish His Deity, and yet, "...not involve any confusion between the Father and the Son the Holy Trinity."

We must also note that this verse speaks of the Virgin Birth in that a "child is born," speaking of the humanity of Jesus, while a "son is given, speaking of the fact that God the Son came in an earthly body.

Micah 5:2

We could also access Micah 5:2.

> "But thou, Bethlehem Ephratah, though thou be little among the thousands of Judah, yet out of thee shall he come forth unto me that is to be ruler in Israel; whose goings forth have been from of old, from everlasting."

Notice, especially the two words used to describe the pre-existence of Jesus. First, His "goings forth" date from old. This makes His activity from the very beginning of time. This takes His activity from the very creation of the world. This, of course, means that the "Babe of Bethlehem" was not "born" in that ancient stable; He came into the human existence at that point in time although He predates that time.

He is also from "everlasting." This simply means that Jesus even predates time in that He is from eternity. Don't misunderstand; this does not mean that He "began" in eternity. The verse says that He was **in** eternity.

Thus, even the Old Testament, written before Jesus was born of woman in Bethlehem, argues for the eternal pre-existence of Jesus. This would show His Divine nature.

We can now move our discussion into the New Testament.

John 1:1

Zodhiates (*God Became Man*) looks at John 1:1.

> "In the beginning was the Word, and the Word was with God, and the Word was God."

"In the beginning 'was' the Word..." The word "was" is "een," which is a durative imperfect tense; it simply means that Jesus existed at the beginning, not that He came into existence. In verse 6 the verb "egento" is used of John the Baptist. This word means "became" or "came." Had John meant to say that Jesus came into being, or became a god, he could have used - would have used, as that word was in his vocabulary - the word "egento."

Anyone who would argue that Jesus is simply a "created god" would be mistaken in their understanding of the fourth Gospel.

We could look a little further in this first chapter of John and consider verse fourteen. "And the Word was made flesh, and dwelt among us, (and we beheld his glory, the glory as the only begotten of the Father,) full of grace and truth."

Matthew Henry's Commentary comments that Jesus was in the world via His Divine Presence and, "...by the prophets *came unto his own*..." (v. 10) But now He came in the Flesh. He was not a man who *became a god*; He was **The** God Who became a man.

Philippians 2:6

Alford (*The New Testament for English Readers*) looks at Philippians 2:6.

> "Who being in the form of God, thought it not robbery to be equal with God."

He sees that Jesus is God.

This, of course, is part of the passage which shows us the great doctrine of the Kenosis. Jesus became one of us. He emptied Himself of the outward glory of Deity so He could not only save our souls but also, as an example of humanity, teach us the way to live even closer to God.

CHAPTER 54: THE OT ATTESTS TO THE ETERNALITY OF JESUS

The great glory and wonder of it all!

Criswell (*Criswell Study Bible*) also comments upon this passage. He notes three rather important facts. The first of course, and the most germane to our present discussion, is that the pre-existence of Jesus is a proof of His eternal nature.

The second is that Jesus is immortal. He died once - for our sins as The Perfect Sacrifice. He rose from the grave. Jesus proved, as Paul points out in the fifteenth chapter of First Corinthians, that He has conquered death and the grave. Jesus will never die again! He is our Savior so that we need not die spiritually. He is our Guide and Friend as we approach The Valley of the Shadow. He went through that valley, physically, as part of the great price He paid to offer us salvation

Finally, Criswell saw that Jesus is invisible. Now, the meaning is not that Jesus is into some "special effects" trick from an old "B movie." What this simply means is that Jesus has more than just the physical nature which walked those dusty roads of two thousand years ago. Jesus has more than just the physical nature which cruel men nailed to that rough wooden cross. Jesus has more than just the physical nature which walked out of the grave after only three days.

Jesus has the spiritual nature of God, Almighty.

Jesus is God.

In our next session we will begin to see that Jesus is more than simply eternal. He is the Great Creator God.

CHAPTER 55
JESUS IS THE CREATOR
(Session Fifty-Six)

Genesis 1:1 Compared to John 1:1-3

A reading of the very first words in Scripture, "In the beginning God created the heaven and the earth," (Genesis 1:1) will tell us that God created all that has been created. When these words are compared with the very first passage in the Gospel of John, "In the beginning was the Word, and the Word was with God, and the Word was God. The same was in the beginning with God. All things were made by him; and without him was not any thing made that was made," (John 1:1-3) we are introduced to the fact that Jesus, the Word, was the Creative Agent.

If "God created" and "Jesus created," then we must argue that Jesus is very God.

We are beginning a new section of our study with this session. We are considering the fact that Jesus is the Creator of all that has been created. As in our last section, considering this fact points out the eternality of Jesus since in order to be Creator it is necessary that Jesus predate everything else. This means, also, that Jesus, since He is the Creator of all cannot be a created Being, Himself.

The Logos

Zodhiates (*God Becomes Man*) looks at John 1:1 and finds facts relating to "logos," the Greek from which "Word" is translated. He sees that,

> "Jesus Christ was not merely 'a' logos but 'the logos.' He was the intelligence behind everything that was created. He is the Person responsible for the creation of the world. That is why the definite article is used before Logos. He is the Master Mind of all creation."

That is really the picture given even before the Scripture speaks definitively about Jesus being the Creator. To the Greek culture the "Logos" was that active participation of deity into the world of men. We could have simply referenced that Jesus was God incarnate (In a human body) in the sacrifice of Calvary. This would have qualified Jesus as the "Logos" into the world of men. But, Jesus was ("**IS**" would be a more correct statement). Jesus is not simply a figure of history. He is the Ultimate Author of History and remains the Constant Contemporary of all in all times in this physical and time centric world.) the Very Creator God.

He Is THE Creative Force of the Godhead

Alford (*The New Testament for English Readers*) reminds us some of the facts of Jesus illustrated in the first verse of John's Gospel. As the Creator, Jesus is not merely the speech of God. Jesus is not the speech (word) of God; He is that active reality which is the First Cause of all later effect. He is **THE** creative force of the Godhead."

When I was first married I didn't realize what I prize I had gotten. I had known that Linda was a pretty good cook. Of course, being the oldest of eleven children she had a little problem our first few meals in cutting down the size of the menu! I knew she could sew a little. After all she was working for a clothing manufacturer when we were dating. When she made me a complete suit, tie included, to wear to church I began to understand she was even better than I'd expected. She also knew how to manage money. She made my E-4 pay in the army last all month. That was an impressive task. Later on she began to be chosen to sit on various boards in the town. I realized that she had married far below herself!

The point I'm making here is that I had greatly underestimated the wonder that was Linda. I knew I loved her. I just didn't know how really wonderful was this person I had met in eighth grace and married a few years out of high school.

So too, it seems, do we fail to consider all the grandeur and majesty of He Who has saved our souls. We understand that we will never fully appreciate all He is while we are this side of Glory. It is just that even our limited understanding is further limited by our view of Him. Do we think we know how great He is? He is a thousand, a million, a billion, more times greater than we could ever think or even imagine.

Jesus Is No Part of Creation, He Is the Creator

Jesus Christ, the Savior of our souls, is the very Creator God of Eternity!

Clarke (*Adam Clarke's Commentary*) reminds us that as the Creator, Jesus is not Himself created.

> "...Jesus Christ is **no part** of **the creation**, as he existed when no part of that existed..."

This being so, and because He made all things (John 1:3), He must be the eternal God.

We can say, in the negative, that Jesus is no "created god." But there are several things to positively consider about the Deity of Jesus. The first verse which we will consider has already been well addressed in this work. John 1:3,

> "All things were made by him; and without him was not any thing made that was made."

The "him" of this verse is easily seen in the context. John was speaking of the Word, the Logos. The Gospel of John was written to appeal to the Gentile readers more than were the synoptic gospels of Matthew, Mark and Luke. John begins by taking a page from Greek philosophy without subjugating the Gospel Message to Greek theologies. He uses the term, familiar to Greek thought, of "Logos" when presenting Jesus.

As the Logos, as we've already considered above, was considered to be the active participation of the deity into the world of humanity, John presents a very active Jesus. So active is the picture presented that we find that it was Jesus who originally formed the physical universe and all that is therein.

Alford (*The New Testament for English Readers*) comments on this fact of Jesus being the Creator of all. "All things..." The Father created through the Son. The Son acts according to the will of the Father - the Father wills creation so the Son creates. Therefore the Son could not have been created by the will of the Father as the Father acts through the Son - i.e. No Son at any point in time = no creative actions (the creative will mobilized) = no Son at any subsequent point in time (or in eternity). Therefore the Son is eternally co-existent with the Father.

My son's car has died. Well, it hasn't really died; it's still setting out there in our parking area. He has a major leak in his gas tank. I think someone may have put a

CHAPTER 55: JESUS IS CREATOR

screwdriver through the tank in order to steal his gas. He drove to the gas station a few blocks from our house and put twenty dollars' worth of gas (A "thimble fill" at today's prices!). He was already out of gas when he returned home - although there was a nice trail of gas on the road coming home.

On a much grander scale is the concept of the Father and the Son. The Father wills to create (My son stepping on his gas pedal.) and the Son creates (The car moving forward.). No gas and the car remains where it is. It exists but it has no real mobility. In a likewise symbiotic relationship the Father wills that the universe and all that is within comes into existence. The Son then moves the will of the Father into active completion. The Two work together. Neither is above, nor below, in order of grandeur or importance. Both work in perfect harmony.

As there is One God, although in the harmony of the Trinity of the Godhead, the Two do not work independently of the Other. We also see, in Genesis 1:2, that the Spirit moved over the creation. This fully suggests His Own active participation in the creative acts. The Spirit seems to be the Godly interaction with the newly created universe. Therefore the Spirit is also eternally co-existent with the Father and the Son.

Adam Clarke (*Adam Clarke's Commentary*) considers this from another angle. He notes that Jesus made all things. This is not a delegated task from God to a subordinate being. Only the Eternal existed before "all" was created. Thus, Jesus must be The Eternal - i.e. God. Also, creation is,

> "...causing that to exist that had no previous being; this is evidently a work which can be effected only by **omnipotence**. Now, God cannot delegate his **omnipotence** to another; were this possible, he **to** whom this omnipotence was delegated would, in consequence become GOD; and he **from** whom it was delegated would **cease to be such**: for it is impossible that there could be **two** omnipotent beings."

The word, "omnipotence," is one of those theological words we don't use a whole lot in our everyday conversation. It simply means "all powerful."

Let me try to explain what Clarke was saying. Back in the days before Mixed Martial Arts became a popular spectator sport, about the only Martial Arts sport was boxing. Now, I'm not going to get this quote exact; I'm pulling it from my musty memory. Muhammad Ali was once asked what it meant to be the Heavyweight Champion of the World. He said, again I am paraphrasing from my memory, "It means that I am the best fighter in the world. It means that I can beat up anybody in the world because I am the greatest."

Omnipotence means a power so great that there is no other power in the universe that can match that power. It means "all powerful." Now, once again, all means all and that's all that all means. If God had created another "God," it would mean that God was no longer omnipotent. God has said,

> "I am the LORD: that is my name: and my glory will I not give to another, neither my praise to graven images." (Isaiah 42:8)

Therefore, besides the philosophic incongruity of the matter, we see from the Biblical standpoint that God would not have created a "co-god." The concept of Jesus being a "created god" is not supportable by either the best of human reasoning (General Revelation) nor by the inspired and preserved Words of God from the Scripture (Special Revelation).

This is a hard concept to grasp with our human reasoning. We have problems understanding the fact of One God in Three Eternal and Co-Existent "Persons." Peter commented on our lack of understanding.

> *"As all in all his epistles, speaking in them of these things; in which are some things hard to be understood, which they that are unlearned and unstable wrest, as they do also the other scripture, unto their own destruction." (II Peter 3:16)*

Peter was speaking of the epistles of Paul in this verse. But, he expanded the thought to the entirety of the Scriptural record. He said that some things are hard for us to understand. He also said that it is much better to accept, even when we have problems understanding everything, the clear message of Scripture.

That's why we say that Christianity is a "faith medium." We simply trust God to be true. What we don't understand - well, we don't understand. We need to continue to study.

The old story is told of a little six year old boy in school. He told his teacher that he was done with school because, "Me and my dad already know everything there is to know."

The teacher said, "How much is two and two?"

The boy said, "Four."

"Four and four?"

"Eight."

"Eight and Eight?"

The boy thought for a moment and said, "That's one my dad knows."

Sometimes we just have to allow our spirits to say, "That's one my Father knows." The Father knows that the Son, Jesus, is God.

CHAPTER 56
JESUS IS THE CREATOR AND MIRACLE WORKER
(Session Fifty-Seven)

Most of the Miracles Jesus Performed Were a Restoration

The *Life Application Bible* makes an interesting point from John 2:11.

> "This beginning of miracles did Jesus in Cana of Galilee, and manifested forth his glory; and his disciples believed on him."

About this verse Beers has observed that most of the miracles which Jesus performed were a restoration of things lost in the fall - i.e. Health, sight, life, etc. The Creator was simply renewing His creation.

This is an especially apt observation when we consider that this was the very point for which Jesus entered into the physical and time centric world of humanity. Jesus said,

> "...I am come that they might have life, and that they might have it more abundantly." (John 10:10b)

In context Jesus was here speaking of eternal life. But when we consider that humankind was originally created to have a relationship with the Creator - and that the thus created humankind was placed in a physical garden on this physical earth - we do not do any violence to this verse by expanding the meaning to include the physical life of mankind.

Jesus was constantly giving physical examples, be it in parable or in actual action, in order that the people, bound to this earth of time would better understand eternal values and realities. When Jesus cleansed the Temple a little later in this same second chapter of John, He overturned the money changers tables and removed even the sacrificial animals from their place. In so doing, He was giving prophecy to the fact that salvation was free and the sacrificial animals, as pictures of His coming sacrifice at Calvary, were not needed. People could approach Him for salvation as He was the true and abiding Temple of the Living God even while being the True and accepted Sacrifice for the sins of those who would accept Him.

Jesus Miracles Were the Setting Aside of the Laws of Nature

As for the miracles, they were often simply the setting aside of the laws of nature. This Jesus could do by right as those laws remain His by virtue of His having created them for His Own good pleasure. This miracles were also the setting aside of the plague of sin brought upon the natural creation, man included, by the sin of Adam.

When Linda and I bought our first car the dealer asked for a "surety," or deposit, while we continued on to the bank to secure financing for the vehicle. The physical healings were an overturning of the effects of sin upon people's lives. I don't mean to say that the blind eyes or lame limbs were the direct result of any specific sin in these people's lives. What I mean is that the fact of sin had brought death, disease and such into the world. This is part of the price of the sin of Adam upon the natural creation of God.

When Linda was diagnosed with cancer the doctor said, "The only consolation I can give is that this type of cancer is not tied to any 'lifestyle' issues such as smoking or anything like that. This cancer just happens." That, of course, was small consolation at the time. But it did help in a strange way that we were guiltless of any human malfeasance in her contracting of the malady.

Sin Causes All the Ill That Befalls Mankind

Sin, in the world - looking at it from the "macro" view - causes all the ill that befalls mankind as a race. Jesus said, "Sin, you've done your work. Now I'm doing mine. Be gone!" In doing so He healed. This was a small "down payment" of the total victory over sin He would offer by His death on the Cross. Our physical bodies may still reel from the effects of Adam's sin upon nature. But our souls, being spiritual, are completely healed by the miracle of the Blood of Jesus Christ shed for us on the Cross of Calvary.

I am preparing to go to the Veteran's Administration hospital near here next week. The doctors and staff at this hospital will be "checking me out" and offering medical treatment for some of the maladies which age has brought to my body. I often tell people that the only thing that causes my ailments is based on heredity: My parents had me way too long ago!

The truth is that the medical professionals can do wonderful things. They can diagnose and prescribe just what is needed to bring my body into its optimal function. But, in the final and true analysis they *cannot* really "heal" anything. They must rely upon medical knowledge and procedure to allow my body to "heal" itself.

Jesus the "Great Physician." He is More. He is God Almighty

We call Jesus the "Great Physician." He is more. He is God Almighty. He can heal with only the power of His Own prerogative as the Lord of Glory.

Colossians 1:16-17: The Glory Which Is His

Colossians 1:16-17 informs us about some of the Glory which is Jesus Christ.

> "For by him were all things created, that are in heaven, and that are in earth, visible and invisible, whether they be thrones, or dominions, or principalities, or powers: all things were created by him, and for him. And he is before all things, and by him all things consist."

Albert Barnes (*Barnes' Notes on the New Testament*) observes that this passage is universal in concept. This passage is an explicit statement that Jesus created the universe and all that it contains.

Since the statement is universal in the application of Jesus as the Creator of all, there is no room for any concept of Jesus as a created being. Since the passage says that Jesus predated, and produced, all of creation, the only logical conclusion allowed is that Jesus is the Great Creator God. There is no other conclusion allowed under the facts provided.

Further, Adam Clarke (*Adam Clarke's Commentary*) also follows the logical progression of fact from the above passage. First, Jesus created the universe. This takes omnipotent, not delegated power. Therefore, Jesus was omnipotent. Only one Being may be all powerful. Since this refers to Jesus, He is God.

Second, since all things were created for Him, He receives the glory which can only

CHAPTER 56: JESUS IS THE CREATOR AND THE MIRACLE WORKER

be the Glory of God. He is God.

Third, we see that Jesus is in existence prior to any creation. All existence must come from God. To be in existence before any of creation is to be God. Jesus is God.

Fourth, Jesus preserves and governs all things. The power to preserve belongs to God. Since Jesus does this Jesus is God.

Fifth, not only did Paul say, and obviously believe, all of this, he received this message via inspiration as he was writing Scripture. Jesus is God.

Barnes also notes that

> "The phrase here employed of 'creating all things in heaven and in earth,' is never used elsewhere to denote a moral or spiritual creation."

Therefore the passage simply means what is says. Jesus created everything. He is the Creator God.

We can add verse fifteen to the above.

> "Who is the image of the invisible God, the firstborn of every creature."

Revelation 1:11, 3:14, 4:11

We have already noted that the concept of "firstborn" does not refer to Jesus as having any sort of "beginning." In Revelation 1:11 Jesus is introduced as the "Alpha and Omega." These are the first and last letters of the Greek alphabet. As such the entire alphabet is contained within these letters. This is a statement of the eternality of Jesus. To refer to Him as the "firstborn" is to refer to His position of eminence over all.

We must also note that Jesus is called the "express image" of God. An express image is not a copy; it is the very image of the object named. Once again, Jesus is God.

Alford (*New Testament for English Readers*) considers Revelation 3:14.

> "And unto the angel of the church of the Laodiceans write; These things saith the amen, the faithful and true witness, the beginning of the creation of God."

Since this speaks of Jesus, He is called the beginning of the creation of God. Again, this phrase does not imply that Jesus was the first of the created beings. As Alford points out, this verse speaks of Jesus as the Beginning, or the Agent which set in motion, of the creative acts of the Godhead.

When Revelation 4:11 is considered we see that the Agent of Creation is God.

> "Thou art worthy, O Lord, to receive glory and honour and power: for thou hast created all things, and for thy pleasure they are and were created."

We have already seen that Jesus is the Creative Agent of <u>ALL</u> creation. We now see that He is, as the Creator, worthy to receive that glory and honor which is the rightful possession of God. Therefore, again, we see that Jesus is God.

We could note that Satan attempts to appropriate this praise and honor. Satan, however, is not worthy to receive this glory. That is the right and privilege of Jesus as the Eternal and Creative God.

May we return one more time to Colossians 1:17.

> "And he is before all things, and by him all things consist."

More than just the Creator of all things, as if this were not more than enough to give Him all praise, Jesus is seen to be the Energizing Force which sustains creation.

Strong (*Systematic Theology*) reminds us that Jesus continues to work in His creation.

> "'In him all things consist,' or 'hold together,' means nothing less than that Christ is the principle of cohesion in the universe, making it cosmos instead of chaos."

I have just read an article where scientists were discussing the force of gravity. It remains a not fully understood force. It is there. It works. But, the "how" and "why" are still being debated.

While not understanding all the facts about gravity, I can understand the confusion. After all we are told that the universe is expanding. Objects are apparently flying away from other objects even while gravity is at work. It must be quite confusing to those who have not understood the fact that God is in charge of His creation.

CHAPTER 57
THE PERSONALITY OF JESUS
(Session Fifty-Eight)

Personality is that which defines a person as who they are in reality. Personality is the manner in which one reacts not only with others but also with events and stimuli within his experiences. In short, personality is who a person is.

Three Errors

Zodhiates (*Who Created Evil?*) looks at the first two verses in the Book of John and finds correction about three mistakes about just who Jesus is.

> "In the beginning was the Word, and the Word was with God, and the Word was God. The same was in the beginning with God." (John 1:1-2)

The Arian Error

The Arian error is to mistake Jesus as a sort of "secondary god." They view Him as a created being who is inferior to God. A prospective pastor of the church I presently attend came into our pulpit with this error. He said, "When God created Jesus..." I stopped him in the middle of his sermon and asked if I had heard him correctly. He assured me that I had.

We had a quick pulpit search committee after the service ended. I brought up the above passage. This prospective pastor said that "the beginning" referred to the beginning of creation and that, in his opinion, and those of the "Baptist" university he had attended, this meant that Jesus was not present in eternity past but was only created as the beginning of the creation of God.

There are two serious problems with this view. The first is the logical inconsistency of having two "supreme beings." In such a case as this there is no "supreme being" as neither is all powerful. Only the Trinitarian concept makes sense in this situation: One God eternally present in three "Persons." If God had divested Himself of His perfect omnipotence with the creation of another "God," He is no longer the All Powerful One. God is a single God eternally existent as a tripartite Entity of One in Three "Persons." I cannot explain that. I have no real understanding of the "math" of the spiritual and eternal realms. But, I rest assured that God understands. He has given us this truth within the pages of His Self-Revelation of Scripture.

The second inconsistency within this prospective pastor's theological consideration is that the passage speaks of Jesus being One with God. Since Jesus is God, the consideration must be that the Father did not exist, under the construct of a "created Jesus," until He had created the Son. After all each is God.

We could add another inconsistency. The view of a created "god" does not line up with the revealed Word of God. That in itself is enough to settle the matter. Our theology is only so many gossamer strands floating in a wind of inconsistency unless it is tethered to the Book of the Ages – the inspired and preserved Words of God.

Sabellians

The error of the Sabellians is also answered in this passage. The Sabellians see God as presenting Himself only in different roles as a cosmic Actor upon the stage of human existence. The picture is much as I am "son" to my father, "father" to my son, and "old fat grampa" to my grandson. The picture is one person assuming different postures with different people.

I prefer the illustration of a cup of coffee with cream and sugar. All are joined into one beverage and yet all give a distinctive flavor to the cup. God is three eternally existent "Persons" and "Personalities" within one essence of individuality.

These first two verses of John also correct the error of the Socinians who see Jesus as simply another man. To this could be added the error of the "New Age" practitioners who view Jesus as just another "Ascended Master."

We could add many more errors which this passage would correct. Islam sees Jesus as a great prophet while the Scripture presents Jesus as the Lord of Eternity. History sees Jesus as a great religious reformer and leader while the Scripture presents Jesus as the Eternal God of Creation. Religious leaders and scholars see Jesus as a great teacher and moralist while the Scripture presents Jesus as the only possible sacrifice for sin.

Jesus is more. He is the Lord of Glory.

Strong (*Systematic Theology*) searches the Scripture and finds that Jesus has a compound relationship with Jehovah. Jesus is distinct from Jehovah (Psalms 45:5-7; Malachi 3:1) and yet Jesus is One with Jehovah (Isaiah 9:6; Micah 3:2).

> "Thine arrows are sharp in the heart of the king's enemies, whereby the people fall under thee. Thy throne, O God, is for ever and ever: the scepter of thy kingdom is a right scepter. Thou lovest righteousness, and hatest wickedness: therefore God, thy God, hath anointed thee with the oil of gladness above thy fellows." (Psalm 45:5-7)

This Psalm is a "Messianic Psalm." As such it speaks of Jesus. It is the Messiah, Jesus, Who inherits the Throne of David. This "inherits" is possibly confusing in that Jesus, in His Deity, predates David. Nonetheless, in His humanity, Jesus inherits the Throne as the Rightful Heir of David.

The point to be noticed in this verse in our present discussion is that Jesus, the Messiah, is referred to as "God." "Thy throne," the throne of Messiah, "O God," that Messiah, Jesus, Who sits on the throne and wields the Sceptre, is God. The anointing of "God" is performed by God.

> "Behold, I will send my messenger, and he shall prepare the way before me: and the Lord, whom ye seek, shall suddenly come to his temple, even the messenger of the covenant: whom ye delight in behold, he shall come, saith the LORD of hosts." (Malachi 3:1)

John the Baptist came as a messenger to prepare the way for the entrance of Jesus into the world. (see John 1:--) Jesus is that Lord, the Messiah, whom the Jewish people had so long sought. Note, importantly, that Jesus comes to "his temple" as "the messenger of the covenant." Both of these phrases identify Him as God. The phrase "'he' shall come, saith the 'LORD' of hosts" gives the picture that Someone else is speaking of Jesus. That someone is "the LORD of hosts." The LORD of hosts is Jehovah. Again, the picture is given that Jesus is distinct from Jehovah.

CHAPTER 57: THE PERSONALITY OF JESUS

Now, keeping all of these *"distinct forms"* in mind we move to first Isaiah 9:6: "For unto us a child is born, unto us a child is given: and the government shall be upon his shoulders: and his name shall be called Wonderful, Counsellor, The mighty God, The everlasting father, The Prince of Peace."

I would add verse seven to this:

> "Of the increase of his government and peace there shall be no end, upon the throne of David, and upon his kingdom, to order it, and to establish it with judgments and with justice from henceforth even forever. The zeal of the LORD of hosts will perform this."

From verse six we see the duality of nature of Jesus. He is human in that "...unto us a child is born." But, at the same time He is not only human in that, in His humanity, He is a "...child given."

His Messiahship

In verse six we also see His Messiahship in that the government, the throne of David, sits upon His shoulders. He establishes this government with His judgments and with perfect justice for "ever and ever" as we see in verse seven.

Notice the descriptive names which Jesus is given. He is the mighty God. He is The everlasting Father. He is The Prince of Peace. In these verses we see the uniting of Jesus with Jehovah as described in the Old Testament.

We look also at Micah 5:2:

> "But thou Bethlehem Ephratah, though thou be little among the thousands of Judah, yet out of thee shall he come forth unto me that is to be ruler in Israel, whose goings forth have been from of old, from everlasting."

In this verse we see a picture of Messiah. He was to be born in Bethlehem in Ephratah. But, at the same time He is from "old, from everlasting." Here we again see the duality of nature of Jesus. He is human in that He was born in Bethlehem. But He is also from eternity. The phrase "old, from everlasting" can be said only of God. Only God is eternal in nature, which is what the phrase means.

What we find is a picture of the Trinity. There are three distinct "Persons," if we may use a phrase which our physical ears can seem to understand, but there is only One essence of The God of Creation.

This Oneness of Jesus with Jehovah is Necessary to Our Very Salvation

Pendleton (*Christian Doctrine*) reminds us that this oneness of Jesus with Jehovah is necessary to our very salvation. If Jesus had been only a created being He would owe His Own allegiance to God. He could not, then, act in our stead as a representative sin bearer for our salvation. No matter how exalted Jesus may have been, if He were not God it would not be possible for Him to die in our place to become a substitute for us. If, likewise, he were not also human, He would not have been a substitute for us.

Jesus is the Only God/Man from eternity unto eternity. We owe our very soul salvation to that fact.

CHAPTER 58
JESUS' TEACHING REVEALS THE DIVINE MIND
(Session Fifty-Nine)

We may now note that the teaching of Jesus reveals the Divine mind. As such, Jesus is God, eternal.

Alford (*The New Testament for English Readers*) points out that Jesus knew the audience to whom He was speaking. John 10:16 tells us,

> "And other sheep I have, which are not of this fold: them also I must bring, and they shall hear my voice; and there shall be one fold, and one shepherd."

One of the cults has taken this verse and made it apply to the "ten lost tribes." They then use the faulty *history* of "British Israelitism" to claim that Jesus was speaking of them as being those "ten lost tribes." We could access James 1:1, where James speaks of his writing as to "the twelve tribes scattered abroad," that even a "scattered ten" tribes are of the same fold. That Jesus here speaks of "other folds," especially when speaking to a Jewish audience, would speak to a group which was outside the House of Israel." The "lost sheep" are the Gentiles of the Christian Church which have been "engrafted" as a people of God.

I might note that the above statement of "engrafted" does not mean that the Christian has replaced the Jew as the people of God. We, of the Christian Churches, are the recipients of promises as believers and worshippers of God. The Jew still has his place in the economy of God as there are distinct promises to the offspring of Abraham which have yet to be fully fulfilled.

We may also see that the method of the teaching of Jesus displays the marks of Deity.

The teaching of Jesus was direct, deep, and touching on the soul need of His audience whether that audience was large, such as the "Sermon on the Mount" in Matthew 5:1 and following into chapters six and seven, or just to an individual such as Nicodemus in John three or the woman at the well in John four.

The Truths of the Illumination of the Spirit

We might note that in the third chapter of John, Jesus was speaking with a well-trained theologian as He taught the truths of the illumination of the Spirit. In the fourth chapter of John, Jesus was speaking with a simple Samaritan woman as He taught the truths of His all sufficiency.

In the third chapter of John we see Jesus speaking with a "master of Israel" (John 3:10) while in the fourth chapter of John we see Jesus speaking with a foreigner, even an outcast, from the view of the pious Jew. Yet, He spoke with both the message of sin and salvation. Jesus knew both of their hearts and gave them the invitation to follow Him.

As the Creator God, Jesus saw all people as unworthy in that they were sinners while, at the same time, He saw all people as worthy of His great love if they would only accept that love He offered to them and that sacrifice He was to offer on their behalf.

The Teaching of Jesus Was Personal and Pointed

Not only was the teaching of Jesus personal and pointed in that the teaching was intended to draw sinners to Himself, as Orr (*Can We Be Sure That Jesus is God?*) reminds us, the teaching of Jesus was a teaching which displayed the hallmark of authority. Not only was the teaching of Jesus authoritative, that authority was centered in His Own Person. Where the prophets had always said, "Thus saith the Lord!," Jesus said, "Verily, verily, I say unto thee..." (John 3:3a)

The Authority That Jesus taught was Either Divine or He Was an Egomaniac

The authority with which Jesus taught was either Divine or it was simply the brag of an egomaniac. At first blush one might be willing to consider that Jesus was speaking from an inflated ego. That is until, as Orr continues, we consider some of the areas over which Jesus more than simply talked with authority, He also displayed that authority.

Jesus Teaching to Pilate

When Jesus stood before the judgment seat of Pilate, Jesus was reminded of His place as the accused.

> "Then saith Pilate unto him, Speakest thou not unto me? knowest thou not that I have power to crucify thee, and have power to release thee?" (John 19:10)

The answer of Jesus displayed His complete authority over human reasoning.

> "Jesus answered, Thou couldest have no power at all against me, except it were given thee from above: therefore he that delivered me unto thee hath the greatest sin." (John 19:11)

Jesus explained to Pilate that he had no real power over Jesus. The old song says that "He could have called ten thousand angels..." And, indeed He could have! The salient point here, however, is that Jesus told Pilate that his very place of judgment over Jesus was in reality a place of sin. Judas may have borne the "greater sin" in that he conspired to deliver Jesus to judgment but Pilate was also condemned as a sinner in his own area of operation.

Jesus Teaching That He Had Authority Over Demons

Orr also notes that Jesus exercised power over demons. In Mark 1:32-34, among many other New Testament examples, Jesus exercised this authority.

> "And at even when the sun did set, they brought unto him all that were diseased, and them that were possessed with devils. And all the city was gathered together at the door. And he healed many that were sick of divers diseases, and cast out many devils; and he suffered not the devils to speak, because they knew him"

I want you to notice something very important here: Not only did Jesus "exorcise" the demons from the people, He also forbid the demons to speak of Him. His time was not yet come when He would offer Himself as King to the Jews. Jesus had such complete authority over those demons that their mouths where shut as His command.

Jesus Taught Authority Over the Religious Leaders of the Jewish People

Orr further notes that Jesus exercised authority in matters of religious discussion. We may recall that Jesus corrected some of the religious misconceptions of the woman at the well in John, the fourth chapter. Jesus also exercised that same authority over

CHAPTER 58: JESUS' TEACHING REVEALS THE DIVINE MIND

the religious leaders of the Jewish people.

> "Then certain of the scribes and of the Pharisees answered, saying, Master, we would see a sign from thee. But he [Jesus] answered and said unto them, An evil and adulterous generation seeketh after a sign; and there shall no sign be given to it, but the sign of the prophet Jonas. For as Jonas was three days and three nights in the whale's belly, so shall the Son of man be three days and three nights in the heart of the earth. The men of Nineveh shall rise in judgment with this generation, and shall condemn it because they repented at the preaching of Jonas, and, behold, a greater than Jonas is here. The queen of the south shall rise up in the judgment with this generation, and shall condemn it: for she came from the uttermost parts of the earth to hear the wisdom of Solomon, and, behold, a greater than Solomon is here." (Matthew 12:38-42)

Jesus rebuked these leaders for not believing in Him. They demanded a sign while Jesus sought faith. Notice also that Jesus spoke of some of the past judgments of God and compared them as nearly trivial in light of these men's lack of faith in Him. Jesus went further, still. He compared Himself to one of the great Jewish prophets and one of the greatest of the Jewish kings. He found them to be of less importance than was He.

Jesus Taught Authority Over Religious Observances

Earlier in the chapter, as Orr again points out, Jesus even displayed His authority over religious observances.

> "At that time Jesus went on the sabbath day through the corn, and his disciples were an hungered, and began to pluck the ears of corn, and to eat. But when the Pharisees saw it, they said unto him, Behold, thy disciples do that which is not lawful to do upon the Sabbath day. But he said unto them, Have ye not read, what David did, when he was an hungered, and they that were with him. How he entered into the house of God, and did eat the showbread, which was not lawful for him to eat, neither for them which were with him, but only for the priests? Or have ye not read in the law, how that on the Sabbath days the priests in the temple profane the Sabbath, and are blameless? But I say unto you, That in this place is one greater than the temple. But, if ye had known what this meaneth, I will have mercy, and not sacrifice, ye would not have condemned the guiltless. For the Son of man is Lord even of the sabbath day. (Matthew 12:1-8)

It might be instructive for us to consider that Jesus was challenging the understanding of the very men whose job it was, and they did it extremely well, to read and study the Scripture. We must understand that the Scripture is more than simple words on paper. It is the Words of God on paper and on our hearts as He illumines us by the ministry of The Spirit.

We have a desperate need to be familiar with the Words of God in Scripture. By the same token, may we never treat those Words with anything other than the utmost reverence. May we read the Scripture often. May we always read the Scripture in an attitude of prayer and communion with the Author of those Words.

Jesus claimed absolute Deity. There is no question about that when He asserted that He was the Lord of the Sabbath. This is the Holy Day of God reaching all the way back to creation. None other than Deity could claim to be the Lord of the Sabbath. No created being could have that right. Either Jesus is Deity, as He has demonstrated, or He is guilty of blasphemy and heresy of the highest order.

Jesus Taught Authority Over Sickness

Orr continues by noting that Jesus displayed divine authority over sickness.

> "And Jesus went about all the cities and villages teaching in their synagogues, and preaching the gospel of the kingdom, and healing every sickness and every disease among the people." (Matthew 9:35)

There are times even in our day when we will witness the true miracle of true physical healing from God. When this does happen we go about and relate the incident to others. We are excited to have seen the power of God displayed. Jesus went about doing this as a daily course of action. I have every respect for doctors. I am under Veteran's Administration care and find those doctors to be wonderful persons whose skill and ability to diagnose and treat with medicine to be simply amazing. But, Jesus is The Healer because only He has complete authority over disease.

Jesus Taught Authority Over Human Relationships

Orr also takes us to the cross where we witness the authority of Jesus over the tenderest of human relationships. Mary, the mother of Jesus, was one of those watching the events of the crucifixion. We can only imagine the excruciating pain and dismay that ate away at her heart as she watched this crucifixion in horror.

On a practical note we must note that, in all probability, Mary was a widow. We have no reference to Joseph after the time Jesus was at the Temple when He was twelve, in human terms. Although she had given birth to other sons and daughters, she had been traveling with Jesus. As her first-born it is likely that He had taken the responsibility for her. Now nearing 50 years of age, Mary was losing her temporal support along with, as she probably supposed, the son of her youth.

Jesus, still full of compassion even during this agony, looked over at her and told His disciple John to take care of His earthly mother. (see John 19:26-27) Even during the time of His execution Jesus exercised His authority in this closest of human relationships.

Jesus Taught Authority Over Heavenly Things

Finally, Orr reminds us that Jesus exhibited authority even over Heavenly things to come.

> "Verily, verily, I say unto thee, We speak that we do know, and testify that we have seen, and ye receive not our witness. If I have told you earthly things, and ye believe not, how shall ye believe if I tell you of heavenly things? And no man hath ascended up to heave, but he that came down from heaven, even the Son of man which is in heaven. And as Moses lifted up the serpent in the wilderness, even so must the Son of man be lifted up; That whosoever believeth in him should not perish, but have eternal life." (John 3:11-15)

Jesus was speaking prophecy of His coming death on the cross. But, I want you to closely notice something in that thirteenth verse: "...*even* the Son of man which is in heaven." Jesus was in Heaven even as He was speaking with Nicodemus! Think of that! Only God has the attribute of "Omnipresence." That means being everywhere at the same time. You can't do it. I can't do it. It is a reality in the life of Jesus. Therefore Jesus is God.

CHAPTER 58: JESUS' TEACHING REVEALS THE DIVINE MIND

The Teaching of Jesus Was Factual

We must note that the teaching of Jesus was factual. In Matthew 17:14-18 we read the story of a man who brought his son to Jesus. The man claimed that his son was a "lunatick." Dake (*Dake Annotated Bible*) reminds us that most people of the day believed that the moon could cause insanity. Some people still do believe that. I have heard of people who are hesitant to venture out in their car on nights when the moon is full.

Jesus knew that this was not the case. Jesus expressed disdain for this false belief in verse seventeen:

> "...O foolish and profane generation, how long shall I be with you? how long shall I suffer you? bring him hither to me."

Jesus then ordered a demon within the boy to leave. Jesus knew the real cause of the young man's malady. The moon was not a cause; the devil was the cause.

When will we ever learn that the religion of the far ancient region of Babylon is a false religion? The moon, the stars, and the planets have no effect on our lives. These are simply parts of the creation of God. It is He Who is in ultimate control of all things. That old serpent, Satan, desires to lead us to doom and destruction. The sin nature within unsaved humanity follows Satan blindly toward the abyss. If Satan can get us to seek "readings" of the "heavens" rather than putting our complete faith and trust in the God Who loves us, he will readily do so.

The Lie That Jesus Taught What He Knew to Be Error

The facts related in these few verses from Matthew should show the lie of those who say that Jesus taught what He knew to be error in some cases because His hearers believed it and He didn't want to "shake their faith." We are told this is the reason that He taught that Daniel wrote the Book of Daniel. (consider Matthew 24:15) We are told that the people believed it was so and this colored His attempts to reach them.

Hogwash! Jesus came to set people free from error and superstition. He came to teach the true way of life. When Jesus (see Matthew 5:17) announced that He had come to fulfill the law the misconceptions of the people were shaken to their very foundations. When He went to the cross to die as a final and effective sacrifice for sin the people were able to finally see that those yearly sacrifices were a thing of the past as the Perfect Lamb of God (see John 1:29) had come to die – once and for all – as the Only Sin Offering for humanity.

If Jesus had taught that which He knew to be false He would be guilty of teaching error. He would be a liar and untrustworthy.

Instead, Jesus is very God and very man. He is our Only and Perfect Savior.

Chapter 59

THE CHARACTER OF JESUS REVEALS THE DIVINE MIND

(Session Sixty)

The Character of Jesus Compared With the Claims of Jesus

The character of Jesus reveals the Divine mind.

In John 8:57 the Jewish leadership said to Jesus,

"...thou art not yet fifty years old, and hast thou seen Abraham?"

This was after Jesus had said, "Your father Abraham rejoiced to see my day: and he saw *it*, and was glad."

We have no real idea how old Jesus was when the above incident happened. The closest we could surmise is that He was around thirty since this was the age that His public ministry began and He was crucified at thirty-three. Whatever was His age at this time we know that Jesus was, in the natural, a mature adult.

The ancient Jews, according to Alford (*New Testament for English Readers*) reckoned fifty years to be the completion of manhood. Apparently what the Jewish leadership was saying was the Jesus was not even old enough to wear the mantle of "elder." It was certain that He was not old enough to have seen, or been seen by, Abraham. This was their contention.

What these men failed to understand was the concept of a "Theophany" whereby Jesus, long before Bethlehem, would appear in a physical form as the "Angel of the Lord." Remembering what we said in the last session about the Omnipresence of Jesus we must consider that He has residence in the eternal realms where, there being no past or present, He would easily step in history in the time of Abraham as He could in the events of Bethlehem.

All that being said in the previous paragraph, and I do believe it to be true, I believe that the real joy of Abraham was seeing Jesus come as Messiah during this earthly sojourn. I do believe that residents of Heaven are well able to see the events of time. This would have been a joyous time for Abraham as he would have offered praise to God at the fulfilling of yet another of the promises seeing fulfillment.

Even more promises to the Jew await their time of earthly fulfillment. May we rejoice that God keeps all His covenants with the Jew. This is an earthly proof of the truth of the promises of God to the Christian, as well.

The Character of Jesus Displays the Marks of the Divine

Little (*Know What and Why You Believe*) compares the character of Jesus with the claims of Jesus. He finds that the character of Jesus also displays the marks of the Divine.

One thing Little notes is that Jesus never prayed for forgiveness of sins. This would be a startling lack in anyone else. Jesus was, in His teaching and life, a moralist. The only rational excuse for the lack of confessional prayer in the life of Jesus is that He was sinless in all His acts and pronouncements.

His Miracles Display His Divine Character

This consideration is borne further along by the simple fact that no one ever charged Him with any sort of wrong doing. Even at His "trial" we find false witnesses as to the meaning of His teaching.

Also, Little reminds us of the power which Jesus displayed over natural forces. To consider the cessation of the storm, and the waves which were already in motion, on the Sea of Galilee is a miracle which only God, Who had created those natural forces, could have accomplished.

Another miracle, the feeding of the five thousand must be considered – in the simple multiplication of those elements – an act of God.

The changing of the water into wine, not just wine colored but drinkable and fresh wine, could have been done by none other than God.

It is hardly possible to read five pages in the New Testament Gospels and not find the wonder of the Healing Hand of Jesus as He displayed His power over, and mastery of, the forces of sickness and disease.

This power over sickness and disease even extended to power and authority over death. I'm certain that many were the funeral processions which were changed into parades of joy as Jesus called the dead back to life. Even Lazarus, dead for several days with decomposition setting in upon his mortal body, obeyed the call of the Savior to "come forth" as he was loosed from the bonds of human death into healthful and complete life.

We must stand in amazement at the picture of the open garden tomb where Jesus had been laid. He fully defeated even the death of His Own human shroud. None but the Creator of humanity and human life could have taken His physical life back from the hands of the reaper. Jesus is God. There is no other explanation for the force of His wonders and Person.

John 5:19 Explained

Even beyond this Clarke (*Clarke's Commentary*) looks at John 5:19 where Jesus said,

> "Then answered Jesus and said unto them, Verily, verily, I say unto you, The Son can do nothing of himself, but what he seeth the Father do: for what things soever he doeth, these also doeth the Son likewise."

Simply, the Son does what the Father does. Anyone could do what the Father does not do (err and sin). "If Jesus can do nothing but what God does, then He is no creature – He can neither sin nor err, nor act imperfectly." Therefore we must conclude that Jesus is not just a man. He is man but He is more. He is the very Creator God.

Two Prophecies in One Verse

We read in Malachi 3:1 that Jesus was the Messenger of the Old Covenant – the Old Testament.

> "Behold, I will send my messenger, and he shall prepare the way before me; and the Lord, whom ye seek, shall suddenly come into the temple, even the messenger of

CHAPTER 59: THE CHARACTER OF JESUS REVEALS THE DIVINE MIND

the covenant, whom ye delight in: behold, he shall come, saith the LORD of hosts."

Notice that there are two prophecies in this verse. The first considers the ministry of John the Baptist as the "forerunner" of the Messiah. Notice that the second is "the Lord whom ye seek." Jesus is the Lord whom the Jew sought. He was the promised and long awaited Messiah. He is also identified as "the messenger of the covenant." He is also the One "whom ye delight in."

In reading this verse we cannot doubt that the Messiah, Who is "the messenger of the covenant," is very God. Who is the Author and Lord of the covenant to the Jew? This is the description which is given of Jesus in this passage. Since God is that Author and Lord of the covenant this Old Testament prophecy of Jesus describes Jesus as God.

Jesus Character Displayed in the Announcement: Animal Sacrifice Is Out

Now we turn to the New Testament. At the "Last Supper" Jesus described the wine as a symbol.

> *"For this is my blood of the new covenant, which is shed for many for the remission of sins." (Matthew 26:28)*

In the old covenant the sins of the people had been covered by the blood of animal sacrifice. Now, in the new covenant we find that the blood of Jesus, shed at the cross, is better than the Old Testament sacrifice. The blood of Jesus is effective for the REMISSION of sin for those who accept.

The same Jesus is in both the Old and New Testaments. He is the Subject of the entire Bible record. He is the Lord of Glory and God, eternal.

Clarke (*An Outline of Christian Theology*) points out that Jesus showed God to us. When Jesus came into the world we learned much more about God.

> "More of his inmost character was shown by Christ, and more of the relation that he bears to men."

Jesus was in the position to show us more of God because He is God. The personality He showed to humanity is the Personality of God.

Chapter 60
JESUS ADMITS HIS DIVINITY
(Session Sixty-One)

Christianity Is Different From All Other Religions of the World

There is something different about Christianity. The religions of the world are all interested in telling us how to placate, or appease, an angry deity who relishes the prospect of bringing judgment upon those who have offended him. The religions of the world all tell us that we must do, do, and do some more. Christianity is the good news that Jesus has already done all that needs to be done. Indeed, any attempt to "do" on our part is a rejection of the salvation which He purchased at the cross of Calvary.

When it comes to our relationship with God we are not ordered to "do." We are fully expected to accept salvation as a free gift because of that which Jesus has already done.

Christianity is different on another level. The founders of the religions of the world see themselves as teachers showing the way to God. Even Moses falls into this category. Jesus is unique among this group because as McDowell (Answers to Tough Questions) points out, Jesus makes a claim to Divinity about Himself.

Is Jesus a Liar?

The claim to be God, made by Jesus, is a true claim. Several other things must be true if the claim of Jesus was false. First, if the claim is patently false, and Jesus knew the claim to be false, then Jesus is a liar. The ethical nature with which Jesus lived and taught would suggest that this is not so. He is not a liar.

Second, as McDowell (*Evidence That Demands a Verdict*) points out, if the claim was not true but Jesus believed it to be true, we have other problems. One of these would be that Jesus, Himself, was deluded. This would make him delusional and all of His teaching would be rendered suspect.

The other possibility is that Jesus was a lunatic. This, of course, would mean that the very base of His teaching was untenable. We could not call Him a teacher or reformer because He would be flawed in all of His teaching. Therefore His teaching would be flawed and unworthy of consideration by rational people.

On the Basis of the Claims of Jesus, We Must Either Accept Him or Reject Him

Again, McDowell makes the point that there is truth in the claims of Jesus. We must either accept Him or reject Him on that basis.

The claim of Jesus to make the claims He made in assuming that he had the power of God would have been courageous claims to make. As McDowell (*Answers to Tough Questions*) states in his use of the following illustration such claims from anyone in our own time would be greeted with more than quiet derision.

> "Suppose this very night the President of the United States appeared on all the major networks and proclaimed that, 'I am God Almighty. I have the power to forgive sin. I have the authority to raise my life back from the dead.' He would be

quickly and quietly shut off the air, led away and replaced by the Vice-President. Anybody who would dare to make such claims would have to be either out of his mind, or a liar, unless he was God."

Others Understood the Claims of Jesus to Deity

Others understood the claims of Jesus to Deity.

The Demons Understood

Certainly the demons understood the Deity of Jesus as they interacted with Him. Barnes (Barnes' Notes on the New Testament) has some observations on this subject from Mark 1:23. I add verses 24-26 to this.

> *"And there was in their synagogue a man with an unclean spirit, and he cried out, Saying, Let us alone, what have we to do with thee, thou Jesus of Nazareth? art thou come to destroy us? I know who thou art, the Holy One of God. And Jesus rebuked him, saying, Hold thy peace and come out of him. And when the unclean spirit had torn him, and cried with a loud voice, he came out of him."*

As Barnes tells us, the evil spirits understood Who Jesus Is. Those evil spirits well knew the power of Jesus. They did not ask, as they might have a mere human, that He would leave them alone. Instead they asked what they had done to Him. Their implied answer was, "nothing." The argument of the unclean spirits seemed to be that if He did cast them out of the man that it would be an "improper interference" of their work.

If this were the argument of those unclean spirits it was not a correct assumption on their part. They had attacked the very creation of God. Now before them stood God, the Son, the Creator of all. Again, Barnes notes that Satan will still use this argument against the soul which would flee to Jesus for salvation.

I would only add that Jesus once again commanded the evil spirits to cease all speaking about Who He was. It was not yet His time to present Himself as the Messiah of Israel to the people. In that we have an instruction. Satan will often speak the truth to us but in such a way as to mislead. This being a national campaign season I am tempted to call Satan a "master politician" as he will "spin" even a nugget of truth to produce a meal of error.

We see an example of this sort of thing in the eighth chapter of John when the religious elite brought a woman taken "in the very act" of adultery. I've always wondered where the man was hiding when they caught her. After all, the Law prescribed the same punishment for him as for her. (see Leviticus 20:10) My suspicion is that he was one of them; he had approached her only to use her very life as a tool to attack Christ.

May we never allow our lives to be used to demean the message of the cross!

When these men brought the woman to Jesus they knew the Law of God. They also knew the law of the Romans. According to their understanding of the Scripture the woman was to be stoned to death. But, if such were done it would be a capital offense under the law of Rome. The men figured that they had Jesus between a stoning and a hard sentence. They felt that they could not lose this argument.

The men did not understand that the very God Who gave that Law was now standing before them. They also did not understand that Jesus came to offer mercy to those still under the Law. His challenge to the men to go ahead and stone her if they were without sin themselves was greeted by a general departure of the woman's accusers.

CHAPTER 60: JESUS ADMITS HIS DIVINITY

If, as I feel, those very men were involved in her "act of adultery," they would also be guilty under the Law of Moses. They would be under a sentence of death. We would do well to note that in verse eleven we see that Jesus did not condone the acts of the woman; He demanded of her that she "sin no more."

Jesus' Antagonists Understood

The antagonists of Jesus among the Jewish leadership certainly understood His claims to Deity. Jesus had healed a sick man at the pool of Bethesda. (see John 5:1-8) Upon finding that Jesus had performed this miracle of healing on the Sabbath the Jewish leadership in the Temple accosted Him, actually (v. 16) wanted to kill Him, for this – they believed – sacrilege of healing "work" on the Sabbath. More than that, Jesus had bid the man to take up his bed and walk! In the minds of the leadership Jesus was even guilty of inducing others to sin.

Jesus answer to these charges only added fuel to the fire of these men's indignation.

> "But Jesus answered them, My Father worketh hitherto, and I work. Therefore the Jews sought the more to kill him, because he not only had broken the sabbath, but said also that God was his Father, making himself equal with God." (John 5:17-18)

Clarke (*Adam Clarke's Commentary*) notices that the understanding of His hearers is that He was calling Himself equal with God – i.e. that "He and the father were ONE." It is well to note that since Jesus did nothing to say that these men were in error in this view, He gives implicit agreement to their consideration. In this He is either claiming Divinity or teaching error.

If Jesus were teaching error by implication He cannot be rightly called a prophet of God. If He agrees because the assessment is correct He is God.

Another display of this same type happens in John 8:58.

> "Jesus saith unto them, Verily, verily, I say unto you, Before Abraham was I am."

In the very next verse these leaders took up stones to kill Him. They understood the significance of the use of God's Covenant Name, "I Am," from the lips of Jesus.

At the Mount of The Burning Bush God had said to Moses,

> "And God said unto Moses, I AM THAT I AM: and he said, Thus shalt thou say unto the children of Israel; I AM hath sent me unto you." (Exodus 3:14)

Jesus had claimed the eternal name of God.

His hearers were so upset by the use of this Covenant Name that they were ready to invoke the wrath of Rome. This is not a small thing.

Once again, if these men had been in error of understanding, Jesus did nothing to correct that understanding. He accepted it as truth.

The Jewish Leaders Understood Jesus

The Pulpit Commentary speaks on John 10:30-39 where Jesus had said that He and God were One. He meant that,

> "...the Father's Personality and his own Personality are merged into one essence and entity."

The Jewish leaders (verse 33) understood this to be Jesus' meaning.

> "I and my Father are one. Then the Jews took up stones again to stone him. Jesus

answered them, Many good works have I shewed you from my Father; for which of those works do ye stone me? The Jews answered him, saying, For a good work we stone thee not; but for blasphemy, and because that thou, being a man, maketh thyself God. Jesus answered them, Is it not written in your law, I said, Ye are gods? If he called them gods, unto whom the word of God came, and the scripture cannot be broken; Say ye of him, whom the Father hath sanctified, and sent into the world, Thou blasphemest; because I said I am the Son of God? If I do not the works of my Father, believe me not. But if I do, though ye believe not me, believe the works that ye may know, and believe, that the Father is in me, and I in him. Therefore they sought again to take him, but he escaped out of their hand." (John 10:30-39)

Jesus further argued that others, who had stood in the place of power – both political and religious, had been called "gods." But, He the very Son of God (verse 36), Who was sanctified before He was sent into the world (verse 36), had the right to that title.

He also argued that this thesis was proven because He did the same works as did the Father. The Jewish leadership felt the same as before He had defended Himself. He had not repudiated, nor weakened, His claim that He and the Father were One.

When the Scripture says that He escaped out of their hand there is no suggestion that He ran and managed to escape. Indeed, had a mob formed planning to stone Him, there was no physical, or *Hollywood* escape. He simply walked away and they, for some reason or the other of spiritual dimension, could not follow or accomplish their intent.

About this, I am reminded of those who sought to attack the angels at the home of Lot.

"And they smote the men that were at the door of the house with blindness, both small and great: so that they wearied themselves to find the door." (Genesis 19:11)

The Power of God is greater, far, than the power of man.

At the "trial" of Jesus He was accused of saying He was God.

"The Jews answered him, We have a law; and by our law he ought to die, because he made himself the Son of God." (John 19:7)

Jesus didn't "make Himself" anything. He was, and is, Who He is: He is God, the Son and The Son of God. Had this been otherwise, He could have spared Himself the trip to Golgotha. All Jesus would have had to do would have been to admit that He was not the Son of God and the trial would have been over. He would have been acquitted. But, that would not have been the Truth. Jesus died for the Truth and for our sins. A liar and a martyr are not made of the same "stuff."

Thomas Understood

After His resurrection Jesus came to the disciples. In John 20:28 Thomas saw Jesus for the first time since the crucifixion.

"And Thomas answered and said unto him, My Lord and my God."

Thomas was not swearing. Jesus did not rebuke him for this. Neither was Thomas wrong in his assessment that Jesus was both Lord and God. Jesus did not correct him for this, either.

CHAPTER 61
JESUS STRONGLY INFERS HIS DEITY
(Session Sixty-Two)

Passages Where Jesus Infers His Deity

Matthew 14:33

There are several places in the New Testament where Jesus strongly infers His deity. One of these is in Matthew 14:33. This happened shortly after He had stilled the wind and the waves of a storm. More than this, He had walked on the water out to the boat and even bade Peter to do the same.

> "Then they that were in the ship came and worshipped him, saying, Of a truth thou art the Son of God." (Matthew 14:33)

Not one place in the entire library of Scripture does any righteous person ever accept worship intended for God. Not even the angels will do this. Jesus did. Jesus must be considered by all to have been, in His humanity, a righteous person. Since Jesus did accept this worship we are left with no other rational conclusion except to admit that Jesus is Divine.

Mark 2:1-11

Mark 2:1-11 gives another instance in which Jesus strongly inferred His deity.

> "And again he entered into Capernaum after some days, and it was noised that he was in the house. And straightway many were gathered together, insomuch that there was no room to receive them, no, not so much as about the door: and he preached the word unto them. And they come unto him, bringing one sick of the palsy, which was borne of four. And when they could not come nigh unto him for the press, they uncovered the roof where he was and when they had broken it up, they let down the bed wherein the sick of the palsy lay. When Jesus saw their faith, he said unto the sick of the palsy, Son, thy sins be forgiven thee. But there were certain of the scribes sitting there, and reasoned in their hearts, why doth this man thus speak blasphemies? who can forgive sins but God only? And immediately when Jesus perceived in his spirit that they so reasoned within themselves, he said unto them, Why reason ye these things in your hearts? Whether is it easier to say to the sick of the palsy, Thy sins be forgiven thee, or to say, Arise, and take up thy bed, and walk? But that ye may know that the Son of man hath power on earth to forgive sins, (he saith to the sick of the palsy,) I say unto thee, Arise, and take up thy bed, and go thy way into thine house."

McDowell (*More Than a Carpenter*) well notes that the fact Jesus forgave the sins of this man is a claim to Deity. I can easily forgive someone else for a wrong done to me. Jesus forgave a man for wrongs committed against God.

The Pulpit Commentary makes note that the Jewish scribes may well have reasoned that it was easy for Jesus to simply say that the man's sins were forgiven. This, after all, is not something easy to prove has been done. Jesus does prove His power to forgive sins when He instructs the man to pick up his bed and walk to his home.

Another thing we must note here is that those scribes had not voiced their suspicions and charges. The fact that Jesus knew what was in the minds of these men is a mark of Deity on His part. No mere man could have thus known the minds of his hearers. The fact that the scribes did not dispute the fact with Jesus is a testament that His knowledge was correct.

Matthew 28:19-20

When we consider the Great Commission we see that Jesus asserts His deity.

"Go ye therefore, and teach all nations, baptizing them in the name of the Father, and of the Son, and of the Holy Spirit." (Matthew 28:19)

Note closely this baptismal formula. In the 'name,' singular, but in the 'Name' of the Father, Son, and Holy Spirit, plural. This is no intimation; this is a statement of the Trinity of the Godhead. The Father is God. Jesus is God. The Holy Spirit is God. Yet, the Three remain One.

Barnes (Barnes' *Notes on the New Testament*) speaks of this fact. He claims that it would be blasphemy to unite the Name of Jesus thus with God, the Father, if He were not Deity. Further, it would be absurd to claim the unity of the Holy Spirit if He were only an attribute of God.

We must also consider the verse following, also part of the Great Commission.

"Teaching them to observe all things whatsoever I have commanded you: and, lo, I am with you alway, even unto the end of the world. Amen." (Matthew 28:20)

Jesus is here speaking prophetically to the prototype of the churches He had established. These churches would someday be spread throughout the world. Even if there had been only a few scattered churches, the words of Jesus, "Lo, I am with you..." speak of His Omnipresence. No mere man or angel could be with each of these groups, not even considering at this point the fact that He dwells with each individual believer, at the same time. Only God has the ability to be at all places at all times. Therefore Jesus was asserting His Deity at this point.

Jesus also gave a time frame for His involvement with the believers and churches. He said, "Alway." This word points out His eternality. Again, this is an attribute of God.

John 16:28

Jesus also makes several assumptions as to His essential deity in John 16:28.

"I come forth from the Father, and am come into the world: again, I leave the world, and go to the Father."

Clarke (*Clarke's Commentary*) examines these words of Jesus. Jesus said that He came forth from the Father. This means that He had existed with the Father from eternity since He was come into time as He spoke with His disciples at this point.

Clarke sees that Jesus says that He is come into the world. This is a plain statement of His incarnation within a human body.

John 10:17-18

When Jesus says that He will leave this world, Clarke mentions that this will be by His own volition via the cross. We would note John 10:17-18 in reference.

"Therefore doth my Father love me, because I lay down my life, that I might take it again. No man taketh it from me, but I lay it down of myself. I have power to lay it

CHAPTER 61: JESUS STRONGLY INFERS HIS DIVINITY

down, and I have power to take it again. This commandment have I received of my Father."

The death of Jesus on the cross was within the plan of God. (see Revelation 13:8) Even this horrible physical death was a victory under the complete control of Jesus. So, we must recall, was His resurrection. In each resurrection from the dead within the Scriptural record we see that such resurrection was presided over by one who accessed the power of God. All but one... Jesus was the Author and Power of His Own resurrection from physical death. He was able to Personally access the power of God because He IS God.

Jesus also, as Clarke notes, said that He would go to the Father. We see this prophecy fulfilled at His ascension in Acts 1:9.

John 16:15

Clarke also asks that we consider John 16:15 where Jesus was speaking with His disciples.

"All things that the Father hath are mine: therefore said I, that he shall take of mine, and shall shew it unto you."

Clarke asks,

"If Christ had not been equal to God, could he have said this without blasphemy?"

The answer, of course, is "No." Once again we see that Jesus claimed Deity before any who would honestly consider His words.

Matthew 5:21-22

Take a look at the claim of Jesus in the Sermon on the Mount.

"Ye have heard that it was said by them of old time, Thou shalt not kill, and whosoever shall kill shall be in danger of the judgment. But I say unto you, That whosoever is angry with his brother without a cause shall be in danger of the judgment: and whosoever shall say to his brother, Raca, shall be in danger of the council: but whosoever shall say, Thou fool, shall be in danger of hell fire." (Matthew 5:21-22)

Read (*The Christian Faith*) asks that we consider the uproar that might come about if a young preacher in one of our churches were to say, "The Bible says, but I say..." This is exactly what Jesus did at this point. He took the Words and Scripture and added illumination to them. Note that He did not change those Words. He merely explained their meaning. This is what the Holy Spirit does for us in this day as we prayerfully read the Words of Scripture.

Again, this is an example of Jesus inferring His Deity by taking to Himself the prerogatives of God in displaying the attributes of God.

CHAPTER 62
JESUS' ESSENCE PROCLAIMS THE POWER OF HIS DEITY
(Session Sixty-Three)

Examples

Most of today's session will consider a record given by Anthony Zeoli (*Is Jesus God – Book Number Two*) where he lists numerous examples where Jesus claimed the Power of Deity in His essence.

John 3:31 & 8:23: Jesus Is Above All

First we will consider John 3:31,

> *"He that cometh from above is above all: he that is of the earth is earthly, and speaketh of the earth: he that cometh from heaven is above all."*

and John 8:23,

> *"And he said not them, Ye are from beneath, I am from above: ye are of this world, I am not of this world."*

where Jesus made the claim that He was from above rather than from earth.

Although Jesus, in His humanity, was *born* in Bethlehem, He does not say that He was *from* Bethlehem. He claims that He had actually come into this world from Heaven. What does the old song say? "This world is not my home." This world was really not the home of Jesus. This world is His creation.

His actual home was in Heaven. We may, as Christians long for our "home" in Heaven. But, we are from the earth. Time and earth are the realities of our nativities. Jesus, as God, is from Heaven and above all from the earth.

John 3:12-13: Jesus Makes the Claim That He Is From Heaven

Jesus had made this very point to Nicodemus in the third chapter of John.

> *"If I have told you earthly things and ye believe not, how shall ye believe, if I tell you of heavenly things? And no man hath ascended up to heaven but he that came down from heaven, even the Son of man which is in heaven:" (John 3:12-13)*

Jesus told Nicodemus that He had the right to speak of Heavenly things because of a first-hand knowledge of them as a resident of Heaven. Could any mere man have said this in truth?

John 6:38: Jesus Claims to Be From Heaven For a Purpose

Second, Jesus directly claimed to have come from Heaven for a purpose.

> *"For I come down from heaven, not to do mine own will, but the will of him that sent me." (John 6:38)*

Jesus made a dual claim to Divinity in this verse. Jesus not only made the claim that He was from Heaven, He also made the claim that He had come into time and physicality for a specific purpose. That purpose was, as He said on many occasions, to go to the cross to die as a sacrifice for the sin of the people. Since no angel or mere human could ever die as a sacrifice for the sin of others, this is a clear statement of His Divinity.

John 8:42: Jesus Claims to Be From God

Third, Jesus claimed to be from God.

> "Jesus said unto them, If God were your father, ye would love me: for I proceeded forth and came from God, neither came I of myself, but he sent me." (John 8:42)

In this verse Jesus claims God as the Father and Himself as the Son. This could not be said of the others to whom He spoke.

Matthew 28:18 & John 17:2: Jesus Claims Omnipotence

Fourth, Jesus claimed the attribute of omnipotence. This is a word which means "All Powerful."

> "And Jesus came and spake unto them saying, All power is given unto me in heaven and in earth." (Matthew 28:18)

> "As thou hast given him power over all flesh, that he should give eternal life to as many as thou hast given him." (John 17:2)

If it is true that Jesus had "all power," including over "all flesh," it must follow that He is God. There can only be One Supreme Being. That One is the Triune God of the Scripture. God, the Father. God, the Son. God, the Holy Spirit. The Three are eternally One in Power, Authority, Grandeur, and Essence.

Luke 9:47 & John 2:24-25, 1:1-3: Jesus Claims to be Omniscient

Fifth, Jesus claimed to be omniscient. This is a word which means "All Knowing," or "Possessing All Knowledge."

> "And Jesus, perceiving the thoughts of their heart, took a child, and set him by him." (Luke 9:47)

> "But Jesus did not commit himself unto them, because he knew all men; And needed not that any should testify of man, for he knew what was in man." (John 2:24-25)

Jesus knew even the 'thoughts and intents" of the hearts of men. (see Hebrews 4:12) we could further consider Hebrews 4:13 in this conversation. "Neither is there any creature that is not manifest in his sight: but all things *are* naked and opened unto the eyes of him with whom we have to do."

Besides the understanding of the creature, as the Creator of all that is in the physical realms (consider John 1:1-3) we must also consider that Jesus would understand all the mysteries of the universe as a whole.

Matthew 18:20, 28:20, & John 3:13: Jesus Claims to be Omnipresent

Sixth, He claimed to be omnipresent. This is a word which means "Being at all places at all times."

> "For where two or three are gathered together in my name, there am I in the midst of them." (Matthew 18:20)

> "Teaching them to observe all things whatsoever I have commanded you: and, lo, I am with you alway, even to the end of the world. Amen." (Matthew 28:20)

We must note the spread of the Christian churches over the world. As we have mentioned before, for Jesus to be with each of these churches – and with each individual Christian – is an ability which could only be performed by God.

John 3:13 could be added to the list of verses in this regard.

> "And no man hath ascended up to heaven, but he that came down from heaven even the Son of man which is in heaven."

I draw your attention to the fact that Jesus was in Heaven even as He spoke with Nicodemus on earth.

Mark 14:61-62 & John 9:35-37: Jesus Claims to Be the Son of God

Seventh, Jesus claimed to be the Son of God.

> "But he held his peace, and answered nothing. Again the high priest asked him, and said unto him, Art thou the Christ, the Son of the Blessed? And Jesus said, I am: and ye shall see the Son of man sitting on the right hand of power, and coming in the clouds of heaven." (Mark 14:61-62)

"...Dost thou believe on the Son of God? he answered and said, Who is he, Lord, that I might believe on him? And he [Jesus] said,

> "Thou hast both seen him, and it is he that talketh with thee." (John 9:35b-37)

Jesus never wavered in His proclamation that He was the Son of God. Even knowing full well what this meant to His hearers (consider Mark 14:64) He continued to assert the Truth that He was Deity in the fullest sense of the word.

Jesus was not claiming a "demigod" status as in the Greek myths. He was no mere human descended from the "gods." Jesus was claiming full essence as God Who had inserted Himself into the human race. (consider John 10:33)

John 4:25-26: Jesus Claims He Is the Messiah

Eighth, Jesus claimed to be the Messiah.

> "The woman saith unto him, I know that Messias cometh, which is called Christ, when he is come, he will tell us all things. Jesus saith unto her, I that speak unto thee am he." (John 4:25-26)

The theme of the Old Testament had been the coming of Messiah. Jesus is the fulfillment of those Old Testament prophecies that God would visit His people.

John 14:6: The Way to God

Ninth, Jesus claimed to be the Way to God.

> "Jesus saith unto him, I am the way, the truth, and the life: no man cometh unto the Father, but by me." (John 14:6)

Consider carefully these words of Jesus. He did not come into the world to show us the way to God. He came into the world to BE the Way to God. We do not follow a creed in order to stand before God. If we have any possibility of standing in righteousness before God we must do so in Christ. His sacrifice at Calvary is that which makes it possible for our sins to be forgiven. We must accept Him, not simply His teaching and "life style" to find Salvation.

John 10:9: Jesus Claims to Be the Door to Heaven

Tenth, Jesus claimed to be the Door to Heaven.

> "I am the door: by me if any man enter in, he shall be saved, and shall go in and

out, and find pasture." (John 10:9)

Jesus is here using the illustration of sheep entering into a pasture. His statement "and shall go in and out" does not suggest any possibility of the loss of salvation. Speaking of "in and out" is only intended to show the free access of the sheep to the pasture. When we come to Jesus in faith, accepting His sacrifice as our means of finding salvation and peace with God, we have come to the "Door" which opens the portals of Heaven for our redeemed soul.

John 10:10, 28: Jesus Claims to Be the Giver of Life

Eleventh, Jesus claimed to be the Giver of Life.

"The thief cometh not, but for to steal, and to kill, and to destroy: I am come that they might have life, and that they might have it more abundantly." (John 10:10)

"And I give unto them eternal life; and they shall never perish, neither shall any man pluck them out of my hand." (John 10:28)

Life came to the human race when God created the first human. God then breathed the breath of life in Adam. All human life from that time has been a continuation of that first created life which God placed upon the earth. There has never been a "test tube" baby *created* without the material of human life first accessed. Only God could give life. This is exactly what Jesus had claimed the authority to do. He is God.

John 14:27: Jesus Claimed to Be the Giver of Peace

Twelfth, Jesus claimed to be the Giver of Peace.

"Peace I leave with you, my peace I give unto you: not as the world giveth, give I unto you. Let not your heart be troubled, neither let it be afraid." (John 14:27)

Jesus does not promise us freedom from trials and tribulations. He promises peace in the midst of them. Noah was not saved from the judgment of God upon the world of the deluge. He was saved in the midst of that judgment. I would suppose that the ark rocked somewhat violently from time to time. I would suppose that the work was dreary in caring for all those animals. Still, Noah was given great peace in that he was spared from the effects of that judgment.

Martyrs of the churches have been known to face the flames of torture and death with praise for the Savior upon their lips. My wife was given a sentence of death at the age of just fifty-two. The doctors had found an inoperable cancer in her brain. So great was her peace that her doctors were amazed. Even a reporter from a newspaper some fifty miles away marveled at her trust in her Lord at this time.

Matthew 11:28: Jesus Claims to Be the Giver of Rest

Thirteenth, Jesus claimed to be the Giver of Rest.

"Come unto me, all ye that labour and are heavy laden, and I will give you rest." (Matthew 11:28)

I have witnessed the death of several people. Some have cried out in fear. They've asked me to intercede with God for "just one more day." Others have simply "gone to sleep in Jesus."

It is an amazing sight to witness the saint of God as he attempts to give comfort to those around his death bed. It is only Jesus Who can give this peace.

CHAPTER 62: JESUS' ESSENCE PROCLAIMS THE POWER OF HIS DEITY

John 8:34, 36: Jesus Claims to Be the Giver of Liberty

Fourteenth, Jesus claimed to be the Giver of Liberty.

> "If the Son therefore shall make you free, ye shall be free indeed." (John 8:36)

The setting for this statement is set forth in verse 34 of the same chapter.

> "Jesus answered them, Verily, verily, I say unto, Whosoever committeth sin is the servant of sin."

Jesus was clearly speaking of making one free from sin. This He does though the redemption of the cross.

We might add here that the evil of slavery was not eradicated even within those of the early churches. However, the slaves were allowed equal access to the ministry and leadership of those churches. Many of those slaves became ministers in the same churches in which their masters would worship. Although the seeds of emancipation were obviously in existence, the eradication of slavery would wait nearly two millennia before those of "christianized" nations set free the slave from his servitude.

Cultures of many other backgrounds still practice a form of slavery even unto this day!

John 1:9, 8:12: Jesus Claims to Be the Light of the World

Fifteenth, Jesus claimed to be the Light of the World.

> "Then spake Jesus again unto them, saying, I am the light of the world: he that followeth me shall not walk in darkness, but shall have the light of life." (John 8:12)

John the Baptist had also said this of Jesus.

> "That was the true Light, which lighteth every man that cometh into the world." (John 1:9)

The sacrifice of Jesus offered men the opportunity to come from the darkness of sin and into the Light of the Truth of God. Jesus could offer this view of God because Jesus was God in the human form.

Luke 19:10, John 3:17: Jesus Claims to Be the Savior of the World

Sixteenth, Jesus claimed to be the Savior of the World.

> "For the Son of man is come to seek and save that which was lost." (Luke 19:10)

> "For God sent not his Son into the world to condemn the world; but that the world through him might be saved." (John 3:17)

Jesus did that which no morality, culture, education, or religion of man could ever accomplish. The death of Jesus on the Cross of Calvary gave man the means to renounce the stranglehold of sin upon his life and accept the free salvation offered by Jesus. The resurrection of Jesus from that garden tomb was proof that he was more than man. He is God.

Matthew 20:28 7 John 10:11: Jesus Claims to Be the Substitute of the World

Seventeenth, Jesus claimed to be the Substitute of the World.

> "Even as the Son of man came not to be ministered unto, but to minister, and to give his life a ransom for many." (Matthew 20:28)

> "I am the good shepherd: the good shepherd giveth his life for the sheep." (John 10:11)

Jesus Christ died in time so that men could live in eternity. He died as our substitute. In doing so He made it possible for us to approach God. He made it possible for us to reverse the curse of the sin of Adam and once again be accepted into the presence of God. This rapprochement could not have been effected by any mortal man bound by a nature of sin. God, the Son, only could do this on our behalf. This was the plan of God even before creation. (see Revelation 13:8b)

John 5:22: Jesus Claims to Be the Judge of the World

Eighteenth, Jesus claimed to be the Judge of the World.

> "For the Father judgeth no man, but hath committed all judgment unto the Son." (John 5:22)

None but God could rightly judge the world of sin because sin is an affront to God. He is the Aggrieved Party from the sin of Adam and all who followed him into the world.

Matthew 16:18: Jesus Claims to Be the Builder of the Church

Nineteenth, Jesus claimed to be the Builder of the Church.

> "And I say also unto thee, That thou art Peter, and upon this rock I will build my church, and the gates of hell shall not prevail against it." (Matthew 16:18)

First we must explain that upon which the churches have been built. There is a play on words here. The meaning of Peter is "a small stone;" Jesus says that He will build His church upon the great rock of the confession which Peter made. It isn't Peter; it is that great confession that Jesus is "The Christ, the Son of the living God." (see verse 16) This is the basis of the Christian churches. Jesus is Divine.

It might be well to note at this place that even this great confession of faith was not of Peter, alone. It was given him from God. (see verse 17)

Since Jesus built His Church upon this confession it must be important to acknowledge the Divinity of Jesus. The Divinity of Jesus is also shown through the fact that He has been building this church for nearly two thousand years. This fact alone is testament to His full Divinity.

I have only one other statement to make regarding this passage. I find it strange that people who claim to be followers of Jesus would fail to populate the very institution He founded.

Matthew 16:27 & Revelation 22:12: Jesus Claims to Be the Rewarder of Men

Twentieth, Jesus claimed to be the Rewarder of Men.

> "For the Son of man shall come in the glory of the Father with his angels, and then he shall reward every man according to his works." (Matthew 16:27)

> "And, behold, I come quickly; and my reward is with me, to give to every man according as his work shall be." (Revelation 22:12)

The rewards are twofold. 1) To the individual who has accepted salvation from the Blood of Christ, the rewards are tied to our works of obedience to the Spirit. And, 2) To the unsaved who has not accepted Jesus as his Savior, the rewards are tied to dead works and sin. There is no salvation attached to any work of man. These verses do not suggest such a thing as a "works salvation" for there is none hinted at in Scripture.

CHAPTER 62: JESUS' ESSENCE PROCLAIMS THE POWER OF HIS DEITY

John 11:25: Jesus Claims to Be the Resurrection

Twenty-first, Jesus claimed to be the Resurrection.

> "Jesus saith unto her, I am the resurrection, and the life: he that believeth in me, though he were dead, yet shall he live." (John 11:25)

This was at the grave of Lazarus. He had been dead four days when Jesus arrived. It would have been possible for Jesus to have arrived before Lazarus had died. Martha had seemed to gently chide Jesus for not having arrived earlier. She didn't seem to understand the power of He Who stood before her.

This passage seems to have reference to the resurrection of Lazarus which was shortly to happen. I believe there to be a deeper meaning. Jesus is saying that all things, even death, are in His hands. Not only will He rise from the dead after Golgotha. He shall raise those of us who have not lived physically to see His Second Appearing.

Also, we must consider that His Own resurrection was of His Own volition. He is the Agent of Resurrection because He is God.

Mark 2:10-11: Jesus Claims to Be the One Who Forgives Sin

Twenty-second, Jesus claimed to be the One Who forgives sin.

> "But, that ye may know that the Son of man hat power on earth to forgive sins, (he saith to the sick of the palsy,) I say unto thee, Arise, and take up thy bed, and go thy way into thine house." (Mark 2:10-11)

Jesus didn't just say that He had power to forgive sins; He gave proof of the matter. Remember, forgiving sins is the prerogative of God only. This is an instance where Jesus clearly stated His Divinity.

John 14:14: Jesus Claims to Be the One Who Answers Prayer

Twenty-third, Jesus claimed to be the One Who answers prayer.

> "If ye shall ask any thing in my name, I will do it." (John 14:14)

Since prayer is always to be made to God, and Jesus is here claiming the ability to answer prayer in the affirmative, Jesus has said that He is God. If this is not so He has promised to do what He cannot do and He, by claiming the prerogative of God, is guilty of blasphemy. The only option of understanding at this point is that Jesus very clearly has claimed absolute Deity.

John 15:26: Jesus Claims to Be the One Who Sent the Holy Spirit

Twenty-fourth, Jesus claimed to be the One Who sent the Holy Spirit.

> "But when the comforter is come, whom I will send unto you, from the Father, even the Spirit of truth, which proceedeth from the Father, he shall testify of me." (John 15:26)

Notice again the wonderful symmetry of Scripture. As The Father had sent The Son, so does the Son send the Spirit. The Spirit then speaks of The Son Who showed The Father unto men. All the "Persons" of the Godhead are seen as working in perfect harmony among the creatures of God's creative acts.

John 14:3: Jesus Claims to Be the One Who Would Come Again

Twenty-fifth, Jesus claimed to be the One Who would come again.

"And if I go and prepare a place for you, I will come again, and receive you unto myself, that where I am, there ye may be also." (John 14:3)

Notice that not only does Jesus promise to return He promises to return from Heaven where He had been working for us. How wonderful it is that Jesus concerns Himself with our well-being. He is truly a caring God.

CHAPTER 63
JESUS CLAIMED DEITY IN HIS VERY WORDS
(Session Sixty-Four)

Two Verses to Consider

We have considered that Jesus claimed Deity by inference in the attributes He displayed. But Jesus also claimed deity in His very words. Orr (*Can We Be Sure That Jesus Christ Is God?*) asks that we consider just two verses. The first of these is John 10:30 where Jesus said that He and the Father were One.

John 10:30: Jesus Said That He and the Father Were One

Some of the cultist's will argue that Jesus simply meant that He and God were of one accord in purpose. This consideration fails as we read the extended passage. In verse 33 we find that the people to whom Jesus was speaking understood Him to be claiming full equality with God. Had they misunderstood it would have been necessary for Jesus to correct their impression of His words.

Instead of correcting an erroneous view on the part of these men, Jesus gave illustration of men, in the Old Testament Scriptures, who had been called "gods" because they spoke the words of God. Then He clinched the meaning which they had assumed in verse 36 when He said that He had the right to the title, not because He was acting as a representative of God in the world but because He was uniquely sent into the world. In verse 38 He cleared any confusion which might have remained by claiming the unity of essence with The Father.

Once again the very next verse gives the meaning as understood, and not challenged, of those to whom Jesus had spoken.

Hebrews 1:3: The Shared Glory of the Father and the Son

Orr then considered the first chapter of Hebrews and sees that inspiration also speaks of the Truth of the Divinity of Christ. Verse three of that chapter speaks of the shared glory of both the Father and the Son. Express image is a limiting phrase which means a shared, not merely a closely copied, image.

Also, the fact that Jesus is "upholding all things by the word of his power" means that Jesus is both the cause (see John 1:1-3) and power behind the entire creation. "Sitting at the right hand" is a phrase symbolic of power. The power of Jesus is the power of God.

We see the phrase "Thou art my Son, this day have I begotten thee..." in verse five. To the casual reader this may be a confusing sentence. Once again we must consider the dual nature of Jesus. He is from eternity. But, in His humanity He was born into the human race in Bethlehem. God is His father but not His Creator since Jesus has existed from eternity.

Jesus became a human in Bethlehem in order to become the Perfect Sacrifice, as one of us, for those created beings of the human race.

The phrase "first begotten" in verse six speaks of His position as the Ultimate Leader of the redeemed of the human race. Notice also in this verse that the angels worship Him. None but God can accept worship. None but God will be offered worship by the angels of God.

Jesus Claims the Authority of God In Three Specific Areas

Little (*Know What and Why You Believe*) sees that Jesus claims the authority of God in three specific areas.

Mark 2:10 Jesus Said "The Son of Man Hath Power on Earth to Forgive Sin"

The first of these is in Mark 2:10 where Jesus healed a lame man by saying that his sins were forgiven. The scribes in attendance were horrified that Jesus had taken the prerogative of God to forgive sin. Jesus knew that this was in their minds. (This is another attribute of God – not of man!) Jesus challenged the reasoning of these scribes and proved His power, and His Divinity, by telling the man to arise, take his bed, and go home. (see verses 11-12)

John 5:22: All Judgment Is Committed Unto the Son

Little also refers us to John 5:22 where Jesus makes this statement.

> *"For the Father judgeth no man, but hath committed all judgment unto the Son."*

Once again, as we stated in a previous session, God is the Aggrieved Party when any person sins. Sin is an offense against the created order of God. For Jesus to judge people for sin is for Him to be seated as the very power of God.

John 5:21, 6:39-40, 54; John 10:17-18: Jesus Has Authority to Raise the Dead

Little understands that Jesus claimed the authority to raise the dead. Jesus is seen as the Giver of Life. Little considers three passages in relation to this.

> *"And this is the Father's will which hath sent me, that of all which he hath given me I should lose nothing, but should raise it up again at the last day. And this is the will of him that sent me, that every one which seeth the Son and believeth on him, may have everlasting life: and I will raise him up at the last day." (John 6:39-40)*

In this we see not only that many, most!, of the saints will die physically. But, the physical death of the Christian is not as the death of others. I Thessalonians 4:13 reminds us, "...sorrow not, even as others which have no hope." We have hope because we have the Giver of Hope. Jesus will raise up again those who have fallen into the sleep of earthly death. This is the power of God.

This concept is repeated in verse 54 of the sixth chapter of John. Jesus promises that those who die in Him will be raised by Him.

The most, from our human standpoint, amazing life which Jesus resurrected from physical death was His Own.

> *"Therefore doth my Father love me, because I lay down my life, that I might take it again. No man taketh it from me, but I lay it down of myself: I have power to lay it down, and I have power to take it again. This commandment have I received of my Father." (John 10:17-18)*

Never, at any time in Scripture does a man resurrect Himself from death. There are many resurrections. All of these were performed in the power of God. So, too, was the resurrection of Jesus in the power of God as God, the Son, brought physical life, robust physical life, back to His beaten, bloodied and crucified Body. Jesus rose from the dead. No other "religious leader" can make such a claim because Jesus is alone in

CHAPTER 63: JESUS CLAIMS DEITY IN HIS VERY WORDS

this as He is God in the flesh of humanity.

Clarke (*Clarke's Commentary*) looks at John 5:21.

> "For as the Father raiseth up the dead and quickeneth them, even so the Son quickeneth whom he will."

Note well the phrase "whom he will." The Son raises the dead by His Own "...sovereign power and independence." He did not do so as did the prophets who had to gain privilege from Deity.

The verse, obviously, means exactly what it says. But we can easily see that the meaning is much deeper than we would think at first glance. The word "quicken" means to be made alive, revived, or enlivened, according to the Defined King James Bible. That term is used both of the physical and the spiritual.

> "And you hath he quickened, who were dead in trespasses and sins." (Ephesians 2:1)

It is through Jesus that our sin darkened hearts are made alive to the light of fellowship with God. This is due to His sacrificial death, for us, on the Cross of Calvary.

Falwell (*The Annotated Study Bible*) looks at John 10:17-18 (see above) and finds that "Jesus does more than predict His crucifixion and resurrection. He also shows that He had the power to lay down His life and to take it up again, once more asserting His deity."

Jesus claimed to be Deity in various situations.

Matthew 26:63-64: Jesus Tells the Truth About Who He Was and Is

A trial, especially a trial where a capital offense is involved meaning that life and death are the issues involved, is a time of duress for any human being. For Jesus this was another opportunity to tell the truth about Himself.

> "And the high priest answered and said unto him, I adjure thee by the living God, that thou tell us whether thou be the Christ, the Son of God. Jesus saith unto him, Thou hast said, nevertheless I say unto you, Hereafter shall ye see the Son of man sitting on the right hand of power, and coming in the clouds of heaven." (Matthew 26:63-64)

John 10:30; Jesus Said, "I and the Father Are One"

The Jamison, Fausset, and Brown Commentary finds Jesus asserting His Deity while under scrutiny. Note in John 10:30, "'Are' is in the masculine gender – 'we (two persons) are'; while 'one' is neuter – 'one thing....'"

Rather than claiming that He and The Father were only on the same "mission," Jesus made the statement that "I and the Father" (we – plural) are one (singular) thereby claiming the unity of the Triune Godhead.

Revelation 1:8; 21:6-7: Jesus Claims the Be Deity With Authority

Understanding that the speaker is Jesus, Revelation 21:6-7 shows us that Jesus claims to be Deity with authority.

> "And he said unto me, It is done. I am Alpha and Omega, the beginning and the end. I will give unto him that is athirst of the fountain of the water of life freely. He that overcometh shall inherit all things, and I will be his God, and he shall be my son." (Revelation 21:6-7)

We could consider Revelation 1:8 at this point. Jesus had claimed the title of "Alpha and Omega" at this point so we know Who It Is that is speaking. We must not make the mistake of assuming that Jesus is the "beginning" in the sense of the first creation of God. He is much more than this. He is God Who began that creation.

> "All things were made by him, and without him was not any thing made that was made." (John 1:3)

All the Claims Leave Us With a Choice

Little (*Know What and Why You Believe*) shows us that all of these claims to Deity made by Jesus will leave us with a choice.

We may choose to believe that these claims are lies. But, to lie such as this is completely inconsistent with the moral force by which Jesus taught.

We may choose to believe that He may have been sincere in His claims and yet self-deceived. There is a problem with this view. His life exhibited great calm. This was true even in the face of the death of crucifixion. He did not give the appearance of insanity.

We may choose to believe that He was only a legend. This was taught often early in the last century. The results of further study about His life and the movement He birthed have nearly moved this theory to the dustbin of outrageous fiction. For instance, parts of Mark are available that were written when there were still people alive who would have known if these things were true or untrue. This does not mean that parts of Mark were written at differing times; the meaning is that there are fragments of the Book of Mark available from that time period.

A lie does not forge a movement among people where even the first purveyors of the lie would have been martyred.

Isn't it simply more reasonable and probable that He spoke the Truth? I hesitate to place a question mark at the end of the previous sentence as it is so obviously a statement of fact rather than a query.

CHAPTER 64
OTHERS ADMIT TO THE DEITY OF CHRIST
(Session Sixty-Five)

Many modern day skeptics will argue that the first Christians did not consider Jesus to be Divine. They assert that the Divinity of Christ was a late addition to the simple story of a young Jewish preacher who never considered such about himself.

Many Persons Recognized Who Jesus Was

These skeptics are wrong. Many persons in the inspired and preserved Scripture recognized Who Jesus was as He walked among them and is even unto this day. Still, the skeptic continues to deride the notion of the Divinity of Jesus. These skeptics will argue that the Scriptures themselves are unreliable. "Those Scriptures have changed so much during the centuries that we have only a scant inference as to what they originally said," we are told by the skeptic, the false religions of mankind, and – sadly – many who profess themselves to be followers of Jesus.

The Claim That Scripture Has Changed So Much We Cannot Know is False

These, too, are wrong. The entire cannon of Scripture was completed about 95 A.D. There were still some who could look back from the twilight years and remember from their own youth the Man from Galilee. Others had parents and grandparents who still told the story in hushed tones of the wonder of the life, death and resurrection of Jesus.

A short fifty years from the completion of the cannon we see a Syrian translation of the Words of Life. Within ten years from this the first Latin translation entered upon the scene. Then the floodgates opened and translation upon translation would follow of the Scriptural message. Add to this the writing of the various "Church Fathers," who were writing even before those first translations, and we are shown a wealth of evidence that the Scripture has not changed and been "mythicized;" the Scripture has been preserved just as Jesus said that it would. (consider Matthew 5:18)

What we have is an accurate, historical, record of what people said about Jesus in His human lifetime on the earth.

Nine Instances of Contemporaries Who Recognized His Divinity

Orr (*Can We Be Sure that Jesus Christ is God?*) lists nine such instances of the contemporaries of the human Jesus who recognized His divinity.

First, John 1:36: John the Baptist

The first example is found in John 1:36. This is John the Baptist speaking.

"And looking upon Jesus as he walked, he saith, Behold the Lamb of God."

This statement would have been easily understood by the first century Jew who would go yearly to the Temple to offer sacrifice. Beyond this we must consider just who was John. Go back to the first chapter of Luke and we will find that John was from the priestly caste.

John knew what the phrase "Lamb of God" meant. The lamb was more than a beast of livestock. Oh, the lamb was that. But, more than this the lamb was a primary sacrificial animal. In saying that Jesus was the "Lamb of God" John was saying that Jesus was the sin bearer Who would take away the sins of the repentant.

Even more than the sacrifice offered by the people, this phrase meant that Jesus was the sacrifice offered by God for the sins of the people. In order to fulfill this office and responsibility it would be necessary that the Sacrifice have the legal "standing" to do so. The Sacrifice could have no sin of His Own. The Sacrifice must be of the "family" of humanity in order to be the representative of humanity. The Sacrifice must also be "outside" the family of man or the very sin of Adam would have made him unable to fulfill those duties.

None but the Virgin Born Son of God could be the True "Lamb of God." Only true Deity could fulfill the Office.

Second, Matthew 16:16: The Apostle Peter

The second example is found in Matthew 16:16. This is the apostle Peter speaking.

> *"And Simon Peter answered and said, Thou art the Christ, the Son of the living God." We must also realize this was not a case of Peter simply speaking excitedly or over enthusiastically. The very next verse informs us that, "...flesh and blood hath not revealed it unto thee, by my Father which is in heaven." (Matthew 16:17b)*

Peter was calling Jesus the very Messiah of God prophesied in the Old Testament. He also admitted that Jesus was no mere human but the Son of God. In doing so Peter attributed Deity to Jesus.

Third, John 20:28: The Apostle Thomas

The third example is found in John 20:28. This is the apostle Thomas speaking.

> *"And Thomas answered and said unto him, My Lord and my God."*

Jesus did not rebuke Thomas for this statement. We may also dismiss the error of those who would argue that Thomas was "swearing" in surprise. Jesus would have rebuked Thomas has this been the case.

> *"Thou shalt not take the name of the LORD thy God in vain..." (Exodus 20:7a)*

Thomas had spoken those words in wonder and in worship. By His Own silence Jesus affirmed the words of Thomas as correct.

Fourth, John 20:31; The Apostle John

The fourth example is found in John 20:31. This is the apostle John speaking. This is also inspired speech as it is written into the record of God.

> *"But these are written that ye might believe that Jesus is the Christ, the Son of God, and that believing ye might have life through his name."*

Adding to the argument that Jesus is more than a mere man, John includes the fact that salvation is available only through Jesus.

Fifth, John 4:29: The Samaritan Woman

The fifth example is found in John 4:29. This is the Samaritan woman speaking.

> *"Come, see a man, which told me all things that ever I did: is not this the Christ?"*

Whatever else might be said of this woman, she was changed through her encounter with Jesus. She recognized that He was more than a man. So certain was

CHAPTER 64: OTHERS ADMIT TO THE DEITY OF CHRIST

she that she even gave up her "dignity" (She brought to the minds of people what type of woman she had been,) and became an "evangelist" for the Good News that Jesus died in time so that others could live in eternity.

Sixth, John 9:33: The Blind Man Healed

The sixth example is found in John 9:33. This is one who had felt the healing touch of Jesus in his own life who is speaking. "If this man were not of God, he could do nothing." The religious "professionals" did not believe in Jesus. They argued,

> "We know that God spake unto Moses: as for this fellow, we know not from whence he is." (John 9:30)

Even the religious "leaders" could not shake the faith of this man who had experienced the Truth of Jesus as exhibiting the power of God.

Seventh, Matthew 27:54: The Centurion and His Men

The seventh example is found in Matthew 27:54. The multitude and the hardened military men who took part in the crucifixion are speaking of Jesus in this place.

> "Now when the centurion, and they that were with him watching Jesus, saw the earthquake, and those things that were done, they feared greatly, saying, Truly this was the Son of God."

There were frequent crucifixions. Many had been witnessed. None of those who had met with this fate had displayed the power of this man. Truly He was not just another human being. He was God.

Eighth, John 7:46: The Enemies of Jesus

The eighth example is found in John 7:46. The enemies of Jesus were speaking here. These were officials who had been tasked with bringing Jesus to the religious authorities. The answer as to why they had not done so? "The officers answered, Never man spake like this." The authority incumbent within the teaching of Jesus was so powerful as to set Him apart from all others. Even the authority of the Pharisee's, probably heard daily by these men, paled in comparison to the Divine Son of God.

Ninth, Matthew 26:59-66: The Witnesses

The ninth example is found in Matthew 26:59-66. At His "trial" before His crucifixion paid informants had to be found to testify against Him.

> "Now the chief priests, and elder's, and all the council, sought false witness against Jesus, to put him to death; But found none: Yea, though many false witnesses came, yet found they none. At the last came two false witnesses. And said, This fellow said, I am able to destroy the temple of God, and to build it in three days. and the high priest arose, and said unto him, Answerest thou nothing? what is it which these witness against thee? But Jesus held his peace. And the high priest answered and said unto him, I adjure thee by the living God, that thou tell us whether thou be the Christ, the Son of God. Jesus saith unto him, Thou hast said: nevertheless I say unto you, Hereafter shall ye see the Son of man sitting on the right hand of power, and coming in the clouds of heaven. The high priest rent his clothes, saying, He hath spoken blasphemy, what further need have we of witnesses? behold, now ye have heard his testimony. What think ye? They answered and said, He is guilty of death."

Neither the false witnesses, nor the "true" witnesses who completely misunderstood what Jesus had said about His death, burial and resurrection (consider John 2:19-21 - Even here the witnesses were not correct. He had not said that He would destroy even the Temple of His Body [wherein God dealt in all His fullness – consider Colossians 1:19]; Jesus had prophesied that the religious elite would kill Him.); it took words of Truth from the lips of Jesus concerning the Glory of His Deity, for the sentence of death to be pronounced by this Jewish "court."

Eight Example of Those Who Testified to the Deity of Jesus

Continuing on in the same consideration, we see that Zeoli (*Is Jesus God? – Book Number Two*) has eight examples of those who testified to the Deity of Jesus.

First, Hebrews 1:8: God Himself

First, Zeoli notes that God, Himself, attests to the Deity of Jesus. "But unto the Son *he saith*, Thy throne, O God, *is* for ever and ever: a scepter of righteousness *is* the scepter of thy kingdom." (Hebrews 1:8) In the first seven verses of this chapter from Hebrews the Father had shown His Own mighty works and spoke of the glory of the Son. Now, lest there be any doubt from what has gone before, the Father addresses the Son as "God."

The fact that the throne is "for ever and ever" also speaks of the eternality of God as a trait of Jesus. Note that this is not a bestowed or applied eternality. This is an eternality of eternal possession by He Who IS God.

Second, John 10:30; Jesus Himself

Second, Zeoli notes that Jesus testified to His Own deity. "I and *my* father are one." (John 10:30) We have commented on this verse numerous times. I would only point out again that "I and my father" – plural, "are" – singular, "one." Jesus is not simply claiming a unity of purpose as the, uncorrected, view of His hearers shows. Jesus is claiming full Deity.

Third, Isaiah 9:6: Isaiah

Third, Zeoli notes that Isaiah testified to the Deity of Jesus.

> *"For unto us a child is born, unto us a son is given: and the government shall be upon his shoulder: and his name shall be called Wonderful, Counsellor, The mighty God, The everlasting Father, The Prince of Peace." (Isaiah 9:6)*

Isaiah is an Old Testament prophet speaking Words inspired by God. These are not simply things said *about* Jesus, these are descriptive phrases and names applied to Who He IS. Note that He is called the mighty God and the everlasting Father. He is not called a "created" or "secondary" god. Jesus is called God in every eternal and powerful sense of the word.

Fourth, Luke 1:46-47: Mary

Fourth, Zeoli notes that even Mary, His mother in the natural, testified to His Deity.

> *"And Mary said, My soul doth magnify the Lord. And my spirit hath rejoiced in God my Savior." (Luke 1:46-47)*

Mary, please notice, needed a Savior. Mary is way too highly exalted by the Roman Church and way to lowly esteemed by most protestant and Baptist churches. She was a wonderful woman, even a heroine of the faith. But, even she knew that she was just a woman who needed the salvation Jesus came to offer.

CHAPTER 64: OTHERS ADMIT TO THE DEITY OF CHRIST

Fifth, John 20:28: Thomas

Fifth, Zeoli notes that Thomas testified to His Deity.

> "And Thomas answered and said unto him, My Lord and my God." (John 20:28)

Once again we have already spoken on this verse. May we continue to consider that this was not a profane exclamation by Thomas. This was an act of worship by a man who knew in Whose presence he stood. Had it been otherwise Jesus would have rebuked him. "Thou shalt not take the name of the LORD thy God in vain." (Exodus 20:7a)

Sixth, John 1:1; Revelation 19:13: The Apostle John

Sixth, Zeoli notes that John, the beloved apostle, testified to the Deity of Jesus.

> "In the beginning was the Word, and the Word was with God, and the Word was God." (John 1:1)

> "And we know that the Son of God is come, and hath given us an understanding that we may know him that is true, and we are in him that is true, even in his Son Jesus Christ. This is the true God, and eternal life." (I John 5:20) "And he was clothed with a vesture dipped in blood: and his name is called The Word of God." (Revelation 19:13)

John the apostle never wavered in asserting that Jesus Christ was God Incarnate.

Seventh, Ephesians 2:6; Colossians 2:9; 1 Timothy 3:16: Paul

Seventh, Zeoli notes that Paul testified to the Deity of Jesus.

> "And hath raised us up together, and made us sit together in heavenly places in Christ Jesus." (Ephesians 2:6)

> "For in him dwelleth all the fulness of the Godhead bodily." (Colossians 2:9)

> "And without controversy great is the mystery of godliness: God was manifest in the flesh, justified in the Spirit, believed on in the world, received up into glory." (I Timothy 3:16)

These are three powerful verses. In the first (Ephesians 2:6), we are told that we are raised to be in Heaven in the presence of Jesus. This would be rank blasphemy if Jesus were not God. To be called into Heaven to be in the presence of a mere mortal would be an affront to God. It would be to consider the Creator only after the creature.

In the second verse (Colossians 2:9) we see that Jesus, in His essence, was – and IS! – fully God while being fully man. The wonder of the incarnation is beyond our mortal ability to fully grasp.

In the third verse (I Timothy 3:16) we see the same theme as in Colossians 2:9. But, we see this more fully as the Trinity of God is displayed. 1) God was manifest in the flesh. 2) Justified in the Spirit. 3) Believed on in the World.

Further, we are shown the ascension of Jesus in this verse from Timothy.

Eight, Jude 25: Jude

Eighth, Zeoli notes that Jude testifies to the Deity of Jesus.

> "To the only wise God our Saviour, be glory and majesty, dominion and power both now and forever. Amen." (Jude 25)

Jude calls Jesus both Savior and God. Further, Jude sees all power throughout eternity to be the domain of Jesus. Jude sees Jesus as God.

CHAPTER 65
THOSE WHO KNEW JESUS BEST KNEW HE WAS GOD
(Session Sixty-Six)

A man can easily fool someone who is not familiar with him. That is the basis on which the "con man" operates. Anyone can be fooled once. Some will not "catch on" to the lies and misdirection's of a false leader until much later. Some, as witnessed by the mass suicide of the followers of Jim Jones, will follow a false prophet to their death. These never really know the man they follow.

Christianson (*Why We Believe in the Deity of Christ*) says that this was not so of Jesus. Indeed,

> "Those who knew Him best were convinced that He is God."

This is not a late addition of "after the fact" theologians of the Christian church. This was the rational consideration of the contemporaries of Jesus.

First, Nathanael

The first example used is not really a good example of the concept "those who knew Him best" as it looks at Nathaniel even before he, himself, had become a disciple. This is, however, a very good example of the impact which a true examination of Jesus would have upon and individual.

> *"Jesus saw Nathanael coming to him, and saith of him, Behold, an Israelite indeed, in whom is no guile. Nathanael saith unto him, Whence knowest thou me? Jesus answered and said unto him, Before that Philip called thee, when thou wast under the fig tree, I saw thee. Nathanael answered and saith unto him, Rabbi, thou art the Son of God; thou art the King of Israel. Jesus answered and said unto him, Because I said unto thee, I saw thee under the fig tree, believest thou? Thou shalt see greater things than these. And he saith unto him, Verily, verily, I say unto you, Hereafter ye shall see heaven open, and the angels of God ascending and descending upon the Son of man."* (John 1:47-51)

The passage goes just beyond the very first of that first meeting of Jesus and Nathanael. Nathanael was impressed to the point of worship when Jesus described to him where he had been and what he had been doing when Philip bade him come to meet Jesus. We could easily do quite a bit of preaching about the importance of, and the power of the Holy Spirit within the Christian witness at this point. But such is best held for another time.

That first impression of Nathanael could have been quickly abandoned by the subsequent claims of Jesus in this first meeting. If I made a claim to you that if you followed me you would see "heaven open, and the angels of God ascending and descending," you might answer as did Martha at the grave of Lazarus, "I know. In the end times we will see such things."

But Jesus continued and said that the angels would be "ascending and descending" upon him. If I said this you would quietly excuse yourself and call for the nice men in the white jackets with the butterfly net. You would assume me, rightly so in my case, to be insane.

Nathanael did not do so. He followed Jesus, and continued to do so for the entirety of the public ministry of Jesus. The force of Jesus upon him was so great that He did accept that Jesus was exactly Who He had said He was. He, Jesus, still is!

Second, John

The second example used is that of John.

> "That which we from the beginning which we have heard, which we have seen with our eyes, which we have looked upon, and our hands have handled, of the Word of life. (For the life was manifested, and we have seen it, and bear witness, and shew unto you that eternal life, which was with the Father, and was manifested unto us.)" (I John 1:1-2)

In this verse John is talking about a man Who had been intently examined. John says that this is an old story which we have investigated in many ways. This isn't a fable that we've heard and accepted. This is something, Someone, with Whom we've traveled and conversed in all manner of ways. We have seen Him in hunger. We have seen Him in fatigue. We have seen Him in danger of the elements. We have seen Him reasoning publicly with experts in His field; and, He has been the more knowledgeable. We have seen Him in betrayal. We have seen Him falsely accused. We have seen Him stand before the court of religion and state. We have seen Him before His executioners. We have seen Him brutally beaten and crucified. And, we have seen Him rise from the dead. We know what we are talking about.

Jesus is from eternity. The life of Jesus is eternal. This is testament to the fact that Jesus is not created. The only conclusion to be reached from the testimony of John is that Jesus is God.

Another verse is referenced to the view of John. Jesus is here the speaker,

> "I am he that liveth, and was dead, and, behold, I am alive for evermore; Amen, and have the keys of hell and of death." (Revelation 1:18)

This verse reinforces the concepts of the previous passage. John completely accepts Jesus as Divine.

Third, Peter

The third example used is that of Peter.

> "And Simon Peter answered and said, Thou art the Christ, the Son of the living God. And Jesus answered and said unto him, Blessed art thou Simon Barjona: for flesh and blood hath not revealed it unto thee, but my Father which is in heaven." (Matthew 16:16-17)

In this instance Peter is influenced by the Father to voice an affirmation of the Deity of Jesus. We might note that it was Jesus Who found this affirmation to be true. Jesus even said that Peter was "blessed" by this contact with the Spirit of Truth. How did Jesus know this was true? Was it just a pretty phrase made to encourage Peter? No. This was truth spoken by the very God Who was bringing that blessing to Peter.

Fourth, Thomas

The fourth example is that of Thomas. Thomas had doubted that Jesus was raised from the dead. Thomas said that he wouldn't believe it was true unless he could feel

CHAPTER 65: THOSE WHO KNEW JESUS BEST KNEW HE WAS GOD

those nail prints and touch the wound made by the spear. This was the attitude of Thomas, who when he saw the risen Jesus was moved to say,

"And Thomas answered and said unto him, My Lord, and my God." (John 20:28)

Thomas was not simply taken by surprise and giving forth an oath. Thomas was taken in wonder and faith. Thomas simply gave worshipful assent that Jesus is, indeed, God.

Fifth, Pilate

The fifth example is Pilate at the trial of Jesus. Pilate was convinced that Jesus was, at the least, more than a mere man.

"Then Pilate therefore took Jesus, and scourged him. And the soldiers platted a crown of thorns, and put it on his head, and they put on him a purple robe. And said, Hail, King of the Jews! and they smote him with their hands. Pilate therefore went forth again, and saith unto them, Behold, I bring him forth unto you, that ye may know that I find no fault in him. Then came Jesus forth, wearing the crown of thorns, and the purple robe. And Pilate saith unto them, Behold the man! When the chief priests therefore and officers saw him, they cried out, saying, Crucify him, crucify him. Pilate saith unto them, Take ye him, and crucify him for I find no fault in him. The Jews answered him, We have a law, and by our law he ought to die, because he made himself the Son of God. When Pilate therefore heard that saying, he was the more afraid; And went again into the judgment hall, and said unto Jesus, Whence art thou? But Jesus gave him no answer. Then saith Pilate unto him, speakest thou not unto me? knowest thou not that I have power to crucify thee, and have power to release thee? Jesus answered, Thou couldest have no power at all against me, except it were given thee from above: therefore he that delivered me unto thee hath the greater sin. And from thenceforth Pilate sought to release him: but the Jews cried out, saying, If thou let this man go, thou art not Caesar's friend: whosoever maketh himself a king speaketh against Caesar." (John 19:1-12)

Pilate, the Roman rulers of the province, was convinced of the fact that Jesus was not just another miscreant to stand before him. Pilate, the Roman ruler of the province, was so afraid of the true power of Jesus that he refused to pronounce sentence upon Him. Pilate did not give official sanction to the crucifixion but, instead, gave Jesus over to the crowd for execution.

Pilate was not without fault. He could have released Jesus; such was his legal and judicial right. Also, Pilate apparently furnished a Roman army detachment to carry out the crucifixion.

Sixth, One of the Men Crucified with Jesus

The sixth example is of one of the men who were crucified with Jesus.

"And he said unto Jesus, Lord, remember me when thou comest into thy kingdom." (Luke 23:42)

This man accepted that Jesus was the King of Heaven. He saw Jesus as returning to His Own kingdom after death. After death comes the spiritual realm. This man would have understood this. He asked that Jesus remember him in the spiritual and eternal realm. This would only have been an effective prayer, and the man would have known this, if Jesus were God and had the power and right to give mercy to him. This was a point of repentance and acceptance for this man.

Seventh, the Apostle Paul

The seventh example is of Paul the apostle. Paul was convinced, and taught, that Jesus was, and IS, God.

> "Looking for that blessed hope, and the glorious appearing of the great God and our Saviour Jesus Christ." (Titus 2:13)

That word "and" is a connective word. Paul said that God *and* Jesus are One in the same.

> "To wit, that God was in Christ, reconciling the world unto himself, not imputing their trespasses unto them; and hath committed unto us the word of reconciliation." (II Corinthians 5:19)

The thrust of the context of this verse is the great grace by which Jesus died on the Cross and resurrected from the tomb to give us freely salvation from our sins. The salient part of this verse is that Paul understands that Jesus was God in the flesh.

We also need to consider that the work of giving forth the message of sin and salvation has been given to us. It is our duty to take the message out into the world that Jesus Christ died in time so that others could live in eternity.

> "Who, being in the form of God, thought it not robbery to be equal with God: But made himself of no reputation, and took upon him the form of a servant, and was made in the likeness of man. And being found in fashion as a man, he humbled himself, and became obedient unto death, even the death of the cross." (Philippians 2:6-8)

This passage deals with the Kenosis. I would encourage you to look back at our sections on the dual nature of Christ and His voluntary submission for further consideration of this topic. The Kenosis is a theological term which deals with the fact that Jesus laid aside His outward glory associated with His Divinity. He did not at any time cease to be God.

This is important. Jesus had to become one of us in order to offer Himself as a sin offering on our behalf. Jesus also had to be God for that sin offering to be effective.

Eighth, The Executioner

The eighth example is that of the executioner who was convinced that Jesus was God.

> "And when the centurion, which stood over against him, saw that he so cried out, and gave up the ghost, he said, Truly this man was the Son of God." (Mark 15:39)

The standard theological argument made about this verse is that this Roman guard was speaking out of his pagan background. I disagree. This man was stationed in the capitol of the Jewish faith. He had surly heard stories about the healing and miracles of Jesus. Several of the healings of Jesus listed in the New Testament concerned the families of military men. He may have heard such stories about the campfire from those who had experienced firsthand the power of God. I believe that this was a true statement of faith by this Roman soldier.

Ninth, The Writer of Hebrews

The ninth example is of the writer of Hebrews. He was convinced that Jesus was God. We must also note that this Book was written by inspiration from God.

> "Thy throne, O God, is for ever and ever: the scepter of thy kingdom is a right

scepter. Thou lovest righteousness, and hatest wickedness: therefore God, thy God hath anointed thee with the oil of gladness above all thy fellows." (Psalm 45:6-7)

This is a psalm of prophecy concerning Messiah. Note that Messiah, Jesus, is called God in this passage. Not only is He called God, He is also ascribed as having the throne of God and the scepter of the power of God. Even the Kingdom is said to be His. The Messiah is God.

Now, consider Hebrews 1:8.

"But unto the Son he saith, Thy throne, O God, is for ever and ever: a scepter of righteousness is the scepter of thy kingdom."

The writer of Hebrews, via inspiration, has written that Jesus, the Son, is that Messiah prophesied in the Old Testament. Since Messiah is God, and Jesus is that Messiah, Jesus is God.

We also see that the human penman of Hebrews quotes from the Old Testament Book of Psalms. This means, of course, that this writer considered that the Old Testament Book had been preserved and was, thus, authoritative. This also means that this concept of Jesus being Divine was not the province of some New Testament "followers" of Him. This verse fully puts the imprint of Divine authority into the New Testament belief that Jesus is "very God while being very man."

The Testimony of Zacharias and His Wife, Elizabeth

Kelly (*The Deity of Christ*) comments upon the testimony of Zacharias. Zacharias was a priest. It fell to him on one special occasion the duty to burn incense in the Temple. While in the labor of his duties Zacharias was visited by the angel Gabriel. Gabriel told Zacharias that his wife would deliver a child to be named John. This child would be a great prophet in like power as Elijah (Compare Luke 1:17 and Malachi 4:5).

Zacharias asked how this should be since both he and his wife were of advanced age and, in the natural, unable to produce children. The angel upbraided Zacharias for his lack of faith. Zacharias would be struck dumb until the child was born.

Elisabeth was the wife of Zacharias. She was also a cousin of Mary. Mary had her own visitation from an angel to inform her that she was to be the mother of the Messiah. The story of Mary at the home of Elisabeth is found in Luke 1:41-56.

Upon the birth of John Zacharias had his power of speech returned. He said,

"Blessed be the Lord God of Israel; for he hath visited and redeemed his people. And hath raised up an horn of salvation for us in the house of his servant David; As he spoke by the mouth of his holy prophets, which have been since the world began." (Luke 1:68-70)

In this Zacharias spoke of his son, who would be a prophet to speak, and of Jesus Who would be that "Horn of Salvation." Zacharias could not have made the entire phrase to be about John because John was not in the house (lineage) of David as was Jesus.

By saying these things Zacharias was speaking of the Messiahship of Jesus. First, Jesus was that "Horn of Salvation;" only deity could fill that office. Second, Zacharias applied that prophecy from Malachi 4:5 to John. John, himself, would later say,

"And I saw, and bare record that this [Jesus in the context of the narrative, v. 33] is the Son of God." (John 1:34)

The Testimony of Thomas

Barnes (*Barnes' Notes on the New Testament*) considers also the statement of Thomas.

> "And Thomas answered and said unto him, My Lord and my God." (John 20:28)

Although we've been over this verse several times in the recent pages I believe it well that we consider Barnes comments.

First, Barnes notes that this could not have been a mere expression of surprise as it was said to the very face of Jesus. Jesus did not rebuke Thomas for either profanity or mistake. Neither was Thomas charged with blasphemy for stating the Divinity of Jesus.

Second, Barnes notes that Thomas was commended for his statement. This would not have been the case with a profane outburst.

> "Jesus saith unto him, Thomas, because thou hast seen me, thou hast believed: blessed are they that have not seen and yet have believed." (John 20:29)

Clarke (*Clarke's Commentary*) adds that if Jesus were not God He could not have allowed this statement from Thomas. He could not have been a prophet or even an

> "...honest man, to permit his disciple to indulge in a mistake so monstrous and destructive..."

We must note that this affirmation of Thomas was not corrected by Him Who is Truth. (consider John 14:6)

Further, Criswell (*The Criswell Study Bible*) comments that Thomas said, "My Lord and my God." The former is the title of Jesus; the latter is a title of Deity. Thomas affirmed that this was Jesus and that Jesus is God.

CHAPTER 66

HIS ENEMIES UNDERSTOOD THE CLAIMS OF JESUS TO DEITY

(Session Sixty-Seven)

The Scribes

McDowell (*Answers to Tough Questions*) reminds us that not only did the friends of Jesus but also His enemies understood the claims of Jesus to deity.

In the second chapter of Mark we have the incident related of the lame man who was let down through the roof into the presence of Jesus. The crowd had been too large to allow the friends of this man to directly approach Jesus with the man. Jesus said,

"Thy sins be forgiven thee." (Mark 2:5b)

Although the scribes didn't verbalize it, they did consider "in their hearts" an objection.

"Why doth this man thus speak blasphemy? who can forgive sins but God only?" (Mark 2:7)

A question naturally arises here. If these scribes did not verbalize their objection but only considered it within their hearts, how did the human writer of Mark know what had happened? There are two possible answers. First, it could be that Jesus told His disciples later. Second, it could be that some of the scribes later spoke in wonder and confusion: "How did He know what I was thinking?"

There is, of course, a third answer to the question: Inspiration could have revealed the fact as the human instrument wrote the Words of God.

Be the answer as it may, the fact remains that Jesus did not dispute the reasoning of those scribes. As a matter of plain fact Jesus agreed with those scribes in His answer in verses ten and eleven. Jesus had claimed to be God in His power and in His actions. Although I am rather certain that they would not have agreed, the scribes own reasoning attested to this fact.

The *Pulpit Commentary* asks that we consider John 5:17-18 where the Jewish interpretation of what He had said was that Jesus was, by what He had said, "making himself equal with God." (John 5:18b) Rather than correcting this view Jesus argues for it.

In verse nineteen Jesus says that the Father and the Son are equal in will and operation. This is to say that the Father and the Son are acting in concert both in intent and in application. For this to be so it is necessary that the Two act from the same Divine will. The inference must be that the Two are One in essence and nature. To be merely One in purpose would not produce the simultaneous actions as described.

Jesus argues that there is, in Him, an equality based on unity with God. This unity comes from their sameness of nature and essence.

In verse twenty we see that the Father communicates with the Son. Again, this communication is instantaneous and purposeful. The context of the narrative will show us that this is not a matter of separateness but flows from the unity of essence of the Father and the Son.

The very next verse (twenty-one) gives an example of the unity of essence when Jesus relates that both the Father and the Son are joined in the quickening (making alive) of the dead. Since real life can only come from God, and since both Father and Son are active in establishing life, the only conclusion possible is that Jesus is God.

A further example of the Divinity of Jesus is shown in the fact that verse twenty-two informs us that all judgment belongs to Jesus. Sin is an affront to the Creator. Only He Who created humanity has the option to judge humanity for sin. Since Jesus is given that work, it must follow that Jesus is God.

The Jews Who Tried to Stone Him

Barnes (*Barnes' Notes on the New Testament*) makes comments in reference to John 10:35-39. In this extended passage we see that Jesus had claimed that He and the Father were one. (John 10:30) The Jews then took up stones to stone Jesus to death. Jesus asked why they were doing so. The answer was that "...thou [Jesus] being a man, makest thyself God." (John 10:33) Note carefully that Jesus did not deny that the Term applied to Him.

Jesus did not deny that the term "God" was properly applied to Him.

Jesus did not deny that the application of the term to Him implied that He was, indeed, God.

Jesus did argue with the inconsistency of charging Him with blasphemy. There were Old Testament examples of men who were called "god" because they stood in the place of giving forth the Words of God or carried forth judgment upon people in the Name and Authority of God. Since He Who stood before them was very God, and these others who had only acted as ambassadors of God were called "god," Jesus had every right to the Title which was rightfully His.

Jesus followed this defense with proofs that He was God. (John 10:37-38) As the men again began to pick up stones to stone Him to death Jesus simply walked away from them. This was a mighty act of God.

My son has two rather large dogs. A few weeks ago these dogs got into an argument over some food that had been given them. It is hard to break up a dog fight. Men are not all that much different in their tenacity when they have decided to do violence to a fellow human being. This being especially so when a "mob" is involved. Who can argue the displayed power of God when Jesus just walked away from an angry mob?

The Demons

Jamison, Fausset, and Brown (*Commentary Practical and Explanatory on the Whole Bible*) use Mark 1:24 to show that the demons understood the deity of Jesus.

> "Saying, Let us alone; what have we to do with thee, thou Jesus of Nazareth? art thou come to destroy us? I know thee who thou art, the Holy One of God."

Jesus was teaching at Capernaum on the Sabbath. A demon possessed man was brought to the synagogue to seek a healing. At the sight of Jesus, even before He had spoken to the man, these demons recognized Jesus. Jesus told the demons to not speak as He was not yet ready to present Himself to the Jews as their Messiah and

CHAPTER 66: HIS ENEMIES UNDERSTOOD THE CLAIMS OF JESUS TO DEITY

King. Then He cast the demon out of the man.

Had the Jews accepted Jesus as their Messiah and King before Calvary that trip may have been avoided. But, so also could the wonderful salvation offered through that sacrifice have been avoided. However, the plan of God was always the cross. (consider Revelation 13:8)

Paul, speaking of the mystery of the church addressed this very thing:

> "For I would not, brethren, that ye should be ignorant of this mystery, lest ye should be wise in your won conceits; that blindness in part is happened to Israel, until the fullness of the Gentiles be come in." (Romans 11:25)

God knew that Israel would reject her Messiah. This brought in the great mystery of the Church Age in which the gospel is to be preached to all nations. Scofield (*The Scofield Reference Bible*) calls this time "the great parenthesis" as it is a time when His program for His chosen people of the earth, the Jew, is set aside until He calls them back to Himself. Their promises are not forfeit. The promises to the Jew are only held in abeyance until the time when they will recognize their king.

> "And as all Israel shall be saved, as it is written, There shall come out of Sion the Deliverer, and shall turn away ungodliness from Jacob. For this is my covenant unto them, when I shall take away their sin." (Romans 11:26-27)

It is suggested that the demon may have told the people Who He was so that they would accept Jesus as a temporal Messiah. This is of the same order as Satan tempting Jesus in the wilderness when Satan offered Jesus the kingdoms of the world. (see Matthew 4:8-10)

Most of the Jews

At the time that Jesus first came into the world via the incarnation the Jewish people were under the thumb of the Roman Empire. They longed for a leader who would come as a physical ruler to bring freedom and political power to Israel. Many pseudo Messiahs would grace the scene of the history of the time. Many of the people followed these leaders in revolts that led to death. The messiah for which the people were looking was a temporal and military messiah. True, they saw the Messiah as a spiritual leader but this was a secondary consideration at the time.

Jesus did come to set the people free. But He came to set the people free from their sin. The people would not have understood this.

When the Jews rejected Jesus as Messiah and King, the crucifixion was provided as an offer to the entire world of men to accept Him as King in salvation. We have the ability to accept Him as Savior because He died for us, in our place, on that cross.

This rejection does not mean that God has closed the book on His dealings with the Jew. Far from that! Paul says,

> "I say then, Hath God cast away his people? God forbid. For I am also an Israelite, of the seed of Abraham." (Romans 11:1)

We have neither space nor time to address all the passages which relate to the glorious future of Israel as the People of God. Suffice at this time to say that there are yet many unfulfilled promises which God has made to the people of Abraham. God will keep His promises to Israel just as He will keep His promises to the people of the churches of Jesus. We can count on His Word because He always fulfills that which He has promised!

There is also the possibility that the demon said what he said so that the people might begin to believe that Jesus was in league with Satan.

The Magistrates at the Trial of Jesus

The magistrates at the trial of Jesus fully understood His claims to Deity. McDowell (*More Than a Carpenter*) says that the trial of Jesus was not concerned with what He had done but over Who He was. Jesus said as much in John 10:32.

> "...many good works have I shewed you from my Father; for which of those works do ye stone me?"

The answer to His question was,

> "For a good work we stone thee not, but for blasphemy, and because that thou, being a man, makest thyself God." (John 10:33)

Jesus could not be legally put to death for bringing life back to Lazarus. Yet the religious leadership was so upset with this miracle that they even considered killing Lazarus.

> "But the chief priests consulted that they might put Lazarus also to death." (John 12:10)

The Religious Elite

Another man, a man born blind, was healed by Jesus. The reaction of the religious elite was to question both the man and his parents about this healing. It seems that they were upset that Jesus had done good on the Sabbath. The religious leaders went so far as to cast this formally blind man from the Temple. (John 9:34)

No. It wasn't for any act of Jesus that these men hated Him. They hated Him for Who He was – and still is. Jesus is God in human flesh.

Read (*The Christian Faith*) reminds us that these "church authorities" who had heard Jesus speak knew, as they asserted at His trial, that He did not claim to be only a prophet. (Luke 22:70-71) A reading of the tenth chapter of John will bring an understanding of Who it was He claimed to be.

The Antagonists of Jesus

Alford (*The New Testament for English Readers*) looks at the antagonists of Jesus. Consider John 8:46. They could find no sin in Him. He daily stood in public to speak the Truth. Yet these religious leaders did not accept Him for Who He said He was. Why is this? There are plenty of natural answers to that question. Jesus was a threat to their political system. Jesus was a threat to their social standing. Jesus was a threat to their religious system. The bottom line, however, is that their foolish hearts were darkened by sin. (consider Romans 1:21)

Jesus' Executioners

Barnes (*Barnes' Notes on the New Testament*) saw that the executioners of Jesus understood His claims to Deity. (see Matthew 27:54) The Romans soldier may not have known all the implications of what he said. He may have spoken from a heathen form of reference, with a plethora of Deity. But, he definitely knew the charge against the accused; the sign atop the cross asserted, "This is Jesus, the King of the Jews." The charge against Jesus was blasphemy – claiming to be the Messiah of the Jews and, therefore, Divine. This soldier, at the very least, said that Jesus was Who He said He was.

CHAPTER 66: HIS ENEMIES UNDERSTOOD THE CLAIMS OF JESUS TO DEITY

For the reasons stated above I do not agree with Barnes' assessment. I believe that this executioner may have even been a believer. If so, to have made the statement he made took real moral courage. Jesus was being crucified for saying that He was Divine and this very soldier is agreeing with Him.

Read (*The Christian Faith*) argues that the early church completely understood the claims of Jesus to Deity in its creeds. This belief in the Deity of Jesus was not a "late addition" to the belief system; it was the reason for that belief system of the churches.

The earliest Christian creed was, "Jesus is Lord." The Greek word for "Lord" is "Kyrios." Although I have some trouble with the concept of the Septuagint, it was an early Greek translation of the Hebrew Scriptures. The word used in the Septuagint (Kyrios) was used "...as the translation of 'Jehovah.'" Therefore, to the religious mind, to call Jesus "Lord," was to give the sort of obedience and honor which should only be given to God."

Yes, the earliest beliefs of the Christian churches was that Jesus was, and is, God.

Judas

Alford asks us to compare John 6:70,

> "Jesus answered them, Have not I chosen you twelve, and one of you is a devil?"

where Jesus claimed to have chosen the twelve disciples – including Judas, with Acts 1:24,

> "And they prayed, and said, Thou, Lord, which knowest the hearts of all men, shew whether of these two thou hast chosen."

where the disciples prayed for guidance over the calling of a disciple to replace Judas. We see in the incident in Acts that prayer is offered to Jesus. Surely these of the earliest church considered Jesus to be both Lord and God.

CHAPTER 67

THE PROPHETS SPEAK OF THE MESSIAH

(Session Sixty-Eight)

John the Baptist, a Preacher of Righteousness

John the Baptist was about six months, in the natural, older than Jesus. The ministry of John was prophetic in that he spoke of the coming Messiah. John was a preacher of righteousness who baptized people as a sign of their repentance. We must consider that John was born into the priestly caste. (see the first chapter of Luke) he would have been well versed in the Scripture of the Old Testament.

When questioned about his ministry by members of the priests and Levites, John gave a Scriptural answer.

> "He said, I am the voice of one crying in the wilderness, Make straight the way of the Lord, as said the prophet Esaias." (John 1:23)

When John said this he was hearkening back to the writing of Isaiah.

> "The voice of him that crieth in the wilderness, Prepare ye the way of the LORD, make straight in the desert a highway for our God." (Isaiah 40:3)

John claimed that he was a prophet foretold in the Scripture of the Old Testament.

It might be instructive at this point to consider some of the Scripture associated with this prophecy from Isaiah as it pertains to John the Baptist.

> "Behold, I will send my messenger, and he shall prepare the way before me: and the LORD, whom ye seek, shall suddenly come to his temple, even the messenger of the covenant, whom ye delight in: behold, he shall come, saith the LORD of hosts." (Malachi 3:1)

Please note that this One Who would follow this messenger was very God. God spoke this and God said that this messenger would "...prepare the way before me..." "Me," in this case is very God. That One Who would follow this messenger was to be God.

Consider well that the speaker here is God. He says that He will come to the land and Temple. He also says that there will be a "messenger" who will come before He does. This messenger will work to prepare the way for God to enter into human history.

The ministry of John was, time wise, before the public ministry of Jesus. Of his own ministry John said,

> "He it is, who coming after me is preferred before me, whose shoe's latchet I am not worthy to unloose." (John 1:27)

John claimed only to be the forerunner of One Who would be much greater than himself. John also identified this One.

> "And looking upon Jesus as he walked, he saith, Behold the Lamb of God." (John 1:36.)

It is important to notice that John said the One Who was coming after him "...is preferred before me..." This speaks of the pre-existence of Jesus. Again, Jesus is God.

He took upon Himself a human body some six months after the birth of John the Baptist. But, in His Deity Jesus predates ("preferred before me") John as Jesus is God from all eternity. This was the message of John as to his own role.

> *"Behold, I will send you Elijah the prophet before the coming of the great and dreadful day of the LORD. And he shall turn the heart of the fathers to the children, and the heart of the children to their fathers, lest I come and smite the earth with a curse." (Malachi 4:5-6)*

This is a verse, I believe, with a dual meaning. The one meaning is for the end times. That meaning is not germane to our present discussion.

What is germane is the fact that God said He would sent Elijah, the prophet, before His Messiah would enter into human history. But, you may well ask, are we not speaking of John the Baptist and not Elijah? Well, yes and no.

> *"And his disciples asked him, saying, Why then say the scribes that Elias must first come? And Jesus answered and said unto them, Elias truly shall first come, and restore all things. But, I say unto you, That Elias is come already, and they knew him not, but have done unto him whatsoever they listed. Likewise shall also the Son of man suffer of them. Then the disciples understood that he spake unto them of John the Baptist." (Matthew 17:10-13)*

To step slightly back we see that Malachi 3:1 records a familiar prophecy. "Behold, I will send my messenger, and he shall prepare the way before me: and the Lord who ye seek, shall suddenly come to his temple, even the messenger of the covenant, whom ye delight in: behold, he shall come, saith the LORD of hosts."

John was that one who should come as a forerunner to the Christ.

Elijah

In Matthew, chapter seventeen, we see Jesus and the disciples discussing those prophecies of Malachi concerning this forerunner. Jesus told His disciples that Elijah, the forerunner prophesied in Malachi 4:5, was personified by John.

Some have confused these verses to suppose that the Scripture teaches reincarnation. That is not the case. Hebrews 9:27 very clearly tells us,

> *"And as it is appointed unto men once to die, but after this the judgment."*

Elijah was one of two persons in Scripture to be *translated* directly (removed directly without having to suffer physical death) into Heaven. Elijah did not taste death upon this earth. (see II Kings 2:11) The other person was Enoch. (see Genesis 5:21-24) When comparing these happenings with Hebrews 9:27 one is drawn to chapter eleven of Revelation where the two witnesses are described as having supernatural power and result during the Great Tribulation.

Many will disagree with me, and I may be way off base, but I believe that the two witnesses of Revelation are to be Elijah and Enoch. It is appointed unto men once to die and these two have not yet died. I believe that they will suffer physical death through martyrdom (and supernatural resurrection) during this time of tribulation.

Since John the Baptist died ("...once to die...") during the ministry of Jesus I do not believe that he was the physical restoration of Elijah. Jesus was pointing out the dual nature of the Malachi prophesies. This was something that was missed by many of the contemporaries of the physical Jesus here on earth. Most of the people were looking for a restoration of the Kingdom in connection with the coming of the Messiah.

CHAPTER 67: THE PROPHETS SPEAK OF THE MESSIAH

Some may argue, "But what about Lazarus, for example, and the others who were resurrected from the dead through the ministry of Jesus?" Could not the Elijah/John connection fit in with these? No. In all the examples suggested, those people who were resurrected by the power of God were resurrected in their own physical bodies. In the first chapter of Luke we are told of the conception and birth of John the Baptist. This was a supernatural event in that his parents were elderly; but, this was a purely physical event in every other sense. John the Baptist had his own body which fell under the Hebrews 9:27 code. His was **not** the physical body of Elijah. Neither was the spirit of Elijah "resurrected" within the body of John the Baptist.

Also, in Scripture we are looking at two appearances of the Messiah upon the earth. The first time He came physically - as a ransom for our sin. The second time He will also come physically. But this second time He will come in the glory that is rightfully His as Deity. At that point He will restore a physical kingdom on earth as He assumes the Throne of David according to the prophets.

The forerunner in His first coming was also a physical man. John the Baptist was so physical that Herod killed him by decapitation.

The second forerunner will also be physical. But, he will be supernaturally human as his resurrection from the death of martyrdom will show. There are two different comings of Jesus. These are of two different circumstances. Thus we see that there are two different men as forerunners.

Along with this we must consider that Jesus came the first time as the Babe of Bethlehem. What we often refer to as His "Second Coming" is actually His second appearing as He comes in the clouds to call His Own in the event known as the Rapture. His actual second coming will not occur until He returns in Glory to judge the world at the end of the Great Tribulation. These prophets in Jerusalem of the Tribulation period will predate that physical return of the second coming.

Now, considering the ministry of John the Baptist, his was the task to prepare the way before God. This Person for Whom the way was prepared is the Owner of the Temple – "his temple" is mentioned in Malachi 3:1. Since Malachi 4:6 states that this One Who is coming is powerful in that He can smite the earth with a curse, we must conclude that this One is the Lord of Hosts.

Considering all this, since the preparer – John the Baptist – came to prepare the way for Jesus, it must follow that Jesus is God.

OT Prophecies of the Ministry of the Messiah

Now we will consider some things about the ministry of the Messiah.

Kelly (*The Deity of Christ*) notes that the Old Testament prophecies indicate that a King will sit upon the throne of David forever. That King will be Messiah. This is a very important consideration especially in this day when some would dismiss the people of Abraham as dispossessed of their promises which God has given them. Many see the Jew as replaced by the church in the economy of God. We have discussed this at other areas; if there is to be a King on the throne of David it naturally follows that the Jew still has a future place in the prophetic economy of God.

Psalm 2:8-9

Psalm 2:8-9 says,

"Ask of me, and I shall give thee the heathen for thine inheritance, and the uttermost parts of the earth for thy possession. Thou shalt break them with a rod of iron: thou shalt dash them in pieces like a potter's vessel."

When this passage is compared with the visions of prophecy in the Book of Daniel we see that the reference concerns an eternal kingdom which will be set in place at the end of the Gentile domination of Jerusalem.

II Samuel 7

This concept of a Gentile domination of Jerusalem gives us insight on one of the first promises to David. In the seventh chapter of II Samuel the prophet Nathan spoke with David about the plan which David had to build a House (Temple) for the Lord. God told Nathan that David was not to build the Temple. That would be a task for the son of David who would succeed him on the throne.

Then, in verse 16 of the seventh chapter, David was given a very important prophecy concerning his throne.

"And thine house and thy kingdom shall be established for ever before thee: thy throne shall be established for ever."

The question could easily be asked as to why, if the house (lineage) and throne of David were to be established forever, is there no king from the house of David in Jerusalem today.

The Times of the Gentiles

The answer has to do with a theological concept called "The Times of the Gentiles." Since the sacking of Jerusalem until this day the entire city of Jerusalem has never been under the complete control of the Jewish people. They have, during the time of the revolt against Antiochus Epiphanies, ruled over the city for a short time but never over the entire Land of Promise.

Schofield, in his *Reference Bible*, makes mention that the age of the church is a "great parenthesis" in God's timetable for this world. That it is as the Church Age is a great age of grace due to the sacrifice of Jesus. His sacrifice has fulfilled the "type" of the sacrificial system of the Old Testament as He has become the True Sacrifice that takes away sin. But, an even longer "parenthesis" is the "Times of the Gentiles" in which the program of God for Israel is under the dominion of the Gentile. God is still in charge. Make no mistake about that. But, He allows for Gentile powers to fill the stage of human history until their own cup of sin is filled.

Israel remains the covenant people of God. The people of the churches remain the redeemed of the Lord. The nations of the world have their own opportunity to turn to God and own Him as Lord and King; in this they will fail miserably. This is all true to the prophetic word.

Psalm 93:2

We could ask just who is that king promised to sit eternally on the throne of David. If we do we need to understand that this King is God's Own anointed. We are told Who this King to Come is in Psalm 93:2. "Thy throne *is* established of old: thou *art* from everlasting." "Everlasting" means "from eternity." Therefore the King to Come, Who will sit on the eternal throne of David is Messiah. That the Messiah is "from everlasting" means that He is God, Eternal.

CHAPTER 67: THE PROPHETS SPEAK OF THE MESSIAH

Isaiah 9:7

Isaiah 9:7 is a prophecy about Jesus. On this point all agree.

> "Of the increase of his government and peace there shall be no end, upon the throne of David, and upon his kingdom, to order it, and to establish it with judgment and with justice from henceforth even for ever. The zeal of the LORD of hosts will perform this."

What does this word "establish" mean? It means to institute, or start, or set up, or found. It does not mean "to recognize the existence of" as many overt secularists in our nation presently claim in relation to the Christian Religion in the public arena.

This may give us a seeming problem. How can Messiah establish the throne of David and yet sit as in the lineage of David? Quite simply there has to be a break in the existence of that throne which is followed by a reestablishment into perpetuity. This is the situation as we now see it to be. Jesus will, as a descendant of David in His humanity, reestablish the throne of David which will never again falter.

Psalm 45:6

Psalm 45:6 also established the Deity of this King.

> "Thy throne, O God, is for ever and ever: the scepter of thy kingdom is a right scepter."

Some may argue that the Psalmist was only giving "royal deference" to the present king by calling him "god." This seems not an argument from logic. Psalm 45:2 says that "God hath blessed thee forever." Therefore Psalm 45:6 is speaking of God, Himself, rather than a mere representative of Him.

Hebrews 1:8

We must also note that the writer of Hebrews makes reference to Psalm 45:6 when speaking of Jesus.

> "But unto the Son he saith, Thy throne, O God, is for ever and ever: a scepter of righteousness is the scepter of thy Kingdom." (Hebrews 1:8)

This is once again an indication that the early churches, and certainly the human penmen of the New Testament, understood that Jesus was God.

The *Concordia Study Bible* looks at Psalm 2:7.

> "I will declare the decree: the LORD hath said unto me, Thou art my Son; this day have I begotten thee."

The Messiah will be God's Servant/Son. "'Son ... Father.' In the ancient Near East the relationship between a great king and one of his subject kings, who rules by his authority and owed him allegiance was expressed not only by the words 'lord' and 'servant' but also by 'father' and 'son.' The Davidic king was the Lord's 'servant' and his 'son.'"

Both of these, servant and son, are true of Messiah in relation to the Father. Jesus came in His humanity to both be our Savior via the cross and our example as to how we are to live as Christians in the world by His life. Jesus is God. In His essential Deity He is equal with the Father as One in the Godhead. But, as a human He showed deference always to the Father. In this He is our example as to how we must relate to God.

Revelation 22:16

Jesus, Himself, declares both His humanity and His deity in Revelation 22:16.

> "I Jesus have sent mine angel to testify unto you these things in the churches. I am the root and the offspring of David, and the bright and morning star."

Clarke (*Clarke's Commentary*) notes that Jesus claiming to be the "root" of David speaks of the fact that Jesus created all – including the Davidic line. By claiming to be the "offspring" of David, Jesus is speaking of His being the descendent of David via Mary.

Isaiah 53 with John 3:16

Kelly (*The Deity of Christ*) asks that we compare the fifty-third chapter of Isaiah with John 3:16. John 3:16 is one of the most beloved and quoted verses in the entire Scripture. The verse speaks of the great love of God for humanity. But there are few details included in the verse as to the meaning of "He gave His only begotten Son."

That fifty-third chapter of Isaiah fills in the blanks. The terrible agony which Jesus went through on the cross was only one of indignities He suffered. He was tired. He was hungry. He saw some of His closest followers desert Him at the time, humanly speaking, they would have been most needed. He was betrayed by one of His inner circle. He was reviled by His most strident critics and, I would assume, others who simply went to Golgotha for the spectacle of another crucifixion. Even His executioners, and one who was crucified with Him, mocked Him. Worst of all, the Father turned His back on the Son as the Son became sin for us so that we could find salvation from our own sins. (see II Corinthians 5:21)

Acts 8:26-39

This passage in Isaiah was that which was being read by Ethiopian official on the way from Jerusalem toward the desert of Gaza. It was from this passage that Phillip led this man to a saving knowledge of Jesus. (see Acts 8:26-39)

The story of the suffering Messiah was the text used to bring salvation to this palace official.

Romans 9:5

Clarke (*Clarke's Commentary*) reminds us that the nature of the Messiah is that He is God. Romans 9:5 says,

> "Whose are the fathers. And of whom all concerning the flesh, Christ came, who is over all, God blessed forever. Amen."

Clarke reminds us that Jesus appeared in the flesh to receive His physical and human Being from these fathers in the incarnation. But He, in His Eternal Self, is over them all as He is God.

Isaiah 9:6

The Pulpit Commentary looks back to Isaiah 9:6.

> "For unto us a child is born, unto us a son is given: and the government shall be upon his shoulder; and his name shall be called Wonderful, Counsellor, The mighty God, The everlasting Father, The Prince of Peace."

This verse is a prophecy of Jesus. That Isaiah calls Him, "...the mighty God...," is significant. Isaiah was no polytheist. This was also spoken under inspiration. As such

CHAPTER 67: THE PROPHETS SPEAK OF THE MESSIAH

every word is beyond question true. It is a statement of Isaiah of the Divinity of the Messiah. Jesus Christ is God but, as surely as the terms, "child" and "son" are used, He is also humanity

CHAPTER 68

THE OLD TESTAMENT AND THE NEW TESTAMENT SPEAK OF THE DIVINITY OF JESUS

(Session Sixty-Nine)

Many of the New Testament passages concerning Jesus use Old Testament passages concerning God as their base.

Isaiah 40:3 With Matthew 3:3

Simmons (*A Systematic Study of Bible Doctrine*) notes two passages which regard God in the Old Testament which are applied to the Son in the New Testament. One of these illustrations concerns the prophecy of Isaiah concerning the ministry of John the Baptist.

"The voice of him that crieth in the wilderness: Prepare ye the way of the LORD, make straight in the desert a highway for our God." (Isaiah 40:3)

Compare this with Matthew's account of the ministry of John the Baptist as a forerunner of Jesus.

> "For this is he that was spoken of by the prophet Esaias, saying, The voice of one praying in the wilderness, Prepare ye the way of the Lord, make his paths straight." (Matthew 3:3)

The word Isaiah used for "Lord" is "Yahovah." This is 03068 in Strong's where it is described as meaning The "Self-Existent or Eternal Jehovah. [This is the] Jewish national name of God – Jehovah, the Lord." All admit that the passage in Isaiah is a prophecy of the coming of Jesus. Since the term means "God" in the fullest sense it must follow that Jesus is God.

Isaiah 6:1 With John 12:41

Simmons also makes an appeal to Isaiah 6:1. This is the vision which Isaiah had of the Glory of God which so impressed him as to lead to spread the Word of the Lord. "In the year that king Uzziah died I saw also the Lords setting upon a throne, high and lifted up, and his train filled the temple." (Isaiah 6:1) The word used for "Lord" in this passage is 01360; it is used "as a proper name of God only..."

Now we are directed to consider John 12:41.

> "These things said Esaias, when he saw his glory, and spake of him."

Isaiah 53:1 With John 12:37-43

Once again the glory of God is ascribed to Jesus by a New Testament reference to an Old Testament prophecy.

Hogan (*Trinitarian Adumbration*) looks at the extended passage above from John.

> "But though he had done so many miracles before them, yet they believed not on him: That the saying of Esaias the prophet might be fulfilled, which he spake, Lord who hath believed our report? and to whom hath the arm of the Lord been revealed? Therefore they could not believe, because that Esaias said again, He hath blinded their eyes, and hardened their heart, that they should not see with their

eyes, nor understand with their heart, and be converted, and I should heal them. These things said Esaias when he saw his glory, and spake of him. Nevertheless among the chief rulers also many believed on him; but because of the Pharisees they did not confess him, lest they should be put out of the synagogue. For they loved the praise of men more than the praise of God." (John 12:37-43)

There are several passages from Isaiah referenced above. Isaiah 53:1 is referenced in this passage. "Who hath believed our report? and to whom is the arm of the LORD revealed.") Isaiah 6:10 is referenced in this passage. ("...lest they see with their eyes, and hear with their ears, and understand with their heart...") the salient reference in our present discussion is Isaiah 6:1. that is where Isaiah saw the Glory of God. This entire passage contains Old Testament references to God which are applied by Holy Spirit inspiration to Jesus.

The "Rock" in Various OT Passages With 1 Cor. 10:4 & Other NT Passages

Alford (*The New Testament for English Readers*) asks that we consider I Corinthians 10:4, where Jesus is called the Rock.

"And did all drink the same spiritual drink: for they drank of that spiritual rock that followed them: and that rock was Christ."

Alford then cites several verses where this term "Rock" was used so we can better understand the Biblical meaning and use of the word.

First we go all the way back to Deuteronomy.

"He is the Rock, his work is perfect: for all his ways are judgment: a God of truth and without iniquity, just and right is he." (Deuteronomy 32:4)

Here, obviously, Moses was speaking of God. We are told here an evident truth: God is without sin. Here God is called "the Rock."

Next we go just a few verses further into this chapter.

"But Jeshurun waxed fat, and kicked: thou are waxen fat, thou art grown thick, thou are covered with fatness; then he forsook God which made him, and lightly esteemed the Rock of his salvation." (Deuteronomy 32:15)

This is a story about a man who was, to all appearances, slothful and lazy. Further, he was intemperate as he could not control his gluttony.

It is clear that his slovenly physical life was carried over into his spiritual life. He forsook God Who was the Rock of his salvation.

Folks, if I can get personal for just a minute. I am not just fat, I am obese. I consider this a terrible testimony before the world. If I cannot control my physical, over which I have great control about what I eat and how I exercise the excess of that calorie intake, why should anyone consider that I have exercised either faith or study in the spiritual things? I can claim that this is physical and has no bearing on the spiritual. But, the physical is the only thing about which anyone can judge my spiritual vigor. It is not a good testimony for my Savior that I am in this state. I admit it. I confess it. It is too my shame and personal dismay that such remains the case.

And now back to our regular commentary.

We move further forward in this chapter.

"And he shall say, Where are their gods, their rock in whom they trusted." (Deuteronomy 32:37)

CHAPTER 68: THE OT AND NT SPEAK OF THE DIVINITY OF JESUS

Even the false gods were called "rocks." In these ancient times rocks were weapons. David slew Goliath with some smooth stones and the power of God. When Saul was pursuing David, David was known to hide in the rocks of caves. Rocks were both offensive and defensive in the art of war. God was the Rock that protected His people and the Rock that could defeat their enemies.

We are now sent to I Samuel 2:2.

> "There is none holy as the LORD for there is none beside thee: neither is there any rock like our God."

The verse asserts that there is no god which is equal to the true God. The other, supposed, gods are but false images of false trust. Only in the true God is there true power and majesty.

Next we move into II Samuel. This is a rather large passage (II Samuel 22:2-23:3ff) which I would ask that you read. I will only comment on three or four representative verses.

This is David speaking in worship of God.

> "The God of my rock; in him will I trust: he is my shield, and the horn of my salvation, my high tower, and my refuge, my saviour; thou savest me from violence." (II Samuel 22:3)

Here David revels in the power of God to protect him even in the trying of circumstances.

> "For who is God, save the LORD? and who is a rock, save our God." (II Samuel 22:32)

Once again God is set in opposition to the false gods of the world and shown to be not only superior but true as opposed to those false gods of the heathen. Once again God is identified as a "Rock."

> "The LORD liveth, and blessed be my rock; and exalted be the God of the rock of my salvation." (II Samuel 22:47)

Again God is called a "Rock" and is worshipped. Who but God could be the "Rock of my salvation?" It is, of course, Jesus Who is the Rock upon which our salvation rests.

> "The God of Israel said, the Rock of Israel spake to me, He that ruleth over men must be just, ruling in the fear of God." (II Samuel 23:3)

In verse two we see that it was the voice of the LORD who was speaking to David. David was reminded that a just ruler must be attuned to the Voice of God. "The Rock of Israel" is a reference to God.

The background of the following verse concerns the Children of Israel as they journeyed from slavery in Egypt to freedom in the land of promise.

> "Behold, I [the LORD] shall stand before thee there upon the rock in Horeb, and thou shalt smite the rock, and there shall come water out of it, that the people may drink. And Moses did so in the sight of the elders of Israel." (Exodus 17:6)

Here the rock was a river of life giving water for the people.

> "Behold, he smote the rock, that the waters gushed out, and the streams overflowed, can he give bread also? can he provide flesh for his people?" (Psalm 78:20)

We must be reminded that Jesus fulfilled this prophecy on at least two occasions as

He fed the multitudes with an abundance from just a few fish (flesh) and loaves (bread).

We further see of Jesus,

> "But whosoever drinketh of the water that I shall give him shall never thirst, but the water that I shall give him shall be to him a well of water springing up into everlasting life." (John 4:14)

The New Testament also speaks of this Rock. Romans 9:33 calls Jesus a "Rock of Stumbling" to those who do not believe.

> "As it is written, Behold, I lay in Sion a stumblingstone and rock of offense and whosoever believeth on him shall not be ashamed."

This verse can be compared with Psalms 118:22.

> "The stone which the builders refused is become the head stone of the corner."

Jesus was that "Stone" which was rejected by the religious leadership. That same Jesus is now become the Head of the churches of God. Isaiah 8:14 also speaks to this conclusion where He is a sanctuary to those that trust Him but a "rock of offence" to those that do not.

The last verse we will consider in this portion is I Peter 2:8. The verse continues the same thought as does the previous.

> "And a stone of stumbling, and a rock of offense even to them which stumble at the word, being disobedient: whereunto also they were appointed."

These religious leaders were appointed to positions of leadership to show the way to God. Instead they refused God and looked away from Him in the Person of Jesus.

What we are seeing here is that Jesus is described as a "Rock" in the New Testament. Since the human penmen of the New Testament were all Jewish men, versed in the Old Testament texts, Jesus was seen as God by the earliest of the early churches and those who were His disciples.

We might consider that the concept of the Sonship of Jesus is a New Testament concept. But, as Zeoli (*Is Jesus God? – Book Number One*) points out there are many Old Testament references to the Sonship of Jesus, the Messiah.

Genesis 49:10 With Psalm 2:7

Shortly before his death Jacob called together his twelve sons. He gave synopses of the character of these patriarchs and prophesied as to some future events. Among these prophecies is the following.

> "The scepter shall not depart from Judah, nor a lawgiver from between his feet, until Shiloh come; and unto him shall the gathering of the people be." (Genesis 49:10)

"Shiloh" is another term for "Messiah."

This prophecy was made about Judah. In the New Testament we find that Jesus did come from the tribe, or family, of Judah. In this Shiloh was seen as a son, although many generations removed, of Judah. This is a prophecy which speaks of the humanity of Jesus as Messiah.

In Psalm 2:7 we see the human penman quoting God.

> "I will declare the decree: the LORD hath said unto me, Thou art my Son; this day have I begotten thee."

CHAPTER 68: THE OT AND NT SPEAK OF THE DIVINITY OF JESUS

This verse speaks of the humanity of Messiah; but, it also speaks of the Divinity of Messiah. In the humanity of Jesus he is a "son" born through Mary into the human race. Still, the Divinity of Jesus is well shown in that He is truly the Son of God.

Proverbs 30:4 With John 3:13

Proverbs 30:4 is another prophecy of Jesus as Messiah.

> "Who hath ascended up into heaven, or descended? who hath gathered the wind in his fists? who hath bound the waters in a garment? who hath established all the ends of the earth? what is his name, and what is his son's name, if thou canst tell?"

This verse is quite obviously awaiting the answer of "God, only!" Nonetheless, Jesus applied this verse to Himself when He spoke to Nicodemus.

> "And no man hath ascended up to heaven, but he that came down from heaven, even the Son of man which is in heaven." (John 3:13)

Jesus, to answer the question of Proverbs 30:4, is the Son of God. How quick are most of us to overlook this important verse (John 3:13) on our way to John 3:16. The fact is that the power of the earlier verse, where the omnipresence of Jesus as God is fully displayed, is that which gives power and meaning to the latter's great promise of love and redemption.

Isaiah 9:6

We are all familiar with Isaiah 9:6.

> "For unto us a child is born, unto us a son is given: and the government shall be upon his shoulder: and his name shall be called Wonderful, Counsellor, The mighty God, The everlasting Father, The Prince of Peace."

Again, this verse of prophecy shows both the humanity and the Divinity of Jesus, the Messiah. A child is born to Mary; this is his humanity without the inherited sin nature from Adam. A son is given; this speaks of His eternality as very God.

Daniel 3:23, 25

We all remember the historical story of the three Jewish men who were thrown into a fiery furnace because they refused to bow down before a pagan idol. What did the king see when he looked in amongst them?

> "He answered and said, Lo, I see four men loose, walking in the midst of the fire, and they have no hurt; and the form of the fourth is like the Son of God." (Daniel 3:25)

Once again the stock theological exegesis on this event is that Nebuchadnezzar spoke from the point of view of a pagan with no understanding of the concept of a "Son" of God. That much may be true. But, Who was that fourth Person? Look back at verse 23:

> "And these three men, Shadrach, Meshach, and Abednego, fell down bound into the midst of the burning fiery furnace."

I would suggest that these three did not "trip." The men who threw them into the furnace were killed by the heat of the flames. Obviously, these three men did not die at the point of entering the fire. I would submit that the three fell down in worship at the feet of the preincarnate Jesus. How else could they have survived even that long unless they were in the loving presence of the Son of God.? Nebuchadnezzar may well have gotten the context incorrectly but inspiration provided those Words of Truth.

CHAPTER 69

I. JEHOVAH AS SHOWN IN THE OLD TESTAMENT IS COMPARED WITH JESUS AS SHOWN IN THE NEW TESTAMENT

(Session Seventy)

We continue to compare statements in the Old Testament as to Jehovah with the testimony of the New Testament to Jesus. Bancroft (Elemental Theology) sees that Jesus fulfills at least eight Old Testament statements regarding Jehovah.

First, the Unchanging Nature of Jehovah: Psa. 102:24-27 With Heb. 1:10-12

First we will look at the unchanging nature of Jehovah.

> "I said, O my God, take me not away in the midst of my days: thy years are throughout all generations. Of old hast thou laid the foundations of the earth: and the heavens are the work of thy hands. They shall perish, but thou shalt endure: yea, all of them shall wax old like a garment, as a vesture shalt thou change them, and they shall be changed: But thou art the same, and thy years shall have no end." (Psalm 102:24-27)

Now let us consider what the human penman, under the inspiration of the Holy Spirit, wrote about Jesus. Consider that this was written early – perhaps only thirty years, or so, after the Crucifixion and Resurrection of Jesus.

> "And, Thou, Lord, in the beginning hast laid the foundation of the earth, and the heavens are the works of thine hands. They shall perish; but thou remainest, and they all shall wax old as doth a garment. And as a vesture shalt thou fold them up, and they shall be changed: but thou art the same, and thy years shall not fail." (Hebrews 1:10-12)

Note the phrasing. The writer is clearly using Old Testament prophecy and imagery to show that Jesus is God. The meaning is the same in both as both are describing deity.

The concept that "they" shall change could well be prophecy of the New Heavens and the New Earth as prophesied in II Peter 3:7 and Revelation 21:1. I believe, however, that this is a secondary application. The primary prophetical application seems to relate to the life times and generations of humanity. I Corinthians 15:51 gives us a hint of the glory that awaits the believer.

> "Behold, I shew you a mystery. We shall not all sleep, but we shall all be changed."

We are gloriously changed but the unsaved are changed ingloriously as they are cast into the pit of Hell.

Second, A Messenger Goes Before Him: Isa. 40:1-4

Second, we will consider that a messenger goes before Him. We have visited this conception at earlier times. One more short look should not hurt our understanding.

> "Comfort ye, comfort ye my people, saith your God. Speak ye comfortably to Jerusalem, and cry unto her, that her warfare is accomplished, that her iniquity is

pardoned: for she hath received of the LORD'S hand double for all her sins. The voice of him that crieth in the wilderness, Prepare ye the way of the LORD, make straight in the desert a highway for our God. Every valley shall be exalted, and every mountain and hill shall be made low and the crooked shall be made straight, and the rough places plain." (Isaiah 40:1-4)

Zacharias Prophesied About John, the Baptist: Luke 1:68-76

Now consider what Zacharias prophesied about his son John, the Baptist.

"Blessed be the Lord God of Israel; for he hath visited and redeemed his people, And hath raised up an horn of salvation for us in the house of his servant David; As he spake by the mouth of his holy prophets, which have been since the world began: That we should be saved from our enemies, and from the hand of all that hate us, To perform the mercy promised to our fathers, and to remember his holy covenant; The oath which he sware to our father Abraham, That he would grant unto us, that we being delivered out of the hand of our enemies might serve him without fear, In holiness and righteousness before him, all the days of our life. And thou, child, shall be called the prophet of the Highest, for thou shalt go before the face of the Lord to prepare his ways." (Luke 1:68-76)

Reflect on the fact that the father of John, after stating all the good that would come from He about Whom John would speak, spoke directly to the child and used the same phraseology as had the Old Testament prophet in regard to God. There is no difference here because this is applying the prophecy to Jesus as Messiah.

Third, Jesus Fulfills those OT Statements In His Own Actions: Jer. 17:10

Third, we will consider that Jesus fulfills those Old Testament statements in His Own actions. The Old Testament says,

"I the LORD search the hearts, I try the reins, even to give men according to his ways, and according to the fruit of his doings." (Jeremiah 17:10)

Revelation 2:23

Now we turn to Revelation 2:23 in the New Testament. Jesus is speaking of Himself in this verse.

"And I will kill her children with death; and all the churches shall know that I am he which searcheth the reins and hearts: and I will give unto every one of you according to your works."

About the "kill her children with death." Jesus is speaking of a woman called Jezebel who claims to be a prophetess but in actuality is seducing the churches into fornication. (v. 20) He has given her ample time to repent but she has refused to do so. (v. 21)

It is suggested by many that this applies to many of the so-called *churches* of the end time who have a faithless faith which seduces many into a false spiritual security which ends in a Christless eternity. At the time of the rapture of the saints such would be left behind to face the horrors of God's wrath in the Great Tribulation.

The relevant point in our present discussion is that Jesus is here fulfilling those things of which it was said that God would do. He could not do so were He not, Himself, God. If it was otherwise Jesus would be in the same position as the woman called Jezebel in Revelation. But, He is not a false prophet; He is God.

CHAPTER 69: I. JEHOVAH IN THE OT IS COMPARED WITH JESUS IN THE NT

Fourth, Jesus Fulfills the Statements About Light and Glory From the OT

Fourth, we see that Jesus fulfills the statements in Light and Glory from the Old Testament.

Isaiah 60:19

"There shall be no more light by day; neither for brightness shall the moon give light unto thee: but the LORD shall be unto thee an everlasting light, and thy God thy glory." (Isaiah 60:19)

Luke 2:32 & John 1:9

This passage is compared with Luke 2:32 where Jesus is identified as

"A light to lighten the Gentiles, and the glory of thy people Israel."

We could add to this the words of John the Baptist, *"That was the true Light, which lighteth every man that cometh into the world."* (John 1:9)

The meaning in these verses is that Jesus is the spiritual light which draws men from the darkness of sin.

Revelation 21:23

I would add Revelation 21:23 which speaks of the holy city of the new Jerusalem.

"And the city had no need of the sun, neither of the moon, to shine in it: for the glory of God did lighten it, and the Lamb is the light thereof."

Pay close attention to the comparison of God and the Lamb, Jesus. Jesus is God for He is the light of the city.

Fifth, Jesus Fulfills the Statements of Temptation

Fifth, we see that Jesus fulfills the statements of temptation. Bancroft does not see in this particular case the temptation of Jesus on the Mount from Matthew 4:1-11. He refers to those which would tempt Christ by their ungodly lusts and actions. We have many people in our day who are often quite vicious in their demands that we accept their perverted life styles. They demand that this is their right. I would suppose that a civil, political, case *could* be made. But, spiritually, such is an affront to God. Our spiritual voices are being cast as evil even when we simply give forth the Truth of God.

Of course, some who call themselves "Biblical" Christians work outside of the known will of God and very violently and hatefully do try to give forth the Truth. I would remind them that hate is of the deceiver while love is from God. A spirit of holy love, with the backing of prayer and the Holy Spirit, can do what hate never can do!

Numbers 21:6-7 Is Considered

"And the LORD sent fiery serpents among the people, and they bit the people, and much people of Israel died. Therefore the people came to Moses and said, We have sinned, for we have spoken against the LORD, and against thee; pray unto the LORD, that he take away the serpents from us. And Moses prayed for the people."

These people were sincere in their repentance. They named their sins just as they had committed those sins. They went to the man who was the representative of God, Moses. They petitioned for forgiveness. That forgiveness was granted in the form of a serpent of brass. This serpent was set up high enough for all the camp to get a glimpse of it. Even though this may have seemed just too easy for some, those who did look at the serpent in faith were healed.

This incident is a prophecy of the crucifixion of Jesus.

John 3:14

"And as Moses lifted up the serpent in the wilderness, even so must the Son of man be lifted up." (John 3:14)

In this day, after the cross, we do not go to a "religious" man to find salvation; we go to Jesus, Who IS salvation.

1 Timothy 2:5

"For there is one God, and one mediator between God and men, the man Christ Jesus. (I Timothy 2:5)

This does not mean that Jesus is not God – because He is God. What it means is that our salvation is dependent upon a faith relationship with Jesus Who died in time that we might live in eternity. He is our only access to salvation.

Bancroft also directs our attention to I Corinthians 10:9 to warn us about tempting Jesus as these ancient Israeli's had tempted God. "Neither let us tempt Christ, as some of them also tempted, and were destroyed of serpents."

Tempting Christ is spoken of in the New Testament in the same manner as was tempting God in the Old Testament. Unless we consider the Paul, the human penman of I Corinthians, was engaging in blasphemy, and doing so as he wrote under inspiration, we must conclude that Jesus is God.

Sixth, Jesus Is Called the "Stone of Stumbling"

Sixth, Jesus is called the "Stone of Stumbling" in the New Testament even as this was said of God in the Old Testament. Isaiah warns us,

Isaiah 8:13-14 With 1 Peter 2:7-8

"Sanctify the LORD of hosts himself, and let him be your fear, and let him be your dread. And he shall be for a sanctuary; but for a stone of stumbling and for a rock of offense to both the houses of Israel; for a gin and for a snare to the inhabitants of Jerusalem." (Isaiah 8:13-14)

Now we find the same phrase in the New Testament. But, this time it will speak of Jesus.

"Unto you therefore which believe he is precious: but unto them which be disobedient, the stone which the builders disallowed, the same is made the head of the corner, And a stone of stumbling, and a rock of offence, even to them which stumble at the word, being disobedient: whereunto also they were appointed." (I Peter 2:7-8)

What we have found here is that Isaiah said that the "LORD of hosts" was the Stone of Stumbling. That most definitely refers to God. Meanwhile, Peter claims that Jesus is "a stone of stumbling." Since there can only be One "Stone" of Stumbling, "one" being a limiting factor in that it speaks of a single entity, then Both cannot be this "Stone" unless Jesus is God. Realizing this shows us that both the Old and the New Testament passages speak of the Same One Who is God.

CHAPTER 69: I. JEHOVAH IN THE OT IS COMPARED WITH JESUS IN THE NT

Seventh, Jesus Fulfills the OT Statements as Shepherd

Seventh, Jesus fulfills the Old Testament statements as Shepherd. The Old Testament statement comes from one of the most beloved of the Psalms. "The LORD *is* my shepherd, I shall not want." (Psalms 23:1) Once again the word translated "LORD" is number 03068 in Strong's. The word is defined as the "...self-Existent or Eternal Jehovah, Jewish national name of God..."

Once again we see that the word means "God" and nothing else.

Bancroft gives us three verses to consider at this place. In John 10:11 Jesus describes Himself as the good Shepherd Who dies for His sheep. Jesus did this, of course, on the cross when He literally gave His life for us. We are only allowed salvation because of His sacrificial death. He literally died physically so that we might literally live spiritually.

It is instructive that He called Himself the "good" shepherd. In the eighteenth chapter of Luke a man came to Jesus and called Him "Good Master." The reply of Jesus was,

Luke 18:19 & Hebrew 13:20 With John 10:18

"And Jesus said unto him, Why callest thou me good? none is good, save one, that is God." (Luke 18:19)

In calling Himself the "good shepherd," by Jesus' Own terminology, He is stating that He is God.

Our attention is next drawn to Hebrews 13:20.

"Now the God of peace, that brought again from the dead our Lord Jesus, that great shepherd of the sheep, through the blood of the everlasting covenant."

We must consider John 10:18 in context of this verse from Hebrews. Of His life Jesus said,

"No man taketh it from me, but I lay it down of myself. I have power to lay it down, and I have power to take it again. This commandment I have received of my Father."

What we see in Hebrews 13:20 are two statements as to the Deity of Jesus. First, Jesus is called a shepherd. Since this is a title of God, from the 23rd Psalm we must consider that Jesus is God. Second, this verse says that God brought Jesus from the dead. In John 10:18 Jesus said that He, Himself, would take His life back up. Putting those two concepts together we must see that Jesus is God.

1 Peter 5:4

Peter also calls Jesus the chief Shepherd.

"And when the chief Shepherd shall appear, ye shall receive a crown of glory that fadeth not away." (I Peter 5:4)

These New Testament instances show that Jesus fulfills the Office of Shepherd. By fulfilling that Old Testament Office in His New Testament role we must conclude that Jesus is God.

Eighth, Jesus Fulfills the OT Statements That He Seeks and Saves the Lost

Eighth, Jesus fulfills the Old Testament statements in that He seeks and saves the lost.

Ezekiel 34:11-12 With Luke 19:10

"For thus saith the Lord GOD, Behold, I, even I, will both search my sheep and seek them out. As a shepherd seeketh out his flock in the day that he is among his sheep that are scattered, so will I seek out my sheep; and will deliver them out of all the places where they have been scattered in the cloudy and dark day." (Ezekiel 34:11-12)

When we compare the above passage with what Jesus said of Himself in Luke 19:10 we find that Jesus was fulfilling exactly what had been said of God in this Old Testament passage. "For the Son of man is come to seek and to save that which was lost."

Jer. 2:13 & 17:13 With John 4:10 & 17:13

Criswell (*The Criswell Study Bible*) asks that we compare John 4:10 with Jeremiah 2:13 and 17:13,

"...where Yahweh is referred to as the fountain of living waters..."

"For my people have committed two evils; they have forsaken me the fountain of living waters, and hewed them out cisterns, broken cisterns, that can hold no water." (Jeremiah 2:13)

In this verse we see that the people have forsaken the God of Abraham. Not only that, they have begun to cling to a "god" and "religion" which cannot offer any hope or salvation.

"O LORD, the hope of Israel, all that forsake thee shall be ashamed, and they that depart from me shall be written in the earth, because they have forsaken the LORD, the fountain of living waters." (Jeremiah 17:13)

The phrase "written in the earth" suggests two things to me. The first is that the only hope which these people, who have forsaken the LORD, can possibly have is bound in this earth. Thus, they have no hope or place of eternal reward and joy. It is a sad existence which bounds into an eternal Hell.

The second thing suggested to me is that even the heathen would see the folly of a people who had forsaken their national God.

"Jesus answered and said unto her, If thou knewest the gift of God, and who it is that saith to thee, Give me to drink; thou wouldest have asked of him, and he would have given thee living water." (John 4:10)

This is the story of the Samaritan woman at the well. Her biggest theological concern was the proper place to worship. Should she worship in the mountain or in Jerusalem? (v. 20) She was so very far away from the God she claimed as her "religion."

She was also one who, I would suppose, was not well spoken of. Her five marriages and current adulterous liaison were most likely the stuff of unkind gossip.

For all her seeming faults and unworthiness, Jesus came to her with the message of life eternal. He identified Himself as Messiah. He also identified Himself as God by claiming to be the "living water" which had been spoken of in the Old Testament.

CHAPTER 70

II. JEHOVAH AS SHOWN IN THE OLD TESTAMENT IS COMPARED WITH JESUS AS SHOWN IN THE NEW TESTAMENT

(Session Seventy-One)

In our last visit to this section we will see that Jehovah as shown in the Old Testament is compared with Jesus as shown in the New Testament. Zeoli (*Is Jesus God? – Book Number Two*) shows that both are the Same in Their essence.

First, Jehovah In the OT and Jesus In the NT are From Everlasting

First, Both are from everlasting. Consider this reference to Jehovah in Psalm 90:2.

> "Before the mountains were brought forth, or ever thou hadst formed the earth and the world, even from everlasting to everlasting, thou art God."

Micah 5:2 speaks in prophecy of the Messiah Who should come. We know, of course, that Jesus is the prophesied Messiah written of in the New Testament. "But thou, Bethlehem Ephratah, though thou be little among the thousands of Judah, *yet* out of thee shall he come forth unto me *that is* to be ruler in Israel; whose goings forth *have been* from of old, from everlasting."

Note that both God and His Messiah are from "everlasting." This is existent from eternity, past. Neither can be called a created being for "everlasting" predates any creation. Therefore both God and His Messiah are eternal in essence. If must then follow that Messiah is very God for none but God could predate, a poor choice of words but fitted to our human understanding, creation and yet have an existence from the eternal realms.

It was from this eternal realm which the entire creation was decreed and accomplished by God.

Second, Both Shall Remain Even After Heaven and Earth Perish

Second, Both shall remain even after Heaven and Earth perish.

> "Of old hast thou laid the foundation of the earth: and the heavens are the work of thy hands. They shall perish, but thou shalt endure, all of them shall wax old like a garment; as a vesture shalt thou change them, and they shall be changed. But thou art the same, and thy years shall have no end. The children of thy servants shall continue, and their seed shall be established before thee." (Psalm 102:25-28)

I have added one more verse to that which Zeoli suggested. I will explain my purpose in doing so in a moment. But first we need to consider the point in reference to our current discussion. The human penman of Hebrews uses the same phraseology of Jesus in the New Testament as was used of God in the Old Testament.

> "And, Thou Lord, in the beginning hast laid the foundation of the earth, and the heavens are the works of thine hands. They shall perish, but thou remainest, and they all shall wax old as doth a garment, And as a vesture shalt thou fold them up, and they shall be changed: but thou art the same, and thy years shall not fail." (Hebrews 1:10-12)

Once again the very same thing is said of Jesus in the New Testament as was said of God in the Old Testament. Therefore it seems quite obvious that These are both God. Since God is One this is an intimation of the Triune Godhead. There is but One God eternally existent in the Father, the Son, and the Holy Spirit. It is beyond our finite understanding to comprehend this fact. The fact that is clear is that the Son is spoken of with the same concepts of His essence as is the Father. Therefore it must follow that the Son is God.

The extra verse I added above from the passage in Psalms concerns the people of God. In the Book of II Peter we are told, "But the day of the Lord will come as a thief in the night; in the which the heavens shall pass away with a great noise, and the elements shall melt with fervent heat, the earth also and the works that are therein shall be burned up." (II Peter 3:10) This event is also foretold in Revelation 21:1. "And I saw a new heaven and a new earth: for the first heaven and the first earth were passed away; and there was no more sea."

It is important to note that these passages are not speaking of the Heaven of God's abode. These verses speak of entities of creation. In this event the sin of Adam, which polluted the entire creation (consider Romans 8:22), will be purged and purified. This could present a scenario where all humanity would be purged as well. Such is not a prospect for the children of God as we are comforted that "The children of thy servants shall continue, and their seed shall be established before thee." (Psalm 102:28)

What about the rest of humanity - those who are not the redeemed of the Lord? Revelation 20:10 says this,

> "And the devil that deceived them was cast into the lake of fire and brimstone, where the beast and the false prophet are, and shall be tormented day and night for ever and ever."

Some may argue that this verse speaks of spiritual beings being preserved in the torments of Hell for all eternity. Those who thus argue could make the claim that there is an annihilation of the souls of the human wicked. I would caution those who hope for this to consider that the beast and false prophet, although energized by Satan, are of human essence. These will suffer the same fate as does Satan.

To those who would argue that such eternal torment is only for those listed in the above verse, I would also note Revelation 20:15.

> "And whosoever was not found written in the book of life was cast into the lake of fire."

It would behoove all of us to consider this certain future and heed the words of II Corinthians 6:2 - "...now *is* the day of salvation."

Third, Jehovah and Jesus Are From the Beginning

Third, Both are from the beginning. The Old Testament begins with four sublime words: "In the beginning God..." (Genesis 1:1) There is no attempt to explain God. There is no attempt to prove the existence of God. There is no attempt to explain the existence of God as is done in nearly every other religion of early man. The Bible only makes the observation that God does exist.

Likewise the New Testament Gospel of John begins with a sublime statement. "In the beginning was the Word, and the Word was with God, and the Word was God." (John 1:1) There is no "cover story," such as was popular in the Greek religious culture

CHAPTER 70: II. JEHOVAH IN THE OT IS COMPARED WITH JESUS IN THE NT

of the day, to explain the existence of Jesus. There is only the sublime statement that He was in the beginning just as the Old Testament argues that God was in the beginning. We are not asked to draw inference that Jesus is God. The verse clearly states that Jesus is God.

This is as clear a statement as any honest inquirer would need. Two of the Three Members of the Triune Godhead are clearly defined. In verse thirty-two of this same chapter we see the Third Member of the Trinity is also introduced. "And John bear record, saying, I saw the Spirit descending from heaven like a dove, and it abode upon him [Jesus]."

I would only add that the same word used for "Spirit" in John 1:32 is also used in Matthew 1:18 of "the Holy Ghost."

> "Now the birth of Jesus Christ was on the wise, When as his mother Mary was espoused to Joseph, before they came together, she was found with child of the Holy Ghost."

Since Both Jesus, of the New Testament, and God, of the Old Testament, are described as existent at the beginning – actually before the beginning since They Both were there at "the beginning" – they must both be considered as God. Since we know that Jesus, in His humanity, is the Son of God and Matthew 1:18 (and v. 20 in a vision to Joseph) clearly states that Mary was with child "of the Holy Ghost," we must also confess that the Holy Spirit is God. We are then presented with the Scriptural case, the inspired and preserved Words of God, for the Triune Godhead of Father, Son, and Holy Spirit.

Fourth, Jehovah and Jesus Speak of Themselves as Being The First

Fourth, Both speak of Themselves as being The First. "Then saith the Lord the king of Israel, and his redeemer, the Lord of hosts, I *am* the first, and I *am* the last, and beside me *there is* no God." (Isaiah 44:6) This was spoken by God of Himself in the Old Testament.

Meanwhile, this is spoken by Jesus of Himself in the New Testament.

> "And when I saw him, I fell at his feet as dead. And he laid his right hand upon me, saying unto me, Fear not, I am the first and the last." (Revelation 1:17)

This phrase and thought is repeated several times throughout the Revelation. It is clear that Jesus was ascribing the Old Testament phrase from Isaiah to Himself. Once again it is clear that either Jesus is God or Jesus was speaking blasphemy as was the accusation of His enemies at His trial before His crucifixion.

Jesus, who is Truth, was speaking Truth. He is God. The great power He displays throughout the Book of Revelation is testament to that fact.

Fifth, Jehovah and Jesus Are The Creator

Fifth, Both are the Creator. The beginning verse in the entire Bible gives one undisputable fact.

> "In the beginning God created the heaven and the earth." (Genesis 1:1)

This is about as plain a statement of fact as can be made. Surely this was an understood fact among those human penmen of the New Testament.

Certainly Paul, a Pharisee (see Philippians 3:5), would understand that God, Alone, was the Creator. Paul wrote,

"For by him were all things created, that are in heaven, and that are in earth, visible and invisible, whether they be thrones, or dominions, or principalities, or powers: all things were created by him, and for him." (Colossians 1:16)

Just two verses previous to this Paul had mentioned of Whom he was speaking. Paul was speaking of Jesus.

Paul considered Jesus to be God.

Sixth, Jehovah and Jesus Are the Supporter and the Preserver

Sixth, Both are the Supporter and the Preserver. Of God in the Old Testament Nehemiah wrote,

"Thou, even thou, art LORD alone; thou has made heaven, the heaven of heavens, with all their host, the earth, and all things that are therein, the seas, and all that is therein, and thou preservest them all, and the host of the heaven worshippeth thee." (Nehemiah 9:6)

This is a strong statement of trust in God and His creative and sustaining power.

Paul, a Pharisee well versed in understanding the Old Testament scripture, wrote this of Jesus in the New Testament.

"And he is before all things, and by him all things consist." (Colossians 1:17)

The Defined King James Bible informs us that this word "consist" is an archaic word meaning "hold together."

To hold something together is to preserve that object. Once again Jesus of the New Testament and God of the Old Testament are shown to be of One essence.

Seventh, Jehovah and Jesus Are Unchanging

Seventh, Both are unchanging.

"For I am the LORD, I change not, therefore ye sons of Jacob, are not consumed." (Malachi 3:6)

Compare this, said of God in the Old Testament, with this, said of Jesus in the New Testament.

"Jesus Christ the same yesterday, and to day, and for ever." (Hebrews 13:8)

The Book of Hebrews has been called the "most Jewish Book in the New Testament." Most of the subject matter in the Book has to do with the Temple order and the sacrificial elements of that worship. Surely the human penman of Hebrews was familiar with the Old Testament Book of Malachi when He ascribed the eternality of Jesus in the same terms as was the eternality of God in the Old Testament.

We must always consider that Hebrews, as are all the Books of Scripture, is inspired and preserved for the Christian's throughout history. Jesus is clearly equated with God.

Eighth, Jehovah and Jesus Are Almighty

Eighth, Both are almighty. In the Old Testament God describes Himself to Abram as almighty.

"And when Abram was ninety years old and nine, the LORD appeared to Abram, and said unto him, I am the Almighty God; walk before me, and be thou perfect." (Genesis 17:1)

CHAPTER 70: II. JEHOVAH IN THE OT IS COMPARED WITH JESUS IN THE NT

In the New Testament Jesus describes Himself to John as almighty.

> "I am Alpha and Omega, the beginning and the ending, saith the Lord, which is, and which was, and which is to come, the Almighty." (Revelation 1:8)

There can only be One Almighty. If there were two neither would be All Mighty since the "almightiness" of the one would offset the "almightiness" of the other. A simple working in concert would not change that equation. That One Almighty is the Triune God Who exists eternally as One in Three.

Ninth, Jehovah and Jesus Are to Whom the Angels Cry

Ninth, Both are to Whom the angels cry, "Holy, Holy, Holy." Isaiah saw his great vision of God in the sixth chapter of the Book which bears his name.

> "And one cried unto another, and said, Holy, holy, holy, is the LORD of hosts: the whole earth is full of his glory." (Isaiah 6:3)

In the New Testament we read another account of this same activity.

> "And the four beasts had each of them six wings about him, and they were full of eyes within: and they rest not day and night, saying, Holy, holy, holy, Lord God Almighty, which was, and is, and is to come." (Revelation 4:8)

The actions are the same. The words are the same. Our only question might consider just Who It Is sitting on the throne in Revelation. That question is answered in the context. As we read down we find the certain identification.

> "And one of the elders saith unto me, Weep not: behold, the Lion of the tribe of Judah, the Root of David, hath prevailed to open the book, and to loose the seven seals thereof." (Revelation 5:5)

The One sitting on the throne, hearing the worship of "Holy, holy, holy" directed toward Himself is none other than Jesus. Since the spiritual beings are offering worship of God directed toward Jesus, and He is accepting such worship, Jesus is God.

Tenth, Jehovah and Jesus Are Righteous

Tenth, Both are Righteous. Jeremiah says,

> "In his days Judah shall be saved, and Israel shall dwell safely: and this is his name whereby he shall be called THE LORD OUR RIGHTEOUSNESS." (Jeremiah 23:6)

> "But of him are ye in Christ Jesus, who of God is made unto us wisdom, and righteousness, and sanctification, and redemption." (I Corinthians 1:30)

Here we see that both of the statements ascribe righteousness. In the Old Testament this is said of God. In the New Testament this is said of Jesus. Note further that this is not the mere righteousness of man. This is a righteousness which effects salvation and redemption to others. This could only be said of God. it would be impossible that this would be said of any human being.

> "But we are all as an unclean thing, and all our righteousnesses are as filthy rags, and we do all fade as a leaf, and our iniquities, like the wind, have taken us away." (Isaiah 64:6)

Eleventh, Jehovah and Jesus Are the Only Savior

Eleventh, Both are the Only Savior. Isaiah looks and God and hears Him say,

> "I, even I, am the LORD; and beside me there is no saviour." (Isaiah 43:11)

Meanwhile Peter preached to the religious panel which had only weeks before sent

Jesus to the death of crucifixion.

> "Neither is there salvation in any other: for there is none other name under heaven given among me, whereby we must be saved." (Acts 4:12)

By the way, we might note that Peter was not talking about morality or ethical standards. He was speaking about salvation from sins and a right standing with God.

Is it possible that God would be the "only" savior while Jesus is the "only" savior? Of course. Because Jesus is God.

Twelfth, Jehovah and Jesus Are Above All

Twelfth, Both are above all. The Psalmist praises God.

> "For thou, LORD, art high above all the earth: thou art exalted far above all gods." (Psalm 97:9)

John the Baptist said this of Jesus.

> "He that cometh from above is above all: he that is of the earth is earthly, and speaketh of the earth: he that cometh from heaven is above all." (John 3:31)

John was admitting to the divinity of Jesus. He spoke of Jesus as from Heaven not from Bethlehem. It was thus proper and reasonable for John to use a phrase describing God when he was speaking of Jesus.

Thirteenth, Jehovah and Jesus Are to Whom Every Knee Shall Bow

Thirteenth, Both are to Whom every knee shall bow. In the Old Testament God said of Himself,

> "I have sworn by myself, the word is gone out of my mouth in righteousness, and shall not return, That unto me every knee shall bow, every tongue shall swear." (Isaiah 45:23)

In the New Testament Paul says of Jesus,

> "That at the name of Jesus every knee should bow, of things in heaven, and things in earth, and things under the earth." (Philippians 2:10)

Since "every knee" must include every single being except the object of such worship, the Object of that worship must be the same in both instances. This object of worship must be God.

Paul actually expands on the concept as put forth by the writing of Isaiah. All includes all things in heaven – all of the angelic beings, all things on earth – all of humanity, and all things under the earth would include the fallen angels and also fallen humanity. All will eventually give God the glory and honor due Him. To some this worship will be of their Savior. To some this worship will be of their Captain and Lord. To some this worship will be of their very Judge.

Fourteenth, Jehovah and Jesus Are the Last

Fourteenth, Both are the Last. This is a continuation of number four, above, where Both were considered first. Isaiah 44:6 and Revelation 1:17 also confirm that Jesus is the finality of Wonder and Greatness. He is of eternity. This is said of God in Isaiah and of Jesus in Revelation.

What we have seen in this section is that Jesus is God. This fact is confirmed by the Old Testament references to God examined in the light of the New Testament references to Jesus.

Chapter 71
THE SCRIPTURES DECLARE THAT JESUS IS DIVINE
(Session Seventy-Two)

We are continuing somewhat the same consideration as in the previous section as we examine Biblical passages which confirm that Jesus is, indeed, God.

Jesus Is God

Isaiah 9:6-7

The first passage we will consider in this section is from Isaiah as we continue to note that the Old Testament Scriptures prophecy that Messiah, Jesus, is God.

> *"For unto us a child is born, unto us a son is given: and the government shall be upon his shoulder: and his name shall be called Wonderful, Counsellor, The mighty God, The everlasting Father, The Prince of Peace. Of the increase of his government and peace there shall be no end, upon the throne of David, and upon his kingdom to order it, and to establish it with judgment and with justice from henceforth even for ever. The zeal of the LORD of hosts will perform this." (Isaiah 9:6-7)*

Lindsell (*The People's Study Bible*) observes that

> "This constellation of names clearly indicates the Messiah is God himself, the second person of the Trinity."

I would like to note that when theologians speak of the "First" or the "Second" or "Third" Members of the Trinity we are not speaking of rank or grandeur; we are speaking only of the order in which Each was introduced to humanity in the inspired and preserved Scripture.

Lindsell further notes that Isaiah uses the term "mighty God" in Isaiah 10:21 when he is speaking of Yahweh. This gives added weight to the use of the term in reference to Messiah in the ninth chapter.

Falwell (*The Annotated Study Bible*) that the term "The Mighty God (El Gibor)" is unique in its application by Isaiah. As noted above, Isaiah only used "El" when speaking of God. "El" means God while "Gibor means 'Hero.' Together they describe one Who is indeed God Himself."

For Isaiah to have used this term for a mere man would have been to diminish the phrase when he used it to speak of God. This is not something which could have happened in the inspired and preserved Scripture as Isaiah was penning the very Words of God.

The *Pulpit Commentary* comments on the phrase "Everlasting Father." Once again Deity is surely ascribed to the Messiah as He is described as the progenitor and protector of humanity.

We must also consider that the phrase "everlasting" would include the concept of ultimate eternality. Only God could be considered as residing in ultimate eternality since all other entities are the result of His creative acts. Even those who might misunderstand the concept of "Son" and "Father" could not mistake the fact that by calling Jesus the "everlasting Father" would completely disallow any possibility of considering Him as a "created," or "secondary" deity.

Jesus is the God of Eternity – The Creator of all. (consider John 1:1-3 and Colossians 1:16)

The Divinity of Christ

Matthew 1:23: Emmanuel

Now we move forward to consider several New Testament passages which consider the Divinity of Christ.

We look first to Matthew 1:23.

"Behold a virgin shall be with child, and shall bring forth a son, and they shall call his name Emmanuel, which being interpreted is God with us."

The New Scofield Reference Bible makes note that this particular name is not used as a name with regard to Jesus.

> "According to Hebrew usage the name does not represent a title but a characterization, as in Isaiah 1:26 and 9:6. The name 'Immanuel' shows that He really was 'God with us.' Thus the Deity of Christ is stressed at the very beginning of Matthew."

I would invite you to consider Isaiah 9:6 where there is that list of Names for Messiah. The particular name of Immanuel is not listed in that place. Scofield asks that we consider this, along with the verse above from Matthew, in light of Isaiah 1:26. Isaiah was speaking of Jerusalem when he spoke of a future, restored to righteousness, glory of the city.

> *"And I will restore thy judges as at the first, and thy counselors as at the beginning: afterward thou shall be called, The city of righteousness, the faithful city."*

In Revelation 21:2 we see this description of this city.

> *"And I John saw the holy city, new Jerusalem, coming down from God out of heaven, prepared as a bride adorned for her husband."*

Note that the name of the city remains Jerusalem. It has not been renamed as "The city of righteousness, the faithful city." That is a term, not a name, which will be used to describe the city. It will be righteous and faithful in that day.

By the same token, Jesus is not *named* Immanuel. He **IS** Immanuel: That is "God with us."

May (*Am I Not Free?*) asks that we consider Matthew 1:16. Jesus is described as born unto Mary. Joseph is not listed as father because he was not. Jesus is the Son of God; He was born into humanity as a representative of our race so that He could be an Effectual Sacrifice for us. Adam, the only other human mentioned in Scripture as being born without father and mother, was created; but Jesus was begotten into the race to redeem the race even though we are sinners.

Melchizedek

There is one other person in Scripture of whom there is specifically no mention of father and mother. This person is Melchizedek.

> *"And Melchizedek king of Salem brought forth bread and wine: and he was the*

CHAPTER 71: THE SCRIPTURES DECLARE THAT JESUS IS DIVINE

priest of the most high God. And he blessed him, and said, Blessed be Abram of the most high God; possessor of heaven and earth. And blessed be the most high God; possessor of heaven and earth. And blessed by the most high God, which hath delivered thine enemies into thine hand. And he gave him tithes of all." (Genesis 14:18-20)

The situation here was just after Abram had marshaled his own forces and rescued Lot and some of the people of both Sodom and Gomorrah from the kings who had taken them in a raid. This had much to do with Lot, the nephew of Abram. It was, of course, before the wicked cities were judged by God for their wickedness.

This is a great illustration of the mercy of God even to the vilest of sinners. He extends His great mercy toward all.

"But God commendeth his love toward us, in that, while we were yet sinners, Christ died for us." (Romans 5:8)

No one is too vile to approach God in repentance and be accepted by Him.

There are those who see Melchizedek as a Theophany. They would believe that this incident is an event featuring the preincarnate Jesus. The arguments are several. Melchizedek offered bread and wine; these are indicative of the Last Supper where Jesus used these elements as illustrations of His Body and Blood which was offered on the Cross for our salvation.

The elements are, however, given to Abram and his armed men to refresh them after battle. There is no mention that this was considered in any way as a worship event. Melchizedek was acting as king, not as priest, in supplying these.

I might add that this, the Lord's Table, is the only celebration specifically sanctioned in the New Testament. While a celebration of the new life in Christ, baptism is an ordinance of the church rather than a celebration.

Also, Melchizedek received tithes from Abram. Many have equated this with receiving worship. Such is not the case. Abram gave tithe to Melchizedek as a priest of God. Abram was also showing due human reverence to a human king in doing this. Paying taxes to a human government is not offering worship toward that human government. Consider the bread and wine. Abram was actually paying for service rendered rather than worshipping.

Melchizedek is also referenced as the king of Salem. Salem is an ancient name for Jerusalem. It is true that Jesus will reign *from* Jerusalem but He is King over all not just the city of Jerusalem.

So we see that Melchizedek was both a priest of God and a king of man. He would have been denied the office of priest had this been the worship as shown by Moses. The Tabernacle, and later the Temple, duties were to come only to the Levitical tribe and then only to those who were descendants of Aaron.

"To be a memorial unto the children of Israel, that no stranger, which is not of the seed of Aaron, come near to offer incense before the LORD, that he be not as Korah, and as his company: as the LORD said to him by the hand of Moses." (Numbers 16:40)

There are other references to Melchizedek in Scripture.

"The LORD hath sworn, and will not repent, Thou art a priest for ever after the order of Melchizedek." (Psalm 110:4)

Another reference is from the New Testament.

> "As he saith also in another place, Thou art a priest for ever after the order of Melchisedec." (Hebrews 5:6)

Just a few verses further the human penman of Hebrews says,

> "Called of God an high priest after the order of Melchisedec." (Hebrews 5:10)

Later, in the seventh chapter of Hebrews, the priesthood of Melchizedek is mentioned as above the Levitical priesthood in that Abram had offered tithe to God by Melchizedek acting as a priest. The purpose of the is to show by Old Testament illustration that Jesus is a priest superior to both Melchizedek and the Aaronic priesthood.

It is clear that Melchizedek was a type of Christ. That is Melchizedek was used of God as an illustration of Messiah to come. As Jesus was born, on His divine "side," from outside the human race and yet was fully human in His maternal side, so was Melchizedek fully human but there is neither father nor mother credited to him.

We might well note that both the Heavenly Father and the earthly mother of the human Jesus are mentioned often in Scripture.

Also, Melchizedek was a priest of God yet was not of the Priestly tribe of the Levites. Jesus, humanly speaking, was from the tribe of Judah. Jesus is also both Priest and King. Jesus also fulfills the Office of Prophet in that He taught the Truth of God while on His earthly sojourn.

Matthew 18:20

Clarke (*Clarke's Commentary*) turns our attention to the familiar promise of Jesus in Matthew 18:20.

> "For where two or three are gathered together in my name, there am I in the midst of them."

Many Biblical churches today can take great comfort from this verse. The promise of God is not to great numbers but to great faith and fidelity to His inspired and preserved Words.

Clarke says,

> "None but God could say these words, to say them with truth, because God alone is **every where present,** and these words refer to his **omnipresence**... But, Jesus says these words: **ergo** – Jesus is God."

John 1:1

Next we will consider John 1:1.

> "In the beginning was the Word, and the Word was with God, and the Word was God."

Zodhiates (*God in Man*) tells us that the word "with" is "pros." This,

> "...could be considered as 'forward' to express the idea of motion. It is as if the Logos and the Father were facing each other. There is no suggestion of the Son following the Father, for then the Son would not be co-equal with the Father."

What we see, then, is that Jesus is not a subordinate God or a created God. Jesus, in His Divinity within the Triune Godhead, is the God of Eternity.

Strong (*Systematic Theology*) speaks of the verse.

CHAPTER 71: THE SCRIPTURES DECLARE THAT JESUS IS DIVINE

"Theos (God) en (is) o (the) logos (word)."

There is no article before "Theos." This word comes before the verb to show the train of thought – not only was "Logos" with God, but Logos was God. "The Logos" is the subject as the entire passage refers not to God, the Father, but to Him Who is the Logos.

Indeed, those first five verses of John speak almost exclusively of Jesus. Even when the Father is mentioned that mention has to do with the relationship of the Father and the Son.

Ryrie (*Basic Theology*) also speaks of the first verse in the Gospel of John. He says that while it is true that there is no article with the word translated "God," that this is not needed unless John chose to use the indefinite. This is "highly improbable" on grammatical grounds. This is especially so since it would be the only time which John would have used that form in his gospel. It is also improbable that John would have used such an imprecise way of expressing a truth if Jesus were only "a god." Again, this is especially true considering the preciseness of John in the rest of the chapter.

John 1:14

We next move to the fourteenth verse of this first chapter of John.

"And the Word was made flesh, and dwelt among us, (and we beheld his glory, the glory as of the only begotten of the Father.) full of grace and truth."

The phrase "dwelt among us" could have also been translated "tabernacled." This would take us back to Exodus when the Glory of God dwelt among men in the Tabernacle in the wilderness.

We might also note that the phrase "made flesh" in the verse presupposes an existence before His birth into humanity in Bethlehem. This fact points to His eternal pre-existence as God.

John 1:18

We now move to the eighteenth verse of this first chapter of John.

"No man hath seen God at any time, the only begotten Son, which is in the bosom of the Father, he hath declared him."

Monogenes

About this verse Zodhiates (*Can Man See God?*) sees just three ways that the meaning of "monogeneses," the word from with "only begotten" is translated, can be viewed.

This could refer to an only child who has no sisters or brothers. We know that this is not the meaning because Jesus had sisters and brothers who were born of Joseph and Mary. These were not divine as was Jesus, of course. I would guess it might be more proper, and less confusing, if we referred to these as "half" sisters and "half" brothers in the natural. (see Matthew 13:55-56)

I know that the Roman Church will consider these as only cousins. But, had that been the case there is a perfectly good word for cousin (see Luke 1:36) had it been the intention of the Spirit to make that case under inspiration.

The word "monogenesis" could mean "the only one of its kind, unique." This is obviously a true meaning. Jesus is unique and the only One of His kind. But, while this is true it is not entirely correct.

It is the third meaning of "monogenes" which Zodhiates claims is true in the fullness of the meaning of the text. This meaning is "of the same nature." While Jesus was "unique," He was more. The entire thrust of this first chapter of John is to show that He was divine in His essence and nature.

Zodhiates (*God in Man*) further notes of this verse and this word:

> "There is no definite article before the adjectival noun monogenes, 'only begotten,' and the noun petros, 'of the Father.' But, the absence of the definite article could not render them indefinite, and therefore this phrase could not be translated 'glory as an only begotten of a father.' Nouns which speak of persons or objects of which only one exists need no article."

John 5:23

Dake (Dake Annotated Bible) asks that we look at John 5:23.

> *"That all men should honour the Son, even as they honour the Father. He that honoureth not the Son honoureth not the Father which sent him."*

Dake said,

> "This absolute equality with the Father in honour proves His Deity and membership in the Trinity..."

I must mention that I would not generally "bet the farm" on the theological stances of Dake. This time, however, he is right on target. I have a large battery operated clock on the wall over my desk. The batteries are long dead. I don't use that clock because I have one in the computer on the very page where I am typing, on my cell phone in my pocket, and as a watch on my wrist. Still, that wall clock is right two times a day! Dake is certainly right in this instance about the Character and Person of Christ!

John 8:56

The Pharisees were speaking with Jesus one day when He said,

> *"Your father Abraham rejoiced to see my day: and he saw it, and was glad." (John 8:56)*

The Pharisees probably got a momentary chuckle out of that. They did deride Him by saying that He wasn't old enough to have seen, or been seen by, Abraham.

But, Abraham did see Jesus. He saw Him in the eye of faith as he trusted the promises of God. Abraham saw Jesus in His Old Testament appearances in Theophanies (see section on "The Angel of the Lord" in this study) as the Lord spoke with him face to face. (see Genesis 12:1-3; 17:1-22)

CHAPTER 72
JESUS IS THE ANOINTED KING
(Session Seventy-Three)

The hour of Jesus' earthy demise was fast drawing upon Him. Jesus spoke to the crowds which would not believe His words. They just could not understand the concept of the suffering Savior. It seems they were looking for a Messiah Who would free them from the bonds of the Roman occupation. They just did not see the Messiah Who could free them from the bonds of sin.

John 12:45: He That Seeth Me Seeth Him That Sent Me

Finally Jesus spoke to the people a Truth they, most of them, were not prepared to hear. "And he that seeth me seeth him that sent me." (John 12:45) *The Life Application Bible* states the Truth of this verse is an easily understood phrase. If one wants to know what God is like he must only study Jesus. Jesus is God. That is what Jesus was saying. He claimed a complete equality and essence with God.

The Life Application Bible also speaks of Acts 17:22-27 where Paul preached to the Greeks on Mars' Hill. It was at this place that the Greeks had placed many idols. So careful were they to not offend any of the "gods" that they even set up an altar to "The Unknown God" lest they would offend.

I read an article today about "speed traps." Many of these are arbitrarily set not to provide for the public safety but to produce revenue. Such municipal shenanigans do not foster a respect for the law; these foster a fear of the law.

This is still the view of most religions of the world. The Biblical concept that "God is Love" is not accepted. These religions instead have a view of God that sees Him as simply waiting and hoping that the people will make a mistake so He can swoop down and beat them with His "Stick of Righteousness and Reproof."

Far too many Christians have set themselves up as "God's Policemen" and see themselves are manning a celestial speed trap rather than the rescue and aid station which says that Jesus Christ died in time so that others could live in eternity.

We do need to preach and teach standards in faith. That is a certainty. But we are the "Town Criers," not the "High Executioner." Our job as Christians is to give forth the message of Jesus is love – even to vile sinners. That is what Jesus did in the New Testament. We do not condone sin; but we do not usurp the prerogative of God and condemn sinners.

It is one thing to simply point out what the Scripture has to say about sin. It is quite another to put that verse on a placard and march around the sinner to point out his sin. Love calls.

Love does call in truth. It is one thing to point out to a motorist on a dark night that the bridge is out. It is quite another to herd that driver towards the chasm and then say, "If he hadn't been out here driving at night he might not have died. It's all his fault for not stopping."

Acts 17:22-27: How Paul Preached

Let's look at this passage in Acts.

> "Then Paul stood in the midst of Mars' hill, and said, Ye men of Athens, I perceive that in all things ye are too superstitious. For as I passed by, and beheld your devotions, I found an altar with this inscription, TO THE UNKNOWN GOD. whom therefore ye ignorantly worship, him declare I unto you. God that made the world and all things therein, seeing that he is Lord of heaven and earth, dwelleth not in temples made with hands. Neither is worshipped with men's hands, as though he needed any thing, seeing he giveth to all life, and breath, and all things; And hath made of one blood all nations of men for to dwell on all the face of the earth, and hath determined the times before appointed, and the bounds of their habitation; That they should seek the Lord, if haply they might feel after him, and find him, though he be not far from every one of us." (Acts 17:22-27)

Notice the methodology of Paul. He didn't berate these men. He did point out their error by noting that they were "too superstitious." He also pointed out that these persons were worshipping in error. Then Paul began to speak to them of Jesus.

The salient point of this passage as concerns our current discussion is that Paul ascribed the acts of God (creation), the attributes of God (omnipresence), the abilities of God (giving life), the anthropology of God (one blood), the area of God (all the earth), the attraction of God (they should seek the Lord), the acceptance of God (find him), and the allure of God (not far from every one), to Jesus. Thereby Paul was saying that Jesus was this "God" who was unknown to the Athenians. It was Jesus Whom Paul would have the people of Athens to worship.

Romans 1:3, 4: Jesus Declared to Be the Son of God

We now turn our attention to Romans 1:4. Albert Barnes (*Barnes' Notes on the New Testament*) has made several references to this verse in relation to the Deity of Jesus.

> "And declared to be the Son of God with power, according to the spirit of holiness, by the resurrection from the dead."

I would quickly note that this verse is speaking of Jesus as is shown when verse three is also read:

> "Concerning his Son Jesus Christ our Lord, which was made of the seed of David according to the flesh."

Note the phrase "...made of the seed of David..." This speaks of the Virgin Birth as this expression shows that Jesus, Who *became* flesh, was preexistent in another form – that of Deity – before He became flesh. Although He sprang from David in his humanity via his human mother, the Person of Jesus predated David as Jesus was existent from eternity past even before there was any creation.

Jesus remained God in His eternal essence even as He *became* flesh in order to effect our salvation.

As to verse four, Barnes notes that others have been called sons of God. Adam, created without father or mother has been called a son of God. John 1:12, and other verses (see Romans 8:14-15, II Corinthians 6:18, Galatians 3:26, I John 3:1), note that the born again Christian is a son of God. Strong men, whose physical strength was above others, were sometimes called sons of God as were kings because of their rule

CHAPTER 72: JESUS IS THE ANOINTED KING

over others. Even angels, as spirit beings, are sometimes called sons of God.

But, only Jesus – as Barnes notes – is given the New Testament Title of Son of God. This is more than a "name" of Jesus in that it is a description of Jesus as Deity. This title designated His special relationship within the Triune Godhead.

As the Messiah of the Jews, as prophesied throughout the Old Testament, this title designates the status of Jesus as the Anointed King of the Jews.

This title also refers to His special and unique virgin birth.

Romans 1:20: Jesus Eternal Power as God

The title of one of Spiros Zodhiates' books asks a question: *"Was Christ God?"* One of the verses which Zodhiates' uses to answer that question is Romans 1:20.

> *"For the invisible things of him from the creation of the world are clearly seen, being understood by the things that are made, even his eternal power and Godhead; so that they are without excuse."*

This verse is set in a section where Paul is describing that the wickedness of humanity is not excused through a lack of understanding. The proof of God and His Creative Hand is evident all around us in nature. Even one who would reject the Book of God cannot reasonably reject the fact of God. To do so is to make a conscious choice to reject God.

This verse speaks of the "Godhead" being seen by the world at large. The Greek word, "theiotes," meaning, "divinity," is used. "It refers to the majesty and glory of God in His creation but not to the essence of His personality. Colossians 2:9 speaks of the 'Godhead' with the Greek word 'theotes.'" The difference is that this reference is "...not to the manifestation of Christ in His external acts, but to His essential nature."

Romans 9:5: Jesus Is God

> *"Whose are the fathers, and of whom as concerning the flesh Christ came, who is over all, God blessed for ever. Amen."*

Some have altered the meaning by placing a period after "Christ came," thereby making the second clause of the sentence to be a doxology to God, the Father. In this they seek to downgrade the Glory which rightfully belongs to Jesus as God, the Son.

Alford (*The New Testament for English Readers*) sees that

> "The Fathers (Abraham, Isaac, Jacob, etc.) are given their due as to whom promises were given. Jesus is called their descendant – according to the flesh. But, He is above them due to His Divinity."

The *Pulpit Commentary* well notes that the ancients agreed that the reading here is that Jesus is God. However many modern scholars find other meanings by looking at what they believe Paul was *likely* to mean as opposed to what he *did* say. This commentary considers this to be "a very unsafe principle of interpretation."

Barnes (*Barnes' Notes on the New Testament*) says that He came in the flesh Who has supreme domination over all. This is God. The pious Jew of the day added "Blessed for ever" after the mention of Deity.

What Paul, through inspiration, shows us in this passage is the dual nature of Jesus. He was – **_IS_** – God. Yet He came to earth as one of us that He might save us from our sins.

1 Corinthians 12:4-6: Jesus is One of the Trinity and Thus God

An important passage relating to the Deity of Christ is I Corinthians 12:4-6.

"Now there are diversities of gifts, but the same Spirit. And there are differences of administration, but the same Lord. And there are diversities of operations, but it is the same God which worketh all in all."

The primary thrust of the extended passage (to the end of the chapter) is that each person in the church has been gifted to some purpose within that body of believers. As in the military, each soldier must be ready to pick up his weapon when called upon but his day to day objective may be to cook, or to work in the motor pool, or to work in administration. Whatever his primary job he remains a soldier. All hands must work together to form an efficient unit.

Clarke (*Adam Clarke's Commentary*) sees an intimation of the Trinity within the passage. "He who may think this *fanciful* must account for the very evident *distinctions* here in some more satisfactory way." Clarke notes that the gifts speak of the Holy Spirit. The administration speaks of the Son. And, the operations speak of the Father.

Alford (*The New Testament for English Readers*) also finds the Trinity of the Godhead in this passage. One Spirit is The Bestower of gifts as mentioned. One Lord is The Appointer of gifts as mentioned. One God is The Worker of gifts as mentioned. Alford rightly notes that what we see here is the Trinity acting in harmony.

Philippians 2:6: Speaks of the Kenosis of Christ

Philippians 2:6 speaks of the Kenosis of Christ.

"Who, being in the form of God, thought it not robbery to be equal with God."

The Kenosis is a theological term which means that Jesus, in His humanity, put off from – or emptied – himself the outward glory of His essential Godhead while on His sojourn as a man. Scofield (*The Scofield Reference Bible*) observes that

"Nothing in this passage teaches that the Eternal Word (John 1:1) emptied himself of either His divine nature, or His attributes, but only of the outward and visible manifestation of the Godhead."

Note that this verse teaches that Jesus is the "form" of God. The study at my home is a room situated within a structure which is in the "form" of a house. Some years ago that same structure was in the "form" of a nursing home. Then, for a time, that same structure was in the "form" of a church and parsonage. Now the structure has reverted to the "form" of a home. The structure itself never really changed except for some additions built on. The use of that structure has changed. The basic "structure" of Jesus has never changed. He took upon Himself a human body so that He might redeem fallen mankind but that "structure," that "form" of God never departed. He remains God because that is His Divine nature and essence.

Unger (*Unger's Bible Handbook*) reminds us that Jesus has this equality as God simply because of His Divine Being as God.

CHAPTER 73
JESUS IS THE IMAGE OF THE INVISIBLE GOD
(Session Seventy-Four)

When We Look at Jesus We See the Person of God Who Is Invisible
Colossians 1:15-17

We begin this session with a consideration of Colossians 1:15-17.

> "Who is the image of the invisible God, the firstborn of every creature: For by him were all things created, that are in heaven, and that are in earth, visible and invisible, whether they be thrones, or dominions, or principalities, or powers: all things were created by him, and for him: And he is before all things, and by him all things consist."

We have already seen that the phrase "firstborn," when it pertains to the Person of Jesus does not refer to His physical birth but to His privileged position as the Head of all. Verse eighteen, which we did not reference above, gives testimony to that fact. This is a simple cultural reference which the people of the day in which this passage was originally penned could readily understand. Those in our day who are familiar with the Scriptural stories of the patriarchs will understand this as well.

We could also note that Jesus is referred to as "the image of the invisible God." This is important in our discussion since the meaning is not that Jesus looks like "the invisible God." If that were so we would be compelled to consider Jesus as invisible as well. The meaning of the phrase is that when we look at Jesus we see the Person of God Who could not before be seen with physical eyes.

Jesus Is the Author of All Creation

Another important fact brought out by this passage is that Jesus is the Author of all creation. As such Jesus can be no created being. This is rendered an impossibility as we consider that Jesus created all and could not, therefore, be a created being of any sort. The act of creation is an act of God alone. Had Jesus been a created being he would have been unable to create.

We are often assaulted with the old question "Can God create a rock too large for Him to lift?" The atheist antagonist will assume that he has painted the theist into the proverbial corner. His theory is that we will have to admit that there is something which God cannot do.

Is There Nothing That God Cannot Do?

Well, is there nothing that God cannot do? He cannot sin. He also cannot act in a way that is inconsistent with His attributes as God. When my daughter was very young she took a fish out of our aquarium for a little walk around the block. One of the attributes of a fish is that it cannot breathe outside the water. That is just who the fish is. God cannot be other than God; that is just Who He is.

It would be foreign to the nature of God for Him to act so illogically as to comply with that atheist's question. Thus the question is an absurdity which needs no real reply. The question is on the order of, "Does the sky look purple with pink polka dots to you?" It is the musings of one not connected to reality.

All Things Were Created *For* Him

We also note from the verse that not only were all things created *by* Him, all things were created *for* Him. Thus the fallacious argument that Jesus is a subordinate to an *original* God is shown to be in error. This argument would postulate that Jesus was only able to create because He had been given this prerogative and power. If this had been so then all things created would have been at the ultimate order of, and for the pleasure of, that presumed *original* God. But, all things were created for Jesus; therefore Jesus is that all powerful God of Creation rather than a subordinate being.

As the Father is God so also is the Son God. So also is the Spirit God. Each, Unique and Inseparable, is fully God in the Triune unity of the Godhead. I cannot understand the concept of the Trinity as One God in three separate *Persons*. This is an eternal and spiritual principle which those of us of a physical and time centric experience are unable to comprehend.

The Disconnect of Humanity to the Realities of the Spiritual

Jesus speaks of this disconnect of humanity to the realities of the spiritual when He is speaking with Nicodemus in the third chapter of John.

> *"If I have told you earthly things, and ye believe not, how shall ye believe, if I tell you of heavenly things?" (John 3:12)*

I cannot fully understand the mystery of the Trinity. That is where faith comes in. God said it and I believe it whether I can understand it or not.

All Things Consist by the Power of Jesus

The passage also says that all things consist by the power of Jesus. Henry (Matthew Henry's Commentary) asks that we consider, "Things not only subsist in their beings, but consist in their order and dependencies." Not only did Jesus create all but it is He Who continues to uphold all created things, even societal things, else they would cease to exist.

Unger (*Unger's Bible Handbook*) bids us to consider I Timothy 3:16.

> *"And without controversy great is the mystery of godliness: God was manifest in the flesh, justified to the Spirit, seen of angels, preached unto the Gentiles, believed on in the world, received up unto glory."*

Unger notes that this passage affirms that Jesus was God in human flesh. Jesus died and then rose from the dead to vindicate and to prove true this claim. That He did rise again from the dead is attested to in the fact that He appeared to many after His resurrection. It is His gospel message that is preached in His churches throughout the history of the world from that time forward. He has ascended into Glory; again there were witnesses to this fact still alive when Paul penned this Book.

New T*ranslations* on the Market Have Changed This Verse

I do know that there are many new *translations* on the market which have changed this verse to read "He was manifest in the flesh." To be simply manifest in the flesh is to simply exist as a human. Jesus goes far beyond this simple formula. He is God as this verse properly states.

CHAPTER 73: JESUS IS THE IMAGE OF THE INVISIBLE GOD

Titus 2:13

We now move on to Titus 2:13.

> *"Looking for that blessed hope, and the glorious appearing of the great God and our Saviour Jesus Christ."*

The Phrase "Great God and Our Saviour" Apply As One to "Jesus Christ

The Commentary Practical and Explanatory on the Whole Bible notes of this verse that the word "'...appearing' (epiphaneia) is never used by Paul to predicate God the Father or His glory. It always applies to Jesus' coming." The meaning here is that Paul was not speaking of two separate persons in this verse. The wording of Paul indicates that the phrase "great God and our Saviour" apply as one to "Jesus Christ."

Falwell (*The Annotated Study Bible*) also considers the grammatical meaning of the verse. "The use of the definite article 'the' with the first noun 'God' and the connection 'and' indicates that the first and second 'Savior' [nouns] are one and the same person. Our 'great God and our Savior Jesus Christ' is thus one and the same person, clearly proving the deity of Christ."

Henry (*Matthew Henry's Commentary*) also weighs in on the grammatical consideration of the verse as it applies to the Deity of Jesus. "The great God and our Saviour Jesus Christ." There is only one subject as "the" is a single article in the Greek."

Those who would deny that this verse clearly states the full Deity of Jesus Christ are guilty of putting their own doctrinal distinctions ahead of the clear grammatical statement of Paul under the inspiration of the Spirit.

Hebrews 1:3

We now move into the Book of Hebrews as we consider what the Scripture has to say about the deity of Jesus.

> *"Who being the brightness of his glory, and the express image of his person, and upholding all things by the word of his power, when he had by himself purged our sins, sat down on the right hand of the Majesty on high." (Hebrews 1:3)*

The Brightness of the Glory of God Emanates from Jesus, Himself

Ryrie (*The Ryrie Study Bible*) says that

"The word [brightness] means an outshining, not a reflection."

The word "brightness" is "apaugasma," number 541 in Strong's. It is a compound word used only here in the New Testament. The first part of the word is "apo," number 575 in Strong's. Strong defines this word as:

> "a primary particle, 'off,' i.e. away (from something) near, in various senses (of place, time, or relation, literal or figurative)...(X here-)after, ago, at, because of, before, by (the space of), from, in, (out) of, off, (up-)on)-ce, with. In composition (as a prefix) it usually denotes separation, departure, cessation, completion, reversal, etc."

The word is commonly used in the New Testament. It means to be "from" some thing. The great slaughter of the innocents by Herod in the second chapter of Matthew (2:16) uses this word when it speaks of the children *from* two years old and under being killed.

In the third chapter of Matthew (verse four) the word is used to describe raiment made of camel's hair. Which, quite obviously, is hair *from* a camel

The second part of the compound word is "augazo," number 826 in Strong's. Strong defines the word as "to beam forth (figuratively)—shine." The word appears only here and in Acts 20:11 where it refers to the "break of day."

Putting the two words together we do not get a picture of a glory either reflected or bestowed upon Christ. What we see is the brightness of the glory of God as emanating from Jesus, Himself. This, of course, means that the human penman of Hebrews wrote that Jesus is God in that the Glory of God emanates from Him.

The *Pulpit Commentary* weighs in on the verse.

> "The rays which stream from the sun reveal the sun itself; so Christ is the ever-visible radiance of the unapproachable light."

The Apostle John said the same thing in different words.

> "No man hath seen God at any time; the only begotten Son, which is in the bosom of the Father, he hath declared him." (John 1:18)

Hebrews 1:8

Next we move on to Hebrews 1:8.

> "But unto the Son he saith, Thy Throne, O God, is for ever and ever: a sceptre of righteousness is the sceptre of thy kingdom."

Wrong Interpretations

Adam Clarke (*Adam Clarke's Commentary*) sees that some argue for a reading that says "God is thy throne forever." This reading would deny the Deity of Jesus as He is only seen as seated in the Throne of God rather than seated as God on the Throne of God. This is a reading based on the theology of the critic rather than on the true reading of the text.

Clarke states that,

> "It is a rule of the Greek language, that when a substantive noun is the subject of a sentence, and something is predicated on it, the article, if used at all, is prefixed to the subject, but omitted before the predicate. The Greek translators of the Old, and the authors of the New Testament, write agreeable to this rule."

We must note that when Clarke speaks of the Greek translators of the Old Testament he is speaking of the LXX.

Clarke also asks that we consider Hebrews 1:2-14. Verse two is the first considered.

> "Hath in these last days spoken unto us by his Son, whom he hath appointed heir of all things, by whom also he made the worlds."

I would note that the phrase "by whom also he made the worlds" does not speak to an order of power or preeminence within the Godhead. As stated above the work of creation was a work of the creative power of God. Only the power of God could have created the entirety of the universe. This is a simple restatement of the fact that Jesus was the Creative Agent Who called the physical universe into existence.

Clarke notes that Jesus is a Son, born under the Law, of a woman. This does not lessen the fact that Jesus is God, Eternal. Jesus is the Eternal Son; that He was Virgin

CHAPTER 73: JESUS IS THE IMAGE OF THE INVISIBLE GOD

Born of a woman speaks to His dual nature of God and man. See our section on the dual nature of Jesus for a further review of this consideration.

Clarke also notes that Jesus is Heir to ALL THINGS. This does not mean that Jesus never held title deed to all. As God Jesus has always, from eternity, been Heir and Possessor of all. The meaning, once again, refers to the humanity of Jesus where He is the heir of all by His right as the son of David and His redemptive role as Savior of all who believe.

A Phrase Shows Jesus to be Divine in His Very Being and Existence

Clarke also bids us to consider verse three.

> "Who being the brightness of his glory, and the express image of his person, and upholding all things by the word of his power, when he had by himself purged our sins, sat down on the right hand of the Majesty on high."

The first thing to note is that Clarke finds Jesus as the Brightness of the Divine Glory. This is an attribute of Jesus; as such this is just a part of Who He Is. This does speak to the Divinity of Jesus.

Jesus is also shown to be the "express image of His person, or character of the Divine Substance." This is a statement of the full Deity of Jesus as the phrase shows Him to be Divine in His very being and existence.

Clarke notes that Jesus, by the "word of His power," is the sustainer of the universe. Not only would the physical universe not have come into existence without the word of the power of Jesus, that physical universe would cease to exist were Jesus not continually upholding that physical universe by His Own Power.

The Theories of "Theistic Evolution" and "Deism" Fall by the Wayside

The popular view that God just created the universe and then sat back to see what would happen is a false view. With the deconstruction of this view the theories of "theistic evolution" and "Deism" fall by the wayside. Jesus not only created the universe, He also continues to take an active and controlling interest in the affairs and applications of the workings of that universe.

So active and interested is Jesus in the affairs of this world that He, Personally, came to offer Himself as The Atonement for the sins of those who would believe.

Clarke sees that Jesus sits upon the right hand of the Majesty on high. This is a place of power which illustrates that Jesus is above all created beings. This is also a position where He is worshipped by the angelic hosts.

Hebrews 1:8-14: The Messiah Will Have an Eternal Throne and Dominion

Next we move to verses eight through fourteen.

> "But unto the Son he saith, Thy throne, O God, is for ever and ever: a sceptre of righteousness is the sceptre of thy kingdom. Thou hast loved righteousness, and hated iniquity; therefore God, even thy God, hath anointed thee with the oil of gladness above thy fellows. And Thou, Lord, in the beginning hast laid the foundation of the earth; and the heavens are the works of thine hands: And they shall perish; but thou remainest, and they all shall wax old as doth a garment; And as a vesture shalt thou fold them up, and they shall be changed: but thou art the same, and thy years shall not fail. But to which of the angels said he at any time, Sit on my right hand, until I make thine enemies thy footstool? Are they not all

ministering spirits, sent forth to minister for them who shall be heirs of salvation?"
(Hebrews 1:8-14)

Clarke notes two very important things in this passage. The first is that Messiah will have an eternal throne. Never throughout the ageless ages of eternity will His Person or His dignity ever change or even decay.

I am about three weeks from my 66th birthday. Even at this age my body will constantly assault my dignity. I cannot do that which I often wish to do. I went on a short walk yesterday to do some church "cold calling." I went to some strangers homes, introduced myself, and invited them to church. After only a couple of blocks of walking I was very glad to find my car. I was exhausted! This old body let me know just how old it is! Such a thing will never happen to the Lord of Glory. He does not change.

I was listening to some old music on the internet a few days ago. I enjoyed many of the groups from the "war years" of the forties. These were major "stars" in their day. Their day was long past. Very few remember them. Just last Sunday I mentioned "Will Rogers" during a sermon and was met with many blank faces who had no idea about whom I was speaking. Fame and the power of popularity fail. Such a thing will never happen to the Lord of Glory. He does not change.

Clarke also notes that Jesus will continue to "exercise dominion when the earth and the heavens are no more." There are many who are dissatisfied with our present president in this nation. It matters not when you might read this words or what location your nation might occupy. There are always some who are dissatisfied with their present temporal ruler. That is simple human nature. But, Jesus will exercise dominion and rule throughout eternity to the delight and joy of the inhabitants of eternity.

Clarke notes of the above that only God in the flesh, Jesus, could fit the above description.

Chapter 74
JESUS WAS GOD IN THE FLESH
(Session Seventy-Five)

Hebrews 2:14: The Self-Existent Jesus Took On Flesh and Blood

We start this section, the last section in this chapter, with a look at Hebrews 2:14.

"Forasmuch then as the children are partakers of the flesh and blood, he also himself likewise took part of the same, that through death he might destroy him that had the power of death, that is, the devil."

As to our discussion, the important part here is that Jesus is shown as having had an existence prior to Bethlehem. That He took upon himself "flesh and blood" means that He was existent in a form which was not "flesh and blood" at some point prior to His humanity. Carrying this point out to the logical conclusion we must admit that Jesus had the power to modify, or expand, His mode of existence at His Own volition. This demands that we must consider Jesus as God. As we have seen in the pages from Scripture, that point prior was eternity and that other form was, and still is, as the God of Creation.

The Mystery of Godliness

For the God of Creation to take upon Himself the body and likeness of humanity is called "the mystery of Godliness" in I Timothy 3:16. Jesus came into humanity with the express purpose of giving up the life of that humanity as a sacrifice for fallen humans. He gave us the opportunity to be saved from our burden of sin and to have peace and fellowship with God. He then took up once again the life of that mortal body to fully defeat the power of sin, Satan, and death. Jesus Christ died in time so that we could live in eternity.

Such a construct is only possible for One Who is the Son of God and God, the Son.

Hebrews 3:1-4: The Apostle and High Priest

We now consider Hebrews 3:1-4.

"Wherefore, holy brethren, partakers of the heavenly calling, consider the Apostle and High Priest of our profession, Christ Jesus; Who was faithful to him that appointed him, as also Moses was faithful in all his house. For this man was counted worthy of more glory than Moses, inasmuch as he who hath builded the house hath more honour than the house."

Some may see some confusion by the title of "Apostle" being given to Jesus. The word "apostle" simply means "one who is sent." Since Jesus was sent forth by the Father the term is properly applied. Continue reading the rest of the Book of Hebrews and there will be light shed on the fact that Jesus is The High Priest to the Christian.

The Ultimate Builder

Moses was a faithful worker in the house, that is the church (Both the Old Testament Jewish and the New Testament Christian assemblies are "churches" in the sense that they are "called out" of the world for a specific purpose by God.), but Jesus built the house as He is the Creator, or Ultimate Builder, of all things. In this verse the human penman of Hebrews clearly and plainly shows Jesus to be God.

1 John 5:7: The Verse, One of the Clearest Statements, Was In the Early Writings

We will take a short look at I John 5:7.

"For there are three that bear record in heaven, the Father, the Word, and the Holy Ghost: and these three are one."

This is a much maligned verse in today's newer English Language Versions. We are constantly reminded by footnote and margin reference, and sometimes buy deletion and bracket, that much of modern "critical text" study finds this verse as an insertion not originally part of the text.

For now I would just remind the reader that the verdict of the early church fathers validate the verse. Tertullian quoted the verse in about 200 AD in his *"Apology Against Praxeas."* The verse is in the original *Latin Vulgate* which was translated about 157 AD. Both of these point to a still earlier text from which they worked.

This verse is one of the clearest statements in Scripture as to the deity of Jesus.

1 John 5:20: The True God and Eternal Life

Next we move to I John 5:20.

"And we know that the Son of God is come, and hath given us an understanding that we may know him that is true, and we are in him that is true, even in his Son Jesus Christ. This is the true God, and eternal life."

The phrase "This is the true God, and eternal life" is our focus in this verse. The immediate antecedent of this statement is "Jesus," thus causing one to assume on simple grammatical grounds that Jesus is being called "the True God." Such an assumption would be correct. To have called the Father the True God would have been redundant and unnecessary. Consider that this was, humanly speaking, penned by a Jewish man brought up with the Old Testament Scriptures which constantly remind the reader that ",,,the LORD our God *is* one LORD." (Deuteronomy 6:4b) He, and most of those to whom this epistle was written understood that God was God.

John 1:4: In Him Was Life

Consider, also that the human penman, John, was also the human author of the Book which bears his name. In John 1:4 John wrote, "In him was life, and the life was the light of men." Therefore the obvious connection is that the True God, Who was eternal life, would be Jesus. Barnes (Barnes' Notes on the New Testament) states the obvious when he tells us that both the "True God" and "Jesus" here refer to eternal life.

Revelation 1:8: The Beginning and the conclusion

We also need to consider Revelation 1:8.

"I am Alpha and Omega, the beginning and the ending, saith the Lord, which is, and which was, and which is to come, the Almighty."

Salem Kirban (*Salem Kirban Reference Bible*) asks us to consider that Jesus is here described as both the beginning and the conclusion. Since this could only be said of the Self-Existent One, God, this is a statement that Jesus is God.

Revelation 4:8: Note the Singular Verb

Next we look at Revelation 4:8.

> "And the four beasts had each of them six wings about him, and they were full of eyes within: and they rest not day and night, saying, Holy, holy, holy, Lord God Almighty, which was, and is, and is to come."

Note the use of "is." It is a singular verb placed after three uses of the word "Holy." The creatures are proclaiming the Trinity of God. The Trinity **IS** one singular Being.

We must also see in Scripture that terms denoting Deity are ascribed to Jesus. Barnes (Barnes' Notes on the New Testament) mentions two such passages.

Matthew 3:17: The Special Connectedness of Jesus and the Father

At the baptism of Jesus God, Himself, called Jesus His Son.

> "And lo a voice from heaven, saying, This is my beloved Son, in whom I am well pleased." (Matthew 3:17)

The term used in this instance shows the special connectedness of Jesus and the Father.

Jesus and the religious leaders were locked in controversy when He called Himself the Son of the Father. "If I do not the works of my Father, believe me not. But if I do, though ye believe not me, believe the works; that ye may know, and believe, that The Father *is* in my, and I in him." (John 10:37-38)

The extended passage had begun back in verse twenty-nine where Jesus had claimed this Sonship. He said that He and the Father were one. The religious leaders knew full well that by claiming to be the Son of God Jesus was claiming Divinity for Himself. There then followed a short review from Jesus that several Old Testament persons were called "god" when they stood in the place as God's representative.

In the passage printed just above Jesus again claimed a special relationship with the Father which extended unto all of His works. Jesus even claimed that the works He was doing were works of God.

Three Instances Where the Son Is Specifically Called God

Simmona (*A Systematic Study of Bible Doctrine*) cites three instances where the Son is specifically called "God."

> "In the beginning was the Word, and the Word was with God, and the Word was God." (John 1:1)

I know that one of the cult groups has made their own translation where they call Jesus "a god" but that is not correct. As we have this in our Authorized Version, Jesus was God. As a Personage of eternity and the Sovereign God, Jesus is still God – and He always will be.

Paul was speaking of the history of the Jewish people when he said the following.

> "Whose are the fathers, and of whom as concerning the flesh Christ came, who is over all, God blessed for ever. Amen." (Romans 9:5)

Jesus came to earth in the form of a human being of the Jewish people. He came to offer himself as their Messiah. He came to die for the sins of the world. He is God over all.

We've just gone over this verse about a page above but it still bears consideration.

> *"And we know that the Son of God is come, and hath given us an understanding that we may know him that is true, and we are in him that is true, even in his Son Jesus Christ. This is the true God, and eternal life."* (I John 5:20)

Once again, "This is the true God" hearkens back to show facts about Jesus Christ.

In this chapter we have been considering that the Scriptures will affirm that Jesus is, indeed, God. This fact is well summarized by this excerpt from the Confession of Faith of the Lenard Street Baptist Church.

> "...if it is true that [the attributes of God] apply to God, then it is equally true that if they are true of Christ, then Christ is God. If they are applied to the Holy Spirit, then the Holy Spirit is God. If they apply to the Father, then the Father is God. And so they are all three God, yet one."

Chapter 75
THE TRUTH OF HIS DIVINITY
(Session Seventy-Six)

Some Facts About Jesus Which Point to His Deity

In this final chapter of our book we will look again at some of the facts about Jesus which point to His Deity. One of these facts concerns some circumstantial evidence that Jesus is Divine. Circumstantial evidence is a flimsy evidence until it is gathered together and observed as a "complete package." This "package" of circumstantial evidence to the Deity of Jesus becomes quite substantial when examined.

Zeoli (*Is Jesus God? Book Number One*) has listed several instances of this circumstantial evidence.

The Times of the Nations

The first bit of evidence concerns the times of the nations. Time is dated from the birth of Jesus. AD stands for "the year of our Lord" while BC stands for "before Christ." I know that this has been changed to "CE" (Common Era) and "BCE" (Before the Common Era) in deference to the secularists of the world. But, while the nomenclature may have changed the substance remains the same: Time is still dated from the birth of Christ. His life and teaching have had that much influence upon the world of mankind.

Second, Scriptural Prophecies Concerning Jesus

We must also consider the Scriptural prophecies concerning Him. Micah 5:2, for instance, records a precise prophecy concerning His birth.

> "But thou, Bethlehem Ephrata, though thou be little among the thousands of Judah, yet out of thee shall he come forth unto me that is to be ruler of Israel, whose goings forth have been from of old, from everlasting."

The human penman makes it clear that he is speaking of Bethlehem Ephrata. This is near Jerusalem. This is done because there is another Bethlehem near the Sea of Galilee.

As for being the ruler of the Jews, even the Roman government put its stamp of approval on that consideration when Jesus was crucified as "The King of the Jews." Rome did not, obviously, agree but Rome, probably unwittingly, acknowledged the fact of truth under the writing placed by Pilate. (see John 19:19)

The virgin birth was foretold in Isaiah 7:14.

> "Therefore the Lord himself shall give you a sign; Behold, a virgin shall conceive, and bear a son, and shall call his name Immanuel."

Matthew 1:23 specifically applies this prophecy to the birth of Jesus.

Daniel 9:25-26 specifically points to the time when Jesus would be born. There can be little doubt that the adoration of Simeon and Anna (Luke 2:25-38) is united to an understanding of the passage in Daniel.

The twenty-second Psalm is a remarkable prophecy concerning the crucifixion of

Jesus. In this Psalm is given a clear picture of a death by crucifixion. This was a Psalm of David as stated in the notes given before the Psalm proper. Since David lived from 1085 to 1015 BC, we have a date of about 1000 years before the death of Christ for the composition of this Psalm. Since crucifixion was unknown at that time the influence of inspiration upon the words of this Psalm is extraordinarily evident.

I call your attention to just one verse, the sixteenth.

> "For dogs have compassed me: the assembly of the wicked have inclosed me: they have pierced my hands and my feet."

Thus, in the prophecy of David, even the death of Jesus is foretold.

There are many prophecies concerning the trial, crucifixion and resurrection of Jesus. We will list just a few of these. First, concerning His trial we find that he was betrayed for thirty pieces of silver.

> "Then Judas, which had betrayed him, when he saw that he was condemned, repented himself, and brought again the thirty pieces of silver to the chief priests and elders." (Matthew 27:3)

Zechariah 11:12 prophecies this:

> "And I said unto them, if ye think good, give me my price, and if not, forbear. So they weighed for my price thirty pieces of silver."

Mark 14:55-56 tells us of false witnesses at the trial of Jesus.

> "And the chief priests and all the council sought for witnesses against Jesus to put him to death; and found none. For many bare false witness against him, but their witness agreed not together."

The Psalmist agreed with this hundreds of years before the trial of Jesus.

> "Deliver me not over unto the will of mine enemies: for false witnesses are risen up against me, and such as breathe out cruelty." (Psalm 27:12)

Isaiah gives a picture of the events of the trial of Jesus. "I gave my back to the smiters, and my cheeks to them that plucked off the hair. I hid not my face from shame and spitting." (Isaiah 50:6)

It was worse at the hands of the soldiers who were schooled in cruelty, but even before the Jewish council we see this verse fulfilled. "Then did they spit in his face, and buffeted him, and others smote *him* with the palms of their hands." (Matthew 26:67)

> "He was wounded for our transgressions, he was bruised for our iniquities: the chastisement of our peace was upon him; and with his stripes we are healed. All we like sheep have gone astray; we have turned every one to his own way; and the LORD hath laid upon him the iniquity of us all. He was oppressed, and he was afflicted, yet he opened not his mouth: he is brought as a lamb to the slaughter, and as a sheep before her shearers is dumb, so he openeth not his mouth. He was taken from prison and from judgment: and who shall declare his generation? for he was cut off out of the land of the living: for the transgression of my people was he stricken." (Isaiah 53:5-8)

It was the Roman guards who gave Him the stripes by "scourging" Him with their whips. "And *so* Pilate, willing to content the people, released Barabbas unto them, and delivered Jesus, when he had scourged *him*, to be crucified." (Mark 15:15)

Jesus did stand silent for a period before His accusers. This amazed Pilate.

> "And the chief priests accused him of many things: but he answered nothing. And

CHAPTER 75: THE TRUTH OF HIS DIVINITY

Pilate asked him again, saying, Answerest thou nothing? behold how many things they witness against thee. But Jesus yet answered nothing; so that Pilate marveled." (Mark 15:3-5)

From prison and judgment Jesus was taken to the place of execution. Notice that both places were part of the flow of the incidents. It was in prison where He was scourged by the soldiers and the judgment, initially, took place before the Jewish council. Jesus was also before the civil judgment seat when He was before both Pilate and Herod.

There are many prophecies concerning the crucifixion of Jesus.

One of these prophecies is from Psalm 69:19.

"Thou hast known my reproach, and my shame, and my dishonor: mine adversaries are all before me."

Who could argue that this is not a picture of the trial and crucifixion of Jesus? He was reproached by those who wished Him dead. These men attempted to shame Him by the death of the crucifixion. They wanted Him and His message to be dishonored before men. Even during His death agonies these adversaries continued to taunt and berate Him.

The Psalmist also says,

"They gavest me also gall for my meat: and for my thirst they gave me vinegar to drink." (Psalm 69:21)

Then, when we look at Jesus on the cross we see that this is so.

"After this, Jesus knowing that all things were now accomplished, that the scripture might be fulfilled, saith, I thirst. Now was set a vessel full of vinegar: and they filled a spunge with vinegar, and put it upon hyssop, and put it to his mouth." (John 19:28-29)

The Psalmist also tells us that the death of Jesus was not as other men.

"Into thine hand I commit my spirit: thou hast redeemed me, O LORD God of truth." (Psalm 31:5)

Jesus said,

"Therefore doth my Father love me, because I lay down my life, that I might take it again. No man taketh it from me, but I lay it down of myself. I have power to lay it down, and I have power to take it again. This commandment have I received of my Father." (John 10:17-18)

Now, anyone could have said that but only the Divine Son of God could actually fulfill that statement.

"And when Jesus had cried with a loud voice, he said, Father, into thy hands I commend my spirit: and having said thus, he gave up the ghost." (Luke 23:46)

There were several statements about the Passover Lamb. The Passover Lamb was a type of Christ. It was illustrative of the sacrifice of the Lamb of God, Jesus.

"In one house shall it be eaten; thou shalt not carry forth ought of the flesh abroad out of the house: neither shall ye break a bone thereof." (Exodus 12.46)

"They shall leave none of it unto the morning, nor break any bone of it: according to all the ordinances of the Passover shall they keep it." (Numbers 9:12)

"He keepeth all his bones: not one of them is broken." (Psalm 34:20)

This seems to be a pretty important point: no bones broken. There was a problem. A crucifixion would normally rupture the diaphragm. Since the diaphragm is used to breathe this meant that those being crucified would use their legs to expand and contract the chest to allow breath. This was agony of course. Thus when the Romans wanted to hasten the demise of the victim they would break the legs to make death accelerate.

This was a time when they wanted to hasten the death of those crucified. But, when they soldiers came to Jesus they found Him already dead.

> *"But when they came to Jesus and saw that he was dead already, they break not his legs: But one of the soldiers with a spear pierced his side, and forthwith came there out blood and water." (John 19:33-34)*

Isn't it amazing how prophecy works? By the way, there is more. Zechariah was talking about the future restoration of Israel in the Millennial Kingdom when he said the following of God.

> *"And I will pour upon the house of David, and upon the inhabitants of Jerusalem, the spirit of grace and of supplications: and they shall look upon me whom they have pierced, and shall mourn for him, as one mourneth for his only son, and shall be in bitterness for him, as one that is in bitterness for his firstborn." (Zechariah 12:10)*

Also since we are considering the Divinity of Jesus we might well note that God said, "...they shall look upon me whom they have pierced..."

The dead bodies of the crucified were normally left upon the crosses so that the population could look and consider the fruitlessness of any rebellion against Rome. However the prophecies of the Bible would take precedence over the Roman custom once again.

> *"His body shall not remain all night upon the tree, but thou shalt in any wise bury him that day: (for he that is hanged is accursed of God;) that the land be not defiled which the LORD thy God giveth thee for an inheritance. (Deuteronomy 21:23)*

> *"And after this Joseph of Arimathaea, being a disciple of Jesus, but secretly for fear of the Jews, besought Pilate that he might take away the body of Jesus: and Pilate gave him leave. He came therefore, and took the body of Jesus." (John 19:38)*

This same Joseph of Arimathaea also gave his grave as a burying place for Jesus.

> *"Therefore will I divide him a portion with the great, and he shall divide the spoil with the strong, because he hath poured out his soul unto death: and he was numbered with the transgressors, and he bare the sin of many, and made intersession for the transgressors." (Isaiah 53:12)*

Jesus was crucified between two criminals but was buried in the grave of a rich man.

And, lest we forget, Jesus did make intercession for the repentant thief on the cross next to Him.

The disciples, not yet understanding the impending resurrection of Jesus, began to make preparations for His burial.

> *"And there came also Nicodemus, which at the first came to Jesus by night, and brought a mixture of myrrh and aloes, about an hundred pound weight." (John 19:39)*

Even this was no surprise to prophecy.

CHAPTER 75: THE TRUTH OF HIS DIVINITY

"All thy garments smell of myrrh, and aloes, and cassia, out of the ivory palaces, whereby they have made thee glad." (Psalms 45:8)

Neither was the resurrection of Jesus a surprise to the prophetic record. Even Job understood that his Redeemer would live.

"For I know that my redeemer liveth, and that he shall stand at the latter day upon the earth." (Job 19:25)

The Psalmist also prophesied the resurrection of Jesus.

"For thou wilt not leave my soul in hell; neither will thou suffer thine holy One to see corruption. Thou will shew me the path of life in thy presence is fullness of joy; at thy right hand there are pleasures for evermore." (Psalm 16:10-11)

"Thou which hast shewed me great and sore troubles, shall quicken me again, and shall bring me up again from the depths of the earth." (Psalm 71:20)

Even though the disciples did not understand the fact, the Scripture had already given testimony to the fact that the Messiah would rise from the dead.

CHAPTER 76
CIRCUMSTANTIAL EVIDENCE THAT POINTS TO THE DIVINITY OF JESUS
(Session Seventy-Seven)

In this session we will continue to consider Zeoli's list of circumstantial evidence that points to the Divinity of Jesus.

Mark 6:2-3: Jesus Came From Relative Obscurity

We consider that Jesus rose from a relative obscurity. Look at Mark 6:2-3.

> "And when the Sabbath day was come, he began to teach in the synagogue: and many hearing him were astonished, saying, From whence hath this man these things? and what wisdom is this which is given unto him, that even such mighty works are wrought by his hands: Is not this the carpenter, the son of Mary, the brother of James, and Joses, and of Judas, and Simon? and are not his sisters here with us? And they were offended at him."

I used the term "relative obscurity" because Jesus was obviously known in the vicinity. After all, His entire earthly family was known by name. As an aside, Joseph is not mentioned. It is assumed that he died some time soon after the family went to the Passover observance recorded in Luke 2:41-52 since he is never mentioned again after that time.

Following this assumption we are led to assume that Jesus, "the carpenter," was the family breadwinner. His half-brothers would have been approaching the age where they could assume this burden. His half-sisters would have been fast approaching, as we used to say down South, "Marrying Age." This would have especially so in this culture.

We see, then, that Jesus cared for, and provided for, His earthly family while in this body of clay. We see further evidence of this when Jesus saw to it, even during His agony on the Cross!, that His earthly mother would be cared for in her approaching old age. (see John 19:25-27)

There is a lesson in this. We must not shirk our earthly responsibilities. This is not the way of Christ for us to fail to provide for those of our own families. This would give a terrible testimony and a great cause for the world at large to find grounds to attack our profession and outreach of faith. It is not a sin to fail in this regard; it is a sin to make no effort!

We must also notice that these people did not see Jesus as a great theologian. Quite to the contrary they were "offended at Him." Even after seeing some of His "mighty works" and hearing His teaching these people were loath to accept Him. Again we have an illustration from Christ. Our following the leading of God may not lead to the praise of men. We must still follow the will of God for our lives.

Jesus Came from Adversity and Opposition

What we see in Jesus is more than a simple rise from obscurity. We see a rise in the face of adversity and opposition. Continue on in the course the Lord has given.

Only therein is real peace and contentment. Only therein is true spiritual power and peace.

Real Authority Comes From the Words of God

Jesus also had great authority in His message. Mark 1:22 records one time when Jesus was teaching in the synagogue at Capernaum. The people said,

> "And they were astonished at his doctrine: for he taught them as one that had authority, and not as the scribes."

Folks, real spiritual authority always comes from the Words of God. We may instruct in morality and lifestyle, but real authority comes from the Words of God. We may pontificate on our political and cultural concerns, but real authority comes from the Words of God. We may even build spectacular castles of profound theological structure, but real authority comes from the Words of God!

There was one instance when some officers were sent out from the chief priests and Pharisees with orders to bring Jesus back with them. When these officers were asked why they had failed to apprehend Jesus, their defense was, "…Never man spake like this man." (John 7:46b)

Jesus Is the Word of God and Is God and Therefore the Real Authority

Jesus spoke with the Authority incumbent to Him as God.

The authority of Jesus extended to His power of death and His power of miracle.

Someone has said that Jesus never passed a funeral procession without changing lamentation into laughter. There are many recorded instances of Jesus raising the dead in the New Testament. One of these, Lazarus, had been dead for four days and decomposition had already set in upon his body. The significant point as regards our study is that He did this on His Own volition. There are several resurrections recorded in the Old Testament. Each of these was accomplished as a prophet was infused with the power of God for that particular miracle. Jesus, as God, carried within His Own Self the power to accomplish this great miracle.

The greatest resurrection miracle in the sacred history is that first Easter Morning when Jesus raised Himself from the dead.

> "Therefore doth my Father love me, because I lay down my life, that I might take it again. No man taketh it from me, but I lay it down of myself. I have power to lay it down, and I have power to take it again. This commandment have I received of my Father." (John 10:17-18)

The miracle of walking on the water was a great display of power and authority. The miracle of feeding thousands with just a few loaves and fish was a great display of power and authority. The stilling of the storm, the winds, and the waves which were already in motion was a great display of power and authority. The power of His resurrection of Lazarus and the others was a great display of power and authority. Somehow even these mighty acts seem to pale in comparison to the fact of the empty tomb and the realization that Jesus performed this miracle of resurrection Himself.

This is power which could only belong to God. Jesus is God.

Jesus Is the Spirit of Prophecy

Jesus also displayed the power of reading tomorrow's headlines today. He didn't

CHAPTER 76: CIRCUMSTANTIAL EVIDENCE THAT POINTS TO THE DEITY OF JESUS

guess at the future. He knew it. He didn't make predictions or dwell in possible scenarios. He spoke of the future with the accuracy and assurance which others might have spoken of the past. The difference is that He is always right while we might just make a mistake or two.

He saw, and foretold, the fall of Capernaum, Chorazin and Bethsaida.

> "Woe unto thee, Chorazin! Woe unto thee, Bethsaida! for if the mighty works, which were done in you, had been done in Tyre and Sidon, they would have repented long ago in sackcloth and ashes. But I say unto you, It shall be more tolerable for Tyre and Sidon at the day of judgment, than for you. And thou, Capernaum, which art exalted unto heaven, shalt be brought down to hell: for if the mighty works, which have been done in thee, had been done in Sodom, it would have remained until this day." (Matthew 11:21-24)

So completely have these cities been devastated that even the exact locations of Chorazin and Capernaum are in dispute. Bethsaida, once a fishing village located at the point where the Jordan River enters into the Sea of Galilee, is little more than ruins.

Consider that from Bethsaida came Peter, Andrew and Philip. Capernaum was nearly a "home base" for Jesus in large portions of His ministries. He did perform miracles in that location. Bethsaida is near where Jesus fed the multitudes with a few loaves and fish.

Chorazin is only mentioned in the above passage and in a parallel passage in Luke 10:13. It may have been a suburb of Bethsaida. If so it may have shared in the rejection of Christ with that city. I do not know, could not find, what sins were counted to these cities accounts. God does know. I think the lesson for us is that great sins, public sins, and even private sins are all alike to God. Judgment comes not from our actions but from our inaction of refusing to accept Jesus as Savior and Lord.

How can we expect to please God when we refuse the Gift He has already offered us of free salvation in Christ? We can never do better than He has done. It is a great insult, and sin!, to refuse His Gift as unworthy and attempt to consider our own work as superior!

Jesus foretold the fall of Jerusalem, and its time.

> "And when he was come near, he behold the city, and wept over it, Saying, If thou hadst known, even thou, at least in this thy day, the things which belong unto thy peace! but now they are hid from thine eyes. For the days shall come upon thee, that thine enemies shall cast a trench about thee, and compass thee round, and keep thee in on every side; And shall lay thy children within thee, and they shall not leave in thee one stone upon another, because thou knewest not the time of thy visitation." (Luke 19: 41-44)

To see the complete accuracy of this statement it is only necessary to look at nearly any history book about this time and region. It was only about forty years after Jesus had said this, less than a single generation, that Titus and his Roman legions completely leveled the city as they defeated a Jewish insurrection against Rome.

Jesus speaks of another indignity suffered by the "City of David." It is a continuing indignity. "And they shall fall by the edge of the sword, and shall be led away captive into all nations: and Jerusalem shall be trodden down of the Gentiles, until the times of the Gentiles be fulfilled." (Luke 21:24)

The Jewish people carried out several revolts against the Roman Empire. None of these succeeded. After one to many, from the view of Rome, of these revolts the Jews were again defeated and forced, in 136 AD, to depart from Judea. Thus began the Diaspora which continues to this day. Unable to return to their own land the people wandered the world to establish homes on "foreign" grounds.

We might also note that never again has Jerusalem been under the complete control of the Jewish people. Even today, as the capital of modern Israel, the city continues to be "trodden down of the Gentiles" as Israel does not enjoy a complete rule of the city.

Jesus Lived a Sinless Life

Jesus lived a sinless life. That seems like such a simple statement. It isn't. Consider just what that means. It means that Jesus never sinned, indeed never could sin since He is God in human flesh, even once in His entire life and ministry on this earth.

This is an important point. First, that Jesus did not sin while He walked this earth in a human body. This means that He had no sin of His Own. Therefore His death was not any sort of sacrifice for Himself. He died for us. (consider II Corinthians 5:21) He died in our place so that the judgment of His non-sin could be applied to our sin.

It is also important that He could not sin. God cannot sin. Sin is that antithesis of His Divine nature. Had Jesus been capable of sin it would mean that He is not God. If Jesus were not God He would owe His Own allegiance to God. In such a case His death would be meaningless to us in that He could not impart grace. His death in such a case could not impart grace as His Own allegiance to God would preclude His ability to offer grace to anyone else.

More simply stated, if Jesus were not fully God He would lack legal *standing* to forgive sins and offer grace. He would not have that authority since that authority belongs to God, alone. Sin is an affront to God. Therefore only God can forgive sin and impart grace. Had Jesus ever sinned, if He had been capable of sin, He would not be of the Divine Nature.

This fact, from a negative viewpoint, is one more indication that Jesus is God.

Jesus Became Sin, He Was Not a Sinner

I understand what II Corinthians 5:21 says. Look closely at that verse.

> "For he hath made him to be sin for us, who knew no sin, that we might be made the righteousness of God in him."

It might be good to consider this verse in light of Romans 8:3.

> "For what the law could not do, in that it was weak through the flesh, God sending his own Son in the likeness of sinful flesh, and for sin, condemned sin in the flesh."

Jesus became sin for us. He did not become a sinner. He took upon Himself our sin while He was on the cross so that when the Father looked at Him what was seen was all the sins which humanity would ever, or had ever, commit. Those sins were judged in the humanity of Jesus. In His divinity He was still righteous to forgive those sins on behalf of those who would accept Him in faith.

> "But this man [Jesus], after he had offered one sacrifice for sins for ever, sat down on the right hand of God." (Hebrews 10:12)

Verse four of this same chapter had said, "For *it is* not possible that the blood of

CHAPTER 76: CIRCUMSTANTIAL EVIDENCE THAT POINTS TO THE DEITY OF JESUS

bulls and of goats should take away sin." This tenth chapter of Hebrews was showing the superiority of the sacrifice of Jesus over the Old Testament sacrifice. Those Old Testament sacrifices had been effectual in covering the sins of those Old Testament faithful. The faith of those people in the Words of God had made them righteous. They were not sanctified, or set apart holy, until the greater sacrifice of Jesus Christ removed and cleansed those sins.

Dr. DeWitt's Commentary on Luke 16:19

The following from my commentary on Luke 16:19 will serve to explain this concept:

> "First, it would be wise for us to consider that this was not a parable. Jesus never mentioned a person by name when He taught by parable. This is a true incident concerning two "certain" people – one named, the other not named.
>
> "Even if this passage had been a parable, we must remember that the spiritual facts would still be true as Jesus never taught error.
>
> "Jesus was acting as a Gentleman when He named the one but not the other. Lazarus, the man in Paradise was named. His family and friends could take comfort in this. The rich man is not named; rather, Jesus simply described the situation of that man. Two things were accomplished in this. The surviving relatives of this man were not unduly given even more grief at the death of their family member. At the same time that family, and all other families with similar circumstance, were given the warning about their own souls.
>
> "We need to compare other passages in relation to this story. The first concerns the rich man, Revelation 20:14-15,
>
> *"And death and hell were cast into the lake of fire. This is the second death. And whosoever was not found written in the book of life was cast into the lake of fire."*
>
> "We also need to consider several verses in relation to the beggar, Lazarus. While on the cross Jesus was asked by one of the malefactors who were being crucified alongside Him that He would remember the man when He came into His kingdom. (Luke 23:43) In the very next verse Jesus replied, "...To day shalt thou be with me in paradise."
>
> "Strong (3857) refers to paradise as a place of happiness. Since Jesus said that this man would be with Him this may refer to Heaven. I would suggest that this may not be so. The ancient Talmud describes one of these [places of the abode of the dead] is Hell, the place of punishment for the sinner, and the other is Paradise, the place where the righteous go. Jesus gives credence to this teaching in this incident.
>
> "To the sinner this was a time prior to the final judgment when they are cast into the Lake of Fire which was originally prepared for the devil and his angels. (Matthew 25:41) These [the devil and his angels] sinned before the creation of humanity. The unregenerate who are consigned to the Lake of Fire will be there as followers of Satan and thus share in his judgments.
>
> "The Blood of Jesus, superior to the blood of those Old Testament sacrifices in that His Blood has the capacity to cleanse sin rather than to cover sin in accordance with the sacrifices which were a shadow of Him to come, had not yet been shed as a full atonement for the sins of the believer. Therefore these saints, made righteous by faith, could not yet be in the full presence of God.
>
> "This explains Ephesians 4:8-10.

> *"Wherefore he saith, When he ascended up on high, he led captivity captive, and gave gifts unto men. (Now that he ascended, what is it that he also descended first into the lower parts of the earth? He that descended is the same one that ascended up far above the all heavens, that he might fill all things."*

"The picture is that Jesus went to Paradise and, as His shed blood was effective to cleanse those Old Testament saints, He led them from Paradise to be ever with Him in Heaven. Now, in this Dispensation of Grace, we depart from this life to be with Him in Heaven. (see Acts 7:56-60; II Corinthians 5:8; Philippians 1:23)"

The point being made is that only the sacrifice of Jesus is effective in cleansing sin. All who have had their sins cleansed owe that to Jesus. It is only He, as God, Who has the power to remove sins and make any person clean before God.

The Sinlessness of Jesus Proves His Divinity and Saves Our Souls!

The sinlessness of Jesus proves His Divinity and saves our souls!

Jesus had an insightful knowledge of humanity. By this it is not meant that He could "read the tea leaves" and understand a person. This is an intimate knowledge which transcends the mere "Sherlock Holmes" observational understanding of a person. Jesus understood all about a person.

An example of this is shown in John 2:24-25 where many people were ready to follow Jesus.

> *"But Jesus did not commit himself unto them, because he knew all men, and needed not that any should testify of man: for he knew what was in man."*

Jesus knew that these people were not true followers of Him. They had been attracted by miracles. (see v. 23) Rather than being attracted to His message of sin and repentance, these were attracted only to the spectacle of His miracle. Like the followers of a "rock star" in our day these would only follow until the next "entertainer" came upon the public stage.

The testimony of the Truth of Jesus is within the heart of His true followers, the believers.

> *"The Spirit itself beareth witness with our spirit, that we are the children of God." (Romans 8:16)*

The Spirit, the Third Person of the Trinity, bears witness to Jesus, the Second Person of the Trinity.

The truth, and the manner of His Own control over His death and resurrection, that Jesus did raise from the dead is another statement toward His true Divinity.

While being interrogated by Pilate Jesus spoke of His kingdom.

> *"...My kingdom is not of this world: if my kingdom were of this world, then would my servants fight, that I should not be delivered to the Jews: but now is my kingdom not from hence." (John 18:36)*

The "other worldly" kingdom of which Jesus spoke is a spiritual kingdom. Jesus could have no such kingdom unless He was possessor of spiritual power. Since we have already seen Jesus tempted of Satan in the wilderness in the fourth chapter of Matthew, we must conclude that Jesus is the Righteous King. Therefore Jesus must be God.

It could well be argued that the evidence above is of a circumstantial nature. After

CHAPTER 76: CIRCUMSTANTIAL EVIDENCE THAT POINTS TO THE DEITY OF JESUS

all, these do not plainly state the Divinity of Jesus. However, each piece of evidence does point to the fact that Jesus is Divine. Cumulatively the evidence presented is a proven case about the true Godhood of Jesus.

CHAPTER 77

THE MIRACLES WHICH JESUS PERFORMED POINT TO THE FACT OF HIS DIVINITY

(Session Seventy-Eight)

Several Reasons to Believe Jesus Is Divine

Josh McDowell and Don Stewart (Answers to Tough Questions) give several reasons from the Scriptural story to believe that Jesus is Divine.

The Miracles

The miracles which Jesus performed certainly point to the fact of His Divinity. Consider the resurrection of Lazarus in the eleventh chapter of John. This was no mere resuscitation of a man merely in a coma or passed out. Lazarus had been dead for four days. The process of decomposition had already begun. (see John 11:39) Yet, at the voice of Jesus Lazarus came out of the tomb still encumbered by his burial wrappings. (John 11:44)

We could also consider the story of Jesus in a small boat on the sea during a storm.

> "And there arose a great storm of wind, and the waves beat into the ship, so that it was now full. And he was in the hinder part of the ship, asleep on a pillow: and they awake him, and say unto him, Master, carest thou not that we perish? And he arose, and rebuked the wind and said unto the sea, Peace, be still. And the wind ceased, and there was a great calm." (Mark 4:37-39)

Certainly the calming of the storm was a great miracle. But, greater still in my mind, the calming of the waves so that there was a great calm seems a still greater miracle. Even the sea waves, set into motion by the high winds, were calmed at the voice and command of Jesus. Could any but God have wrought such a miracle? There is no other answer for this miracle than to admit that Jesus is God in the flesh.

The Fulfilled Prophecies About Jesus

The many fulfilled prophecies concerning the birth, life, ministry, death and resurrection of Jesus point to His Divinity.

Some could argue, and many have, that these fulfilled prophecies were fulfilled by design. The argument is that Jesus intended to appear as though He had fulfilled the Old Testament Scriptures so He would appear to be the Messiah.

This argument falls apart when we consider that some of those prophecies concern things over which a mere mortal would have had no control. The place of birth comes quickly to mind as one of these things.

I would suppose that some skeptics might argue that there was a "happy coincidence" of Jesus being born in Bethlehem which would make the rest of the prophecies easier to accomplish. I would turn your attention to Psalm 22:7 and 8 as examples where Jesus' death on the cross is foretold. "All they that see me laugh me to scorn: they shoot out the lip, they shake the head, *saying*, He trusted on the LORD *that* he could deliver him: let him deliver him, seeing he delighted in him."

Consider this passage in relation to Luke 23:35.

> "And the people stood beholding. And the rulers also with them derided him, saying, He saved others; let him save himself, if he be Christ, the chosen of God."

Consider the passage in Psalms with Mark 15:31.

> "Likewise also the chief priests mocking said among themselves with the scribes, He saved others, himself he cannot save."

Consider, also, the passage in Psalms with Matthew 27:41-43.

> "Likewise also the chief priests mocking him, with the scribes and elders said, He saved others, himself he cannot save. If he be the King of Israel, let him now come down from the cross, and we will believe him. He trusted in God, let him deliver him now, if he will have him: for he said, I am the Son of God."

Jesus fulfilled the prophecies of the Old Testament because He really is the promised Son of God – the Messiah of Israel. Those prophecies were not fulfilled in a calculated ruse to establish Himself in that office. For that scenario to be considered one must also conclude that the very group which worked for His death was willing to help Him fulfill those prophecies.

Those fulfilled prophecies offer compelling and irrefutable evidence that Jesus is Divine.

Must Consider That Jesus Said He Was Divine

We must also consider that Jesus said He was Divine. Jesus, in John 10:30 plainly said that He was God. I know that some have argued that He was only claiming to work in concert with God but that is not the meaning which His hearers understood. In verse thirty-three their reason for wanting to stone Him was that, "...thou, being a man, makest thyself God."

Jesus spent the next several verses explaining that He deserved to be known as God. Others, in the Old Testament times, had been called "god" in deference to their ministry of position in a theocratic government. Jesus asked His accusers why they would then, "Say ye of him, whom the Father hath sanctified, and sent into the world, Thou blasphemest; because I said, I am the Son of God?" (John 10:36)

The important thing to notice in this passage is the reason that the Jewish leaders wanted to kill Jesus over what He had said and the fact that He never disavowed that statement. Jesus asserted His Deity as this point.

For a further discussion of this point see our chapter on "'gods' With a Small 'g.'"

Most Important Is the Fact of His Resurrection

Most importantly, of course, is the fact of the resurrection of Jesus. No one raised Him up from the dead. No one, even among His followers it seems, expected Him to walk out of that grave as a living Person. This only could have happened because Jesus has power over death. The Only Person with such power is God.

The reaction to the resurrected Jesus was nothing short of miraculous. Those sorrowful disciples were made joyous. The doubting of Thomas was turned into faith and praise. The former emphasis on the physical gave was to an emphasis on the spiritual realities. The fearful were made bold in His Name and Message.

That the group of believers was still willing to accept teaching and instruction from Jesus is testament to the reality of His resurrection. They all went to wait for the Spirit.

CHAPTER 77: THE MIRACLES BY JESUS POINT TO THE DEITY OF JESUS

They all rejoiced. They all loved His appearing. They all went to the mount to witness His ascension into heaven. The entire world was changed due to the energized message from these followers of a first century Teacher from a mostly insignificant Roman province.

Such is the power which could only emerge from the truth of the life, death and resurrection of the empowering presence of the Son of God.

The Attributes of Jesus Illustrate That He Is God

We see through just these four short illustrations that the Bible speaks of Jesus as God in that He has the attributes of God. Only God, or someone energized by the Spirit of God, could have performed the miracles which Jesus performed. Since Jesus performed these miracles upon His Own initiative in that He had no need to pray for that power as the power was already incumbent within His Own Person, His Deity is evidenced. Therefore He is God.

Only God's Anointed could possibly have fulfilled all of those Old Testament prophecies about the coming Messiah. Since Jesus fulfilled all those prophecies, excepting only those which He has promised to fulfill in His second advent, He is that Messiah. Since Jesus has the prophetic power to claim those promises yet to be fulfilled at His Own Word, He is God.

Since Jesus claimed Divinity and His teaching was always truth, He is God.

Since Jesus died and then rose from the dead by His Own power, He is Master over the temporal forces of created life. Since Jesus is that Master over created life, He is demonstrated to be the Creator of that life. Since Jesus is the Creator of life, He is God.

CHAPTER 78
THE IMPORTANCE OF THE SONSHIP OF JESUS
(Session Seventy-Nine)

Zeoli (*Is Jesus God? – Book Number One*) asks that we consider the Sonship of Jesus, as the Son of God, as a very important point. As Jesus is called the son of man in relation to His identification as a man, in His humanity, so is Jesus called the Son of God in relation to His ultimate Deity as God.

Several Examples

Zeoli gives several examples of the importance of the Sonship of Jesus and our need to understand this as we seek to understand the glories and majesty of Jesus.

First, The Sonship Is Important to Our Understanding of the Trinity

First, the Sonship of Jesus is important to our understanding of the Trinity. In the Great Commission we are given a command in relation to the baptism of the believer. That command contains information as to the Trinity and the Sonship of Jesus.

> "Go ye therefore and teach all nations, baptizing them in the name of the Father, and of the Son, and of the Holy Ghost." (Matthew 28:19)

Notice that the baptism is to be in the "name" (singular) of three "Persons." Once again, the use of the word "persons" is not accurate to reflect the grandeur or the majesty of the Eternal Godhead. Our finite minds are wholly unable to grasp the magnitude of God. He is One God eternally existent in three "Persons" of equal and unlimited power and splendor. What our minds are unable to understand due to our physical and time centric limits of understanding, our faith must be willing to accept simply because the Triune God of all Glory has said this is true.

The Son of God is Jesus. If we are to deny His Godhood we are limiting the true spiritual knowledge of God. As such, we are substituting a false picture of just Who God is in spiritual reality. To do this is to demean Jesus, and the entire Godhead, in our minds and hearts.

Paul mentions the Trinity of the Godhead in another place.

> "The grace of our Lord Jesus Christ, and the love of God, and the communion the Holy Ghost, be with you all. Amen." (II Corinthians 13:14)

Please notice the totality of our acceptance by God. It is through the grace of Jesus Christ in His great sacrifice on Calvary that we are allowed a fellowship in the love of God. It is through the grace of this great love that we are granted communion by the Holy Spirit. It is a great privilege that we are allowed to have this relationship with the Triune God. It is only by the grace of the Son of God, Jesus Christ, that we are allowed to enter into this privileged relationship.

For our present discussion I would ask that we notice the Trinitarian formula given by Paul, via the inspiration of the Spirit, in this passage. Jesus is the Son of God because He is God, the Son.

Second, The Concept of the <u>Eternal</u> Sonship of Jesus Is Very Important

This concept of the eternal Sonship of Jesus is very important. Were He not the Son of God He would be only the son of Joseph. Were He only the son of Joseph, He would be simply another human being. Even as the son of Joseph, Jesus could have worked seeming miracles. It is known that many dismissed Him as a "magician." As the son of Joseph, Jesus could have been an ethical teacher of righteousness; was not John the Baptist an ethical and religious teacher? As the son of Joseph, Jesus could have been a charismatic teacher and speaker. Throngs could have clamored for the chance to hear His insights.

But, as the son of Joseph, Jesus could never have been the Savior of my soul. If Jesus were simply another human being His death on the cross would have been tragic and final. He could not have risen from the grave as The Victory over sin and death. It is only as the Divine Son of God that Jesus was able to secure salvation for those who would believe.

Had Jesus been simply another man upon the earth He would have had the same sin nature as all men born of Adam. He could not have been the spotless Lamb of God. He could not have died for the sins of any other as He would have been a sinner by birth into the human race of man. It is only the sinless Son of God, born of a virgin without the stain of sin upon His soul and life who could have died as a sacrifice for the sin of humanity. It is only Jesus Christ, very man and Very God, Who has the right to forgive sin – which is a trespass and offense against God – and offer salvation and fellowship with God.

Third, The Sonship Is Important to Jesus' Sinlessness

The Sonship is important to Jesus' sinlessness. If He were not the Son of God He cannot be sinless since all men are sinners both by heredity from the sin of Adam and by experience from their own trespasses and guilt.

The Book of Proverbs gives Godly counsel on dealing with our fellow creatures.

"He that goeth about as a talebearer revealeth secrets: therefore meddle not with him that flattereth with his lips." (Proverbs 20:19)

There is a well-known old story about a preacher at a rural church. The preacher said, "Woe unto them that drink that hard liquor and harm their fellow man." An elderly woman, from the back of the congregation said, "Preach it, Brother."

The preacher said, "Woe unto them that sneak in by night and rustle the cattle from their neighbor." The woman answered, "Yes, Lord. Preach the Word, Brother."

The preacher said, "Woe unto them that gossip and tell tales about their neighbor." The woman said, "Now you've quit preaching and started meddling."

Why are we like this? It's because we are sinners as a race of human beings.

The writer of Proverbs reminds us that, "An high look, and a proud heart, *and* the plowing of the wicked, *is* sin." (Proverbs 21:4) We could all assume sin is in the first two things in that verse, "a high look and a proud heart." But, the Scripture goes so far as to call even the plowing of the wicked as a sin. Why?

It is because a man who is a sinner, and all are until such time as they receive the free grace of Jesus Christ, is a sinner in every act he might do. That is one reason why we, as a race of humanity, are unable to save ourselves by "good works." We can

CHAPTER 78: THE IMPORTANCE OF THE SONSHIP OF JESUS

perform no "good works," no matter how noble the deed might seem to other unregenerate men, as long as we remain in a state of sin.

The writer of Ecclesiastes observed, "For *there is* not a just man upon the earth, that doeth good, and sinneth not." (Ecclesiastes 7:20) As it was in the days when Ecclesiastes was first penned, it remains a spiritual truth forever among humanity born of this earth.

As Romans 3:23 reminds us, "For all have sinned, and come short of the glory of God." All men are sinners by nature and by experience.

The exception to this rule is Jesus Christ. "Who did not sin, neither was guile found in his mouth." (I Peter 2:22) Jesus was not born as are others of this race of Adam. He is the only begotten Son of God. Jesus was Virgin Born into this world of physicality. He had no sin either in experience or in nature. He experience tempting to sin, most notably on the mount of temptation by Satan, but never succumbed to the experience of sin.

Fourth, The Sonship of Jesus Is Important to Jesus' Ability to Save Sinners

The Sonship of Jesus is important to Jesus' ability to save sinners. As mentioned above, if Jesus had sinned He would not have had the power to save others. Had Jesus sinned He would have been simply another man born of woman in the natural manner. As God the possibility of sin did not reside within Jesus. He was a wholly and righteous Person in that He was God. He still is God! It is not in the divine nature of God to sin. As the eternal Son of God it is not within the Divine nature of Jesus Christ to sin.

Since Jesus did not sin, indeed as God He was not capable of sin, He has standing to impart grace and forgiveness to those who come to Him by faith and accept His substitutionary death on the cross as payment for the sin of the penitent.

Since Jesus declared on many occasions that He was the Son of God, the concept of His Sonship is important to the very truthfulness of the Savior. Since Jesus did not sin, He always told the complete truth. He did not lie. Therefore, by His own testimony, He is the Son of God.

Since the Bible declares on many occasions that Jesus was the Son of God, the concept of His Sonship is important to the very truthfulness of the Scripture. Since the Scripture is the inspired and preserved Words of God, we know that the Scripture is not capable of error. Therefore, by the testimony of Scripture Jesus is the Son of God.

Things Inferred, Stated, or Contained Within Any Denial of the Sonship of Jesus

Zeoli also notes several things that are inferred, stated or contained within any denial of the Sonship of Jesus.

First, To Deny the Sonship Is to Call God a Liar

We might well consider just what God said of Jesus at His baptism by John. As the baptism of Jesus concluded John the Baptist heard the voice of God, the Father.

> "And lo a voice from heaven, saying, This is my beloved Son, in whom I am well pleased." (Matthew 3:17)

John, the apostle, wrote the following.

> "He that believeth on the Son of God hath the witness in himself: he that believeth not God hath made him a liar; because he believeth not the record that God gave of

his Son." (I John 5:10)

Simply put: To refuse to accept the Divine Sonship of Jesus is to call God, the Father, a liar.

Earlier in the short epistle of I John, John had written the following.

"Who is a liar but he that denieth that Jesus is the Christ? He is antichrist, that denieth the Father and the Son." (I John 2:22)

Not only does one call the Father a liar, one also calls the Son, Jesus, a liar when the Sonship of Jesus is denied.

We must add I John 4:3 at this point.

"And every spirit that confesseth not that Jesus Christ is come in the flesh is not of God: and this is that spirit of antichrist, whereof ye have heard that it should come; and even now already is it in the world."

We are used to hearing of the Antichrist who shall come in the last days during the Tribulation Period. There are those who have displayed the same spirit of evil and opposition to the things of God throughout this dispensation of grace.

It is an antichrist spirit which denies the truth of the Sonship and Deity of Jesus.

We are all familiar with John 3:16. This is, probably, the most beloved and well known verse in Scripture. But, look just two verses further.

"He that believeth on him is not condemned: but he that believeth not is condemned already, because he hath not believed in the name of the only begotten Son of God." (John 3:18)

To deny the Sonship of Jesus is to stand condemned by God.

Second, The Severity of Refusing to Accept Jesus as the Son of God

At the end of this third chapter of John we are reminded of the severity of refusing to accept Jesus as the Son of God.

"He that believeth on the Son hath everlasting life: and he that believeth not the Son shall not see life; but the wrath of God abideth on him." (John 3:36)

Consider all that Jesus endured when He came to this earth. He knew that the cross was on His path. Yet, He still came to offer salvation to all who would accept Him. What an affront to God it is that any should refuse to accept this gracious offer of salvation.

Is it any wonder that the wrath of God is upon those who would refuse to accept that Jesus is the Son of God. I understand that the person who rejects Jesus is simply continuing on his path as a sinner. Still, the person who rejects the Sonship of Jesus stands under the wrath of God.

Third, To Deny the Sonship Is to Die in Sin

Finally, Zeoli asks that we consider John 8:24.

"I [Jesus speaking] said therefore unto you, that ye shall die in your sins, for if ye believe not that I am he, ye shall die in your sins."

To deny the Sonship of Jesus is to die in sin.

I left the power on to my coffee pot on last night. The bottom of the coffee pot is now stained with burnt coffee. I don't know if I will ever be able to clean the pot to its original condition. Our souls are stained with sin. We can never clean them to the point

CHAPTER 78: THE IMPORTANCE OF THE SONSHIP OF JESUS

where they would be clean unto God. Jesus has offered the Cleansing Agent of His Own Blood to clean our souls. Our condition will remain besmirched and sinful unless we meet Him at the cross and accept Him as our Savior.

There is no need for any to die in their sin. Jesus will cleanse your sin.

> *"Wherefore he is able also to save them to the uttermost that come unto God by him, seeing he ever liveth to make intercession for them."* (Hebrews 7:25)

Fourth, Even the Demons Admit That Jesus Is Divine

Orr (*Can We Be Sure that Jesus Christ is God?*) notes that even the demons admit that Jesus is Divine.

We see this fact in the power which Jesus possessed over Satan. Shortly after His temptation by Satan on the mountain, Jesus continued on His earthly ministry. Satan could not defeat Him by a myriad of temptations.

As He went about His ministry the following was written of Jesus by Matthew.

> *"And his fame went throughout all Syria: and the brought unto him all sick people that were taken with divers diseases and torments, and those which were possessed with devils, and those which were lunatic, and those that had the palsy, and he healed them."* (Matthew 4:24)

Not only did Jesus heal disease, He also healed spiritually in that His power over demons removed them from their attacks upon people. The demonic forces were powerless against the Divine God-man, Jesus Christ.

Shortly after Jesus had displayed His power over the natural elements by stilling the storm on the sea, He encountered spiritual forces and displayed His power there as well.

> *"And when he was come to the other side into the country of the Gergesenes, there met him two possessed with devils, coming out of the tombs, exceeding fierce, so that no man might pass by that way."* (Matthew 8:28)

Once again Jesus commanded these two men to become whole by banishing the evil spirits from them. One this occasion the demonic forces were sent into a herd of swine. Sadly, notice (verse 34) that the people of the area seemed more interested in the pigs than they were in the two men who were healed!

We also see that the demons were not only exorcised by Jesus. They were also forced to obey His instructions.

> *"And he healed many that were sick of divers diseases, and cast out many devils, and suffered not the devils to speak, because they knew him."* (Mark 1:34)

Jesus knew that it was not His time to confront the religious leaders. His time of teaching His disciples, that they might carry forth His message when He was departed from the earthly scene was not complete. His time of sacrifice was not yet. So He commanded the demons that they would not report of Him at this time. Those demons were forced to submit to His will and voice even in this point.

There is another report of this sort of ministry by Jesus in relation to the demonic forces.

> *"Saying, Let us alone, what have we to do with thee, thou Jesus of Nazareth? art thou come to destroy us? I know thee who thou art; the Holy one of God."* (Luke 4:34)

The demons recognized the power and Person of Jesus Christ, the Son of God.

I would only make note here that the demonic forces did not understand the purpose of this first coming of Jesus. It seems that the majesty of the love of God toward us, who are the called according to His grace, is so great that the demonic forces had no concept of that redemptive love. Even the holy angels are not able to fully comprehend this majesty and glory of God which is shed upon us who have been washed in His Blood.

> "Unto whom it was revealed, that not unto themselves, but unto us they did minister the things, which are now reported unto you by them that have preached the gospel unto you with the Holy Ghost sent down from heaven, which things the angels desire to look into." (I Peter 1:12)

Jesus also delegated this power over demons to His disciples.

> "And when he had called unto him his twelve disciples, he gave them power against unclean spirits, to cast them out, and to heal all manner of sickness and all manner of disease." (Matthew 10:1)

Fifth, The Delegation of Power By Jesus Is A Sign of His Deity

The delegation of power by Jesus is another sign of His Own Deity. Had He simply been another man, even though empowered by God, He could not have passed on this power of His Own volition. He could have called upon God, had He been simply a man, to also endow those disciples with power over the demons. He could not have simply given them this power on His Own.

At one point some considered that Jesus was working in concert with Satan in the casting out of demons. Jesus argued that this was not reasonable even on a natural level. This incident is recounted in Luke 11:14-20. Students of American history may read this account and remember the words of Abraham Lincoln and his "House Divided" speech. Jesus cast out those demons because, as God, He was in opposition to the devices of Satan.

The Words of God and the reality of the life of Jesus are powerful because He is the virgin born Son of God. Even the secular history pays homage to the Man from Galilee.

CHAPTER 79

THE FACTS OF JESUS' LIFE AND BIRTH POINT TO THE FACT THAT HE IS DIVINE

(Session Eighty)

Christianson (*Why We Believe in the Deity of Christ*) makes note that the facts of Jesus' life and birth point to the fact that He is Divine.

Fact One, The First Prophecy of Jesus Points to His Deity

We note the first prophecy of Jesus in the Scripture. In the Garden, after the fall of Adam and Eve into sin, God made a promise to all humanity when He spoke to Satan who was in the form of a serpent.

> "And I will put enmity between thee and the woman, and between thy seed and her seed; it shall bruise thy head, and thou shalt bruise his heel." (Genesis 3:15)

There is not another place in the Scripture where any person is considered as the seed of a woman. This is a prophecy of the virgin birth of Jesus Christ. As the story is read here in the third chapter of Genesis we are struck with the fact that there is no mention of anything happening when Eve took part of the fruit. According to the Words of God we must understand that Eve was lost, spiritually dead, at the point of her sin. But, the great upheaval of creation did not happen until Adam partook of the fruit.

I would believe that there are two things at work. Adam was the first of the human creation of God. It was into Adam that God breathed the breath of life. As we read the expanded version of the creation of man as given in chapter two, we see that the Garden was prepared for the man before woman had been created as a "helper" and "companion" for man. It was to man that the command was given to not eat of the Tree of the Knowledge of Good and Evil.

It is obvious that Eve understood this command of God. It is possible that God may have repeated the prohibition to Eve after her creation. It is also possible that Adam may have "witnessed" the fact to her. However the fact was communicated to Eve, she was without excuse before God when she departed from His Words to her.

Man was the head of the race and carried with him the responsibility to oversee, have dominion over, the temporal creation.

It could be argued that Eve was cajoled, or tempted, to partake of the fruit. There is no such temptation related in reference to Adam. It seems that Adam made a cold and calculated decision to disobey God. In this decision, and in his responsibilities, the sin of Adam caused a great upheaval in the perfect creation of God.

> "For we know that the whole creation groaneth and travaileth in pain together until now." (Romans 8:22)

We read some of the curse upon the earth in the middle of the third chapter of Genesis.

At this point the creation was cursed from the sin of Adam. From that time forth every person born of Adam carried the curse of sin within them as an inheritance from Adam. Eve, who had her own sin for which to account, would not have been a recipient of this "sin nature" as she was taken from Adam before he had sinned.

Thus, for the Savior of humanity to be born as a human – in order to be representative of the race of humanity – it would be necessary that He not be born of Adam. Jesus, the virgin born offspring of humanity in the natural, was therefore free from the stain of the inherited sin of Adam. As God He could not sin; as man He did not sin.

Fact Two, The Names of Jesus Are the Names of God

We see that the names of Jesus are the names of God.

> "Therefore the Lord himself shall give you a sign; Behold, a virgin shall conceive, and bear a son, and shall call his name Immanuel." (Isaiah 7:14)

"Immanuel," of course, means "God with us."

Isaiah 9:6 adds information as to the names of Jesus.

> "For unto us a child is born, unto us a son is given: and the government shall be upon his shoulder: and his name shall be called, Wonderful, Counsellor, The mighty God, The everlasting Father, The Prince of Peace."

We might note, especially in this latter verse, that Jesus was never actually called by these names. These are not intended to be mere monikers; these are descriptions of Who Jesus is in reality.

Fact Three, Jesus Would Do a Perfect and Supernatural Work

Of Jesus it was prophesied that He would do a perfect and a supernatural work.

> "Behold my servant, whom I uphold; mine elect, in whom my soul delighteth, I have put my spirit upon him: he shall bring forth judgment to the Gentiles. He shall not cry, nor lift up, nor cause his voice to be heard in the street. A bruised reed shall he not break, and the smoking flax shall he not quench he shall bring forth judgment unto truth. He shall not fail nor be discouraged, till he have set judgment in the earth: and the isles shall wait for his law." (Isaiah 42:1-4)

Jesus continued His work of His first advent until He was able to say, "It is finished. (see John 19:30) Still, there is more work that Jesus will do in the future.

> "The Spirit of the LORD is upon me, because the LORD hath anointed me to preach good tidings unto the meek; he hath sent me to bind up the brokenhearted, to proclaim liberty to the captives, and the opening of the prison to them that are bound; To proclaim the acceptable year of the LORD, and the day of vengeance of our God; to comfort all them that mourn, To appoint unto them that mourn in Zion, to give unto them beauty for ashes, the oil of joy for mourning, and garment of praise for the spirit of heaviness, that they might be called trees of righteousness, the planting of the LORD, that he might be glorified." (Isaiah 61:1-3)

There is a very old play in baseball. It is called the sacrifice bunt. The idea is to advance a runner on first to second, or on second to third, by having the batter simply bunt the ball so that he is thrown out at first while that the runner on base can advance. This play would not be attempted if there were no runner on base. There is a time and a place for this strategy.

Jesus well understood this concept. He came to call sinners to repentance in His first advent. He came to offer Himself a sacrifice for the sins of many in His first advent. It is in His second advent that He will come to judge the world and set up His Own Kingdom of Righteousness as He rules the world from the Throne of David for one

CHAPTER 79: THE FACTS OF JESUS' LIFE AND BIRTH POINT TO THE FACT HE IS DIVINE

thousand years.

> "And he came to Nazareth, where he had been brought up: and, as his custom was, he went into the synagogue on the sabbath day, and stood up for to read. And there was delivered unto him the book of the prophet Esaias. And when he had opened the book, he found the place where it was written, The Spirit of the Lord is upon me to preach the gospel to the poor; he hath sent me to heal the brokenhearted, to preach deliverance to the captives, and recovering of sight to the blind, to set at liberty them that are bruised, To preach the acceptable year of the Lord. And he closed the book, and he gave it again to the minister, and sat down. And the eyes of all them that were in the synagogue were fastened on him. And he began to say unto them, This day is this scripture fulfilled in your ears." (Luke 4:16-21)

Jesus stopped in mid-sentence. He did not move on the discussion to the "day of vengeance." This day of vengeance would await His second advent. Isaiah had not seen the mystery of the church. Isaiah had seen, in his prophecy, the first advent and the second advent as one.

As Isaiah looked at the mountain peaks of God's prophetic plan he was able to see the Spiritual Reconciliation of sinful humanity at the cross of the first coming of Christ. Isaiah was also able to see the National Reconciliation of Israel at the second coming of Christ. What Isaiah could not see was, as Paul puts it (see Ephesians 5:32), the *mystery* of the church wherein both Jew and Gentile would join as a people of God in the redemption of Christ.

This does not mean that the Jewish national identity and their special place in the earthly plan of God were to be dismissed. The rest of the passage from Isaiah, which Jesus did not quote at the time, was to come just as God had promised in His prophecies. That Jesus was able to see this is further proof of the Divinity of Jesus.

Fact Four, The Eternality of Jesus Is a Statement of His Full Deity

The eternality of Jesus is a statement of His full Deity. Isaiah 9:7 speaks of the eternality of Jesus. "Of the increase of *his* government of peace *there shall be* no end..." Even when Adolph Hitler spoke of his "thousand year Reich," no one, not even his demented followers considered that Hitler would be in charge of that government for one thousand years. They knew that others would have followed him in his government of tyranny and murder if that Reich were to last one thousand years.

The government of the reign of Jesus is not slated for just one thousand years. That may be the "Millennial Reign;" but the rule of Jesus shall never end. That is what the verse says, is it not? The old song said that we would have no less time to praise Jesus even after we had been there for ten thousand years. The duration of the reign of Jesus is, as is He, eternal in scope. It will never end.

That this is called "his government" which will never end means that Jesus will be an eternal ruler. He will never be replaced by a succession of others because He will eternally be the ruler of His government.

Micah 5:2 tells us, of Jesus, that His "...goings forth *have been* from of old, from everlasting." If Jesus has always existed, meaning that He is no created being in any sense of the world, and will always exist, we have no other option that to accept Him as God because He is God.

We must also consider that His virgin birth was supernatural. This event was prophesied in Genesis 3:15 where He is called the seed of woman. This is the oldest prophecy in Scripture concerning the coming Redeemer of humanity. He is shown to be Divine in the fact of His miraculous birth which was outside the normal laws of human conception. His humanity is also shown in that He was born of woman. This union of Divine and human, in order to give full reconciliation between God and man, could only be possible by Divine decree.

Fact Five, The Announcements of His Birth Were Supernatural Events

The angelic announcements to both His parents, in the natural, and to the shepherds at the time of His birth were supernatural events.

When the angel came to Mary he was met with incredulity. I would not ascribe doubt to Mary; she only wondered how such a thing could possibly happen. After all she said, "...I know not a man." (Luke 1:34b) The concept of a virgin birth appeared not to have been in Mary's vocabulary.

Although Mary could not understand the words of the angelic messenger, she did agree with God. Sometimes we of the Protestant or Baptist theological stance will fail to give due honor to Mary. May we never overlook the fact that Mary stands high in the pantheon of Biblical heros and heroines. Her faith and attitude of submissiveness to the Word and Will of God ought to stand as an example to all!

We also need to consider the great courage of Mary. In the time in which she lived the concept of a "single mother" was not one of admiration. This was an extremely patriarchal society. You may recall the incident from the eighth chapter of John where an adulteress was taken to Jesus. Read the story again and you'll find that the man involved was not brought forward. Such was the reality of the culture of the day that the woman was brought forward for stoning while the man, who was guilty of the same sin, was not even named.

How could Mary explain her situation of pregnancy? Her explanation would, of necessity, begin with the words, "There was this angel with whom I talked..."

Should she survive the censure of her condition the next problem would be as to how she and the child would survive. There were few career opportunities for women at this time. Fewer still were the opportunities available for women in her situation. She had to consider that Joseph would probably not be willing to keep her as wife when he found her condition. Mary understood that her total faith and reliance for the future were in the Hands of God. Nonetheless Mary said, "...Behold the handmaid of the Lord; be it unto me according to thy word..." (Luke 1:38)

There can be few examples of faith, confidence in God, and righteous courage in the history of the world than that of Mary, the virgin mother of our Lord.

Then we have the situation of Joseph. Joseph appears to have been a just and compassionate man. When Joseph found out about the pregnancy he was, in all likelihood, appalled.

> *"Then Joseph her husband, being a just man, and not willing to make her a publick example, was minded to put her away privily."* (Matthew 1:19)

Joseph was a just man. When he found what he perceived as sin in the life of his betrothed he was no longer willing that she be his wife. Still, Joseph did not seek full punishment brought to bear against her; he was willing to set her aside with as little "fanfare" as possible.

The angel then came to Joseph and explained the situation.

CHAPTER 79: THE FACTS OF JESUS' LIFE AND BIRTH POINT TO THE FACT HE IS DIVINE

> *"But while he [Joseph] thought on these things, behold, the angel of the Lord appeared unto him in a dream, saying, Joseph, thou son of David, fear not to take unto thee Mary thy wife: for that which is conceived in her is of the Holy Ghost. And she shall bring forth a son, and thou shalt call his name JESUS: for he shall save his people from their sins. Now all this was done, that it might be fulfilled which was spoken of the Lord by the prophet, saying, Behold, a virgin shall be with child, and shall bring forth a son, and they shall call his name Emmanuel, which being interpreted is, God with us. Then Joseph being raised from sleep did as the angel of the Lord had bidden him, and took unto him his wife. And knew her not till she had brought forth her firstborn son: and he called his name JESUS,"* (Matthew 1:20-25)

This may be an appropriate place to explain something about the marriage custom of the day. The couple would become betrothed, or engaged. At this point the two were considered as legally married in the eyes of society. But, they did not begin to live together. The woman would return to her parent's home to await the return of her husband. The husband, meanwhile, would begin to prepare a home in which the couple would reside.

When his work on their abode was complete the husband would gather together some of his friends and go to the home of his wife's parents so that the husband could take his bride to her, and his, new home.

Does not this understanding of the marriage ritual in the time of the earthy abode of Jesus give us fuller understanding of the words and return of Jesus.

> *"In my Father's house are many mansions; if it were not so, I would have told you. I go to prepare a place for you. and if I go and prepare a place for you, I will come again, and receive you unto myself, that where I am, there ye may be also."* (John 14:2-3)

Fact Six, Jesus Came Into the World In "the Fullness of Time"

Galatians 4:4 tells us that Jesus came into the world of men in "the fullness of time." That fullness included the ease and safety of travel of the Roman peace and system of roads. Part of that fullness included the fact that the world had been conditioned by the prophecies of God from the Old Testament Scripture, the political and religious system of the day, and even the culture of the day to accept the message that Jesus Christ died in time so that others could live in eternity. Surely these facts point to the Divinity of Jesus.

The announcement to the shepherds must also be considered. How often in Scripture have we seen such an angelic choir report the birth of any man? Abraham was the father of the entire Jewish nation. There was no such choir at his birth. Moses was the great law giver (Actually Moses only passed on the laws which God had given to him.) of the Jewish nation. There was no such choir at his birth. Aaron was the first of the priestly line and he assisted Moses in preparing the Exodus from slavery in Egypt. There was no such choir at his birth. David is known as the "Sweet Psalmist of Israel..." Still no such heavenly announcement of his birth is mentioned or suggested. Go down the line of prophet, priest and king and there is no such heavenly choir assembled to announce their birth. Not Daniel. Not Isaiah. Not Ezekiel. Not Jeremiah. None.

Only at the birth of Jesus was a heavenly choir assembled to announce the birth. The choir even praised God for this birth. Surely Jesus was no simple man born into this earth. Surely Jesus is God incarnate.

Many commentators will argue that the flocks being watched were of sheep prepared for sacrifice at the Temple. How appropriate this would be if it is indeed true. Jesus is Himself the Lamb of God prepared and accepted for the sacrifice of sins!

CHAPTER 80
WHY WE BELIEVE IN THE DEITY OF CHRIST
(Session Eighty-One)

In this session we will continue to follow the list which Christianson (*Why We Believe in the Deity of Christ*) gave in showing the fact that Jesus is Divine. As in our last session, I will give explanatory comments.

The Supernatural Star

The star which the wise men followed in their visit was supernaturally arraigned. Most commentators are agreed that these Magi were from Persia. We may well recall that the Jewish prophet Daniel was an official of the Persian royal court. The writings of Daniel, with his specific prophecies of the seventy weeks until the time of Messiah would have been known by the people of this land.

We may also recall that Esther was a Jewess who became the Queen of Persia and we find a rich testimony to the Jewish faith and people in the history of Persia. The Jews of the Diaspora would have continued to carry on this tradition throughout the Greek and Roman empires which followed the Persians.

This witness would have brought to mind the fact and the time of the entrance of Messiah into the world. It is likely that these Magi were astrologers. If so they were versed in the constellations of the night sky. A new star would have drawn their interest. They would have consulted the ancient writings and concluded that this star was an indication of the birth of the Jewish Messiah.

These men were apparently not as well versed in the Scripture. Upon arriving in Jerusalem, the capitol of the Jews, they were forced to inquire of Herod just where they might find the infant "King of the Jews." This precipitated two things. The first was that Herod worried that a "new" king would threaten his own rule. In a brutal act of "self-preservation" Herod ordered the killing of all children two years old and under in Bethlehem. This act fulfilled the prophecy of Jeremiah 31:15. "Thus saith the LORD, A voice was heard in Ramah, lamentation, *and* bitter weeping, Rachel weeping for her children refused to be comforted for her children, because they *were* not."

The second thing was that Joseph was warned by God in a dream of the danger to Jesus. From this came the flight of Joseph, Mary, and Jesus into Egypt as prophesied by Hosea.

"When Israel was a child, then I loved him, and called my son out of Egypt." (Hosea 11:1)

Thus we are shown two instances of God displaying His concern for the Gentile world through Christ. The Magi were foreigners, called to worship Jesus through the witness of God's people and through Scripture. The former false worship of these men was replaced by a worship of the true Savior of humanity. Even as a two year old child the prophecy of Jesus was shown to be true.

"And I, if I be lifted up from the earth, will draw all men unto me." (John 12:32)

Also, Israel was called back into the land of bondage from which a fresh "Exodus of Righteousness" was shown through the life of Jesus.

So many things came together with just this one incident of worship that we must consider these to be more than mere coincidence. These are pictures of the Truth of the God-man, Jesus Christ.

The Temptation of Jesus

The temptation of Jesus by Satan points out the Deity of Christ. James tells us,

> "But every man is tempted, when he is drawn away of his own lust, and enticed. Then when lust hath conceived, it bringeth forth sin: and sin, when it is finished, bringeth forth death." (James 1:14-15)

Humans are burdened with a nature which is disposed to sin. Sin is a natural act for humanity. Jesus was pure; being virgin born Jesus had no sin nature to drag Him down. In this case we see that Satan reverted to the same plan as he had used in the Garden. Satan came with subtlety and argument to tempt Jesus. Jesus did not meet the temptations of Satan on human ground with human wisdom. Jesus reverted, under each temptation, to Scripture to give an unassailable answer to Satan. When Satan attempted to pervert the meaning of Scripture Jesus was ready to answer with pure Scripture.

Satan was defeated. The true Divinity of Jesus was shown not only through the manner of the temptations but, also, through the manner and power of His rejection of those temptations.

Likewise should we, the Christian, resort to Scripture – and the God of that Scripture – to uphold us in the hour of temptation.

John the Baptist's Announcement

The announcement made by John the Baptist of the Savior was supernatural.

First, the birth of John had been supernatural. His was not a virgin birth. But, John was born to parents who were past the time of life of bearing children. (see Luke 1:18) Also, the birth of John was announced to his father by an angel. (see Luke 1:11-20) Further, John was to be the prophesied "forerunner" of Messiah. (see Luke 1:17) Finally, John was to be a mighty prophet of God. (see Luke 1:15-16)

Even before his birth John showed joy at the presence of Jesus. (see Luke 1:39-45) John was hesitant to baptize Jesus as he recognized the superiority of Jesus. (see Mark 1:8) John saw a representation of the Triune God at the baptism of Jesus (see Mark 1:10-11) as he saw the Son, heard the Father, and witnessed the Spirit descend as a dove.

John said of Jesus,

> "And I saw, and bare record that this is the Son of God." (John 1:34)

The voice which John witnessed from Heaven at the baptism of Jesus was a supernatural sign of the Divinity of Jesus.

The Compassionate, Sinless, Sacrifice of Himself Displayed Love

Jesus led a sinless life. He knew no sin; He was incapable of sin. At the cross He sacrificed Himself as the Only Remedy to take away our sin. Surely these are all marks of the true and full Divinity of Jesus Christ!

Jesus displayed love and compassion to the vilest of sinners. Even concurrent with His great love, Jesus was never tolerant of sin. After removing her accusers Jesus told

CHAPTER 80: WHY WE BELIEVE IN THE DEITY OF CHRIST

the woman taken in adultery to go "...and sin no more." (John 8:11)

While we see Jesus as always acting in a loving manner toward the sinners He called to repentance, we sometimes see Him angry toward the false religious leaders who would keep people from finding grace in Him.

This gracious and balanced approach indicates the Divine mind of Jesus.

Christianson (*Why We Believe in the Deity of Christ*) reminds us that whenever Jesus spoke,

> "He spoke with certainty concerning subjects beyond the range of human knowledge."

Jesus Never Wavered

Jesus never wavered in the certainty of His pronouncements.

At one point Jesus was asked about divorce. The purpose was not to gain information but was an attempt to cause Jesus to stumble. The attempt failed because of the certainty and power of the answer of Jesus.

> "The Pharisees also came unto him, tempting him, and saying unto him, Is it lawful for a man to put away his wife for every cause? And he answered and said unto them, Have ye not read, that he which made them at the beginning made them male and female, And said, For this cause shall a man leave father and mother, and shall cleave to his wife: and they twain shall be one flesh? Wherefore they are no more twain, but one flesh. What therefore God hath joined together, let not man put asunder. They say unto him, Why did Moses then command to give a writing of divorcement, and to put her away? He said unto them, Moses because of the hardness of your hearts suffered you to put away your wives: but from the beginning it was not so. And I say unto you, Whosoever shall put away his wife, except, it be for fornication, and shall marry another, committeth adultery: and whoso marrieth her which is put away doth commit adultery." (Matthew 19:3-9)

Jesus Never Dismissed the Words of the OT

Did you notice that Jesus expanded upon the words of Moses? Moses wrote under the inspiration of the Holy Ghost. What right did Jesus have to expand on those words? Note that Jesus never dismissed the writing of Moses and inspiration. Jesus only gave more information about that Scripture. This is following the concept of progressive revelation. This is where God gives more information than was previously given.

This is a right that is only applicable to God.

We could also argue that this expanded teaching is simply an illumination of the Scripture. It is God, the Spirit, Who illumines Scripture. Once again we see Jesus claiming the prerogative of God.

Jesus Unsurpassed Understanding of Scripture

Another time some came to Jesus to argue about the resurrection of the dead. The Pharisee believed in this resurrection. The Sadducee did not. It was the Sadducee's who approached Jesus on this occasion.

> "Then came to him certain of the Sadducees, which deny that there is any resurrection; and they asked him, Saying, Master, Moses wrote unto us, If any man's brother die, having a wife, and he die without children, that his brother should take his wife, and raise up seed unto his brother. There were therefore seven

brethren: and the first took a wife, and died without children. And the second took her to wife, and he died childless. And the third took her, and in like manner the seven also: and they left no children, and died. Last of all the woman died also. Therefore in the resurrection whose wife of them is she? for seven had her to wife. And Jesus answering said unto them, The children of this world marry, and are given in marriage: But they which shall be accounted worthy to obtain that world, and the resurrection from the dead, neither marry, nor are given in marriage: Neither can they die any more: for they are equal unto the angels, and are the children of God, being the children of the resurrection. Now that the dead are raised, even Moses shewed at the bush, when he calleth the Lord the God of Abraham, and the God of Isaac, and the God of Jacob. For he is not a God of the dead, but of the living: for all live unto him." (Luke 20:27-38)

Jesus answered them so well, and with so much authority that, "...after that they durst not ask him any *question at all*." (Luke 20:40) Jesus showed an understanding of the Scripture above that of a group of men who had made a lifetime of study therein. This is not surprising since, as God, He is the Ultimate Author of that Scripture.

Just before this incident some of the chief priests and scribes had given Jesus another question designed to "trip Him up." They brought for a coin for Him to examine. They then asked if it was proper to pay taxes to Rome. If He had said, "No," the Roman occupiers would have found Him guilty of treason. If He had said, "Yes," the Jewish population would have felt the same about Him; they would have seen Him as a traitor to the Jewish people.

Jesus simply asked whose picture was on the coin. The questioners said that the image was of Caesar. The answer of Jesus was sublime, authoritative and correct. He said to give to Caesar what is his and to God what is His. The authority and reasoning of Jesus was beyond human reproach.

The Lord of the Sabbath

Another incident concerns Jesus' healing of a woman on the Sabbath.

"And he was teaching in one of the synagogues on the Sabbath. And, behold, there was a woman which had a spirit of infirmity eighteen years, and was bowed together, and could in no wise lift up herself. And when Jesus saw her, he called her to him, and said unto her, Woman, thou art loosed from thine infirmity. And he laid his hands on her, and immediately she was made straight, and glorified God. And the ruler of the synagogue answered with indignation, because that Jesus had healed on the Sabbath day, and said unto the people, There are six days in which men ought to work: in them therefore come and be healed, and not on the sabbath day. The Lord then answered him, and said, Thou hypocrite doth not each one of you on the sabbath loose his ox, or his ass from the stall, and lead him away to watering? And ought not this woman, being a daughter of Abraham, whom Satan hath bound, lo, these eighteen years, be loosed from this bond on the sabbath day? And when he had said these things, all his adversaries were ashamed: and all the people rejoiced for all the glorious things that were done by him." (Luke 13:10-17)

Sometime before this Jesus had declared Himself to be the "Lord of the Sabbath." Certainly this designation means that Jesus claimed fully Divinity!

Jesus Proclaims the Preservation of the Scripture

Jesus also spoke of the preservation of the Scripture.

CHAPTER 80: WHY WE BELIEVE IN THE DEITY OF CHRIST

"For verily I say unto you, Till heaven and earth pass, one jot or one tittle shall in no wise pass from the law, till all be fulfilled." (Matthew 5:18)

It is sad that today even some who claim to revere and trust the Scripture cannot see that God has preserved His Words to man!

Supernatural Miracles

The miracles of Jesus were supernatural. He raised the dead and healed all manner of illness. He had miraculous power over demonic forces. In the stilling of the wind and waves He displayed a power over the very physical laws of nature. Can He be other than God? The answer is a resounding "NO!"

His Knowledge of Future Events: The Divine Mind and Power of Jesus

We must not fail to consider the prophecies of Jesus. His knowledge of future events was surely supernatural. We will look at just a few samplings of these. In the first of these samples we will note the lament of Jesus over Jerusalem.

"Nevertheless I must walk to day, and to morrow, and the day following: for it cannot be that a prophet perish out of Jerusalem. O Jerusalem, Jerusalem, which killest the prophets, and stonest them that are sent unto thee; how often would I have gathered thy children together, as a hen doth gather her brood under her wings, and ye would not! Behold, your house is left unto you desolate: and verily I say unto you, Ye shall not see me, until the time come when ye shall say, Blessed is he that cometh in the name of the Lord." (Luke 13:33-35)

Notice that in this place Jesus predicted His Own death. He hurried to get back to Jerusalem because the hour was coming for which He had entered time and the community of humanity. He knew that He was coming to the cross.

The Prophecy of His Triumphal Return

In this place Jesus also predicted His triumphal return at the last day when He would return to earth to assume the throne of David. He would return to a Jewish people who had been redeemed by the Lord to rule the earth from Jerusalem.

Until that day of His return the Jewish people would suffer displacement from the full program of God as the church age would take center stage in God's plan for the redemption of the world. On that day of His return the Jewish people would once again have been called back into their special covenant relationship to receive those earthly promises guaranteed to Abraham, Isaac, Jacob, David and the rest of His people.

The Betrayal

The twenty sixth chapter of Matthew has more prophecies given by Jesus.

"And as they did eat, he said, Verily I say unto you, that one of you shall betray me. And they were exceeding sorrowful, and began every one of them to say unto him, Lord, is it I? And he answered and said, He that dippeth his hand with me in the dish, the same shall betray me. The Son of man goeth as it is written of him: but woe unto that man by whom the Son of man is betrayed! it had been good for that man if he had not been born. Then Judas, which betrayed him, answered and said, Master, is it I? He said unto him, Thou hast said. And as they were eating, Jesus took bread, and blessed it and brake it, and gave it to the disciples, and said, Take, eat; this is my body. And he took the cup, and gave thanks, and gave it to them, saying, Drink ye all of it; For this is my blood of the new testament, which is shed for

many for the remission of sins. But I say unto you, I will not drink henceforth of this fruit of the vine, until that day when I drink it new with you in my Father's kingdom." (Matthew 26:21-29)

The Future Kingdom

In this passage Jesus correctly saw the betrayal of Judas. He also correctly notes that He would die before there would be another meal with His disciples. He also made reference to the future kingdom of God on the earth.

"Then said Jesus unto them, All ye shall be offended because of me this night: for it is written, I will smite the shepherd, and the sheep of the flock shall be scattered abroad. But after I am risen again, I will go before you into Galilee. Peter answered and said unto him, Though all men shall be offended because of thee, yet will I never be offended. Jesus said unto him, Verily I say unto thee, That this night, before the cock crow, thou shalt deny me thrice." (Matthew 26:31-34)

Disciples Scattered

We see in this passage that Jesus knew His disciples would be scattered. We see the fulfillment of this in verse fifty-six. Also, although He had not yet been to the cross, Jesus spoke of His resurrection. And, Jesus informed the impetuous Peter that Peter would deny Him before men three times by the break of the next day.

His Return

Consider what Jesus said of His return in Luke.

"I tell you, in that night there shall be two men in one bed; the one shall be taken, and the other shall be left. Two women shall be grinding together; the one shall be taken, and the other left. Two men shall be in the field; the one shall be taken, and the other left." (Luke 17:34-36)

The Understanding of the Rotating Earth

Even beyond the predictive element of this prophecy I would have you to notice the time element. The first two are sleeping; it is nighttime. The second two are grinding food for the coming day. It is early. In the final group we see them working the fields. What Jesus has described, even past the predictive, is the rotation of the earth. Jesus understood the concept of "time zones" even before there were established time zones. He knew earth science in a time when the even the word "earth science" had not been invented.

The Warning About Persecution

I would have us to look at only one more prediction of Jesus.

"These things have I spoken unto you, that ye should not be offended. They shall put you out of the synagogues: yea, the time cometh, that whosoever killeth you will think that he doeth God service. And these things will they do unto you, because they have not known the Father nor me. But these things have I told you, that when the time shall come, ye may remember that I told you of them. And these things I said not unto you at the beginning, because I was with you." (John 16:1-4)

In this passage Jesus is warning His disciples of persecution – even unto death. Brethren, in that nation wherein I reside we have not seen real persecution as yet. It is coming. This, too, is one of the promises and predictions of Jesus. It should not come upon us unexpected for the world still hates Jesus and the message that Jesus died in

CHAPTER 80: WHY WE BELIEVE IN THE DEITY OF CHRIST

time so that others could live in eternity.

These predictions show the Divine mind and power of Jesus.

The Manner of His Death

Further evidence of the supernatural in the life of Jesus is seen in His manner of death. We know, as an article of faith, that Jesus died as a sacrifice for the sins of repentant humanity. Even beyond this we must acknowledge the supernatural in His death when we consider that His death was upon His Own volition. He released His Own spirit.

> "And when Jesus had cried with a loud voice, he said, Father, into thy hands I commend my spirit: and having said thus, he gave up the ghost." (Luke 23:46)

We might ascribe the death of Jesus, on natural terms, from the trauma of the Roman crucifixion. We might ascribe the death of Jesus, on natural terms, from hate, envy and fear of the Jewish authorities. We might ascribe the death of Jesus, on theological terms, to the sin of mankind. We might ascribe the death of Jesus, on theological terms, to God's determinative will. But, on observational terms we must ascribe the death of Jesus to His Own supernatural power as God.

Those events which followed the death of Jesus were decidedly supernatural.

> "And, behold, the veil of the temple was rent in twain from the top to the bottom, and the earth did quake, and the rocks rent; And the graves were opened, and many bodies of the saints which slept arose, And came out of the graves after his resurrection, and went into the holy city, and appeared unto many." (Matthew 27:51-53)

The veil of the temple kept all but the high Priest, and him but once a year, from the Mercy Seat of God. Now, with the death of Jesus, all Christian have direct access to God. More than this, we have the invitation – nay! The obligation! – to come boldly before the Throne of God in prayer. "Let us therefore come boldly unto the throne of grace, that we may obtain mercy, and find grace to help in the time of need." (Hebrews 4:16)

The earthquakes were an illustration that even the natural creation was touched by the power of the sacrificial death of Jesus. His power reached into heaven, earth, time and humanity. The opened graves were not that different from His miraculous healings during His ministry on earth. Notice that only the saints were called forth into Jerusalem as witnesses of His grace.

About the above, I would remind you that the Old Testament is filled with physical manifestations of spiritual truths. That these resurrections and earthquakes were real is beyond doubt. Among other things these events are reminders that, even before His Own resurrection, Jesus has defeated death and the dominion of Satan. Only God could have performed these things. Jesus is God.

The only thing I would add to the above would come from John 5:39. Jesus told the doubters, "Search the scriptures, for in them ye think ye have eternal life: and they are they which testify of me." Could any argue that the Scriptures speak of God? If, then, the Scriptures speak of Jesus, it must follow that Jesus is God. Salvation may indeed be found in the Scripture because the Scripture speaks of Jesus.

CHAPTER 81
OTHER PROOFS THAT JESUS WAS GOD
(Session Eighty-Two)

Jesus' Resurrection Is Incontrovertible Proof of His Deity

John R. Rice (*The Rice Reference Bible*) made comment as to the Deity of Jesus from John 2:19. "Jesus answered and said unto them, Destroy this temple, and in three days I will raise it up." The comment of Jesus came in response to the Jewish leadership who had asked Him by what right He had cleansed the Temple of the moneychangers.

Jesus answered that the sign of His authority would be seen in His resurrection from the dead. Others had performed miracles in the power of God. Jesus, however, would rise from the dead as an incontrovertible proof of His Deity.

Jesus' Flesh Was A "Temple" Where God Dwelt

We might also make an observation on the fact that Jesus compared His body to the Temple. Although even the Old Testament (see Psalm 139:7-12 for an example) makes the case that God is Omnipresent, or everywhere present at all times, it was understood that the Temple – with the Mercy Seat and the daily sacrifices – was the "special place of His residence." When Jesus spoke of His body as a Temple He was speaking the Truth that He was very God in the flesh. His flesh *was* a Temple in that God dwelt therein.

> "For in him dwelleth all the fullness of the Godhead bodily." (Colossians 2:9)

On the Deity of Jesus, Christianson (*Why We Believe in the Deity of Christ*) quoted C. S. Lewis.

> "The late C. S. Lewis put the matter succinctly when he wrote in <u>Mere Christianity</u>, 'A man who was merely a man and said the sort of things Jesus said would not be a great moral teacher. He would either be a lunatic – on the level with the man who says he is a poached egg – or else he would be the Devil of Hell. You must make your choice. Either this man was, and is, the Son of God; or else a madman or something worse.'"

Even the Death of Christ Is Proof of His Divinity

Orr (*Can We Be Sure That Jesus Christ is God?*) argued that even the death of Christ is proof of His Divinity. At least three times, just in the Book of Matthew (16:21; 17:22-23; 20:17-19), Jesus told His disciples that He would die. It is worth noting that each of these incidents also includes His statement of resurrection from the dead.

Though the disciples seemed to miss the point of His teaching after His death, they fully understood after He had risen from the dead! This foreknowledge, and power over death, shows Jesus to be much more than just another ordinary man. He is even more than simply an extraordinary man as He is God.

Jesus came to die. He knew He was going to die. He understood the pain, the humiliation, the degradation of the manner of death He was to suffer. Yet, He came for that very purpose. "Jesus' death was no ordinary death. He was paying the penalty for the sins of a world of man. His death as the Lamb of God was anticipated before the foundation of the world." (Revelation 13:8)

More Comments On Jesus' Resurrection

Orr also sees the resurrection as proof that Jesus is Divine.

> "This was no resuscitation of one who had fainted. Christ had laid down His life, and now He had taken it again. He was in His glorified resurrection body; He appeared and disappeared at will; He entered closed doors. Yet, He was the same Jesus; He invited His disciples to handle Him and convince themselves. He called for food and ate before them. Who was the Person who had conquered death but the very Son of God Himself?"

Ryrie (*The Ryrie Study Bible*) comments on Romans 1:4 where Jesus is declared (shown to be) Deity by His resurrection from the dead.

> *"And declared to be the Son of God with power, according to the spirit of holiness, by the resurrection from the dead."*

The "Spirit of Holiness" could be either His Own holiness which shows this fact to be true or the Holy Spirit Who shows this to be true. Ryrie also argues that the reference could be to both.

I would agree with this third assessment. The fact that Jesus rose from the dead is proof of His Deity. The Spirit then spoke the Truth of the Deity of Jesus to the human penmen of Scripture and to the churches.

Over 520 Individuals Saw Jesus After He Rose From the Dead

The title of Orr's book, *Can We Be Sure Jesus Christ is God?*, asks a question. The book well answers that question. Over 520 individuals, some who did not seem to want to believe the resurrection (ex: Thomas) saw Jesus after He rose from the dead.

Jesus' Present Life Saves Us From Sin

The life of Jesus in the present shows that He is divine.

Jesus, today!, saves us from the penalty of our sins.

> *"And, behold, they brought to him a man sick of the palsy, lying on a bed: and Jesus seeing their faith said unto the sick of the palsy, Son, be of good cheer; thy sins be forgiven thee. And, behold, certain of the scribes said within themselves, The man blasphemeth. And Jesus, knowing their thoughts said, Wherefore think ye evil in your hearts? For whether is easier, to say, Thy sins be forgiven thee, or to say, Arise, and walk? But that ye may know that the Son of man hath power on earth to forgive sins, (then saith he to the sick of the palsy,) Arise, take up thy bed, and go unto thy house. And he arose, and departed to his house."* (Matthew 9:2-7)

Jesus' Ability to Forgive Sin

Lindsell (*The Harper Study Bible*) observes that this passage proves the Jesus has the authority to forgive sins rather than simply to say that they are forgiven. Any preacher or priest can declare that sins are forgiven. Only Jesus can actually forgive sins!

Christianson (*Why We Believe in the Deity of Christ*) has commented about the ability of Jesus to forgive sin.

> "Only if Jesus Christ is God could Christ's atoning work be effective for us... Only a

CHAPTER 81: OTHER PROOFS THAT JESUS WAS GOD

holy, sinless person could become an effectual sacrifice for those guilty of sin."

Forgiveness Is Proof of the Divinity of Jesus

I would go further than Christianson. I don't argue with his assessment; it's just that I would go further. Sin is an affront to God. Only the person offended by an action could really forgive the offender. This is a proof of the Divinity of Jesus. Also, any person other than the virgin born Son of God would not have legal standing to be an effective sacrifice for the sin of mankind. A simple "person," no matter how holy and seemingly pure, could not be sinless if born of man and woman as such a person would inherit the sin nature of Adam.

Jesus also, in this day, saves us from ourselves. We are able to have transformed lives though His offered and accepted salvation. Although we may not be perfect (Just ask anyone who knows me!) we have, at the very least, a "mark" for which to strive! The "Church World," even the counterfeits in her, recognizes the need to be different from the "world at large." We are to accept and assume a higher standard than are others.

Alford (*The New Testament for English Readers*) comments upon this principle in relation to John 14:6.

> "Jesus said unto him, I am the way, the truth, and the life: no man cometh unto the Father, but by me."

Jesus is more than an example to follow. He is The Way – the Path, the Mode, the Means of our Journey.

Surely, as the old catechism tells us, **Jesus is very man and Very God**.

BIBLIOGRAPHY

Adam Clarke's Commentary (Vols. 1 - 5): Adam Clark, LL.D., F.S.A.; Abingdon Press, Nashville, TN - New York, NY; No date given

Am I Not Free?; John S. May; Self Published; Linton, IN 1974

Annotated Study Bible, The; Jerry Falwell, D.D., D. LITT., LL.D., Ex. ed.; Thomas Nelson Publishers; Nashville, TN; 1988

Answers To Tough Questions; Josh McDowell & Don Stewart; Here's Life Publishers, Inc.; San Bernadino, CA; 1980

Baptist Way- Book, The; Ben M. Bogard, LL.D.; Bogard Press; Texarkana, AR-TX; 1946

Barnes' Notes on the New Testament; Albert Barnes (Ingran Cobbin, ed.); Kregel Publications; Grand Rapids, MI; 1972

Basic Christian Faith; C. Donald Cole; Crossway Books; Westchester, IL; 1985

Basic Theology; Charles C. Ryrie; Victor Books; Wheaton, IL; 1986

Biblical Standard for Evangelists, A; Billy Graham; World Wide Publications; Minneapolis, MN, 1984

Book of Discipline of the United Methodist Church - 1968, The; Emory Stevens Bucke, Curtis A. Chambers, Charles C. Parlin, Paul A. Washburn, Lovick Pierce, Donald A. Theuer; The Methodist Publishing House; Nashville, TN; 1968

Can Man See God; Spiros Zodhiates; AMG International; Chattanooga, TN; No date given

Can We Be Sure Jesus Christ Is God?; William B. Orr, AB, MA, ThB, D.D.; Scripture Press Pub., Inc.; Wheaton, IL; 1968

Chosen People Ministers; _____; International Headquarters; Orangeburg, NY; No Date given

Christian Doctrine; James M. Pendleton; Judson Press; Valley Forge, PA; 1971

Christian Faith, The; David H. C. Read; Abingdon Press; Nashville, TN - New York, NY; 1956

Christian Unity; John S. May; Self Published; Terre Haute, IN; 1984

Commentary Practical and Explanatory on the Whole Bible; Rev. Robert Jamieson, D. D., Rev. A. R. Fausset, A.M., Rev. David Brown, D.D.; Zondervan Publishing House; Grand Rapids, MI; 1973

Concordia Self-Study Bible; Robert G. Hoerber, Gen. Ed.; Concordia Publishing House; St. Louis, MO; 1986

Confession of Faith, Lenord St. Baptist Church; _____; Lenord St. Baptist Church; Grand Rapids, MI; No date given

Constitution and Articles of Faith of the General Association of Regular Baptist Churches; _____; General Association of Regular Baptist Churches; Schaumburg, IL; 1980

Constitution of Berean Fundamental Church Council, Inc.; _____; Berean Fundamental Church Council, The; North Platte, NE; 1983

Criswell Study Bible, The; W. A. Criswell, Ph.D.; Thomas Nelson, Publishers; Nashville, TN - Camden, NJ; 1979

Dake's Annotated Reference Bible; Finis Jennings Dake; Dake Bible Sales, Inc.; Lawrenceville, GA; 1983

Defined King James Bible, The; Dr. D. A, Waite, Gen. Ed.; The Bible for Today Press; Collingswood, NJ;

Deity of Christ, The; Prof. Howard A. Kelly, M.D., LL.D.; The Biblical Evangelist (v. 18, n. 16), pp. 3-4; Aug. 3, 1984

Discipline of the Wesleyan Church - 1972, The; _____; The Wesleyan Publishing House; Marion, IN; 1972

Elemental Theology; E. H. Bancroft (Ronald B. Meyers, ed. and rev.); Zondervan Publishing House; Grand

Rapids, MI; 1977

Every Prophecy of the Bible; John F. Walvoord; David C. Cook; Colorado Springs, Co; 2011

Evidence that Demands a Verdict; Josh McDowell; Campus Crusade for Christ; San Bernadino, CA; 1977

Exposition of Genesis (Vol. 1); H. C. Leupold, D.D.; Baker Book House; Grand Rapids, MI; 1979

Fundamentals, The (Vol. II); R. A. Torrey, A. C. Dixon, et. al. eds.; (The Deity of Christ; Prof. Benjamin B. Warfield, D.D., LL.D.); Baker Book House; Grand Rapids, MI; 1980

Full Gospel Christian Church Constitution & By laws; _____; Full Gospel Christian Church; Streetsboro, OH; No date given

God Becomes Man; Spiros Zodhiates; AMG International; Chattanooga, TN; No date given

God in Man; Spiros Zodhiates; AMG Publishers; Chattanooga, TN; no date given

Halley's Bible Handbook; Henry H. Halley; Zondervan Publishing House; Grand Rapids, MI; 1965

Harper Study Bible; Harold Lindsell; Ph.D., D.D., ed.; Zondervan Publishing House; Grand Rapids, MI; 1965

Have You Ever Walked Through These Doors?; _____; Mt. Olive Missionary Church; Peoria, IL; No date given

Hebrew-Greek Key Study Bible; Spiros Zodhiates, ThD; AMG Publishers; Chattanooga, TN' 1984

Introducing the Orthodox Church: Its Faith and Life; Anthony M. Coniaris; Light and Life Publishing Company; Minneapolis, MN; 1982

Iowa Yearly Meeting of Friends Book of Discipline; _____; Oskaloosa Herald Printers; Oskaloosa, IA; 1891

Is Jesus God? (Books no. 1 & 2); Anthony Zeoli; The Cedar Book Store; Waterloo, IA; 1943

Jerusalem Bible, The; Alexander Jones, L.S.S., S.T.L., I.C.B.M Gen. ed.; Doubleday and Co., Inc.; Garden City, NY; 1966

Jesus: Son of God; Calvin Burrell; Bible Advocate (v. 122, n. 6) pp. 10-13; June 1968

Know What and Why You Believe (Special Billy Graham Evangelistic Crusade Edition); Paul Little; Victor Books; Wheaton, IL; 1960

Life Application Bible; Ronald A. Beers, Gen. ed.; Tyndale House Publishers, Inc., and Youth For Christ / USA; Wheaton, IL; 1987

Luther's Small Catechism; _____; Concordia Publishing House; St. Louis, MO; 1971

Manuel of the Church of the Nazarene; John Riley, S. T. Ludwig, Leslie Parrott, Roy E. Swim, W. T. Purkiser, eds.; Nazarene Publishing House; Kansas City, MO; 1960

Matthew Henry's Commentary on the Whole Bible (Vol. 1 - 2); Matthew Henry; Sovereign Grace Publishers; Wilmington, DE; 1972

More Than A Carpenter (Special Billy Graham Evangelistic Association Crusade Edition); Josh McDowell; World Wide Publications, Minneapolis, MN; 1977

New Hyde Park Baptist Church Articles of Faith; _____; New Hyde Park Baptist Church; New Hyde Park; NY; No date given

New Scofield Reference Bible, The; E. Schuyler English, ed.; Oxford University Press; New York, NY; 1967

New Testament for English Readers, The; Henry Alford, D.D.; Moody Press; Chicago, IL; No date given

New World Translation of the Holy Scriptures; _____; Watch Tower Bible and Tract Society of New York, Inc.; Brooklyn, NY; 1961

Our Eternal God; Paul A. Henderson; The Biblical Evangelist (v. 19, n. 16); p. 3; Aug. 16, 1985

Outline of Christian Theology, An; William Newton Clarke, D.D.; Charles Scribner's Sons; New York, NY; 1898

BIBLIOGRAPHY

People's Study Bible, The; Harold Lindsell, Ph.D., D.D., Gen. ed.; Tyndale House Publishers, Inc.; Wheaton, IL; 1986

Pentecostals, The; John Thomas Nichol; Logos International; Plainfield, NJ; 197

Prison Fellowship Statement of Faith; _____; Prison Fellowship; Washington, DC; No date given

Pulpit Commentary, The; H. D. M. Spense and Joseph S. Exell, eds.; Wm. B. Eerdmans Publishing Co.; Grand Rapids, MI; 1977

Rice Reference Bible, The; John R. Rice, D.D., Litt.D., S.T.D.; ed.; Thomas Nelson Publishers; Nashville, TN - Camden, NJ; 1981

Ryrie Study Bible, The; Charles Caldwell Ryrie, Th.D., Ph.D.; Moody Press; Chicago, IL; 1978

Salem Kirban Reference Bible; Salem Kirban, ed.; Salem Kirban, Inc.; Location not noted, 1980

Scofield Reference Bible, The; Rev. C. I. Scofield, D.D., ed.; Oxford University Press; New York; NY; 1917

Spurgeon's Devotional Bible; C. H. Spurgeon; Baker Book House; Grand Rapids, MI; 1978

Statement of Faith; _____; Toledo Home Fellowship; Toledo, OH; No date given

Systematic Study of Bible Doctrine, A; Thomas Paul Simmons; Associated Publishers; Daytona Beach, FL; 1969

Systematic Theology; Augustus Hopkins Strong, D.D., LL.D.; Judson Press; Valley Forge, PA; 1979

This is the Church of God of Prophecy; Public Relations Department; Church of God of Prophecy; Cleveland, TN; No date given

Trinitarian Adumbration; Ronald F. Hogan; The Biblical Evangelist (v. 18, n. 17); p. 3; Aug. 17, 1984

Truth of the Gospel, The; G. B. Caird; Oxford University Press; London, GB; 1950

Unger's Bible Handbook; Merrill F. Unger; Th.D., Ph.D.; Moody Press; Chicago, IL 1967

Was Christ God?; Spiros Zodhiates; AMG Publishers; Chattanooga, TN; No date given

What is the American Baptist Association?; Dr. I. K. Cross; Baptist Sunday School Committee of the American Baptist Association; Texarkana, AR-TX; 1965

Who created Evil?; Spiros Zodhiates; AMG Publishers; Chattanooga, TN; No date given

Who We Are and What We Believe; _____; Community Christian Fellowship; Moline, IL; No date given

Why We Believe in the Deity of Christ; Wayne Christianson; Moody Monthly (v. 79, n. 11); pp. 16-19; Jul. / Aug. 1979

OUTLINE STUDIES

In The Deity of Jesus, The Christ

Prepared, 1989, by Dr. E. E. DeWitt, D.D.

Revised 2012

THE DEITY OF JESUS, THE CHRIST - WHAT THE CHURCHES SAY

I. The testimony of the historical church:
   A. From the Council of Chalcedon 451: "We acknowledge one and the same Christ so to be perfect God and perfect man; of the same substance with the Father as regards His Godhead, and of the same substance with us as regards His manhood - in all things like unto us, sin only excepted; begotten of the Father from everlasting, but in the last days born of the Virgin; subsisting of separation; the distinction between the natures not being destroyed by the union, but each preserving its own properties and both culminating in one Person and Hypostasis: one and the same Christ, not divided into two Persons." (Basic Christian Faith p.142)
   B. From the early part of the 20th century in a series of position papers which shaped early Fundamentalism: Luke 15:10 - In answering the Pharisees murmurings at His meetings with sinners, Jesus points out that the very nature of the Heavenly, which He Himself is, is to meet and call sinners. (The Fundamentals v. II p. 243)

II. The testimony of the liturgical church:
   A. The Church of England: (Entire section: Basic Christian Faith p. 141)
      1. From the Thirty-ninth Article of the Church of England, 1563: "The Son, which is the Word of the Father, begotten from everlasting of the Father, the very and eternal God, and of one substance with the Father, took man's nature in the womb of the Blessed Virgin, of her substance; so that two whole and perfect natures, that is to say, the Godhead and manhood, were joined together in one Person, never to be divided."
      2. From the Westminster Confession of Faith: "The Son of God, the second person of the Trinity, being very and eternal God, of one substance, and equal with the Father, did, when the fulness of time was come, take upon him man's nature, with all the essential properties and common infirmities thereof, yet without sin; being conceived by the power of the Holy Ghost, in the womb of the Virgin Mary, of her substance. So that the two whole, perfect, and distinct natures, as Godhead and the manhood, were inseparably joined together in one person, without conversion, composition, or confusion, which is the very God and very man, yet one Christ, the only Mediator between God and Man."
   B. The Lutheran Church:
      1. "I believe that Jesus Christ is true God because the Scriptures ascribe to Him A. Divine names... B. Divine Attributes... C. Divine works... D. Divine honor and glory." (Luther's Small Catechism pp. 103-104)
      2. It is necessary that Christ be divinity so that: A) His fulfilling of the Law would be effectious for all men (Ps. 49:7-8; Rom. 5:19), B) His life and death would be sufficient for our redemption (Mk. 10:45), and C) He could defeat both death and Satan (II Tim. 1:10; Heb. 2:14; I Cor. 15:57). (Luther's Small Catechism pp. 106-107)
   C. The Orthodox Church - "Jesus is Lord - absolute and undisputed creator and

possessor of the entire universe... Then the title 'Christ' (meaning the Anointed One or the Messiah) is applied to Jesus it becomes a confession of faith indicating our faith that Jesus, the Son of God, the Second Person of the Trinity, is the Messiah." (Introducing the Orthodox Church: Its Faith and Life p. 20)

III. The testimony of the Pentecostal Church:
 A. "The Full Gospel Christian Church gladly accepts the fact that the Bible emphatically and unequivocally teachers the union of three (3) persons in the Godhead, correctly called in theology, the Trinity. The Three (3) persons of the Godhead are (1) God, The Father, (2) Jesus Christ, The Son, (3) The Holy Spirit, The Comforter." (Full Gospel Christian Church Constitution and By-Laws p. 9)
 B. Statement number 2 from the "Statement of Truth adopted by the Pentecostal Fellowship of North America... We believe that there is one God, eternally existent in three persons: Father, Son and Holy Ghost." (The Pentecostals p. 4)

IV. The testimony of Baptist Churches:
 A. Article of faith "a" - "We believe that the Godhead eternally exists in three persons: Father, Son and Holy Spirit, and that these three are One God." (New Hyde Park Baptist Church Articles of Faith; New Hyde Park, New York)
 B. "We believe that there is (a) one, and only one, living and true God, and infinite, intelligent Spirit, the maker and supreme ruler of the heaven and the earth; (b) inexpressibly glorious in holiness, and worthy of all possible honor, confidence and love; (c) that in the unity of the Godhead there are three persons, the Father, the Son, and the Holy Ghost, equal in every divine perfection, and executing distinct but harmonious offices in the great work of redemption... (C) Matt.28:19; John 15:26; I Cor. 12:4-6; I John 5:7; John 10:30; 17:5; Acts 5:3-4; Phil. 2:5-6; Eph. 2:18; II Cor. 13:14." (Confession of Faith, Lenord Street Baptist Church; Grand Rapids, Michigan p. 14)
 C. "...in unity of the Godhead there are three persons, the Father, the Son and the Holy Spirit, equal in every divine perfection, and executing distinct but harmonious office in the great work of redemption (Exod. 20:2, 3: I Cor. 8:6; Rev. 4:11)." (Constitution and Articles of Faith of the General Association of the Regular Baptist Churches p. 5)
 D. "We believe... that in the unity of the Godhead there are three persons, the Father, the Son, and the Holy Spirit; (Matt. 28:19; John 15:16) equal in every divine perfections (John 10:30), and executing distinct but harmonious offices in the great work of redemption. (Eph. 2:18; II Cor. 13:14)" (The Baptist Way-Book pp. 49-50)
 E. Listed under "Beliefs" is number 5 - "The Deity of Jesus Christ." (What is the American Baptist Association? pp. 11-12)

V. The testimony of various protestant churches:
 A. The Berean Fundamental Church: Article of Faith number II - "We believe that the Godhead Eternally exists in three persons: the Father, the Son, and the Holy Spirit. These three are one God, having precisely the same nature, attributes, essence and perfections, and worthy of precisely the same homage, confidence and obedience. (Mark 12:29; Gen. 1:26; Matt. 28:19; John 14:16, 17, 26; II Cor. 13:14)" (Constitution of the Berean Fundamental Church p. 15)
 B. The Church of God of Prophecy: "The Trinity is recognized as one Supreme Godhead in three persons - the Father, the Son, and the Holy Ghost." (This is the Church of God of Prophecy p. 6)
 C. The Missionary Church: "We believe that Jesus Christ was and is both God and man, and that He came to earth in the form of a man to pay the penalty of sin. By faith in His sacrificial death, man is forgiven of his sin and is reunited into fellowship with God." (Tract entitled: "Have You Ever Walked Through These Doors?)

    D. Friends: "Meetings on Ministry and Oversight shall be careful to recommend no one to be recorded as a minister or elder whose doctrinal views are not clearly in accord with the affirmative of the following question. [Question number 3] Did thou believe in the Deity and Manhood of the Lord Jesus Christ...?" (Iowa Yearly Meetings of Friends Book of Discipline pp. 111-112)
    E. The United Methodist Church: "The Son, who is the Word of the Father, the very eternal God, of one substance with the Father, took man's nature in the womb of the blessed Virgin; so that two whole and perfect natures, that is to say, the Godhead and Manhood, were joined together in one person, never to be divided; whereof is one Christ, very God and very Man..." (The Book of Discipline of the United Methodist Church, 1968 Paragraph 91, Article II p. 37)
    F. The Wesleyan Church: "There is but one living and true God, everlasting, of infinite power, wisdom and goodness; the Maker and Preserver of all things, visible and invisible. And in unity of this Godhead there are three persons of one substance, power, and eternity - the Father, the Son (the Word), and the Holy Ghost. (Gen. 1:1; 17:1; Ex. 3:13-15; 33:20; Deut. 6:4; Ps. 90:2; 104:24; Isa. 9:6; Jer. 10:10; John 1:1-2; 4:24; 5:18; 10:30; 15:13; Acts 5:3-4; Rom. 16:27; I Cor. 8:4, 6; II Cor. 13:14; Eph. 2:18; Phil. 2:6; Col. 1:16; I Tim. 1:17; I John 5:7, 20; Rev. 19:13)." (The Discipline of the Wesleyan Church, 1972 Paragraph 103 p. 25)
    G. The Church of the Nazarene: "We believe in Jesus Christ, the Second Person of the Triune Godhead; that He was eternally one with the Father..." (Manual of the Church of the Nazarene Paragraph 2 p. 26)
VI. The testimony of para-church agencies:
    A. Chosen People Ministries: "We believe in the Triune nature of the one true God, and in the Deity of the Lord Jesus Christ, the only begotten Son of God, born of a virgin." (Doctrinal Statement number 2 of the Chosen Peoples Ministries)
    B. Prison Fellowship: "We believe in one God, Creator and Lord of the Universe, the co-eternal Trinity: Father, Son and Holy Spirit... We believe that Jesus Christ...[is] truly God and truly man..." (Prison Fellowship Statement of Faith)
    C. Toledo Home Fellowship: "We believe in the Trinity of the Father, Son and the Holy Spirit, one God and Creator of all things, seen and unseen. (Matt. 28:19 and I John 5:7)" (Number 2 in the Statement of Faith of the Toledo Home Fellowship)
    D. The proof that Jesus was Who He said He was is:
        1. His perfect life (He was without sin);
        2. His power over nature at the storm on Galilee (Matt. 8:23-27), over sickness and death;
        3. The prophecies which were fulfilled in His life;
        4. His resurrection from the dead; and,
        5. The lives that have been changed by Him. (VI,E,1 -5: A Biblical Standard for Evangelists pp. 14-16)
VII. The result of the testimonies:
    A. "...Christianity is Christ..." (The Christian Faith p. 35)
    B. "Christian unity demands acceptance of His perfect deity and at the same time His perfect humanity... Jesus' mother, Mary, is a bona fide member of the human race, and His Father, God, is the one, true, and living God... [Those] who consider Him to be a great prophet and the greatest teacher who ever lived, but deny His deity, are not eligible for Christian Fellowship. Likewise, those who consider Jesus to be divine but who deny His humanity are also ineligible to be a part of the Christian community." (Christian Unity p. 4)

THE DEITY OF JESUS, THE CHRIST - TERMS

I. The Deity of Jesus is important.

STUDIES IN THE DEITY OF JESUS, THE CHRIST

- A. The Deity of Jesus is the foundation of the Christian Faith. John 20:28 - "The deity of Christ is the foundation of the Christian faith. The denial of it invalidates the entire structure of Christian theology." (Harper Study Bible p. 1621)
- A. The Deity of Jesus is the center of the Christian Faith. "Confucianism is a set of teachings; Confucius is not important. Islam is the revelation of Allah, with Mohammed being the prophet, and Buddhism emphasizes the principles of Buddha, not Buddha himself. This is especially true of Hinduism, where there is no historical founder. However, at the center of Christianity is the person of Jesus Christ. Jesus did not just claim to be teaching mankind the truth. He claimed that **He** was the truth (John 14:6)." (Answers To Tough Questions p. 40)
- B. The Deity of Jesus is the hope of the Christian's salvation.
    1. If Jesus were not Divine, He is only a man.
        a. His death, then, cannot be substitutionary.
        b. His teachings, then, stem from a false basis of authority.
        c. His leadership, then, is flawed.
    2. If Jesus were not Divine, He is not a good man.
        a. He taught that He was Divine. If He believed this and it were untrue, He was insane.
        b. He taught that He was Divine. If He knew this to be false and still taught it, He was a liar.

II. Some do not accept the Divinity of Jesus.
- A The acceptance or rejection of the Divinity of Jesus ought to be a test of fellowship.
    1. Those who do not accept the Divinity of Jesus should be rejected. I John 4:3 - "This is a very useful test in many cases. If any form of doctrine denies or dishonours the Godhead or Messiahship of the Lord Jesus, or makes his incarnation to be a mere myth, it is to be rejected with abhorrence. Errors which touch the person or work of Jesus are fatal. (The Spurgeon Devotional Bible p. 758)
    2. There are many who do not accept and believe the Divinity of Jesus. In his book **Is Jesus God** (Book Number One, p. 23), Evangelist Zeoli makes note, in discussing the Virgin Birth, that many do not accept the Virgin Birth because it is, "...not believed by present day scholars." That, he reminds us, is simply not true; many conservative scholars do accept the Virgin Birth. By the same token, many conservative scholars do accept the Divinity of Jesus.
        a. These people believe and trust the Bible of God.
        b. These people believe and trust the God of miracle.
    3. The important point here is not what one does or does not accept as doctrine; what is important is what God has said is true in His Own Book and man's acceptance of this - simply put, is that we either take God's Word or man's theory.
- B. Worldly wisdom may not accept the Divinity of Jesus. Worldly wisdom is:
    1. Foolish - Rom. 1:22; I Cor. 1:20
    2. Conceited - Rom. 12:16 (II, B, 1-2 – Can We Be Sure That Jesus is God? P. 1)
    3. Deceived - I Cor. 3:19 (Is Jesus God, Book Number One, p. 23)
    4. The wisdom of God is above that of man. "If Jesus is not God, the world is irreparably lost. If He is not God, the entire structure of truth collapses. If He is not God, the Bible is a lie, the Gospel is a farce, and heaven is just a jest." (Can We Be Sure That Jesus Christ is God? p. 1)

OUTLINE STUDIES

III. There are many false views of Jesus.
- A. Any view of Jesus which denies Who He is, in reality, presents a false view of Him.
  1. A false view of Jesus will produce a false Christ. As only the True Christ can offer salvation to mankind, the false view must lead to damnation.
  2. A view which denies Jesus, Himself, will give false view of other truths as well.
- B. Examples of false views of Jesus (III, B, 1 - 7: Elemental Theology p. 146):"
  1. "Cerinthianism held that there was no union of the two natures (of Jesus) until after baptism, thus establishing Christ's deity upon His baptism rather than upon His birth."
  2. "Eutychianism held that the two natures of Christ were mingled into one which was predominantly divine, though not the same as the original divine nature."
  3. "Nestorianism denied the union of human and divine natures, making Christ two persons."
  4. "Apollinarianism made Christ only two parts human, denying to Him a human soul, which they claimed is sinful."
  5. "Arianism regarded Christ as the highest of created beings, thus denying His deity and misinterpreting His temporary humiliation."
  6. "Ebionism denied the divine nature of Christ and held Him to be only man."
  7. "Docetism denied the reality of Christ's body on the ground that His purity could not be linked with matter, which was thought by Docetists to be inherently evil."
- C. Col. 2:9 - Jesus is not simply "God-Like," He **is** God. (Commentary Practical and Explanatory on the Whole Bible p. 1321)

IV. Explanation of some confusing terminology:
- A. Jesus referred to as "Son:"
  1. Rom. 1:3-4 - Note that Jesus was **made** the son of David but **declared** the Son of God. The former applies to His humanity while the latter refers to His Divinity. (Commentary on the Whole Bible p. 1140)
  2. Luke 1:35 - "Sonship with Christ always refers to humanity, not to deity. As God, He had no beginning (Mic. 5:2; Jn. 1:1-2); was not begotten or He would have had a beginning, was begotten, and was God's Son (Ps. 2:7, 12; Mt. 1:18; Lk. 1:35; Heb. 1:5-6)." Scripture teaches that there was a day in history when the Father had a Son and the Son a Father. Yet the same Scripture teaches the eternality of the Son. Rather than a contradiction, this is a clear teaching of the Biblical concept of the dual nature of Jesus Christ. As God, the Son, He is eternal; as the Son of God, He is human with beginning. (Dake Annotated Bible p. 57 [NT])
  3. Different Sonships are ascribed to Jesus:
     a. "Son of David" refers to His Messiahship. This speaks of His office in the Redemptive plan.
     b. "Son of Man" speaks of His Humanity. This speaks of His Representation of us in the Redemptive plan.
     c. "Son of God" alludes to His Deity. This speaks of His Authority in the Redemptive plan.
- B. Jesus is referred to as "First Born" - Col. 1:15
  1. The term "First Born" does not relate to beginnings; rather it relates to His position of honor. (Halley's Bible Handbook p. 622)
  2. The term "First Born" refers to His position of eminence over

creation.

- C. Jesus is referred to as "Christ." This is not a name; it is an office or title. Christ is the New Testament Greek equal to the Old Testament Hebrew word Messiah. It simply means that He is the promised Savior.

- D. The First, Second, and Third Person of the Trinity do not refer to the rank of the Father, Son, or Holy Ghost. They are equal; the reference is in relation to their manifestation to mankind.

- E. The term "Trinity" refers to that essential truth that there is only One God but that His essence is in the three distinct "Persons" of the Father, the Son, and the Holy Ghost. These three, while distinct, are nonetheless, **ONE**.

    1. The Father is neither the Son nor the Holy Spirit. Still, He is God.
    2. The Son is neither the Holy Spirit nor the Father. Still He is God.
    3. The Holy Spirit is neither the Son nor the Father. Still He is God.

THE DEITY OF JESUS, THE CHRIST - JESUS: THE SON OF GOD

I. Jesus is the Son of God.
- A. Many have said that Jesus is the Son of God. (Entire section: Is Jesus God - Book Number One, pp. 76-84)
    1. God said so - Matt. 3:16-17
    2. Jesus said so
        - a. To the woman at the well - Jn. 4:25-26
        - b. To blind men - Jn. 9:35-37
        - c. To His disciples - Jn. 11:4
        - d. To the Jews - Jn. 5:17-18; 10:36; 19:7
        - e. To the Father - Jn. 17:1-5
        - f. To the High Priest - Mk. 14:61-62
    3. The Holy Spirit said so - Rom. 1:4
    4. The Scripture said so - Jn. 20:31
    5. Gabriel said so - Lk. 1:26-27; 35
    6. Demons said so - Matt. 8:29; Mk. 3:11; Lk. 4:41
    7. John the Baptist said so - Jn. 1:32-34
    8. Matthew said so - Matt. 1:20; 23
    9. Mark said so - Mk. 1:1
    10. Luke said so - Lk. 1:35
    11. John said so - Jn. 20:31
    12. Nathaniel said so - Jn. 1:49
    13. Andrew said so - Jn. 1:41
    14. The blind man said so - Jn. 9:35-38
    15. The Disciples in the ship said so - Matt. 14:33
    16. Peter said so - Matt. 16:15-16
    17. Martha said so - Jn. 11:27
    18. Judas said so - Matt. 27:3-5
    19. The Roman Centurion said so - Matt. 27:54
    20. Paul said so - Acts 9:20
    21. The eunuch said so - Acts 8:37-38
    22. The empty tomb said so - Rom. 1:4
- B. The Person of Jesus testifies that He is the Son of God. (Entire Section: Is Jesus God - Book Number 1 pp. 64-68)
    1. He is the revealer of the Father - Matt. 11:27
    2. He is the object of the Father's love - Jn. 3:35

OUTLINE STUDIES

        3.   He is the object of faith - Jn. 3:36; 14:1; Acts 16:30-31
        4.   He is the One to Whom the Father shows all - Jn. 5:20
        5.   He is the One Who quickens - Jn. 5:21
        6.   He is the Judge - Jn. 5:22
        7.   He is the Object of Honor - Jn. 5:23
        8.   He is the One Who has Life in Himself - Jn. 5:26
        9.   He is the Liberator - Jn. 8:36
        10. He is the object of the Father's Glory - Jn. 14:13
        11. He is the Lover of Righteousness - Heb. 1:8-9
        12. He is the Test of Truth - I Jn. 2:22
        13. He is the Sent One - I Jn. 4:14
        14. He is the Assurance of Life - I John 5:12
        15. He is the Ticket to the Father's abode - I Jn. 4:15

    C.   The actions of Jesus testify that He is the Son of God. (Entire Section: Is Jesus God - Book Number 1 pp. 68-73)
        1.   He is the Savior of the world - Jn. 3:17
        2.   He is glorified - Acts 3:13
        3.   He is the Person of the Gospel - Rom. 1:9
        4.   He is the Reconciler of men - Rom. 5:10
        5.   He is our Role Model - Rom. 8:29
        6.   He is the Person of fellowship - I Cor. 1:9
        7.   He is the Deliverer from wrath - I Thess. 1:10
        8.   He is the One through Whom the Father spoke - Heb. 1:2
        9.   He is the propitiation for our sin - I Jn. 4:10
        10. He is the cleanser from sin - I Jn. 1:7
        11. He is the Repository of Life - I Jn. 5:11-12
        12. He is known to demons - Matt. 8:29
        13. He is the Repository of the Promises of God - I Cor. 1:19-20
        14. He is the Stronghold of our faith - Gal. 2:20
        15. He is the Great High Priest - Heb. 4:14
            a.   The Son of God is the Great High Priest
            b.   The Son of God is passed in Heaven.
            c.   The Son of God is Jesus
        16. He was mistreated by men - Heb. 10:29 pp. 68-73

II.   The term "son of" may have several different meanings in Scripture.(Entire section: Basic Theology p. 248)
    A.   "Son of" can mean "offspring," but it can also mean "of the order of."
        1.   "Sons of the prophets" (I Kg. 20:35) meant "of the order of the prophets."
        2.   "Sons of the singers" (Neh. 12:28) meant "of the order of the singers.
    B.   "Son of" can mean "offspring," but it can also mean or imply the essential nature of an individual.
        1.   "Sons of consolation" (Acts 4:36) meant "one who encourages."
        2.   "Sons of thunder"(Mk. 3:17) meant "thunderous men."
    C.   "Son of Man" refers to Jesus' representing us before the Father.

III.   When the Scripture speaks of Jesus as the "Son of God," It speaks of His Divinity.
    A.   Jesus said that He was Divine.
        1.   Jesus said that He was Divine in words about Himself. "In no summary should one omit the testimony of the fifth, the divinity chapter of John's

Gospel, where our Lord Himself cites six testimonies to His sonship..." (Entire section: The Deity of Christ p. 3)
- a. "His own claim...
- b. "The witness of John the Baptist...
- c. "The witness of the Father...
- d. "His works...
- e. "The testimony of the Scriptures, and,...
- f. "Moses' testimony...
- g. "I only cite further the 'I am's' of this Gospel, as identifying Him with Jehovah in His infinite, unfathomable nature; note but one, Before Abraham was, I am,' and reflect upon it."

2. Jesus said that He was Divine in the hearing of others. John 19:7 - "When Christ called himself <u>the</u> <u>Son</u> <u>of</u> <u>God</u>, they [the religious leaders] understood it to imply positive <u>equality</u> to the Supreme Being; and, if they were wrong, our Lord never attempted to correct them." (Adam Clarke's Commentary v. 5 p. 649)
- a. If this were a misconception on their part, His failure to correct them means that He believed it true. It is therefore either true of He was in error to the extent of madness.
- b. If this were a misconception on their part, His failure to correct them, if He knew it false, makes Him a deceiver and a false teacher who cannot be trusted.
- c. If this is not a misconception on their part, and He did not correct them, He is God.

B. The Scripture declares that Jesus is the Son of God.
1. The Messiah, who Jesus clearly was, is recognized as the Son of God in the Old Testament - Ps. 2:7; Dan. 3:24-26 (Is Jesus God - Book Number One, pp. 53-54)
2. The New Testament declares that Jesus is the Son of God - Jn. 20:31.

THE DEITY OF JESUS, THE CHRIST - JESUS AS THE ANGEL OF THE LORD

I. We note in Exodus 3:2 & 6 that the "Angel of the Lord" is the same as the "God of the Fathers." When this fact is compared with Jn. 1:18 (No one has seen God except as He is revealed by Jesus) we are led to conclude that the "Angel of the Lord" is an Old Testament appearance of Jesus as the second "Person" of the Trinity.
- A. The Angel of the Lord identified His name as "secret" to the parents of Sampson. Judges 13:18 - The name is secret because it is wonderful. That is the meaning of the word "secret." It is thus translated in Is. 9:6 with reference to Jesus. The name, the implication, is so "transcendently wonderful (cf. II Cor. 12:4)," that it could not be uttered. Compare this with the custom of the ancients in not speaking the name of Jehovah. (*Pulpit Commentary* v. 3 [Judges] p. 139)
- B. The Angel of the Lord is identified as Jehovah.
    1. The Angel of the Lord identifies Himself as Jehovah - Gen. 22:11, 16; 31:11, 12. (Systematic Theology p. 319)
    2. The actions of the Angel of the Lord identify Him as Jehovah in that He accepts worship - Ex. 3:2-5; Jud. 13:20-22. (Systematic Theology p. 319)

II. Others identify the Angel of the Lord as Jehovah.
- A. Genesis 16:7-14 - Hagar identifies the Angel of the Lord as Jehovah. (Entire section: Is Jesus God - Book Number 1 pp. 48-49)

OUTLINE STUDIES

      1.   The Angel claims the power to multiply Hagar's seed (v. 10).
      2.   The Angel has knowledge of Hagar's pregnancy (v. 11).
      3.   The Angel uttered prophecy (v. 12).
      4.   The Angel was called God without rebuke (v. 13)

B.   Exodus 3:2-7 - Moses identifies the Angel of the Lord as Jehovah .(Entire section: Is Jesus God - Book Number One, p. 50)

1.   The Angel appeared to Moses in a supernatural manner (v. 2).
2.   The Angel called to Moses with authority (v. 4).
3.   The Angel gave Moses instruction in worship (v. 5).
4.   The Angel claimed to be God (v. 6)

C.   Joshua 5:13-15 - Joshua identifies the Angel of the Lord as Jehovah

      (Dake Annotated Bible p. 243 [OT] entire section)

1.   The Angel claimed to be Captain of the Host of the Lord. God is identified as the Captain of Israel.
2.   The Angel accepted worship from Joshua.
3.   The Angel allowed Joshua to call Him Lord.
4.   The Angel commanded Joshua to remove his shoes in the same manner as had God done with Moses at the burning bush.

D.   Judges 13:7-22 – Manoah knew Who he had seen and verbalized the same. (Is Jesus God? – Book Number One, p. 51)

E.   Genesis 32:24-30 - Jacob identifies the One with Whom he wrestled as God. (Dake Annotated Bible p. 21 [OT], entire section)

      1.   Jacob recognized Him as the Blesser (v. 26).
      2.   The wrestler performed a miracle to shrink the sinew (v. 25).
      3.   God acknowledged that He was there (v. 28).
      4.   Only God could have blessed Jacob (vv. 28-30).
      5.   Jacob claimed that he had seen God (v. 30).

F.   Judges 6:21-23 - Gideon was not corrected when he called this Messenger, "God'" he was comforted. (Is Jesus God - Book Number One, pp. 50-51)

G.   Genesis 22:11-18 - Abraham identifies the Angel of the Lord as Jehovah.
      1   The Angel gives instruction in worship (vv. 10-12).
      2   The Angel calls Himself, "Lord" - (v. 16).
      3   Vv. 17-18 show a knowledge beyond that of a mere human.

H.   Genesis 32:24-30 - The Person here mentioned is not a mere man. (Entire section: Is Jesus God - Book Number One, pp. 52-53)
      1.   The man gave Jacob a new (and a prophetic) name (v. 28).
      2.   The man blessed Jacob (v. 29).
      3.   The man was God (v. 30).

I.   Joshua 5:13-15 - The action of the Angel of the Lord indicates His Deity.

      1.   The Person here is Captain of the Lord's Host.

      2.   The Person here accepted worship.

      3.   The Person here had authority to instruct in worship. (Is Jesus God - Book Number One, p. 52)

      4.   God did visit man in the days of the Old Testament. He did so in the form of a man.

      5.   The view of the early church fathers is that Joshua 5:13-15 speaks of the pre-incarnate Jesus. (*Pulpit Commentary* v. 3 [Joshua] p. 91)

           a.   Partly, the view is inference. Gen. 16:10 - "Since the angel of the Lord ceases to appear after the incarnation, it is often inferred that the angel in the O. T. is a preincarnate appearance of the

                    Second Person of the Trinity [Jesus]." (Ryrie Study Bible p. 29)
- b. Much of this view is based on Scriptural principles. Gen. 16:7 - "The organic unity of Scripture would be broken if ... the central point in the Old Testament revelation was a creature angel, while that of the New is the incarnation of the God-Man." (Exposition of Genesis v. 1 p. 501)
- c. Mainly, this view is of Scriptural pronouncement. I Cor. 10:4 - "As a matter of [historical] fact, the Word, the Wisdom of God, was the Angel of the Church in the Wilderness." (*Pulpit Commentary* v. 19 [Corinthians] p. 336)

THE DEITY OF JESUS, THE CHRIST - gODS WITH A SMALL "g"

I. Jesus is called "God" in a unique sense. Adam is the son of God by creation. The nation of Israel was called God's son by election. All Christians are children (sons) of God by regeneration. Only Jesus Christ is the "monogenas" - the unique, one-of-a-kind, only-begotten, Son of God. (Jesus: Son of God pp. 10-12)

II. Others, in Biblical times, were called "god."
- A. Rulers were often called "god."
    1. The Egyptian people considered their pharaohs to be real gods.
    2. The Egyptians expected others to so address their pharaoh. "The pharaohs of Egypt were sometimes addressed as 'my god' by their vassal kings in Palestine, as evidenced by the Amarna letters..." (Concordia Study Bible p. 831)
    3. Since the Jews saw themselves as special representatives of the True God, it is not surprising that they would follow the linguistic traditions of the day by using the term "god" to address their own king, who ruled - albeit temporally - over the chosen people of God. But, if this were done, the central truth of the Jewish religion is that there is only One true Creator God. They would not have considered their kings divine. To dismiss the many messianic passages in the Psalms (ex. 45:6) as simply cultural statements about temporal rulers (or worse yet, as mistaken religious observations) is both unwarranted and unwise.
- B. Religious leaders (as well as political leaders in the near-Theocracy of Israel) were sometimes called "god." Often Scripture calls those who are representatives of God, "god" themselves. This is done since they stand in the place of representing God (Example: Ex. 4:16; 7:1; Ps. 82:6). But, the connection leaves no doubt as to what is meant. These are men standing as representatives of God. In this passage, however, Jesus is ascribed as having the creative attributes of God. This is clearly higher than the references to mere man. (Systematic Theology p. 307)

III. Jesus stands far above the sense of merely being called "god."
- A. John 10:34-36 -
    1. Jesus is defending Himself from the religious leaders. Note (v. 38) that He does not back from His unique position. He does not merely work for God; He claims equality. For this He is nearly stoned.
    2. "If there is any sense in which men can be spoken of as 'gods' (as Ps. 82:6 speaks of human rulers or judges), how much more may the term be used of him whom the Father set apart and sent!" (Concordia Study Bible p. 1627)
    3. Jesus is alluding to the Hebrew judges who interpret God's Law and justice. He is not denying His Deity. That, Jesus has just affirmed.

He is: (Entire section: Annotated Study Bible p. 1630)
- a. Showing that His words did not necessarily constitute blasphemy.
- b. "...demonstrating His superior knowledge of Scripture."

B. When Jesus is called "God," there is no reference to either title or position; this would not have raised the extreme ire of the religious leaders which led to the crucifixion. The term "God," when applied to Jesus speaks of His Person - i.e., Who He is!

THE DEITY OF JESUS, THE CHRIST - GOD: HE IS ONE

I. We accept the concept of the Trinity.
- A. The Bible teaches that there is only one God - Deut. 6:4; Is. 44:6; Jn. 17:3; I Cor. 8:4; I Tim. 1:17 (A Systematic Study of Bible Doctrine p. 62)
- B. The belief in the Trinity is not polytheism; such a concept is foreign to Christianity. The concept is Trinitarianism not Tri-Theism. There is only one God. "The three Persons of the Trinity are one as to substance, yet three as to individuality. ... There are ...no inequalities... each of the three is God." Yet there is only one God. (Basic Christian Faith p. 61)
- C. In the singleness of the Godhead there is a unity of multiplicity.
  1. The are three "Persons" but only one God.
     - a. We use the term "Person" figuratively when we speak of the Godhead as the Father, the Son and the Holy Ghost. "In the case of three human beings there is a division of nature, essence, and being... Such a conception of God is forbidden by the teaching of the Scripture as to the unity of God." (A Systematic Study of Bible Doctrine p. 78)
     - b. An Old Testament example of the concept of the unified multiplicity of God: Gen. 1:1 - the word for God is plural (There are three tenses in the Hebrew: Single - pertaining to one, dual - pertaining to two, and plural - pertaining to three or more.), yet the verb translated "created" is singular. One God in three Persons equals one act in harmony. (Can We Be Sure that Jesus Christ is God p. 3)
     - c. A New Testament example of the concept of the unified multiplicity of God: Matt. 28:19 - "Baptizing them **in** the name" speaks of a singular act by the "Father, Son, and Holy Ghost." (The New Testament for English Readers p. 216)
  2. The concept of the unity within the Trinity is a hard concept for man to grasp. "...the unity of God does not preclude His trinity, and His trinity is in no way inconsistent with His unity." (A Systematic Study of Bible Doctrine p. 63)
  3. Deut. 6:4 - There cannot be Two who are absolute. In such a case, **neither** would be **absolute**. (Annotated Study Bible p. 309)

II. We accept Jesus as God.
- A. God resided in the body of the Babe of Bethlehem.
  1. John 2:21 - The body of Jesus was **The Temple** where resided the **Eternal God**. (Adam Clarke's Commentary v. 5 p. 529)
  2. Colossians 2:9 - Men may have God in their lives, but Jesus has **all of God** (the fulness of Him) in His body. (*Pulpit Commentary* v. 20 [Colossians] p. 144)
  3. God resided in the body of Jesus in fact, not in either image or type.
     - a. Colossians 2:9 - There were representations of God in the Temple, but the reality of God is in Jesus. (Adam Clarke's

STUDIES IN THE DEITY OF JESUS, THE CHRIST

            Commentary v. 6 pp. 523-524)
- b. Colossians 2:9 - Not simply as an image did God exist in the Body of Jesus. He is bodily in the Babe of Bethlehem; this is true God, Himself. (*Pulpit Commentary* v. 20 [Colossians] p. 103)
- c. Colossians 1:15 - "...the term 'image'... must not be restricted to Christ corporeally visible in the Incarnation, but understood of Him as the manifestation of God in His Whole Person and work..." (New Testament for English Readers p. 1286)
- d. Philippians 2:6 - "Lit. 'Who subsisting in the form of God.' Here 'form' means all the attributes that express and reveal the essential 'nature' of God: Christ, being God, had all the divine prerogatives by right." (Jerusalem Bible p. 339 [NT])
- e. John 10:30 - "This speaks more than the harmony, and consent, and good understanding that were between the Father and the Son in the work of man's redemption... It must be meant of the **oneness of the nature** of Father and Son, that they are the same in substance, and equal in power and glory." (Matthew Henry's Commentary v. 2 p. 600)
- f. Isaiah 44:6 - Two Persons are mentioned:
  - (1). The Lord, the King of Israel, and,
  - (2). The Redeemer, the Lord of Hosts.
  - (3). Both are called by the personal name of "Yahweh." Yet, there is only One ("...beside me there is no God.") The Father and the Son equal One God. (Annotated Study Bible p. 1072)
  - (4) Added to the above, it must be remembered that the Father, and the Son, <u>and</u> the Holy Spirit, equal the One God!

B. Jesus, Himself, is the One True God.
1. I John 5:20 - There are not three Gods. Jesus is the "one, true God." (Christian Doctrine pp. 79-80)
2. Jesus is fully God. Colossians 2:9 - We do not worship a plurality of Gods. In Jesus is the fulness of God. (*Pulpit Commentary* v. 20 [Colossians] pp. 144-145)
3. John 1:1 - Jesus is fully God. Yet, He has a distinct Personality. The same could be said of the Father, and of the Holy Spirit. Each is fully God; each has a distinct Personality. Note John 1:1 in relation to Jesus:
   - a. "The Word was with God" - This speaks of the distinct personality of Jesus.
   - b. "The Word was God" - This speaks of the unity of the Godhead.

THE DEITY OF JESUS, THE CHRIST - GOD: HE IS PLURAL

I. God is a Trinity.
    A. "The Divine Trinity is God's triune mode of existence." (An Outline of Christian Theology p. 161)
        1. Augustine noted that the Scriptures declare that, "God is love." Love requires a lover, an object of that love, and love itself. Since God existed before creation (from eternity), the fact that He is love suggests the Trinity. (The Truth of the Gospel pp. 117-118)
        2. Although the Trinity is beyond our human comprehension, a cup of coffee, with cream and sugar, gives a simple illustration of this Truth. Each ingredient may be tasted distinctly, yet not as though it were the entire cupful in and of itself. Together they form one drink and *cannot* be

divided. Yet, each is a distinct ingredient. Such, on a much grander scale of course, is the Trinity.
3. Although a Trinity, God is yet One.
   a. The use of the term, "3 Persons in One God," is misleading. Our concept of "person" is "individual." But, God is three personalities in One Individual. (Christian Doctrines pp. 64-65)
   b. The Bible gives many examples of several persons being considered as one. (I, A, 3, b, [1] - [4], Our Eternal God p. 3)

   (1) Adam and Eve - Gen. 2:24
   (2) The people at the Tower of Babel - Gen. 11:6
   (3) He that planteth and he that watereth - I Cor. 3:6-8
   (4) All Baptized believers - I Cor. 12:13
   (5) The Scripture often give physical example to provide spiritual truth.
       (a) Adam and Eve's aprons of leaves vs. God's coat of skin in relation to the blood atonement vs. man's works.
       (b) Jacob wrestling with God in relation to the Christian and prevailing in prayer.
       (c) Joseph thrown into the pit by his brothers, sold in slavery, and becoming the magistrate of Egypt in relation to Jesus being rejected by His Own, killed, and risen to sit in majesty in Heaven.
       (d) David, the shepherd boy become king, in relation to Jesus, the Shepherd of our Faith.

B. Scripture begins with the proclamation of the truth of the trinity.
   1. Genesis 1:1 - "The original word [Hebrew] **Elohim**, God, is certainly the plural form of El, or Eloah, and has long been supposed, by the most eminently pious men, to imply a **plurality** of Persons in the Divine nature." (Adam Clarke's Commentary v. 1 pp. 27-28)
   2. We see the Trinity in Genesis 1 - "...God is viewed as creating... the 'Spirit' is seen hovering, and... the 'Word' is heard speaking." (Trinitarian Adumbration p. 3)

II. The Trinity is the manner in which God presents Himself.
   A. God is Three Equals, but only One Being. "There is that in God which defies all human thought and formulae..." (The Christian Faith p. 120)
      1. There is only one God manifest in three "persons."
         a. The Bible teaches the unity of God.
         b. The Father, the Son, and the Holy Spirit are each recognized as God.
         c. The Father, the Son, and the Holy Spirit are each recognized as equal. (A Systematic Study of Bible Doctrine p. 81)
      2. The doctrine of the trinity is expressed:
         a. Scripture recognizes three as being God.
         b. The Three are described as distinct Persons.
         c. This Trinity is not three gods as there is only One Essence.
         d All Three "Persons" are equal.
         e. "Inscrutable yet not self-contradictory, this doctrine furnishes the key to all other doctrines." (Systematic Theology p. 304)

STUDIES IN THE DEITY OF JESUS, THE CHRIST

   3. "The Divine Trinity is God's threefold self-manifestation." (An Outline of Christian Theology p. 161)
   B. Scripture proclaims the Truth of the Trinity.
   1. Matthew 28:19 - Note the Trinity. People are to be baptized in the Name (Singular) of the Father, the Son, and the Holy Ghost. (Rice Reference Bible p. 1053)
   2. "Not only does the opening text of the Word of God allow for a trinity of Persons in the Godhead, but it also supplies its own proper emphasis to the essential unity of the true and living God. This is implied in the fact that the very verb 'created' (**bara** in Hebrew) is in the singular. Hence our Bible commences with the sublime peculiarity of a plural substantive with a singular verb, thus laying the groundwork for the progressive unfolding of the grand truth concerning the one infinite, unique, eternal, and transcendental God who subsists as a trinity of divine Persons." (Trinitarian Adumbration p. 3)
   3. Genesis 1:26 - The early readers may have seen "us" as a plurality of majesty. Also, they may have envisioned God "...consulting with his angelic court..." (Harper Study Bible p. 5)
      a Plurality of majesty - This may be one meaning, but by comparing Scripture with Scripture (as II Peter 1:20 commands), we find a deeper meaning. Also, earlier peoples misunderstanding does not detract from the Truth.
      b The Angelic Court - The creation was of His Will, alone.
   4. Deuteronomy 6:4 - "'The Lord (YHWH) our Elohim is one Lord (YHWH),' the **one 'ehadh**, expressing **compound unity** not **yahid**, meaning a **single** one, thus not supporting [any] ... denial of the Trinity." (Unger's Bible Handbook p. 142)

III. Jesus is not the Father.
   A. The Hebrew word translated "God" in Genesis 1:1 is "Elohim" which is the plural form of "Eloah." "Being in the specific Hebrew plural form which applies to more than two, it lays the foundation at the very commencement of revelation for the subsequent disclosure of three divine Persons in the one Godhead." (Trinitarian Adumbration p. 3)
   B. John 1:14 - Jesus is a separate personality from the Father. He is not the Father but in constant "fellowship and proximity with the Father." (God in Man p. 8)
   C. "The Son is not God as such; for God is not only Son, but also Father and Holy Spirit. 'The Son' designates that distinction in virtue of which God is related to the Father, is sent by the Father to redeem the world and with the Father sends the Holy Spirit." (Systematic Theology p. 334)

IV. Jesus is God.
   A. Jesus is equal with the Father in the passions of humankind.
      1. John 15:23 - The Two are One. To hate One is to hate the Other. (Barnes' Notes on the New Testament p. 340)
      2. Ephesians 6:23 - Note that the Father and the Son are equally the givers of peace, love and faith. (Barnes' Notes on the New Testament p. 1016)
   B. Jesus is equal with the Father in essence. John 12:45 - "In no other can it be true that he who saw Jesus saw him that sent him, unless he were the same in essence." To say it of anyone else, even of a prophet, would be blasphemy." (Barnes' Notes on the New Testament p. 327)
   C. Jesus is Divine. Titus 2:13 - "There is but one **Greek** article to 'God' and 'Saviour,' which shows that both are predicated on one and the same Being..." (Commentary Practical and Explanatory on the Whole Bible p. 1388)

OUTLINE STUDIES

THE DEITY OF JESUS, THE CHRIST - THE DUAL NATURE OF JESUS

I. The Divine Nature of Jesus:
   A. The Divine nature of Jesus is eternal.
      1. Before Bethlehem, Jesus had: (Entire section: Is Jesus God - Book Number One, pp. 59-60)
         a. A place of abode - Jn. 6:62; 14:2
         b. Creative power - Jn. 1:3-4 ("He who created all things must have existed **before** all things, or otherwise He could not have created all things.")
         c. Knowledge - Jn. 6:64 ("Notice please that Jesus knew this from the beginning, from all eternity.")
         d. Glory - Jn. 17:5
         e. Riches - II Cor. 8:9
      2. John 8:58 - "The 'I am' denotes absolute eternal existence, not simply existence prior to Abraham. It is a claim to be Yahweh of the O. T. That the Jews understood the significance of this claim is clear from their reaction (v. 59) to the supposed blasphemy." (Ryrie Study Bible p. 1512)
      3. Before Bethlehem, Jesus was: (Entire section: Is Jesus God - Book Number One, pp. 59-60)
         a. Foreordained - I Pet. 1:20
         b. With the Father - Prov. 8:22-30; Jn. 1:1
         c. Of Old - Micah 5:2
         d. Worshipped by Angels - Is. 6:1-5
         e. Called "Lord" by David - Matt. 22:41-46
         f. A Rock of Refreshment - I Cor. 10:1-4
         g. Sent by God - Jn. 5:23
         h. Known by Abraham - Jn. 8:56-58
         i. Before John the Baptist - Jn. 1:15
         j. In the past - Heb. 13:8
            (1) Yesterday - His Pre-existence
            (2) Today - His Present Existence
            (3) Forever - His Permanent Existence
   B. The Divine nature of Jesus is holy. Romans 1:4 - "The Spirit of Holiness" is not the same as the Holy Spirit. The intent is to show that the essence of the Spirit of Christ is holiness - i.e. Divine, in opposition of, as well as an amplification to, His human nature in v. 3. Thus the dual nature of Christ is shown. (The New Testament for English Readers   pp. 842-843)

II. The Human Nature of Jesus:
   A. The human nature of Jesus united with the Divine nature even before Bethlehem - Luke 1:43.
      1. He developed as a normal child; this was His human nature.
      2. He was the Savior even before His birth; this is His Divine Nature.
   B. The human nature of Jesus is now united with His Divine Nature.
      1. "Divinity and humanity are united in Him, but they are not blended. Humanity is not deified and divinity is not humanized. ... Divinity cannot take into its essence anything finite, and the human is finite." (Christian Doctrine pp. 198-199)
      2. "There is no mixture of divine and human attributes (as Eutchians taught), no change in either complex (as Appollinarians taught), no dividing of them, and no separating them so as to have two Persons (as Nestorianism taught). Orthodoxy says two natures comprising one Person

or hypostasis forever. It is correct to characterize Christ as a theoanthropic Person. But not accurate to speak of theoanthropic natures [since that would mix the divine and human attributes.]" In His incarnation, Jesus Christ is One Person with both a complete and an unadulterated Divine nature and a complete and unadulterated human nature: Two natures - one individual. (Basic Theology p. 251)

III. Jesus is God manifest to humanity as man.
    A. This is God revealed to man. John 1:18 - "...God chose to reveal Himself physically in Christ." (Criswell Reference Bible p. 1239)
    B. This is God in fellowship with man.
        1. Ephesians 4:10 - He fills all things with His Sovereignty and workings by the Spirit. As God, Jesus can be everywhere; yet as man, He can be anywhere. (The New Testament for English Readers p. 1231)
        2. Matt. 28:20 - Jesus promises, taking on the attribute of God, to be with His church - everywhere and at all times.
    C. This is God as God and man. Micah 5:2 - (Entire section: Commentary Practical and Explanatory on the Whole Bible pp.816-817)
        1. "out of thee shall come..." - the human side of Jesus.
        2. "...goings forth from everlasting..." - the Divine side of Jesus.
        3. This is the dual nature of Jesus.

THE DEITY OF JESUS, THE CHRIST - HIS VOLUNTARY SUBMISSION

I. He laid aside His great glory. This is called His "Kenosis."
    A. The process of Kenosis - Philippians 2:5-11
        1. The outward glory He laid aside:
            a. V. 6 - Jesus only removed the "outward and visible manifestation of the Godhead." He did not empty "...Himself of either His divine nature or His [divine] attributes..." (Scofield Reference Bible p. 1258)
            b. V. 7 - He did not empty Himself of His "...essential glory, but [of] its manifested [or visible to humankind] possession..." (The New Testament for English Readers p. 1263)
        2. The power of glory He did not lay aside.
            a. V. 6 - He did not, could not as God, give up the prerogatives and power of Deity. But only gave up that "...visible glorious light in which the Deity is said to dwell..." as evidenced by the many Old Testament presentations - i.e. the Burning Bush; Isaiah's vision; Ezekiel's visions; etc." (Adam Clarke's Commentary v. 6 p. 495)
            b. Note, from the passage, that "...He never empties Himself of the fulness of His Godhead, or His 'Being **on an equality with God**'; but between His being 'in the FORM (i.e., the outward glorious self-manifestation) of God,' and His 'taking on Him **the form of a servant**,' whereby He in a great measure emptied Himself of His precedent 'form' or outward self-manifesting glory as God." (Commentary Practical and Explanatory on the Whole Bible p. 1305)
    B. The purpose of Kenosis:
        1. The Kenosis is the manifestation of His dealing with sinful humanity.
            a. Officially, the President of the United States is superior to us, but his nature, being human, is essentially ours. (Christian Doctrine p. 70)
                (1) The essential nature of Jesus remained Divine in the incarnation. He was still God.

                (2) The human nature, which Jesus assumed in the incarnation, is that which allows Him to be our Perfect Substitute.
            b. Colossians 2:9 - "Before His incarnation [the fullness of the Godhead] dwelt in Him, as the Word non-incarnate, but not bodily, as now that He is the Word Incarnate." (The New Testament for English Readers p. 1296)
            c. Our Lord sometimes speaks of Himself as God and
            d. Sometimes as the Ambassador of God. As he had a human and a Divine nature, this distinction was essentially necessary. Many errors have originated from want of attention to this circumstance." (Adam Clark. Commentary v. 5 p. 551)
        2. The Kenosis is the method of His dealing with sinful humanity.
            a. The Son, by virtue of being in subjection to the Father, assumes an "...inferiority ... in office, not in nature; the subordination is official and does not touch the divine substance." (Christian Doctrine p. 69)
            b. Jesus is the Redeemer of sinful humanity.
                (1) Jesus laid aside His equity with God to purchase our redemption - Phil. 2:5-11; Jn. 10:29; 16:28; 17:21 (Can We Be Sure that Jesus Christ is God p. 22)
                (2) Matthew 3:17 - Besides His being the Son of God by the miracle of the Virgin Birth, Jesus is the Son "...by special designation to the work and office of the world's Redeemer." (Matthew Henry's Commentary v. 2 p. 17)
            c. Jesus is the Mediator between God and a sinful world.
                (1) Hebrews 1:10 - Jesus had original title to govern the world as He is the creator; He also has that right as mediator by commission. (Matthew Henry's Commentary v. 2 p. 1243)
                (2) Matthew 28:18 - As God, the Son, Jesus has title as creator to all things (Jn. 1:3; Col. 1:16-17; Heb. 1:8). But, He had just, with His death and resurrection, assumed the office of Mediator. The authority spoken of in this passage is in reference to that office. (Barnes' Notes on the New Testament P. 145)

II. The Kenosis displayed the great power of Jesus.
    A. Jesus exercised great power before Bethlehem. Jesus was free from creatureship and could, by His Own Volition, place Himself under the Law (Gal. 4:4-5). He could then satisfy the Law and yet be able to offer grace as One Who administered the Law. (Christian Doctrine p. 75)
    B. Jesus exercised great power while He was on earth. John 5:19 - The Trinity acts in unison. While on earth Jesus acted in union with the Father and His will. (Dake Annotated Bible p. 98[NT])
    C. Jesus continues to exercise great power after His resurrection. John 17:5 and Philippians 2:5-11 - Jesus took up again the glory which He had laid aside in the incarnation.

THE DEITY OF JESUS, THE CHRIST - THE GLORIFICATION OF JESUS

I. The proof of the Glory of Jesus:
    A. The proof of His Glory shines from His Person - Heb. 1:3
        1. The proof of his glory shines through His sinless life and resurrection.

STUDIES IN THE DEITY OF JESUS, THE CHRIST

      2.   The proof of His glory shines through the lives He touches yet today.
      3.   The verse here speaks of the "Brightness of His Glory." One cannot look at the sun and not see the light. The light is of the same essence as is the sun. (Concordia Study Bible p. 1876)
      4.   "Skeptics ask, 'Why did not Jesus by reasoning prove His deity?' But amid the blaze of His miracles, this would be like placing a label on the sun. Does the sun need a label?" (God in Man p. 21)
  B.   The proof of His glory is shown to His disciples. Matthew 17:2 - Even His clothing shone with the glory.
      1.   When Moses came down from Mt. Sinai, after being in the presence of God, his face shone with the glory of God to such an amount that his face had to be hidden with a cloth (Ex. 34:29-33).
      2.   As God, Jesus' glory was much more than just His face. (Matthew Henry's Commentary p. 139)
  C.   The proof of His glory is shown through His disciples.
      1.   At His death the disciples scattered in apparent fear. But, after His resurrection those same disciples became fearless propagators of His story.
      2.   His disciples, mostly drawn not from the *religious elite* but from the working class - among people whose status in a nation occupied by a foreign power and from a culture which was not mobile in which they would not be expected to travel very far from their childhood homes and families - took His Message of sin and salvation to the corners of the world.
  D.   The proof of His glory is shown by the work He did for us. Philippians 2:6 - In order to fully understand the "magnificence" of what Jesus did for us in coming into this world, we need to understand the glory which He voluntarily laid aside. (*Pulpit Commentary* v. 20 [Philippians] p. 78)

II.   The power of the Glory of Jesus:
  A.   The power of the Glory of Jesus was His Own Glory.
      1.   The Power His in His Pre-existence. Philippians 2:6 - His pre-existence was as God. He was (and is) equal with the Father. (The New Testament for English Readers pp. 1262-1263)
      2.   The Power was His in His Person. Colossians 2:9 - "The language is such as would be obviously employed on the supposition that God became incarnate, and appeared in human form; and there is no other idea which it so naturally expresses, nor is there any other which it can be **made** to express without a forced construction." "Theotas," the word translated "Godhead," does not simply mean an attribute (morality, holiness, knowledge, etc.), "...but that whole Deity thus became incarnate, and appeared in human form." (Barnes' Notes on the New Testament pp. 1068-1069)
      3.   The power was in His "Para." In John 1:14 and 17:5, the Greek preposition, "para." is used in speaking of the glory of Jesus. Para means, "beside, alongside." We, therefore, see that the Glory of Jesus was not derived from the Father but was His [Jesus'] Own Glory which was **alongside** that of the Father. (God in Man pp. 29-30)
  B.   The power of the Glory of Jesus is His Own Glory.
      1.   The power is His in His Own Person - What and Who He is. Philippians 2:6 - Form, here, can mean only either splendor, majesty, glory or nature as in essence. (Barnes' Notes on the New Testament p. 1030)

        2.   The power of His glory is shown in His performance. Matthew 17:3 - In the Transfiguration we catch a glimpse, although a veiled glimpse, of the glory which was the property of Jesus before He "laid it aside" in the Kenosis.

        3.   The power of His glory is His in prophecy. John 17:5 - We see, here, a reversal of the emptying of Himself at the incarnation. What He lays aside He has the power to gather to Himself again.

III.   The performance of the Glory of Jesus:
    A.   The glory of Jesus is seen in that He gave the message of God to man. John 1:18 - The Word has "...announced the Divine oracles unto men..." (Adam Clarke's Commentary v. 5 pp. 516-517)
    B.   The glory of Jesus is seen in that He received worship.
        1.   Hebrews 1:4-6 - The ancient Jews had the highest regard for the angels. They considered them the highest council of God. The angels could even be worshipped as God's representatives (although not for themselves). None but God was thought to be entitled to the worship of angels. Paul in saying that Jesus is above the angels, and that the angels are instructed to worship Jesus, is claiming Deity for Jesus. (Adam Clarke's Commentary v. 6 p. 687 [Reference is made, by Clarke, to the **Targum** of Jonathan ben Uzziel])
        2.   If Jesus were not God, the above would be the highest blasphemy.
        3   If Jesus were God, the above would be most reasonable. John 11:4 - The glory that was for God is properly applied to the Son. By that action it **does** go to God.

THE DEITY OF JESUS, THE CHRIST - JESUS HAS THE ATTRIBUTES OF DEITY

I.   Jesus claimed the rights reserved for God.
    A.   Jesus forgave sins - Matt. 9:6
    B.   Jesus claimed he could raise the dead - Jn. 5:21
    C.   Jesus said He would judge the world - Jn. 5:22-27
    D.   Jesus claimed to have all power in Heaven and in Earth - Matt. 28:18 (I. A. - I. D.] Why We Believe in the Deity of Christ p. 18)
    E.   Jesus claimed to have power over the Sabbath.
        1.   John 5:17 - There is no need for Jesus to rest as must a mortal human. Mortal man is in danger of losing his attentiveness to God. Worship is the operative stance of Jesus even in His work. (The New Testament for English Readers p. 506)
        2.   As God, Jesus has the right to do whatever He wishes in relation to the Sabbath. He no more breaks the Sabbath in doing good than in His sustaining the universe.
    F.   Jesus claimed to be more than a mere man. John 14:6 - Jesus does not claim to simply **show** or **teach** the way, the truth and the life. He **is** the Way, the Truth and the Life. (Criswell Study Bible p. 1262)
    G.   Jesus taught man how to worship.
        1.   This is honor due God; Jesus received it. The Son receives the honor and worship due God - Jn. 5:23; Heb. 1:6; I Cor. 11:24-25; II Pet. 3:18; II Tim. 4:18 (A Systematic Study of Bible Doctrine p. 79)
        2.   Jesus taught that only God could be worshipped (Matt. 4:10), yet He accepted, and called for (Jn. 5:23), worship from man. (Christian Doctrine pp. 86-66)
        3.   Jesus, Himself, accepted worship from many. (Entire section: Is Jesus God - Book Number Two, pp. 40-42)
            a.   He accepted worship from angels - Heb. 1:6

STUDIES IN THE DEITY OF JESUS, THE CHRIST

        b.   He accepted worship from the wise men - Matt. 2:11
        c.   He accepted worship from the men in the ship - Matt. 14:33
        d.   He accepted worship from the ruler (a military man) - Matt. 9:18
        e.   He accepted worship from a leper (an outcast) - Matt. 8:2
        f.   He accepted worship from the Woman of Tyre (a woman not of His race, humanly speaking) - Matt. 15:25
        g.   He accepted worship from the blind man (a handicapped person) - Jn. 9:38
        h.   He accepted worship from the disciples (devout men) - Matt. 28:17; Lk. 24:32
        i.   He accepted worship from all - Phil. 2:10-11

II.   Jesus displayed the power of His Deity.
     A.   He is the Word - John 1:1
         1.   "'The Word' is not an attribute of God, but an acting reality, by which the Eternal and Infinite is the first great cause of the created and finite." (The New Testament for English Readers p. 453)
         2.   Both the Written and the Living Word came through human instrument. The Written Word via the prophets, etc., and the Living Word via Mary. Both are of God and His essence. (Rice Reference Bible p. 1130)
     B.   He is superior. (Entire section: Is Jesus God - Book Number Two, pp. 44-45)
         1.   Jesus is superior to created beings.
             a.   Jesus is superior to the angels - Heb. 1:4-9
             b.   Jesus is superior to Moses - Heb. 3:1-6
             c.   Jesus is superior to Solomon – Matt. 12:42
             d.   Jesus is superior to Jonah - Matt 12:41
         2.   Jesus is superior in the essence of Who He is.
             a.   The Name of Jesus is superior - Phil. 2:9
             b.   The Sacrifice of Jesus is superior - Heb. 9:26-28; 10:11-12
             c.   The Blood of Jesus is superior.
                 (1)   The Blood of Jesus is superior to that of Abel - Heb. 12:24
                 (2)   The Blood of Jesus is superior to that of the Old Testament sacrifices - Heb. 9:12
                 (3)   The Blood of Jesus is superior in its cleansing Power - I Jn. 1:7
     C.   His Name is associated with God.
         1.   The Name of Jesus is associated with God in the prayers of the pious. He is on equal footing in their prayers and statements. (Entire section: Systematic Theology p. 312)
             a.   The Name of Jesus is included in the Baptismal formula - Matt. 28:19; Acts 2:38; Rom. 6:3 (It would be absurd and profane to speak of baptizing in the name of the Father and of Moses, to use an example.)
             b.   The Name of Jesus is used in Apostolic Benedictions - II Cor. 13:14; I Cor. 1:3; Gal. 1:3; Eph. 3:14; Eph. 6:23
             c.   The Name of Jesus fits in other miscellaneous passages - Jn. 5:23; Jn. 14:1; Jn. 17:3; Matt. 11:27; I Cor. 12:4-6; Rom. 10:17; Col. 3:17; II Thess. 2:16-17; Eph. 5:5; Col. 3:1; Rev. 10:6; 22:3, 16
         2.   The Name of Jesus is associated with God in the essence of Who Jesus Is.

(Entire section: Is Jesus God - Book Number Two pp. 38-46)
- a. Jesus is One with the Godhead - Col. 2:9
- b. Jesus is One with God in Image - Heb. 1:3; Jn. 12:45; Jn. 14:9
- c. Jesus is One with God in Glory - Jn. 17:5
- d. Jesus is One with God in Honor - Jn. 5:23
- e. Jesus is One with God in Possessions - Jn. 16:15
- f. Jesus is One with God in Saving Faith - Jn. 14:1; Jn. 17:3
- g. Jesus is One with God in Abiding with Believers - Jn. 14:23
- h. Jesus is One with God in being hated by the World - Jn. 15:23
- i. Jesus is One with God in Baptism - Matt. 28:19
- j. Jesus is One with God in Raising the Dead - Jn. 5:21
- k. Jesus is One with God in Benediction - II Cor. 13:14

D. His knowledge displays the power of God.
1. His knowledge of others displays the power of God. (Entire section: Can We Be Sure Jesus Christ Is God? p. 21)
   - a. He knew what was thought under the fig tree - Jn. 1:48
   - b. He knew the healing of the son - Jn. 4:46-53
   - c. He knew the need of Nicodemus - Jn. 3:1-16
   - d. He knew the answer to His antagonist - Mk. 12:17
2. His knowledge of sinners displayed the power of God. Mark 5:30 - As with Adam in the Garden, the request was not made in order to receive information. It was made to give the woman of whom it was asked the opportunity to make a public confession. (Barnes' Notes on the New Testament p. 157)
3. His knowledge of Himself displayed the power of God. He even knew the manner of His Own earthly end - Matt. 16:21

E. His power of life displays the power of God - Jn. 1:4; 6:48; 14:6; Matt. 9:18-25; Lk. 7:12-15; I Jn. 5:11) (Can We Be Sure That Jesus Christ Is God? p. 26)

F. He is the Lord of nature. (Entire section: Can We Be Sure That Jesus Christ Is God? pp. 10-13)
1. He displayed the power of God at the marriage in Cana - Jn. 2:11
2. He displayed the power of God at the feeding of the 5000 - Jn. 6:13
3. He displayed the power of God at Peter's fishing - Jn. 21:11
4. His many healings, both physical and mental (demonic, etc, display the power of God.

G. His holiness displays the power of God. ([II,G,1,a - II,G,3,h] Is Jesus God - Book Number Two, pp. 35-48)
1. The fact of His holiness.
   - a. Jesus was Holy before the foundation of the world - I Pet. 1:19-20
   - b. Jesus was Holy at His birth in Bethlehem - Lk. 1:35 (Note: "That Holy thing" could read "That Holy One.")
   - c. Jesus was Holy as a child - Acts 4:20
   - d. Jesus was Holy at His death - Acts 3:4-15
2. The testimonies to His holiness:
   - a. The testimony of God, the Father, to His Holiness - Heb. 1:8-9
   - b. The testimony of the unclean spirits to His Holiness - Mk. 1:23-25
   - c. The testimony of Judas to His Holiness - Matt. 27:3-4
   - d. The testimony of Pilate to His Holiness - Jn. 19:4
   - e. The testimony of Pilate's wife to His Holiness - Matt. 27:19
   - f. The testimony of the thief on the cross to His Holiness - Lk. 23:41

STUDIES IN THE DEITY OF JESUS, THE CHRIST

                g.   The testimony of the Centurion to His Holiness - Matt. 27:54

        3.   He challenged men concerning His Holiness - Jn. 8:46

    H.   His works display the power of God.

        1.   His works of miracle display the power of God. Mark 4:36-41 - Even more of a miracle than we usually consider happened here. Supposing He had only stopped the winds; it would have taken some time for the sea to calm. But He calmed **Both**!

        2.   He displayed works of power. (Entire section: Can We Be Sure That Jesus Christ Is God? p. 20)

                a   He forgave sins - Mk. 2:10

                b   He healed disease and cast out demons - Matt. 10:1

                c   He lay down, and reclaimed again, His life - Jn. 10:18

        3.   His works display the Divinity of God.

                a.   The works of God are performed by Jesus: (Entire section: A Systematic Study of Bible Doctrine p. 79)

                      (1)   Jesus does the work of creation - Jn. 1:3; I Cor. 8:6; Col. 1:16; Heb. 1:10; Heb. 3:3-4; Rev. 3:14

                      (2)   Jesus does the work of upholding the universe - Col. 1:17; Heb. 1:3 (Systematic Theology p. 310)

                      (3)   Jesus does the work of bringing life - Jn. 5:28-29 (Christian Doctrine pp. 84-86)

                      (4)   Jesus does the work of raising and judging the dead - Jn. 5:27-28; Matt. 25:31-32

                b.   The works of God are performed by Jesus as God. It may be true that anyone may compose music; but, only Chopin could compose a work of Chopin. There may be many composers but there is only One God. I almost put "only One **True** God," but that is a false statement: There is only **One** God; any others who assume the title are, by definition, **false** gods.

III.   In Jesus are displayed the attributes of God.

    A.   Jesus claimed the power of God. John 10:30 - This answer was occasioned by a discussion not of plan or of purpose, but of power. Jesus was claiming the Omnipotent Power of God - an attribute of God. He was, therefore, claiming Deity. The hearers (v. 31) understood this. If it were not His intention to say this, He is guilty of moral dishonesty in that He did not correct the hearers. (Barnes' Notes on the New Testament p. 317)

    B.   Jesus is the Wisdom of God. Proverbs 8:22-30 - Wisdom here is more than merely an attribute of God. This Wisdom "...has personal properties and actions..." This is the Son of God. (Matthew Henry's Commentary v. 1 p. 495)

    C.   The essence of Jesus contains the attributes of God.

        1.   He is immortal - I Tim. 6:16; Heb. 7:25; Rev. 1:18 (Is Jesus God - Book Number Two, p. 45)

        2.   Jesus is from eternity - Jn. 8:57-58 ([II,C,2 - II,C,4] Know What and Why You Believe p. 60)

        3.   Jesus is the sustainer of all - Heb. 1:3

        4.   Jesus is everything - Col 2:9

        5.   Jesus is Omniscient. ([III,C,5,a - III,C,5,(9)] Is Jesus God? - Book Number Two, pp. 26-31)

                a.   He knows all - Jn. 16:30

                b.   He knows the thoughts of man - Lk. 5:22

                c.   He knows the hearts of men - Acts 1:24; Mk. 2:8

                d.   He knows the lives of men - Jn. 4:16-19

OUTLINE STUDIES

        e.   He knows the craftiness of men - Lk. 20:19-26
        f.   He knows the love of man - Jn. 5:42
        g.   He knows the whereabouts of man - Jn. 1:48
        h.   He knows the future.
            (1)   He knew the catch of fish - Lk. 5:4-9
            (2)   He knew Peter's denial - Matt. 26:75
            (3)   He knew Peter's death - Jn. 21:18-19
            (4)   He knew His Own death - Mk. 10:34 with Matt. 27:29-31
            (5)   He knew Judas' betrayal - Jn. 6:64
            (6)   He knew His disciples reaction to His arrest - Jn 16:32 with Matt. 26:56
            (7)   He knew of the Passover accommodations - Lk. 22:10-12
            (8)   He knew His ascension into Heaven - Jn. 6:62 with Acts 1:11
            (9)   He knows what is in all men - Jn. 2:24-25
6.   Jesus is immutable - Heb. 13:8([III,C,6 -III,C,10] A Systematic Study of Bible Doctrine p. 79)
7.   Jesus is Self-existent - Jn.. 5:26
8.   Jesus is Truth - Jn. 14:6
9.   Jesus is Love - I Jn. 3:16
10.   Jesus is Holy - Luke 1:35; Jn. 6:39; Heb. 7:26
11.   Jesus is the Creator. (Entire section: Is Jesus God? - Book Number Two, pp. 33-35)
        a.   He created all things - Jn. 1:3; Eph. 3:9
        b.   He created all things out of nothing - Heb. 11:3
        c.   He created all things in Heaven and in Earth - Col. 1:16
        d.   He created the worlds - Heb. 1:2; Jn. 1:10
        e.   He laid the foundation of the world - Heb. 1:10
12.   Jesus is omnipresent. (Is Jesus God - Book Number Two, pp. 31-33)
        a.   He is where two or three are gathered - Matt. 18:20
        b.   He is with His people, always - Matt. 28:20
        c.   He is in Heaven and in Earth - Jn. 3:13 Note here that Jesus was in Heaven even as He spoke on earth.
        d.   He is in the Father and the believer - Jn. 14:20
        e.   He is everywhere, filling all - Eph. 1:23; 4:10
        f.   He is near to all - Acts 17:27 (Is Jesus God - Book Number 2 pp. 31-33)
13.   In Jesus is life - Jn. 1:4; 14:6 ([III,C,13 - III,C,14] Systematic Theology pp. 309-310)
14.   In Jesus is eternality - Jn. 1:1; 8:58; 17:5; Eph. 1:4; Col. 1:17; Rev. 21:6
15.   Jesus is Omnipotent. (Entire section: Is Jesus God - Book Number Two, pp. 13-26)
        a.   Jesus had the power of life and death - Jn. 10:7-10
        b.   Jesus has the power of healing
            (1)   He healed the deaf and dumb - Mk. 7:33-35
            (2)   He healed the blind - Matt. 9:27-30
            (3)   He healed sickness - Jn. 5:5-10; 4:46-54; Matt. 4:23
            (4)   He healed a withered hand - Matt. 12:10-13
            (5)   He healed dropsy (an unnatural accumulation of fluids in any body cavity) - Lk. 14:2-4

STUDIES IN THE DEITY OF JESUS, THE CHRIST

	(6)	He healed paralysis - Mk. 3:12
	(7)	He healed leprosy Matt. 8:1-4
	(8)	He healed palsy - Matt. 8:14-15
	(9)	He healed fever - Matt. 8:14-15
	(10)	He healed the insane - Matt. 17:15
	(11)	He healed the issue of blood - Matt. 9:20-22
	(12)	He healed infirmity - Lk. 13:11-13
	(13)	He heaved the severed ear - Lk. 22:50-51

    c.   He had power over the fig tree - Matt. 21:19-20
    d.   He had power over Satan.
        (1)   He had power over Satan in temptation - Matt. 4:1-11
        (2)   He had power over Satan's works - I Jn. 3:8
        (3)   He had power over Satan, the destroyer of life - Heb. 2:14; Jn. 10:18
        (4)   He had power over Satan at Calvary - Col. 2:14-15
    e.   Jesus had power over death and the grave.
        (1)   He rose from the dead, Himself - Jn. 2:19-22; 10:18; II Tim. 1:10
        (2)   He raised the widow's son - Lk. 7:11-17
        (3)   He raised the daughter of Jarius - Matt. 9:18-26; 28:18
    f.   Jesus has power over the elements - Matt. 8:26-27
    g.   Jesus has the power to uphold all things - Heb. 1:3
    h.   Jesus has the power to change our bodies - Phil. 3:20-21
    i.   Jesus has power over principalities and powers - Col 2:10
    j.   Jesus has power over demons - Matt. 8:16
    k.   Jesus has power over Hell and death - Rev 1:18 ([III,C,15,a - III,C,15,1] Is Jesus God - Book Number 2 pp. 13-26)

THE DEITY OF JESUS, THE CHRIST - THE AUTHORITY OF JESUS

I.   He exercised His Authority.
    A.   He exercised His Authority as an opportunity. Philippians 2:7 - "He used His equality with God as an opportunity ... self-abasement." The method He chose was as a servant in the form of a man. (The New Testament for English Readers p. 1263)
    B.   He exercised His Authority in every situation.
        1   In His private life He withstood the temptations of Satan - Matt. 4:1-11
        2.   In His public life He withstood the wiles of His accusers - Lk. 19:39-40
        3.   In His ministerial life He met the needs of the inquirer - Jn. 3:1-21
        4.   In His trial He maintained His control. John 19:10 - Even at the trial we find Jesus in control. Pilate vacillated while the Jews only reacted out of hatred and anger. (Life Application Bible p. 283)
        5.   In His death we see His authority. Luke 23:46 - His death was due to **His** command. (The New Testament for English Readers p. 442)

II.   He displayed His Authority.
    A.   He displayed His Authority as a Judge. Matthew 25:32 - This is not the Great White Throne Judgment of Rev. 20. Here those Gentiles who are still alive after the Tribulation are judged. "Nations" is "ethnos," which means "Gentiles." The acts of the sheep and the goats are acts of individuals, not of national groups. (Rice Reference Bible p. 1045)
    B.   He displayed His Authority in His miracles. John 4:51 - The miracles of Jesus

were not simply illusions or done by the power of suggestion. Jesus was 20 miles from the child He healed. (Life Application Bible p. 246)
- C. He displayed His authority in His commands. John 8:37 - "My words hath no place in you..." The prophets always said, "The Word of the Lord," but here was The Lord, The Word, speaking. (Commentary Practical and Explanatory on the Whole Bible p. 1046)

THE DEITY OF JESUS, THE CHRIST - THE ETERNALITY OF JESUS

I. He claimed eternity - John 8:58
- A. He claimed to have existed prior to Abraham. (Can We Be Sure That Jesus Christ is God? p. 18)
- B. He claimed to have always existed. Note the tense change: "...before Abraham was (past tense) I am (present tense)." As a man Abraham has a place in history - both past and present as a contemporary and a historical figure. Jesus, as God, is the Eternal Contemporary.
- C. "'Before Abraham was, I am' - the words rendered 'was' and 'am' are quite different. The one clause means, 'Abraham was **brought into being**;' the other '**I exist**.' The statement therefore is not that **Christ came into existence before Abraham did**..., but that He never **came** into being at all, but existed before Abraham had a being; in other words, existed before **creation** or **eternally**..." (Commentary Practical and Explanatory on the Whole Bible p. 1047)

II. His attributes exhibit eternality.
- A. He pre-dates **all** creation (Col. 1:17) and, therefore is not, Himself, created.
- B. He has a glory, as does the Father - John 17:5
  - 1 Jesus has glory that is "co-eternal with the Father" before the world - i.e. in eternity.
  - 2. Both the glory and the existence of Jesus are from everlasting. (Matthew Henry's Commentary v. 2 p. 667)
- C. His consecration exhibits eternality. Matthew 3:16 - The Holy Spirit descended upon Him. As parts of the "...indissoluble union of the Divine Persons, the Holy Three are One." Thus, He did not **become** God (or 'a god') at this point as **He always was God**. This was consecration of the "God / Man" to His sacred office of Redeemer. (*Pulpit Commentary* v. 15 [Matthew] pp. 80-81)

III. The Old Testament attests to His eternality
- A. Proverbs 8:22 – (Entire sections: Unger's Bible Handbook pp. 292-293)
  - 1. Wisdom here is the preincarnate Jesus (As He is the "Word" of John 1:1)
  - 2. Note that He is "possessed" not "created." Wisdom (Jesus) is eternally in "the beginning." This "...is an absolute timeless beginning.") He is co-existent with the Father
- B. The Old Testament attests to His eternality. Isaiah 9:6 - In this prophecy of the coming of Jesus, "Everlasting Father" could be translated as "Father of Eternity" which would designate the role of the Son in creating all things, establish His deity, and yet, "...not involve any confusion between the Father and the Son in the Holy Trinity." (Harper Study Bible p. 1013)

IV. The New Testament attests to His eternality.
- A. John 1:1 – "In the beginning 'was' the Word..." The word "was" is "een," which is a durative imperfect tense; it simply means that Jesus existed at the beginning, not that He came into existence. In verse 6 the verb "egento" is used of John the Baptist. This word means "became" or "came." Had John meant to say that Jesus came into being, or became a god, he could have used - would have used, as that word was in his vocabulary - the word "egento." (God Became Man pp. 11-12)

- B. John 1:14 - Matthew Henry argues that Jesus was in the world via His Divine Presence and, "...by the prophets **came unto his own**..." But, now, He came in the Flesh. He was not a man who **became** a god; He was **The** God Who became a man. (Matthew Henry's Commentary v. II p. 493)
- C. Philippians 2:6 - The existence here is from eternity. (The New Testament for English Readers p. 1262)
    1. Jesus is eternal - He pre-existed. (IV, C, 1-3: Criswell Study Bible p. 1412)
    2. Jesus is immortal - He will never die.
    3. Jesus is invisible - He has a spiritual, as well as a physical, nature.

THE DEITY OF JESUS, THE CHRIST - JESUS IS THE CREATOR

I. The fact that Jesus is the Creator, negatively considered - John 1:1
- A. As the Creator, Jesus in not merely "a" word, or "a" representative of God. "Jesus Christ was not merely 'a' logos but 'the logos.' He was the intelligence behind everything that was created. He is the Person responsible for the creation of the world. That is why the definite article is used before Logos. He is the Master Mind of all creation." (God Becomes Man p. 27)
- B. As the Creator, Jesus is not merely the speech of God. Jesus is not the speech (word) of God; He is that active reality which is the First Cause of all latter effect. He is **THE** creative force of the Godhead. (The New Testament for English Readers p. 453)
- C. As the Creator, Jesus is not, Himself, created. "...Jesus Christ is **no part** of **the creation**, as he existed when no part of that existed..." This being so, and because He made all things (v. 3), He must be the eternal God. (Adam Clarke's Commentary v. 5 p. 511)

II. The fact that Jesus is the Creator, positively considered:
- A. John 1:3 -
    1. "All things..." The Father created through the Son. The Son acts according to the will of the Father - the Father wills creation so the Son creates. Therefore the Son could not have been created by the will of the Father as the Father acts through the Son - i.e. No Son at any point in time = no creative action (will mobilized) = no Son at any subsequent point in time (or eternity). Therefore the Son is eternally co-existent with the Father. (The New Testament for English Readers p. 457)
    2. Jesus made all things. This is not a delegated task from God to a subordinate being. Only the Eternal existed before "all" was created. Thus, Jesus must be The Eternal - i.e. God. Also, creation is, "...causing that to exist that (which) had no previous being: this is evidently a work which can be effected only by **omnipotence**. Now, God cannot delegate his **omnipotence** to another: were this possible, he **to** whom this omnipotence was delegated would, in consequence become GOD; and he **from** whom it was delegated would **cease to be such**: for it is impossible that there could be **two** omnipotent beings." (Adam Clarke's Commentary v. 5 p. 512)
- B. John 2:11 - Most of the miracles which Jesus performed were a restoration of things lost due to the fall - i.e. Health, sight, life, etc. The Creator was simply renewing His creature. (Life Application Bible p. 238)
- C. Colossians 1:16-17 -
    1. The phrase is universal in concept. This is an explicit statement that Jesus created the universe and all that it contains. (Barnes' Notes on the New Testament p. 1062
    2. Note the clear statements of Paul: (Entire section: Adam Clarke's Commentary v. 6 pp. 516-517)

a. Jesus created the universe - this takes omnipotent, not delegated power. So, Jesus was omnipotent. Only one being may be **ALL** powerful; since this is Jesus, He is God.
b. All things were created for Him - He receives the glory which can only be the Glory of God - He is God.
c. Jesus exists prior to creation - All existence must come from God. To be before **any of creation** is to be God. Jesus is God.
d. Jesus preserves and governs all things. The power to preserve belongs to God, therefore, Jesus is God.
e. Not only did Paul say, and believe, all the above, he said this under inspiration.
3. "The phrase here employed of 'creating all things in heaven and in earth,' is **never** used elsewhere to denote a moral or spiritual creation." Therefore the passage simply means what it says: Jesus created everything; He is the Creator-God. (Barnes' Notes on the New Testament p. 1063)
D. Revelation 3:14 - Jesus began, was the working agent of, creation. (The New Testament for English Readers p. 1811)
E. Revelation 4:11 - Note that the One Who created all things, Who we have just seen to be Jesus, is called "GOD."

III. Jesus continues to work in His creation. Colossians 1:17 - "'In him all things consist,' or 'hold together,' means nothing less than that Christ is the principle of cohesion in the universe, making it cosmos instead of chaos." (Systematic Theology p. 311)

THE DEITY OF JESUS, THE CHRIST - THE PERSONALITY OF JESUS

I. He is Divine.
  A. John 1:1-2 - The first two verses of John correct three mistakes about the person of Jesus. (Entire section: Who Created Evil p. 3)
    1 The first two verses of John correct the mistaken view of the Arians; they see Jesus as a created being who is inferior to God.
    2. The first two verses of John correct the mistaken view of the Sabellians; they do not see the Trinity. They only see God as presenting Himself in different manifestations.
    3. The first two verses of John correct the mistaken view of the Socinians. They see Jesus as simply a man.
  B. The relationship of Jesus to Jehovah is compound.
    1. Jesus is distinct from Jehovah - Ps. 45:5-7; Mal. 3:1 (Systematic Theology pp. 321-322)
    2. Jesus is one with Jehovah.
      a. The Messiah (Jesus) is one with Jehovah - Is. 9:6; Mic. 5:2 (Systematic Theology pp. 321-322)
      b. The oneness of Jesus with Jehovah is necessary if we are to have salvation. If Jesus were a created being He would owe His Own allegiance to God. He could not act in our stead for salvation - no matter how exalted He might be. (Christian Doctrine pp. 73-74)

II. The teaching of Jesus reveals the Divine mind.
  A. He knew His audience. John 10:16 - Jesus was speaking to a Jewish audience. The "other sheep" of which He speaks are not scattered as the, supposed, ten lost tribes (Cf. James 1:1 where James writes to **all twelve tribes**), but are "in other folds." These "lost sheep" are the Gentiles of the Christian church. (The New Testament for English Readers p. 556)
  B. The method of His teaching.

STUDIES IN THE DEITY OF JESUS, THE CHRIST

        1.   He spoke much to few or even to one - Jn. 3:18; 4:1-42; Matt. 5:1
        2.   He taught with great authority - Mk. 12:37 (Entire section: Can We Be Sure That Jesus Christ Is God? P. 14)
            a.   His authority was of Himself. Where the prophets had said, "Thus saith the Lord," He said, "Verily, verily, I say unto thee..." (John 3:3)
            b.   His authority extended over:
                (1)   Human reasoning - Jn. 19:11
                (2)   Demons - Mk. 1:32-34
                (3)   Religious discourse - Matt. 12:38-42
                (4)   Religious observance - Matt. 12:2-8
                (5)   Physical disease - Matt. 9:35
                (6)   The closest of human relationships - Jn. 19:26-27
                (7)   Heavenly things to come - Jn. 3:11-15
    C.   His teaching was true and factual despite popular misconception.
        1.   Matt. 17:15-18 - The people believed that a man's insanity was caused by the phases of the moon (luatick). This was the wisdom of the day. Jesus knew better than this. (Dake Annotated Bible p. 19 [NT])
        2.   This fact will show the lie of those who say that Jesus taught what He knew to be in error in some cases ("He only taught that Daniel wrote the Book of Daniel because the people believed it was so.", is a popular example of this type of heresy.) Because His hearers believed it so and He didn't want to "shake their faith."
            a.   Jesus did shake their misconceptions and faith when He announced that He had come to fulfill the Law - Matt. 5:17
            b.   If Jesus had taught what He knew to be wrong, He would be guilty of teaching error. He would be a liar and untrustworthy.

III.   The character of Jesus reveals the Divine mind.
    A.   The character of Jesus was that of a mature adult. John 8:57 - No inference is made to the actual age of Jesus. Fifty years was reckoned as the completion of manhood by the ancient Jews. (The New Testament for English Readers p. 437)
    B.   His character compared with His claims. ([III,B,1 - III,B,2] Know What and Why You Believe pp. 168-170)
        1.   His character compared with His claims.
            a.   He was sinless. He never asked forgiveness even though He was a moralist.
            b.   No one ever charged Him with wrong doing.
        2.   His character displayed power.
            a.   Over natural forces.
            b.   Over sickness and disease.
            c.   Over death.
        3.   Jesus claimed that His character was Divine. John 5:19 - The Son does what the Father does. Anyone could do what the Father does not do (err and sin). "If Jesus can do **nothing** but what God does, then He is no creature - He can neither **sin** nor **err**, not act **imperfectly**." (Adam Clarke's Commentary v. 5 p. 551)

IV.   The Personality of Jesus showed man the message of God.
    A.   Malachi 3:1 - Jesus was the Messenger and Lord of the Old Covenant (Old Testament) and - as He said in Matthew 26:28 - He was also the Messenger of the New Covenant.
    B.   He showed us God. When Jesus came into the world we learned much more about God. "More of his inmost character was shown by Christ, and more of the

THE DEITY OF JESUS, THE CHRIST - JESUS ADMITS HIS DIVINITY

I. The grandeur of His claim.
    A. It is a singular claim. Neither Buddha, Moses, Mohammed, nor Zoroaster claimed to be God. Jesus is unique in His claim of Deity. (Answers To Tough Questions p. 39)
    B. It is a true claim. If Jesus' claims to Deity are untrue, then one of the following must be true:
        1. He knew the claim was false and He was a liar. This He, due the ethical nature with which He taught, did not appear to be.
        2. He did not know that His claim was false. If this is true, then one of the following must also be true: (Entire section: Evidence that Demands a Verdict pp. 109-111)
        3. He was deluded. This would make all of His teaching suspect.
        4. He was, Himself, a lunatic.
    C. But, since His claims to Deity are true, we must either accept or reject Him on that basis. (Evidence that Demands a Verdict p. 109)
    D. It is a courageous claim. "Suppose this very night the President of the United States appeared on all the major networks and proclaimed that, 'I am God Almighty. I have the power to forgive sin. I have the authority to raise my life back from the dead.' He would be quickly and quietly shut off the air, led away, and replaced by the Vice-President. Anybody who would dare to make such claims would have to be either out of his mind, or a liar, unless he was God." (Answers To Tough Questions p. 40)

II. Others understood His claims.
    A. Mark 1:23 - The evil spirits understood. They knew His power. They asked, not that He leave them alone - as they might have demanded of a mere human, but what they had done to Him. The implied answer they expected was, "Nothing." Therefore, their argument seemed to be, if He cast them out it would be "improper interference." This argument is not correct. The evil spirits had attacked the creation of God. God, the Son, the Creator, now stood before them. Satan still uses this argument against the soul who flees to Jesus for salvation. (Barnes' Notes on the New Testament p. 148)
    B. John 5:17-18
        1. The understanding of His hearers is that He was calling Himself equal with God - i.e. that "He and the father were ONE." (Adam Clarke's Commentary v. 5 p. 550)
        2. Note that Jesus did nothing to say that they were in error in this view. He does not dispute their view.
    C. John 8:58 - Jesus claims the eternal Name of God. In the next verse we see that the Jewish leaders grasped the significance.
    D. John 10:30-39 - When Jesus said that He and God were One, He meant that, "...the Father's Personality and his own Personality are merged into one essence and entity." The Jewish leaders (v. 33) understood this to be His meaning. Jesus argued that others, who had stood in places of power - both political and religious, had been called "gods." But, He, the very Son of God (v. 36), Who was sanctified before He was sent into the world (v. 36), had right to that title. He further argued that this unity was proven because He did the same works as did the Father. The Jews still felt as before. He had not repudiated, nor weakened, His claim that He and the Father were One. (*Pulpit Commentary* v. 17 [John II] pp. 51-53)
    E. John 19:7 - His claims of Deity were brought forth at His trial. He could have

saved His life if this were untrue; all He had to do was admit the truth. The truth was that He is God. A liar and a martyr are not of the same character.
- F. John 20:28 - Jesus did not rebuke Thomas for calling Him both Lord and God.

III. He inferred His Deity.
- A. He inferred His Deity in His works.
    1. Matthew 14:33 - Jesus accepts worship.
    2. Mark 2:1-11 -
        a. The fact that Jesus forgave his sins is a claim of Deity. I can forgive someone only for a wrong done me. Christ was forgiving a man for a wrong committed against God. (More Than a Carpenter pp. 10-11)
        b. Jesus argues that the Jewish Religionist may well reason that it is easy for Him to simply say that He forgives sin; this is not something easy to prove that one has done. However, He does prove that He can, in fact, forgive sins when He bids the man walk. (*Pulpit Commentary* v. 16 [Mark] pp. 84-85)
        c. Jesus knew what was in the minds of the scribes
- B. He inferred His Deity in His words.
    1. Matthew 28:19 - It would be blasphemy to unite the Name of Jesus thus with God, the Father, if He were not Deity. It would be absurd to claim unity the Holy Spirit if He were only an attribute of God. (Barnes' Notes on the New Testament p. 145)
    2. Matthew 28:20 - This verse speaks of the divine attributes of Jesus.

        a. "Lo, I am with you" - His Omnipresence
        b. "Alway" - His Eternality
- C. John 16:28 - Note the assumptions of Jesus in this passage: (Entire section: Adam Clarke's Commentary v. 5 p. 635)
    1. "I came forth from the Father" - with Whom I had existed from eternity.
    2. "Am come into the world" - by the incarnation
    3. "I leave this world" - of My Own will by the cross
    4. "And go to the Father" - by the ascension
- D. John 16:15 - "If Christ had not been equal to God, could he have said this without blasphemy?" (Adam Clarke's Commentary v. 5 p. 633)
- E. Matthew 5:21-22 - In the Sermon on the Mount Jesus says, "Ye have heard it said, but I say unto you..." Imagine if a young preacher said, "The Bible says, but I say..." (The Christian Faith p. 42)

IV. He claimed the Power of Deity.
- A. Jesus claimed the Power of Deity in His essence.
    1. He claimed to be from above - Jn. 3:31; 8:23 (Entire section: Is Jesus God - Book Number Two, pp. 47-51)
    2. He claimed to be from Heaven - Jn. 6:38
    3. He claimed to be from God - Jn. 8:42
    4. He claimed to be omnipotent - Matt. 28:18; Jn. 17:2
    5. He claimed to be omniscient - Lk. 9:47; Jn. 2:24-25
    6. He claimed to be omnipresent - Matt. 18:20; 28:20
    7. He claimed to be the Son of God - Mk. 14:61-62; Jn. 9:37
    8. He claimed to be the Messiah - Jn. 4:25-26
    9. He claimed to be the Way to God - Jn. 14:6

            10. He claimed to be the Door to Heaven - Jn. 10:9
            11. He claimed to be the Giver of Life - Jn. 10:10, 28
            12. He claimed to be the Giver of Peace - Jn. 14:27
            13. He claimed to be the Giver of Rest - Matt. 11:28
            14. He claimed to be the Giver of Liberty - Jn. 8:36
            15. He claimed to be the Light of the World - Jn. 8:12
            16. He claimed to be the Savior of the World - Lk. 19:10; Jn. 3:17
            17. He claimed to be the Substitute of the World - Matt. 20:28; Jn. 10:11
            18. He claimed to be the Judge of the World - Jn. 5:22
            19. He claimed to be the Builder of the Church - Matt. 16:18
            20. He claimed to be the Rewarder of Men - Matt. 16:27; Rev. 22:12
            21. He claimed to be the Resurrection - Jn. 11:25
            22. He claimed to be the One Who forgives sin - Mk. 2:10-11
            23. He claimed to be the One Who answers prayer - Jn. 14:14
            24. He claimed to be the One Who sends the Holy Spirit - Jn. 15:26
            25. He claimed to be the One Who would come again - Jn. 14:3
        B. Jesus claimed the Power of Deity in His words.
            1. Jesus is equal with god. (Entire section: Can We Be Sure That Jesus Christ Is God? P. 22)
                a. He said this is true - Jn. 10:30
                b. Inspiration says this is true - Heb. 1:1-14
            2. Jesus claimed the authority of God. (Entire section: Know What And Why You Believe p. 60)
                a. He claimed the authority to forgive sin - Mk. 2:10
                b. He claimed the authority to judge men - Jn. 5:22
                c. He claimed the authority to raise the dead (to give life) - Jn. 6:39-40, 54; 10:17-18
        C. Jesus claimed the Power of Deity in His actions.
            1. John 5:21 - Note: "Whom he will." The Son raises the dead by His Own "...sovereign power and independence." He did not do so as did the prophets who had to gain privilege from Deity. (Adam Clarke's Commentary v. 5 p. 551)
            2. John 10:17-18 - "Jesus does more than predict His crucifixion and resurrection. He also shows that He had the power to lay down His life and take it up again, once more asserting His deity." (The Annotated Study Bible p. 1269)
V. Jesus claimed to be Deity.
    A. Jesus claimed to be Deity while under duress - Matt. 26:63-64
    B. Jesus claimed to be Deity while under scrutiny. John 10:30 - "'**Are**' is in the **masculine** gender - 'we (two persons) are'; while '**one**' is neuter - '**one thing**.'" (Commentary Practical and Explanatory on the Whole Bible p. 1050)
    C. Jesus claimed to be Deity with authority. Revelation 21:6-7 - The speaker claims Divinity; the speaker is Jesus (cf. Rev. 1:8).
VI. The claims of Jesus leave us with a choice. (Entire section: Know What And Why You Believe pp. 166-167)
    A. His claims may have been lies, but He taught with great moral force.
    B. He may have been sincere in His claims and yet self-deceived. But, His life exhibited great calm. He did not appear to be insane.
    C. He may have been only a legend. But, parts of Mark are available that were written when there were still people alive who would have known if this were true or untrue.

STUDIES IN THE DEITY OF JESUS, THE CHRIST

    D.   It is much more probable that He spoke the truth.

THE DEITY OF JESUS, THE CHRIST - OTHERS ADMIT TO THE DEITY OF CHRIST

I. Many testify to the Deity of Jesus.
- A. Jesus was not a recluse. He was seen, and known, by crowds and - at least - twelve intimates. How was He viewed by His contemporaries? (Entire section: Can We Be Sure That Jesus Christ Is God? p. 7)
    1. John the Baptist called Him, "The Lamb of God" - Jn. 1:36
    2. Peter called Him, "The Christ, the Son of God" - Matt. 16:16
    3. Thomas called Him, "My Lord, and My God" - Jn. 20:28
    4. John, the Beloved, called Him, "The Christ" - Jn. 20:31
    5. The Samaritan woman called Him, "The Christ" - Jn. 4:29
    6. The healed blind man called Him, "of God" - Jn. 9:33
    7. The multitude called Him, "The Son of God" - Matt. 27:54
    8. His enemies said that, "Never a man spake like this" - Jn. 7:46
    9. Even at His trial, paid informers had to be found to testify against Him - Matt. 26:59-66
- B. Many testified to His Deity.(Entire section: Is Jesus God - Book Number Two pp. 46-47)
    1. The Father testified to His Deity - Heb. 1:8
    2. He testified to His Own Deity - Jn. 10:30
    3. Isaiah testified to His Deity - Is. 9:6
    4. Mary testified to His Deity - Lk. 1:46-47
    5. Thomas testified to His Deity - Jn. 20:28
    6. John testified to His Deity - Jn. 1:1; I Jn. 5:20; Rev. 19:13
    7. Paul testified to His Deity - Eph. 2:6; Col. 2:9; I Tim. 3:16
    8. Jude testified to His Deity - Jd. 25
- C. "Those who knew Him best were convinced that He is God." (Entire section: Why We Believe in the Deity of Christ   p. 19)
    1. Nathanael, even before he became a disciple, was convinced that He is God - Jn. 1:47-51
    2. John was convinced that He was God - I Jn. 1:1-2; Rev. 1:18
    3. Peter was convinced that He was God - Matt. 16:16-17
    4. Thomas was convinced that He was God - Jn. 20:28
    5. Pilate was convinced that He was, at the least, more than a mere man - Jn. 19:1-12
    6. One crucified with Him was convinced that He was God - Lk. 23:42
    7. Paul was convinced that He was God - Titus 2:13; II Cor. 5:19; Phil. 2:6-8
    8. His executioner was convinced that He was God - Mk. 15:39
    9. The writer of Hebrews was convinced that He was God - cf. Ps. 45:6-7 with Heb. 1:8

II. His friends testified to His Deity.
- A. Zacharias testified to His Deity - Lk. 1:68-70 (The Deity of Christ p. 3)
- B. John 20:28 -
    1. This is not a mere expression of surprise.
    2. This was said to the face of Jesus.
    3. Jesus did not rebuke Thomas for either profanity or mistake.
    4. Thomas was commended for his statement. ([II, B, 1 - II, B, 4] Barnes' Notes on the New Testament   p. 357)
    5. If Jesus were not God He could not have allowed this statement from Thomas. He could not have been a prophet or even an, "...honest man, to permit his disciple to indulge in a mistake so monstrous and destructive..." (Adam Clarke's Commentary v. 5   p. 659)

OUTLINE STUDIES

        a.   The affirmation of Thomas was not corrected by Him Who **is** Truth - Jn. 14:6

        b.   Thomas said, "My Lord and my God." The former is a title of Jesus; the latter is a title of Deity. Thomas affirmed that this was Jesus and that Jesus is God. (Criswell Study Bible p. 1272)

III. Not only did Jesus' friends, but also His enemies, understood His claim to Deity. (Answers To Tough Questions p. 39)
- A. The religious foes of Jesus understood that He claimed Deity.
    1. Mark 2:7-10 - Jesus does not condemn the reasoning of the scribes; it is correct. He admits to this in His answer.
    2. John 5:17-18 - The Jewish interpretation of what Jesus had said was that He was "making himself equal with God." Rather than correcting this view, He argues for it.
        - a. He says that the Father and the Son are equal in will and operation - v. 19 (III, A, 2, a - d: *Pulpit Commentary* v. 17 [John] p. 227)
            - (1) The equality is based on their unity
            - (2) This unity stems from their "sameness of nature."
        - b. He says that the Father communicates with the Son - v. 20
        - c. He says that the Father and the Son are joined in quickening the dead - v. 21
        - d. He says that judgment belongs to the Son - v. 22
    3. John 10:35-39 - (III, A, 3. a - d: Barnes' Notes on the New Testament p. 318)
        - a. He did not deny that the Term applied to Him.
        - b. He did not deny that the term was properly applied to Him.
        - c. He did not deny that the application of the term to Him implied that He was God.
        - d. He did argue with the inconsistency in charging Him with blasphemy.
        - e. He followed with proofs of His true Divinity.
- B. The demons understood His Deity - Mark 1:24   (Entire section: Commentary Practical and Explanatory on the Whole Bible   pp. 952-953)
    1. "I know thee ... the Holy One of God." This was possibly spoken so that people would accept Him as a temporal Messiah.
        - a. This would negate the trip to Calvary.
        - b. This would be the same temptation as when Satan offered Christ the kingdoms of the world - He could accept a throne now and forsake Calvary.
    2. "I know thee ... the Holy One of God." This may have been spoken so that He would appear in league with Satan.
- C. The judges at His trial understood His claims to Deity.
    1. The trial of Jesus was not over what He had done but over Who He was. (More Than a Carpenter p. 12)
    2. The church authorities who had heard Jesus speak knew, as they asserted at His trial, that He did not claim to be only a prophet. (The Christian Faith p. 43)
    3. John 8:46 - They could find no sin in Him. Therefore, He spoke only Truth. Why did they not believe that He was Who He said He was. (The New Testament for English Readers p. 545)
- D. The executioners understood His claims to Deity. Matt. 27:54 - The Roman soldier may not have known all the implications of what he said. He may have

STUDIES IN THE DEITY OF JESUS, THE CHRIST

spoken from a heathen form of reference, with a plethora of Deity. But, he definitely knew the charge against the accused; the sign atop the cross asserted, "This is Jesus, the King of the Jews." The charge against Jesus was blasphemy - claiming to be the Messiah of the Jews and, therefore, Divine. This soldier, at the very least, said that Jesus was Who He said He was. (Barnes' Notes on the New Testament p. 131 [NT])

IV. The early church understood the claim of Jesus to Deity.
- A. The early church understood the claim of Jesus to Deity in its creeds. The earliest Christian creed was, "Jesus is Lord." The Greek word for "Lord" is "Kyrios." This word was used in the Septuagint (A translation of the Hebrew Scripture into Greek), "...as the translation of 'Jehovah.'" To the religious mind, to call Jesus, "Lord," was to give the sort of obedience that should only be given to God. (The Christian Faith pp. 37-38)
- B. The early church understood the claim of Jesus to Deity in its prayers. Compare Acts 1:24 with John 6:70 where Jesus says that He chose the Twelve. We see, in Acts, an example of prayer addressed to Jesus. (The New Testament for English Readers P. 653)

THE DEITY OF JESUS, THE CHRIST - THE PROPHETS SPEAK OF THE MESSIAH

I. The ministry of John the Baptist comes before the Messiah - Malachi 3:1 (Cf. With Mal. 4:5-6 and Matt. 17:10-13)
- A. John the Baptist came in the spirit of Elijah. Note what he is to do:
  - 1 He prepares the way before Yahweh.
  - 2 The Person Who has the way prepared is the Owner of the Temple.
  - 3 The Person Who has the way prepared is the Lord of Hosts.
- B. Since the preparer, John the Baptist, came to prepare the way for Jesus (John 1:22-24), then Jesus is God.

II. The ministry of the Messiah:
- A. The Old Testament prophecies indicate that a King will sit on the throne of David forever - Ps. 2:8-9, 27-29, 45; cf. Heb. 1:8 (The Deity of Christ p. 3)
- B. Psalm 2:7 - The Messiah will be God's Servant / Son. "'Son ... Father.' In the ancient Near East the relationship between a great king and one of his subject kings, who ruled by his authority and owed him allegiance was expressed not only by the words 'lord' and 'servant' but also by 'father' and 'son.' The Davidic king was the Lord's 'servant' and his 'son.' (2 Sa. 7:5, 14)." (The Concordia Study Bible p. 788)
- C. Revelation 22:16 - The Messiah is both man and God. (Entire section: Adam Clarke's Commentary v. 6 p. 1064)
  - 1 The "root" of David speaks of His creating all - including the Davidic line.
  - 2 The "offspring" of David speaks of His being the descendent of David via Mary.

III. The nature of the Messiah.
- A. In prophecy One is to come to bear the sins of the world - Is. 53 cf with Jn. 3:16; Acts 8:30-31 (The Deity of Christ p. 3)
- B. He will be God. Romans 9:5 - Jesus appeared, in the flesh to receive His Being from these fathers in the incarnation, but He is, in His Eternal Self, over them all, God. (Adam Clarke's Commentary v. 6 p. 109)
- C. He will be both God and man. Isaiah 9:6 - This is a prophecy of Jesus. That Isaiah calls Him, "...the mighty God...," is significant. Isaiah was no polytheist. This is also spoken under inspiration. It is a statement of Isaiah of the Divinity of the Messiah - Jesus Christ, as surely as the terms "child" and "sons" speak of His humanity. (*Pulpit Commentary* v. 10 [Isaiah] p. 170)

OUTLINE STUDIES

THE DEITY OF JESUS, THE CHRIST –
THE OLD TESTAMENT AND THE NEW TESTAMENT SPEAK OF THE DIVINITY OF JESUS

I. New Testament passages equate Jesus with Old Testament passages about God.
   - A. Many Old Testament passages regarding God are applied to the Son in the New Testament. Examples: Matt. 3:3 with Is. 40:3 and Jn. 12:41 with Is. 6:1 (A Systematic Study of Bible Doctrine   p. 79)
   - B. Under inspiration John equated Jesus with Old Testament references to God - John 12:37-43 (Trinitarian Adumbration   p. 3)
   - C. Compare I Corinthians 10:4 ("The rock was Christ") with Deuteronomy 32:4, 15, 18, 30-31, 37; I Samuel 2:2; II Samuel 22:2-23:3 ff; Psalms 78:20; Romans 9:33; I Peter 2:8. God is the Rock and Jesus is the Rock. The equation follows that Jesus is God. (The New Testament for English Readers p. 1033)
   - D. There are many Old Testament references to the Sonship of Jesus - Genesis 49:10 (Shiloh is the Messiah and the Messiah is Jesus.); Psalms 2:7; Proverbs 30:4; Isaiah 9:6; Daniel 3:25 (Is Jesus God - Book Number One   pp. 62-63)

II. Jesus (New Testament) and Jehovah (Old Testament) compared:
   - A. Jesus fulfills Old Testament statements made regarding Jehovah. (II, A, 1 - 8: Elemental Theology   pp. 145-146)
     1. His is unchanging - Ps. 102:24-27 / Heb. 1:10-12
     2. A messenger goes before Him - Is. 40:1-4 / Lk. 1:68-76
     3. He fulfills the statements in His actions - Jer. 17:10 / Rev. 2:23
     4. He fulfills the statements in Light and Glory - Is. 60:19 / Lk. 2:32
     5. He fulfills the statements in temptation - Num. 21:6-7 / I Cor. 10:9
     6. He is the Stone of Stumbling - Is. 8:13-14 / I Pet. 2:7-8
     7. He fulfills the statements as Shepherd - Ps. 23:1 / Jn. 10:11; Heb. 13:20, I Pet. 5:4
     8. He fulfills the statements in that He seeks and saves the lost - Ezek. 34:11-12 / Lk. 19:10 (II, A, 1 - 8: Elemental Theology   pp. 145-146)
     9. Compare John 4:10 with Jeremiah 2:13 and 17:13, "...where Yahweh is referred to as the fountain of living waters..." (Criswell Study Bible p. 1244)
   - B. Jehovah compared in Essence with Jesus: (Entire section: Is Jesus God - Book Number Two, pp. 51-61)
     1. Both are from everlasting - Ps. 90:2 / Micah 5:2
     2. Both will remain after Heaven and Earth - Ps. 102:25-27 / Heb. 1:10-12
     3. Both are from the beginning - Gen. 1:1 / Jn. 1:1
     4. Both are first - Is. 44:6 / Rev. 1:17
     5. Both are the Creator - Gen. 1:1 / Col. 1:16
     6. Both are the Supporter and Preserver - Neh. 9:6 / Col. 1:17
     7. Both are unchanging - Mal. 3:6 / Heb. 13:8
     8. Both are almighty - Gen. 17:1 / Rev. 1:8
     9. Both are to Whom the angels cry, "Holy, Holy, Holy" - Is. 6:3 / Rev. 4:8
     10. Both are our Righteousness - Jer. 23:6 / I Cor. 1:30
     11. Both are the Only Savior – Is. 43:11 / Acts 4:12
     12. Both are above all - Ps. 97:9 / Jn. 3:31
     13. Both are to Whom every knee shall bow - Is. 45:23 / Phil. 2:10
     14. Both are the Last - Is. 44:6 / Rev. 1:17 (Is Jesus God - Book Number Two, pp. 51-61)

THE DEITY OF JESUS, THE CHRIST - THE SCRIPTURES DECLARE THAT JESUS IS DIVINE

STUDIES IN THE DEITY OF JESUS, THE CHRIST

I. The Old Testament speaks on the Divinity of Christ - Isaiah 9:6-7
   A. "This constellation of names clearly indicates the Messiah is God himself, the second person of the Trinity." (The People's Study Bible p. 1083)
   B. The title "Mighty God" is used in Isaiah 10:21 for Yahweh. (The People's Study Bible p. 1083)
   C. "The Mighty God (El Gibor)." Isaiah used "El" only of God. "Gibor means 'Hero.' Together they describe one Who is indeed God Himself." (The Annotated Study Bible p. 1031)
   D. "Everlasting Father" - Again Deity is surely ascribed to the Christ. He is the Progenitor and Protector of humanity. (*Pulpit Commentary* v. 10 [Isaiah] p. 170)

II. The New Testament speaks on the Divinity of Christ:
   A. Matthew 1:23 - Jesus was not called by the name "Immanuel." "According to Hebrew usage the name does not represent a title but a characterization, as in Isaiah 1:26 and 9:6. The name 'Immanuel' shows that He really was 'God with us.' Thus the Deity of Christ is stressed at the very beginning of Matthew." (The New Scofield Reference Bible p. 992)
   B. Matthew 1:16 - "Adam was made; Jesus was begotten." (Am I Not Free? P. 4)
   C. Matthew 18:20 - "None but God could say these words, to say them with truth, because God alone is **every where present**, and these words refer to his **omnipotence**... But, Jesus says these words: **ergo** - Jesus is God. (Adam Clarke's Commentary v. 4 p. 185)
   D. John 1:1 -
      1. The word "with" is "pros." This, "...could be translated as 'forward' to express the idea of motion. It is as if the Logos and the Father were facing each other. There is no suggestion of the Son following the Father, for then the Son would not be co-equal with the Father." (God in Man p. 6)
      2. "Theos (God) en (is) o (the) logos (word)" There is no article before "Theos." This word comes before the verb to show the train of thought - not only was "Logos" with God, but Logos was God. "The Logos" is the subject as the entire passage refers not to God but to Him Who is the Logos. (Systematic Theology pp. 305-306)
      3. True, there is no article with the word translated "God." This is not needed unless John chose to use the indefinite. This is "highly improbable" on grammatical grounds - especially since it would be the only time John used that form in his gospel. It is also improbable that John would have used such an imprecise way of expressing a truth if Jesus were only "a god," especially considering his preciseness in the rest of the chapter. (Basic Theology p. 53)
   E. John 1:14 - The phrase, "dwelt among us," could as well have been translated "tabernacled." This, is as in Exodus when the Glory of God dwelt among men in the Tabernacle in the wilderness.
   F. John 1:18 -
      1. The word translated "only begotten" is "monogenees." Its meanings are three, with Spiros Zodhiates arguing for the third. (Entire section: Can Man See God? Pp. 25-26
         a   It could mean an only child, i.e. One without sister or brother.
         b   It could mean, "the only one of its kind, unique."
         c   It could mean, "of the same nature."
      2. "There is no definite article before the adjectival noun monogenes, 'only begotten,' and the noun petros, 'of the Father.' But the absence of the definite article could not render them indefinite, and therefore this phrase

OUTLINE STUDIES

could not be translated 'glory as an only begotten of a father.' Nouns which speak of persons or objects of which only one exists need no article." (God in Man p.23)

G. John 5:23 - "This absolute equality with the Father in honour proves His deity and membership in the Trinity..." (Dake Annotated Bible p. 99 [NT])

H. John 8:56 - This could apply to two separate interpretations. Either of theses would point to the Deity of Jesus.
   1. This could refer to the eyes of faith.
   2. This could refer to Theophanies (see section on "The Angel of the Lord") - Gen. 12:1-3; 17:1-22

I. John 12:45 - If one wants to know what God is like, he must only study Jesus. Jesus is God. (Life Application Bible p. 269)

J. Acts 17:22-27 - Note that Paul speaks of the unknown **GOD**, and equates this with the Lord - i.e. Jesus. Jesus is God. (Life Application Bible p. 269)

K. Romans 1:4 - Others were called the sons of God. (Entire section: Barnes' Notes on the New Testament p. 545)
   1. Adam, who was created without mother or father, is called a son of God.
   2. Christians, who are adopted into the family of God, are called sons of God.
   3. Strong men, whose physical strength is above others, were sometimes called sons of God.
   4. Kings, because of their rule over others, were sometimes called sons of God.
   5. Angels, as spirit beings, are sometimes called sons of God.
   6. Only Jesus is given the New Testament Title of Son of God.
      a. This designates His special relationship with God.
      b. This designates His status as the Anointed King - The Messiah.
      c. This refers to His special virgin birth.

L. Romans 1:20 - This speaks of the "Godhead" being seen by the world at large. The Greek word, "theiotees," meaning, "divinity," is used. "It refers to the majesty and glory of God in His creation but not to the essence of His personality. Colossians 2:9 speaks of the 'Godhead' with the Greek word 'theotees.'" The difference is that this reference is "...not to the manifestation of Christ in His external acts, but to His essential nature." (Was Christ God? Pp. 10-11)

M. Romans 9:5 -
   1. "The Fathers (Abraham, Isaac, Jacob, etc.) Are given their due as to whom promises were given. Jesus is called their descendent - according to the flesh. But, He is above them due to His Divinity." (The New Testament for English Readers p. 920)
   2. The ancients agree that the reading here is that Jesus is God. Many modern scholars find other meanings by looking at what they believe Paul was **likely** to mean as opposed to what he **did** say - "a very unsafe principle of interpretation." (*Pulpit Commentary* v. 18 [Romans] pp. 262-265)
   3. He came in the flesh Who has supreme domination (over all). This is God. The Pious Jew of the day added "Blessed for ever" after the mention of Deity. (Barnes' Notes on the New Testament p. 614)

N. I Corinthians 12:4-6 -
   1. This is an intimation of the Trinity. "He who may think this **fanciful** must account for the very evident **distinctions** here in some more satisfactory way." (Entire section: Adam Clarke's Commentary v. 6 p. 259)

                a. The gifts speak of the Holy Spirit.
                b. The administration speaks of the Son.
                c. The operations speak of the Father.
            2. There are three Personages mentioned here. (Entire section: The New Testament for English Readers pp. 1050-1051)
                a. One Spirit - The Bestower of gifts as mentioned.
                b. One Lord - The Appointer of gifts is mentioned.
                c. One God - The Worker of gifts is mentioned.
                d. We see here the Trinity acting in harmony.
O. Philippians 2:6 -
    1. "Nothing in this passage teaches that the Eternal Word (John 1:1) emptied Himself of either His divine nature, or His attributes, but only of the outward and visible manifestation of the Godhead." (Scofield Reference Bible p. 1258)
    2. Jesus is the "form" of God.
    3. Jesus has this equality simply by nature of His Divine Being. (Unger's Bible Handbook p. 686)
P. Colossians 1:17 - "Things not only **sub**sist in their beings, but **con**sist in their order and dependencies." (Matthew Henry v. 2 p. 1160)
Q. I Timothy 3:16 - This verse centers on Jesus. (Entire section: Unger's Bible Handbook p. 720)
    1. He was God in the flesh.
    2. He rose from the dead to vindicate and to prove true His claims.
    3. He appeared to many after His resurrection.
    4. His gospel is preached.
    5. His church continues throughout history.
    6. He has ascended to His glory.
R. Titus 2:13 -
    1. "...appearing" (epiphaneia) is never used by Paul to predicate God the Father or His glory. It always applies to Jesus' coming." (Commentary Practical and Explanatory on the Whole Bible p. 1388)
    2. "The use of the definite article 'the' with the first noun 'God' and the connection 'and' indicates that the first and second 'Savior' [nouns] are one and the same person. Our 'great God and our Savior Jesus Christ' is thus one and the same person, clearly proving the deity of Christ." (The Annotated Study Bible p. 1905)
    3. "The great God and our Saviour Jesus Christ." There is only one subject as "the" is a single article in the Greek. (Matthew Henry's Commentary v. 2 p. 1228)
S. Hebrews 1:3 -
    1. "The word [brightness] means an outshining, not a reflection" (Ryrie Study Bible p. 1730)
    2. "The rays which stream from the sun reveal the sun itself; so Christ is the ever-visible radiance of the unapproachable Light." (*Pulpit Commentary* v. 21 [Hebrews] p. 19)
T. Hebrews 1:8 - Some would argue that the verse should read: "God is thy throne forever." This is based on their theology rather than on the text. "It is a rule in the Greek language, that when a substantive noun is the subject of a sentence, and something is predicated on it, the article, if used at all, is prefixed to the subject, but omitted before the predicate. The Greek translators of the Old, and the authors of the New Testament, write agreeable to this rule." (Adam Clarke's Commentary v.. 6 p. 692)

OUTLINE STUDIES

- U. Hebrews 1:2-14 - A progressive revelation of Jesus: (Entire section: Adam Clarke's Commentary v. 6 p. 686)
    1. Verse 2 -
        a. He is a Son, born under the Law, of a woman.
        b. He is Heir of **ALL THINGS**.
        c. He is Creator of all.
    2. Verse 3 –
        a. He is the brightness of Divine Glory
        b. He is the "**express image of His person, or character of the Divine Substance**."
        c. He, by the "word of His power," is the sustainer of the universe.
        d. He made atonement for sins.
        e. He is on the right hand of God.
            (1) Since He is on the right hand of God, He is above all created beings.
            (2) Since He is on the right hand of God, He is worshipped by angelic hosts.
    3. verses 8 - 14 -
        a. He has an eternal throne; neither His person nor His dignity ever changes or decays.
        b. He continues to "**exercise dominion** when the earth and the heavens are no more."
    4. Only God in the flesh could fit the above description.
- V. Hebrews 2:14 - That He "partook" of our humanity means several things.
    1. He had an existence prior to Bethlehem.
    2. He was so constituted in this prior existence that he was not "flesh and blood" at that point.
    3. He had the power to modify, or expand, His mode of existence at **His Own volition**.
- W. Hebrews 3:1-4 - Moses was a faithful worker in the house, that is the church (Both the Old Testament Jewish and the New Testament Christian assemblies are "churches" in the sense that they are "called out" of the world, for a purpose, by God.), but Jesus built the house. "...he that built all things is God." Paul plainly calls Jesus, "God."
- X. I John 5:7 – Many newer versions cast doubt on the validity of this verse
    1. Tertullian quoted the verse in about 200 A.D. in his "Apology Against Praxeas.'
    2. The original Latin Vulgate, translated 157 A.D. contained the verse.
    3. These must both be acknowledged as giving evidence of a still earlier template.
- Y. I John 5:20 - "This is the true God."
    1. The immediate antecedent of this statement is "Jesus."
    2. Both the "True God" and "Jesus" here refer to eternal life. (Barnes' Notes on the New Testament p. 1497)
- Z. Revelation 1:8 - Jesus is the beginning and the conclusion. Since this could be said only of the Self-existent One - God, Jesus is God. (Salem Kirban Reference Bible p. 38 [Revelation])
- AA. Revelation 4:8 - Note, "**Holy, Holy, Holy, is...**" the creature proclaim the Trinity of God (The Trinity **is** - one, singular.)

III. The terms of Deity are ascribed to Jesus.

- A. The term "Son of God" implied Deity - Matt. 3:17; Jn. 10:29-36 (Barnes' Notes on the New Testament p. 75)
- B. The Son is called God - Jn. 1:1; Rom. 9:5; I Jn. 5:20 (A Systematic Study of Bible Doctrine p. 79)
- C. "…if it is true that [the attributes of God] apply to God, then it is equally true that if they are true of Christ, then Christ is God. If they are applied to the Holy Spirit, then the Holy Spirit is God. If they apply to the Father, then the Father is God. And so they are all three God, yet one." (Confession of Faith, Lenord Street Baptist Church p. 15)

THE DEITY OF JESUS, THE CHRIST - THE TRUTH OF HIS DIVINITY

I. The circumstantial evidence shows that He is Divine. (Entire section: Is Jesus God? - Book Number One, pp. 2-15)
- A. Time is dated from His birth.
- B. There are many prophecies of Him Scripture.
  1. His birth is foretold - Micah 5:2
  2. His Virgin Birth is foretold - Is. 7:14
  3. The time of His birth is foretold - Daniel 9:25-26
  4. The Death He suffered is foretold - Psalm 22:16
  5. His trial, death, and resurrection are foretold.
- C. He rose from obscurity - Mark 6:2-3
- D. He had great authority of message.
- E. He had great power.
  1. He had power over death.
  2. He had power to work miracle.
- F. He foretold the fall of Capernaum, Chorazin and Bethsaida - Matt. 11:21-24
- G. He foretold the fall of Jerusalem, and its time - Luke 19:41-44
- H. He foretold the Diaspora - Luke 21:24
- I. He lived a sinless life.
- J. He had insightful knowledge of humanity - John 2:24-25
- K. The testimony of Him lies within the Christian – Romans 8:16
- L. He rose from the dead.
- M. He has a Kingdom - John 18:36

II. The Bible says that He is Divine.
- A. There are several reasons to believe that Jesus is Divine. (Entire section: Answers To Tough Questions pp. 40-41)
  1. The miracles which He performed point to His Divinity.
  2. Fulfilled prophecy about His birth, life, ministry, death and resurrection point to His Divinity.
  3. Jesus said He was Divine.
  4. Most importantly, His resurrection proves His Divinity.
- B. His Sonship proves His Divinity.
  1. The Sonship of Jesus is important. (Entire section: Is Jesus God - Book Number One pp. 85-90)
     - a. The Sonship of Jesus is important to the Trinity. If One is removed it is not a Triune God. "God is one!" - compare Matt. 28:19; II Cor. 13:14.
     - b. The Sonship is important to Jesus' Deity. If Jesus were only another man, He would not be Deity.
     - c. The Sonship is important to Jesus' sinlessness. If He were not the Son of God, then He is not sinless. All mere men are sinners - Prov. 20:19; Eccl. 7:20; Rom. 3:23; I Pet. 2:22
     - d. The Sonship is important to Jesus' ability to save sinners. If He sinned, Himself, He had no right or power to save others.

OUTLINE STUDIES

        e. The Sonship is important to Jesus' truthfulness. He said that He was the Son of God.
        f. The Sonship is important to the credibility of God's Word. The Bible says that He is the Son of God.
    2. To deny the Sonship of Jesus is to do several things. (Entire section: Is Jesus God - Book Number One pp. 90-91
        a. To deny the Sonship of Jesus is to call God a liar - Matt. 3:17; I Jn. 5:10
        b. To deny the Sonship of Jesus is to be a liar - I Jn. 2:22
        c. To deny the Sonship of Jesus is to be in the spirit of the Antichrist - I Jn. 4:3
        d. To deny the Sonship of Jesus is to be condemned - Jn. 3:18
        e. To deny the Sonship of Jesus is to be under the wrath of God - Jn. 3:36
        f. To deny the Sonship of Jesus is to die in sin - Jn. 8:24

III. The Demons say that Jesus is Divine. (Entire section: Can We Be Sure That Jesus Christ Is God? p. 17)
    A. This shows His power over Satan.
        1. He had power over Satan - Matt. 4:24; 8:28; Mark 1:34; Luke 4:34
        2. His disciples did not cast our demons except in His power - Matt. 10:1
    B. This shows His opposition to Satan. He would not be able to cast out demons if He were in collusion with Satan - Luke 11:14-20

IV. The life of Jesus shows that He is Divine.
    A. The facts of Jesus' life and birth point to His Divinity. (IV, A, 1-17: Why We Believe in the Deity of Christ p. 18)
        1. He is the seed of woman, not man and woman - Gen. 3:15
        2. His names are God's Names - Is. 7:14; 9:6
        3. He did a perfect and Supernatural work - Is. 42:1-4; 61:1-3
        4. He is eternal - Is. 9:7; Mic. 5:2
        5. His conception was supernatural.
        6. The angelic announcement of His birth to the shepherds and to His parents was supernatural.
        7. The Star and the wise men's visit were supernaturally arranged.
        8. His temptations by Satan, and His reaction to them, were supernatural.
        9. John's announcement of Him was supernatural.
        10. The voice from Heaven at His Baptism was supernatural.
        11. He led a sinless life.
        12. His love and compassion were balanced with "His wrathful indignation against hypocrisy and all evil."
        13. "He spoke with certainty concerning subjects beyond the range of human knowledge."
        14. His miracles were supernatural.
        15. His knowledge of the future was supernatural.
        16. His manner of death was supernatural in that He released His Own Spirit.
        17. The events which followed His death were supernatural - Matt. 27:32
        18. The Scriptures speak of Jesus – this is supernatural – John 5:39 (Added by editor)
    B. John 2:19 - The miracles only proved that the message was of God. Others had performed miracle. The resurrection proved His Deity. (Rice Reference Bible p. 1133)
    C. He claimed to be God. "The late C. S. Lewis put the matter succinctly when he wrote in *Mere Christianity,* 'A man who was merely a man and said the sort of

things Jesus said would not be a great moral teacher. He would either be a lunatic - on the level with the man who says he is a poached egg - or else he would be the Devil of Hell. You must make your choice. Either this man was, and is, the Son of God; or else a madman or something worse.'" (Why We Believe in the Deity of Christ   pp. 18-19)

V. The death of Jesus shows that He is Divine.   (Entire section: Can We Be Sure That Jesus Christ Is God? p. 28)
- A. Jesus knew that He came to die. He even warned His disciples that He was to die - Matt. 16:21; 17:22-23; 20:17-19
- B. "Jesus' death was no ordinary death. He was paying the penalty for the sins of a world of man. His death as the Lamb of God was anticipated before the foundation of the world." Revelation 13:8

VI. His resurrection shows that He is Divine.
- A. "This was no resuscitation of one who had fainted. Christ had laid down His life, and now He had taken it again. He was in His glorified resurrection body; He appeared and disappeared at will; He entered closed doors. Yet, He was the same Jesus; He invited His disciples to handle Him and convince themselves. He called for food and ate before them. Who was this Person who had conquered death but the very Son of God Himself?" (Can We Be Sure That Jesus Christ Is God? p. 29)
- B. Romans 1:4 - His Deity is declared (shown to be true) by His resurrection. The "Spirit of Holiness" could be interpreted three ways: (Entire section: Ryrie Study Bible p. 1594)
    1. The "Spirit of Holiness" could be His Own holiness showing this.
    2. The "Spirit of Holiness" could, of course, be the Holy Spirit.
    3. The "Spirit of Holiness" could be both of the ABOVE.
- C. Over 520 individuals, some who did not seem to want to believe the resurrection (example: Thomas), saw Jesus after He rose from the dead. (Can We Be Sure Jesus Christ Is God? P. 29)

VII. His life **now** shows that He is Divine.
- A. He saves us from our sins.
    1. Matthew 9:6 - Note that He has the authority to forgive sins, not merely to declare that they are forgiven. (Harper Study Bible   p. 1450)
    2. "Only if Jesus Christ is God could Christ's atoning work be effective for us... Only a holy, sinless person could become an effectual sacrifice for those guilty of sin." (Why We Believe in the Deity of Christ p. 19)
- B. He saves us from ourselves.
    1. The transformed lives - not that they are perfect - testify to His Divine Influence. We, at the very least, have a "mark to reach." The Church, even the counterfeits in her, recognizes the need to be different from the "world."
    2. John 14:6 - "The way" - Jesus is more than an example to follow; He is the Way - the Path, the Mode, the Means of our journey. (The New Testament for English Readers   p. 584)

ABOUT THE AUTHOR

Dr. DeWitt was born in north central Illinois after the War in Europe (WW II) had ended. He was one of the first of the "Baby Boomer" generation. As had been his father in WWII, Dr. DeWitt was a combat infantryman during the Vietnamese Conflict. He won his Combat Infantry Badge less than three weeks after entering the war zone.

Dr. DeWitt has written books on Inspiration (Study in Inspiration), a defense of the Textus Receptus (God Keeps His Word), and the Virgin Birth of Jesus (Study in the Virgin Birth). He has also written verse by verse commentaries on Daniel and Nahum.

From 1985 - 1995 Dr, DeWitt taught the fundamentals of the Christian Religion over WGPA-TV 7 in Galesburg, Illinois. He also published a newsletter, BQM Reports..., during the decade of the 1990's. This started out to be simply a newsletter of his activities. It soon morphed into a bi-monthly journal of theological thought and teaching. Although the magazine had only a press run of about 1000 every two months, copies were sent to every state in the U.S. and all the provinces of Canada. Copies were sent to every continent except Antarctica.

Dr, DeWitt has been a member of high IQ societies MENSA and Intertel. He has graduated both from private and public colleges and universities.

Dr. DeWitt was married to the former Linda Guenther for over thirty years until her Home Going to Glory in May of 2000. They are the parents of two children, Amy and Ethan and have two grandchildren, Shandi and Elijah.

In the past 50 years Dr. DeWitt has pastored four churches in Louisiana and Illinois. He is currently pastor of the Allen Park Baptist Church in Galesburg, Illinois.

INDEX OF WORDS AND PHRASES

200 AD, 386
30 A.D., 226
Aaronic priesthood, 372
Abel, 156
Abiding, 167
Abraham, 58, 71, 78, 81, 82, 86, 88, 114, 117, 135, 183, 202, 203, 230, 269, 272, 295, 301, 307, 339, 345, 358, 362, 374, 377, 410, 415, 420, 421
absolute, 36, 45, 97, 114, 137, 142, 170, 174, 179, 191, 202, 211, 216, 218, 236, 279, 297, 319, 374
accident, 266
AD, 35, 134, 386, 389, 398
Adam, 78, 91, 100, 106, 107, 113, 115, 120, 124, 126, 138, 139, 142, 157, 161, 165, 168, 172, 173, 178, 181, 182, 195, 214, 218, 219, 221, 223, 229, 230, 251, 256, 279, 284, 285, 287, 288, 307, 316, 318, 326, 355, 364, 370, 376, 378, 382, 406, 407, 411, 412, 427, 429
Adam Clarke, 100, 107, 124, 126, 138, 139, 284, 285, 288, 307, 378, 382, 429
Alford, 96, 100, 118, 120, 123, 126, 137, 145, 153, 263, 266, 280, 283, 284, 289, 295, 301, 340, 341, 352, 377, 378, 427, 430
all power, 142, 143, 222, 233, 257, 285, 288, 291, 314, 330, 380
Allah, 45
almighty, 366
Alpha and Omega, 232, 289, 323, 324, 367, 386
altered, 112, 377
Amarna letters, 91
amazing symmetry of Scripture, 215
answers, 99, 251, 264, 271, 319, 337, 340, 426
antagonists, 307, 340
Anthony Zeoli, 149, 165, 185, 221, 239, 313, 430
apaugasma, 381
apo, 381

Apollianarianism, 52
apostolic benedictions, 160
Arian error, 291
Arianism, 52
Articles of Faith, 37, 429, 430
ascension, 113, 182, 201, 215, 311, 329, 403
astrologers, 417
atomic construction, 222
Attributes, 5, 36, 92, 113, 141, 201, 202, 257, 403
Author of Evil, 244
Author of Life, 250
Bancroft, 51, 357, 359, 360, 361, 429
baptism, 51, 61, 65, 129, 159, 160, 277, 371, 387, 405, 407, 418
Baptismal formula, 159
Baptist Churches, 37, 429
Barnes, 112, 130, 137, 138, 172, 199, 288, 289, 306, 310, 336, 338, 340, 376, 377, 386, 387, 429
basic sin of Satan, 146
BCE, 134, 389
became sin, 182, 348, 398
Beers, 268, 287, 430
benediction, 168, 202
Benjamin B. Warfield, 36, 430
Bethlehem, 56, 79, 81-83, 85, 99, 100, 113-119, 121, 128, 130, 139, 182, 196, 199, 201, 203, 215, 223, 231, 280, 293, 301, 313, 321, 345, 363, 368, 373, 385, 389, 401, 417
Bethsaida, 397
betray, 114, 214, 216, 421
Billy Graham, 39
biographers, 199
blasphemy, 46, 61, 92, 112, 114, 139, 161, 206, 231, 271, 297, 308, 310, 311, 319, 327, 329, 336-338, 340, 360, 365
blessed hope, 112, 256, 334, 381
Blesser, 88
blind, 61, 64, 151, 234, 287, 340, 413
blind man, 61, 64, 151, 340
blood atonement, 107
Bogard, 37, 429

born again, 72, 74, 100, 119, 160, 171, 201, 216, 217, 226, 265, 376
bow, 123, 128, 150, 152, 161, 166, 355, 368
Bread of Life, 174
British Israelitism, 295
Buddha, 45, 51
Buddhism, 45
burning bush, 87, 161, 173, 202, 230, 272
Burrell, 91, 430
Caiaphas, 79
Caird, 105, 431
cancer, 48, 287, 316
Capernaum, 170, 235, 268, 309, 338, 396, 397
capital offense, 306, 323
Catechism, 36, 430
CE, 134, 389
centurion, 65, 189, 327, 334
cessation of existence, 246
character, 47, 89, 154, 155, 167, 206, 214, 215, 261, 301, 303, 354, 383
Chorazin, 397
Chosen Peoples Ministries, 38
christianized, 317
Christianson, 141, 142, 331, 411, 417, 419, 425-427, 431
Christology, 45
chronological term, 149
church, 35, 37, 38, 40, 45, 57, 72, 73, 89, 91, 105, 107, 119, 121, 146, 159, 160, 170, 178, 196, 205, 206, 208, 214, 219, 225, 275, 276, 284, 289, 291, 318, 331, 339, 340, 341, 345, 346, 371, 378, 384,-386, 406, 413, 421
circumstantial evidence, 389, 395
Clarke, 78, 100, 105, 107, 124, 126, 138, 139, 284, 285, 288, 302, 303, 307, 310, 311, 323, 336, 348, 372, 378, 382-384, 430
coats of skins, 107, 157
coincidence, 401, 418
Cole, 35, 36, 96, 429
combat veteran, 235
coming to Jesus, 167
comparing Scripture with Scripture, 110, 116, 156
compassion, 175, 214, 253, 255, 298, 418
con men, 77
Confucianism, 45
Congestive Heart Failure, 259
Coniaris, 36, 430
Constant Companion, 74
Constant Contemporary, 74, 229, 244, 272, 283
conveyance from one duty station to another, 247
convicting power, 241
Council of Chalcedon, 35
cousin of Mary, 335
created god, 57, 195, 257, 276, 280, 284, 285
Criswell, 120, 281, 336, 362, 429
Cross, 37, 47, 55, 72, 99, 119, 127, 129, 138, 146, 156, 157, 172, 174, 178, 187, 188, 226, 230, 231, 233, 247, 249, 250, 257, 266, 288, 317, 323, 334, 371, 395, 431
Cross of Calvary, 47, 72, 127, 156, 157, 174, 178, 230, 231, 233, 247, 249, 250, 266, 288, 317, 323
cult, 45, 57, 101, 111, 128, 149, 257, 387
cultist, 135, 231, 321
cup of coffee, 41, 95, 105, 292
Dake, 56, 86-88, 130, 299, 374, 429
daughter of Jarius, 254, 255
decay, 264, 384
Defined King James Bible, 196, 212, 323, 429
Deism, 383
demons admit, 409
denial, 45, 47, 48, 111, 212, 213, 407
derivative life, 230
destroyer, 246
devious, 246
DeWitt, 1-3, 5, 43, 258, 399, 479
disconnect, 380
Divine mind, 295, 301, 419, 423
Divine Suicide, 249
Docetism, 52
doctrine of the Godhead, 129
dropsy, 236

INDEX OF WORDS AND PHRASES

dual nature, 56, 82, 112, 113, 118, 121, 126, 321, 334, 344, 377, 382
E-4, 284
Ebionism, 52
ecumenical fervor, 69
Edward F. Hills, 43
een, 280
egento, 280
elements, 41, 95, 174, 211, 222, 258, 264, 268, 276, 302, 332, 364, 366, 371, 409
Eli, 153
Elijah, 335, 344, 345, 479
Elisabeth, 119, 335
Eloah, 107, 111
Elohim, 107, 110, 111
empty tomb, 65, 396
endowed with the Christ Spirit, 61
engrafted, 295
Enoch, 344
Ephratah, 56, 116, 121, 280, 293, 363
EPT (Ed's Paraphrased Translation, 271
Erasmus, 42
essence, 38, 40, 56, 96, 100, 105, 109, 111, 112, 118-121, 123, 125, 129, 134, 137-139, 154, 155, 163, 165, 174, 187, 200, 201, 226, 257, 275, 292, 293, 307, 313, 315, 321, 329, 337, 338, 363, 364, 366, 373, 375-378
Ethan, 96, 133, 149, 479
Ethiopian eunuch, 65
Eutychianism, 51
evidences, 71, 157, 243
evolutionary mutations, 229
executioner, 334, 341
existed prior to Abraham, 272
express image of his person, 133, 134, 165, 166, 197, 203, 258, 381, 383
false religious concepts, 175
false religious professionals, 175
Falwell, 92, 97, 102, 323, 369, 381, 429
feeding, 153, 178, 302, 396
fever, 170, 235, 239, 268
fig tree, 170, 208, 243, 331
First Born, 58, 59
Firstbegotten, 57, 149

firstborn, 58, 72, 100, 101, 276, 289, 379, 392, 415
five thousand men, 178
flotilla, 191
foot washing, 160
force of gravity, 290
foreordained, 115, 181
foundation, 45, 106, 111, 115, 130, 156, 181, 196, 223, 231, 267, 279, 357, 363, 383, 425
fractured skull, 171
funeral, 253, 256, 302, 396
future, 89, 134, 209, 211, 217, 244, 339, 345, 354, 364, 370, 392, 397, 412, 414, 421, 422
Gabriel, 62, 81, 335
Garden, 107, 120, 172, 229, 241, 256, 411, 418, 430
General Association of the Regular Baptist Churches, 37
Gergesenes, 409
Gnostic sect, 169
God Almighty, 231, 254, 255, 288, 305, 367, 387
God cannot be tempted, 246
God encased in that human form, 165
God in the flesh, 46, 91, 142, 150, 159, 179, 267, 269, 323, 334, 384, 401, 425
God Keeps His Word, 43, 479
Graham, 429, 430
Great Commission, 35, 74, 121, 130, 142, 225, 257, 260, 310, 405
Great Physician, 171, 233, 288
great power of Jesus, 130
greatest need of man, 171
Hagar, 85, 86
Halley, 58, 430
He lay down His life, 193
He received worship, 139, 151
Henderson, 106, 430
Henry, 101, 129, 130, 136, 277, 380, 381, 430
High Priest, 62, 79, 154, 182, 219, 385
Hills, 40-42
His name is superior, 155
His Own Glory, 136-138
His Words, 46, 59, 154, 208, 269, 411,

421
Hogan, 108, 110, 111, 351, 431
home church, 214
home was in Heaven, 313
hoopla, 191
human origin, 78
hypocrite, 244, 420
I AM, 161, 230, 272, 307
I AM THAT I AM, 272, 307
I *am* the first, 102, 365
I *am* the last, 102, 365
identification with Jesus, 160
illumination, 110, 295, 311, 419
image, 58, 59, 72, 100, 101, 110, 134, 166, 207, 258, 276, 289, 321, 379, 383, 420
imperfect tense, 280
In him was life, 113, 150, 173, 201, 229, 250, 272, 386
incontrovertible proof, 425
indwelt, 100, 159
infirmity, 234, 240, 420
inglorious, 249
insane, 46, 79, 240, 332
inspiration, 39, 63, 86, 99, 206, 221, 289, 321, 334, 335, 349, 352, 356, 357, 360, 373, 377, 381, 390, 405, 419
inspiration of God, 63
inspired Scripture, 63, 264
instruct in worship, 89
Isaiah, 41, 81, 95, 102, 116, 124, 266, 268, 275, 279, 285, 292, 293, 328, 343, 347, 348, 351, 352, 354, 355, 358-360, 365, 367-370, 389, 390, 392, 412, 413, 415
Islam, 45, 292
issue of blood, 175, 240, 254
Jacob, 71, 81, 82, 86-89, 107, 183, 339, 354, 366, 377, 420, 421
Jamison, Faussett, and Brown, 338
Jarius, 254, 255
Jehovah, 57, 78, 82, 85, 86, 88, 91, 101, 102, 111, 114, 195, 221, 257, 276, 292, 293, 341, 351, 357, 361, 363-368
Jerusalem Bible, 101, 430
Jesus IS Righteousness, 155
Jesus never ceased being Who He Is, 125
Jesus of Nazareth, 79, 99, 102, 186, 306, 338, 409
Jesus, Who IS salvation, 360
Jewish people, 61, 91, 99, 155, 172, 292, 297, 339, 346, 387, 397, 398, 420, 421
Jezebel, 358
Johannine Comma, 41, 42
John R. Rice, 110, 267, 425, 431
John the Baptist, 63, 65, 77, 78, 118, 119, 277, 280, 292, 303, 317, 325, 343, 344, 345, 351, 359, 368, 406, 407, 418
Jonah, 40, 155
Jonathan ben Uzziel, 139
Joseph, 57, 62, 63, 107, 298, 365, 370, 373, 392, 395, 406, 414, 415, 417, 431
Josh McDowell, 45, 401, 429, 430
Joshua, 55, 86, 87, 89
Judas, 64, 65, 114, 160, 186, 187, 193, 206, 214, 249, 296, 341, 390, 421, 422
judgment for sin, 250
Kelly, 77, 78, 335, 345, 348, 429
Kenosis, 101, 123, 125-131, 138, 166, 185, 217, 231, 276, 277, 280, 334, 378
keys, 202, 260, 332
King Solomon, 155
Laban, 82
Lamb, 65, 115, 163, 199, 223, 279, 299, 325, 326, 343, 359, 391, 406, 416, 425
lame man, 142, 183, 322, 337
Latin Vulgate, 41, 386
Lawful Commander of the Army of the Redeemed, 74
laws of nature, 287, 421
Lazarus, 78, 139, 255, 256, 302, 319, 331, 340, 344, 396, 399, 401
Leonard Street Baptist, 37
leprosy, 239
Leupold, 90, 430
Levites, 343, 372

INDEX OF WORDS AND PHRASES

Lewis, 425
Liberator, 68
lie, 49, 234, 246, 256, 299, 324, 407
Linda, 3, 174, 179, 212, 245, 251, 283, 284, 287, 479
Lindsell, 45, 110, 279, 369, 426, 430, 431
lineage of David, 347
literal interpretation, 35
Little, 202, 211, 301, 302, 322, 324, 430
liturgical churches, 36
logos, 283, 372
Longfellow, 244
Lord of the Sabbath, 145, 236, 297, 420
lost for a thousand years, 169
Louie, 133
Lover of Righteousness, 68
Ludwig, 38, 430
Magi, 417
magistrate, 107
manner of His impending death, 172
Manoah, 82, 87
Martha, 64, 255, 319, 331
Martial Arts, 285
Mary, 36, 39, 57, 62, 63, 119, 150, 154, 182, 219, 255, 298, 328, 335, 348, 355, 365, 370, 373, 395, 414, 415, 417
Master, 64, 134, 136, 159, 160, 177, 178, 191, 192, 207, 208, 212, 215, 234, 237, 239, 241, 255, 260, 264, 283, 292, 297, 361, 401, 403, 419, 421
Master of time and botany, 177
Matthew Henry, 101, 129, 130, 136, 199, 277, 280, 380, 381, 430
May, 39, 74, 75, 133, 207, 208, 214, 289, 297, 301, 306, 329, 370, 414, 429, 479
McDowell, 305, 309, 337, 340, 430
mechanics of the Kenosis, 125
Mediator, 36, 129, 130, 219
Melchisedec, 58, 371, 372
Merrill Unger, 279
Messianic Psalm, 292
mighty works of Deity, 192

miracle of multiplication, 178
miscreant, 333
mission, 62, 101, 118, 125, 136, 145, 240, 245, 246, 250, 323
mistreated, 74
Mohammed, 45, 51
Monogenes, 91, 373
Monotheist, 97
Mormonism, 45
Moses, 77, 78, 81-83, 86, 87, 117, 135, 136, 154, 159, 161, 169, 171, 173, 196, 202, 230, 239, 265, 272, 298, 305, 307, 327, 352, 353, 359, 360, 371, 385, 415, 419
mother of Peter's wife, 239
Mount of Transfiguration, 117, 135, 136, 277
Muhammad Ali, 78, 285
My wife, 127, 179, 316
mystery of the Godhead, 102
mythicized, 325
Nathaniel, 63, 64, 331
natures, 35, 36, 38, 51, 120, 245, 264
near to all, 227
Negro League, 225
Nestorianism, 51, 120
net, 178, 179, 212, 332
New Birth, 91, 156, 160, 264
New Hyde Park Baptist Church, 37, 430
newlyweds, 245
Newton, 110, 430
Nicodemus, 106, 143, 155, 171, 216, 226, 264, 265, 269, 295, 298, 313, 315, 355, 380, 392
Nixon, 211
object of faith, 67
Object of Honor, 68
object of the Father's Glory, 68
occultism, 169
offspring, 77, 163, 165, 219, 233, 245, 295, 348, 412
old manuscripts, 42
Omega, 232
omnipotent, 222, 285, 288
omnipresence, 99, 167, 224-227, 355, 372, 376
Omnipresence, 99, 120, 121, 143, 216,

225, 235, 298, 301, 310
omnipresent, 165, 225, 314
omniscient, 205, 206, 314
One Who *is* God, 277, 360
only laid aside, 123
only mediator, 219
Orr, 48, 96, 128, 169-173, 177, 192, 193, 272, 296-298, 321, 325, 409, 425, 426, 429
Orthodox Church, 36, 430
orthodoxy, 68, 275
outward glory of the Godhead, 123
Own Person, 66, 138, 143, 243, 258, 296, 403
palsy, 141, 168, 192, 237, 239, 309, 319, 409, 426
para, 38, 138, 285
para-church agencies, 38
Passover, 215, 391, 395
Paul, 35, 65, 107, 112, 117, 161, 162, 201, 206, 222, 247, 256, 260, 269, 281, 286, 289, 329, 334, 339, 360, 365, 366, 368, 375-377, 380, 381, 387, 405, 413, 429-431
Pendleton, 102, 106, 119, 125, 127, 130, 147, 197, 293, 429
penman, 196, 222, 335, 354, 357, 360, 363, 366, 371, 382, 386, 389
Pentecostal, 37, 159
Pentecostal Church, 37
Pentecostal style churches, 159
Perfection of Jesus, 174
Persia, 417
Person of Jesus Christ, 5, 51, 52, 55, 64, 113, 120, 133, 179, 409
Pharisees, 36, 116, 145, 171, 206, 236, 264, 265, 297, 352, 374, 396, 419
physical examples, 287
Pilate, 55, 71, 183, 187, 188, 247, 265, 266, 296, 333, 389, 390-392, 400
plural, 96, 106, 107, 109-111, 310, 323, 328
plurality, 102, 107, 109, 110
Plurality of Majesty, 110
polytheism, 96
post Christian days, 69
power over Satan, 244-247
preacher of righteousness, 63, 155, 343

pregnancy, 85, 119, 414
pre-incarnate appearances, 79, 83, 90
prerogatives, 101, 124, 145, 259, 311
present tense, 118, 217, 229, 272
preserved, 6, 40, 41, 42, 57, 59, 87, 89, 135, 139, 146, 151, 152, 170, 176, 245, 264, 267, 273, 285, 291, 325, 335, 364-366, 369, 372, 407, 421
presidential politics, 185
principality, 259
Prison Fellowship, 38, 431
promise, 42, 85, 113, 121, 142, 143, 213, 316, 320, 353, 355, 372, 411
prophets, 42, 77, 123, 133, 135, 154, 168, 175, 179, 193, 214, 243, 247, 250, 269, 280, 296, 297, 323, 335, 345, 358, 421
propitiation, 73
Protector, 146
psychic, 211
pulpit supply, 275
quicken, 67, 323, 393
Rabbi, 63, 171, 265, 331
race, 39, 59, 83, 95, 106, 151, 155, 157, 165, 182, 218, 219, 230, 250, 251, 288, 315, 316, 321, 355, 370, 372, 406, 407, 411, 412
Raising the Dead, 168
Read, 39, 109, 311, 340, 341, 414, 429
rebelled, 183
reclaimed it, 193
redeemed by the Blood of Jesus, 246
redemption, 36, 37, 101, 117, 128, 157, 266, 317, 355, 367, 413, 421
reflected, 382
representative of humanity, 124, 128, 154, 165, 223, 245, 326
resurrections, 65, 66, 322, 396, 423
resuscitation, 256, 401, 426
revealer, 67
Rice, 110, 154, 267, 425, 431
Rock, 5, 116, 117, 352-354
Roman Church, 42, 328, 373
Ryrie, 77, 89, 114, 120, 373, 381, 426, 429, 431
Sabellians, 292
Salvation is, 130, 169, 178

INDEX OF WORDS AND PHRASES

Samaritan woman, 295, 326, 362
Saving Faith, 167
Scofield, 86, 123, 339, 370, 378, 430, 431
secondary god, 291
seed, 55, 85, 88, 211, 219, 269, 339, 363, 364, 371, 376, 411, 414, 419
Self-existent, 217
sent forth, 207, 245, 383, 385
Sermon on the Mount, 295, 311
Simmona, 387
Simmons, 95-97, 109, 146, 195, 217, 351, 431
sin bearer, 52, 293, 326
sin eradicator, 52
singular, 41, 96, 106, 107, 110, 159, 163, 168, 196, 201, 219, 273, 310, 323, 328, 387, 405
singular verb, 110, 387
sinless life, 134, 191, 398, 418
sleeping, 255, 258, 422
social christians, 216
Socinians, 292
Sonship, 56, 354, 387, 405-408
sonships, 58
space, 226, 268, 269, 339, 381
Spurgeon, 47, 431
stick outline, 257
stolen valor, 77
stone, 46, 92, 101, 231, 245, 255, 263, 271, 306-308, 318, 338, 340, 354, 360, 397, 402
Stone of Stumbling, 360
storm, 39, 78, 191, 192, 258, 302, 309, 396, 401, 409
Strong, 82, 92, 96, 109, 112, 159-161, 196, 229, 230, 289, 292, 351, 361, 372, 376, 381, 382, 399, 431
Study on the Virgin Birth, 245
subordinate, 127, 217, 285, 372, 380
Substitute of the World, 317
superior, 92, 125, 154-156, 257, 258, 353, 372, 397, 399
supernatural power, 243, 344, 423
Supreme Godhead, 38
symbiosis, 119
symbolism, 160
system, 99, 127, 156, 235, 244, 340, 341, 346, 415
Targum, 139
Temple, 99, 100, 181, 183, 205, 216, 287, 298, 307, 325, 328, 335, 340, 343, 345, 346, 366, 371, 416, 425
temptation, 245, 246, 264, 359, 407, 409, 411, 418
temptation of Jesus, 245, 359, 418
ten lost tribes, 295
Terminology, 55
Tertullian, 43, 386
testimony of the unclean spirits, 186
Textus Receptus, 42
the Assurance of Life, 68
the Captain of Israel, 86
the cleanser from sin, 73
the Creative Agent, 72, 81, 85, 92, 130, 154, 163, 203, 221, 230, 231, 276, 283, 289, 382
The Defined King James Bible, 73, 259, 366
the Deliverer from wrath, 72
The First Lady, 58
the Great High Priest, 74
the purpose of the Kenosis, 125
the Repository of Life, 73, 201
the Repository of the Promises of God, 73
the Sent One, 68
the Stronghold of our faith, 74
the Test of Truth, 68
the Ticket to the Father's abode, 69
theistic evolution, 229, 383
theoanthropic, 120
theological term, 101, 109, 276, 334, 378, 423
Theophanies, 82, 374
Theophany, 58, 301, 371
Theos, 372
Thirty-ninth Article, 36
Thomas, 45, 308, 326, 329, 332, 333, 336, 402, 426, 429, 431
thoughts, 41, 141, 170, 175, 192, 206, 254, 314, 426
Three distinct, 59
time/space continuum, 174
tithes, 58, 371
tools of Satan, 247

Tower of Babel, 106
Traditional Text, 169
tri theism, 137
Tribulation, 223, 267, 344, 345, 358, 408
Trinitarian, 95, 96, 105, 108, 110, 111, 161, 186, 226, 231, 291, 351, 405, 431
Trinity, 36-41, 59, 81, 90, 96, 97, 100, 105-111, 115, 116, 119, 130, 161, 162, 168, 202, 231, 273, 276, 277, 279, 285, 293, 310, 329, 365, 369, 374, 378, 380, 387, 400, 405
two or three are gathered, 225, 314, 372
unchanging, 217, 357, 366
Unger, 111, 279, 378, 380, 431
United Methodist Church, 38, 429
unity, 37-39, 90, 96, 97, 100, 102, 105-107, 109-111, 161, 310, 321, 323, 328, 337, 338, 380
utter holiness of Jesus, 186
Veil, 99
Victor, 266, 429, 430
Viet Nam War, 35
Virgin Birth, 46-48, 51, 52, 56, 82, 116, 124, 139, 157, 217, 245, 279, 376, 479
Voluntary Submission, 5, 121
Watchtower Bible & Tract Society, 221
Watergate Era, 211
Wesleyan Church, 38, 429
wine, 58, 87, 170, 174, 177, 235, 268, 302, 303, 370, 371
witch of Endor, 169
withered, 234, 236, 243
withered hand, 236
Woman at the Well, 207
Woman of Tyre, 151
wonderful, 81, 133, 187, 259, 284, 288, 298, 319, 320, 329, 339
Words of God, 40, 42, 48, 57, 130, 135, 136, 151, 169, 177, 203, 219, 246, 264, 269, 285, 291, 297, 337, 338, 365, 369, 396, 399, 407, 410, 411
worship by the angels, 146, 322
Wrestler, 88, 89
Yahovah, 351
Zacharias, 335, 358
Zeoli, 47, 48, 61, 67, 69, 71, 79, 85-89, 113-118, 150, 151, 154-157, 181-183, 185-189, 201, 205, 211, 213, 215, 216, 221-223, 225, 226, 233, 243, 245, 249, 253, 257, 328, 329, 354, 363, 389, 395, 405, 407, 408
Zodhiates, 111, 134, 138, 280, 283, 291, 372, 373, 377, 429-431

www.ingramcontent.com/pod-product-compliance
Lightning Source LLC
Chambersburg PA
CBHW081413230426
43668CB00016B/2221